The Good Hotel Guide 2015

GREAT BRITAIN & IRELAND

Editors:
Desmond Balmer
and Adam Raphael

Editor in chief:
Caroline Raphael

Founding editor:
Hilary Rubinstein

THE GOOD HOTEL GUIDE LTD

The Good Hotel Guide Ltd

This edition first published in 2014 by
The Good Hotel Guide Ltd

Copyright © 2014 Adam and Caroline Raphael
Maps © 2014 David Perrott

Managing director: Richard Fraiman

Contributing editors:
Bill Bennett
Astella Saw

Production: Hugh Allan
Managing editor: Alison Wormleighton
Designer: Lizzy Laczynska
Text editor: Daphne Trotter
Computer consultant: Vince Nacey
Website design: HeadChannel

A CIP catalogue record for this book may be found in the British Library.

ISBN 978 0 9549404 9 2

Cover photograph: *Gravetye Manor*, East Grinstead

Printed and bound in Spain by Graphy Cems

*'A good hotel is where
the guest comes first'*

Hilary Rubinstein (1926–2012)

Milebrook House, Knighton

CONTENTS

INTRODUCTION

The print edition of the *Good Hotel Guide* is the cornerstone on which our ever-expanding multi-media activity is based. For nearly 40 years, we have given unbiased advice on the best hotels in Great Britain and Ireland, selecting hotels on merit alone, and making impartial judgments based on reports from inspectors and readers. Readers' reports are vital to the *Guide*'s well-being. Reports can be sent via email, our website or post. The best reports win a prize of a free night's stay in one of our selected hotels.

Unlike reader-review websites, which are open to abuse from unscrupulous hoteliers and guests with a grudge, we monitor and track every report sent to us. That helps us to filter out both collusive praise and malicious complaints.

Our independent hotel reviews, which are rewritten every year, are now carried on several platforms including free apps for iPhone, Android and Windows smartphones. We are increasing our social media presence, so please follow us on Twitter and 'like' us on Facebook. *The Huffington Post* has been featuring top ten selections from the *Guide* in recent months.

We have also launched a *Good Hotel Guide* club which offers a monthly newsletter with prizes of a free hotel night, special deals on the best hotels, pre-publication discounts, and advice if you are in dispute with a hotel.

Our website carries the entries for most, but not all, of our selected hotels. Hotels are asked to make a modest payment if they wish their entry to appear on the web. If they choose not to pay, the listing remains, but without the details or photographs.

We have ambitious plans to expand our European selection of hotels. Watch this space. This year also marks our return to the North American market with a special edition of the *Guide*.

One thing that doesn't change is the character of the places we select, which are as independent as the *Guide*. Most are small and family owned and managed. Our choices reflect the changing face of hospitality: pubs- and restaurants-with-rooms are listed alongside simple B&Bs as well as many full-service hotels.

Desmond Balmer and Adam Raphael
July 2014

HOW TO USE THE *GOOD HOTEL GUIDE*

MAIN ENTRY

The 405 main entries, which are given a full page each, are those we believe to be the best of their type in Great Britain and Ireland.

Colour bands identify each country; London has its own section.

An index at the back lists hotels by county; another index lists them by hotel name.

Hotels are listed alphabetically under the name of the town or village.

The maps at the back of the book are divided into grids for easy reference. A small house indicates a main entry, a triangle a Shortlist one.

This hotel is making its first appearance or returning after an absence.

The wheelchair symbol indicates whether or not a hotel can accommodate wheelchair users. Phone the hotel to check details.

We name the readers who have endorsed a hotel; we do not name inspectors, readers who ask to remain anonymous, or those who have written a critical report.

The panels provide the contact details, number of bedrooms and facilities.

422	WALES

TAL-Y-LLYN Gwynedd
Map 3:B3

THE OLD RECTORY ON THE LAKE *NEW*

On the shore of Lake Tal-y-llyn beneath Cadair Idris in southern Snowdonia, this peaceful stone-built house has lake views from every window. 'Wonderful our visit is an annual highlight,' says a regular correspondent, whose comment brings a full entry for *The Old Rectory*. The house is run in personal style by the owners, John Caine, 'a welcoming and chatty host', and Ricky Francis, who cooks the 'very good' evening meals. There are two double bedrooms on the first floor; one has a free-standing bath and a separate walk-in shower in the bathroom. A smaller (and cheaper) room is on the ground floor. A self-contained ground-floor apartment, *The Rectory Retreat*, is equipped for visitors with mobility issues. It can be booked on a B&B basis; dogs are allowed to share this room with their owners. There is no mobile phone signal but free Wi-Fi is available. In the *Orangery* dining room, Ricky Francis uses Welsh produce for his four-course dinners. Typical dishes: locally smoked trout salad; slow-roasted Welsh lamb shank; banoffee pie. There is good walking, mountain biking and fishing. (*David Lipsey*)

25% DISCOUNT VOUCHERS

Tal-y-llyn LL36 9AJ

T: 01654-782225
E: enquiries@rectoryonthelake.co.uk
W: www.rectoryonthelake.co.uk

BEDROOMS: 3, 1 on ground floor, plus *Rectory Retreat*, a self-catering apartment on ground floor suitable for & (also available for B&B).
OPEN: all year except Jan, dining room closed Wed.
FACILITIES: lounge, *Orangery* dining room, free Wi-Fi, 2-acre grounds, outdoor hot tub.
BACKGROUND MUSIC: none.
LOCATION: on lake 9½ miles E of Tywyn.
CHILDREN: not under 18.
DOGS: allowed in Rectory Retreat only.
CREDIT CARDS: MasterCard, Visa.
PRICES: [2014] per room B&B single £60–£90, double £90–£120. Set dinner £30. Only 2-night bookings accepted at weekends.

---

www.goodhotelguide.com

This hotel has agreed to give *Guide* readers a discount of 25% off their normal bed-and-breakfast rate for one night only, subject to availability; terms and conditions apply.

We give the range of prices per person for 2015, or the 2014 prices when we went to press. The price for dinner is for a set meal, or (as full alc) the cost of three courses with wine.

HOW TO USE THE *GOOD HOTEL GUIDE*

SHORTLIST ENTRY

The Shortlist includes untested new entries and places we think should be appropriate in areas where we have limited choice. It also has some hotels about which we have not had recent reports. There are no photographs; many of these hotels have chosen to be included on our website where pictures are carried.

In some cases we list the entry under the nearest town.

Many readers tell us that they find background music irritating. We tell you if music is played, and where you might encounter it.

Dinner prices are either for set menus or an estimate of the likely price of a meal.

These are abbreviated descriptions listing the essential facilities.

This hotel has agreed to give *Guide* readers a discount of 25% off their normal bed-and-breakfast rate for one night only, subject to availability; terms and conditions apply.

CÉSARS 2015

We give our *César* awards to the ten best hotels of the year. Named after César Ritz, the most celebrated of hoteliers, these are the Oscars of hotel-keeping.

⚜ FAMILY HOTEL OF THE YEAR
FOWEY HALL, FOWEY
Part of Nigel Chapman's Luxury Family Hotels group, this Victorian mansion is run by staff committed to making sure that guests, young and old, have a good time.

⚜ DOG-FRIENDLY HOTEL OF THE YEAR
OVERWATER HALL, IREBY
Dogs, who are 'genuinely welcomed', are allowed to sit in one of the lounges and have the freedom of the grounds at this country hotel run by owners Stephen Bore and Angela and Adrian Hyde.

⚜ SMALL HOTEL OF THE YEAR
YALBURY COTTAGE, LOWER BOCKHAMPTON
Hands-on owners Ariane and Jamie Jones run their small hotel, a row of 350-year-old thatched cottages, in a friendly manner; he produces memorable meals using fresh, local produce.

⚜ COUNTRY HOUSE HOTEL OF THE YEAR
LORDS OF THE MANOR, UPPER SLAUGHTER
Unstuffy and impeccable, this 17th-century former rectory is a superlative country house hotel which has class without ostentation. The cooking of chef Richard Edwards is much admired.

⚜ PUB-WITH-ROOMS OF THE YEAR
THE TALBOT INN, MELLS
In a Domesday village, this former coaching inn has been remodelled with feeling and flair by the owners, Charlie Luxton, Dan Brod and Matt Greenlees (the manager). It is run with cheerful informality.

♔ COUNTRY HOTEL OF THE YEAR

THE PEAR TREE AT PURTON, PURTON

In lovely gardens, this sympathetically extended 16th-century former vicarage is run in personal style by Anne Young and her daughter, Alix. The excellent service and good food impressed inspectors.

♔ NEWCOMER OF THE YEAR

MOOR OF RANNOCH HOTEL, RANNOCH STATION

At the end of the road, on the edge of the moor, this 19th-century hotel has been reinvigorated by the personable new owners, Scott Meikle and Stephanie Graham.

♔ SCOTTISH HOTEL OF THE YEAR

THE GREEN PARK, PITLOCHRY

A remarkable attention to detail and an impressive level of personal service stand out at the McMenemie family's impressive traditional hotel on the banks of the River Tummel.

♔ WELSH HOTEL OF THE YEAR

MILEBROOK HOUSE, KNIGHTON

Three generations of the Marsden family run this small hotel in the Teme valley with aplomb. Beryl Marsden, endlessly on duty, is assisted by her daughter, Joanne; her granddaughter, Katie, is the chef.

♔ IRISH GUEST HOUSE OF THE YEAR

NEWFORGE HOUSE, MAGHERALIN

Owned by the Mathers family for six generations, this Georgian house is run in hands-on fashion by John and Louise Mathers, whose care of guests and cooking are of the highest order.

REPORT OF THE YEAR COMPETITION

Readers' contributions are the lifeblood of the *Good Hotel Guide*. Everyone who writes to us is a potential winner of the Report of the Year competition. Each year twelve correspondents are singled out for the helpfulness of their reports. They win a copy of the *Guide* and an invitation to our annual launch party in October. This year's winners are:

PHILIP AND ANN CARLISLE of Ashburton

GWYN MORGAN of Beaconsfield
KATE MACMASTER of Bewdley
WILLIAM K WOOD of Bolton
SHEILA ROBINSON of Cork
IAN MALONE of Ferndown
PETER ROGERS of Hereford
JANE AND MARTIN BAILEY of London
PETER ANDERSON of Newbury
MARY HEWSON of Oldham
ANNE LAURENCE THACKERAY of Oxford
JILL AND MIKE BENNETT of St Albans

JOIN THE *GOOD HOTEL GUIDE* READERS' CLUB

Send us a review of your favourite hotel.

As a member of the club, you will be entitled to:

1. A pre-publication discount offer
2. Personal advice on hotels
3. Advice if you are in dispute with a hotel
4. Monthly emailed *Guide* newsletter

The writers of the 12 best reviews will each win a free copy of the *Guide* and an invitation to our launch party. And the winner of our monthly web competition will win a free night, dinner and breakfast for two at one of the *Guide*'s top hotels.

Send your review via:
our website: www.goodhotelguide.com
or email: editor@goodhotelguide.com
or fax: 020-7602 4182
or write to:

In the UK
Good Hotel Guide
Freepost PAM 2931
London W11 4BR
(no stamp needed)

From abroad
Good Hotel Guide
50 Addison Avenue
London W11 4QP
England

EDITOR'S CHOICE

A visit to a hotel should be a special occasion. Here are some of our favourite hotels in various categories. Turn to the full entry for the bigger picture.

ASKHAM HALL
ASKHAM

At their family home, a Grade I listed Pele Tower expanded in Elizabethan times, Charles Lowther and his artist wife, Juno, have created a hotel of character with a seriously good restaurant. Original features, some of architectural significance, have been retained in the bedrooms which have all the necessary modern technology. Juno Lowther's bold artwork is displayed in the hall. In the restaurant, Cumbrian-born chef Richard Swale serves a short seasonal menu

Read more, page 76.

THE LORD CREWE ARMS
BLANCHLAND

The owners of *Calcot Manor*, Tetbury, have given this old inn in a medieval village a thorough make-over. It has a dramatic entrance with contemporary sofas around a large stone fireplace. The bedrooms, in the inn and converted buildings facing the village square, have been carefully furnished with contemporary colours and antique pieces. In the high-ceilinged dining room, chef Simon Hicks serves an interesting menu.

Read more, page 100.

THE RED LION FREEHOUSE
EAST CHISENBURY

In a peaceful country village, chef/patron Guy Manning and his American wife, Brittany, have updated this unpretentious thatched pub. He has a *Michelin* star for his innovative cooking of dishes with unusual combinations of ingredients. The bedrooms, in a converted bungalow across the road, are decorated in restful colours and are well equipped. Some have a private decking area.

Read more, page 150.

THE TALBOT INN
MELLS

Owners Charlie Luxton, Dan Brod and Matt Greenlees (the manager) have remodelled this former coaching inn in a Domesday village with flair. It is run with an enjoyable informality by a helpful young staff. The comprehensively equipped bedrooms are decorated in a simple, modern style. Local produce is nicely cooked by the chef, Pravin Nayar.

Read more, page 211.

THE PIG NEAR BATH
PENSFORD

Experienced hoteliers Robin and Judy Hutson have reinvented the country house hotel at this honey-stoned mansion, debunking the tradition of formality to create a fresh and appealing style. The bedrooms have bare floorboards, shabby chic or distressed furnishings, feature wallpaper. All the ingredients in the restaurant come from within 25 miles. Loud music plays in the public areas; service is uninhibited and friendly.
Read more, page 240.

IDLE ROCKS
ST MAWES

On the harbour front, this 100-year-old hotel has been brought up to date by David and Karen Richards. They have given it a well-chosen nautical decor – bright colours (lots of blue), big vibrant paintings, huge planters full of orchids. Everyone has a sea view in the cleverly planned restaurant where Mark Apsey, the chef, serves modern dishes on a daily-changing menu.
Read more, page 265.

POPPIES HOTEL AND RESTAURANT
CALLANDER

Within the Loch Lomond and The Trossachs national park, this small hotel is run in unhurried and efficient style by owners, John and Susan Martin, who are ever-present hosts. In the dining room, chef Jim O'Reilly serves first-class contemporary dishes, nicely presented. The Victorian mansion faces west to the River Teith. Spotless bedrooms are clean and warm.
Read more, page 325.

MOOR OF RANNOCH HOTEL
RANNOCH STATION

Close to the railway station on a line that runs across the moor, this 19th-century hotel has been renovated by new owners Scott Meikle and Stephanie Graham. Friendly and full of information about the area, they have created cosy and light interiors. The views from the public rooms and the bedrooms are magnificent. Beautifully prepared, well-balanced dishes are served on an appetising menu.
Read more, page 366.

LLWYN HELYG
LLANARTHNE

In countryside near the National Botanic Garden of Wales, Caron and Fiona Jones have furnished their newly-built stone house in lavish style. Granite, marble and limestone feature throughout. There are many sitting areas for guests, who are welcomed on a B&B basis; they have use of a listening room which has a remarkable sound system. An impressive oak staircase leads to the bedrooms which have Italianate furnishings; a luxurious bathroom.
Read more, page 404.

THE OLD RECTORY ON THE LAKE
TAL-Y-LLYN

There are lake views from every window of this stone-built house (*pictured opposite*) on the shore of Lake Tal-y-llyn beneath Cadair Idris. The owners, John Caine, 'welcoming and chatty', and Ricky Francis, who cooks the evening meals, run the house in personal style. There is good walking, mountain biking and fishing in the immediate vicinity.
Read more, page 422.

CHURCH STREET HOTEL
LONDON

Greek/Spanish brothers José and Mel Raido have decorated their south London hotel in 'extravagant' Latino style with sculptures and religious artefacts. The 'vividly coloured' bedrooms are up 'steep, warren-like' staircases. There's a selection of teas and coffee plus an honesty bar in a lounge/breakfast room. Tapas meals are served in the *Angels & Gypsies* restaurant. Room £90–£155. Continental breakfast £5, dinner £28.
Read more, page 50.

BIGGIN HALL
BIGGIN-BY-HARTINGTON

Within the Peak District national park, James Moffett runs his Grade II* listed 17th-century manor house as an unpretentious hotel. The simple bedrooms have tea-making facilities and a bottle of fresh milk in a fridge. Dinner orders are taken while guests enjoy a complimentary aperitif in the sitting room and library. Classic English dishes are served in the dining room. Per room D,B&B £122–£174.
Read more, page 96.

CASTLEMAN
CHETTLE

A former dower house in a feudal village, this informal restaurant-with-rooms is run by Barbara Garnsworthy and her brother, Brendan. Fans admit that there might be an air of 'faded gentility' about the two period drawing rooms and that some bedrooms are better than others. But everyone admires the 'first-class' cooking and the service (guests 'are looked after as individuals'). Per room B&B single £70, double £95–£110. Dinner £28–£30.
Read more, page 133.

THE OLD STORE
HALNAKER

Close to the Goodwood estate, Patrick and Heather Birchenough's Grade II listed Georgian flint-and-brick house is well placed for exploring Chichester and the countryside around. Guests are welcomed with tea and cake in a lounge or the garden; the bedrooms are well equipped. Breakfast has a varied menu. Per person B&B £35–£50.
Read more, page 170.

THISTLEYHAUGH FARM
LONGHORSLEY

On the family's working farm in the rolling Cheviot hills, this Georgian farmhouse is run in a friendly fashion by Enid Nelless. In the public rooms, there are nooks and crannies for guests to sit. After a glass of complimentary sherry, a 'delicious' dinner is taken communally in the dining room. Breakfasts are generous. Per room B&B single £70, double £100. Set dinner £25.
Read more, page 196.

THE NAG'S HEAD
PICKHILL

'Everything a country inn should be', this old coaching inn in a village just off the A1 near Thirsk has been run by the Boynton family for more than 40 years. Vegetarians are well catered for in the meals which can be taken in the tap room, the lounge bar or the 'lovely' dining room. The bedrooms are simple but 'perfectly adequate'. Per room B&B single £60–£75, double £80–£95. Dinner £28.
Read more, page 245.

THE BLACK SWAN
RAVENSTONEDALE

'Unstuffy and dependable', Alan and Louise Dinnes's village inn is 'remarkable value for money'. Chef Kev Hillyer's comfort foods can be taken in the dining rooms or the bar, accompanied by an ale from a local microbrewery. 'Everything is made on the premises and is nicely presented, delicious and served in generous portions.' Per room B&B single £65, double £80–£130. Dinner £22.
Read more, page 250.

HOWTOWN HOTEL
ULLSWATER

In an unspoilt part of the Lake District, this stone house appeals to those who prefer conversation to surfing the Internet – there is no Wi-Fi and only one television. The simple bedrooms have excellent storage, sheets and blankets on the beds; most rooms have a view of Lake Ullswater. A gong summons guests to a four-course dinner at 7 pm. Per person D,B&B £89.
Read more, page 293.

BEALACH HOUSE
DUROR

Reached by a challenging forestry track, Jim and Hilary McFadyen's small guest house is the only dwelling in Salachan Glen. The welcome is warm, and the communal dinners are liked by visitors. The bedrooms are not large but are well equipped (a tea and coffee tray, fresh chilled milk on the landing, a decanter of whisky). Per room B&B £90–£110. Set dinner £30.
Read more, page 332.

AEL Y BRYN
EGLWYSWRW

Near the Pembrokeshire coast, this former prisoner-of-war camp has been transformed into a striking guest house by Robert Smith and Arwel Hughes. There are unusual objects and furnishings; a spectacular chandelier in a baronial-style hall, a grand piano, an organ in the music room. Tables are 'well dressed' for dinner, a meal of 'traditional home cooking'. Per room B&B £96–£120. Set dinner £24–£28.
Read more, page 397.

WOOLLEY GRANGE
BRADFORD-ON-AVON

In extensive, rambling grounds, this Jacobean stone manor house is liked for its 'happy, relaxed attitude'. Part of the Luxury Family Hotels group, it has facilities for all ages; a giant trampoline, cheery play houses, and an indoor swimming pool. Children can choose from a variety of tasty dishes in the *Orangery*; adults can dine in style in the evening.
Read more, page 108

THE EVESHAM HOTEL
EVESHAM

Children will enjoy the happy atmosphere at John and Sue Jenkinson's quirky, informal hotel. There is much for them to do indoors (a play area, a swimming pool designed with younger visitors in mind) and outdoors (slides, a trampoline). Themed bedrooms add to the fun: an Alice in Wonderland-inspired family suite has a play nook under the beams. Children under 12 are included in the price of a family suite.
Read more, page 159.

MOONFLEET MANOR
FLEET

'A million out of a million,' said the *Guide*'s five-year-old inspector about this child-friendly Georgian house overlooking Chesil beach. A crèche (two sessions a day) is included in the cost of the stay; older children have play areas; there are three swimming areas (to accommodate different ages). Snoopy, the resident spaniel, likes to be taken for a walk in the grounds.
Read more, page 162.

FOWEY HALL
FOWEY

The inspiration for Toad Hall in *The Wind in the Willows*, this Victorian mansion has plenty to keep children occupied. The Four Bears Den is a crèche for the under-8s; older children have a games room, an outdoor play area and an indoor swimming pool. In the grounds are a trampoline and a play area with slides and swings. Baby-listening and baby-sitting can be arranged.
Read more, page 164.

AUGILL CASTLE
KIRKBY STEPHEN

Simon and Wendy Bennett welcome visitors in a laid-back manner to their family home, an eccentric neo-Gothic Victorian folly. Many of the bedrooms are big enough for a family; some are interconnected. Children are warmly welcomed ('my two-year-old daughter said she loved her castle'). Outdoors, there is a playground, a fort in a forest, a tree house. Early suppers, baby monitors and cots are available.
Read more, page 186.

CALCOT MANOR
TETBURY

The generations can happily co-exist at this luxury hotel, a converted 14th-century farmhouse in the Cotswolds. It combines many activities for children of all ages alongside separate spa sessions and fine dining for adults. Older children have the run of the *Mez*, which has games consoles, a cinema and an outdoor swimming pool. Little ones are looked after in the Ofsted-registered *Playzone*.
Read more, page 286.

SWINTON PARK
MASHAM

Falconry displays, mountain biking and a jungle gym are among the attractions at Mark and Felicity Cunliffe-Lister's 19th-century Gothic castle. The needs of younger visitors are catered for in the accommodation; a new family suite has a large bedroom for the parents, a seating area and a connected room for the children. Downstairs, a play room converts into a private cinema.
Read more, page 207.

LOCH MELFORT HOTEL
ARDUAINE

Toys, books and games are supplied in the family-friendly rooms at Calum and Rachel Ross's country hotel on Asknish Bay. Children have a playground with swings, slides and plenty of climbing. They can engage with the 'resident' Highland cattle and feed the ducks on the pond. The bistro has a child-friendly menu. A small beach is within walking distance.
Read more, page 316.

BEDRUTHAN HOTEL AND SPA
MAWGAN PORTH

Every member of the family is looked after at this large hotel which stands above a sandy beach. There are free child-care sessions, kids' clubs and entertainment (magicians and visits from nearby sea life centre). Toddlers have their own supervised club; older siblings can try out the swimming pools, playgrounds, a jungle gym. Family meals can be taken in the 'relaxed' *Wild Café*.
Read more, page 208.

PORTH TOCYN HOTEL
ABERSOCH

Children sharing their parents' bedroom are not charged at the Fletcher-Brewer family's unstuffy hotel in a magnificent setting above Cardigan Bay. Younger visitors have an 'area to escape' with television, books and a games room. There is an outdoor heated swimming pool and a 'makeshift' football pitch; many other activities are available nearby. The youngest can take high tea; the dinner menu can be adapted for the over-6s.
Read more, page 385.

THE CARY ARMS
BABBACOMBE

In a dramatic setting on a bay close to Torquay, Lana de Savary's small hotel has been given a nautical look suited to the setting. There are stripy deckchairs on a sea-facing terrace (*pictured above*) where meals can be taken alfresco. The bedrooms are decorated in New England style; all face the sea. There is a sandy beach in the bay, and other hidden coves are nearby.

Read more, page 81.

THE HENLEY
BIGBURY-ON-SEA

A private cliff path (recently restored) descends from the garden of this unpretentious Edwardian villa to the beach below on the tidal Avon estuary. Guests can take in the splendid view (binoculars provided) from the comfort of a Lloyd Loom chair in the lounge. Martyn Scarterfield and his wife, Petra Lampe, run the popular small hotel with relaxed informality. His cooking is much admired.

Read more, page 95.

THE WHITE HORSE
BRANCASTER STAITHE

The Norfolk Coastal Path runs at the bottom of the landscaped garden of Cliff Nye's small hotel above the tidal sea marshes. Bedrooms in a garden annexe, which have direct access to the path for walkers and dog owners, are furnished in appropriate seaside colours. Fish and shellfish brought in by local fishermen supply the kitchen for chef Avrum Frankel's 'very good' modern menus.

Read more, page 111

THE BEACH
BUDE

In a spectacular position above Summerleaze beach, this small hotel has been upgraded by its owner, William Daniel. He has introduced a bar with a 'rude cocktail' menu, and opened a restaurant with a Cuban chef. The beach is renowned for the good surfing for beginners and experts alike, and has a seawater swimming pool beneath the cliff.

Read more, page 122.

MULLION COVE HOTEL
MULLION COVE

On a cliff above Mullion Cove, this former railway hotel has been 'rescued and revived' by the Grose family. Most of the bedrooms face the sea (they are equipped with binoculars). Surrounded by National Trust land, the hotel is on the Coastal Path which leads to beaches and dramatic scenery. Dinner can be taken in the *Atlantic View* restaurant or an Art Deco-inspired bar.
Read more, page 219.

DRIFTWOOD HOTEL
PORTSCATHO

'The sea seems to stretch for ever' at Paul and Fiona Robinson's seaside-inspired hotel in an 'idyllic' setting overlooking Gerrans Bay on the Roseland peninsula. A path (with steep steps) leads through woodland to a 'blissful' private beach. There are hidden seating areas in the landscaped gardens. Bedrooms are decorated in shades of sand and sky; most are sea-facing.
Read more, page 247

SOAR MILL COVE HOTEL
SOAR MILL COVE

Family-run and child-friendly, Keith Makepeace's single-storey stone and slate hotel stands above a sandy beach framed by cliffs (good rock pooling). The well-equipped bedrooms, many with coastal views, have French doors opening on to a private patio. Within the grounds are a heated indoor saltwater pool and a play area. Coasteering, sailing and surfing expeditions can be arranged; good walking from the door.
Read more, page 269.

BALCARY BAY HOTEL
AUCHENCAIRN

On a coastline once populated by smugglers, Graeme Lamb's white-painted hotel has a 'beautiful setting' on the shore of the Solway Firth. It is well placed for exploration of the coast with its cliffs and quiet bays. Many rooms overlook the bay, others face the mature gardens. In the dining room, which faces the sea, chef Craig McWilliam serves 'delicious' meals.
Read more, page 317

DUNVALANREE IN CARRADALE
CARRADALE

At the end of a quiet road with beaches on both sides, Alan and Alyson Milstead's small hotel looks across Kilbrannan Sound to the Isle of Arran. A ground-floor room, which has French doors and a patio with tables and chairs, gives direct access to the shore. Alyson Milstead (the chef) is a founder member of the Scottish Seafood Trail, which promotes a West Coast culinary journey.
Read more, page 326.

THE COLONSAY
COLONSAY

On a hillside above the harbour, Jane and Alex Howard's renovated mid-18th-century inn is the only hotel on a 'magical' island which has more than a dozen beaches. It is run in a 'relaxed, unpretentious' style that is just right for the setting. The bedrooms, which vary in size and outlook, are simply furnished. At low tide, a mile-long stretch of sand joins Colonsay with the Isle of Oronsay.
Read more, page 328.

ROTHAY MANOR
AMBLESIDE

In large, landscaped gardens, a short walk from Lake Windermere, this Regency mansion (built for a wealthy Liverpool merchant) has been run in traditional style by the Nixon family for 45 years. The spacious bedrooms are 'immaculate and beautifully furnished'; the best have a balcony with views towards Wansfell Pike. In the refurbished dining room, Jane Binns uses local produce for her daily-changing menu.

Read more, page 72.

FARLAM HALL
BRAMPTON

The Quinion family's Victorian manor house recalls the 'heyday of country house hospitality', creating nostalgia for 'a more gracious era'. Sheltered by tall trees, it stands in landscaped grounds. There are open fires in the ornate public rooms which are furnished in extravagant Victorian style. In an elegant dining room, which has a 'warm satisfied buzz', Barry Quinion cooks 'imaginative but unfussy' dishes.

Read more, page 110.

GIDLEIGH PARK
CHAGFORD

In large grounds with formal gardens and marked walks on the River North Teign, Andrew and Christina Brownsword's luxurious hotel was built in Arts and Crafts style in the 1920s. Original features (wood panelling, leaded windows, a magnificent staircase) have been preserved in the public rooms. Executive chef Michael Caines has two *Michelin* stars for his sophisticated cooking

Read more, page 131.

GRAVETYE MANOR
EAST GRINSTEAD

In beautiful countryside, Jeremy and Elizabeth Hosking's 16th-century Elizabethan manor house stands in gardens designed by William Robinson, the pioneer of the English natural garden. The gardens and house have been extensively restored. The Arts and Crafts public rooms have dark wood panelling and bold floral displays, easy chairs on thick carpets. The bedrooms have antique furniture and modern technology.

Read more, page 151.

HAMBLETON HALL
HAMBLETON

'The perfect country house', Tim and Stefa Hart's luxury hotel (*pictured opposite*) is on a peninsula jutting into Rutland Water. The public rooms have antiques, spectacular flower arrangements. The best bedrooms have views of the water. In the candlelit restaurant, the chef, Aaron Patterson, has a *Michelin* star for his 'magnificent' cooking. Breakfast has 'divine' bread from Tim Hart's nearby bakery.
Read more, page 171.

LIME WOOD
LYNDHURST

The lack of airs and graces is liked at this relaxed country house hotel (with a modern twist) in extensive grounds in the New Forest. The bedrooms are in a 'stunning' Regency manor house and several 'beautifully designed' newer buildings. Angela Hartnett and Luke Holder are the chefs in the 'vibrant, buzzy' restaurant, *Hartnett Holder & Co*, which has British dishes with a strong Italian influence.
Read more, page 204.

CHEWTON GLEN
NEW MILTON

'Top drawer', this luxurious country house hotel stands out for 'sheer attention to detail'. Most of the bedrooms in the main house, which have antiques and modern fabrics, have a terrace, balcony or private garden. Tree-house suites in a wooded valley have a whirlpool tub on a wrap-around terrace and woodland views from a free-standing bathtub; breakfast hampers are delivered to the door.
Read more, page 223.

LORDS OF THE MANOR
UPPER SLAUGHTER

The staff are 'pleasant and courteous with just the right degree of interaction with the guests' at this 17th-century former rectory in superb gardens on the edge of a Cotswold village. Impeccable interiors have elegant antiques and modern furniture. In the formal dining room (white tablecloths, classic silverware and china), chef Richard Edwards has a *Michelin* star for his 'perfect' cooking.
Read more, page 295.

GLENAPP CASTLE
BALLANTRAE

Rescued from a state of disrepair by the owners, Graham and Fay Cowan, this baronial castle is run as a luxurious hotel. There is intricate plasterwork, an Austrian oak-panelled entrance and staircase, a parquet-floored library; 'beautiful' furnishings and fine paintings. The bedrooms are spacious. Chef Tyron Ellul uses garden and foraged produce for his modern dishes. Guests can wander in the wooded grounds, which have a magnificent Victorian glasshouse.
Read more, page 320.

LLANGOED HALL
LLYSWEN

'Everything is lovely' at this 17th-century mansion (redesigned by Sir Clough Williams-Ellis), which stands in large grounds on the River Wye. It was once owned by the late Sir Bernard Ashley, whose art collection is displayed throughout. Chef Nick Brodie combines produce from the garden with local ingredients for his modern dishes.
Read more, page 412.

THE ZETTER
LONDON

Full of retro styling, this quirky hotel is a conversion of the former headquarters of Zetter Pools. The bedrooms have been decorated with wit: bright, sometimes shocking colours, perhaps dark pink walls, olive fittings, a citrus yellow rug. They range from bijou to rooftop studios, each with a private terrace. All rooms have state-of-the-art technology and entertainment. The acclaimed restaurant, *Bistrot Bruno Loubet*, has picture windows facing St John's Square.
Read more, page 53.

THE ZETTER TOWNHOUSE
LONDON

The sister of the *Zetter*, this small town house hotel has been styled with equal flair. Modelled on the imagined jumble found in the house of an eccentric aunt, it is filled with portraits, old postcards, stuffed animals, Staffordshire dogs. Reclaimed furnishings, such as a wildly coloured and patterned bedhead made from an old fairground merry-go-round, give the bedrooms a zany look.
Read more, page 54.

THE LEVIN
LONDON

David Levin's sophisticated small town house hotel has a pistachio-coloured lobby with a dramatic 18-metre-long light installation cascading down the stairwell of a spiral staircase. The bedrooms are decorated in a discreet contemporary style; they have Art Nouveau furnishings, blocks of bold colour, designer lighting by Sarah Marsden, under-floor heating in a splendid marble bathroom. Deluxe rooms have an alcove seating area.
Read more, page 58.

THE GRAZING GOAT
LONDON

On a quiet street near Marble Arch, this pub has been given a modern rustic look: oak floors, coir carpets, pale woods, open fires. The bedrooms on the top three floors have an uncluttered, fresh feel with thoughtful furnishings; a superb bathroom. Under the watch of two stuffed, bearded goats, the ground-floor bar heaves with after-work drinkers. A British bistro menu is served in the oak-panelled first-floor dining room.
Read more, page 59.

THE QUEENSBERRY
BATH

Four 18th-century town houses with high ceilings and Georgian proportions have been given a surprisingly modern interior. The owners, Laurence and Helen Beere, have created bedrooms to look 'like the guest room in the house of some stylish friends'; each has its own character, and might be decorated with feature wallpaper, brown and taupe colours; a transparent plastic armchair. The split-level *Olive Tree* restaurant in the basement is 'a real draw'.
Read more, page 89.

JESMOND DENE HOUSE
NEWCASTLE UPON TYNE

At the head of a forested valley close to the city centre, Peter Candler's 'very good' hotel is a conversion of an Arts and Crafts mansion. Original features stand alongside modern designs and retro furnishings. There are ornate fireplaces, stained glass, oak panelling; contemporary art. The bedrooms, which vary in size and view, are decorated in muted shades with bursts of colour.
Read more, page 226.

38 ST GILES
NORWICH

On a street of independent shops, Jan and William Cheeseman's restored Grade II listed Georgian building 'has all the essential features of a boutique B&B: a stylish interior with quality bedding and bathroom fittings; and breakfast with tasty home-made things on the menu'. The 'spotless' bedrooms are reached by a fine square central staircase with a modern chandelier.
Read more, page 232.

HART'S HOTEL
NOTTINGHAM

In an elevated position overlooking the city, a quiet cul-de-sac on the site of a medieval castle, Tim and Stefa Hart's purpose-built hotel has modern lines with curved buttresses and lots of glass; much contemporary art on the walls. The bedrooms are 'small but well equipped'; garden rooms have French doors leading to a terrace with outdoor seating.
Read more, page 233.

OLD BANK
OXFORD

Many bedrooms have views of the city's dreaming spires at Jeremy Mogford's modern conversion of three old stone buildings (one was a bank) on the High, opposite All Souls. The well-appointed bedrooms have original artwork (many Stanley Spencer prints) from the owner's extensive collection; a marble bathroom. The former banking hall houses *Quod*, a lively bar/brasserie.
Read more, page 238.

THE PIG IN THE WALL
SOUTHAMPTON

Between medieval gates in the city wall, this white-painted building, brightly lit at night, is an 'eye-opening treat'. Robin Hutson and his wife, Judy, who was the designer, have turned it into a B&B hotel (*pictured opposite*), on the 'stylish side of shabby chic'. Everything in the bedrooms is modern and well thought out; each has a larder with snacks and drinks. Light meals and snacks are served at a ground-floor deli counter.
Read more, page 271.

BARNSLEY HOUSE
BARNSLEY

The Cotswold home of the late Rosemary Verey, acclaimed garden designer and author, is now run as a luxury hotel. The gardens remain true to her creation of layered (sometimes self-seeding) planting that provides colour and interest in every season. Her bold approach is reflected in a mix of features, including a laburnum walk, a temple with a pool, an ornamental fruit and vegetable garden and a knot garden.
Read more: page 82.

THE BATH PRIORY
BATH

Like a country house on the outskirts of the city, Andrew and Christina Brownsword's graceful building backs on to large and beautiful gardens. There are three acres of lawn, a wild meadow dominated by a 350-year-old cedar of Lebanon, Victorian gardens, an Italian garden with a water feature, and a sun terrace facing a croquet lawn. Country house comfort is combined with impeccable service in the hotel.
Read more: page 88.

LINDETH FELL
BOWNESS-ON-WINDERMERE

The Kennedy family's Edwardian house stands in lovely grounds overlooking Lake Windermere. The gardens were laid out by Thomas Mawson (a renowned Windermere landscape gardener), who filled them with rhododendrons, azaleas and specimen trees. When at their best, in spring and early summer, they are open to the public. A small lake is a haunt for wildlife. Lawns are laid for bowls and croquet.
Read more: page 106.

GIDLEIGH PARK
CHAGFORD

The River North Teign runs through the extensive grounds of this Arts and Crafts country house, now a luxurious hotel. Its gardens are full of colour throughout the year; wooden benches supply seating. There are marked walks along the river, and a water garden with pathways, bridges and miniature waterfalls. The kitchen garden supplies vegetables and herbs for the *Michelin*-two-star chef, Michael Caines.
Read more: page 131.

GRAVETYE MANOR
EAST GRINSTEAD
The pioneer of the English natural garden, William Robinson, created the fine gardens (*pictured opposite*) at this creeper-clad Elizabethan manor house, which is now run as a country house hotel. Much work has been done to restore the house (which was given an Arts and Crafts interior by Robinson) and the gardens. Head gardener Tom Coward writes a weekly blog on the planting.
Read more: page 151.

HOTEL ENDSLEIGH
MILTON ABBOT
Humphry Repton was commissioned by the Duchess of Bedford to design the gardens for this shooting and fishing lodge in an extensive wooded estate running down to the River Tamar. It is now run by Olga Polizzi as a luxury hotel. Repton created forested walks, wild meadows, a rose and jasmine walkway. There are rare and grand trees, a parterre beside the veranda, and a shell-covered summer house.
Read more: page 212.

MILLGATE HOUSE
RICHMOND
Just off the town's cobbled square, this Georgian house has an award-winning sheltered walled garden renowned for its clever planting. Owners Austin Lynch and Tim Culkin open it to the public from April to October. Residents can enjoy the garden in all seasons. Meandering paths lead through luxuriant planting; two of the three bedrooms overlook the garden and beyond to the River Swale and the Cleveland hills.
Read more: page 252.

STONE HOUSE
RUSHLAKE GREEN
Visitors to Jane and Peter Dunn's 15th-century house (with 18th-century modifications) are encouraged to explore the huge grounds. They have an ornamental lake, gazebos, a rose garden, a 100-foot herbaceous border, a walled herb, vegetable and fruit garden. In warm weather, guests can sit in the summer house, and visit the greenhouses.
Read more: page 257.

CLIVEDEN HOUSE
TAPLOW
In magnificent grounds managed by the National Trust, this stately home is run as a luxurious country house hotel. On chalk cliffs above a bend of the River Thames, it stands within 376 acres of formal gardens and woodlands, which have a celebrated parterre (created by John Fleming in 1855), distinctive floral displays, topiary and the Astor family's outstanding sculpture collection. Other features include an octagonal temple on the cliff edge, a maze and an amphitheatre.
Read more, page 281.

BODYSGALLEN HALL AND SPA
LLANDUDNO
In a wonderful situation, in parkland and gardens with views of Snowdonia and Conwy, this Grade I listed 17th-century mansion is now owned by the National Trust. A parterre of box hedges is filled with sweet-scented herbs; there's a walled rose garden; unusual trees including medlar and mulberry; a rockery with a cascade.
Read more: page 406.

LITTLE BARWICK HOUSE
BARWICK

In wooded grounds near the Somerset/
Dorset border, Tim (the chef) and
Emma Ford run their popular
restaurant-with-rooms (*pictured above*)
in a listed Georgian dower house.
He uses local produce for his 'well
presented but not over-elaborate' dishes,
perhaps marinated saddle of wild
venison, braised red cabbage, beetroot
purée, rösti potato. The smart bedrooms
are decorated in country style.
Read more, page 83.

READ'S
FAVERSHAM

Rona Pitchford is the 'warm,
professional host' at this handsome
Georgian manor house; her husband,
David, is the highly regarded chef. In
the candlelit restaurant ('not spoiled' by
background music), he serves seasonal
dishes like breast of corn-fed chicken,
galette potatoes, bacon lardons, lemon
thyme sauce. Each dish on the menu is
accompanied by a quotation, eg, 'no
man can be wise on an empty stomach
(George Eliot)'.
Read more: page 161.

THE GREAT HOUSE
LAVENHAM

The setting could not be more English –
a Georgian house on the market square
of a medieval wool town – but the food
and ambience are distinctly French at
Régis and Martine Crépy's restaurant-
with-rooms. Chef Enrique Bilbault
presents classic dishes like mint and
marjoram marinated lamb saddle,
garden pea 'cremeux', lamb jus, port
reduction. It is cooking 'of a high
standard', said an inspector.
Read more, page 189.

MR UNDERHILL'S
LUDLOW

In a conservation area by the River
Teme, Christopher and Judy Bradley
have created a distinctive restaurant-
with-rooms. She supervises the service
of his eight-course set meal (no choice
until dessert), which is presented on a
handwritten personalised menu. The
dishes have 'playful' combinations,
perhaps smoky aubergine custard,
sweet pepper cream, balsamic glaze.
The accommodation is in suites.
Read more, page 202.

MORSTON HALL
MORSTON

There is an air of anticipation when guests gather for canapés and pre-dinner drinks at Galton and Tracy Blackiston's Jacobean flint-and-brick mansion on the north Norfolk coast. Dinner is taken at a single sitting at 8 pm from a no-choice seven-course daily-changing menu of inventive dishes (perhaps longshore cod, girolles, pork crackling, warm egg yolk dressing, pork and Calvados jus).
Read more, page 217.

THE BLACK SWAN AT OLDSTEAD
OLDSTEAD

The 'welcoming' Banks family, who have farmed in the North Yorkshire Moors for generations, supervise all aspects of this restaurant-with-rooms. Tommy Banks is the young chef whose modern cooking is much praised. His menus have simple descriptions of dishes that are full of flavour, eg, pigeon, celeriac, hazelnut and savoy cabbage. The peaceful bedrooms overlook the countryside.
Read more, page 235.

THE YORKE ARMS
RAMSGILL-IN-NIDDERDALE

By the green in a village below the moors, this 17th-century former shooting lodge is run as a restaurant-with-rooms by Frances Atkins, the chef, and her husband, Bill, an affable and caring host. She uses the moors as a larder for her creative menus of seasonal dishes like local roast grouse, greens, bread sauce, bramble, heather-scented jus. The well-furnished bedrooms have high-tech fittings.
Read more, page 249.

THE ALBANNACH
LOCHINVER

On a hill above the fishing port, this handsome white-painted building is run in hands-on style by Lesley Crosfield and Colin Craig who share the cooking of 'exquisite' meals. They 'construct' the five-course (no-choice) menu daily, using herbs and vegetables 'grown organically to order' and local produce. Typical dishes: Assynt chanterelle risotto; roast saddle of wild roe deer, candied beetroot, croft baby turnip, game port sauce.
Read more, page 355.

TYDDYN LLAN
LLANDRILLO

'A truly lovely place', this pretty Georgian house facing the Berwyn Mountains is run by Bryan (the acclaimed chef) and Susan Webb, who runs front-of-house with 'allure and dynamism'. He dismisses the trend for foams and jellies in his presentation of modern dishes like grilled wild sea bass, laverbread butter sauce, Jersey royals, monk beards.
Read more, page 405.

PLAS BODEGROES
PWLLHELI

Visitors are drawn to the remote Lleyn peninsula by the superb cooking of Chris Chown, whose wife, Gunna, has styled the Georgian house in clean Scandinavian lines. He is assisted in the kitchen by Hugh Bracegirdle, producing imaginative menus of modern dishes like crispy belly pork, black pudding scotch egg; fillet of Faroese plateau cod, parsnip purée, beurre rouge.
Read more: page 419.

THE VICTORIA
LONDON

A popular local gathering place, this pub-with-rooms near Richmond Park is owned by celebrity chef Paul Merrett and restaurateur Greg Bellamy. In the handsome conservatory restaurant, the menus are imaginative with dishes like pan-seared hake fillet, potato and nettle purée, brown shrimp butter. The simple bedrooms have modern furnishings.
Read more, page 61.

THE BILDESTON CROWN
BILDESTON

'A must for foodies', this handsome old inn in a Suffolk village is owned by local farmer James Buckle and run by Chris Lee, the chef, and his wife, Hayley, the manager. 'Cooking is of a high standard' in *Ingrams* restaurant where the dishes include beef from the owner's herd of Red Poll cattle (perhaps beef fillet, braised shin, crispy bone marrow, creamed parsley, roasted garlic). Drinks and informal meals are taken in two 'congenial' bar areas.
Read more, page 97.

THE HORSE AND GROOM
BOURTON-ON-THE-HILL

In a honey-stone Cotswold village, this former coaching inn is run as a pub-with-rooms by brothers Tom and Will (the chef) Greenstock. The food is of a 'consistently high standard' in the 'cheerful' dining room. Vegetables from the garden and local produce are used for the 'imaginative yet unpretentious' menus in dishes like braised shin of Dexter beef, garlic, ginger, steamed greens, sesame noodles. Smart, modern bedrooms 'have all the essentials'.
Read more, page 105.

THE TROUT AT TADPOLE BRIDGE
BUCKLAND MARSH

By a narrow bridge over the River Thames, Gareth and Helen Pugh's 'unpretentious' 17th-century stone inn (*pictured above*) has an informal atmosphere. In the restaurant, chef Pascal Clavaud's modern dishes might include guinea fowl cooked three ways (roasted breast, confit leg and beignets), caramelised shallots. The well-equipped bedrooms are individually designed.
Read more, page 121.

THE SUN INN
DEDHAM

Opposite St Mary's church on Dedham's main street, this friendly inn has been sympathetically restored by the owner, Piers Baker. It has a beamed and wood-panelled interior with open fires and an inviting low-ceilinged dining room. The chefs, Ugo Simonelli and Ewan Naylon, serve a daily-changing modern menu with an Italian influence, with dishes like calf's liver, Marsala, sage, olive oil potato purée, spinach.
Read more, page 148.

THE ROYAL OAK
EAST LAVANT

In a village at the foot of the South Downs, Charles Ullmann's 200-year-old inn has a rustic decor. Chef Paul Tansley keeps the journey from field to fork short for his modern dishes (eg, duo of Funtington pork, marmalade, crackling and local vegetables). In warm weather, meals can be taken on a terrace or in the small garden. The well-equipped bedrooms are in the main building and a converted cottage and barn.
Read more, page 153.

THE FEATHERED NEST
NETHER WESTCOTE

In a quiet village, Tony and Amanda Timmer's rural inn has views of the verdant Evenlode valley. A kitchen garden supplies herbs and vegetables for chef Kuba Winkowski's 'excellent' modern dishes, perhaps poussin, duck liver, girolles, smoked mash potato, shallot. Informal meals may be taken in the popular bar or, in warm weather, on the terrace. The 'peaceful' bedrooms have many extra touches.
Read more, page 221.

THE CAT INN
WEST HOATHLY

In a pretty hilltop village on the Sussex Weald, Andrew Russell's 16th-century inn is a 'modern take on the traditional pub'. The cooking of the chef, Max Leonard, is much admired: a typical dish might be middle white pork schnitzel, gremolata, aïoli, fries and salad. The wine list has several Sussex wines. The bedrooms are 'simply but pleasantly furnished'.
Read more, page 302.

THE GURNARD'S HEAD
ZENNOR

Local growers are invited to bring their fruit and vegetables to the kitchen of Charles and Edmund Inkin's laid-back inn in an isolated coastal position near Land's End. Matt Smith is now the chef, cooking a seasonal menu that might include brill, crushed potatoes, spinach, mussel and dill cream. 'There are lovely Cornish beers and gulpable wines.' The simple bedrooms 'lack for nothing'.
Read more, page 314.

THE FELIN FACH GRIFFIN
FELIN FACH

'A modern version of a traditional inn', this old roadside hostelry is managed by Julie Bell for Charles and Edmund Inkin (who also own the *Gurnard's Head*, above). Ross Bruce, the chef, works closely with the kitchen gardener, Joe Hand, to secure vegetables, fruit and herbs for his seasonal menus of dishes like Bryn Derw chicken breast, spring greens, hash brown. There are books and a Roberts radio in the bedrooms.
Read more, page 398.

BLAGDON MANOR
ASHWATER

Dogs are warmly welcomed at Liz and Steve Morey's restaurant-with-rooms in rolling countryside near Dartmoor. 'The kings of the place are the Moreys' friendly Labradors, who are the first to welcome you.' Visiting dogs (charged at £10 a night) are given a fleece blanket, bowl and treats 'to make their stay as comfortable as yours'.
Read more, page 75.

THE TRADDOCK
AUSTWICK

Dogs are welcome to stay in all the bedrooms (£5 per day charge) at the Reynolds family's small country hotel in the Yorkshire Dales national park. Towels and dog-washing facilities are provided. Dogs may sit with their owners in the lounges provided they are on a lead. The grounds have plenty of space for a gambol. Wonderful walking all around.
Read more, page 78.

COMBE HOUSE
HONITON

Dogs are welcomed in certain rooms (£12 a night) at Ken and Ruth Hunt's Grade I listed Elizabethan manor house on a large country estate. In the thatched cottage in the grounds, dogs can play in a secure garden. A K9 survival box is given to visiting dogs, as well as an illustrated book of dog-friendly walks.
Read more, page 180.

OVERWATER HALL
IREBY

There is no extra charge for visiting dogs, who are 'genuinely welcomed' at this castellated Georgian mansion in the northern Lake District. They can join their owners in one of the lounges ('not on chairs, please') and in the bedrooms. For exercise, there is no need to leave the 18-acre grounds which have a woodland boardwalk. A dog-sitting service can be arranged for 'those rainy days when your four-legged friend might not be welcome at an art gallery'.
Read more, page 184.

THE CROWN AND CASTLE
ORFORD

'We love our doggie visitors, who give us very little trouble,' says Ruth Watson, co-owner of this Suffolk hotel/restaurant. Arriving dogs are welcomed with home-made treats. They may stay in one of the five garden rooms (£6 per dog, per night charge). Organic cheese biscuits, poop bags, feeding bowls, dog food, spare leads, towels and an extra bed cover over can be provided. There is a (bookable) doggie table in the restaurant area.
Read more, page 236.

PLUMBER MANOR
STURMINSTER NEWTON

'Dogs are always welcome because there are two lovely resident black Labradors,' say the Prideaux-Brune family. There is a £10 per visit charge for canines staying in one of four courtyard bedrooms which have direct access to the grounds. They are not allowed in the main house. Staff will take dogs 'for a quick walk whenever necessary'.
Read more, page 278.

PRINCE HALL
TWO BRIDGES

Polo, the resident host, warmly welcomes other canines to Fi and Chris Daly's small hotel high on Dartmoor. 'Doggy decadence' (at no extra charge) is promised, with exceptional opportunities to romp in the grounds and on the moors. Bedrooms have space for 'a pet bed or two'; treats are provided. Polo can advise on the 'best spots to curl up while the owners enjoy lunch or dinner'.
Read more, page 292.

KILCAMB LODGE
STRONTIAN

'The outdoor life of the Highlands simply has to be shared with your best pal, so don't leave it at home,' say Sally and David Ruthven-Fox. Spike, the resident dog, welcomes canine visitors; his Facebook entry gives helpful advice. He recommends walks in the ancient forests, and splashing in the loch. Four pet-friendly rooms are close to an exit that leads directly into the grounds for 'calls of nature'. £10 per night charge.
Read more, page 372.

THE FALCONDALE
LAMPETER

The 'friendly and inquisitive' Pudgeley and Major welcome canine guests to this Italianate hotel in landscaped gardens above the Teifi valley. The owners, Chris and Lisa Hutton, have a flexible approach to number and size of dogs in each room (£10 a night charge). Bowls and treats are provided; torches are available for early-morning and/or late-night walkies.
Read more, page 403.

RATHMULLAN HOUSE
RATHMULLAN

Brushie, the resident Jack Russell, welcomes visiting canines to the Wheeler family's handsome white mansion on the shores of Lough Swilly. 'But be warned,' says Mark Wheeler, 'she is known as the MD.' A special doggie room (€20 per night) adjoins the human bedroom in the courtyard extension; it has a bed, doggie pics and a coat hook; there is direct access to the gardens. There is good walking on the beach.
Read more, page 459.

BRIDGEHOUSE
BEAMINSTER
Three public rooms are licensed for wedding ceremonies at this lovely old hotel, a 700-year-old building by a bridge over the River Brit. Up to 50 guests can attend the ceremony and as many as 80 can join the wedding breakfast in the dining room; in summer, the garden brasserie offers an alfresco alternative. Exclusive weekend wedding parties can be arranged.
Read more, page 91.

MONTAGU ARMS
BEAULIEU
A red-carpet welcome awaits couples who make an exclusive booking for their wedding at this 22-bedroom Georgian country house in the New Forest. A master of ceremonies will guide the couple through the day which includes the ceremony and dinner in the *Michelin*-starred *Terrace* restaurant. More intimate weddings can be held in the Paris room which has an ornate fireplace.
Read more, page 92.

AUGILL CASTLE
KIRKBY STEPHEN
'No two weddings are the same at *Augill Castle*,' say Simon and Wendy Bennett who arrange bespoke events at their eccentric neo-Gothic Victorian folly in the upper Eden valley. A marquee can be pitched in the two-acre grounds for a two-day wedding house party for 30 adults and 10 children; many of the bedrooms are inter-connected for a family.
Read more, page 186.

LANGAR HALL
LANGAR
The first venue in Nottinghamshire to be licensed for civil weddings, Imogen Skirving's honey-stone Georgian mansion specialises in intimate weddings for up to 50 guests. There are 12 bedrooms (each decorated to an individual theme) to accommodate guests for house-party weddings; a marquee on the lawn allows for larger events. Ed Miliband, the Labour Party leader, chose Langar Hall for his wedding in 2011.
Read more, page 187.

SWINTON PARK
MASHAM

A two-night exclusive wedding package at Mark and Felicity Cunliffe-Lister's 19th-century Gothic castle opens with an activity evening, perhaps a game of cricket or a treasure hunt followed by a barbecue. The family-friendly house stands in extensive grounds with parkland, a lake and a walled garden. Blessings and alfresco celebrations can take place in the Deerhouse a short distance from the castle.
Read more, page 207.

ROSE IN VALE
ST AGNES

'Country house weekend weddings' can be organised at this elegant Georgian manor in a wooded Cornish valley. This includes accommodation for 45 people, a Friday night supper and the ceremony and the wedding breakfast. The ceremony can be held in a summer house in the garden or in the Valley room. More intimate events can also be organised.
Read more, page 259.

ARDANAISEIG
KILCHRENAN

In a remote and romantic setting, in wooded grounds by the shores of Loch Awe, this late Georgian baronial manor has an opulent interior. The wedding ceremony can be held in the hotel or in a small 18th-century stone church just four miles away; in summer, an amphitheatre by the water provides an unusual alternative. Up to 50 guests can take the wedding breakfast in the dining room which has picture windows facing the loch.
Read more, page 348.

KNOCKINAAM LODGE,
PORTPATRICK

Destination weddings, which include the ceremony, celebration and honeymoon, can be arranged by the wedding planners at this grey stone 19th-century hunting lodge, which faces a small curved bay by the Irish Sea. Help will be given in booking the registrar for a Scottish wedding. Special rates are available for exclusive use of the ten-bedroom hotel. The chef, Tony Pierce, has a *Michelin* star for his modern Scottish menus.
Read more, page 364.

YNYSHIR HALL
EGLWYSFACH

The bride and groom can arrive by helicopter if they choose at this luxury hotel/restaurant, a pretty manor house in large and lovely grounds by an RSPB reserve. Wedding packages for up to 35 guests can be arranged. There are dramatic artworks in the public rooms; bedrooms, named after famous artists, have a colourful decor. In the restaurant, chef Gareth Ward serves elaborate modern dishes.
Read more, page 396.

BALLYMALOE HOUSE
SHANAGARRY

In the lush countryside of east Cork, the Allen family's renowned hotel/restaurant has been at the forefront of relaxed Irish hospitality for 50 years. Wedding parties of various sizes can be hosted in one of the cheerful dining rooms; larger parties have use of the recently converted grain store in the grounds. The family farm supplies produce for the restaurant where the cooking is highly regarded.
Read more, page 462.

HARTWELL HOUSE
AYLESBURY

In the grounds of this stately home, which is owned by the National Trust, this purpose-built spa has been styled like an orangery with high arch windows. It has a large swimming pool, spa bath, steam room, sauna. On a sun terrace, an all-weather hot tub has 28 hydro jets. There is a gymnasium and four treatment rooms. Drinks and light meals are served all day in the spa café and bar.

Read more, page 80.

BARNSLEY HOUSE
BARNSLEY

A winding path through the gardens leads to a spa and skincare centre at this relaxed country hotel, a William and Mary house in a Cotswold village. Designed to reflect the gardens, it has floor-to-ceiling windows, plants and aromatic herbs which hang from wooden beams. Inside is a steam room, a sauna and five treatment rooms (for holistic and beauty treatments). On the terrace is a heated hydrotherapy pool.

Read more, page 82.

PARK HOUSE
BEPTON

A 15-metre mother-of-pearl swimming pool with a marble entry shower is at the centre of the spa at this country hotel in rural Sussex. Other facilities include a gym and fitness studio (personal trainer on request), a whirlpool bath, saunas and relaxation room. A 'decadent champagne experience' allows use of the facilities, followed by a glass of bubbly, afternoon tea and a massage or facial.

Read more, page 93.

DART MARINA
DARTMOUTH

Holistic and luxurious treatments (including organic hand, nail and foot therapies) are available in the spa at this smart hotel beside the River Dart. A fitness suite has cycles, treadmills and a cross-trainer; in the exercise pool you can swim against the current; there's a spa bath and a steam room, a gym and a heated indoor swimming pool.

Read more, page 145.

LIME WOOD
LYNDHURST

'We don't do average,' is the claim at *Lime Wood*, a contemporary hotel in the New Forest. *The Herb House* spa combines relaxation opportunities with serious health and fitness facilities. Guests can do yoga in a herb garden on a roof. Couples can escape to one of the two double treatment rooms; each has a steam room and a private bath (one outdoor, the other indoor). A walkway through the trees leads to the Mintarium, a sun deck meditation area anchored by ancient olive trees.

Read more, page 204.

THE SCARLET
MAWGAN PORTH

Luxurious tented treatment rooms are lit by lanterns at the spa at this adults-only hotel above an Atlantic beach. The focus is on holistic well-being and the nourishment of the mind, body and soul. A Cornish twist is added to Ayurveda treatments. 'Messy mineral mud sessions' can be taken in a hammam; outside is a natural chemical-free swimming pool.

Read more, page 209.

CHEWTON GLEN
NEW MILTON

A state-of-the-art gymnasium and a dance studio with daily programmes of exercise and relaxation classes are among the attractions of the spa (*pictured opposite*) at this luxurious country house hotel on the edge of the New Forest. Manicures and zen pedicures can be taken in the grooming lounge. The 17-metre swimming pool is ozone treated; there are aromatherapy saunas and crystal steam rooms.

Read more, page 223.

CALCOT MANOR
TETBURY

In the grounds of this luxury Cotswold hotel, the spa has a soft-lit courtyard, floor-to-ceiling windows and a heated outdoor swimming pool surrounded by stone-green slate. Indoors is a larger swimming pool, and a separate pool for children to splash in; rooms for relaxation and beauty treatments; and a gym with top-of-the-range equipment.

Read more, page 286.

ISLE OF ERISKA HOTEL
ERISKA

As much a resort as a luxury hotel, this baronial mansion is on a private island which has a nine-hole golf course, a driving range and a sports hall with badminton and table tennis. On the first floor of a converted stable block is a spa with a heated outdoor swimming pool, sauna and steam room. Treatments include therapeutic detoxification. Holistic and luxury day packages come with a voucher for a Bento box for a light lunch.

Read more, page 339.

THE LAKE
LLANGAMMARCH WELLS

Once the only barium spa resort outside Germany (Kaiser Wilhelm II visited in 1912), this country house hotel stands by a lake on the River Irfon. A short walk from the main building, the spa has a swimming pool and outdoor tub on a balcony overlooking the lake. The energetic can use the gym or play tennis; for relaxation, a wide range of health and beauty treatments can be taken. These include Indian head massage, reflexology and hot-stone massage.

Read more, page 409.

BUDOCK VEAN
MAWNAN SMITH

The Barlow family's traditional hotel has its own nine-hole golf course (with 18 tees) running through the grounds on the banks of the Helford river. The parkland course presents a challenge with a lengthy par 5 and several dog-leg par 4s. Unlimited golf is free to guests, who also have access to two nearby courses.

Read more: page 210.

ST ENODOC
ROCK

Above the Camel estuary, this seaside hotel is close to St Enodoc golf club, one of the most evocative links courses in England. Designed by James Braid, doyen of golf architects, it has undulating fairways, firm greens, blind shots and superb sea estuary views. Hidden fairway bunkers will catch out the unwary player. The tenth hole, which winds past the 11th-century church where John Betjeman is buried, is the toughest on the course. The poet was a keen, if not accomplished, golfer.

Read more: page 254.

GLENAPP CASTLE
BALLANTRAE

Some of Scotland's best links courses are within easy reach of this 19th-century baronial castle (now a luxury hotel) in South Ayrshire. They include Turnberry, a regular venue for the Open championship. Tee times can be arranged here and at Royal Troon, another historic Open venue. Guests have access to the private course at nearby Caley Palace, a fine parkland layout.

Read more: page 320.

KILMICHAEL COUNTRY HOUSE
BRODICK

Golf might not be the main topic of conversation in the drawing rooms of this period house in the main village on the Isle of Arran, but the island has some outstanding courses. Brodick has an 18-hole layout ribboned by two burns. Don't miss the 12-hole Shiskine course, a quintessential links experience with roller-coaster fairways and blind shots across dunes; this is links golf in its purest form.

Read more: page 324.

THE DOWER HOUSE
MUIR OF ORD

Robyn and Mena Aitchison are friendly hosts at their gabled cottage-orné in a large garden bordered by two rivers. A keen golfer, he can advise guests on the 25 courses within an hour's drive. Try the championship links at Nairn, which has hosted the Walker Cup: you can see the Moray Firth from every hole, and it is possible to strike the ball into the sea on the first seven.
Read more: page 356.

ISLE OF ERISKA HOTEL
ERISKA

On a private island near Oban, the Buchanan-Smith family's luxury hotel has its own nine-hole course fashioned in true links style to blend with the natural terrain. Practice facilities include a putting green, a short game area and a full-size driving range. For other challenges, try the nearby Glencruitten course, a short but testing parkland course on a hilly estate near Oban.
Read more: page 339.

TREFEDDIAN HOTEL
ABERDYFI

Guests at this large, traditional Edwardian hotel have only to cross the road to play at Aberdyfi links course, which lies below the hotel on the dunes of Cardigan Bay. The toughest test is the 12th, a par 3 to an elevated green with the sea to the right, and a steep bank to the left that kicks away anything other than the correct shot. Younger players can limber up on the pitch-and-putt course in the grounds.
Read more: page 383.

CASTLE COTTAGE
HARLECH

Guests at this restaurant-with-rooms run by chef/proprietor Glyn Roberts and his wife, Jacqueline, receive a ten per cent discount at Royal St David's, Harlech, perhaps the finest links course in Wales. The drive from the elevated 14th tee has to carry sand dunes and rough ground to reach the green; this heralds a tough finish through the dunes.
Read more: page 401.

CARRIG COUNTRY HOUSE
CARAGH LAKE

On the lakeshore, Frank and Mary Slattery's small hotel is within easy distance of a host of fine courses. The nearest, Dooks, is one of Ireland's oldest links, combining stunning views with testing golf. The famous lakeside courses at Killarney will examine a golfer's technique: Killeen might be the flagship course, but the 18th at the shorter Mahony's Point, a par 3 across the corner of the lake, will linger long in the memory.
Read more: page 438.

RATHSALLAGH HOUSE
DUNLAVIN

The O'Flynn family's 'low-key' yet 'totally spoiling' country house hotel has its own championship golf course. Designed by Christie O'Connor Jnr and Peter McEvoy, it is a parkland course across rolling countryside through which small streams meander. Greens are firm and true.
Read more: page 445.

BIGGIN HALL
BIGGIN-BY-HARTINGTON

High in the Peak District, this small
hotel is popular with walkers for its
simple, unfussy style. Footpaths lead in
all directions over beautiful countryside;
disused railway tracks nearby provide
flat walking. The 17th-century house
has antiques, mullioned windows.
Bedrooms in a barn conversion have a
porch. 'Sustaining' packed lunches of
'well-filled sandwiches, fresh fruit and
crisps' are included in the room rate.
Read more: page 96.

BATTLESTEADS
HEXHAM

In a sparsely populated area on the edge
of the Northumberland national park,
this excellent small hotel and restaurant
is well placed for visitors walking on
Hadrian's Wall or the moors; Kielder
water and forest park, the largest
working forest in England, is nearby. A
large communal drying room is useful
for walkers, as are the 'excellent
sandwiches for picnics, with generous
filling, and flavour'.
Read more: page 178.

UNDERLEIGH HOUSE
HOPE

There is good walking from the door at
Philip and Vivienne Taylor's barn and
cottage conversion in the Hope valley
in the Peak District national park. The
'generous' hosts will provide advice on
the best walks, a packed lunch, and a
complimentary tray of tea and cakes
to returning walkers (waterproofs
will be dried). The award-winning
breakfast will sustain even the hardiest
of walkers.
Read more: page 181.

OVERWATER HALL
IREBY

A booklet of local walks can be
purchased and Ordnance Survey maps
can be borrowed by guests at this
castellated Georgian mansion beside
Overwater Tarn, close to Bassenthwaite
Lake. There is good walking, from a
lakeside ramble to a more demanding
mountain climb. Because this is the
quieter Northern Lakes, 'you often
have it all to yourself'. In the 18-acre
grounds, a boardwalk snakes through
nursery woodland.
Read more: page 184.

LASTINGHAM GRANGE
LASTINGHAM

In large grounds on the edge of the
North York Moors national park, this
traditional hotel is run by Bertie Wood,
helped by his mother, Jane, and brother,
Tom. From the door, there is superb
walking in the moors and dales. Guided
walks are available: perhaps a llama trek
on the moors, or a dawn safari through
forest and woodland, returning in time
for breakfast.
Read more: page 188.

PEN-Y-DYFFRYN
OSWESTRY

A folder of walks, all starting from the
front door, is available to guests at this
small hillside hotel which is surrounded
by hills and mountains on the English/
Welsh border. The walks range from
30 minutes to all-day treks (with a
recommended pub stop). Packed
lunches can be provided. The long-
distance Offa's Dyke footpath is just a
mile away.
Read more: page 237.

THE BURGOYNE
REETH

At the top of the green in a village on
Alfred Wainwright's coast-to-coast
walking route, this small hotel, a listed
Georgian house, provides ready activity
for the casual walker and the serious
rambler alike. Packed lunches are
available for guests who can set off from
the village to walk along the River
Swale or to spend a day on the moors.
Read more: page 251.

HOWTOWN HOTEL
ULLSWATER

A car-free holiday is possible at this
unsophisticated hotel on the quiet
eastern shore of Lake Ullswater. It is
run in relaxed style by Jacquie Baldry
and her son, David. Walkers can ask for
a substantial picnic before heading out
along the shores of the lake, or on to the
wooded hillside. There is no phone, TV
or radio in the simple bedrooms.
Read more: page 293.

TIRORAN HOUSE
TIRORAN

On the island of Mull, Laurence and
Katie Mackay's white-painted Victorian
hunting lodge is liked for its house-
party atmosphere. There are walks on
the island to suit all tastes. The hotel is
in the foothills of Ben More, the island's
only Munro. A track above the house
leads to a shoreline walk along the
remote Ardmeanach peninsula. This
walk is challenging but rewarding.
Read more: page 375.

THE MANOR TOWN HOUSE
FISHGUARD

The Pembrokeshire Coastal Path can be
joined in the wooded valley below this
B&B, a Georgian house near the town
square of the ferry port. The excellent
local bus services allow walkers to tackle
the Coastal Path further afield and
return in comfort for teas and home-
baked cakes on the sea-facing terrace.
The Poppet Rocket runs along the coast
to Cardigan; the Strumble Shuttle to
St David's.
Read more: page 399.

THE COTTAGE IN THE WOOD
BRAITHWAITE

Within England's only mountain forest, this converted 17th-century coaching inn has fine views to the Skiddaw mountain range (with sightings of the red squirrels and roe deer that populate the woodland). The converted 17th-century whitewashed coaching inn is run as a restaurant-with-rooms by Kath and Liam Berney. The conservatory restaurant overlooks the surrounding forest.
Read more, page 109.

SWINSIDE LODGE
NEWLANDS

At the foot of Cat Bells and surrounded by Lake District peaks, this white-painted Georgian house is run as a small hotel by Mike and Kath Bilton. All the bedrooms have 'thrilling' views towards Cat Bells and Causey Pike, or Skiddaw and Blencathra mountains. The only disturbance in the morning is from the dawn chorus or possibly the bleating of lambs on the hills.
Read more, page 227.

PEN-Y-DYFFRYN
OSWESTRY

In beautiful countryside on the last hill in Shropshire, this former Georgian rectory is run as a small country hotel by the owners, Miles and Audrey Hunter. Most of the 'delightful' bedrooms have splendid views of the Welsh hills. Rooms in the coach house have a private patio opening on to the garden. The restaurant has south-west facing sash windows.
Read more, page 237.

TIGH AN DOCHAIS
BROADFORD

Designed by award-winning architects to make the most of the views across Broadford Bay, this contemporary building is entered by a bridge to the upper floor, where the guest lounge and dining room have full-length picture windows facing the tidal bay. Each of the three bedrooms on the floor below has an equally inspiring aspect. It is run as a B&B by 'friendly' owners Neil Hope and Lesley Unwin.
Read more, page 323.

THE THREE CHIMNEYS AND HOUSE OVER-BY
DUNVEGAN

In the remote north-west corner of Skye, this restaurant-with-rooms has long been popular with gourmet travellers prepared to go the extra mile. They can savour unfettered views of Loch Dunvegan as they enjoy the Isle of Skye showcase menu. Each of the bedrooms has a sea view and direct access to the garden with a pathway to the shore. Breakfast is taken in a light-filled room with a telescope.
Read more, page 331.

KYLESKU HOTEL
KYLESKU

In a 'setting few hotels can equal' (a comment by *Guide* inspectors), this white-painted inn is run as a small hotel by Tanja Lister and Sonia Virechauveix. It stands beside a working harbour on a sea loch. The bar, restaurant and lounge all have an unrivalled outlook over the sea where seals and birdlife can be watched. Four of the bedrooms face the sea.
Read more, page 353.

MOOR OF RANNOCH HOTEL
RANNOCH STATION

'A place to get away from it all', this recently renovated hotel stands at the end of the road on the edge of the moor. Although it is 16 miles from the nearest settlement, it is close to a station on the West Highland railway line. In two of the bedrooms, the bed is on a raised platform to enable a view of the magnificent scenery. The outlook is as good from the dining room.
Read more, page 366.

SCARISTA HOUSE
SCARISTA

On the 'beautiful' and remote Isle of Harris, this white-painted Georgian manse (*pictured opposite*) looks across fields to the white shell sands of a three-mile-long beach. The sense of peace and the views of the sea and the surrounding hills are 'remarkable', say visitors. The bedrooms are in the main house and in a converted outbuilding.
Read more, page 368.

BURRASTOW HOUSE
WALLS

In a 'magnificent' setting on the western edge of the island, this small, 'very comfortable' guest house is run in personal style by the owner, Pierre Dupont. Built in 1759 as a 'Haa' house for the local laird, it looks across a sandy-bottomed bay to the island of Vaila. A silent night is guaranteed in the bedrooms.
Read more, page 379.

BRYNIAU GOLAU
BALA

In an elevated position on the eastern edge of Snowdonia national park, this Victorian house has 'wonderful' views over Lake Bala to the Arenig Mountains. 'Breathtaking' sunsets over the mountains can be watched from the terrace. Each of the bedrooms has a view of the lake. In fine weather, guests can take tea on the terrace or explore the gardens which have lots of corners for relaxation.
Read more, page 387.

Each of these hotels has
a tennis court (T) and/or a
swimming pool (S)

LONDON
One Aldwych,
  Strand (S)

ENGLAND
Deans Place,
  Alfriston (S)
Askham Hall,
  Askham (S)
Hartwell House,
  Aylesbury (T,S)
Bath Priory,
  Bath (S)
Park House,
  Bepton (T,S)
Burgh Island,
  Bigbury-on-Sea (T,S)
Blakeney,
  Blakeney (S)
Woolley Grange,
  Bradford-on-Avon (S)
Hell Bay,
  Bryher (S)
Gidleigh Park,
  Chagford (T)
Tor Cottage,
  Chillaton (S)
Rectory,
  Crudwell (S)
Dart Marina,
  Dartmouth (S)

Old Whyly,
  East Hoathly (T,S)
Starborough Manor,
  Edenbridge (S)
Evesham,
  Evesham (S)
Moonfleet Manor,
  Fleet (S)
Fowey Hall,
  Fowey (S)
Stock Hill House,
  Gillingham (T)
Hambleton Hall,
  Hambleton (T,S)
Augill Castle,
  Kirkby Stephen (T)
Feathers,
  Ledbury (S)
Lime Wood,
  Lyndhurst (S)
Bedruthan,
  Mawgan Porth (T,S)
Scarlet,
  Mawgan Porth (S)
Budock Vean,
  Mawnan Smith (T,S)
Eshott Hall,
  Morpeth (T)
Mullion Cove,
  Mullion Cove (S)
TerraVina,
  Netley Marsh (S)

Chewton Glen,
  New Milton (T,S)
Old Rectory,
  Norwich (S)
Penzance,
  Penzance (S)
St Enodoc,
  Rock (S)
Rose in Vale,
  St Agnes (S)
Star Castle,
  St Mary's (T,S)
Soar Mill Cove,
  Soar Mill Cove (T,S)
Plumber Manor,
  Sturminster Newton (T)
Cliveden House,
  Taplow (T,S)
Calcot Manor,
  Tetbury (T,S)
Nare,
  Veryan-in-Roseland (T,S)
Holbeck Ghyll,
  Windermere (T)
Watersmeet,
  Woolacombe (S)
Middlethorpe Hall,
  York (S)

SCOTLAND
Glenapp Castle,
  Ballantrae (T)
Isle of Eriska,
  Eriska (T,S)
Inverlochy Castle,
  Fort William (T)
Ardanaiseig,
  Kilchrenan (T)
Kirroughtree House,
  Newton Stewart (T)
Skirling House,
  Skirling (T)

WALES
Trefeddian,
  Aberdyfi (T,S)
Porth Tocyn,
  Abersoch (T,S)
Glangrwyney Court,
  Crickhowell (T)
Gliffaes,
  Crickhowell (T)
Bodysgallen Hall and Spa,
  Llandudno (T,S)
St Tudno,
  Llandudno (S)
Lake,
  Llangammarch Wells (T,S)
Portmeirion,
  Portmeirion (S)

CHANNEL ISLANDS
White House,
  Herm (T,S)
Atlantic,
  St Brelade (T,S)
Longueville Manor,
  St Saviour (T,S)

IRELAND
Rathsallagh House,
  Dunlavin (T)
Marlfield House,
  Gorey (T)
Shelburne Lodge,
  Kenmare (T)
Rosleague Manor,
  Letterfrack (T)
Currarevagh House,
  Oughterard (T)
Rathmullan House,
  Rathmullan (T,S)
Coopershill,
  Riverstown (T)
Ballymaloe House,
  Shanagarry (T,S)

Each of these hotels has at least one bedroom equipped for a visitor in a wheelchair. You should telephone to discuss individual requirements

LONDON

Zetter
Clerkenwell

Victoria
Mortlake

One Aldwych
Strand

Goring
Victoria

ENGLAND

Wentworth,
Aldeburgh

Deans Place,
Alfriston

Rothay Manor,
Ambleside

Hartwell House,
Aylesbury

Bath Priory,
Bath

Park House,
Bepton

Bildeston Crown,
Bildeston

du Vin, Birmingham,
Birmingham

Lord Crewe Arms,
Blanchland

Millstream,
Bosham

White Horse,
Brancaster Staithe

Brooks,
Bristol

Hell Bay,
Bryher

George,
Buckden

Northcote Manor,
Burrington

Pendragon Country House,
Camelford

Blackmore Farm,
Cannington

Gidleigh Park,
Chagford

Captain's Club,
Christchurch

Beech House & Olive Branch,
Clipsham

Hipping Hall,
Cowan Bridge

Clow Beck House,
Croft-on-Tees

Dart Marina,
Dartmouth

Dedham Hall,
Dedham

Evesham,
Evesham

Fowey Hall,
Fowey

Manoir aux Quat'Saisons,
Great Milton

Castle House,
Hereford

Battlesteads,
Hexham

Byfords,
Holt

Slaughters Country Inn,
Lower Slaughter

Lime Wood,
Lyndhurst

Swinton Park,
Masham

Bedruthan,
Mawgan Porth

Scarlet,
Mawgan Porth

Midland,
Morecambe

Manor House,
Moreton-in-Marsh

Redesdale Arms,
Moreton-in-Marsh

TerraVina,
  Netley Marsh
Chewton Glen,
  New Milton
Jesmond Dene House,
  Newcastle upon Tyne
Beechwood,
  North Walsham
Hart's,
  Nottingham
Grange at Oborne,
  Oborne
Old Bank,
  Oxford
Old Parsonage,
  Oxford
Pig near Bath,
  Pensford
Old Railway Station,
  Petworth
Black Swan,
  Ravenstonedale
Burgoyne,
  Reeth
Rose in Vale,
  St Agnes
St Cuthbert's House,
  Seahouses
Swan,
  Southwold
Arden,
  Stratford-upon-Avon
Titchwell Manor,
  Titchwell
Tuddenham Mill,
  Tuddenham
Nare,
  Veryan-in-Roseland
Holbeck Ghyll,
  Windermere
Watersmeet,
  Woolacombe

Middlethorpe Hall,
  York

SCOTLAND
Boath House,
  Auldearn
Dunvalanree in Carradale,
  Carradale
Three Chimneys and
  House Over-By,
  Dunvegan
Bonham,
  Edinburgh
Langass Lodge,
  Locheport
Craigatin House,
  Pitlochry
Green Park,
  Pitlochry
Viewfield House,
  Portree
Skirling House,
  Skirling

WALES
Harbourmaster,
  Aberaeron
Ye Olde Bulls Head,
  Beaumaris
Ynyshir Hall,
  Eglwysfach
Penbontbren,
  Glynarthen
Tyddyn Llan,
  Llandrillo
Bodysgallen Hall and
  Spa,
  Llandudno
Lake,
  Llangammarch Wells
Portmeirion,
  Portmeirion

Old Rectory on the Lake,
  Tal-y-llyn

IRELAND
Mustard Seed at Echo
  Lodge,
  Ballingarry
Seaview House,
  Ballylickey
Quay House,
  Clifden
Rayanne House,
  Holywood
No. 1 Pery Square,
  Limerick
Sheedy's,
  Lisdoonvarna
Rathmullan House,
  Rathmullan

LONDON

Westminster and the River Thames

CHURCH STREET HOTEL

'Good fun', this 'flamboyant, friendly' south London hotel, in three converted town houses, is owned by Greek/Spanish brothers José and Mel Raido. It is decorated in 'extravagant' Latino style with sculptures, prints, religious artefacts and bottles of rum; 'vividly coloured' bedrooms are up two 'steep, warren-like' staircases. A high-ceilinged room above the restaurant had electric-blue walls, 'a big bed with good linens, a small desk with chocolates and some interesting books; the bathroom was a riot of Mexican tiles', *Guide* inspectors said. There is no tea tray in the room but, 'more pleasantly', the lounge/breakfast room, accessible all day, has complimentary hot drinks (including a 'good selection' of teas) and an honesty bar. There may be some noise from the corridor and the busy road ('double glazing and earplugs help'). The 'busy and buzzy' *Angels & Gypsies* restaurant is popular locally; the 'excellent' tapas menu might include slow-cooked cuttlefish stew; 'a moist classic tortilla'. Breakfast, served communally on tables covered with cheery oil cloths, has big jugs of 'superb' freshly squeezed orange juice, 'chunky toast brought hot to the table'.
(*Charlotte Bryant*)

29–33 Camberwell Church Street
London SE5 8TR

T: 020-7703 5984
F: 020-7358-4110
E: info@churchstreethotel.com
W: www.churchstreethotel.com

BEDROOMS: 28, 8 with shared bathrooms.
OPEN: all year, restaurant closed 24/25 Dec, 1/2 Jan.
FACILITIES: lounge/breakfast room, free Wi-Fi, restaurant, unsuitable for &.
BACKGROUND MUSIC: 'easy listening' in public areas.
LOCATION: Camberwell Green, underground Oval.
CHILDREN: all ages welcomed.
DOGS: not allowed.
CREDIT CARDS: Amex, MasterCard, Visa.
PRICES: room £90–£155. Continental breakfast £5, à la carte £28.

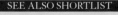

SEE ALSO SHORTLIST

THE DRAYCOTT

In three red brick Edwardian town houses on a quiet street, this luxury hotel has 'lots of character'. It is part of the Mantis Collection owned by Adrian Gardiner. 'It is expensive, but a good base for anyone who can afford it: the impeccable service lives up to the cost,' said *Guide* inspectors. Each of the original houses has 'a fine wooden staircase, a warren of corridors, small lifts'; the high-ceilinged public rooms have antiques and paintings. Bedrooms are named after theatrical personalities (Coward, Shaw, Grenfell, etc); each has a print, photograph or short biography of its namesake. Guests' names are written on a card and placed outside room doors 'like at an Edwardian house party'. 'Our large room, Kean, had a beautiful moulded ceiling, floor-to-ceiling windows with heavy curtains, a sofa facing a gas fire, a table and chairs for meals.' Children are welcomed: adjoining rooms and toy boxes are available for families. Afternoon tea, champagne and hot chocolate (served in the drawing room) are included in the room rates; there is no restaurant, but a room-service menu has light meals and hot dishes.

26 Cadogan Gardens
London SW3 2RP

T: 020-7730 6466
F: 020-7730 0236
E: reservations@draycotthotel.com
W: www.draycotthotel.com

BEDROOMS: 35.
OPEN: all year.
FACILITIES: drawing room, library, breakfast room, free Wi-Fi, 1-acre garden, unsuitable for &.
BACKGROUND MUSIC: classical in breakfast room.
LOCATION: Chelsea, underground Sloane Square.
CHILDREN: all ages welcomed.
DOGS: not allowed in breakfast room.
CREDIT CARDS: all major cards.
PRICES: [to April 2015] per room B&B £260–£398. Set menus £40–£65.

SEE ALSO SHORTLIST

SAN DOMENICO HOUSE

Occupying two Victorian town houses whose original red brick balconies overlook a residential street, this hotel has 'a most pleasing ambience and an emphasis on comfort and service'. It has been owned by the Melpignano family since 2005. 'We had a delightful stay with charming staff who could not have been more helpful,' a visitor said this year. 'Decorations and fittings reveal impeccable taste': beyond the 'imposing' entrance hall, the walls are hung with 'prints of the famous from previous centuries'; the 'luxurious, inviting' lounge has sofas, fresh flowers, an open fire in cool weather. Individually designed bedrooms have antique furnishings, rich fabrics, a marble bathroom; some have a balcony. 'I had a large room filled with beautiful and distinguished antiques – a carved bedhead, a mirror with an extravagant gilded frame, a chaise longue with good-quality cushions.' Drinks and afternoon tea can be taken in the lounge or on the roof terrace; one guest was unimpressed by the presence of tea bags. Breakfast, in a basement room with a marble fireplace, has 'good' coffee and freshly squeezed orange juice.

29–31 Draycott Place
London SW3 2SH

T: 020-7581 5757
F: 020-7584 1348
E: info@sandomenicohouse.com
W: www.sandomenicohouse.com

BEDROOMS: 17.
OPEN: all year.
FACILITIES: lounge, breakfast room, roof terrace, free Wi-Fi, unsuitable for &.
BACKGROUND MUSIC: classical in lounge.
LOCATION: Chelsea, underground Sloane Square.
CHILDREN: all ages welcomed.
DOGS: not allowed.
CREDIT CARDS: all major cards.
PRICES: [2014] (*excluding VAT*) room £255–£390. Breakfast (*including VAT*) £14.40–£21.60.

SEE ALSO SHORTLIST

THE ZETTER

In a converted Victorian warehouse in a fashionable neighbourhood, this 'quirky' hotel has 'imaginatively styled' rooms, a popular restaurant combined with 'a buzzing' bar and 'exceptionally friendly' staff. It is owned by Mark Sainsbury and Michael Benyan. In the entrance lobby, a lively mural creeps up and around the elevator doors; upstairs, the brightly coloured bedrooms vary in size and decor. The largest and best are roof-top studios and suites, which each have a private patio. 'Our corner deluxe room facing Clerkenwell Road had a splendid bed, two 1960s chairs, a bean bag, up-to-date magazines; a smart bathroom. Secondary double glazing on the four sash windows minimised street noise.' Natural light pours through huge windows into the well-regarded restaurant overlooking St John's Square; served on white linens, the modern bistro menu might include octopus terrine, Niçoise style; confit lamb shoulder, white bean and preserved lemon purée, green harissa. Breakfast is served until 11 am at weekends; the 'superb' continental buffet has home-made granola, freshly squeezed juice, 'delicious' croissants. The *Zetter Townhouse* (see next entry) is under the same ownership.

St John's Square
86–88 Clerkenwell Road
London EC1M 5RJ

T: 020-7324 4444
F: 020-7324 4445
E: reservations@thezetter.com
W: www.thezetter.com

BEDROOMS: 59, 2 suitable for &.
OPEN: all year.
FACILITIES: 2 lifts, ramps, cocktail bar/lounge, *Bistrot Bruno Loubet*, 2 function/meeting rooms, free Wi-Fi.
BACKGROUND MUSIC: 'low-volume' eclectic mix.
LOCATION: Clerkenwell, by St John's Sq, NCP garage 5 mins' walk, underground Farringdon.
CHILDREN: all ages welcomed.
DOGS: only guide dogs allowed.
CREDIT CARDS: Amex, MasterCard, Visa.
PRICES: [2014] room (*excluding VAT*) from £195. Continental breakfast £9.50, à la carte £30.

SEE ALSO SHORTLIST

THE ZETTER TOWNHOUSE

❧ *César award in 2012*

On a quiet cobbled square, the exterior of this 'elegant' double-fronted Georgian town house might appear sedate. Through the light blue front door, however, the 'wit and (zany) flair' of Michael Benyan and Mark Sainsbury's intimate hotel become clear. Public rooms are filled with antique ceramics and bronzes, paintings and porcelain figurines, old postcards and fringed lampshades; the 'excellent' cocktail bar, inspired by an old-fashioned apothecary counter, has velvet sofas and armchairs, 'superb' huge vases of fresh flowers. Amid the design flourishes, staff are 'outstanding'. 'It has the small-hotel feel in spades,' visiting *Guide* hoteliers said. 'Attractive' bedrooms range from 'compact' rooms to a grand suite; all have large sash windows, reclaimed and vintage furniture, classic novels, 'good bedside lighting'. A room-service menu is available 24 hours a day; 'small eats' are served in the cocktail lounge. Breakfast can be taken in the bedroom (cooked dishes from the room-service menu); the bar has a continental selection. *Bistrot Bruno Loubet*, in the sister *Zetter* hotel across the square (see previous entry), is 'excellent'. (*D and HA, NP*)

49–50 St John's Square
London EC1V 4JJ

T: 020-7324 4567
F: 020-7324 4456
E: reservations@thezetter.com
W: www.thezettertownhouse.com

BEDROOMS: 13.
OPEN: all year.
FACILITIES: cocktail lounge, private dining room, games room, free Wi-Fi.
BACKGROUND MUSIC: in public areas.
LOCATION: Clerkenwell, underground Farringdon.
CHILDREN: all ages welcomed.
DOGS: only guide dogs allowed.
CREDIT CARDS: Amex, MasterCard, Visa.
PRICES: [2014] room (*excluding VAT*) from £225. Continental breakfast £9.50.

SEE ALSO SHORTLIST

THE FIELDING

On a 'charming' traffic-free lane close to the Royal Opera House, this small hotel has a romantic exterior – window boxes with flowering plants, fairy lights at night. A 'simple, well-located place to stay', it is managed by Grace Langley for private owners. The bedrooms are modest, there are no public rooms and breakfast is not served (a list of the many eating places nearby is provided). 'Superb photographs of ballet adorn the walls, and other decorations reflect the history of Covent Garden.' Reached by narrow corridors, the 'clean and tidy' bedrooms vary in size. 'Our room, on the second floor, had plenty of storage space; the bathroom had a large shower cubicle, plus simple but high-quality toiletries.' They are well equipped: a kettle, biscuits, mineral water; a large flat-screen TV; slippers and an eye mask; 'good toiletries' in the bathrooms. A family room on the top floor can accommodate four people. 'There was little noise at night; in the morning we heard birdsong.' Guests have free access to a nearby spa. 'The staff were most helpful; relatively good value for its position,' is a comment in 2014. (*PV, and others*)

4 Broad Court
Bow Street
London WC2B 5QZ

T: 020-7836 8305
F: 020-7497 0064
E: reservations@
    thefieldinghotel.co.uk
W: www.thefieldinghotel.co.uk

BEDROOMS: 25.
OPEN: all year.
FACILITIES: no public rooms, free Wi-Fi, unsuitable for &.
BACKGROUND MUSIC: none.
LOCATION: central, underground Covent Garden.
CHILDREN: all ages welcomed.
DOGS: not allowed.
CREDIT CARDS: all major cards.
PRICES: [2014] room (*excluding VAT*) single £90–£100, double £140–£180.

SEE ALSO SHORTLIST

THE ROCKWELL

There are 'helpful staff', 'thoughtfully furnished rooms' and a 'relaxed atmosphere' at this modern hotel in west London. Michael Squire and Tony Bartlett are the owners; it is managed by Ocky Paller. In the lobby lounge, heavy burgundy drapes frame the bay window on to the busy road; sofas and armchairs are arranged around a coffee table with newspapers and magazines. In the rear of the building, drinks and meals may be taken in a walled courtyard garden with vast plant pots. The bedrooms vary considerably in size, from compact singles to deluxe doubles with large Victorian windows and a king-size bed; split-level suites have a smart sitting area. 'Our high-ceilinged second-floor room overlooked the road (double glazing eliminated traffic noise). The styling was minimalist without being spare; mineral water and robes were provided (but no tea tray – 24-hour room service).' The continental breakfast buffet has home-made muesli, big jugs of freshly squeezed juices, pastries, salamis, cheese; a freshly baked loaf for toast. Five minutes from the Tube station; 'the prices are modest for such a good position close to the shops and museums'.

181 Cromwell Road
London SW5 0SF

T: 020-7244 2000
F: 020-7244 2001
E: enquiries@therockwell.com
W: www.therockwell.com

BEDROOMS: 40, 1 on ground floor.
OPEN: all year.
FACILITIES: lift, ramps, lobby, lounge, bar, restaurant, conference room, free Wi-Fi, garden.
BACKGROUND MUSIC: in bar.
LOCATION: 1 mile SW of Marble Arch, opposite Cromwell Hospital, underground Earls Court.
CHILDREN: all ages welcomed.
DOGS: not allowed.
CREDIT CARDS: Amex, MasterCard, Visa.
PRICES: room £90–£176. Breakfast £9.50–£12.50, à la carte £28.

SEE ALSO SHORTLIST

THE CAPITAL

🪶 *César award in 2008*

Twin topiaries flank the entrance of this traditional stone and red brick town house hotel on a quiet street minutes from busy Knightsbridge. It is owned by David Levin; his daughter Kate is the manager. Guests enter into a handsome lobby with fresh flowers, paintings, winged armchairs and a grand fireplace. There are immense chandeliers in the intimate *Outlaw's at The Capital* restaurant, where chef Nathan Outlaw has a *Michelin* star for his modern dishes. He specialises in seafood, perhaps scallops and hazelnuts, Jerusalem artichoke, watercress; turbot, crispy oysters, cabbage, bacon. 'Dinner was outstanding, with Mr Levin's Sauvignon [from his organic Loire valley vineyard] to wash it down.' The elegant bedrooms are individually decorated with classic English fabrics, antiques and works of art; each has a marble bathroom. Rooms vary in size: smaller classic rooms may be interconnected for a family; larger deluxe rooms, some in a galleried corridor in the older part of the building, have a sitting area. Guests have access to a private health club nearby. David Levin also owns *The Levin*, next door (see entry).

22–24 Basil Street
London SW3 1AT

T: 020-7589 5171
F: 020-7225 0011
E: reservations@capitalhotel.co.uk
W: www.capitalhotel.co.uk

BEDROOMS: 49.
OPEN: all year (restaurant closed Sun).
FACILITIES: lift, sitting room, bar, restaurant, brasserie/bar next door, free Wi-Fi, access to nearby health club/spa, only restaurant suitable for &.
BACKGROUND MUSIC: soft jazz in bar in evenings.
LOCATION: central, underground Knightsbridge, private car park.
CHILDREN: all ages welcomed.
DOGS: small dogs, on request.
CREDIT CARDS: all major cards.
PRICES: [2014] per room B&B (continental) £310–£575, D,B&B £425–£690. Cooked breakfast £19.50 per person, à la carte £50, tasting menu £75 (*plus 12½% discretionary service charge*).

SEE ALSO SHORTLIST

THE LEVIN

'Everything is just about perfect' at this 'immaculate' small town house hotel close to Harrods and Hyde Park. It is owned by David Levin. Harald Duttine is the long-serving manager; the staff are 'interested and interesting, remembering previous conversations'. The smart, Art Deco-style reception area has fresh flowers, books and botanical prints; upstairs (via a staircase with a dramatic light installation, or a small, characterful lift), contemporary bedrooms have a marble bathroom with under-floor heating. Rooms vary in size and decor: deluxe rooms have an alcove seating area; the top-floor junior suite, ideal for a small family, has two sofas. A standard room 'was not large, but was well appointed; the bed was comfortable, and the lighting was good (we could actually read in bed); an excellent bathroom'. There is an open kitchen in the basement *Metro* bar and bistro; the menu of bar classics might include double-baked spinach and cheese soufflé. The wine list has a Sauvignon Blanc from David Levin's Loire valley vineyard. Breakfast has 'especially good croissants and pastries from the owner's bakery'; cooked dishes cost extra. (*R and SL*)

28 Basil Street
London SW3 1AS

T: 020-7589 6286
F: 020-7823 7826
E: reservations@thelevinhotel.co.uk
W: www.thelevinhotel.co.uk

BEDROOMS: 12.
OPEN: all year, restaurant closed Sun after 5.30 pm.
FACILITIES: lobby, library, honesty bar, bar/brasserie (*Le Metro*), free Wi-Fi, access to nearby health club/spa, unsuitable for &.
BACKGROUND MUSIC: in restaurant.
LOCATION: central, underground Knightsbridge (Harrods exit), private car park (£40 a night).
CHILDREN: all ages welcomed.
DOGS: not allowed.
CREDIT CARDS: all major cards.
PRICES: [2014] per room B&B (continental) £240–£619. Set menu £14–£16, à la carte £30.

SEE ALSO SHORTLIST

THE GRAZING GOAT

In a 'peaceful little zone' minutes from Oxford Street, this stylish pub-with-rooms, decorated with stuffed goats and old London prints, 'will appeal to the young at heart'. It is owned by the small Cubitt House group (see *The Orange*, London, Shortlist). 'It is not cheap, but you get a thoughtfully furnished bedroom and an exceptional bathroom in a good location,' *Guide* inspectors say. There is a modern rustic atmosphere throughout: oak floors, coir carpets, pale woods, open fires. The bedrooms are on the top three floors (no lift, but help with bags is offered). 'Our simple, beautifully furnished room had a huge, firm bed, lots of storage, up-to-date magazines; the excellent, well-lit bathroom had especially good toiletries. We heard no noise from the busy floors below.' The ground-floor bar 'heaves' with after-work drinkers during the week; a British bistro menu (perhaps hot smoked sea trout, Jersey Royals, brown shrimp, tomato and caper butter sauce) is 'promptly and efficiently' served in the panelled first-floor dining room. Breakfast has pots of tea, 'splendid' bacon and eggs, 'generous glasses of orange juice, as fresh as it gets'.

6 New Quebec Street
London W1H 7RQ

T: 020-7724 7243
E: reservations@
    thegrazinggoat.co.uk
W: www.thegrazinggoat.co.uk

BEDROOMS: 8.
OPEN: all year.
FACILITIES: bar, dining room, free Wi-Fi, unsuitable for &.
BACKGROUND MUSIC: in bar and dining room.
LOCATION: central, underground Marble Arch.
CHILDREN: all ages welcomed.
DOGS: allowed on ground floor only, not in bedrooms.
CREDIT CARDS: Amex, MasterCard, Visa.
PRICES: [2014] room £205–£240. Cooked breakfast from £6.50, à la carte £32 (*plus 12½% discretionary service charge*).

SEE ALSO SHORTLIST

DURRANTS

🏆 *César award in 2010*

The Miller family's traditional hotel in the heart of Marylebone village 'lives up to its amiable and quietly efficient reputation', says a guest this year. Earlier visitors liked the 'personal, slightly eccentric' style. Managed by Ian McIntosh, *Durrants* occupies a conversion of four terraced houses with a Georgian facade. It is 'nicely old-fashioned, with creaking irregular floorboards and pleasant sitting rooms'. There are engravings, original paintings and prints, antique furniture in the public rooms; a 'cosy' wood-panelled bar. The bedrooms vary in size, shape and aspect. They are individually designed and have antiques, prints and 'first-rate' beds. Most have air conditioning, all have flat-screen TV and free Wi-Fi. Suites have a private sitting room with sofa and armchairs. In the wood-panelled restaurant, chef Cara Baird's three-course set menu is 'a bargain'; it might include pan-fried sea bass with leek confit and shallot purée. The cooked breakfast is 'first rate', though one visitor found the individual pricing of items (eg, 'additional sausage') 'bizarre'. The last-minute rates on the hotel's website are recommended. (*K Salway, and others*)

26–32 George Street
London W1H 5BJ

T: 020-7935 8131
F: 020-7487 3510
E: enquiries@durrantshotel.co.uk
W: www.durrantshotel.co.uk

BEDROOMS: 92, 7 on ground floor.
OPEN: all year, restaurant closed 25 Dec evening.
FACILITIES: lifts, ramp, bar, restaurant, lounge, 5 function rooms, free Wi-Fi.
BACKGROUND MUSIC: none.
LOCATION: off Oxford Street, underground Bond Street, Baker Street.
CHILDREN: all ages welcomed.
DOGS: only guide dogs allowed.
CREDIT CARDS: Amex, MasterCard, Visa.
PRICES: [2014] room from £195. Set dinner Mon–Fri £19.50–£21.50, Sun £27.50–£32.50, à la carte £55 (*excluding 'optional' 12½% service charge*).

SEE ALSO SHORTLIST

THE VICTORIA

Five minutes' walk from Richmond Park, this 'cheerful' pub-with-rooms is in a leafy residential neighbourhood with 'a pleasant village feel'. It is owned by celebrity chef Paul Merrett and restaurateur Greg Bellamy. A popular local spot with 'friendly' staff and 'a family ambience', the bar has vintage Penguin paperbacks and an open fire. In the conservatory restaurant and garden terrace, 'imaginative' menus, served informally on wooden tables, might include lamb rump, ras-el-hanout, shallot and apple purée. 'We ate on the pleasant terrace: pea soup, a garlic and mushroom risotto and, best of all, delicious sliced blood oranges in Campari.' A light supper (charcuterie board, cheese board, salmon plate) is served on Sunday nights in the winter months; there are evening barbecues in the summer. In a separate building reached by a covered walkway, 'good-value' bedrooms are simply furnished in a modern style; they have magazines and tea- and coffee-making facilities. A continental breakfast buffet – with fresh fruit, yogurts, home-made preserves, and jars of nuts and grains for mix-it-yourself muesli – is included in the room rate; cooked dishes cost extra.

10 West Temple Sheen
London SW14 7RT

T: 020-8876 4238
E: bookings@thevictoria.net
W: www.thevictoria.net

BEDROOMS: 7, 3 on ground floor, 1 suitable for &.
OPEN: all year.
FACILITIES: bar, restaurant, free Wi-Fi, garden.
BACKGROUND MUSIC: 'easy listening' throughout.
LOCATION: Mortlake (10 mins' walk) to Waterloo/Clapham Jct, car park.
CHILDREN: all ages welcomed.
DOGS: allowed in bar.
CREDIT CARDS: MasterCard, Visa.
PRICES: [2014] per room B&B (continental) single £120, double £130. Cooked breakfast from £8.50 per person, à la carte £28 (*including 12½% discretionary service charge*).

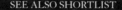

SEE ALSO SHORTLIST

THE ROOKERY   `NEW`

'It was a pleasure to slip into this soothing space bang in the middle of busy Smithfield.' *Guide* inspectors had a 'wicked time' at this small luxury hotel in a neighbourhood once infamous for all manner of villainy (the hotel takes its name from the 18th-century term given to this then-lawless quarter). Occupying three refurbished Georgian houses, the hotel is owned by Peter McKay and Douglas Blain (who also own *Hazlitt's*, Soho, London, see entry). 'Outstanding' staff are 'friendly, helpful, always available'. Public rooms have polished flagstone floors, panelled walls, gilt-framed portraits; 'a club-like calm throughout'. Bedrooms are traditionally decorated, with pictures and antiques. 'Our dark, masculine room had a huge, carved wooden headboard; velvet curtains; a table and two chairs by a window; plenty of storage space. Double doors opened on to the immaculate bathroom; double-glazed windows provided solid soundproofing.' A short breakfast menu, with 'freshly squeezed orange juice and a generous basket of pastries', may be ordered for a timed delivery. There is no restaurant, but a limited room-service menu may be taken in the conservatory or on the terrace.

12 Peter's Lane
Cowcross Street
London EC1M 6DS

T: 020-7336 0931
E: reservations@rookery.co.uk
W: www.rookeryhotel.com

BEDROOMS: 33.
OPEN: all year.
FACILITIES: drawing room, library, conservatory, meeting rooms, free Wi-Fi, courtyard garden, unsuitable for &.
BACKGROUND MUSIC: none.
LOCATION: Smithfield, underground Farringdon, Barbican.
CHILDREN: all ages welcomed.
DOGS: not allowed.
CREDIT CARDS: all major cards.
PRICES: per room B&B £245–£700. À la carte (room service) £25.

`SEE ALSO SHORTLIST`

HAZLITT'S

🥂 *César award in 2002*

'A stunningly individual hotel, unlike any other we have stayed at.' Peter McKay's quirky hotel, in a group of historic Soho buildings, is 'filled with old architectural features, old furniture, old books and paintings – every corridor and every room had much to investigate and appreciate'. Guests ring a bell to enter; inside, 'the welcome is warm'. Elaborately furnished bedrooms have original panelled walls, silk curtains, a period bathroom. 'Our room at the back had a wonderfully comfortable bed; a complex system of light switches; a throne of a toilet in the large bathroom. We slept with two windows ajar and heard no noise during the night – admirable for central London.' Guests have use of a sitting room and a library with an honesty bar; a simple breakfast has fruit salad, pastries and rolls. 'Breakfast in the room was served on a tray, but there was not enough space to eat comfortably.' There is no restaurant, but a small room-service menu is available all day. 'Incredibly convenient for theatres and restaurants; within comfortable walking distance of the British Museum.' (*Harry and Annette Medcalf*)

6 Frith Street
London W1D 3JA

T: 020-7434 1771
F: 020-7439 1524
E: reservations@hazlitts.co.uk
W: www.hazlittshotel.com

BEDROOMS: 30, 2 on ground floor.
OPEN: all year.
FACILITIES: lift, 2 sitting rooms, meeting room, free Wi-Fi, unsuitable for &.
BACKGROUND MUSIC: none.
LOCATION: Soho (front windows triple glazed, rear rooms quietest), NCP nearby, underground Tottenham Court Road, Leicester Square.
CHILDREN: all ages welcomed.
DOGS: not allowed.
CREDIT CARDS: all major cards.
PRICES: per room B&B £245–£700. À la carte (room service) £25.

SEE ALSO SHORTLIST

NUMBER SIXTEEN

🏵 *César award in 2011*

'Conveniently situated' on a quiet side street near the Victoria and Albert Museum, this modern hotel, in a mid-Victorian terrace, is close to the shops and cafés of South Kensington. It is part of Tim and Kit Kemp's small Firmdale Hotels group. The staff are 'helpful'; there is 'a personal, home-from-home feeling' throughout, says a visitor this year. The light-filled sitting rooms have floor-to-ceiling windows, flowers, modern art, stylishly mismatched furnishings: 'no bland corporate anonymity here'. Bedrooms have bold prints, a 'wonderfully comfortable' bed, a writing desk and a 'well-equipped' bathroom; a basement room was less liked. There is no restaurant, but a good room-service menu with snacks and light meals (perhaps crispy duck, mango, cucumber wrap) may be served all day in bedrooms and public areas, including the peaceful private garden. Children receive a welcoming gift and a book of London activities; their own bathrobe and toiletries; milk and cookies at bedtime. Breakfast, normally charged extra, has home-made granola, hot chocolate, a smoothie of the day; a 'good' choice of cooked dishes. (*AL, and others*)

16 Sumner Place
London SW7 3EG

T: 020-7589 5232
F: 020-7584 8615
E: sixteen@firmdale.com
W: www.firmdale.com

BEDROOMS: 41, 5 on ground floor.
OPEN: all year.
FACILITIES: drawing room, library, conservatory, free Wi-Fi, civil wedding licence, garden.
BACKGROUND MUSIC: none.
LOCATION: Kensington, underground South Kensington.
CHILDREN: all ages welcomed.
DOGS: not allowed.
CREDIT CARDS: all major cards.
PRICES: [2014] room (*excluding VAT*) £174–£396. Breakfast £18.50–£24.50 per person (*plus 12½% discretionary service charge*).

SEE ALSO SHORTLIST

ONE ALDWYCH

🎖 *César award in 2005*

In a grand Edwardian building that once housed the offices of the *Morning Post* newspaper, this luxury hotel is liked for its 'helpful' staff, its 'superb' food and its 'elegant' public spaces filled with contemporary art and sculpture. The large double-height lobby has huge flower arrangements and a striking statue of a boatman by London sculptor André Wallace; a 'large and light space with comfortable seating', it is 'a peaceful place for morning coffee'. There are two restaurants: in *Axis*, chef Dominic Teague's seasonal dinner menus might include wild bass, crushed potato, samphire, shellfish vinaigrette; *Indigo*, a 'relaxed' restaurant overlooking the *Lobby Bar*, has modern European dishes. Guests also have use of a residents' lounge with velvet armchairs, cocktails, and an all-day menu. The 'comfortable' modern bedrooms have 'fantastic pillows', original artwork and many thoughtful touches: flowers and fresh fruit are delivered daily; a weather forecast for the following day is placed on the pillow at turn-down. Children are welcomed with their own bathrobe and slippers. (*HRL, and others*)

1 Aldwych
London WC2B 4BZ

T: 020-7300 1000
F: 020-7300 0501
E: reservations@onealdwych.com
W: www.onealdwych.com

BEDROOMS: 105, 6 suitable for &.
OPEN: all year, *Axis* closed Mon.
FACILITIES: lifts, bar, 2 restaurants, guest lounge, free Wi-Fi, function facilities, health club (18-metre heated swimming pool, spa, sauna, gym), civil wedding licence.
BACKGROUND MUSIC: in bar and restaurants.
LOCATION: Strand, valet parking, underground Covent Garden, Charing Cross, Waterloo.
CHILDREN: all ages welcomed.
DOGS: only guide dogs allowed.
CREDIT CARDS: all major cards.
PRICES: [2014] rooms and suites £250–£1,430, breakfast from £19 (continental), pre- and post-theatre menu £20–£25, à la carte (*Indigo*) £30, (*Axis*) £45 (*including 12½% optional service charge*).

SEE ALSO SHORTLIST

THE GORING

♛ *César award in 1994*

'Expensive but excellent', this luxury hotel a minute from Buckingham Palace 'stands out amongst its peers for the attention to detail'. Long the favoured choice of royal visitors, it has elegant bedrooms individually styled with silks, antiques and bespoke furniture; a wood-panelled, silk-wallpapered Edwardian lounge bar with access to private gardens; a charming veranda for alfresco drinks or afternoon tea; gifts and activities for children; complimentary shoe cleaning that is 'a joy to behold'. Run by the Goring family since it was built in 1910, it has a rich history that includes the world's first en suite bathrooms; Prince Charles's christening cake; a flurry caused by Jean Shrimpton's miniskirts; and hosting the Middleton family for the most recent royal wedding. Jeremy Goring is now in charge; David Morgan-Hewitt is the long-serving managing director. Shay Cooper joined as chef in 2013; his modern dinners, served in the candlelit restaurant, might include Scottish halibut, smoked eel barley, parsley and garlic purée. At breakfast, 'hot toast and tea/coffee are brought exactly when you want them'. (*DC, H and AM*)

Beeston Place
Grosvenor Gardens
London SW1W 0JW

T: 020-7396 9000
F: 020-7834 4393
E: reception@thegoring.com
W: www.thegoring.com

BEDROOMS: 69, 2 suitable for &.
OPEN: all year.
FACILITIES: lifts, ramps, lounge bar, terrace room, restaurant, function facilities, Wi-Fi (£15.75 for 24 hours), civil wedding licence.
BACKGROUND MUSIC: none.
LOCATION: near Victoria Station, garage, mews parking, underground Victoria.
CHILDREN: all ages welcomed.
DOGS: not allowed.
CREDIT CARDS: all major cards.
PRICES: [2014] per room (*excluding 12.5% service*) B&B from £400. Set lunch £42.50, pre-theatre dinner £33, set dinner £52.50.

SEE ALSO SHORTLIST

ENGLAND

Yorkshire Dales

ABBOTSBURY Dorset

Map 1:D6

THE ABBEY HOUSE

'A really lovely place to stay', this 14th-century house has been run for 20 years by Jonathan and Maureen Cooke, who are 'most welcoming' (say *Guide* inspectors). It stands next to the remains of an 11th-century abbey in a 'very pretty village' on the Dorset coast. 'The house has great charm, with a spacious garden equipped with pergolas and arbours, overlooking a beautiful tithe barn.' The five bedrooms differ in size and facilities. 'Our room was heavily Victorian, with a rose-covered dado border, flowered curtains and bedspreads in dark red and green chintz. However, it was a generous size and had everything we needed; an ample hospitality tray, chocolates, a good TV and fast broadband.' St Nicholas faces south, looking over the garden, and has its own lounge area with TV and easy chairs; St Catherine's features a half-tester bed; Monks is the smallest and is not en suite but has a private bathroom with shower. Breakfast was 'delicious, with lots of choice'. No evening meals; 'We ate well in a nearby pub, recommended by the Cookes.'

Church Street
Abbotsbury DT3 4JJ

T: 01305-871330
E: info@theabbeyhouse.co.uk
W: www.theabbeyhouse.co.uk

BEDROOMS: 5.
OPEN: all year, tea room open for lunches Apr–Sept, dinners for house parties only.
FACILITIES: reception, lounge, breakfast/tea room, free Wi-Fi, civil wedding licence, 1½-acre garden (stage for opera), sea 15 mins' walk, unsuitable for ♿.
BACKGROUND MUSIC: classical, sometimes.
LOCATION: village centre.
CHILDREN: not under 12.
DOGS: not allowed.
CREDIT CARDS: MasterCard, Visa.
PRICES: [2014] per room B&B £75–£110. 1-night bookings sometimes refused.

ALDEBURGH Suffolk

Map 2:C6

THE WENTWORTH

Opposite the shingle beach in this small coastal town, Michael Pritt's 'well-situated', 'traditional and friendly' hotel attracts many return visitors. They like the 'personal attention of the owner and pleasant staff'. Individually decorated bedrooms, many with sea views, are divided between the main building and *Darfield House* across the road; those in the latter building have access to a sheltered walled garden. 'Our ground-floor room in *Darfield House* was not as large as others we have stayed in, but it was comfortable; the bathroom, with a walk-in shower, was very good.' Afternoon tea is taken in the public rooms (sofas, paintings, an open fire); the cake of the day is announced at Reception. For meals, guests may eat in the bar, the lounge, the elegant sea-facing restaurant or on the terrace in good weather. Chef (since early 2014) Jason Shaw produces dishes like prawn and crayfish salad; Darsham fillet steak medallions, peppercorn jus, gratin potatoes. Breakfast includes 'delicious muesli, good cooked (fine black pudding), superb bread and croissants'. (*Richard and Jill Burridge, Simon Rodway*)

25% DISCOUNT VOUCHERS

Wentworth Road
Aldeburgh IP15 5BD

T: 01728-452312
F: 01728-454343
E: stay@wentworth-aldeburgh.co.uk
W: www.wentworth-aldeburgh.com

BEDROOMS: 35, 7 in *Darfield House* opposite, 5 on ground floor, 1 suitable for &.
OPEN: all year.
FACILITIES: ramps, 2 lounges, bar, restaurant, private dining room, conference room, free Wi-Fi, 2 terrace gardens, shingle beach 200 yds.
BACKGROUND MUSIC: none.
LOCATION: seafront, 5 mins' walk from centre.
CHILDREN: all ages welcomed.
DOGS: not allowed in restaurant.
CREDIT CARDS: all major cards.
PRICES: per room B&B £135–£280, D,B&B £151–£311. Set dinner £25. 1-night bookings refused Sat.

SEE ALSO SHORTLIST

ALFRISTON East Sussex

Map 2:E4

DEANS PLACE

In a 'beautiful area of the South Downs with
lovely walks and attractive villages', this country
hotel has 'a nice traditional feel'. Owned by
Michael Clinch and managed by James Dopson,
it was originally on a large farming estate on the
banks of the Cuckmere river. 'There is plenty of
space for sitting and relaxing,' said a visitor;
'nooks and crannies where you can hide with a
good book.' The staff 'are most helpful, we had
a happy and relaxing stay'. Lunch can be taken
in the *Terrace* lounge, which has views across the
croquet lawn. There are fresh flowers on the
tables in the more formal *Harcourts* restaurant,
where chef Stuart Dunley serves dishes such as
local scallops, tempura oyster; pan-roasted
guineafowl breast, cider-scented fondant potato,
celeriac purée. 'We were impressed by the
dining experience, which had the right mix of
fine dining and being child friendly.' There is an
'excellent' vegetarian menu. 'Our bedroom was
large and well furnished; sheets and blankets on
the bed; a hospitality tray and a good
information pack.' Pets are welcomed (in
selected bedrooms). (*SR, and others*)

25% DISCOUNT VOUCHERS

Seaford Road
Alfriston BN26 5TW

T: 01323-870248
F: 01323-870918
E: reception@deansplacehotel.co.uk
W: www.deansplacehotel.co.uk

BEDROOMS: 36, 1 suitable for &.
OPEN: all year.
FACILITIES: lounge, bar, restaurant,
meeting rooms, free Wi-Fi, civil
wedding licence, heated outdoor
swimming pool (10 by 5 metres,
May–Sept), 4-acre garden.
BACKGROUND MUSIC: classical, jazz
in restaurant.
LOCATION: edge of village.
CHILDREN: all ages welcomed.
DOGS: allowed.
CREDIT CARDS: Amex, MasterCard,
Visa.
PRICES: [2014] per room B&B
£110–£160, D,B&B £180–£230. Set
meals £28–£35.

SEE ALSO SHORTLIST

AMBLESIDE Cumbria

Map 4: inset C2

THE REGENT

Opposite a pier on Lake Windermere ('an excellent position to explore the lakes'), this Hewitt family's hotel is 'friendly and well run', say visitors this year. 'Andrew Hewitt is very much the quiet power behind the throne – he seemed to be everywhere.' Staff are 'attentive and professional'; there is 'a great atmosphere'. Bedrooms range from small singles to family rooms with a bunk bed in a separate sleeping area. Ground-floor courtyard rooms are ideal for dog owners; garden rooms have a large sitting area and a private terrace. 'We were upgraded to a tastefully and thoughtfully furnished garden suite with an excellent king-size bed and two sitting areas.' Books and DVDs are available to borrow. Informal meals (burgers, pies, chips, etc) are taken in the bar or served in the room; in the restaurant, chef John Mathers cooks a seasonal menu that might include Morecambe Bay shrimps, poached egg, crumpet; Lakeland lamb Wellington, beetroot and gratin dauphinoise. 'We ate well at dinner.' Breakfast, served until noon, is 'equally good', with lots of choice: home-made muesli, local Cumberland sausage, Manx kippers. (*Ian and Barbara Dewey, and others*)

25% DISCOUNT VOUCHERS

Waterhead Bay
Ambleside LA22 0ES

T: 015394-32254
F: 015394-31474
E: info@regentlakes.co.uk
W: www.regentlakes.co.uk

BEDROOMS: 30, 10 in courtyard, 5 in garden, 7 on ground floor.
OPEN: all year except Christmas.
FACILITIES: ramp, lounge, sun lounge, bar, restaurant, free Wi-Fi in public areas, courtyard, ¼-acre garden, on Lake Windermere.
BACKGROUND MUSIC: classical/modern in public rooms.
LOCATION: on A591, S of centre, at Waterhead Bay.
CHILDREN: all ages welcomed.
DOGS: not allowed in restaurant.
CREDIT CARDS: Amex, MasterCard, Visa.
PRICES: [2014] per person B&B £52–£79, D,B&B £79–£114. À la carte £28.

SEE ALSO SHORTLIST

ROTHAY MANOR

❦César award in 1992

'Standards are as high as ever: immaculate, beautifully furnished bedrooms and lounges; excellent food; a warm welcome.' In large, landscaped gardens, a short walk from Lake Windermere and the town centre, the Nixon family's 'comfortable', traditional hotel has been in every edition of the *Guide*. 'Everyone thoroughly enjoyed their stay,' said a returning guest this year, who visited with a varied cast of family members. The best bedrooms have a balcony with views towards Wansfell Pike. All have good storage; tea and coffee trays also have drinking chocolate and biscuits. ('Pity the bedside lights were too dim to read by.') The restaurant overlooking the gardens is newly refurbished; head chef Jane Binns's daily-changing menu might include Cumbrian lamb shank, Colcannon potatoes, braised red cabbage. 'I liked the sensible policy of charging by the number of courses taken at dinner, which catered for my small appetite and the teenagers' enormous ones.' Breakfast has home-made jams and 'secret recipe' muesli; hot dishes are cooked to order. (*Margaret H Box, Jill and Mike Bennett*)

Rothay Bridge
Ambleside LA22 0EH

T: 015394-33605
F: 015397-33607
E: hotel@rothaymanor.co.uk
W: www.rothaymanor.co.uk

BEDROOMS: 19, 2 in annexe, 2 suitable for ♿.
OPEN: all year except 3–22 Jan.
FACILITIES: ramp, 2 lounges, bar, 2 dining rooms, meeting/conference facilities, free Wi-Fi, 1-acre garden (croquet), free access to local leisure centre.
BACKGROUND MUSIC: classical/jazz/acoustic in restaurant.
LOCATION: ¼ mile SW of Ambleside.
CHILDREN: all ages welcomed.
DOGS: not allowed.
CREDIT CARDS: MasterCard, Visa.
PRICES: [2014] per room B&B £99–£240, D,B&B £149–£295. À la carte £39.50. 1-night bookings often refused Sat.

SEE ALSO SHORTLIST

AMPLEFORTH North Yorkshire

Map 4:D4

SHALLOWDALE HOUSE

César award in 2005

'It is an unchanging pleasure to stay here.' On the edge of the North York Moors national park, Phillip Gill and Anton van der Horst's hillside guest house attracts many return visitors. 'We enjoyed it as much as ever,' say third-time guests this year. There is a 'restful atmosphere' throughout the house; large picture windows have panoramic views of the Howardian hills. The ground-floor drawing room and first-floor sitting room are filled with antiques and objets d'art, books and comfortable chairs. 'Afternoon tea on the terrace was a real treat. Anton obviously loves his garden and talks knowledgeably about the plants and flowers.' Individually decorated, the bedrooms also have the views. 'Our spacious, elegant room was thoughtfully equipped and well lit; there were binoculars so that we could fully enjoy the lovely outlook.' Phillip Gill's imaginative home cooking (48 hours' notice required) is 'delicious'; the four-course set dinner might have cider-braised pork cheeks, curly kale, celeriac purée. 'Breakfast has a wide choice; the freshly squeezed orange juice deserves a mention.'
(*Richard Creed, Mary Hewson, and others*)

West End, Ampleforth
nr York, YO62 4DY

T: 01439-788325
F: 01439-788885
E: stay@shallowdalehouse.co.uk
W: www.shallowdalehouse.co.uk

BEDROOMS: 3.
OPEN: all year except Christmas/New Year, occasionally at other times.
FACILITIES: drawing room, sitting room, dining room, free Wi-Fi, 2½-acre grounds, unsuitable for &.
BACKGROUND MUSIC: none.
LOCATION: edge of village.
CHILDREN: not under 12.
DOGS: not allowed.
CREDIT CARDS: MasterCard, Visa.
PRICES: [2014] per room B&B single £95–£110, double £115–£140. Set dinner £39.50. 1-night bookings occasionally refused weekends.

ARUNDEL West Sussex

Map 2:E3

THE TOWN HOUSE

'An excellent restaurant with pleasant rooms and welcoming staff.' *Guide* inspectors found much to like at this restaurant-with-rooms, a Grade II listed Regency building at the top of the High Street of an interesting town. It is owned and managed by Lee Williams (the chef) and his wife, Katie, who say 'dining should be fun'. There is no dress code and 'stuffiness is taboo'. An unusual feature of the interior is a late Renaissance gilded walnut ceiling in the dining room, which was imported from Florence. The cooking is equally 'dazzling'. Lee Williams's set dinner menu of modern dishes might include langoustine ravioli, chive butter sauce; fillet of Southdown venison, wild mushroom risotto. The home-baked bread is 'delicious'. The bedrooms are on two floors; those on the second floor have a direct view over the castle wall to the battlements. The suite has a four-poster double bed and a small private balcony. Some rooms have hand-painted original coving and panelling. All have flat-screen TV and tea-/coffee-making facilities. There is no guest lounge so the house is best suited to short stays.

25% DISCOUNT VOUCHERS

65 High Street
Arundel BN18 9AJ

T: 01903-883847
E: enquiries@thetownhouse.co.uk
W: www.thetownhouse.co.uk

BEDROOMS: 4.
OPEN: all year except 25/26 Dec, 1 Jan, 2 weeks Easter, 2 weeks Oct, restaurant closed Sun/Mon.
FACILITIES: restaurant, free Wi-Fi, unsuitable for ♿.
BACKGROUND MUSIC: 'easy listening' in restaurant.
LOCATION: top end of High Street.
CHILDREN: all ages welcomed.
DOGS: not allowed.
CREDIT CARDS: Diners, MasterCard, Visa.
PRICES: [2014] per room B&B £95–£130, D,B&B (midweek) £135–£170. Set dinner £29.50. 1-night bookings refused weekends in high season.

ASHWATER Devon

Map 1:C3

BLAGDON MANOR

César award in 2006

'Our favourite place to stay.' Praise this year comes from trusted reporters returning to Liz and Steve Morey's 'attractive, immaculately maintained' restaurant-with-rooms. Their Grade II listed mansion stands in 'beautifully manicured gardens'. 'Liz and Steve are the best kind of hoteliers – friendly and helpful without being ingratiating.' Dogs are warmly welcomed: 'The kings of the place are the Moreys' friendly Labradors, who are the first to welcome you,' say other trusted correspondents. Bedrooms have views of the 'wonderful' grounds. 'Our tastefully furnished room had many thoughtful touches: sherry, good biscuits, fruit, a selection of quality magazines. Though small, it was well appointed and comfortable.' In good weather, afternoon tea and drinks are taken on a patio overlooking the countryside. The large conservatory dining room has 'well-spaced, elegantly laid' tables; Steve Morey's 'excellent' cooking is 'fresh and pleasant', with dishes such as pan-fried duck breast, duck confit ravioli, port. 'We needed an early breakfast, and this was supplied without a quibble.' (*Bill and Patsy Bennett, Francine and Ian Walsh*)

25% DISCOUNT VOUCHERS

Ashwater EX21 5DF

T: 01409-211224
E: stay@blagdon.com
W: www.blagdon.com

BEDROOMS: 6.
OPEN: all year Wed–Sun, except 2 weeks Jan.
FACILITIES: ramps, lounge, library, snug, bar, conservatory, restaurant, private dining room, free Wi-Fi in lounge, 20-acre grounds (3-acre gardens, croquet, giant chess, gazebo, pond), unsuitable for &.
BACKGROUND MUSIC: none.
LOCATION: 8 miles NE of Launceston.
CHILDREN: not under 12.
DOGS: allowed (£10 charge per night).
CREDIT CARDS: MasterCard, Visa.
PRICES: per room B&B £145–£250. Set dinner £35–£40. 1-night bookings refused Christmas.

ASKHAM Cumbria

Map 4: inset C2

ASKHAM HALL   NEW

In a village on the eastern edge of the Lake District national park, this manor house (a Grade I listed Pele Tower expanded in Elizabethan times) is the family home of Charles Lowther and his artist wife, Juno. In late 2013, they opened the hall as a 'Bohemian home from home'. 'They have created a hotel of character,' say *Guide* inspectors. 'The staff were willing to please and anxious to listen to our comments; the food was excellent.' The bedrooms are in the Pele Tower and a 17th-century wing. 'Our room had a magnificent stone fireplace; a large, comfortable bed; an antique chest of drawers, a circular table with two chairs; a brass rod with hangers in place of a wardrobe.' There is striking artwork by Juno Lowther in the hall. The drawing room has 'books, paintings, framed photographs – the epitome of a wealthy family home'. There's an honesty bar in the library. In the restaurant, Cumbrian-born chef Richard Swale serves a short seasonal menu: 'The cooking was seriously good. We enjoyed well-presented scallops and spring lamb, enhanced by vegetables and herbs from the hotel's garden.'

Askham
Penrith CA10 2PF

T: 01931-712350
E: enquiries@askhamhall.co.uk
W: www.askhamhall.co.uk

BEDROOMS: 13.
OPEN: all year except Christmas/New Year, Jan–early Feb, Sun/Mon (Sun–Thurs Oct–Mar).
FACILITIES: drawing room, library, billiard room, 3 dining rooms, free Wi-Fi in bedrooms, civil wedding licence, 12-acre gardens, small swimming pool, only restaurant suitable for ♿.
BACKGROUND MUSIC: none.
LOCATION: 5 miles S of Penrith.
CHILDREN: all ages welcomed, not under 10 in restaurant.
DOGS: allowed in bedrooms, not in restaurant.
CREDIT CARDS: Amex, MasterCard, Visa.
PRICES: [2014] per room B&B £150–£320. Set dinner £45.

AUSTWICK North Yorkshire

AUSTWICK HALL

'Great company', Michael Pearson and Eric Culley show an 'obvious enthusiasm' for their home, a handsome manor house which they have 'lovingly' restored. The house, parts of which date back to the 12th century, has a mix of Tudor and Georgian influences. It has been furnished with antiques, paintings and a vast collection of ethnic art. Arriving visitors will be greeted with home-made scones and jam in the 'relaxing' lounge, which has a wood-burning stove, bookcases and sofas. The bedrooms are off open landings reached by a curved staircase. 'Our huge room was well lit; the old floorboards and bed frame were polished; a marble fireplace, antique wardrobe, a writing desk.' Rooms are well equipped: a flat-screen TV, DVD/CD-player, a hospitality tray with chocolates. Breakfast is a 'relaxed affair' (served until 10 am): cereals, home-made granola, fruit salad, yogurts and freshly baked croissants are on a side table; there are 'eggs to your liking' and all manner of ingredients for the cooked dish. On Sundays and Mondays from April to October the house and gardens are open to the public.

Townhead Lane
Austwick LA2 8BS

T: 01524-251794
E: austwickhall@austwick.org
W: www.austwickhall.co.uk

BEDROOMS: 4.
OPEN: all year.
FACILITIES: hall, sitting room, drawing room, dining room, free Wi-Fi, 13-acre gardens, hot tub, unsuitable for &.
BACKGROUND MUSIC: none.
LOCATION: edge of village.
CHILDREN: not under 16.
DOGS: not allowed.
CREDIT CARDS: MasterCard, Visa.
PRICES: [2014] per room B&B single £110–£140, double £125–£155 (rates lower Feb/Mar mid-week). 1-night bookings refused bank holiday weekends.

AUSTWICK North Yorkshire

THE TRADDOCK

César award in 2014

In a 'lovely, quiet' village location, the Reynolds family's small hotel has a 'homely' atmosphere and 'pleasant, obliging staff', say visitors this year. The Grade II listed Georgian manor (with Victorian extensions) is 'not grand, not designerish, not shabby either', said *Guide* inspectors. Three 'lovely' lounges have 'big sofas, lots of chairs, board games'; the walled garden terrace, ideal for 'delicious scones in the sunshine', has views over the Yorkshire Dales. 'Pretty' bedrooms vary in size and aspect; a large family room with a Victorian bay window overlooks the gardens. Dogs are welcomed in all rooms: towels and dog-washing facilities are available, the grounds have plenty of room for a gambol. Inspired by the Slow Food Movement, chef John Pratt's 'excellent' cooking features seasonal produce, much of it sourced from within a 50-mile radius. 'The pigeon breast with braised pearl barley is worthy of a special mention.' Breakfast is 'fantastic': home-made lemon curd and 'thick toast', an 'enormous' full English, 'an excellent kipper'. 'Good walking'; guides, maps, packed lunches available. (*Michael Heath, Peter Anderson, and others*)

Austwick, Settle
LA2 8BY

T: 01524-251224
F: 01524-251796
E: info@austwicktraddock.co.uk
W: www.thetraddock.co.uk

BEDROOMS: 12, 1 on ground floor.
OPEN: all year.
FACILITIES: 3 lounges, bar, 2 dining rooms, function facilities, free Wi-Fi, 1½-acre grounds (sun deck), only public rooms accessible to &.
BACKGROUND MUSIC: in 2 lounges and dining rooms.
LOCATION: 4 miles NW of Settle, train Settle, bus.
CHILDREN: all ages welcomed.
DOGS: allowed in bedrooms, public rooms on lead, not in restaurant.
CREDIT CARDS: MasterCard, Visa.
PRICES: [2014] per person B&B £45–£100, D,B&B £77.50–£132.50. À la carte £30. 1-night bookings refused weekends in season.

AYCLIFFE VILLAGE Co. Durham   Map 4:C4

THE COUNTY

'A delight to visit.' Opposite the village green, this refurbished former pub is a 'well-kept', 'bustling' restaurant-with-rooms and 'a really comfortable place to stay'. The front garden is 'especially lovely in contrast to the very busy A1 just five minutes away'. Colette Farrell and Stuart Dale are the 'hands-on' owners; they are supported by a 'friendly and seemingly happy' team. In the 'welcoming' open-plan restaurant, Stuart Dale cooks 'exceptional' food – 'and the place is very busy with locals to prove it'. 'We had a good seafood mixed grill, and sole.' Next to the main building, the bedrooms are simply furnished in modern style; many overlook the green. 'Our room (No. 4) had a large bed, good lighting, two comfortable leather armchairs; a dressing room with plenty of storage led to the good-sized bathroom with a window.' The ground-floor residents' lounge is 'useful if the pub is busy; the small patio, accessed through French doors in the lounge, is probably very popular in the summer'. A 'proper' breakfast has freshly cooked eggs and 'excellent' bacon. 'Easy parking.' (*Lynn Wildgoose*)

13 The Green
Aycliffe Village
Newton Aycliffe
DL5 6LX

T: 01325-312273
F: 01325-317131
E: info@thecountyaycliffevillage.com
W: www.thecountyaycliffevillage.com

BEDROOMS: 7 in annexe.
OPEN: all year except 25/26 Dec, 1 Jan.
FACILITIES: bar, restaurant, free Wi-Fi, unsuitable for &.
BACKGROUND MUSIC: 'easy listening'.
LOCATION: in village 5 miles N of Darlington.
CHILDREN: all ages welcomed.
DOGS: not allowed.
CREDIT CARDS: Amex, MasterCard, Visa.
PRICES: [2014] per room B&B single £49, double £70–£110. À la carte £25.

AYLESBURY Buckinghamshire

Map 2:C3

HARTWELL HOUSE

César award in 1997

In 'beautiful' landscaped grounds with a lake, a church and a Gothic tower, this 'excellent' stately home is run by Richard Broyd's Historic House Hotels for the National Trust. 'Sumptuous' public rooms have antiques, brocaded sofas, marble fireplaces and rococo ceilings; they are a 'pleasant' place for aperitifs. In the elegant dining room, chef Daniel Richardson's seasonal menus might include roasted loin of venison, gingerbread crust, creamed potatoes. (Faced with a sea bass special three evenings in a row, a guest this year would have liked more variety on the menu.) A remarkable staircase, decorated with carved Jacobean figures, leads to the rooms and suites upstairs; all are decorated with fine prints and pictures. 'We were blown away by the size of our royal four-poster room; it had a beautiful, very large and comfortable bed, sofas, a dressing table.' More bedrooms are in the converted coach house and the *Old Rectory*, a restored Georgian house standing in its own two-acre garden. Treatments can be taken in the spa, which has a 'lovely' swimming pool. (*John and Irene Harding, OHS, and others*)

Oxford Road
nr Aylesbury HP17 8NR

T: 01296-747444
F: 01296-747450
E: info@hartwell-house.com
W: www.hartwell-house.com

BEDROOMS: 46, 16 in stable block, some on ground floor, 2 suitable for &.
OPEN: all year.
FACILITIES: lift, ramps, 4 drawing rooms, bar, 3 dining rooms, conference facilities, free Wi-Fi, civil wedding licence, spa (swimming pool, 8 by 16 metres), 90-acre grounds (tennis).
BACKGROUND MUSIC: none.
LOCATION: 2 miles W of Aylesbury.
CHILDREN: not under 4.
DOGS: allowed in some bedrooms.
CREDIT CARDS: Amex, MasterCard, Visa.
PRICES: [2014] per room B&B single £175–£290, double £205–£700. Set dinner £25–£62.

BABBACOMBE Devon

Map 1:D5

THE CARY ARMS

Sheltered behind a headland, this small, secluded hotel, in a dramatic setting below a steep cliff on Babbacombe Bay, emerged unscathed from the battering storms of early 2014. It is owned by Peter and Lana de Savary. There is a modern nautical look throughout, with yachting photographs in the lounge, and stripy deckchairs on the terrace overlooking the beach and bay. All the bedrooms have sea views; most have a terrace or balcony. 'Our lovely, large room had New England-style panelled walls, a big, comfy bed, a decanter of sloe gin; a good bathroom with fluffy towels and flannels. A stick of *Cary Arms* rock was left on each pillow at turn-down.' Menus are written on blackboards in the restaurant; chef Ben Kingdon uses much freshly caught fish and shellfish in his menus. Typical dishes: mackerel fillet, pickled beetroot; garlic-infused lamb 'cooked perfectly pink, as requested'. A 'wholesome' breakfast is 'very good'; there is a buffet with fresh fruit, yogurts, ham on the bone; 'good' cooked dishes are brought to the table. Children are welcomed with a fishing net, bucket and spade.

Beach Road
Babbacombe TQ1 3LX

T: 01803-327110
F: 01803-323221
E: enquiries@caryarms.co.uk
W: www.caryarms.co.uk

BEDROOMS: 8, 2 on ground floor, plus 4 self-catering cottages.
OPEN: all year.
FACILITIES: lounge, bar, restaurant, conservatory, free Wi-Fi, civil wedding licence, garden, terrace, treatment room.
BACKGROUND MUSIC: occasional live jazz.
LOCATION: by beach.
CHILDREN: all ages welcomed.
DOGS: not allowed in 6 bedrooms.
CREDIT CARDS: Amex, MasterCard, Visa.
PRICES: [2014] per room B&B £155–£375. À la carte £29. 1-night bookings refused weekends.

BARNSLEY Gloucestershire

BARNSLEY HOUSE

With 'the smell of wood burning in the cosy lounges', there is 'a romantic air' at this 'relaxed' country hotel in a 'beautiful setting' among historic gardens. The William and Mary house was once the home of celebrated gardener Rosemary Verey; today, it is a luxury hotel run by the owners of *Calcot Manor*, Tetbury (see entry). The extensive grounds have statues, a knot garden and a potager, formal lawns and ancient meadows; head gardener Richard Gatenby works closely with chef Graham Grafton to grow food for the kitchens. Bedrooms are divided between the main house, the stableyard and other buildings in the grounds; 'there are some lovely rooms if you are careful about which you choose,' *Guide* inspectors found. A duplex room in the stable block had a bedroom up a steep flight of steps; a 'charming' bedroom in the main house had a sitting area with a window seat overlooking the garden. 'We liked the flexibility of being able to dine in the *Potager* restaurant or at *The Village Pub*', a short stroll away and under the same ownership (see Shortlist).

Barnsley, nr Cirencester
GL7 5EE

T: 01285-740000
F: 01285-740925
E: info@barnsleyhouse.com
W: www.barnsleyhouse.com

BEDROOMS: 18, 7 in stableyard, 4 in courtyard, 1 in cottage.
OPEN: all year.
FACILITIES: 2 lounges, bar, restaurant, cinema, meeting room, free Wi-Fi, civil wedding licence, terrace, 11-acre garden (spa, outdoor hydrotherapy pool), unsuitable for &.
BACKGROUND MUSIC: 'easy listening', 'lounge' music in restaurant.
LOCATION: 4 miles NE of Cirencester.
CHILDREN: not under 14.
DOGS: allowed in stableyard rooms, not in grounds.
CREDIT CARDS: all major cards.
PRICES: [2014] per room B&B £290–£650. Mid-week set menu £26, à la carte £40. 1-night bookings refused Sat.

SEE ALSO SHORTLIST

BARWICK Somerset

Map 1:C6

LITTLE BARWICK HOUSE

🅦 *César award in 2002*

'Top quality.' In large, wooded grounds close to
the Somerset/Dorset border, Tim and Emma
Ford's restaurant-with-rooms is liked for the
'simple warm welcome, comfort and good,
imaginative cooking'. The listed Georgian
dower house has smart, country-style bedrooms,
'tastefully decorated' by Emma Ford; most
overlook the garden. Well equipped, they have a
flat-screen TV, iPod dock (new in 2014); home-
made shortbread, cafetière coffee, fresh milk.
The 'rolling programme of renovation' is
appreciated by returning guests. The garden
furniture has been replaced and the restaurant
has been recarpeted. Canapés are served before
dinner. Tim Ford's modern English dishes –
'well presented but not over-elaborate' – use
much West Country produce, perhaps Cornish
lemon sole, Kynance crab, pak choi, chive
butter; fillet of local beef, shallot purée, wild
mushrooms. 'Tim's menus have some variation
every day, which is much appreciated for a stay
of a number of nights.' There are walks from
the door. 'It is not extravagantly posh, but
everything that matters is right.' (*Bryan and
Mary Blaxall, Michael and Margaret Cross*)

Barwick, nr Yeovil
BA22 9TD

T: 01935-423902
F: 01935-420908
E: reservations@barwick7.fsnet.co.uk
W: www.littlebarwickhouse.co.uk

BEDROOMS: 6.
OPEN: all year except Christmas,
2 weeks Jan, restaurant closed Sun
evenings, Mon.
FACILITIES: ramp, 2 lounges,
restaurant, conservatory, free Wi-Fi,
3½-acre garden (terrace, paddock),
unsuitable for &.
BACKGROUND MUSIC: none.
LOCATION: ¾ mile outside Yeovil.
CHILDREN: not under 5.
DOGS: allowed in public rooms
subject to other guests' approval.
CREDIT CARDS: MasterCard, Visa.
PRICES: [2014] per person B&B
£70–£95, D,B&B £105–£145. Set
dinner £47.95. 1-night bookings
sometimes refused.

THE CAVENDISH

César award in 2002

Owned by the Duke of Devonshire, this
traditional hotel borders the Chatsworth estate;
guests can walk through a kissing gate to
explore the grounds. The hotel has been run for
more than 30 years by Eric Marsh, who 'remains
much in evidence'. 'We had a lovely welcome.
Our bedroom was pleasant, the bathroom small
but spotless,' said a visitor in 2014. Light meals
are served in the conservatory *Garden Room*,
which overlooks the estate. The chef, Mike
Thompson, cooks 'innovative, modern' dishes in
the *Gallery* restaurant, perhaps tandoori
monkfish cheek, roast pumpkin purée; seared
loin of lamb, mini shepherd's pie, sweetbread.
The largest bedrooms ('quiet and spacious') are
in the oldest part of the building, originally a
coaching inn. Other rooms are in the newer
Devonshire wing; seven were refurbished in
early 2014. Although *The Cavendish* is on a busy
road, all the bedrooms are at the back, shielded
from the noise; they have views across the
Chatsworth estate. The cooked breakfast is
'substantial'. Mr Marsh owns *The George Hotel*,
Hathersage (see entry); Philip Joseph is the
manager of both.

Church Lane
Baslow DE45 1SP

T: 01246-582311
F: 01246-582312
E: info@cavendish-hotel.net
W: www.cavendish-hotel.net

BEDROOMS: 24, 2 on ground floor.
OPEN: all year.
FACILITIES: lounge, bar, 2
restaurants, 2 meeting rooms, free
Wi-Fi, ½-acre grounds (putting),
river fishing nearby.
BACKGROUND MUSIC: classical/'easy
listening' in *Garden Room*
restaurant.
LOCATION: on A619, in Chatsworth
grounds.
CHILDREN: all ages welcomed.
DOGS: not allowed.
CREDIT CARDS: Amex, MasterCard,
Visa.
PRICES: [2014] per room B&B single
£166–£196, double £227–£338.
D,B&B £49 added per person, set
menus £35–£45 (*5% 'service levy'
added to all prices*). 1-night bookings
sometimes refused.

FISCHER'S AT BASLOW HALL

César award in 1998

At the end of a driveway lined by chestnut trees, Max and Susan Fischer's restaurant-with-rooms, an Edwardian manor house, is on the edge of the Chatsworth estate. It is much liked for the 'impeccable service' and 'first-class cooking'. The 'well-equipped' bedrooms are divided between the main house and a garden courtyard. 'Characterful' rooms in the main house are traditionally decorated with ornate fabrics; 'splendidly appointed' rooms in the *Garden House* have 'quality' books, a 'generous' amount of toiletries, and umbrellas in the porch. There is a turn-down service during dinner. Mr Fischer and head chef Rupert Rowley have a *Michelin* star for their cooking, which combines classic favourites with modern combinations. Their 'fantastic' tasting menu might include dishes like Derbyshire oxtail and smoked bone marrow. There are inventive vegetarian options, perhaps pumpkin panna cotta or crispy aubergine cannelloni. Breakfast – with 'good cafetière coffee', 'generous' portions of smoked salmon, and a 'comprehensive' basket of bread, croissants and pastries – is good fuel for the many country walks from the front door.

Calver Road
Baslow DE45 1RR

T: 01246-583259
F: 01246-583818
E: reservations@fischers-baslowhall.co.uk
W: www.fischers-baslowhall.co.uk

BEDROOMS: 11, 5 in *Garden House*.
OPEN: all year except 25/26 and 31 Dec evening.
FACILITIES: lounge/bar, breakfast room, 3 dining rooms, function facilities, free Wi-Fi, civil wedding licence, 5-acre grounds, unsuitable for &.
BACKGROUND MUSIC: none.
LOCATION: edge of village.
CHILDREN: no under-8s in restaurant in evening, no under-5s at lunch, all ages welcomed at Sunday lunch.
DOGS: not allowed.
CREDIT CARDS: Amex, MasterCard, Visa.
PRICES: [2014] per room B&B £150–£250, D,B&B £258–£394. Set dinner £72–£128. 1-night bookings refused in *Garden House* June–Sept weekends.

BASSENTHWAITE LAKE Cumbria

Map 4: inset C2

THE PHEASANT

Well placed for rural walks, this 'beautiful old pub', a 17th-century coaching inn not far from Bassenthwaite Lake, is surrounded by woodland populated by roe deer, red squirrels and natterjack toads. 'It looks almost too "chocolate-boxy" to be true, but it is just as attractive inside.' Matthew Wylie is the long-serving manager. Each of the traditionally decorated bedrooms has views of the gardens or woods; superior bedrooms also have a sitting area. 'Our good-sized room, under the eaves, had an enormous bed with high-quality bedlinen. The bathroom had plenty of storage and the best power shower I've come across.' A residents' lounge, bar and garden are 'a bonus' when the pub, open to locals, is busy. In *The Fell*, the wood-panelled restaurant, chef Alan O'Kane's dishes – perhaps Cumbrian ham hock terrine, quail's eggs, crackling crumbs; cod fillet, shellfish risotto, samphire – are praised: 'Breakfasts were excellent, but the dinners really starred.' The more informal bistro has 'ample and tasty' meals. 'It remains my ideal country hotel – warm, comfortable, good food, log fires and charming staff.' (*Mary Hewson, and others*)

25% DISCOUNT VOUCHERS

Bassenthwaite Lake
nr Cockermouth
CA13 9YE

T: 017687-76234
F: 017687-76002
E: info@the-pheasant.co.uk
W: www.the-pheasant.co.uk

BEDROOMS: 15, 2 on ground floor in lodge.
OPEN: all year except 24/25 Dec.
FACILITIES: 3 lounges, bar, dining room (closed Sun eve and Mon), bistro, free Wi-Fi, 10-acre grounds, lake 200 yds (fishing), unsuitable for &.
BACKGROUND MUSIC: none.
LOCATION: 5 miles E of Cockermouth, ¼ mile off A66 to Keswick.
CHILDREN: not under 8, £30 to share parents' room.
DOGS: allowed in lodge bedrooms (£10 charge) and public rooms.
CREDIT CARDS: MasterCard, Visa.
PRICES: [2014] per room B&B £110–£180. À la carte £35. 1-night bookings sometimes refused Sat.

BATH Somerset

Map 2:D1

APSLEY HOUSE

'Everything is carefully thought out' at Claire and Nicholas Potts's 'delightful' Georgian house built for the Duke of Wellington (and, allegedly, his mistress) after the battle of Waterloo. In February 2014 they were joined by new managers, Miro Mikula and Kate Kowalczyk. This B&B is much liked by readers (and inspectors) who regard it as 'a model of its kind', praising the 'good housekeeping' and 'helpful' service. The bedrooms, some with a four-poster bed, vary in style and size (and are priced accordingly). Salamanca, on the second floor, faces south over the garden; Wellington, on the first floor, has a hand-finished solid wood bed, a chaise longue and a recently refurbished bathroom. There's an honesty bar in the spacious lounge, which has tall windows facing countryside and the garden. This is a good place to enjoy an evening aperitif. A 'generous' breakfast has a buffet of fresh fruit, cereals and Greek yogurt; the cooked items include a daily special. The house is set back from a busy road; it is a 20-minute walk to the centre of the town, or you can catch a bus.

25% DISCOUNT VOUCHERS

141 Newbridge Hill
Bath BA1 3PT

T: 01225-336966
F: 01225-425462
E: info@apsley-house.co.uk
W: www.apsley-house.co.uk

BEDROOMS: 12, 1 on ground floor, plus 1 self-catering apartment.
OPEN: all year except 24–26 Dec.
FACILITIES: drawing room, bar, dining room, free Wi-Fi, ¼-acre garden.
BACKGROUND MUSIC: Classic FM in dining room.
LOCATION: 1¼ miles W of city centre.
CHILDREN: all ages welcomed (under-2s free).
DOGS: only guide dogs allowed.
CREDIT CARDS: Amex, MasterCard, Visa.
PRICES: [2014] per room B&B £80–£215. 1-night bookings refused Sat in peak season.

SEE ALSO SHORTLIST

THE BATH PRIORY

♕ *César award in 2014*

With Edwardian sporting paintings in the lounge, and croquet to be played on the 'immaculate' lawns, there is a 'comfortable country house feel' at Andrew and Christina Brownsword's luxury hotel near Victoria Park (they also own *Gidleigh Park*, Chagford, and *The Slaughters Country Inn*, Lower Slaughter – see entries). *Guide* inspectors in 2013 praised the 'impeccable service and exquisite modern cooking' (while not overlooking the 'excellent' biscuits); later visitors confirmed that 'staff, service and food are of the highest order'. Individually decorated rooms overlook the courtyard or the award-winning gardens; 'thoughtful touches' include overnight shoe cleaning. In the restaurant, Sam Moody has a *Michelin* star for his cooking: 'We made our choices over a delicious cocktail and exquisite canapés.' 'Out of this world,' is this year's comment. Lighter eating options are now offered in *The Pantry*, a casual bar and restaurant, open from 9 am until late and serving an informal menu. The youngest guests are well catered for, too: 'We sat in the lovely garden for children's tea, and our toddlers ate every morsel.' (*Richard Bright, and others*)

Weston Road
Bath BA1 2XT

T: 01225-331922
F: 01225-448276
E: info@thebathpriory.co.uk
W: www.thebathpriory.co.uk

BEDROOMS: 33, 6 in annexe, 3 on ground floor, 1 suitable for &.
OPEN: all year.
FACILITIES: ramps, lounge bar, library, drawing room, 2 restaurants, free Wi-Fi, civil wedding licence, spa (heated indoor pool, 9 by 5 metres), 4-acre grounds (heated outdoor pool, 11 by 4 metres).
BACKGROUND MUSIC: none.
LOCATION: 1½ miles W of centre.
CHILDREN: no under-12s in restaurant at night.
DOGS: allowed in 2 bedrooms, not in public rooms.
CREDIT CARDS: all major cards.
PRICES: [2014] per room B&B £205–£1,050, D,B&B £365–£1,210. À la carte £80. 1-night bookings refused weekends.

SEE ALSO SHORTLIST

BATH Somerset

Map 2:D1

THE QUEENSBERRY

'An excellent place to stay.' Praise this year from *Guide* inspectors for Laurence and Helen Beere's boutique hotel. It occupies four 18th-century town houses, all 'high ceilings and Georgian proportions'. The hotel's location just off the Circus is 'central, but very quiet', enabling 'very easy walking into the centre'. Lauren McCann is the 'ever-present' manager; she leads a team of 'happy, relaxed, helpful' staff. The bedrooms are individually styled. 'Our room at the top was large, with lots of storage and a spacious bathroom; lots of brown and taupe in the decor; a transparent plastic armchair.' A dim view was taken of the lighting in the public areas. 'You cannot read in the lounge, and reading the menu in the restaurant was tricky.' The 'excellent' *Olive Tree* restaurant, where modern dishes are served, is 'a real draw'. 'Our dinner was outstanding: gazpacho, prettily displayed; delicious halibut on vegetables.' Breakfast has 'a good buffet and a good kipper; *Aida* with the cereals'. 'We received chocolates and little goodies, along with a hand-written note from Lauren – a little thing, but it helps.' (*Alec Frank, and others*)

25% DISCOUNT VOUCHERS

4–7 Russel Street
Bath BA1 2QF

T: 01225-447928
F: 01225-446065
E: reservations@
   thequeensberry.co.uk
W: www.thequeensberry.co.uk

BEDROOMS: 29, some on ground floor.
OPEN: all year, restaurant closed Mon–Thurs lunch.
FACILITIES: lift, 2 drawing rooms, bar, restaurant, meeting room, free Wi-Fi, 4 linked courtyard gardens, car-parking service, unsuitable for &.
BACKGROUND MUSIC: in restaurant and bar.
LOCATION: near Assembly Rooms.
CHILDREN: all ages welcomed.
DOGS: not allowed.
CREDIT CARDS: Amex, MasterCard, Visa.
PRICES: [2014] per room B&B £145–£275. À la carte £45. 1-night bookings sometimes refused Sat.

SEE ALSO SHORTLIST

BATH Somerset

Map 2:D1

TASBURGH HOUSE

In a row of imposing mansions on a hill facing the city, this red brick Victorian guest house is owned and run by Susan Keeling, 'an elegant and kind hostess'; Dalila Ganna Nasri is the manager. It stands in large grounds with terraces and a meadow park leading down to the Kennet and Avon Canal (the towpath makes a pleasant walk to the city in daylight). The twelve bedrooms, each named after an English author, vary in size and style: Kipling and Wells can each accommodate three people; Dickens, on the first floor, is a single; Austen, a deluxe double, is on the second floor and has views of the rear garden and 'peaceful' valley. Four of the rooms have been refurbished, and equipped with a new bathroom this year. There is a 'nice' drawing room in which to relax. Music plays all day in public areas but may be muted at the request of guests. Breakfast is served in the dining room and the 'pretty' conservatory. An extensive continental breakfast is included in the room price, cooked dishes cost extra.

Warminster Road
Bath BA2 6SH

T: 01225-425096
F: 01225-463842
E: stay@tasburghhouse.co.uk
W: www.tasburghhouse.co.uk

BEDROOMS: 12, 2 on ground floor.
OPEN: 14 Jan–21 Dec.
FACILITIES: drawing room, dining room, conservatory, free Wi-Fi, terrace, 7-acre grounds (canal walks, mooring), unsuitable for &.
BACKGROUND MUSIC: 'classical/jazz when appropriate'.
LOCATION: on A36 to Warminster, ½ mile E of centre.
CHILDREN: not under 6.
DOGS: only guide dogs allowed.
CREDIT CARDS: MasterCard, Visa.
PRICES: per room B&B (continental breakfast) single £95, double £120–£180. Cooked breakfast £8.50, set dinner (Mon–Thurs for groups of 8 or more by prior arrangement) £35. 1-night bookings sometimes refused Sat.

SEE ALSO SHORTLIST

BEAMINSTER Dorset

Map 1:C6

BRIDGEHOUSE

'Tea and biscuits on arrival get your stay off to a good start' at Mark and Joanna Donovan's 'lovely old hotel' in a pretty market town. Once a priest's house, the 700-year-old building stands by a bridge over the River Brit. The public rooms are in the oldest part; the bar and lounge have inglenook fireplaces, low ceilings, oak beams, lots of seating. They provide 'the perfect backdrop for pre-dinner drinks', say visitors. In the dining room, which has white-painted Georgian panelling and an Adam fireplace, the chef, Stephen Pielesz, serves 'imaginative' dishes. The bedrooms in the main building are 'good sized, well furnished'; they combine the 'charm' of the old building with 'modern comfort'. Two rooms have a four-poster bed; the best face the walled garden. Four smaller rooms are in a converted coach house at the back; it has a family suite (baby-listening devices are available and babysitting can be arranged). Light lunches and breakfasts are taken in a conservatory; all bread, jam, marmalade and ice creams are made in the kitchen. (*S and BP, and others*)

3 Prout Bridge
Beaminster DT8 3AY

T: 01308-862200
F: 01308-863700
E: enquiries@bridge-house.co.uk
W: www.bridge-house.co.uk

BEDROOMS: 13, 4 in coach house, 4 on ground floor.
OPEN: all year.
FACILITIES: hall/Reception, lounge, bar, conservatory, restaurant, free Wi-Fi, civil wedding licence, ¼-acre walled garden, alfresco dining.
BACKGROUND MUSIC: light jazz and classical.
LOCATION: 100 yds from centre.
CHILDREN: all ages welcomed.
DOGS: allowed in coach house, in bar except during food service.
CREDIT CARDS: Amex, MasterCard, Visa.
PRICES: [2014] per room B&B £125–£200, D,B&B £195–£270. 1-night bookings refused weekends and bank holidays.

BEAULIEU Hampshire

Map 2:E2

MONTAGU ARMS

Two stone dogs guard the entrance to this wisteria-clad Georgian country house, in an 'attractive' village in the New Forest national park. Inside, there are oak-panelled public rooms, an old brick fireplace, a log fire in the lounge. 'We had a most enjoyable stay,' says a visitor this year. Many of the traditionally decorated bedrooms overlook Beaulieu Palace or the garden; superior rooms have a seating area. 'Our spacious, comfortable room had its own sitting room and views of the garden.' Tea or coffee is delivered to the room in the morning. In the *Terrace* restaurant, chef Matthew Tomkinson has a *Michelin* star for his cooking, which uses much local and home-grown produce. Typical dishes: slow-poached garden egg, crispy duck croquettes, spiced consommé; grilled Shetland monkfish, buttered wild asparagus, mussel risotto. 'The food matched our high expectations; much care was lavished on presentation.' Informal meals and local ales may be taken in *Monty's Inn*. Guests can use the SenSpa at a sister hotel, *Careys Manor*, in nearby Brockenhurst. 'Right next to the river walk to Buckler's Hard, which makes a pleasant outing.' (*Bryan and Mary Blaxall, and others*)

Palace Lane
Beaulieu SO42 7ZL

T: 01590-612324
F: 01590-612188
E: stay@montaguarmshotel.co.uk
W: www.montaguarmshotel.co.uk

BEDROOMS: 22.
OPEN: all year, *Terrace* restaurant closed Mon.
FACILITIES: lounge, conservatory, bar/brasserie, restaurant, free Wi-Fi, civil wedding licence, garden, access to nearby spa, only public rooms suitable for &.
BACKGROUND MUSIC: none.
LOCATION: village centre.
CHILDREN: all ages welcomed (under-3s stay free), no under-11s in restaurant.
DOGS: allowed in *Monty's Inn*.
CREDIT CARDS: Amex, MasterCard, Visa.
PRICES: [2014] per room B&B £143–£348, D,B&B £243–£448. À la carte £70. 1-night bookings refused Sat in season.

BEPTON West Sussex

Map 2:E3

PARK HOUSE

'A lovely, peaceful place to stay', the O'Brien family's 'pretty' country hotel stands in 'immaculate' gardens between Midhurst and the South Downs. Rebecca Coonan is the manager. 'All the staff were most attentive,' says a visitor this year. The Victorian house is 'intimate and homely'; the drawing room is 'a good place to relax in'. The grounds are 'colourful, well maintained but nicely formal'. The bedrooms are in the main house and three cottages in the grounds. Bay Tree Cottage was 'excellent, amazingly well fitted and comfortable, with a private sitting-out area which had good furniture and a parasol'. A room in the house was furnished in country house style; 'all very smart, newly done and comfortable'. Callum Keir, the head chef, works with locally based producers to prepare his modern menus of dishes like vine tomato, courgette and goat's cheese tart; herb-marinated lamb cutlets with kohlrabi, garden peas and dauphinoise potatoes. Breakfast is 'lavish and good; tasty and fresh'. The 'luxurious' spa has a 'glamorous' swimming pool. There is much to do in the surrounding countryside. (*Diana Blake, Mary Woods, and others*)

Bepton Road
Bepton
Midhurst GU29 0JB

T: 01730-819000
F: 01730-819099
E: reservations@parkhousehotel.com
W: www.parkhousehotel.com

BEDROOMS: 21, 5 on ground floor, 1 suitable for &, 9 in cottages in grounds.
OPEN: closed Christmas.
FACILITIES: drawing room, bar, dining room, conservatory, free Wi-Fi, civil wedding licence, 9-acre grounds, spa, indoor and outdoor swimming pools (both heated, 15 metres), tennis, pitch and putt.
BACKGROUND MUSIC: in dining room.
LOCATION: 2½ miles SW of Midhurst.
CHILDREN: all ages welcomed.
DOGS: allowed in 2 bedrooms, not in dining room.
CREDIT CARDS: Amex, MasterCard, Visa.
PRICES: [2014] per room B&B £135–£270, D,B&B £200–£335. Set dinner £37.50. 1-night bookings refused weekends.

BIGBURY-ON-SEA Devon

Map 1:D4

BURGH ISLAND HOTEL

César award in 2012

'It is so refreshing to leave the world behind.'
Wallis Simpson and Edward Windsor used to
hide away in this Grade II listed 1930s hotel on a
tidal island at the end of Bigbury beach. Today,
restored as an 'Art Deco tour de force' by
owners Deborah Clark and Tony Orchard, it
remains a 'romantic', 'delightful' place to stay. It
is 'quirky but magnificent'; the 'house rules' are
'part of the charm', say visitors. Named after
famous guests (Josephine Baker, Agatha
Christie), 'great' bedrooms have many period
details – a claw-footed bath, a Bakelite radio,
'marvellous wallpaper' – and no TV; tea or
coffee is brought to the room each morning.
Black tie is encouraged (but not obligatory) at
dinner, where chef Tim Hall's daily-changing
menu uses much local produce, including
lobsters and scallops landed at Bigbury itself.
The winter menu might have baked pollack,
leeks à la Grecque, clam velouté; summer could
bring herb gnocchi, asparagus, courgette, truffle
dressing. Pub lunches of 'excellent' oysters and
crab baguettes are available at the 'characterful'
Pilchard Inn. (*Paula Cairns, and others*)

Burgh Island
Bigbury-on-Sea TQ7 4BG

T: 01548-810514
E: reception@burghisland.com
W: www.burghisland.com

BEDROOMS: 25, 1 suite in Beach
House, apartment above *Pilchard Inn*.
OPEN: all year, limited closure
2 weeks in Jan.
FACILITIES: lift, sun lounge, *Palm
Court* bar, dining room, ballroom,
billiard room, table tennis, spa, free
Wi-Fi, civil wedding licence,
17-acre grounds on 26-acre island
(30-metre natural sea swimming
pool, tennis).
BACKGROUND MUSIC: 1930s in bar,
live Wed, Sat with dinner in
ballroom.
LOCATION: 5 miles S of Modbury.
CHILDREN: not under 5, no under-
12s at dinner.
DOGS: not allowed.
CREDIT CARDS: MasterCard, Visa.
PRICES: [to 31 Mar 2015] per room
D,B&B single £310, double
£400–£665. 1-night bookings
refused Sat, some bank holidays.

BIGBURY-ON-SEA Devon

Map 1:D4

THE HENLEY

♀César award in 2003

'The relaxed atmosphere and lack of
pretentiousness bring us back again and again.'
Praise from regular visitors to Martyn
Scarterfield and Petra Lampe's small hotel on a
cliff overlooking the tidal Avon estuary. With
potted palms, antiques, comfortable chairs, and
piles of books and magazines, the 'peaceful'
Edwardian villa has the feel of a private home.
'The lovely house Labrador and the couple's
delightful young daughter are much in
evidence,' says a visitor in 2014. 'This is a place
to savour and to relax in.' Bedrooms are simply
furnished in country style; all have sea views,
and a pair of binoculars to go with them. Pre-
dinner drinks are taken in the lounge; in the
dining room, 'Martyn's cooking continues to
impress with its quality'. His 'delicious' home-
cooked dinners use many locally sourced
ingredients, perhaps pea soup, asparagus and
pea girasole; pan-fried John Dory, lemongrass-
marinated prawns. An 'excellent' breakfast is
cooked individually, 'so it's best not to be in a
hurry in the morning'. A steep private cliff
path through the garden leads to the beach.
(*Jane Savery, Nigel Macintosh*)

Folly Hill
Bigbury-on-Sea TQ7 4AR

T/F: 01548-810240
E: thehenleyhotel@btconnect.com
W: www.thehenleyhotel.co.uk

BEDROOMS: 5.
OPEN: Mar–end Oct.
FACILITIES: 2 lounges, bar,
conservatory dining room, free
Wi-Fi, small garden (steps to beach,
golf, sailing, fishing), Coastal Path
nearby, unsuitable for &.
BACKGROUND MUSIC: jazz, classical
in the evenings in lounge, dining
room.
LOCATION: 5 miles S of Modbury.
CHILDREN: not under 12.
DOGS: well-behaved dogs in lounge
only.
CREDIT CARDS: Amex, MasterCard,
Visa.
PRICES: [2014] per room B&B single
£90, double £120–£150, D,B&B
(2-night min.) single £115, double
£173–£195. Set dinner £36. 1-night
bookings sometimes refused
weekends.

BIGGIN-BY-HARTINGTON Derbyshire   Map 3:B6

BIGGIN HALL

In an 'excellent location for walking' in 'glorious countryside', James Moffett's unpretentious hotel within the Peak District national park offers 'true value for money'. 'The attitude to guests, the food and the accommodation are all brilliant,' says a visitor in 2014. The Grade II* listed 17th-century manor house has an oak-panelled lobby, massive fireplaces and antiques. The 'comfortably furnished' sitting room and library have oriental rugs, paintings and fresh flowers. Individually designed, the simple bedrooms are in the main house, the courtyard, the 'bothy' and the lodge; they have tea-making facilities and a bottle of fresh milk in the fridge. A daily-changing menu of classic English dishes (perhaps seared Cornish scallop, black pudding, apple purée; chicken supreme, wild mushroom risotto, basil oil; vegetarian alternatives available) is served between 6.30 and 8 pm; orders are taken over complimentary aperitifs. 'We were offered a glass of cheering hot punch on a bitterly cold evening.' Breakfast, taken between 8 and 9 am, has a hot and cold buffet. 'Sustaining' packed lunches of 'well-filled sandwiches, fresh fruit and crisps' are included in the room rate. (*Gwyn Morgan, and others*)

Biggin-by-Hartington
Buxton SK17 0DH

T: 01298-84451
E: enquiries@bigginhall.co.uk
W: www.bigginhall.co.uk

BEDROOMS: 21, 13 in annexes, some on ground floor.
OPEN: all year.
FACILITIES: sitting room, library, dining room, meeting room, free Wi-Fi (in sitting rooms), civil wedding licence, 8-acre grounds (croquet), River Dove 1½ miles, unsuitable for &.
BACKGROUND MUSIC: classical, in dining room.
LOCATION: 8 miles N of Ashbourne.
CHILDREN: not under 12.
DOGS: allowed in courtyard and bothy bedrooms, not in public rooms.
CREDIT CARDS: MasterCard, Visa.
PRICES: [2014] per room B&B £90–£142, D,B&B £122–£174. Set dinner £25. 1-night bookings sometimes refused.

BILDESTOŃ Suffolk

Map 2:C5

THE BILDESTON CROWN

On the main street of a Suffolk village, this 'handsomely restored' old coaching inn has 'attractive' beamed walls and ceilings throughout. It is owned by Suffolk farmer James Buckle, and run by Chris Lee, the chef, and his wife, Hayley, the manager. 'A must for foodies', it 'continues to be a popular local restaurant', a *Guide* inspector said in 2014. 'Cooking is of a high standard' in *Ingrams* restaurant: 'The well-presented tasting menu had first-class beef and halibut; a comprehensive wine list.' Drinks and informal meals are taken in two 'congenial' bar areas or in the walled courtyard. Bedrooms vary in size and aspect; a first-floor room facing the street had 'constant' traffic noise. 'Decorated in rococo style, my room had a carved, gold-painted bed frame, an elegant console, an 18th-century-style winged sofa; the tiled bathroom had a freestanding bathtub and an excellent monsoon shower. Tea and coffee were brought to the room on request.' Breakfast has 'moist scrambled eggs, classy toast, delicious butter', 'coffee with a smoky kick'. A decanter of 'good' freshly squeezed orange juice is brought to the table. 'Convenient for exploring Suffolk.'

104 High Street
Bildeston IP7 7EB

T: 01449-740510
E: reception@thebildestoncrown.co.uk
W: www.thebildestoncrown.com

BEDROOMS: 13, 1 suitable for &.
OPEN: all year, except 25/26 Dec and 1 Jan (restaurant is open for lunch on all three).
FACILITIES: lift, bar, lounge, restaurant, 2 meeting rooms, free Wi-Fi, civil wedding licence, courtyard.
BACKGROUND MUSIC: 'jazz/chill-out' in bar and restaurant.
LOCATION: village centre.
CHILDREN: all ages welcomed.
DOGS: allowed (£10 charge).
CREDIT CARDS: Amex, MasterCard, Visa.
PRICES: [2014] per room B&B single (Sun–Thurs) £70–£120, double £100–£195. Set dinner £19.95 (Mon–Thurs), £45 or £70. À la carte £45.

BIRMINGHAM West Midlands

Map 2:B2

HOTEL DU VIN BIRMINGHAM

In a 'fine' Victorian building within walking distance of the cathedral, shops and museums, this branch of the du Vin chain is 'perfectly placed', a *Guide* inspector said. 'It might not be particularly personal, but the staff are excellent, the situation is superb and the food is fine.' It was formerly the city's eye hospital; the 'grand' entrance retains the original granite pillars and 'wonderful' staircase. Bedrooms in the 'rambling' building are 'masculine', with a dark decor in shades of beige, brown and black. 'My spacious room had a black wood wardrobe and an armchair; the large bathroom had a slipper bath, a huge shower area, masses of hot water.' The panelled walls are covered in prints and paintings in the 'charming', high-ceilinged dining room, where French bistro dishes are served, perhaps steak haché, fried duck egg, bois boudran sauce. There are local ales, bar snacks and pub classics (fish and chips, home-made sausage rolls) in the 'lively' basement *Pub du Vin*. Breakfast has a 'country table' buffet; cooked dishes include a healthy option with egg white omelettes, carrot and ginger sausages.

25 Church Street
Birmingham B3 2NR

T: 0121-200 0600
E: info.birmingham@
   hotelduvin.com
W: www.hotelduvin.com

BEDROOMS: 66, 3 suitable for &.
OPEN: all year.
FACILITIES: lift, bistro, 2 bars, billiard room, free Wi-Fi, civil wedding licence, spa, courtyard.
BACKGROUND MUSIC: in public areas.
LOCATION: central, near St Philip's Cathedral.
CHILDREN: all ages welcomed.
DOGS: not allowed in bar/bistro.
CREDIT CARDS: Amex, MasterCard, Visa.
PRICES: [2014] room only £115–£365. Breakfast £13.95–£16.95, set dinner £16.95–£19.95, à la carte £35.

BLAKENEY Norfolk

Map 2:A5

THE BLAKENEY HOTEL

'The setting, combined with the tranquillity, comfort and excellent service, always draws me back.' Praise this year from a regular visitor to the Stannard family's 'relaxing' quayside hotel, with 'wonderful' views over the marshes. Another comment: 'It has lost none of its charm and friendliness.' 'It is a hotel that seems to retain the personal touch,' said a guest, who was offered an alternative room near the lift when the porter noticed that her original room, up several flights of stairs, might be difficult to reach. The traditional hotel has a 'mature clientele' in the off season; it is busy with families during the school holidays. There is 'plenty of room in which to relax' in the two sitting rooms. In the dining room, the 'imaginative' daily-changing menus might include fig-marinated rack of Suffolk lamb, butter fondant potatoes, bean Niçoise. A returning visitor, who found other aspects of the hotel 'excellent', had issues over the dining-room service. The best bedrooms have the views: 'My room in the *Granary* overlooked the estuary and was wonderfully quiet despite the hotel being full.' (*Moira Jarrett, EM Greaves, CT Blackburn, and others*)

Blakeney
nr Holt NR25 7NE

T: 01263-740797
F: 01263-740795
E: reception@blakeneyhotel.co.uk
W: www.blakeneyhotel.co.uk

BEDROOMS: 64, 16 in *Granary* annexe opposite, some on ground floor.
OPEN: all year.
FACILITIES: lift, ramps, lounge, sun lounge, bar, restaurant, free Wi-Fi, function facilities, heated indoor swimming pool (12 by 5 metres), steam room, sauna, mini-gym, games room, ¼-acre garden.
BACKGROUND MUSIC: none.
LOCATION: on quay.
CHILDREN: all ages welcomed.
DOGS: allowed in some bedrooms, not in public rooms.
CREDIT CARDS: Amex, MasterCard, Visa.
PRICES: [2014] per person B&B £83–£133, D,B&B (2-night min.) £95–£157. Set dinner £29, à la carte £29–£45. 1-night bookings sometimes refused Fri/Sat, bank holidays.

BLANCHLAND Northumberland

Map 4:B3

THE LORD CREWE ARMS   `NEW`

In a medieval village on the North Pennine moors, this old inn reopened in 2014 after a thorough renovation by the owners of *Calcot Manor*, Tetbury (see entry). *Guide* inspectors were impressed: 'This place has everything going for it without ever becoming twee or touristy. We were given the most cheerful welcome from a receptionist who lives in the village.' The bedrooms are divided between the inn, miners' cottages facing the square, and *The Angel*, a converted building across the road. 'Our *Angel* room was lovely: it was carefully furnished and had attractive fabrics, contemporary colours and antique pieces; a high, comfortable bed; lighting was good; a huge, stunning bathroom had a claw-footed bath and an enormous power shower.' Umbrellas are provided for the crossing to the main hotel. It has a 'dramatic' entrance – contemporary sofas around a stone fireplace; a large floral display. In the high-ceilinged dining room, chef Simon Hicks serves an 'interesting' menu: 'We much enjoyed delicious Portland crab, pan-fried duck egg and spiced butter; a tasty if large portion of creamed wheat with a crispy fried egg and wild garlic.'

The Square
Blanchland DH8 9SP

T: 01434-675469
E: enquiries@
   lordcrewearmsblanchland.co.uk
W: www.lordcrewearmsblanchland.
   co.uk

BEDROOMS: 21, 7 in adjacent cottages, 10 in *The Angel* across road, some on ground floor, 1 suitable for &.
OPEN: all year.
FACILITIES: 3 lounges, restaurant, free Wi-Fi, civil wedding licence, beer garden.
BACKGROUND MUSIC: 'instrumental' in dining room.
LOCATION: in village, 9 miles S of Hexham.
CHILDREN: all ages welcomed.
DOGS: allowed in bedrooms ('on request').
CREDIT CARDS: Amex, MasterCard, Visa.
PRICES: [2014] per room B&B £140–£180. À la carte £25.

BLEDINGTON Oxfordshire

Map 3:D6

THE KING'S HEAD INN

In a 'lovely position on the village green', this Cotswold stone inn is run in 'informal' style by the owners, Archie and Nicola Orr-Ewing. The low-ceilinged bar has 'an unspoilt rustic charm', say visitors in 2014. With low beams, rugs on flagstone floors, old settles, it is popular with locals ('Morris dancers were singing folk songs by the bar'). A separate dining room, decorated with old hunting prints, has well-spaced tables. Giles Lee, the chef, shows 'interesting modern touches' in his cooking: 'We very much enjoyed our meal: delicious crisp hen's egg, asparagus, pea salsa verde; excellent Mediterranean flavours in the house-salted fishcake with Atlantic prawns.' Six bedrooms are in the main building; they have a mix of antiques, junk-shop finds and painted furniture. Other rooms are across a courtyard with ponds, plants and shrubs: 'We were underwhelmed by our small ground-floor room; it had silver-grey feature wallpaper, a red headboard; the bed was comfortable but the old-fashioned bathroom was tiny.' The Orr-Ewings also manage the nearby *Swan Inn*, Swinbrook (see Shortlist). Bicycle hire and treatments at a nearby spa can be arranged.

The Green
Bledington OX7 6XQ

T: 01608-658365
F: 01608-658902
E: info@kingsheadinn.net
W: www.thekingsheadinn.net

BEDROOMS: 12, 6 in annexe, some on ground floor.
OPEN: all year.
FACILITIES: bar, restaurant, free Wi-Fi, courtyard.
BACKGROUND MUSIC: occasionally.
LOCATION: on village green.
CHILDREN: all ages welcomed.
DOGS: not allowed in bedrooms.
CREDIT CARDS: MasterCard, Visa.
PRICES: per room B&B £95–£135. À la carte £30. 1-night bookings refused Sat.

BLOCKLEY Gloucestershire
Map 3:D6

LOWER BROOK HOUSE

'A lovely Cotswold house in a delightful village with long walks to be had. Perfect for a country weekend away.' Praise this year from *Guide* inspectors for Julian and Anna Ebbutt's wisteria-covered 17th-century stone cottage, in a 'charming' garden bordered by a stream. There is a 'cosy' ambience in the 'comfortable' lounge, where sofas and armchairs surround an open fire. 'A welcoming place to sit; the massive fire basket creates warmth and ambience.' At night, candles are lit in the windows. Bedrooms are named after the village's early 19th-century silk mills; most have views of the garden and surrounding countryside. 'Our room, one of the plainer ones, had a comfortable bed, good linens, blankets; two slices of very good home-made chocolate cake; a basic bathroom, a little on the cool side in winter.' A supper menu of 'excellent' home-cooked food is 'satisfying and good value for money'. Guests this year enjoyed lime- and honey-marinated chicken supreme, mango salsa, new potatoes; an 'excellent' Bakewell tart. 'Breakfast was good, with freshly squeezed orange juice, well-prepared grapefruit halves, good coffee; the cooked options were beautifully done.'

25% DISCOUNT VOUCHERS

Lower Street
Blockley GL56 9DS

T: 01386-700286
F: 01386-701400
E: info@lowerbrookhouse.com
W: www.lowerbrookhouse.com

BEDROOMS: 6.
OPEN: all year except 14–27 Dec and 1–26 Jan, dining room closed Sun night.
FACILITIES: lounge (with free Wi-Fi – spotty coverage 'but we are in the countryside'), restaurant, ½-acre garden, unsuitable for &.
BACKGROUND MUSIC: in restaurant at night.
LOCATION: centre of village.
CHILDREN: not under 10.
DOGS: not allowed.
CREDIT CARDS: Amex, MasterCard, Visa.
PRICES: per room B&B £80–£190. À la carte £20. 1-night bookings usually refused Sat.

BOSCASTLE Cornwall

Map 1:C3

THE OLD RECTORY

'The sound of the birds is so tranquil' at this ecological B&B down winding country lanes near the north Cornwall coast. Chris and Sally Searle are the 'helpful, hospitable' owners; daughter Anna helps run the house, and cooks 'sociable' communal dinners by arrangement. The house and 'magnificent' grounds were the backdrop for the blossoming romance between the writer Thomas Hardy and the rector's sister, Emma Gifford; through these 'most beautiful and romantic gardens', guests may sit and stroll where the poet courted his future wife. The slate-hung house retains many Victorian features; the 'lovely' terrace, sheltered from wind and rain, is ideal for tea or a pre-dinner drink. Decorated in period style, bedrooms have antiques, home-made biscuits and much 'character'. 'We stayed in the Old Stable with our two dogs; it was very comfortable and private.' Dinners and 'plentiful' breakfasts use fruit and vegetables from the walled garden, eggs from the Searles' hens and ducks, bacon, sausages and chops from their pigs, honey from their bees. 'Everywhere is green, from solar panels in a field to waste disposal.' (*Janet Covacic, and others*)

St Juliot, nr Boscastle
PL35 0BT

T: 01840-250225
E: sally@stjuliot.com
W: www.stjuliot.com

BEDROOMS: 4, 1 in stables (linked to house).
OPEN: Mar–Nov.
FACILITIES: sitting room, breakfast room, conservatory, free Wi-Fi, 3-acre garden (croquet lawn, 'lookout'), unsuitable for &.
BACKGROUND MUSIC: none.
LOCATION: 2 miles NE of Boscastle.
CHILDREN: not under 12.
DOGS: only allowed in stables (£8 per stay).
CREDIT CARDS: MasterCard, Visa.
PRICES: [2014] per room B&B £70–£110. 2-course dinner (by arrangement; bring your own bottle) £15. 1-night bookings refused weekends and busy periods.

BOSHAM West Sussex

THE MILLSTREAM

25% DISCOUNT VOUCHERS

On the road leading to the harbour in a Saxon village, this hotel has been owned by the Wild family for almost 40 years. Clare Sherlock, née Wild, is the manager. Originally a row of 17th-century cottages, it has a 'pretty' garden with a millstream and gazebo. The 'high standards of service' were liked by a *Guide* inspector in 2014. 'It appeals strongly to a mature clientele who value the traditional decor and ambience. It also recognises the need to attract a wider guest list by having a young and enthusiastic staff and up-to-date facilities in the bedrooms.' Tables are well spaced in the restaurant where chef Neil Hiskey serves modern dishes. 'We enjoyed twice-baked cheese soufflé; breast of guineafowl with risotto; the cooking was good if not memorable.' Meals can also be taken in the informal *Marwick's Brasserie*. The bedrooms have bold floral prints. 'Our room, which had a small balcony over the garden, had sheets and blankets on the bed as requested; good reading lights; two chairs and a built-in dressing table; fresh milk and water in a small fridge. Housekeeping was excellent.'

Bosham Lane
Bosham, nr Chichester
PO18 8HL

T: 01243-573234
F: 01243-573459
E: info@millstreamhotel.com
W: www.millstreamhotel.com

BEDROOMS: 35, 2 in cottage, 7 on ground floor, 1 suitable for &.
OPEN: all year.
FACILITIES: lounge, bar, restaurant (pianist Fri and Sat), brasserie, conference room, free Wi-Fi, civil wedding licence, 1¼-acre garden, Chichester Harbour 300 yards.
BACKGROUND MUSIC: 'mixed' music 10.30 am–10.30 pm in lounge and restaurant.
LOCATION: 4 miles W of Chichester.
CHILDREN: all ages welcomed, £20 B&B to share adult's room.
DOGS: only guide dogs allowed.
CREDIT CARDS: all major cards.
PRICES: [2014] per room B&B single £99–£139, double £159–£229. D,B&B (min. 2 nights) £92–£147 per person, set dinner £26.50–£34, à la carte £45. 1-night bookings refused Sat.

BOURTON-ON-THE-HILL Gloucestershire   Map 3:D6

THE HORSE AND GROOM

César award in 2012

In a hilltop Cotswold village, this Grade II
listed Georgian coaching inn is now run as a
'delightful' pub-with-rooms by brothers Tom
and Will Greenstock. 'We received a sincere
welcome from Tom', who manages front-of-
house. Will is the chef, whose 'imaginative yet
unpretentious' menus are served in the 'busy',
'cheerful' dining room. 'The food is of a
consistently high standard, with a commitment
to using locally sourced ingredients', perhaps
trio of charcuterie, celeriac remoulade; whole
Cornish lemon sole, brown shrimps, Café de
Paris butter. Smart, modern bedrooms 'have all
the essentials'; one has views over the village,
another has French doors opening on to the
landscaped garden. 'Our spacious bedroom had
an extremely comfortable bed; we loved the
complimentary flapjack and fresh milk – such a
contrast to standard hotel offerings.' Breakfast
has eggs from the Greenstocks' hens, milk from
the local farm, 'gorgeous, buttery croissants'; 'the
yellowest butter we have ever seen'. There is no
lounge, 'but you can sit comfortably and read in
your bedroom'. Some road noise from the busy
A44. (*Jane and Stephen Marshall, and others*)

25% DISCOUNT VOUCHERS

Bourton-on-the-Hill
nr Moreton-in-Marsh
GL56 9AQ

T/F: 01386-700413
E: greenstocks@
    horseandgroom.info
W: www.horseandgroom.info

BEDROOMS: 5.
OPEN: all year except 25/31 Dec,
restaurant closed Sun eve except on
bank holiday weekends.
FACILITIES: bar/restaurant, free
Wi-Fi, 1-acre garden, unsuitable
for &.
BACKGROUND MUSIC: none.
LOCATION: village centre.
CHILDREN: all ages welcomed.
DOGS: not allowed.
CREDIT CARDS: Diners, MasterCard,
Visa.
PRICES: [2014] per room B&B single
£80, double £120–£170. À la carte
£27. 1-night bookings refused
weekends.

BOWNESS-ON-WINDERMERE Cumbria   Map 4: inset C2

LINDETH FELL

♥ *César award in 2009*

'A real country house atmosphere and hands-on proprietors – our sort of hotel.' Praise this year from returning visitors to Diana Kennedy's country hotel, in 'lovely grounds' on the fells overlooking Lake Windermere. A family affair, the hotel is managed by daughters Sheena and Jo. 'The Kennedys are much in evidence, chatting to guests and ensuring that we are being looked after. It is that personal touch that attracts so many regular guests.' Individually styled rooms vary greatly in size; the largest have a super-king-size bed and a seating area. Guests have use of two sitting rooms with deep sofas, books and magazines; afternoon tea may be taken on the terrace in the summer. In the restaurant overlooking the lake, chef Bryan Parsons's 'imaginative' dishes might include beetroot gravlax, potted salmon, horseradish emulsion; Lancashire pork belly, saffron potatoes, pickled apple. One comment: 'We would have liked to see more seasonal vegetables.' There is lots of choice at breakfast, including fresh fruit, home-made marmalade and yogurt, and porridge cooked to order. (*Ken and Mildred Edwards, Jill and Mike Bennett*)

25% DISCOUNT VOUCHERS

Lyth Valley Road
Bowness-on-Windermere
LA23 3JP

T: 015394-43286
F: 015394-47455
E: kennedy@lindethfell.co.uk
W: www.lindethfell.co.uk

BEDROOMS: 14, 1 on ground floor.
OPEN: all year except Jan.
FACILITIES: ramp, hall, 2 lounges, dispense bar, 3 dining rooms, free Wi-Fi, 7-acre grounds (gardens, croquet, putting, bowls, tarn, fishing permits).
BACKGROUND MUSIC: none.
LOCATION: 1 mile S of Bowness on A5074.
CHILDREN: all ages welcomed, but no under-7s in dining rooms in evening.
DOGS: only assistance dogs allowed.
CREDIT CARDS: MasterCard, Visa.
PRICES: [2014] per person B&B £63.50–£110, D,B&B £87.50–£145. Set dinner £32.95–£39.95. 1-night bookings sometimes refused weekends, bank holidays.

SEE ALSO SHORTLIST

BOWNESS-ON-WINDERMERE Cumbria   Map 4: inset C2

LINTHWAITE HOUSE

'Beautifully situated' high above Windermere, with 'magnificent' views across the lake, this 'very comfortable' late Victorian country hotel stands in extensive gardens with 'vast' terraces for taking in the 'superb' scenery. It is owned by Mike Bevans; Andrew Nicholson is the manager. 'Service is impeccable – always attentive but never noticed,' says a visitor this year. The atmosphere is 'relaxed but also elegant, a rare combination'; 'spacious' public rooms 'combine the contemporary with period features' for an 'eclectic' feel. 'On a cold November day, we sat by the fire and enjoyed the landscape of snow-dusted peaks across the valley.' 'Our spotless room with a view was one of the more expensive, but worth every penny.' 'Delicious' canapés are served before dinner. In the smart restaurant, chef Chris O'Callaghan's 'excellent' modern dishes include good vegetarian options, perhaps crispy Allerdale cheese risotto, salt-baked kohlrabi, truffled celeriac purée. One guest thought there were 'too many fancy trimmings' on the fish. Breakfast has fruit, home-made muesli, a wide choice of cooked dishes. (*Brian and Gwen Thomas, Sandra Clark, Vanessa Cameron*)

Crook Road
Bowness-on-Windermere
LA23 3JA

T: 015394-88600
F: 015394-88601
E: stay@linthwaite.com
W: www.linthwaite.com

BEDROOMS: 30, some on ground floor.
OPEN: all year.
FACILITIES: ramp, lounge/bar, conservatory, 3 dining rooms, function facilities, free Wi-Fi, civil wedding licence, 14-acre grounds.
BACKGROUND MUSIC: in bar and dining room.
LOCATION: ¾ mile S of Bowness.
CHILDREN: no under-7s in dining rooms after 7 pm.
DOGS: allowed in two bedrooms.
CREDIT CARDS: Amex, MasterCard, Visa.
PRICES: [2014] per person B&B £95–£285, D,B&B £135–£325. À la carte £52. 1-night bookings sometimes refused weekends.

SEE ALSO SHORTLIST

BRADFORD-ON-AVON Wiltshire

Map 2:D1

WOOLLEY GRANGE

'There is character in spades' at this family-friendly Jacobean stone manor set in extensive, rambling grounds. It is part of the Luxury Family Hotels group, owned by Nigel Chapman; Clare Hammond is the 'warm and ever-present' manager. There is a 'happy, relaxed attitude', *Guide* inspectors said. The public rooms are filled with curios, well-loved furniture and wild flowers. 'Our toddlers loved every minute: the giant trampoline out front, the indoor swimming pool, the cheery play houses, the beautiful walled garden.' Bedrooms vary considerably in size and style; a small room in the eaves has views over the grounds, larger family suites have a separate sitting room. 'Our charming, spacious room, McIntosh, had a comfortable bed, and great views on two sides.' There is a good variety of 'tasty' dishes for children in the *Orangery*; in the beamed restaurant, chef Mark Bradbury's dinners might include an 'extraordinary' roast loin of cod, herb gnocchi, tomato compote. Guests who visited this year found the cooking irregular: 'We had delicious lamb rump one night, but dinner the next evening suggested it was the chef's night off.' (*Richard and Sheila Owen, and others*)

Woolley Green
Bradford-on-Avon BA15 1TX

T: 01225-864705
E: info@woolleygrangehotel.co.uk
W: www.woolleygrangehotel.co.uk

BEDROOMS: 25, 11 in annexes, 2 on ground floor.
OPEN: all year.
FACILITIES: 2 drawing rooms, 2 restaurants, cinema, free Wi-Fi, crèche, spa, heated indoor and outdoor swimming pools (12 metres), civil wedding licence, 14-acre grounds.
BACKGROUND MUSIC: none.
LOCATION: 1 mile NE of Bradford-on-Avon.
CHILDREN: all ages welcomed.
DOGS: not allowed in restaurants.
CREDIT CARDS: Amex, MasterCard, Visa.
PRICES: [2014] per room B&B £120–£500, D,B&B £190–£570. À la carte £39.

BRAITHWAITE Cumbria

THE COTTAGE IN THE WOOD

There are views down to the Skiddaw mountain range, and sightings of the red squirrels and roe deer that populate the woodland, from Kath and Liam Berney's restaurant-with-rooms within Whinlatter forest. Inside the converted 17th-century whitewashed coaching inn, guests like the 'excellent' service and the modern menus showcasing regional, local and foraged produce. Christopher Archer is the new chef; his dishes, served in the conservatory restaurant overlooking the surrounding forest, might include black figs, Curthwaite goat's curd, beetroot; Lakeland lamb loin, artichoke barigoule, mushy peas. The bedrooms vary in size and decor: small cottage-style rooms are simply furnished; larger rooms with views of the mountains have a seating area; the Garden Room has a leather sofa, an 'amazing' wet room and a private patio leading to the terraced garden. Breakfast is 'good': yogurts, fresh fruit, local bacon and sausages, home-made jam and marmalade. In warm weather, drinks may be taken on the terrace; guests also have use of a sitting room with a wood-burner, magazines, books and games. There is a drying room for walkers; secure bicycle storage. (*PH*)

Magic Hill
Whinlatter Forest
Braithwaite CA12 5TW

T: 017687-78409
E: relax@thecottageinthewood.co.uk
W: www.thecottageinthewood.co.uk

BEDROOMS: 9, 1 in the garden with separate entry.
OPEN: all year except Mon, restaurant closed Sun/Mon.
FACILITIES: lounge, restaurant, free Wi-Fi, 5-acre grounds (terraced garden, woodland), only restaurant suitable for &.
BACKGROUND MUSIC: none.
LOCATION: 5 miles NW of Keswick.
CHILDREN: not under 10.
DOGS: not allowed.
CREDIT CARDS: MasterCard, Visa.
PRICES: per room B&B £110–£205. Set menu £45–£60. 1-night bookings refused weekends.

BRAMPTON Cumbria

Map 4:B3

FARLAM HALL

♀ *César award in 2001*

'Going to *Farlam Hall* is like stepping back into the heyday of country house hospitality.' Continuing praise this year for this traditional, ivy-covered country hotel (Relais & Châteaux), which has been owned and run by the Quinion family for 40 years. 'We had a warm and attentive welcome from Helen Quinion. At dinner, staff were proactive and engaged,' said a trusted correspondent. 'The consistent high quality of the service and the food make this a very special place,' is another comment from a returning guest. 'Attention to detail is evident: a comfortable bed with crisp linens; good bathrobes; fluffy towels on a heated towel rail.' In the 'elegant' dining room, Barry Quinion's food is 'imaginative but unfussy, with sprightly variations', perhaps loin of Cumbrian lamb, roasted parsnip purée, ratatouille. 'The satisfied buzz in the restaurant says it all.' 'Excellent breakfasts have lots of choice: fresh and stewed fruit, eggs in all possible ways, toast with good marmalade and plum jam, strong coffee.' 'It certainly makes one nostalgic for a more gracious era.' (*Francine and Ian Walsh, Gillian Todd*)

25% DISCOUNT VOUCHERS

Brampton CA8 2NG

T: 01697-746234
F: 01697-746683
E: farlam@farlamhall.co.uk
W: www.farlamhall.co.uk

BEDROOMS: 12, 1 in stables, 2 on ground floor.
OPEN: all year except 24–30 Dec, 4–22 Jan; restaurant closed midday (light lunches by arrangement) except New Year's Day, Mothering and Easter Sun.
FACILITIES: ramps, 2 lounges, restaurant, free Wi-Fi, civil wedding licence, 8-acre grounds, unsuitable for &.
BACKGROUND MUSIC: none.
LOCATION: on A689, 2½ miles SE of Brampton (*not* in Farlam village).
CHILDREN: not under 5.
DOGS: not allowed unattended in bedrooms.
CREDIT CARDS: Amex, MasterCard, Visa.
PRICES: [2014] per person D,B&B £155–£185. Set dinner £47–£49.50. 1-night bookings refused New Year's Eve.

BRANCASTER STAITHE Norfolk

Map 2:A5

THE WHITE HORSE

♥ *César award in 2014*

Above the tidal sea marshes on the north Norfolk coast, the Nye family's small hotel is liked for its 'relaxing ambience, delicious food, cheerful staff and good management'. A former 1930s pub, the refurbished hotel has 'seaside colours and a simple decor' that *Guide* inspectors found 'just right'. Eight of the bedrooms are in a garden annexe; each has a terrace and access to the Coastal Path at the bottom of the garden. 'The modern rooms are very good: airy, spacious, well equipped, with (praise be) a good-sized bathroom and heaps of storage space,' says a visitor this year. There are 'plenty of options for eating': the conservatory restaurant with a decked area (and panoramic views to Scolt Head Island); the open-plan pub, popular with locals; the landscaped sunken garden with a sun canopy. Chef Avrum Frankel's 'very good' modern menus are influenced by seasonal produce and the fish and shellfish brought in by local fishermen. Typical dishes: Cromer crab tartlet, carrot three ways; local venison and orange sausages, thyme mash, sautéed kale. Breakfast 'has all the right elements: chunky toast, proper butter, freshly squeezed juice'.

Brancaster Staithe
PE31 8BY

T: 01485-210262
F: 01485-210930
E: reception@whitehorsebrancaster.co.uk
W: www.whitehorsebrancaster.co.uk

BEDROOMS: 15, 8 on ground floor in annexe, 1 suitable for &.
OPEN: all year.
FACILITIES: 2 lounge areas, public bar, conservatory restaurant, dining room, free Wi-Fi, ½-acre garden (covered sunken garden), harbour sailing.
BACKGROUND MUSIC: 'subtle' at quiet times, not when busy or in summer.
LOCATION: centre of village just E of Brancaster.
CHILDREN: all ages welcomed.
DOGS: allowed in annexe rooms (£10 per night) and bar.
CREDIT CARDS: MasterCard, Visa.
PRICES: [2014] per room B&B £100–£220, D,B&B (Nov–Mar only) £150–£230. À la carte £27. 1-night bookings sometimes refused weekends.

THE WATERSIDE INN

'A great experience', chef/patron Alain Roux's restaurant-with-rooms has a 'lovely' setting on the bank of the River Thames. The restaurant has held three *Michelin* stars since 1985 for the classic French cooking. In the glass-fronted dining room overlooking the river; the seven-course 'menu exceptionnel', which must be taken by the entire table, is rich but none the less recommended. 'We enjoyed some beautiful flavours, although I started to flag when the pigeon – after the amuse-bouche, the ceviche, the foie gras and the lobster – was brought out,' a visitor said this year. 'The service was very attentive, including a greeting from Alain Roux who took our food order.' The 'impeccable' bedrooms, designed by Robyn Roux, are divided between the main building and a neighbouring cottage; a guest kitchen has coffees, teas and an honesty box for alcoholic drinks. 'Our standard room was small but pretty, with a soft bed and an excellent strong shower.' A 'delicious' breakfast of fresh juice, yogurt and buttery pastries is brought to the room with newspaper ('not the one of our choice'). (*ANR, and others*)

Ferry Road
Bray SL6 2AT

T: 01628-620691
F: 01628-784710
E: reservations@waterside-inn.co.uk
W: www.waterside-inn.co.uk

BEDROOMS: 11, 3 in cottage.
OPEN: 29 Jan–25 Dec, closed Mon/Tues.
FACILITIES: restaurant, private dining room (with drawing room and courtyard garden), free Wi-Fi, civil wedding licence, riverside terrace (launch for drinks/coffee), unsuitable for &.
BACKGROUND MUSIC: none.
LOCATION: 3 miles SE of Maidenhead.
CHILDREN: not under 12.
DOGS: not allowed.
CREDIT CARDS: all major cards.
PRICES: [2014] per room B&B £240–£360. Set lunch £59.50–£79.50, à la carte £150, menu exceptionnel £155.

BRIGHTON East Sussex

Map 2:E4

HOTEL DU VIN BRIGHTON

With a 'state-of-the-art' breakfast buffet and 'big, comfortable beds', this branch of the du Vin chain is a 'favourite in Brighton' for some *Guide* readers. It is in a 'handy' position in the Lanes conservation area, close to the seafront. Bedrooms are in a quirky collection of mock Tudor and Gothic revival buildings with narrow passageways and the odd gargoyle. The staff are 'well motivated and trained; everyone makes an effort to help you'. 'Masculine' bedrooms are individually styled ('dark browns predominate'); some have a balcony with sea views. Rooms facing the street get some noise at night. Bistro classics are served in the 'lively' dining room, perhaps chicken liver parfait, raisin chutney; sole meunière, caper beurre noisette. Pub classics and local ales are taken in the *Pub du Vin* next door (wooden floors, pewter tankards). The wine list is 'varied and interesting'. Breakfast, served until 11 am on weekends, has 'delicious fresh breads, pastries, crisp croissants; two types of fresh fruit salad, a wonderful treacly granola; a big jug of freshly squeezed orange juice. Good cooked dishes.' (*DB*)

2–6 Ship Street
Brighton BN1 1AD

T: 0844-736 4251
E: reception.brighton@
    hotelduvin.com
W: www.hotelduvin.com

BEDROOMS: 49, 6 in courtyard, 11 in connected *Pub du Vin*.
OPEN: all year.
FACILITIES: lounge/bar, bistro, billiard room, function rooms, free Wi-Fi, civil wedding licence, unsuitable for &.
BACKGROUND MUSIC: 'easy listening' in bar all day.
LOCATION: 50 yds from seafront.
CHILDREN: all ages welcomed.
DOGS: allowed, not in bistro.
CREDIT CARDS: Amex, MasterCard, Visa.
PRICES: [2014] room £140–£319. Breakfast £13.95–£16.95, à la carte £31. 1-night bookings sometimes refused in summer.

SEE ALSO SHORTLIST

BROOKS GUESTHOUSE

In a 'good position' in the old town, close to the waterfront and the main shopping areas, this former hostel has been converted into a modern hotel by Carla and Andrew Brooks. The nominator, a former *Guide* hotelier, was impressed by the 'flair and imagination' shown in the conversion of the building. In 2014, the owners introduced the equivalent of inner-city glamping by installing four retro aluminium caravans on the roof; each has a double bed and a small seating area and hanging space; a compact bathroom. In two, the sofa will convert into a bed to create family accommodation. In the building, the small bedrooms have a contemporary decor: 'My room had a good bed, excellent lighting; a quirky 1950s chair; no wardrobe – two wooden hangers sufficed.' The quietest rooms overlook a courtyard. Downstairs is a lounge/dining room with an honesty bar. Breakfast, a leisurely affair, has 'quality coffee, granary toast; a tasty blackcurrant compote; wonderful eggs Benedict'. The building is accessed via a wrought iron gate which opens into a paved courtyard; 'perfect for coffee or sundowners' in good weather.

Exchange Avenue
Bristol BS1 1UB

T: 0117-930 0066
F: 0117-929 9489
E: info@
  brooksguesthousebristol.com
W: www.brooksguesthousebristol.
  com

BEDROOMS: 27, 4 in Airstream caravans on roof, 1 on ground floor suitable for &.
OPEN: all year except 22–26 Dec.
FACILITIES: lounge/dining room, free Wi-Fi, courtyard garden.
BACKGROUND MUSIC: 'easy listening' in lounge.
LOCATION: central.
CHILDREN: all ages welcomed.
DOGS: not allowed.
CREDIT CARDS: Amex, MasterCard, Visa.
PRICES: [2014] per room B&B £70–£119.

BRISTOL

Map 1:B6

NUMBER THIRTY EIGHT CLIFTON

César award in 2013

At the top of Clifton Downs, Adam Dorrien-Smith's luxury B&B, in a refurbished five-storey Georgian merchant's house, has 'wonderful views down to Bristol and beyond'. It has a 'stunning' contemporary interior, striking modern art and sculpture, comfortable and 'interesting' bedrooms; everything shows 'careful attention to detail'. The greeting by the young manager, Jarek Eliasz, is 'cheerful and charming'. Guests were offered complimentary coffee and biscuits while waiting for their room to be ready. The handsome bedrooms are individually decorated. A 'huge' room with wide bay windows had a wooden floor and coir carpeting, 'smart linen fabrics, excellent lighting, plenty of storage'. Its vast bathroom has a roll-top bath by the window, a separate power shower. The ground-floor lounge has 'comfortable sofas and armchairs, coffee tables with magazines, local information'; in good weather, drinks and snacks are served on a smart roof terrace. Breakfast, which can be taken in the room or in a dining room with well-spaced tables, is 'inspiring'. No evening meals; restaurants are within walking distance. (*DB, and others*)

38 Upper Belgrave Road
Clifton, Bristol BS8 2XN

T: 0117-946 6905
E: info@number38clifton.com
W: www.number38clifton.com

BEDROOMS: 10.
OPEN: all year.
FACILITIES: lounge, breakfast room, free Wi-Fi, terrace, unsuitable for &.
BACKGROUND MUSIC: jazz/soul all day.
LOCATION: on edge of Clifton Downs.
CHILDREN: not under 12.
DOGS: not allowed.
CREDIT CARDS: all major cards.
PRICES: [2014] per room B&B £125–£210.

BROADWAY Worcestershire

Map 3:D6

THE BROADWAY HOTEL

Occupying a half-stone, half-timber 16th-century building in the centre of the village, this small hotel, part of the Cotswold Inns and Hotels group, is commended for its 'warm atmosphere' and 'courteous and attentive' service. 'We were shown around the public rooms before being personally taken to our bedroom (our bag was carried),' said a *Guide* inspector. 'Of adequate size, it had a built-in wardrobe, good lighting and a comprehensive hospitality tray. An extremely comfortable mattress ensured a good night's sleep.' The 'focal point' of the building is the 'stunning' high-ceilinged bar, which is popular with locals; a striking minstrels' gallery runs along one side. Afternoon tea and aperitifs can be taken in the 'comfortably furnished' sitting room: 'We thoroughly enjoyed sitting in front of the crackling log fire.' There is a 'good choice' on the menu of *Tattersalls Brasserie*, perhaps confit of salmon, shaved fennel; roasted breast and leg of guineafowl, savoy cabbage. A 'well-stocked' breakfast buffet has fresh juices, hot dishes, and cold meats and cheese; warm toast and cafetière coffee are brought to the table. 'Exceptional value in a fantastic location.'

The Green
Broadway WR12 7AA

T: 01386-852401
F: 01386-853879
E: info@broadwayhotel.info
W: www.cotswold-inns-hotels.co.uk/
broadway

BEDROOMS: 19, 1 on ground floor.
OPEN: all year.
FACILITIES: bar, sitting room, brasserie, free Wi-Fi, small garden.
BACKGROUND MUSIC: gentle in public areas.
LOCATION: village centre.
CHILDREN: all ages welcomed.
DOGS: allowed in some bedrooms (£10 charge), on leads in public rooms.
CREDIT CARDS: all major cards.
PRICES: [2014] per person B&B £80–£110. À la carte £28–£35.

BROADWAY Worcestershire

Map 3:D6

RUSSELL'S

César award in 2006

On the wide main street of this Cotswold village, Andrew Riley has created an 'excellent' restaurant-with-rooms in the former showroom of Arts and Crafts furniture designer Sir Gordon Russell. He has created a chic, contemporary look while retaining original features: huge inglenook fireplaces, broad oak beams, stone walls. In the L-shaped restaurant (wooden tables, grey slate mats, modern cutlery and artwork), chef Neil Clarke serves modern British dishes on a daily-changing menu, perhaps pan-seared sea bass, lemon and herb bonbon, tomato, olives, polenta chips. 'Friendly, attentive service and first-rate food,' said one visitor. The bedrooms are individually designed, and vary in size. A beamed suite has a super-king-size bed and a separate seating area with two-seater sofa. An 'exciting' room on two levels had two armchairs and 'a window on almost every wall'. Some rooms face the village (windows are double glazed). All have air conditioning, good linen and a flat-screen TV. There is an honesty bar on the landing. Two rooms on the ground floor face a courtyard. (*RS, and others*)

The Green, 20 High Street
Broadway WR12 7DT

T: 01386-853555
F: 01386-853964
E: info@russellsofbroadway.co.uk
W: www.russellsofbroadway.co.uk

BEDROOMS: 7, 3 in adjoining building, 2 on ground floor.
OPEN: all year, restaurant closed Sun night.
FACILITIES: ramp, residents' lobby, bar, restaurant, private dining room, free Wi-Fi, patio (heating, meal service).
BACKGROUND MUSIC: 'ambient' in restaurant.
LOCATION: village centre.
CHILDREN: all ages welcomed.
DOGS: not allowed.
CREDIT CARDS: Amex, MasterCard, Visa.
PRICES: per room B&B £110–£305, D,B&B (seasonal) £150–£245. Set menus £13.50–£16.50, à la carte £42. 1-night bookings refused weekends.

BROCKENHURST Hampshire

Map 2:E2

THE PIG

There is a 'lovely' ambience at this 'absolutely charming' hotel, in a former hunting lodge in the New Forest. In the main house and a converted stable block, smart bedrooms overlook the forest or gardens. 'Our cottage-like family room had a large, comfortable bed and a walk-in wardrobe; a small but beautifully appointed bathroom; a larder, fridge and Nespresso machine tastefully hidden behind wooden doors. There were two sofas and a wood-burning stove in a separate sitting room; on a rainy day, we lit the stove and spent a cosy afternoon reading.' An 'impressive' kitchen garden grows much of the produce used in the restaurant. In the 'buzzy, atmospheric' conservatory dining room, chef James Golding serves a 'distinctively rustic, piggy' menu. 'There is a decided bias towards pork, but our meal of crab, trout and pollack was very well executed. The beetroot tart with goat's cheese was delicious.' Breakfast has an 'excellent' buffet (pastries, granola with thick yogurt) and a 'delicious' full English. There are sister hotels, *The Pig in the Wall*, Southampton, and *The Pig near Bath*, Pensford (see entries). (*Aileen Reid, Barbara Watkinson*)

Beaulieu Road
Brockenhurst SO42 7QL

T: 01590-622354
E: info@thepighotel.com
W: www.thepighotel.com

BEDROOMS: 26, 10 in stable block (100 yds), some on ground floor.
OPEN: all year.
FACILITIES: 2 lounges, bar, restaurant, free Wi-Fi, *Potting Shed* spa, kitchen garden, 14-acre grounds.
BACKGROUND MUSIC: in restaurant and lounges.
LOCATION: 2 miles E of Brockenhurst.
CHILDREN: all ages welcomed.
DOGS: allowed in 1 bedroom, some public areas.
CREDIT CARDS: all major cards.
PRICES: [2014] room £139–£269. Breakfast £10–£15, à la carte £35. 1-night bookings refused at weekends.

BRYHER Isles of Scilly

Map 1: inset C1

HELL BAY HOTEL

In a collection of cottage-style buildings on a rugged, virtually traffic-free island – the smallest of the inhabited Scilly Isles – this seaside hotel is part of Tresco Estates, owned by the Dorrien-Smith family. It is reachable only by boat from Tresco or St Mary's; guests are met at the quay. The cheerfully decorated bedrooms, many facing the sea, are individually styled; the best have a balcony, or a terrace with direct access to the garden and beach. Many are suitable for a family, with convertible chair beds or single beds in a connecting room. There is a 'wonderful art collection' of Cornish works in the lofty lounge. In the dining rooms, chef Richard Kearsley's modern menus might include rabbit confit, pickled baby carrots, radishes; fillet of Bryher pollack, crab risotto, lemongrass and ginger bisque. A rustic crab shack operates in the summer months. Nights are ideal for stargazing (there is a Dark Sky Discovery Site beside the island's community centre). A regular boat service operates between the islands (timetable available at reception); fishing trips and seal- and puffin-spotting trips can be arranged.

Bryher, Isles of Scilly
Cornwall TR23 0PR

T: 01720-422947
F: 01720-423004
E: contactus@hellbay.co.uk
W: www.hellbay.co.uk

BEDROOMS: 25 suites, in 5 buildings, some on ground floor, 1 suitable for &.
OPEN: Mar–Oct.
FACILITIES: lounge, games room, bar, 2 dining rooms, free Wi-Fi, gym, sauna, large grounds (heated swimming pool, 15 by 10 metres, children's playground, par 3 golf course), beach 75 yds.
BACKGROUND MUSIC: none.
LOCATION: W coast of island, boat from Tresco (reached by boat/helicopter from mainland) or St Mary's.
CHILDREN: all ages welcomed (high tea at 5.30).
DOGS: not allowed in some public rooms.
CREDIT CARDS: MasterCard, Visa.
PRICES: [2014] per person B&B £100–£285, D,B&B £135–£320. Set dinner £42.50.

BUCKDEN Cambridgeshire

Map 2:B4

THE GEORGE

On the main street of the village, this refurbished 19th-century coaching inn is owned by Anne and Richard Furbank. The 'smart, stylish' public areas have parquet floors, wood and leather furnishings; a wood-burning fire in the entrance hall. The busy bar is popular with locals (background music was not liked by a visitor in 2014). Bedrooms are named after famous Georges (Washington, Eliot, Orwell, etc). 'Our room, Stephenson, was approached via a delightful corridor with a sloping low ceiling, exposed beams, a crooked window. We had a comfortable armchair and a grand bed with a dramatic bedstead; poor lighting for reading. It was remarkably quiet despite overlooking the road off the high street.' Rooms have no tea- or coffee-making facilities, but 'tea was brought promptly, with newspapers, at 7 am'. A biscuit barrel on the landing is 'a nice touch'. In the conservatory-style dining room, chef José Graziosi's modern menus have a Mediterranean touch, perhaps tiger prawns, fennel and citrus salad, chermoula; Barbary duck breast, fondant potato, celeriac purée. Breakfast has home-made granola and a daily cooked special.

25% DISCOUNT VOUCHERS

High Street
Buckden PE19 5XA

T: 01480-812300
F: 01480-813920
E: manager@thegeorgebuckden.com
W: www.thegeorgebuckden.com

BEDROOMS: 12, 3 suitable for ♿.
OPEN: all year.
FACILITIES: lift, bar, lounge, restaurant, private dining rooms, free Wi-Fi, civil wedding licence, courtyard.
BACKGROUND MUSIC: jazz in all public areas.
LOCATION: village centre.
CHILDREN: all ages welcomed.
DOGS: allowed.
CREDIT CARDS: Amex, MasterCard, Visa.
PRICES: [2014] per room B&B £95–£150. D,B&B £75–£99.50 per person, à la carte £30–£40.

BUCKLAND MARSH Oxfordshire

Map 2:C2

THE TROUT AT TADPOLE BRIDGE

On the banks of the River Thames, this 'atmospheric and attractive' pub/restaurant-with-rooms is owned by Gareth and Helen Pugh. The 'unpretentious' 17th-century stone inn has an informal atmosphere and an 'unfussy' decor. The flagstoned bar, with cask ales, log fires and a new all-day tapas menu, is popular with locals (who are 'positively' encouraged). Children are welcomed with toys and games; the large garden that runs down to the river provides much outdoor space in which to explore. Well-equipped bedrooms at the back of the inn are individually designed; one has a claw-footed bath, another a sleigh bed; all were being refurbished as the *Guide* went to press. The information pack in the rooms 'shows much thought'. In the restaurant, chef Pascal Clavaud's modern dishes might include goat's cheese panna cotta, poached pear, beetroot; roast sucking pig, sweet potato Parmentier, garlic spinach. Breakfast has local sausages, home-baked bread and home-made marmalade. Dogs are welcomed. The Thames Path next to the inn leads through the wild flower meadows of the Chimney Meadows nature reserve.

Buckland Marsh
SN7 8RF

T: 01367-870382
F: 01367-870912
E: info@troutinn.co.uk
W: www.troutinn.co.uk

BEDROOMS: 6, 3 in courtyard.
OPEN: all year except 25/26 Dec.
FACILITIES: bar, dining area, breakfast area, private dining room, free Wi-Fi, civil wedding licence, 2-acre garden (pagoda, river, moorings).
BACKGROUND MUSIC: none.
LOCATION: 2 miles N of A420, halfway between Oxford and Swindon.
CHILDREN: all ages welcomed.
DOGS: allowed.
CREDIT CARDS: MasterCard, Visa.
PRICES: per room B&B single £85, double £130, D,B&B single £115, double £190. À la carte £30. 1-night bookings refused Sat.

BUDE Cornwall

Map 1:C3

THE BEACH

Owner William Daniel has made many changes at his small hotel above Summerleaze beach. He has shortened the name and added a bar and restaurant. 'It lived up to the entry in the *Guide*,' said a regular contributor this year. 'The staff worked hard, especially the hands-on manager, Sara Whiteman.' The bar, which is open from midday to late, has a 'rude cocktail' menu; tapas dishes can be taken (eg, Cornish fish tempura, chilli and seaweed salt). In the new restaurant, *Nomada*, Cuban chef Ruben Leon-Acosta serves international dishes like roast sucking pig, Spanish-style potatoes. The bedrooms are 'of different sizes and personality': booking by phone to discuss requirements is recommended. The best overlook the beach; they have a seating area, a bath and a separate walk-in shower. Standard rooms face a courtyard. All rooms are decorated in New England style. The fitted bleached oak furniture, and the Lloyd Loom chairs 'suit the seaside atmosphere'. 'Our ground-floor room had a terrace, a modern bathroom, a coffee machine, and a comfortable bed.' Breakfast has cereals, fruit juices, croissants; a variety of cooked dishes. (*Frank Millen*)

Summerleaze Crescent
Bude EX23 8HJ

T: 01288-389800
F: 01288-389820
E: enquiries@thebeachatbude.co.uk
W: www.thebeachatbude.co.uk

BEDROOMS: 16, 1 on ground floor.
OPEN: all year.
FACILITIES: lift, 2 bars, restaurant, free Wi-Fi, terrace.
BACKGROUND MUSIC: various.
LOCATION: above Summerleaze beach.
CHILDREN: all ages welcomed.
DOGS: not allowed.
CREDIT CARDS: Amex, MasterCard, Visa.
PRICES: [2014] per room B&B £95–£185. À la carte £35.

BURFORD Oxfordshire

Map 2:C2

THE LAMB INN

In a small medieval town, this old inn ('a lovely place') has welcoming log fires in the public areas, and a sheltered wall garden where guests can sit in fine weather. Part of a small group of Cotswold hotels, it is managed by Bill Ramsay. Built in 1420 as a row of weavers' cottages (it became an inn in the 18th century), it has many original features: the flagstones in the bar were laid in 1420, five gables and a Gothic window date back to the late 1400s. The bedrooms are 'slightly old-fashioned'. 'Our room was spacious and comfortable.' Shepherd has a four-poster bed and a sitting area; Allium, the largest room, can be connected to Rosie, a double room with a private garden. Two large lounges, which run the length of the building, have plenty of seating, books and magazines. In the restaurant, freshly decorated in 2014, chef Sean Ducie serves a set menu of modern dishes like goat's cheese and pistachio parfait; sea bass with crab risotto. Dogs are welcomed in some bedrooms, the lounges and bar; they have their own 'dinner menu'.

25% DISCOUNT VOUCHERS

Sheep Street
Burford OX18 4LR

T: 01993-823155
F: 01993-822228
E: info@lambinn-burford.co.uk
W: www.cotswold-inns-hotels.co.uk/
   lamb

BEDROOMS: 17.
OPEN: all year.
FACILITIES: 2 lounges, bar, restaurant, free Wi-Fi, courtyard, ½-acre garden, unsuitable for &.
BACKGROUND MUSIC: 'gentle' in restaurant.
LOCATION: 150 yds from centre.
CHILDREN: all ages welcomed.
DOGS: allowed in allocated bedrooms, not in restaurant.
CREDIT CARDS: all major cards.
PRICES: per room B&B £185–£275, D,B&B £39 added per person. Set menu £39, tasting menu £55 (*10% service added to restaurant bills*). 1-night bookings sometimes refused Sat.

SEE ALSO SHORTLIST

BURNHAM MARKET Norfolk

Map 2:A5

THE HOSTE

In the centre of the village, this 'well-run' hotel, in a 17th-century manor house, has 'helpful' staff and 'very good' food. It is owned by Brendan and Bee Hopkins, who have undertaken much renovation since they bought the hotel in 2012. Bedrooms are in the main building, a courtyard wing, *Vine House* across the green, and *Railway House*, a ten-minute walk away (where one of the rooms is in a refurbished railway carriage on the old train tracks). 'Our courtyard room was slightly over the top – silver furnishings, silvery wallpaper, tassels, pelmets – but the essentials were right: a large, comfortable bed, quality bedlinen, excellent lighting, a decent bathroom,' *Guide* inspectors said. In the main house, the bar is a popular local watering hole; chef James O'Connor's modern dishes are served in the wood-panelled dining room. Typical choices: lobster risotto, bisque sauce; baked halibut, herb crust, clams. Afternoon tea is taken in the lounge and conservatory, or in the walled garden on warm days. Breakfast has local kippers and 'exceptionally good' local sausages; a buffet table has home-baked pastries, freshly squeezed juice. Beaches nearby.

The Green
Burnham Market PE31 8HD

T: 01328-738777
F: 01328-730103
E: reception@thehoste.com
W: www.thehoste.com

BEDROOMS: 61, 6 on ground floor, 6 in courtyard wing, 7 in *Vine House*, 8 in *Railway House*.
OPEN: all year.
FACILITIES: bar, conservatory, restaurant, free Wi-Fi, spa, terrace garden (at *Vine House*).
BACKGROUND MUSIC: in public areas.
LOCATION: village centre.
CHILDREN: all ages welcomed.
DOGS: allowed in some rooms.
CREDIT CARDS: all major cards.
PRICES: [to March 2015] per room B&B £115–£310, D,B&B (midweek only) £170–£290. À la carte £35. 1-night bookings sometimes refused weekends.

BURRINGTON Devon

Map 1:C4

NORTHCOTE MANOR   NEW

'In the middle of nowhere, so totally peaceful', this 18th-century former manor house stands in extensive grounds with views over the Taw valley. Owned by Jean-Pierre Mifsud, who also has *The Lake*, Llangammarch Wells, Wales (see entry), it returns to the *Guide* after a positive report in 2014 by a regular contributor. 'The staff were universally charming, our room had all the necessities, and the food was excellent.' The manor has an elegant country house decor: a studded oak door opens on to a spacious hall with oriental rugs on polished wooden floors. There are large medieval-style murals on the walls of the lounges and the main restaurant. The chef, Richie Herkes, cooks a seasonal menu of modern dishes like tian of Cornish crab and oak-smoked salmon; tournedos of Red Ruby beef, pomme purée, Madeira gravy. 'Although the menu didn't change, we were offered new starters and mains for our third night to give us extra choice, an exceptional gesture.' Each of the bedrooms is individually designed: the Honeysuckle Suite on the ground floor is fully equipped for visitors with a disability. (*Peter Adam*)

Burrington
Umberleigh EX37 9LZ

T: 01769-560501
F: 01769-560770
E: rest@northcotemanor.co.uk
W: www.northcotemanor.co.uk

BEDROOMS: 16, 1 suitable for ♿.
OPEN: all year.
FACILITIES: ramps, 2 lounges, bar, 2 restaurants, free Wi-Fi, civil wedding licence, 25-acre grounds.
BACKGROUND MUSIC: classical in public areas.
LOCATION: 3 miles S of Umberleigh.
CHILDREN: no under-10s in restaurant after 7 pm.
DOGS: not allowed in 5 bedrooms, or in restaurants.
CREDIT CARDS: Amex, MasterCard, Visa.
PRICES: [2014] B&B per room £170–£280, D,B&B £260–£340. Set dinner £45, gourmet menu £90.

CAMELFORD Cornwall

Map 1:C3

PENDRAGON COUNTRY HOUSE

In mature gardens, Nigel and Sharon Reed's 'lovely' guest house occupies a former Victorian rectory 'filled with antique furniture and well-chosen pictures'. 'Nigel is a splendid host; a great deal of thought has gone into the house,' a *Guide* inspector said. Guests are offered tea and home-made biscuits on arrival; the sitting rooms have comfortable seating, books, cards and board games; an honesty bar is 'a good idea'. A guest who travelled alone said she was made to feel 'at home'. 'Elegant' bedrooms have 'high-quality bedding and heavy damask curtains; a tea tray with a mini-cafetière and a proper teapot'. In the dining room overlooking moorland, Nigel Reed cooks a set menu by arrangement (no choices but 'you get a chance in the morning to say what you don't like'), perhaps a 'beautifully prepared' ham hock terrine. 'My wife is a coeliac, and she was well catered for.' Children are welcomed: special meals can be served early for young guests; books, games and toys are available to borrow. Plenty of choice at breakfast, with home-made jams and marmalades, home-baked bread. (*Bryher Raval, Jack Beaumont*)

Old Vicarage Hill
Davidstow
Camelford PL32 9XR

T: 01840-261131
E: enquiries@
   pendragoncountryhouse.com
W: www.pendragoncountryhouse.
   com

BEDROOMS: 7, 1 on ground floor suitable for &.
OPEN: all year except 24–26 Dec, restaurant closed Sun.
FACILITIES: sitting room, bar, Orangery breakfast/dining room, private dining room, free Wi-Fi, civil wedding licence, 1¼-acre grounds.
BACKGROUND MUSIC: if requested.
LOCATION: 3½ miles NE of Camelford.
CHILDREN: all ages welcomed.
DOGS: allowed in downstairs bedroom.
CREDIT CARDS: all major cards.
PRICES: per room B&B single £60–£65, double £95–£140. D,B&B £22.50 added per person, set menu £26.

CAMPSEA ASHE Suffolk

Map 2:C6

THE OLD RECTORY

'A beautiful house in lovely gardens', this former rectory is run as a B&B by the owner, Sally Ball. The 18th-century building stands by the church in a village near the Suffolk coast ('a peaceful place to stay'). The bedrooms are individually designed. Oak has windows on two sides overlooking the garden; it has a sleigh bed and a sofa which converts to a bed, good for a family. Ash is decorated in Scandinavian style with 'cool greys and startling red'. A ground-floor room in a cottage beside the house has a sitting area (with a sofa bed); its own entrance and a small terrace. Afternoon tea, with home-made cakes, is available daily and is free to guests on their first day. Breakfast, served in the conservatory in summer and the dining room (with log fire) in winter, has freshly squeezed fruit juices, yogurts, muesli, porridge ('cooked slowly overnight in the Aga'); eggs 'from our own hens'. Dinner is now served only to parties of eight or more (by prior arrangement). Sally Ball will suggest and book at local eating places. (*AD and JL, and others*)

Station Road
Campsea Ashe
nr Woodbridge IP13 0PU

T: 01728-746524
E: mail@theoldrectorysuffolk.com
W: www.theoldrectorysuffolk.com

BEDROOMS: 7, 1 in garden cottage on ground floor, 1 in coach house.
OPEN: all year except Christmas/New Year.
FACILITIES: sitting room, dining room, conservatory, free Wi-Fi, terrace, garden, unsuitable for &.
BACKGROUND MUSIC: none.
LOCATION: in village 8 miles NE of Woodbridge.
CHILDREN: all ages welcomed.
DOGS: allowed in garden cottage and coach house, not in main house.
CREDIT CARDS: MasterCard, Visa.
PRICES: [2014] per room B&B £90–£120 Mon–Thurs, £180–£270 Fri–Sat (2 nights). Set dinner £28. 1-night bookings refused weekends at busy times.

CANNINGTON Somerset

BLACKMORE FARM

Working farmers with a large dairy herd (as well as cereal crops), Ann and Ian Dyer welcome B&B guests to their Grade I listed 15th-century manor house. It stands at the foot of the Quantock hills. Entry is through an impressive Great Hall, which has a large open fireplace and a long oak refectory table at which breakfast is taken communally. Children love the 'quirky' rooms, nooks and crannies, the lack of formality and the opportunity to watch milking from a viewing room. A small sitting room has books, board games and brochures. Light lunches (salads, quiches, soups) and cream teas with home-made lemon Pavlova and almond gateau can be taken in a café, and there's fresh produce to purchase at the farm shop. The bedrooms, in the main house and a converted barn, are full of character: West, which has a four-poster bed, has original roof trusses with cob-and-lime-plaster walls; the south-facing Gallery looks over the garden and has stairs leading to a bathroom and sitting room. Breakfast has fresh fruit salad, cereals, toast, croissants and any combination of full English. More reports, please.

Blackmore Lane
Cannington
nr Bridgwater TA5 2NE

T: 01278-653442
E: dyerfarm@aol.com
W: www.blackmorefarm.co.uk

BEDROOMS: 5, 2 on ground floor in barn suitable for &.
OPEN: all year.
FACILITIES: lounge/TV room, hall/breakfast room, free Wi-Fi, 1-acre garden (stream, coarse fishing), unsuitable for &.
BACKGROUND MUSIC: none.
LOCATION: 3 miles NW of Bridgwater.
CHILDREN: all ages welcomed.
DOGS: not allowed.
CREDIT CARDS: Diners, MasterCard, Visa.
PRICES: [2014] per person B&B £50–£60. 1-night bookings refused bank holiday weekends.

CARLISLE Cumbria

Map 4:B2

WILLOWBECK LODGE

In a village near Carlisle, this architect-designed guest house is recommended by readers as 'a great place to stop on the way to or from Scotland'. The owners, Liz and John McGrillis, welcome B&B guests, serving dinner by arrangement. They have made changes this year, moving into a cottage in the grounds; their son, Andrew, runs a coffee shop in the house, *Fini's Kitchen*, serving brunch, lunch and afternoon tea (Tuesday–Saturday). 'We received a friendly welcome from Liz who was at the door to greet us,' said a visitor this year. In woodland, with a duck pond, the house is 'modern, with light wood, beige carpets or wooden floors, a big window overlooking the pond and a patio; it feels like a private home, not a hotel. Our room had a good bed, nice white linen, a tea tray with chocolates and biscuits.' The hosts share the cooking of the three-course dinners. 'We had excellent bruschetta; duck breast with marmalade sauce; Eton Mess. It was served with humour by the hosts.' Breakfast has 'proper bread, butter, marmalade; excellent cooked dishes'. (*Carol Jackson, and others*)

Lambley Bank
Scotby, nr Carlisle CA4 8BX

T: 01228-513607
F: 01228-501053
E: info@willowbeck-lodge.com
W: www.willowbeck-lodge.com

BEDROOMS: 4.
OPEN: all year except 22 Dec–2 Jan, restaurant closed Sun.
FACILITIES: lounge, lounge/dining room, conference/function facilities, free Wi-Fi, civil wedding licence, 1½-acre garden (stream, pond), unsuitable for &.
BACKGROUND MUSIC: 'at owners' discretion'.
LOCATION: 2½ miles E of Carlisle.
CHILDREN: not under 12.
DOGS: not allowed.
CREDIT CARDS: MasterCard, Visa.
PRICES: [2014] per room B&B £100–£135 (£10 deduction for single occupancy). Set dinner £25.

CARTMEL Cumbria

Map 4: inset C2

AYNSOME MANOR

♣ *César award in 1998*

In the Vale of Cartmel, this 17th-century manor house is run as a traditional hotel by the Varley family. Chris and Andrea Varley, who took over from his parents, are in charge, assisted by David Autef. '*Aynsome* is alive and well,' says a returning visitor. 'The formula remains the same: it is our home from home and gives the best value for money in the Lake District.' Another fan said: 'A lovely building, a warm welcome and an excellent dinner (without music playing, thank goodness).' A rare dissenter, however, commented this year on 'tired furniture' and the 'dated style and presentation of the food'. Ten of the 'comfortable' bedrooms are built around a courtyard; two others are in a cottage converted from a 16th-century stable. Two bathrooms have been renovated. The lounges have log fires, patterned carpets: 'We sit here with a newspaper or a book and are happy.' In the candlelit Georgian dining room, chef Gordon Topp's daily-changing menu has 'a Lakeland slant', with dishes like roast sirloin of aged Cumbrian beef, red onion marmalade, creamed potato. (*Ken and Mildred Edwards, William Smethurst, and others*)

25% DISCOUNT VOUCHERS

Cartmel
nr Grange-over-Sands
LA11 6HH

T: 01539-536653
F: 01539-536016
E: aynsomemanor@btconnect.com
W: www.aynsomemanorhotel.co.uk

BEDROOMS: 12, 2 in cottage (with lounge) across courtyard.
OPEN: all year except 25/26 Dec, 2–30 Jan, lunch served Sun only, Sun dinner for residents only.
FACILITIES: 2 lounges, bar, dining room, free Wi-Fi, ½-acre garden, unsuitable for &.
BACKGROUND MUSIC: none.
LOCATION: ½ mile outside village.
CHILDREN: no under-5s at dinner.
DOGS: not allowed in public rooms.
CREDIT CARDS: Amex, MasterCard, Visa.
PRICES: per room B&B £85–£125. D,B&B £75–£90 per person, set dinner £29. 1-night bookings occasionally refused weekends.

CHAGFORD Devon

Map 1:C4

GIDLEIGH PARK

Built in the Arts and Crafts style for an Australian shipping magnate in the 1920s, this country house is now a luxurious hotel (Relais & Châteaux), managed by Damien Bastiat for the owners, Andrew and Christina Brownsword. It stands in 'beautiful' grounds with formal gardens and marked walks on the River North Teign within Dartmoor national park. The welcome is 'warm'. Original features (wood panelling, leaded windows, a magnificent staircase) have been preserved in the public rooms. The executive chef, Michael Caines, has two *Michelin* stars for his sophisticated cooking of dishes like shellfish jelly, Beesands crab, cauliflower cream; rosé veal, celeriac and black truffle purée. The bedrooms, all different, have antiques, paintings, fresh flowers. A smaller room at the top of the house ('with an open-plan bathroom') was less liked this year. Guests can order room service or serve themselves in a 'civilised' pantry with a coffee machine, tea, milk and 'delicious' biscuits. 'We found it difficult to drag ourselves away from *Gidleigh*,' said a fan. The Brownswords have a small group of hotels, which includes *The Bath Priory*, Bath (see entry). (*BW, and others*)

Chagford TQ13 8HH

T: 01647-432367
F: 01647-432574
E: gidleighpark@gidleigh.co.uk
W: www.gidleigh.co.uk

BEDROOMS: 24, 2 in annexe (75 yds), 2 in cottage (375 yds), 3 on ground floor, 1 suitable for &.
OPEN: all year.
FACILITIES: ramps, drawing room, hall, bar, loggia, conservatory, 3 dining rooms, free Wi-Fi, 107-acre grounds (gardens, tennis).
BACKGROUND MUSIC: none.
LOCATION: 2 miles from Chagford.
CHILDREN: no under-8s at dinner.
DOGS: allowed in 3 bedrooms, not in public rooms.
CREDIT CARDS: all major cards.
PRICES: [2014] per room B&B £350–£1,225, D,B&B £580–£1,455. À la carte £115, tasting menu £125–£140. 1-night bookings sometimes refused at weekends.

SEE ALSO SHORTLIST

PARFORD WELL

Within Dartmoor national park, this small B&B is run in 'professional but personal' style by Tim Daniel, who used to manage one of London's first town house hotels. 'He is the perfect host,' says a visitor this year. 'We had a delightful stay, in a very comfortable room.' Arriving guests are given afternoon tea and home-made cake in an elegantly furnished lounge, which has original paintings, books, games and a wood-burning stove. The three 'immaculate' bedrooms overlook the garden; there are two queen-size doubles, each with an en suite bathroom; the third room, a smaller double, has a private bathroom across the landing. Tim Daniel prepares a 'superb' breakfast. 'Nothing is packaged'; fruit salad is freshly prepared; all the produce for the hot dishes is local and cooked to order. The meal is generally taken communally, but guests preferring privacy can eat in a small, private room. The host lives in an adjoining cottage. There are 'wonderful' walks in the wooded valley and on the open moor. There is a restaurant in the village, and a pub a short walk away. (*Colin Adams, and others*)

Sandy Park
nr Chagford TQ13 8JW

T: 01647-433353
E: tim@parfordwell.co.uk
W: www.parfordwell.co.uk

BEDROOMS: 3.
OPEN: all year, except Jan/Feb.
FACILITIES: sitting room, 2 breakfast rooms, free Wi-Fi, ½-acre garden, unsuitable for &.
BACKGROUND MUSIC: none.
LOCATION: in hamlet 1 mile N of Chagford.
CHILDREN: not under 8.
DOGS: not allowed.
CREDIT CARDS: none.
PRICES: per room B&B £90–£110. 1-night bookings sometimes refused weekends in season.

SEE ALSO SHORTLIST

CHETTLE Dorset

Map 2:E1

CASTLEMAN

♔ *César award in 2004*

'Excellent food; the able staff are helpful beyond the call of duty.' '*The Castleman* will not suit everyone but we just love it.' This year's praise for this informal restaurant-with-rooms. A former dower house in a feudal village, it is run by Barbara Garnsworthy and her brother, Brendan. Another comment from a regular correspondent: 'They look after their guests as individuals; you never have to ask for anything.' Fans admit that there is an air of 'faded gentility' about the two period drawing rooms. But drinks are provided 'promptly' and the cooking of Barbara Garnsworthy and Richard Morris is 'first class': 'We enjoyed halibut with chorizo and shrimp dressing; excellent local venison; meringues with mascarpone cream.' Everyone likes 'the quiet, away-from-it-all atmosphere'. The doubts are about the bedrooms: 'Housekeeping needs greater attention: paintwork was damaged and burnt-out bedside lights needed replacing.' Breakfast wins fresh plaudits: 'They squeeze their own orange juice, make their own bread, marmalade and wonderful plum jam; and Richard cooks the finest scrambled eggs.'

Chettle
nr Blandford Forum
DT11 8DB

T: 01258-830096
F: 01258-830051
E: enquiry@castlemanhotel.co.uk
W: www.castlemanhotel.co.uk

BEDROOMS: 8 (1 family).
OPEN: Mar–Jan, except 25/26 Dec, 31 Dec, restaurant closed midday except Sun.
FACILITIES: 2 drawing rooms, bar, restaurant, free Wi-Fi, 2-acre grounds (stables for visiting horses), riding, fishing, shooting, cycling nearby, only restaurant suitable for &.
BACKGROUND MUSIC: none.
LOCATION: village, 1 mile off A354 Salisbury–Blandford, hotel signposted.
CHILDREN: all ages welcomed.
DOGS: not allowed.
CREDIT CARDS: MasterCard, Visa.
PRICES: [2014] per room B&B single £70, double £95–£110. À la carte £28–£30.

CHICHESTER West Sussex

Map 2:E3

ROOKS HILL

'Amenable owners, pleasant fellow guests,' were found by a *Guide* inspector visiting Ron and Lin Allen's Grade II listed B&B. Originally a farmhouse, it is at the foot of the South Downs. 'We were offered tea on arrival and our bag was carried to our room. There are nice countryside views; double glazing kept out noise from the road.' The oak-beamed breakfast room and lounge open on to a wisteria-clad courtyard. 'We were given a mini-suite with a super-king-size bed, double-aspect windows and a seating area with two-seater leather sofa and chair. It had cream walls, dark wood furniture, a honey-coloured carpet and a heavily ornate silver mirror.' Free Wi-Fi ('which works well') is available throughout. There are two other bedrooms; each is in 'immaculate order'. All rooms are equipped with a hospitality tray, a small fridge with fresh milk and water; up-to-date magazines; a power shower in the bathroom. The 'nicely laid-out breakfast had a good selection of fresh fruit, home-made jams, home-baked bread and natural yogurts. The full English was beautifully cooked, not at all greasy.' The *Earl of March* pub just across the road is recommended for meals.

Lavant Road
Mid Lavant, Chichester PO18 0BQ

T: 01243-528400
E: info@rookshill.co.uk
W: www.rookshill.co.uk

BEDROOMS: 3, 1 on ground floor.
OPEN: all year, except 25 Dec, 1 Jan.
FACILITIES: lounge, breakfast room, free Wi-Fi, courtyard garden, unsuitable for &.
BACKGROUND MUSIC: classical in breakfast room.
LOCATION: 2 miles N of city centre.
CHILDREN: not under 12.
DOGS: not allowed.
CREDIT CARDS: Amex, MasterCard, Visa.
PRICES: per person B&B £75–£165. 1-night bookings refused weekends Apr–Oct.

SEE ALSO SHORTLIST

CHILLATON Devon

Map 1:D3

TOR COTTAGE

Guests are welcomed with a trug containing sparkling wine, home-made truffles and fresh fruit at Maureen Rowlatt's upmarket B&B in a remote valley in mid-Devon. Her hospitality is 'second to none', said a recent visitor. There are four en suite garden rooms, each with its own log fire, well-equipped kitchenette, private terrace and garden. The Craftsman's Deco has an Art Deco theme and can be arranged as a double or a twin-bedded room. The Cottage Wing is a private wing of Tor Cottage; situated upstairs, it overlooks the valley. The most private room is Laughing Waters, which has steps leading down to a stream; it has a barbecue area with decking and hardwood furniture. Each room has a hospitality area with a fridge and tea- and coffee-making facilities. Breakfast, taken on the terrace or in the conservatory, has home-made muesli, cereals, fresh fruit and an extensive choice of cooked dishes. There are no evening meals but guests may prepare a simple meal in their room. There are abundant flowers and wildlife in the extensive grounds; deer roam the gorse-covered hillside.

Chillaton, nr Lifton
PL16 0JE

T: 01822-860248
F: 01822-860126
E: info@torcottage.co.uk
W: www.torcottage.co.uk

BEDROOMS: 5, 4 in garden.
OPEN: mid-Jan–mid-Dec.
FACILITIES: sitting room, large conservatory, breakfast room, free Wi-Fi (in conservatory only), 28-acre grounds (2-acre garden, heated swimming pool (13 by 6 metres, May–Sept), barbecue, stream, bridleway, walks), river (fishing ½ mile), unsuitable for &.
BACKGROUND MUSIC: none.
LOCATION: ½ mile S of Chillaton.
CHILDREN: not under 14.
DOGS: only guide dogs allowed.
CREDIT CARDS: MasterCard, Visa.
PRICES: per person B&B (min. 2 nights) £75–£77.50. Picnic platter £16. 1-night bookings sometimes refused.

CAPTAINS CLUB HOTEL

A short walk from the attractions of Christchurch Quay, this striking metal-and-glass spa hotel on the banks of the River Stour is 'modern but with character'. It is owned by Tim Lloyd and Robert Wilson. 'We had a fabulous stay in a lovely setting; they couldn't have looked after us better.' Each of the large contemporary bedrooms faces the water; a suite, with a 'huge' lounge, fully fitted kitchen and floor-to-ceiling windows, was 'delightful'. The hospitality tray had 'good coffee, and home-made biscuits' in a Kilner jar. In *Tides* restaurant, chef Andrew Gault's 'excellent' modern dishes – perhaps roast cod, clams, celeriac – are served on 'immaculately laid' tables. 'Our attentive waiter was very knowledgeable about the food.' Light meals and snacks are available all day in the open-plan bar and lounge; the riverside terrace is 'delightful when the sun shines'. Guests have direct access to the spa from their room (robes and slippers supplied). Breakfast is 'good': fresh fruit, yogurts, Dorset cereals, pastries; hot dishes, including home-baked beans, are cooked to order. River trips can be arranged. (*PC, IM*)

Wick Ferry
Wick Lane
Christchurch BH23 1HU

T: 01202-475111
F: 01202-490111
E: enquiries@captainsclubhotel.com
W: www.captainsclubhotel.com

BEDROOMS: 29, 2 suitable for &.
OPEN: all year.
FACILITIES: lifts, lounge, bar, restaurant, function facilities, free Wi-Fi, terrace, spa (hydrotherapy pool, sauna, treatments).
BACKGROUND MUSIC: 'easy listening' in public areas.
LOCATION: on Christchurch quay.
CHILDREN: all ages welcomed.
DOGS: allowed in suites.
CREDIT CARDS: Amex, MasterCard, Visa.
PRICES: [2014] per room B&B £199–£249. À la carte £35.

SEE ALSO SHORTLIST

CLEARWELL Gloucestershire

Map 3:D4

TUDOR FARMHOUSE

'Blissfully quiet; a good bolt-hole from the city.'
Renewed praise comes this year for Hari and
Colin Fell's 'relaxing' hotel in a converted old
farmhouse in the Royal Forest of Dean. 'An
attractive courtyard and imaginative Japanese-
style gardens around the buildings offer scope
for privacy,' says a regular correspondent.
Original features have been retained in the
public rooms where 'unremitting music' might
play. Bedrooms are spread between the main
house, a converted barn and a cider house.
'Our room was lovely, with comfortable beds,
sumptuous linen, good lighting and an
exceptional hot drinks tray including a Nespresso
machine. The bathroom had a washbasin that
looked handsome but was so small that I couldn't
wash my face without flooding the floor; a case
of design over functionality.' In the award-
winning restaurant, chef Martin Adams uses
ingredients from the kitchen garden for his menu.
'Dinner was a triumph. I had the beef cooked
three ways, roasted sirloin, terrine of confit shin
and bone marrow croquettes. Desserts, including
my treacle sponge, were equally impressive.'
Breakfast, 'in peaceful silence', was 'excellent'.
(*Matthew Caminer, and others*)

25% DISCOUNT VOUCHERS

High Street
Clearwell GL16 8JS

T: 01594-833046
E: info@tudorfarmhousehotel.co.uk
W: www.tudorfarmhousehotel.co.uk

BEDROOMS: 23, 5 on ground floor,
11 in barn, 7 in cider house.
OPEN: all year.
FACILITIES: 2 lounges, restaurant,
free Wi-Fi, 14-acre grounds.
BACKGROUND MUSIC: in restaurant.
LOCATION: 7 miles SE of
Monmouth.
CHILDREN: all ages welcomed.
DOGS: not allowed.
CREDIT CARDS: MasterCard, Visa.
PRICES: [2014] per room B&B
£95–£210. À la carte £35–£40.
2-night stays only in selected rooms
weekends May–Sept.

CLEE STANTON Shropshire

Map 3:C5

TIMBERSTONE

In a rural setting within the Clee hills, this 'lovingly extended', restored stone cottage is run as a 'delightful' B&B by 'charming' hosts Tracey Baylis and Alex Read. 'They could not be kinder or warmer,' say returning guests. A large, light public room has a sitting area at one end and a dining table at the other; there are kilim rugs on oak floorboards, books, games and a wood-burning stove. Simple, country-style bedrooms have a tea tray with hot chocolate, infusions and biscuits. A room in the older part of the building had 'old pine furniture, window seats and a big, comfortable bed'. Two newer rooms have been 'beautifully crafted' with oak fittings; one has a freestanding bath in the room. Tracey Baylis cooks a 'delicious' communal dinner by arrangement, 'served elegantly, with canapés, and choice for each course'. Vegetarian alternatives are available. Breakfast has home-made bread, eggs from the house's hens. Tracey Baylis, a reflexologist, can provide treatments in a garden studio. There are country walks from the door, and bicycles are available to borrow; the hosts are 'very helpful' with routes and maps. (*JM*)

Lackstone Lane
Clee Stanton
Ludlow SY8 3EL

T: 01584-823519
E: timberstone1@hotmail.com
W: www.timberstoneludlow.co.uk

BEDROOMS: 4 (plus summer house retreat in summer).
OPEN: all year except 25 Dec and 1 Jan.
FACILITIES: lounge/dining room, free Wi-Fi, ½-acre garden, treatment room, unsuitable for &.
BACKGROUND MUSIC: in lounge/ dining room ('if guests request it').
LOCATION: 5 miles NE of Ludlow.
CHILDREN: all ages welcomed.
DOGS: allowed by arrangement, not in public rooms.
CREDIT CARDS: MasterCard, Visa.
PRICES: per room B&B £95, D,B&B £144. À la carte £24.50.

CLIPSHAM Rutland

Map 2:A3

BEECH HOUSE & OLIVE BRANCH

César award in 2012

The 'light touch' service in the restaurant and the 'comfort and elegance' of the accommodation were applauded by visitors in 2014 to Sean Hope and Ben Jones's restaurant in a pretty Rutland village. Praise for the cooking: 'We could understand why the restaurant was full on a Sunday in November: the wild mushroom and tarragon risotto was perfect; the desserts had a suitably autumnal air, pumpkin pie, maple syrup ice cream.' Another comment: 'Hats off to the attention shown to people in our party with allergies.' The bedrooms are in *Beech House* across the road. 'Ours had a comfortable bed, fine linen; an excellent power shower in the well-lit bathroom. The bedroom lighting was less good; we were quickly given extra lights.' A suite 'had a lounge with two leather settees, two bedrooms with a TV in each, soft bedlinen (the duvet was like a cloud). The roomy bathroom had a powerful shower and large bath; outside was a private patio.' Breakfast, in a 'delightfully restored' barn, had a 'superb selection of hot and cold dishes'. (*Matthew and Miriam Caminer, Mary Hewson*)

Main Street
Clipsham LE15 7SH

T: 01780-410355
F: 01780-410000
E: info@theolivebranchpub.com
W: www.theolivebranchpub.com

BEDROOMS: 6, 2 on ground floor, family room (also suitable for &) in annexe.
OPEN: all year.
FACILITIES: ramps, pub, dining room, breakfast room, free Wi-Fi, small front garden.
BACKGROUND MUSIC: in pub.
LOCATION: in village 7 miles NW of Stamford.
CHILDREN: all ages welcomed.
DOGS: allowed in downstairs bedrooms and bar.
CREDIT CARDS: MasterCard, Visa.
PRICES: [2014] per room B&B £97.50–£195. Set dinner £24.50, à la carte £40.

COLWALL Worcestershire

Map 3:D5

COLWALL PARK HOTEL

From its black-and-white-timbered facade to the log fires burning in the lounges, this Edwardian building on the flank of the Malvern hills has 'a charm all of its own'. Originally built to serve the now-defunct Colwall Park racecourse – a guest ledger from 1907 is on display – it is today owned by Iain and Sarah Nesbitt, who run it as an 'extremely friendly' country hotel and local meeting place. An accordionist might sometimes perform in the *Lantern* bar on a cold winter evening. Individually decorated rooms vary in size; a family suite has a separate bedroom for children. 'Our standard room was pleasantly furnished, and had home-made shortbread biscuits on the tea tray. Fresh milk is available from Reception.' The meals in the *Seasons* restaurant are 'excellent': chef James Garth uses herbs and salads from the garden, produce from local suppliers for his modern dishes (eg, seared plaice, cauliflower purée, crushed potatoes). Light meals are available in the bar, which has real ales. Through the large garden, footpaths lead directly to the hills. 'Very good value; ideal for a walking or sightseeing holiday.'

25% DISCOUNT VOUCHERS

Walwyn Road
Colwall, nr Malvern
WR13 6QG

T: 01684-540000
F: 01684-540847
E: hotel@colwall.com
W: www.colwall.com

BEDROOMS: 22.
OPEN: all year.
FACILITIES: ramp, 2 lounges (1 with TV), library, bar, restaurant, ballroom, free Wi-Fi, business facilities, 1-acre garden, only public rooms suitable for &.
BACKGROUND MUSIC: 'light' music in bar.
LOCATION: halfway between Malvern and Ledbury on B4218, train Colwall.
CHILDREN: all ages welcomed.
DOGS: not allowed.
CREDIT CARDS: MasterCard, Visa.
PRICES: [2014] per room B&B £110–£200, D,B&B £195–£255 (2-night min.). À la carte £40–£45.

CORNHILL ON TWEED Northumberland   Map 4:A3

COLLINGWOOD ARMS

'The open fires in the lounges and the pretty garden are welcome sights on arrival' at Lindie and Richard Cook's Grade II listed Georgian building by the River Tweed in border country. 'You can see the careful transformation from a traditional coaching inn into something more modern,' says a visitor in 2014. Each of the bedrooms is named after a ship in Vice-Admiral Collingwood's van at the Battle of Trafalgar. 'Our large room, on the first floor overlooking the garden, had a good-sized bed, a sofa and plenty of storage. The bathroom was well lit, and had a separate shower and bath. However, lighting in the bedroom was inadequate, with just two bedside lamps and one small desk lamp.' The chef, Gordon Campbell, serves separate menus for the elegant dining room and the informal brasserie, which adjoins the cheerful bar. 'They are flexible about which menu you use, and you can mix and match vegetables and sauces. Cooking was hit and miss: we enjoyed very good roe deer and a decent fish pie.' (*LW, and others*)

25% DISCOUNT VOUCHERS

Main Street
Cornhill on Tweed
TD12 4UH

T: 01890-882424
F: 01890-883098
E: enquiries@collingwoodarms.com
W: www.collingwoodarms.com

BEDROOMS: 15, 1 on ground floor.
OPEN: all year.
FACILITIES: hall, library, bar/brasserie, dining room, free Wi-Fi in public areas only, 3-acre garden.
BACKGROUND MUSIC: in brasserie.
LOCATION: village centre.
CHILDREN: all ages welcomed.
DOGS: allowed in kennels, only guide dogs in restaurant.
CREDIT CARDS: MasterCard, Visa.
PRICES: [2014] per room B&B £130–£200, D,B&B from £185. Set menus £29–£35, à la carte £20.

COWAN BRIDGE Lancashire

Map 4: inset D2

HIPPING HALL

🏆 *César award in 2008*

In 'peaceful, well-kept grounds', this 'sympathetically renovated' 18th-century 'mini-stately home' is run as a hotel/restaurant by owner/manager Andrew Wildsmith. Trusted reporters returning in 2014 enjoyed again 'a warm welcome, and the attention to detail that makes for a comfortable stay'. The bedrooms are 'furnished in country style'; there are 'very comfortable beds'; 'smart' bathrooms are tiled in natural stone. A suite has been created in the roof of the building: 'It has a sitting room, a large bedroom; the spacious bathroom, designed like a conservatory, had a sofa and a bath big enough for two. Good lighting highlighted the original beams.' Andrew Wildsmith takes orders for dinner, which is served in the 15th-century Great Hall. Everyone praises the 'outstanding' cooking of New Zealand chef Brent Hulena: 'Superb: innovative, delicate flavours beautifully presented.' Typical dishes: Lancashire quail, savoy cabbage, foie gras; roast halibut, truffled pomme purée. A 'good' breakfast is 'individually prepared and served hot'. The staff are 'young enthusiastic, attentive'. (*Jane and Martin Bailey, David and Kate Wooff, William Wood*)

Cowan Bridge
nr Kirkby Lonsdale LA6 2JJ

T: 015242-71187
E: info@hippinghall.com
W: www.hippinghall.com

BEDROOMS: 10, 3 in cottages, 1, on ground floor, suitable for ♿.
OPEN: all year.
FACILITIES: lounge, bar, restaurant, free Wi-Fi, civil wedding licence, 3-acre garden.
BACKGROUND MUSIC: jazz in dining hall, bar.
LOCATION: 2 miles SE of Kirkby Lonsdale, on A65.
CHILDREN: all ages welcomed.
DOGS: allowed in 2 bedrooms, not in public rooms.
CREDIT CARDS: MasterCard, Visa.
PRICES: [2014] per room B&B £159–£419. D,B&B £40 added per person, set dinner £55–£65 (£39.50 Sun–Thurs). 1-night bookings normally refused Sat.

CROFT-ON-TEES Co. Durham

Map 4:C4

CLOW BECK HOUSE

César award in 2007

In 'beautifully landscaped and immaculately kept' gardens close to the River Tees, Heather and David Armstrong's small hotel and restaurant occupy a group of converted stone outbuildings on family farmland. 'Housekeeping is excellent: everything is spotless.' The Armstrongs are 'friendly' hosts who 'make their guests feel special'; visitors are greeted with tea and home-made cake or biscuits in the 'bright and comfortable' lounge. It is an 'unusual' place; the theatrical decor and novelty garden ornaments might not be to all tastes, but they are done with 'humour and charm'. The well-equipped bedrooms are individually decorated: one has a bay window and a chandelier, another, dramatic and moody, has a black-painted brass bed. Drinks and canapés are taken in the lounge before dinner; David Armstrong's 'farmhouse' menus, including a separate vegetarian menu, have 'good and wholesome' dishes such as fillet steak, Yorkshire Blue cheese, new potatoes. Breakfast has home-baked nut and apricot bread, home-made yogurt, local cheeses and a large variety of 'excellent' cooked dishes. Good walks from the door.

Monk End Farm
Croft-on-Tees
nr Darlington DL2 2SP

T: 01325-721075
F: 01325-720419
E: david@clowbeckhouse.co.uk
W: www.clowbeckhouse.co.uk

BEDROOMS: 13, 12 in garden buildings, 1 suitable for &.
OPEN: all year except Christmas/New Year.
FACILITIES: ramps, lounge, restaurant, free Wi-Fi, small conference facilities, 2-acre grounds in 100-acre farm.
BACKGROUND MUSIC: classical in restaurant.
LOCATION: 3 miles S of Darlington.
CHILDREN: all ages welcomed.
DOGS: not allowed in bedrooms, public rooms.
CREDIT CARDS: Amex, MasterCard, Visa.
PRICES: per room B&B single £85, double £135. À la carte £37.

CRUDWELL Wiltshire

Map 3:E5

THE RECTORY HOTEL

Children are welcomed at this small hotel, which was once the home of a village rector who had 14 offspring. It is managed by Jenna Tomblin for the owners Julian Muggridge (antiques dealer) and Jonathan Barry (formerly with Hotel du Vin). In the Victorian walled garden there is a croquet lawn, a boules court and a heated outdoor swimming pool. 'Our son loved roaming the grounds,' said a recent visitor. In the large hall/sitting room there are soft chairs, a log fire and magazines; the high-ceilinged bar/lounge has a collection of ornamental glass. Bedrooms have a mix of antique and contemporary furniture, a Roberts radio and an iPod docking station. Leckhampton is large, bright and airy with window seats and a king-size bed; Sudeley has a super-king-size four-poster, and 'his' and 'hers' sinks in the bathroom. In the wood-panelled dining room, which looks over a sunken Victorian pool, chef Peter Fairclough serves a modern menu with dishes like tuna sashimi with salad; roast corn-fed chicken, wild mushroom, potato galette. Children have their own menu. The *Potting Shed* pub across the street is under the same ownership.

25% DISCOUNT VOUCHERS

Crudwell, nr Malmesbury
SN16 9EP

T: 01666-577194
F: 01666-577853
E: info@therectoryhotel.com
W: www.therectoryhotel.com

BEDROOMS: 12.
OPEN: all year, restaurant closed lunchtime.
FACILITIES: lounge, bar, dining room, free Wi-Fi, meeting facilities, civil wedding licence, 3-acre garden (heated swimming pool, 10 by 5 metres), unsuitable for &.
BACKGROUND MUSIC: 'soft jazz' in bar.
LOCATION: 4 miles N of Malmesbury.
CHILDREN: all ages welcomed.
DOGS: not allowed in dining room.
CREDIT CARDS: Amex, MasterCard, Visa.
PRICES: per room B&B £105–£225. Set dinner £31.50. 1-night bookings refused bank holidays.

DARTMOUTH Devon

Map 1:D4

DART MARINA

'An absolute favourite: a lovely setting, fabulous staff, well-appointed accommodation and good food.' Richard Seton's smart hotel by the River Dart continues to win plaudits in 2014. 'The welcome is always enthusiastic; John, the long-serving and always-smiling porter, rushed out to carry our cases.' Another comment: 'All the staff are delightful and clearly get on well together.' There is 'an air of calm in the public rooms, which are dignified and spacious areas with large windows overlooking the river; a shame about the background music'. The 'beautiful, well-equipped' bedrooms have river views; some have a balcony or small private terrace. Peter Alcroft has been appointed head chef; his cooking, served in the bright *River* restaurant, is 'brilliant'. 'We enjoyed a double-baked Sharpham Brie soufflé, vanilla pear salad; an exquisite pork tenderloin, caramelised cauliflower purée, wild mushroom and tarragon risotto.' The 'superb' breakfast has a buffet of compotes, fruit salads, yogurts; 'generous cooked dishes'. A small riverside garden has a maritime theme; garden beds are covered with cockle shells. Ten minutes' walk to town centre. (*Ian Malone, Mary and Eric Woods*)

Sandquay Road
Dartmouth
TQ6 9PH

T: 01803-832580
F: 01803-835040
E: reception@dartmarina.com
W: www.dartmarina.com

BEDROOMS: 51, 3 on ground floor, 1 suitable for ⅍, plus 3 apartments.
OPEN: all year, restaurant closed lunchtime Mon–Sat.
FACILITIES: lounge/bar, bistro, restaurant, free Wi-Fi, river-front terrace, small garden with seating, spa (heated indoor swimming pool, 8 by 4 metres, gym).
BACKGROUND MUSIC: varied.
LOCATION: on waterfront.
CHILDREN: all ages welcomed.
DOGS: in ground-floor rooms (£10 per stay), not during meal times in public rooms.
CREDIT CARDS: MasterCard, Visa.
PRICES: [2014] per room B&B £140–£270, D,B&B £200–£330. Set dinner £30–£37.50. 1-night bookings usually refused Sat.

SEE ALSO SHORTLIST

DARTMOUTH Devon

Map 1:D4

NONSUCH HOUSE

César award in 2000

'Just as good as we remembered,' say guests returning this year, after a five-year gap, to Kit and Penny Noble's Edwardian guest house on a steep, south-facing hill opposite Dartmouth. 'We were warmly welcomed by Kit, who carried our bags to our room.' Views across the estuary are 'glorious', with constant activity to watch on the river. The comfortable residents' lounge has a log fire and books and magazines. The four bedrooms all face south; they are well equipped with flat-screen TV, DVD/CD-player, alarm clock and iPod dock; bathrobes, water and fresh milk are provided. Biscay has a queen-size double bed and a small balcony; Plymouth has a king-size bed and 'stunning' views. Kit Noble prepares evening meals, served in the conservatory/dining room, on four nights a week. His limited menu 'depends on what is fresh on the day', perhaps locally landed fish. Guests are 'encouraged to say what they would like to eat'. No liquor licence, bring your own drinks and the hosts will provide ice, lemon and nibbles. Breakfast has 'wonderful home-made bread and proper tea'. (*Geoffrey Bignell*)

Church Hill, Kingswear
Dartmouth TQ6 0BX

T: 01803-752829
E: enquiries@nonsuch-house.co.uk
W: www.nonsuch-house.co.uk

BEDROOMS: 4.
OPEN: all year except Jan, dining room closed midday, evening Tues/Wed/Sat.
FACILITIES: ramps, lounge, dining room/conservatory, free Wi-Fi, ¼-acre garden (sun terrace), rock beach 300 yds (sailing nearby), membership of local gym and spa.
BACKGROUND MUSIC: none.
LOCATION: 5 mins' walk from ferry to Dartmouth.
CHILDREN: not under 12.
DOGS: not allowed.
CREDIT CARDS: MasterCard, Visa.
PRICES: [2014] per room B&B single £100–£165, double £125–£190. D,B&B £37.50 per person added. 1-night bookings usually refused weekends.

SEE ALSO SHORTLIST

DEDHAM Essex

DEDHAM HALL & FOUNTAIN HOUSE RESTAURANT

In the landscape that inspired Constable's paintings, this 15th-century manor house has long been run as a 'quirky' guest house by Jim and Wendy Sarton. It stands in 'informal English gardens' with a pond; in winter, residential art courses are held in a converted 14th-century barn filled with easels, boards and stools. (The lounge is decorated with paintings by artists who have attended the courses.) 'The whole establishment is wonderfully warm.' Traditionally furnished bedrooms have Persian rugs and antiques; some have exposed original beams. A large room that overlooked a field and lavender bushes had a 'comfortable' bed; 'the sun shone, the bees buzzed; it was beautifully quiet'. There are 'generous portions, nicely presented' in the restaurant ('none of this itsy-bitsy nouvelle cuisine'); typical dishes might include smoked duck breast, red onion marmalade; roast guineafowl, herb stuffing, quince cheese. Dinner is provided for hotel guests when the restaurant is closed. Breakfast is 'perfectly cooked – if you have room for it'. Forest walks nearby; Stour Wood is a ten-minute drive away.

25% DISCOUNT VOUCHERS

Brook Street, Dedham
nr Colchester CO7 6AD

T: 01206-323027
E: sarton@dedhamhall.demon.co.uk
W: www.dedhamhall.co.uk

BEDROOMS: 20, 16 in annexe, some on ground floor, suitable for &.
OPEN: all year except Christmas/New Year, restaurant closed Sun/Mon Nov–Feb.
FACILITIES: ramps, 2 lounges, 2 bars, dining room, restaurant, studio, free Wi-Fi, 6-acre grounds (pond, gardens).
BACKGROUND MUSIC: none.
LOCATION: end of High Street.
CHILDREN: all ages welcomed.
DOGS: not allowed.
CREDIT CARDS: MasterCard, Visa.
PRICES: per room B&B single £65, double £110, D,B&B single £95, double £170. À la carte £35.

DEDHAM Essex

THE SUN INN

Opposite the church in the village associated with John Constable, this 'friendly inn', a 15th-century building restored by the owner, Piers Baker, is much liked by *Guide* readers. 'Highly recommended' by visitors in 2014, it has 'an attractive beamed and wood-panelled interior with open fires; a knowledgeable barman; a cosy sitting room and inviting low-ceilinged dining room with wooden tables and a good art gallery'. The chefs, Ugo Simonelli and Ewan Naylon, serve a daily-changing modern menu with an Italian influence: 'Really good cooking; a delicious focaccia with a pot of olive oil; a fine risotto and chicken cacciatore.' Two bedrooms are accessed by a 'lovely' external Elizabethan staircase: 'Our room had a Victorian-style bedstead, good reading lights; not a lot of space for sitting; an exemplary bathroom had everything you need.' A 'huge' room in the main building had 'low beams and a fireplace; stylish furniture including a very wide four-poster bed'. Breakfast has freshly squeezed orange juice; 'unusual' cooked dishes – 'delicate pancakes encasing pink rhubarb, with crème fraîche'. (*Jill and Mike Bennett, Robin and Sarah McKie*)

High Street, Dedham
nr Colchester CO7 6DF

T: 01206-323351
E: office@thesuninndedham.com
W: www.thesuninndedham.com

BEDROOMS: 7.
OPEN: all year except 25/26 Dec, 4–8 Jan.
FACILITIES: lounge, bar, dining room, free Wi-Fi, 1-acre garden (covered terrace, children's play area), unsuitable for &.
BACKGROUND MUSIC: jazz/blues in bar.
LOCATION: central, 5 miles NE of Colchester.
CHILDREN: all ages welcomed.
DOGS: 'welcomed' in bar, not allowed in bedrooms.
CREDIT CARDS: MasterCard, Visa.
PRICES: per room B&B single £85–£150, double £120–£165, D,B&B £175–£220. À la carte £27.50.

DODDISCOMBSLEIGH Devon

Map 1:C4

THE NOBODY INN

Down narrow country lanes, this 'lovely old pub in a wonderful hidden valley has a happy atmosphere', say *Guide* inspectors. The 17th-century inn is a popular local meeting spot in this rural village; Sue Burdge is the 'hands-on' owner. The 'atmospheric' beamed bars, 'busy on a Friday night', have good cask ales, many wines by the glass, 'an enormous selection of whiskies'; there are books and board games, a log fire in winter. The adjoining restaurant has linen cloths, 'crisp napkins' and 'generous helpings' of chef Rob Murray's cooking, perhaps rabbit tortelloni, carrot purée, pancetta crisps; braised shin of Dartmouth beef, wild mushroom and white bean ragout. Upstairs, the bedrooms ('some noise until closing time, but this is a pub') are decorated in modern country style; one has a four-poster bed; a family room sleeps three. All rooms have bottled water and a decanter of sherry. 'Ours was a reasonable size, light and bright; a good built-in wardrobe (captive hangers, alas); a small shower room.' There is much choice at breakfast, ordered the night before and served at an agreed time. (*Andrew Kleissner, and others*)

Doddiscombsleigh EX6 7PS

T: 01647-252394
F: 01647-252978
E: info@nobodyinn.co.uk
W: www.nobodyinn.co.uk

BEDROOMS: 5, 1 with bathroom across corridor.
OPEN: all year except 1 Jan, restaurant closed Sun/Mon evening.
FACILITIES: 2 bars, restaurant, free Wi-Fi (may be patchy), garden, patio, parking, unsuitable for &.
BACKGROUND MUSIC: none.
LOCATION: in village 6 miles SW of Exeter.
CHILDREN: not under 5 for overnight stays, not under 14 in bar.
DOGS: not allowed in restaurant, bedrooms.
CREDIT CARDS: MasterCard, Visa.
PRICES: [2014] per room B&B single from £50, double from £70. À la carte £30.

EAST CHISENBURY Wiltshire

Map 2:D2

THE RED LION FREEHOUSE NEW

'Unpretentious, well kept and well managed', this thatched pub in a peaceful country village is owned by chef/patron Guy Manning and his American wife, Brittany. They have 'lightly updated' the building 'without losing its integrity', say *Guide* inspectors in 2014. The accommodation is in *Troutbeck*, a converted bungalow across the road. 'We were shown to a spacious, well-equipped room painted in restful olive green; a wardrobe and minibar were enclosed by a sliding opaque-glass door; oak wooden flooring, dark wood bedside tables, brass table lights; a tan leather sofa but no table and chair for laptop users. A small but carefully designed shower room.' Some rooms have a private decking area. Wooden tables are 'nicely set' for dinner in the restaurant. Guy Manning has a *Michelin* star for his 'exciting' menu. 'An excellent dinner with interesting combinations of ingredients: plump mussels came with bacon and cream; agnolotti pasta with truffle, whole hazelnuts and purple sprouting broccoli was a delicious vegetarian option.' The manager, Richard Smith, 'was knowledgeable on wine and food; service was considerate'. Breakfast was 'fresh, hearty'.

East Chisenbury
Pewsey SN9 6AQ

T: 01980-671124
E: enquiries@redlionfreehouse.com
W: www.redlionfreehouse.com

BEDROOMS: 5, on ground floor, in adjacent building.
OPEN: all year.
FACILITIES: pub/restaurant, free Wi-Fi, 1-acre garden.
BACKGROUND MUSIC: in pub/restaurant.
LOCATION: in village.
CHILDREN: 'best suited for babies'.
DOGS: allowed in pub, 1 bedroom.
CREDIT CARDS: MasterCard, Visa.
PRICES: [2014] per room B&B £130–£230. À la carte £35.

EAST GRINSTEAD West Sussex

Map 2:D4

GRAVETYE MANOR

There is a 'lovely smell of wood smoke' from the open fires at this luxury hotel (Relais & Châteaux) set in 'beautiful countryside'. Once the home of William Robinson, the pioneer of the English natural garden, the 16th-century Elizabethan manor house is surrounded by extensive grounds with wild meadows, Victorian glasshouses, a pear orchard and flowerbeds 'full of exuberant colour'. The house and gardens have been extensively renovated by the owners, Jeremy and Elizabeth Hosking; Andrew Thomason is the manager. The Arts and Crafts public rooms have dark wood panelling and bold floral displays, easy chairs on thick carpets. The staff are 'charming', the atmosphere is 'not at all stuffy'. Bedrooms have a mix of antiques and the latest technology; afternoon tea is served 'with ceremony' in the lounges. 'Our splendid corner room overlooked the glorious gardens. We had a comfortable king-size bed and a sitting area.' The cooking in the candlelit dining room is 'of the highest order'; modern British dishes might include roast squab pigeon, confit leg tortellini, salt-baked beetroot. There are freshly squeezed juices and an 'excellent' full English breakfast.

Vowels Lane
East Grinstead RH19 4LJ

T: 01342-810567
F: 01342-810080
E: info@gravetyemanor.co.uk
W: www.gravetyemanor.co.uk

BEDROOMS: 17.
OPEN: all year.
FACILITIES: 2 lounges, bar, restaurant, private dining room, free Wi-Fi, civil wedding licence, 1,000-acre grounds (woodland, ornamental and kitchen gardens, meadow, orchard, lake, croquet lawn), only restaurant suitable for &.
BACKGROUND MUSIC: classical in restaurant at breakfast.
LOCATION: 5 miles SW of East Grinstead.
CHILDREN: babes in arms, and over-7s welcomed.
DOGS: not allowed.
CREDIT CARDS: all major cards.
PRICES: [2014] per room B&B £240–£455. D,B&B £185–£280 per person, set dinner £40, à la carte £65. 1-night bookings sometimes refused at weekends.

EAST HOATHLY East Sussex

Map 2:E4

OLD WHYLY

'Beautiful and comforting, even when it rains', Sarah Burgoyne's upmarket B&B, in a Grade II listed Georgian manor house, is 'better than ever', says a regular *Guide* correspondent this year. 'She always gives a warm welcome. The breakfasts continue to be wonderful.' Deep in the East Sussex countryside, the elegant building is filled with antique furniture and pictures. The drawing room, light and well proportioned, has a large open fire, comfortable seating, paintings, interesting old books. Guests meet here for pre-dinner drinks and canapés. Meals are taken communally at an antique circular table in the candlelit dining room. Sarah Burgoyne, 'a passionate cook', prepares dishes like wild mushroom risotto; roast fillet of pork with mustard sauce. The four bedrooms, two en suite and two with a private bathroom, are decorated in country house style. At breakfast 'the home-made marmalade and jams are always a treat'. Picnic hampers are provided in individual tiffin boxes, a course in each of the layers, for guests going to nearby Glyndebourne. 'Our spirits were lifted by the supper as we sat under umbrellas.' (*Catrin Treadwell*)

London Road
East Hoathly BN8 6EL

T: 01825-840216
E: stay@oldwhyly.co.uk
W: www.oldwhyly.co.uk

BEDROOMS: 4.
OPEN: all year.
FACILITIES: drawing room, dining room, free Wi-Fi, 3-acre garden in 30-acre grounds, heated outdoor swimming pool (10 by 5 metres), tennis, unsuitable for &.
BACKGROUND MUSIC: none.
LOCATION: 1 mile N of village.
CHILDREN: all ages welcomed.
DOGS: allowed throughout.
CREDIT CARDS: none.
PRICES: per room B&B £98–£145. Set dinner £35, Glyndebourne hamper £38 per person. 1-night bookings sometimes refused weekends in high season.

EAST LAVANT West Sussex

Map 2:E3

THE ROYAL OAK

'A busy country pub with a warm and cosy restaurant', Charles Ullmann's 200-year-old inn is in a village at the foot of the South Downs. 'The decor is rustic, with bare brick, flint walls and oak beams,' said a *Guide* inspector. An open fire, close to the bar, is appreciated on winter days, particularly by walkers. The restaurant, adjacent to the bar, has 'subdued lighting, rustic wooden tables and chairs, linen napkins' (background music was found 'intrusive' this year). Paul Tansley, the new chef, tries to keep the journey from field to fork as short as possible for his dishes. 'We enjoyed slow-roasted venison cooked to perfection, accompanied by a mighty wedge of pommes dauphinoise. We were tempted, but too replete to try desserts like Eton Mess or dark chocolate and orange brownies.' Tables are set on a terrace or in the small garden for alfresco dining during fine weather. Bedrooms, some in the main building, others in a converted cottage and barn behind the pub, are well equipped; most look over farmland or the downs. Breakfast has a wide choice.

Pook Lane
East Lavant PO18 0AX

T: 01243-527434
E: rooms@royaloakeastlavant.co.uk
W: www.royaloakeastlavant.co.uk

BEDROOMS: 5, 3 in adjacent barn and cottage, 2 self-catering cottages nearby.
OPEN: all year.
FACILITIES: bar/restaurant, free Wi-Fi, terrace (outside meals), small garden, unsuitable for &.
BACKGROUND MUSIC: jazz in restaurant.
LOCATION: 2 miles N of Chichester.
CHILDREN: all ages welcomed.
DOGS: not allowed in bedrooms.
CREDIT CARDS: all major cards.
PRICES: [2014] per room B&B £125–£220. À la carte £35. 1-night bookings refused weekends, bank holidays.

EASTBOURNE East Sussex

Map 2:E4

BELLE TOUT LIGHTHOUSE

'Highly recommended' by a *Guide* inspector, this decommissioned lighthouse on the chalk cliffs of Beachy Head has been turned into a B&B with, unsurprisingly, 'fantastic views'. It has been restored by the owner, David Shaw, who has given it a 'pleasing' interior 'in sympathy with the building'. Ian Noall is the manager; his staff are 'friendly'. A guest sitting room on an upper floor has wraparound windows looking out towards the Seven Sisters: 'There are comfy chairs and sofas, lots of local information (including suggestions of places to eat), a wood-burning stove and a small fridge for drinks.' Eighty steps up is the former lantern room with a 360-degree view. Three bedrooms on the lowest floor face the sea. Two larger rooms look out on the South Downs; a quirky Keeper's Loft in the tower has a mezzanine loft bed reached by the original fixed ladder. All rooms have a small en suite shower, tea- and coffee-making facilities, TV with a DVD- and CD-player. 'Breakfast is a generous affair: juices, cereals, home-made muffins; a wide range of ingredients for the cooked dishes.'

Beachy Head Road
Eastbourne BN20 0AE

T: 01323-423185
E: info@belletout.co.uk
W: www.belletout.co.uk

BEDROOMS: 6.
OPEN: all year, except 19 Dec–10 Jan.
FACILITIES: lounge, breakfast room, free Wi-Fi, terrace, garden, unsuitable for ♿.
BACKGROUND MUSIC: none.
LOCATION: 3 miles W of Eastbourne.
CHILDREN: not under 15.
DOGS: not allowed.
CREDIT CARDS: MasterCard, Visa.
PRICES: [2014] per room B&B £145–£220. Min. 2-night stay, 1-night bookings only accepted 7–10 days in advance.

SEE ALSO SHORTLIST

EDENBRIDGE Kent

Map 2:D4

STARBOROUGH MANOR

In parkland opposite a small moated castle, this 'beautiful' old manor house is a 'relaxing place, comfortable and informal'. It is the home of Lynn and Jonathan Matthias, who welcome guests on a B&B basis; a kitchen and dining room are available (for a charge of £15) if visitors prefer to prepare their own evening meal instead of heading for a local pub. The bedrooms are 'generously proportioned'. Two rooms, which share a bathroom, are let together as a family suite. Rooms are decorated and furnished in country/traditional style; all have a hospitality tray, mineral water, free Wi-Fi. 'Our room was well appointed, had top-quality bedlinen and a super-king-size bed.' Guests have use of a first-floor sitting room, which has television, a library of books to borrow, games and DVDs. A second sitting room/study is for those wanting to work or to read quietly. Breakfast can be taken communally in a 'large, light oak kitchen' or in the dining room for larger parties. 'The table was laden with generous portions of fresh fruit', yogurts, home-made muesli and granola. 'Excellent' cooked dishes.

Moor Lane, Marsh Green
Edenbridge TN8 5QY

T: 01732-862152
E: lynn@starboroughmanor.co.uk
W: www.starboroughmanor.co.uk

BEDROOMS: 4.
OPEN: all year.
FACILITIES: 2 sitting rooms, dining room, free Wi-Fi, 13-acre grounds, heated outdoor pool (5 by 10 metres), unsuitable for &.
BACKGROUND MUSIC: none.
LOCATION: 1½ miles W of Edenbridge.
CHILDREN: all ages welcomed.
DOGS: not allowed.
CREDIT CARDS: MasterCard, Visa.
PRICES: [2014] per room B&B single £90–£100, double £140. 1-night bookings sometimes refused weekends in summer.

EGTON BRIDGE North Yorkshire

Map 4:C5

BROOM HOUSE

'Excellent,' says a visitor this year to David and Maria White's small guest house near Whitby in the North York Moors national park. Earlier guests found the restored Victorian farmhouse 'a very comfortable and relaxing place to stay'. Bedrooms, in the older part of the house and an extension, vary in size. The Bridge Suite is self-contained, and has a lounge, fireplace and valley view. A compact room in the extension has 'a comfortable bed, good linen, a modern decor in grey, black and white; a good-sized bathroom'. In the candlelit restaurant (open Thursday to Saturday), Maria White uses local suppliers and vegetables and herbs from the garden to prepare dishes which she describes as 'British traditional with a touch of international flavours'. Her menu might include wild mushroom risotto; seared Yorkshire lamb rump, red cabbage, rosemary potatoes. In fine weather meals may be taken al fresco on the patio. An 'excellent' breakfast has home-made bread and local honey. *Broom House* is 'ideally situated for exploring the coast and the moors'. Steam trains pass the perimeter of the garden. (*Roger Bousfield, and others*)

25% DISCOUNT VOUCHERS

Broom House Lane
Egton Bridge YO21 1XD

T: 01947-895279
F: 01947-895657
E: mw@broom-house.co.uk
W: www.egton-bridge.co.uk

BEDROOMS: 8, 1 on ground floor, 2 in cottage.
OPEN: Feb–Dec, restaurant closed Sun–Wed.
FACILITIES: lounge, dining room, restaurant, free Wi-Fi, ½-acre garden.
BACKGROUND MUSIC: in restaurant.
LOCATION: ½ mile W of village.
CHILDREN: all ages welcomed.
DOGS: not allowed.
CREDIT CARDS: MasterCard, Visa.
PRICES: [2014] per room B&B £89–£145. À la carte from £21.50. 1-night bookings sometimes refused Sat.

EMSWORTH Hampshire

Map 2:E3

36 ON THE QUAY

♥*César award in 2011*

In a 'delightful position' opposite the quay of an 'attractive little town', Ramon and Karen Farthing's restaurant-with-rooms occupies a 'sympathetically modernised' 17th-century fishermen's inn. Karen Farthing is a 'welcoming' hostess, who 'presides over a quietly efficient operation'; her husband has a *Michelin* star for his modern French cuisine. In a dining room with 'beautifully laid tables', his sophisticated cooking on a short, seasonal menu is praised by a trusted reporter for the 'contrasting textures and seasonings'. 'Good if elaborate,' is this year's comment. Characteristic dishes: wild sea bass gravadlax, charred asparagus, pickled baby artichokes; brill fillet, creamed parsley root, confit egg yolk, apple biscuit. Most of the bedrooms above the restaurant have views of the harbour; a new two-bedroom cottage has its own garden and parking area. 'Our room had ultra-modern fittings contrasting with the ancient building. It had a comfortable sofa, very good lighting; the small shower room lacked shelf space.' A 'good' continental breakfast has 'muesli, yogurt, fresh fruit, toast, croissants and pastries; decent coffee'.

47 South Street
Emsworth PO10 7EG

T: 01243-375592
E: info@36onthequay.co.uk
W: www.36onthequay.co.uk

BEDROOMS: 6, 1 in cottage (with lounge) across road (can be let weekly), plus 2-bed cottage.
OPEN: all year except 24–26 Dec, first 2 weeks Jan, 1 week May, 1 week Oct, restaurant closed Sun/Mon.
FACILITIES: bar area, restaurant, free Wi-Fi, small terrace, limited parking, only restaurant suitable for ♿.
BACKGROUND MUSIC: none.
LOCATION: on harbour.
CHILDREN: all ages welcomed.
DOGS: allowed in 1 cottage, by arrangement.
CREDIT CARDS: MasterCard, Visa.
PRICES: [2014] per room B&B £100–£200. Set dinner £57.95.

ERMINGTON Devon

PLANTATION HOUSE

In pretty countryside between Dartmoor and the south Devon coast, Richard Hendey's small hotel is 'relaxing and comfortable; no airs and graces here'. The Grade II listed Georgian house, formerly the parish rectory, overlooks the River Erme. There are tropical pot plants, cane furniture, artefacts, fresh flowers, modern artwork in the public areas. A front-facing bedroom on the first floor had 'a large bed, two cane chairs and a coffee table; a small dressing room with an open wardrobe; a well-kitted-out bathroom with under-floor heating'. The extra touches (fresh milk, fruit and biscuits replenished daily, hot-water bottles, flowers from the garden) are appreciated. In the bar, 'Richard Hendey introduced himself, lit a fire and asked about our food likes and dislikes. Over four days he served us with some stunning meals.' The four-course dinner menu might include ballotine of guineafowl, pistachio, prune, duck liver stuffing; puff pastry basket of local seafood, champagne and raspberry cream. Breakfast has a 'wide-ranging array' of cereals, organic fruit juices, etc; real leaf tea; the 'Devon' cooked dish was a 'delight'. (GC, LMcG)

Totnes Road
Ermington, nr Plymouth
PL21 9NS

T: 01548-831100
E: info@plantationhousehotel.co.uk
W: www.plantationhousehotel.co.uk

BEDROOMS: 9.

OPEN: all year, restaurant closed midday, some Sundays.

FACILITIES: lounge/bar, 2 dining rooms, free Wi-Fi, terrace, garden, unsuitable for &.

BACKGROUND MUSIC: if required.

LOCATION: 10 miles E of Plymouth.

CHILDREN: 'well-behaved' children welcomed.

DOGS: allowed in 1 bedroom, not in public rooms.

CREDIT CARDS: Amex, MasterCard, Visa.

PRICES: per room B&B single £70, double £115–£230. D,B&B £36 add per person, set dinner £36. 1-night bookings occasionally refused bank holidays.

EVESHAM Worcestershire

Map 3:D6

THE EVESHAM HOTEL

♀ *César award in 1990*

There is 'a happy atmosphere' at John and Sue Jenkinson's family-friendly hotel, set in large grounds with mulberry trees and 'lovely' gardens. It is full of spirit and likeable eccentricity: John Jenkinson delights in off-beat jokes. David Field has joined as manager: 'He is making gentle changes to our decor,' the Jenkinsons tell us. 'We still keep the quirkiness though some of the extremes have been toned down.' Paul Napper is the new chef: 'everything possible is made on site' for his menus which might include dishes like goat's cheese and beetroot tart, walnut dressing; slow-cooked pork belly, toffee apple purée, mashed potatoes. Sue Jenkinson was creating a salad and herb garden as the *Guide* went to press. Children are positively encouraged and will enjoy the themed rooms, which 'add to the fun'. An Alice in Wonderland-inspired family suite has a play nook under the beams; a room with jockey-print upholstery and horse heads on the bedhead pays tribute to the Cheltenham races. 'Rooms are well furnished; a quiet night's sleep is guaranteed.' Breakfast has local honey, and home-made jams and marmalades.

25% DISCOUNT VOUCHERS

Cooper's Lane, off Waterside
Evesham
WR11 1DA

T: 01386-765566
F: 01386-765443
E: reception@eveshamhotel.com
W: www.eveshamhotel.com

BEDROOMS: 38, 11 on ground floor, 2 suitable for ㅊ.
OPEN: all year.
FACILITIES: 2 lounges, bar, restaurant, private dining room, free Wi-Fi, children's play area, indoor swimming pool (5 by 12 metres), 2½-acre grounds (croquet, putting, swings).
BACKGROUND MUSIC: none.
LOCATION: 5 mins' walk from centre, across river.
CHILDREN: all ages welcomed.
DOGS: allowed (small charge), but only guide dogs allowed in public rooms.
CREDIT CARDS: Amex, MasterCard, Visa.
PRICES: [2014] per room B&B single from £85, double from £115, D,B&B from £105. À la carte £28.

THE CROWN

'Very attractive in that quiet, practical way – no grand statements.' Surrounded by 'splendid' countryside and heather-clad moorland, where deer and Exmoor ponies roam free, Sara and Dan Whittaker's 17th-century coaching inn sits in large grounds with a water garden and trout stream. It is liked for its 'relaxing' ambience and 'hospitable atmosphere'. A popular village pub, it has log fires to accompany real ales and local tales. The hotel and pub have separate entrances; a door from hotel reception opens on to the pub. 'You can enjoy village life simply by walking through.' Individually styled, bedrooms are 'clean and unpretentious'; a lobby lounge is 'nicely furnished for flopping'. Dogs are made welcome; stabling can be provided for horses; there is a gun safe. In the smart restaurant, chef Raza Muhammad's 'excellent' modern dishes might include pan-fried sea bass fillet, saffron beurre blanc; wild boar and apple sausages. Special diets are catered for. There are plenty of walks from the front door; riding, fishing, cycling and shooting can all be arranged. 'Just right.' (*GM, MM, P and KR*)

Exford
Exmoor National Park
TA24 7PP

T: 01643-831554
F: 01643-831665
E: info@crownhotelexmoor.co.uk
W: www.crownhotelexmoor.co.uk

BEDROOMS: 16.
OPEN: all year.
FACILITIES: lounge, cocktail bar, public bar, restaurant, meeting room, free Wi-Fi, 3-acre grounds (trout stream, water garden, terrace garden), stabling, unsuitable for &.
BACKGROUND MUSIC: in bar and restaurant.
LOCATION: on village green.
CHILDREN: all ages welcomed.
DOGS: not allowed in restaurant.
CREDIT CARDS: MasterCard, Visa.
PRICES: [2014] per room B&B single £60–£79, double £105–£159, D,B&B single £80–£115, double £150–£210. Set menu £35.

FAVERSHAM Kent

Map 2:D5

READ'S

✪César award in 2005

'A charming hotel, highly recommended.' More praise this year for Rona and David Pitchford's restaurant-with-rooms, an elegant Georgian manor house near an old market town. Rona Pitchford is the 'warm, professional host'; hotel guests are 'anything but a second thought' even though the dining room might be the focus. The lack of background music in a candlelit room appeals to visitors. David Pitchford is the chef; he uses local ingredients for his seasonal dishes, perhaps sautéed tiger prawns, pan-fried Parmesan gnocchi; Kentish lamb served four ways. The meal 'is served with great care but without fuss by an obviously happy staff'. The tasting menu is 'good value and special'. 'Everything is spotless' in the bedrooms, which are decorated in classic country house style. 'Our room had a super four-poster bed. The well-stocked fridge in the pantry was a good touch.' A room with window seats overlooking a magnificent cedar tree had 'rich fabrics, an inviting sitting area, heaps of good taste'. Breakfast, which 'is kept simple and more enjoyable for that', has home-made jams, 'excellent' hot choices. (*David Soanes, and others*)

Macknade Manor
Canterbury Road
Faversham ME13 8XE

T: 01795-535344
F: 01795-591200
E: rona@reads.com
W: www.reads.com

BEDROOMS: 6.
OPEN: all year except 25/26 Dec, restaurant closed Sun/Mon.
FACILITIES: sitting room/bar, restaurant, private dining room, free Wi-Fi, civil wedding licence, 4-acre garden (terrace, outdoor dining), only restaurant suitable for ♿.
BACKGROUND MUSIC: none.
LOCATION: 1 mile SE of Faversham.
CHILDREN: all ages welcomed.
DOGS: not allowed in public rooms.
CREDIT CARDS: Amex, MasterCard, Visa.
PRICES: [2014] per room B&B single £125–£185, double £165–£195. D,B&B £135–£240 per person. Set dinner £60.

FLEET Dorset

Map 1:D6

MOONFLEET MANOR   NEW

'A hotel that is good at looking after young children and exhausted parents.' Inspectors (a family of four) were impressed by this child-friendly Georgian house, which returns to the *Guide* under the renewed ownership of Luxury Family Hotels. There is 'lots for children to do' indoors and outdoors. A crèche (two sessions a day) is included in the cost of the stay; a playroom is 'full of toys, dressing-up clothes, books, lots of space'. An indoor swimming pool has three areas to accommodate children of different ages. Outside are a climbing frame and a sandpit. 'Our bedrooms had an old-fashioned, characterful decor; an interconnecting door to the children's room, where towels were laid out in the shape of an elephant.' The public rooms have a relaxed, shabby-chic style – 'big sofas, piles of newspapers, lots of colour'. Dining arrangements are 'flexible': high tea for small children at 5 pm; adults can eat with their children until 7.30 pm when parents can dine alone (listening devices available). On Sunday mornings, children can join a breakfast club – 'ours begged to be allowed to go'. 'Amazing,' said a seven-year-old inspector.

Fleet Road
Weymouth DT3 4ED

T: 01305-786948
F: 01305-774395
E: info@moonfleetmanorhotel.co.uk
W: www.moonfleetmanorhotel.co.uk

BEDROOMS: 36, 6 in annexes, 3 on ground floor.
OPEN: all year.
FACILITIES: 4 lounges, restaurant, indoor playroom, crèche, free Wi-Fi, civil wedding licence, indoor swimming pool, terrace, 10-acre garden (play areas).
BACKGROUND MUSIC: 'mixed' in restaurant.
LOCATION: 7 miles W of Weymouth.
CHILDREN: all ages welcomed.
DOGS: allowed in bedrooms, not in public rooms.
CREDIT CARDS: all major cards.
PRICES: [2014] per room B&B £120–£455, D,B&B £190–£525. Set meals £42.50. 1-night bookings sometimes refused weekends, bank holidays.

FLETCHING East Sussex

THE GRIFFIN INN [NEW]

In a pretty village above the Ouse valley, the Pullan family's 16th-century Grade II listed coaching inn has a large garden with extensive views over the South Downs. It returns to the *Guide* after a positive report by inspectors who liked the 'excellent' food and the 'pleasant, relaxed atmosphere'. The 'informal' pub has oak beams, open fires, horse brasses. Lighting is 'subtle' in the L-shaped restaurant. 'Lovely focaccia bread came with a fine olive oil; we enjoyed lemon and garlic chicken breast with chorizo, sherry vinegar; rack of Romney Marsh lamb, anchovy and rosemary dressing. The staff were good at knowing when something was required.' Five of the bedrooms are in *Griffin House* next door: 'Our small room was bright and clean. Nicely decorated in country style, it had an original cast iron fireplace, wardrobe, chest of drawers; a good make-up mirror in the bathroom.' Four beamed rooms are in the main building; others (each with a four-poster bed) in a renovated coach house. Breakfast has 'locally sourced jams, honey'; a 'delicious' full English. Children are welcomed. *The Griffin* has its own cricket team.

Fletching, nr Uckfield
TN22 3SS

T: 01825-722890
F: 01825-722810
E: info@thegriffininn.co.uk
W: www.thegriffininn.co.uk

BEDROOMS: 13, 4 in coach house, 5 in *Griffin House* next door, 4 on ground floor.
OPEN: all year except 25 Dec, restaurant closed Sun evening except bank holidays.
FACILITIES: ramps, 2 lounge bars (1 with TV), restaurant, free Wi-Fi (in main building only), terrace (1-acre garden).
BACKGROUND MUSIC: none.
LOCATION: 3 miles NW of Uckfield.
CHILDREN: all ages welcomed.
DOGS: welcomed.
CREDIT CARDS: all major cards.
PRICES: [2014] per room B&B single £70–£80, double £85–£145. À la carte £35. 1-night bookings refused bank holidays.

FOWEY Cornwall

Map 1:D3

✿ FOWEY HALL

`NEW`

César award: family hotel of the year

'Outstanding: the staff are totally committed to making sure the guest has a good time.' A *Guide* inspector in 2014 was impressed by service at this Victorian mansion at the top of the town, which is part of Nigel Chapman's Luxury Family Hotels group. Families can take advantage of a crèche, baby-listening services, high tea, special menus. Older children have a games room, an outdoor play area and an indoor swimming pool. A 'swish but comfy' drawing room has two log fires; Lloyd Loom chairs are in a glassed morning room; CDs and puzzles in a snug. 'The food is glorious.' Children take high tea from 5 pm. James Parkinson is the chef, serving modern dishes in the restaurant. 'We had a great fish soup; roast loin of cod; duck with truly delicious lentils.' The bedrooms are in the main house, a garden wing and a coach house a short walk away. 'Our large room was a proper retreat: it had a divinely comfortable bed; good lighting, easy chairs, lots of hanging space.' At breakfast 'the buffet table groaned with poached fruits, yogurts, cereals, juices and bread. The porridge and kipper were the stuff of dreams. Super toast, home-made marmalade.'

Hanson Drive
Fowey PL23 1ET

T: 01726-833866
E: info@foweyhallhotel.co.uk
W: www.foweyhallhotel.co.uk

BEDROOMS: 36 bedrooms, 8 in coach house, some on ground floor, 2 suitable for ♿.
OPEN: all year.
FACILITIES: 2 lounges, snug, 2 restaurants, free Wi-Fi, games rooms, civil wedding licence, spa, 12-metre indoor swimming pool, 5-acre grounds.
BACKGROUND MUSIC: in restaurants.
LOCATION: top of the town.
CHILDREN: all ages welcomed.
DOGS: allowed in main house bedrooms (£10), not in restaurant.
CREDIT CARDS: Amex, MasterCard, Visa.
PRICES: [2014] per room B&B £160–£265, D,B&B £220–£325. Set dinner £42. 1-night bookings refused at weekends.

`SEE ALSO SHORTLIST`

GATESHEAD Tyne and Wear

Map 4:B4

ESLINGTON VILLA

In a large garden overlooking the Team valley, Nick and Melanie Tulip's Victorian hotel, converted from two substantial houses, is recommended 'to anyone who wants a family-run place where you feel at home'. The 'attractive' garden has plenty of seats and the terrace is 'ideal for alfresco drinks'. Ground-floor public areas have mainly traditional artwork, some 'nice' old photographs and 'good' antiques. The lounge/bar has 'plenty of seating'. The bedrooms, named after trees and shrubs, have a traditional decor in the older part of the house and a lighter touch in the extension. 'Our room, Lilac, had a lilac-patterned wallpaper behind the bed, other walls were painted in another shade of lilac. It looked bright and contemporary.' The owners say: 'No two bedrooms are the same; there is something to suit everyone.' In the restaurant, chef Jamie Walsh (a former North East Chef of the Year winner), serves dishes like cream of wild mushroom soup, white truffle oil; slow-cooked duck leg, savoy cabbage and cherries. Staff are 'friendly and helpful'. (*JC, and others*)

25% DISCOUNT VOUCHERS

8 Station Road, Low Fell
Gateshead NE9 6DR

T: 0191-487 6017
F: 0191-420 0667
E: home@eslingtonvilla.co.uk
W: www.eslingtonvilla.co.uk

BEDROOMS: 18, 3 with separate entrance on ground floor.
OPEN: all year except 25/26 Dec, 1 Jan.
FACILITIES: ramp, lounge/bar, conservatory, restaurant, private dining room, conference/function facilities, free Wi-Fi, 2-acre garden (patio).
BACKGROUND MUSIC: jazz/pop in public rooms.
LOCATION: 2 miles from centre, off A1.
CHILDREN: all ages welcomed.
DOGS: not allowed.
CREDIT CARDS: Amex, MasterCard, Visa.
PRICES: [2014] per room B&B single £74.50–£79.50, double £94.50–£104.50. Set dinner £22.95–£27.50.

GILLINGHAM Dorset

Map 2:D1

STOCK HILL HOUSE

Once the summer home of cartoonist Osbert Lancaster (an original cartoon hangs in the breakfast room), Nita and Peter Hauser's small hotel/restaurant stands in landscaped grounds with huge trees, lawns and flowerbeds. The late Victorian mansion is richly decorated in period style, with antiques, paintings, curios and fine fabrics; a log fire burns in the lounge. Divided between the main building and the former coach house, bedrooms are flamboyantly styled in bold colours; most have views of the gardens. 'Standards are as immaculate now as on my first visit,' said a recent visitor. In the restaurant, Peter Hauser's 'delicious' home-cooked dinners have a strong Austrian influence, reflecting his heritage. The daily-changing menu – using game and meat from the surrounding countryside, and vegetables from the kitchen garden – has 'a splendid combination of the tried and tested with more innovative dishes', perhaps French guineafowl and roe deer terrine, crab apple jelly, toasted lemon brioche; Aga-roasted lamb rump fillet, rosemary jus. Breakfast has home-made yogurts, and honey from the Hausers' bees; full English or fish. (*DW, IC*)

25% DISCOUNT VOUCHERS

Stock Hill
Gillingham SP8 5NR

T: 01747-823626
F: 01747-825628
E: reception@stockhillhouse.co.uk
W: www.stockhillhouse.co.uk

BEDROOMS: 9, 3 in coach house, 3 on ground floor.
OPEN: all year.
FACILITIES: ramp, 2 lounges, restaurant, breakfast room, private dining room, free Wi-Fi, 11-acre grounds (tennis, croquet, small lake), unsuitable for &.
BACKGROUND MUSIC: none.
LOCATION: 1 mile W of Gillingham.
CHILDREN: all ages welcomed.
DOGS: not allowed.
CREDIT CARDS: MasterCard, Visa.
PRICES: [2014] per room D,B&B single £175, double £265–£325. Set dinner £45.

GRASMERE Cumbria

Map 4: inset C2

THE GRASMERE HOTEL

'High standards of friendliness and helpfulness' are shown by the hosts and their staff at Rob van der Palen and Anton Renac's small hotel in the Lake District. The River Rothay borders the small garden of the three-storey Victorian house. The owners, who provide 'thoughtful attention and fine food', have extensively renovated the building. The 'neutral colours and muted greens' of the dining room 'provide a link' with the secluded garden, which is visible through floor-to-ceiling windows; there are linen cloths on the well-spaced tables, 'subdued background music'. Anton Renac is the chef, serving a four-course menu of European dishes, perhaps rose veal patties, cucumber and yogurt dip; supreme of guineafowl, pancetta, pork sauce. The 'delicious' bread is baked in the kitchen. The bedrooms vary in size: the lighting was 'well thought out' in a spacious room with a king-size bed, two armchairs, a full-length mirror. Breakfast has fresh fruit salad; 'beautifully cooked, well-presented hot dishes'. 'No need to use your car,' say the owners; there are many walks from the door. (*John and Christine Moore, and others*)

Broadgate
Grasmere LA22 9TA

T: 015394-35277
E: info@grasmerehotel.co.uk
W: www.grasmerehotel.co.uk

BEDROOMS: 11.
OPEN: all year except 4–30 Jan.
FACILITIES: lounge, restaurant, free Wi-Fi, 1-acre garden, unsuitable for &.
BACKGROUND MUSIC: 'easy listening'.
LOCATION: on edge of village.
CHILDREN: not under 10.
DOGS: allowed in some bedrooms (£10 per stay), not in public rooms.
CREDIT CARDS: MasterCard, Visa.
PRICES: per person B&B £56–£71, D,B&B £76–£91. Set dinner £20 residents, £26 non-residents. 1-night bookings generally refused Sat.

GRASMERE Cumbria

OAK BANK

Owners Glynis and Simon Wood are 'very hands-on and take pride in their establishment', says a visitor in 2014 to this small hotel. It stands on a quiet road on the village outskirts. The Woods run it 'with passion and flair', and give 'amazing value for money'. Another comment: 'It is not a luxury hotel but it doesn't hold itself out to be one.' There are flowers on the tables in the three dining areas (one a conservatory). The cooking of Darren Comish is widely praised. His daily-changing menu might include grilled mackerel, beetroot purée; Goosnargh duck breast, confit leg tortellini, foie gras. 'The food was superb; many "ohs" and "aahs" from the assembled diners.' The bar stocks local ales: 'I recommend the Collie Wobbles.' The lounge, which has a converted range, has plenty of good seating. The bedrooms are well equipped: a small room overlooking the garden was 'smartly furnished, with a modern decor'; lighting is 'excellent' – guests can read in bed 'without strain'. Staff are 'unobtrusive, but always on hand'. (*Jane Pennington, Rick Holland, and others*)

Broadgate
Grasmere LA22 9TA

T: 015394-35217
F: 015394-35685
E: info@lakedistricthotel.co.uk
W: www.lakedistricthotel.co.uk

BEDROOMS: 14, 1 on ground floor.
OPEN: all year except 20–26 Dec, 3–22 Jan, 2–14 Aug.
FACILITIES: lounge, bar, dining room, conservatory dining room, free Wi-Fi, unsuitable for &.
BACKGROUND MUSIC: during dinner in bar lounge and dining rooms.
LOCATION: outskirts of village.
CHILDREN: all ages welcomed.
DOGS: allowed in 3 bedrooms, 1 lounge.
CREDIT CARDS: MasterCard, Visa.
PRICES: per person B&B £34.50–£82, D,B&B £54.50–£102. Set dinner £35, à la carte £37.50. 1-night bookings usually refused weekends.

GREAT MILTON Oxfordshire

Map 2:C3

LE MANOIR AUX QUAT'SAISONS

𝒬 *César award in 1985*

A good choice for a 'special occasion', say readers about Raymond Blanc's luxury hotel in a village near Oxford. This honey-stone 15th-century manor house stands amid extensive gardens. The food might be the main reason for a visit, but 'equal attention to detail' is shown in the service to hotel guests. Philip Newman-Hall is the long-serving manager. In the main house and garden courtyard, the elegant, imaginative bedrooms vary in style: Botticelli has a hand-painted mural and a spiral staircase linking bedroom and bathroom; Passion Flower has a private terrace leading to the gardens. Each has a writing desk, a seating area, a marble bathroom. In the grounds are an orchard of 800 apple and pear trees, a Japanese garden (with a tea house) and an English water garden. A two-acre organic vegetable garden supplies the kitchen with more than 90 varieties of vegetables and 70 types of herbs; a garden of heritage plants was being completed as the *Guide* went to press. The conservatory restaurant has held two *Michelin* stars for 30 years; vegetarian alternatives are offered for the various five- and seven-course menus.

Church Road
Great Milton OX44 7PD

T: 01844-278881
F: 01844-278847
E: lemanoir@blanc.co.uk
W: www.manoir.com

BEDROOMS: 32, 22 in garden buildings, some on ground floor, 1 suitable for &.
OPEN: all year.
FACILITIES: ramps, 2 lounges, champagne bar, restaurant, private dining room, free Wi-Fi, cookery school, civil wedding licence, 27-acre grounds.
BACKGROUND MUSIC: in the lounges.
LOCATION: 8 miles SE of Oxford.
CHILDREN: all ages welcomed.
DOGS: not allowed in house, kennels provided.
CREDIT CARDS: all major cards.
PRICES: [2014] per room B&B (French breakfast) £555–£635, D,B&B £890–£970. Set dinner £134–£154, à la carte £130.

THE OLD STORE

'Extremely good value', Patrick and Heather Birchenough's B&B is 'in an excellent position for exploring Chichester and the countryside'. Close to the Goodwood estate, the Grade II listed Georgian flint-and-brick house was once the village bakery and shop. 'We were welcomed with tea and cake in the garden, before being shown to our immaculate bedrooms,' said one visitor. Downstairs is a reception room, a lounge and a twin-bedded bedroom; the other rooms are on the first and second floors, reached by fairly steep stairs. All have an en suite shower room, TV, a radio alarm clock and a tea/coffee tray. A beamed family room has two single beds as well as a double. Although the house is close to a busy road, triple glazing 'ensures a good night's sleep'. Breakfast is 'excellent – not only full English but pancakes with bacon and maple syrup or a muffin with smoked salmon and scrambled egg'. Preserves and bread are home made. The *Anglesey Arms*, across the road, is open for evening meals, and nearby Chichester has many restaurants. 'Many larger establishments could learn from the way guests are treated.' (*MW*)

Stane Street, Halnaker,
nr Chichester
PO18 0QL

T/F: 01243-531977
E: theoldstore4@aol.com
W: www.theoldstoreguesthouse.com

BEDROOMS: 7, 1 on ground floor.
OPEN: Mar–Dec.
FACILITIES: lounge, breakfast room, free Wi-Fi, ⅓-acre garden with seating, unsuitable for &.
BACKGROUND MUSIC: none.
LOCATION: 4 miles NE of Chichester.
CHILDREN: all ages welcomed.
DOGS: not allowed.
CREDIT CARDS: MasterCard, Visa.
PRICES: [2014] per person B&B £35–£50 (higher for Goodwood 'Festival of Speed' and 'Revival' meetings). 1-night bookings refused weekends in high season.

HAMBLETON Rutland

Map 2:B3

HAMBLETON HALL

César award in 1985

'The perfect country house. It is practically impossible to fault it.' Praise this year from trusted correspondents visiting this luxury hotel on a slope overlooking Rutland Water. It has been owned and run by Tim and Stefa Hart for 35 years (see also *Hart's Hotel*, Nottingham). Another comment: 'There is a strong sense among the staff of a shared ethos of the pursuit of excellence.' 'Classy, tasteful' public rooms have antiques, 'spectacular' flower arrangements, 'comfortable' sofas. Bedrooms vary in size and aspect; the best have views of the water. 'Our standard room over the front door was warm and very comfortable, with a fantastic bathroom.' In the candlelit dining room, Aaron Patterson has a *Michelin* star for his 'magnificent' modern cooking: 'dainty' dishes, perhaps consommé of wild mushrooms, parsley root panna cotta; hare Wellington, quince purée, cutlets. Breakfast, with 'divine' bread from Tim Hart's Hambleton Bakery, is served at table. On a summer's day, sitting on the terrace overlooking the lake is 'as near to paradise as one can get'. (*Francine and Ian Walsh, Anthony Bradbury, Robert Gower, Julia de Waal*)

Hambleton
Oakham LE15 8TH

T: 01572-756991
F: 01572-724721
E: hotel@hambletonhall.com
W: www.hambletonhall.com

BEDROOMS: 17, 2-bedroomed suite in pavilion.
OPEN: all year.
FACILITIES: lift, ramps, hall, drawing room, bar, restaurant, 2 private dining rooms, free Wi-Fi, civil wedding licence, 17-acre grounds (swimming pool, heated May–Sept, tennis).
BACKGROUND MUSIC: none.
LOCATION: 3 miles SE of Oakham.
CHILDREN: only children 'of a grown-up age' in restaurant in evening.
DOGS: not allowed in public rooms, nor unattended in bedrooms.
CREDIT CARDS: all major cards.
PRICES: [2014] per room B&B £265–£440. Set dinner £65–£75. 1-night bookings sometimes refused weekends.

HARWICH Essex

Map 2:C5

THE PIER AT HARWICH

Two historic buildings on the quayside of this maritime town form Paul Milsom's smart hotel/restaurant. One was built in palazzo style in the 19th century as a waiting room for European ferry passengers, the other is a conversion of a 17th-century pub. Individually decorated bedrooms are divided between the two buildings; the best, in the front, have panoramic views over the quayside and the Stour and Orwell estuaries, where 'ferries and fishing boats come and go'. A 'sophisticated', 'richly coloured' room was decorated with 'quirky pastoral paintings'. Chef Tom Bushell cooks much locally landed seafood in the modern *Harbourside* restaurant, perhaps Harwich crab tacos, guacamole, chipotle; hake fillet, Greek giant beans, baby squid, fennel. Informal meals are served in the *Ha'Penny* bistro, including an interesting children's menu (smoked mackerel pâté, toast fingers); guests write their orders on a provided notepad and take them to the counter. Breakfast has a buffet with cereals, pastries and juices; a 'full regional' has sausages and kippers from Suffolk. Convenient for modern ferries to Esbjerg and the Hook of Holland. (*LW*)

The Quay
Harwich CO12 3HH

T: 01255-241212
F: 01255-551922
E: pier@milsomhotels.com
W: www.milsomhotels.com

BEDROOMS: 14, 7 in annexe, 1 on ground floor.
OPEN: all year, restaurant closed Mon/Tues.
FACILITIES: ramps, lounge (in annexe), restaurant, bistro, free Wi-Fi, civil wedding licence, small front terrace.
BACKGROUND MUSIC: 'easy listening'.
LOCATION: on quay.
CHILDREN: all ages welcomed.
DOGS: not allowed in public rooms.
CREDIT CARDS: all major cards.
PRICES: [2014] per room B&B £115–£225. À la carte £38.

HASTINGS East Sussex

Map 2:E5

BLACK ROCK HOUSE

'This was the nicest hotel we stayed at during our two-week vacation in England,' say American visitors this year to this privately owned B&B. The restored Victorian villa, 'very stylish and in a great location', is managed by Yuliya Vereshchuk, 'a professional and accommodating innkeeper'. The 'immaculate' house has a sitting room with an open fire and an honesty bar 'with a good range of spirits, mixers and well-sourced wines'. An elegant staircase leads to the bedrooms. 'Our beautifully decorated room had a hugely comfortable bed with a goose-down duvet.' The turret room has three white and cream walls and a bold floral feature wall; 'excellent lighting'; a 'splendid' bathroom with a dressing area at one end. The rooms are well equipped: a carafe of filtered water, fresh milk for the tea tray, bathrobes. A 'delicious' breakfast has home-made granola, a fruit compote (perhaps 'wonderful plums'), chunky toast; freshly squeezed fruit juice is brought to the table; hot dishes include smoked salmon and scrambled eggs. (*John Lake, Lis Dennis, and others*)

25% DISCOUNT VOUCHERS

10 Stanley Road
Hastings TN34 1UE

T: 01424-438448
E: enquiries@
  black-rock-hastings.co.uk
W: www.hastingsaccommodation.
  com

BEDROOMS: 5.
OPEN: all year.
FACILITIES: lounge, breakfast room, free Wi-Fi, terrace, unsuitable for &.
BACKGROUND MUSIC: lounge and breakfast room.
LOCATION: central.
CHILDREN: not under 10, family room available.
DOGS: not allowed.
CREDIT CARDS: MasterCard, Visa.
PRICES: [2014] per room B&B single £90–£95, double £130–£145. 1-night bookings refused bank holidays, weekends.

HASTINGS East Sussex

Map 2:E5

SWAN HOUSE

On a narrow street of medieval houses in the old town, this 15th-century cottage has been given a rustic chic interior by the owners, Brendan McDonagh (the 'thoughtful' host) and his partner Lionel Copley (a fashion designer). The big lounge has white walls, a beamed ceiling, two long settees and a huge stone fireplace; it has been filled with an eclectic mix of paintings, antique furniture and bric-a-brac collected by the owners. The bedrooms have original wood beams, white walls and floorboards, 'simple, fresh' furnishings. The double-aspect Renaissance suite, large and sunny, has a second smaller bedroom connected to a shower room; a small balcony above the garden. Church, which faces the 14th-century St Clement's church, has a king-size bed, a hand-printed wall design (by a local artist); shelled grotto panelling in the bathroom. Many of the ingredients for the breakfast are sourced in the town, including handmade strawberry and pomegranate jam, and citrus marmalade. A list of nearby restaurants is available. No parking on the narrow street ('don't take a large car') but permits are provided for nearby car parks.

25% DISCOUNT VOUCHERS

1 Hill Street
Hastings, TN34 3HU

T: 01424-430014
E: res@swanhousehastings.co.uk
W: www.swanhousehastings.co.uk

BEDROOMS: 4, 1 on ground floor.
OPEN: all year except 24–26 Dec.
FACILITIES: lounge/breakfast room, courtyard garden, civil wedding licence, free Wi-Fi, unsuitable for &.
BACKGROUND MUSIC: none.
LOCATION: in old town, near seafront.
CHILDREN: not under 5.
DOGS: not allowed.
CREDIT CARDS: Amex, MasterCard, Visa.
PRICES: per room B&B single £80–£120, double £120–£150.

HATCH BEAUCHAMP Somerset

Map 1:C6

FROG STREET FARMHOUSE

In a 'peaceful' setting in the Somerset countryside, yet only five miles from the county town of Taunton, Louise and David Farrance's small guest house is 'highly recommended' by *Guide* readers. The traditional character of the listed longhouse, which dates back to the 15th century, has been maintained: it has beamed ceilings, flagstone floors, Jacobean panelling and inglenook fireplaces. 'The scenery and setting were idyllic,' is a typical comment. Guests are encouraged to 'unwind' in the lounge in the evening. It has a wood-burning stove, leather seating; there are books, games and a large television. The bedrooms are 'light and airy'; they have a large bed, 'crisp linen'; good technology. Willow has a double brass bedstead, an exposed stone wall and beams; the Garden Room has French-style furniture and a king-size Bergère bed. The Snug has a private entrance, a lounge with a log fire; a roll-top slipper bath in the bathroom. Louise Farrance will cook a simple evening meal, which has to be pre-booked. She uses vegetables from the garden and local produce. The bread and preserves at breakfast are home made.

Hatch Beauchamp
nr Taunton TA3 6AF

T: 01823-481883
E: frogstreet@hotmail.com
W: www.frogstreet.co.uk

BEDROOMS: 4.
OPEN: Jan–15 Mar, Apr–14 Nov.
FACILITIES: 2 lounges, dining room, free Wi-Fi, 150-acre grounds, unsuitable for &.
BACKGROUND MUSIC: optional.
LOCATION: 4 miles NW of Ilminster.
CHILDREN: all ages welcomed.
DOGS: not allowed.
CREDIT CARDS: all major cards (charges may apply).
PRICES: per room B&B £81–£90.

SEE ALSO SHORTLIST

HATHERSAGE Derbyshire

Map 3:A6

THE GEORGE HOTEL

In the centre of a Peak District village, this 15th-century former coaching inn is liked by readers for its 'comforting atmosphere'. Charlotte Brontë is said to have been a patron (the village was used as a model for *Jane Eyre*). 'A good room, excellent food and friendly staff,' says a returning visitor this year. Owned by Eric Marsh (who also runs *The Cavendish* in Baslow – see entry), it is managed by Philip Joseph. There are stone walls, rich fabrics, well-spaced seating with sofas and leather chairs in the large lounge and bar. 'Formality is not on the menu' in the *George*'s restaurant where the chef, Helen Price, serves modern dishes. While she was on maternity leave in 2014, her sous chef produced 'enjoyable, well-balanced and attractively presented dishes'. The bedrooms at the back are 'spacious and quiet'; those at the front have double-glazed windows. Superior rooms are equipped with bathrobes, DVD-player and a private bar. Nineteen bathrooms were renovated this year. Breakfast has a 'well-laid' buffet, 'toast delivered in relays', and hearty cooked dishes. The chef's own marmalade is recommended. The village is a good base for walkers and climbers. (*Peter Anderson, Peter and Kay Rogers, Padi Howard*)

Main Road
Hathersage S32 1BB

T: 01433-650436
F: 01433-650099
E: info@george-hotel.net
W: www.george-hotel.net

BEDROOMS: 24.
OPEN: all year.
FACILITIES: lounge/bar, restaurant, 2 function rooms, free Wi-Fi, civil wedding licence, courtyard, only restaurant suitable for &.
BACKGROUND MUSIC: light jazz in restaurant.
LOCATION: in village centre, parking.
CHILDREN: all ages welcomed.
DOGS: only guide dogs allowed.
CREDIT CARDS: Amex, MasterCard, Visa.
PRICES: [2014] per room B&B single £70–£164, double £80–£198. Set dinner £36.95 (*5% 'service levy' added to all prices*). 1-night bookings occasionally refused.

HEREFORD Herefordshire

Map 3:D4

CASTLE HOUSE NEW

By the castle moat and close to the cathedral, this handsome Grade II listed Regency villa and a Georgian town house on the same street form a small, 'friendly' hotel. It is owned by David Watkins, a local farmer whose pedigree Hereford herd and other produce supply the restaurant menu; Michelle Marriott-Lodge is the manager. *Castle House* gains a full entry thanks to a positive report by regular *Guide* correspondents who enjoyed 'an excellent stay from every point of view' this year. The lounge, bar, restaurant and bistro are in the main house. 'Meals were outstanding, with a good choice at dinner.' The chef, Claire Nicholls, presents dishes in a modern style, perhaps crab, red grapefruit, celery, caviar; fillet of Herefordshire beef, spring onion and horseradish rösti, watercress purée. Bedrooms in the main house are traditionally furnished: 'Our spacious suite, recently refurbished, was spotless; it had a large and comfortable sitting area.' A ground-floor suite, which has a private terrace, is equipped for disabled visitors. Rooms in *Number 25*, a stroll down the street, have a modern decor. (*Richard and Jill Burridge*)

Castle Street
Hereford HR1 2NW

T: 01432-356321
E: info@ castlehse.co.uk
W: www.castlehse.co.uk

BEDROOMS: 24, 8 in *Number 25* (a short walk away), some on ground floor, 1 suitable for &.
OPEN: all year.
FACILITIES: lift, lounge, *Bertie's* bar, restaurant, bistro, free Wi-Fi, civil wedding licence, terrace, garden.
BACKGROUND MUSIC: in restaurant and bistro.
LOCATION: by castle.
CHILDREN: all ages welcomed.
DOGS: not allowed.
CREDIT CARDS: Amex, MasterCard, Visa.
PRICES: [2014] per room B&B single £130, double £150–£190. À la carte £35, tasting menu £50.

HEXHAM Northumberland

BATTLESTEADS

In the 'beautiful' North Tyne valley, Dee and Richard Slade's 'excellent' small hotel and restaurant is well placed for visitors exploring Hadrian's Wall or taking moor walks. It is a 'very comfortable, welcoming place' in a sparsely populated area, say visitors who were walking the Roman wall. The extended 18th-century farmhouse 'flies the flag' for green tourism: the heating and hot-water system is carbon-neutral; three wormeries turn food waste into compost; rainwater for the garden is captured in a huge tank. The chef, Eddie Shilton, cooks 'generous, imaginative meals of a high standard using local produce almost exclusively, with vegetables and salads from the hotel's own sizeable organic garden'. Typical dishes on the seasonal menu: salmon rillette, bread crisps, pickles; dry-cured gammon steak, free-range hen's egg, pease pudding, hand-cut chips. 'The bedrooms are small but attractive and well fitted.' Superior rooms have a seating area; a walk-in shower and spa bath in the bathroom. A family room has a double bed and two single sofa beds. Winston, the resident Labrador, welcomes four-legged friends, who can be accommodated in ground-floor rooms (by arrangement). (*S and PG, DM*)

Wark-on-Tyne
nr Hexham NE48 3LS

T: 01434-230209
F: 01434-230039
E: info@battlesteads.com
W: www.battlesteads.com

BEDROOMS: 17, 4 on ground floor, 2 suitable for &.
OPEN: all year.
FACILITIES: bar, dining room, function facilities, free Wi-Fi, civil wedding licence, 2-acre grounds.
BACKGROUND MUSIC: jazz in public areas.
LOCATION: edge of village, 12 miles N of Hexham.
CHILDREN: all ages welcomed.
DOGS: allowed in public rooms, by arrangement in bedrooms.
CREDIT CARDS: Amex, MasterCard, Visa.
PRICES: [2014] per room B&B £115–£145, D,B&B from £160. Set meals £23.50–£27.50.

SEE ALSO SHORTLIST

HOLT Norfolk

Map 2:A5

BYFORDS

Believed to be the town's oldest building, this Grade II listed property is run by the owners, Iain and Clair Wilson, as a store selling bread and speciality foods, a café/restaurant, and a 'posh' B&B. Inside the flint-fronted building is a 'warren of public rooms and narrow corridors', with exposed brickwork and oak floorboards. Local materials (slate, leather, silk and linen) were used for the bedrooms, which have dark wood bedsteads. Modern bathrooms are tiled in marble; many have a double-ended bath and a drench shower. 'Our room had good reading lights, a lovely antique writing desk, a leather sofa, and tartan throws on the bed'. A ground-floor room is adapted for disabled visitors; a family suite has a separate bedroom for children. *Guide* inspectors were impressed by 'the enthusiasm of the young staff'. Meals are served all day in the café on an extensive menu with sharing plates, pizzas and burgers; ice cream is home made. Breakfast, 'a superior meal', has a 'vast buffet' of freshly squeezed juices, compotes, fresh fruit salads; 'good toast and home-made preserves'; a wide choice of cooked dishes.

1–3 Shirehall Plain
Holt NR25 6BG

T: 01263-711400
E: queries@byfords.org.uk
W: www.byfords.org.uk

BEDROOMS: 16, 3 on ground floor, 1 suitable for &.
OPEN: all year.
FACILITIES: ramps, 5 internal eating areas, free Wi-Fi, deli.
BACKGROUND MUSIC: none.
LOCATION: central, private secure parking.
CHILDREN: all ages welcomed.
DOGS: only guide dogs allowed.
CREDIT CARDS: Amex, MasterCard, Visa.
PRICES: [2014] per room B&B single £120–£130, double £155–£175, D,B&B single £140–£180, double £195–£215. À la carte £35. 1-night bookings refused Sat.

COMBE HOUSE

❦ *César award in 2007*

'Hospitality is a tradition here.' In rolling parkland where Arabian horses and pheasants roam free, Ken and Ruth Hunt's 'stunningly renovated' Elizabethan manor house is 'a delight'. 'The staff genuinely seem to care at all levels.' Beyond the heavy oak door, there are open log fires, 'tastefully furnished' bedrooms, and a long history. Bedrooms vary in size and decor: some country-style rooms overlook the gardens; grander rooms have antiques and family portraits. Half a mile from the main building, a new cob and thatch house (which sleeps eight) stands in woodland with fenced gardens, ancient orchards and a brook. For a couple seeking seclusion, there is a cottage with a private garden. In the candlelit restaurant, chef Hadleigh Barrett's 'excellent' dinners use ingredients from the house's Victorian kitchen garden, perhaps pink grapefruit; grilled brill with a foie gras crust, roasted garden artichokes, girolles. Breakfast has plenty of choice, including home-made yogurt, home-laid eggs; porridge with Devon cream and maple syrup is 'a wonderful, if naughty treat'. (*WA, DH, and others*)

25% DISCOUNT VOUCHERS

Gittisham
nr Honiton EX14 3AD

T: 01404-540400
E: stay@combehousedevon.com
W: www.combehousedevon.com

BEDROOMS: 20, 1 in cottage, 4 in thatch house.
OPEN: all year.
FACILITIES: ramp, sitting room, Great Hall, bar, restaurant, private dining rooms, free Wi-Fi, civil wedding licence, 10-acre garden in 3,500-acre estate (helipad), only public rooms suitable for &.
BACKGROUND MUSIC: occasionally in hall and bar.
LOCATION: 4 miles SW of Honiton.
CHILDREN: all ages welcomed.
DOGS: allowed in some bedrooms, public rooms except restaurant, a booklet of dog-friendly walks is available.
CREDIT CARDS: MasterCard, Visa.
PRICES: [2014] per room B&B £220–£380, D,B&B £328–£488. Set dinner £54. 1-night bookings sometimes refused Fri/Sat in peak season.

HOPE Derbyshire

UNDERLEIGH HOUSE

In an idyllic setting outside a village within the Peak District national park, Vivienne and Philip Taylor's B&B is in a conversion of a Victorian cottage and barn. It is much liked for the good value and their 'generous' hospitality. There is good walking from the door: the Taylors will provide advice on the best walks, a packed lunch, and a complimentary tray of tea and cakes to returning walkers (waterproofs will be dried). The bedrooms, which vary in size, are comprehensively equipped: they have tea- and coffee-making facilities, a silent mini-fridge and a well-written information pack. The first-floor Derwent Suite faces the rear garden and has an adjoining lounge with dual-aspect windows. Shatton, accessed via a passageway from the guest lounge, is on the ground floor and has a glazed door which leads directly to the garden. The award-winning breakfast, served communally in a beamed and flagstoned room, has home-made granary bread, Aga-cooked porridge, unusual fruit compotes (such as sliced mango with lemon and Calvados), free-range eggs and locally made sausages and black pudding. Advice is given on restaurants and pubs; bookings will be made. (*JF*)

Lose Hill Lane
off Edale Road
Hope S33 6AF

T: 01433-621372
F: 01433-621324
E: info@underleighhouse.co.uk
W: www.underleighhouse.co.uk

BEDROOMS: 5.
OPEN: all year except Christmas, Jan.
FACILITIES: lounge, breakfast room, free Wi-Fi, ¼-acre garden, unsuitable for &.
BACKGROUND MUSIC: none.
LOCATION: 1 mile N of Hope.
CHILDREN: not under 12.
DOGS: allowed by arrangement.
CREDIT CARDS: MasterCard, Visa (*both 1.75% surcharge*).
PRICES: [2014] per room B&B £90–£110. 1-night bookings refused Fri/Sat, bank holidays.

SEE ALSO SHORTLIST

HOUGH-ON-THE-HILL Lincolnshire

Map 2:A3

THE BROWNLOW ARMS

'At the top of its game', Paul and Lorraine Willoughby's stone-built 17th-century inn, in a quiet village, 'exceeded expectations' for trusted correspondents in 2014. 'Lorraine's warmth and relaxed organisation made this place for us.' The 'charming', 'impeccably clean' bedrooms are in the main building and a neighbouring barn conversion; 'luxurious fabrics and the tasteful decor create a plush, cosy and classic feel'. 'Our spacious room had a comfortable bed with lovely pillows, good lighting, ample storage; the bathroom had a powerful, hot shower. A perfect room in which to hunker down on a wet weekend.' The public rooms have recently been refurbished. There is a 'buzzy' atmosphere in the bar – 'the sort of space you could comfortably spend hours in'. Chef Ruaraidh Bealby's 'imaginative' dinner menus, served in the 'relaxed, stylish' restaurant, have 'a great deal of choice'. A typical dish: 'perfectly pink' saddle of venison, 'sweet and unctuous' mini-venison shepherd's pie. 'Service was excellent; the friendly staff managed the busy restaurant beautifully.' Breakfast is 'adequate'; 'a shame that the radio was so dominant'. (*Anna and Bill Brewer*)

High Road
Hough-on-the-Hill NG32 2AZ

T: 01400-250234
E: armsinn@yahoo.co.uk
W: www.thebrownlowarms.com

BEDROOMS: 7, 3 on ground floor in barn conversion.
OPEN: all year except 24–26 Dec, restaurant closed midday Mon–Sat, Sun evening, Mon evening.
FACILITIES: bar, 3 restaurants, free Wi-Fi, unsuitable for &.
BACKGROUND MUSIC: 'easy listening' in public areas.
LOCATION: in village 7 miles N of Grantham.
CHILDREN: not under 8.
DOGS: not allowed.
CREDIT CARDS: MasterCard, Visa.
PRICES: [2014] per room B&B single £65–£75, double £98–£110. À la carte £50.

HUNTINGDON Cambridgeshire

Map 2:B4

THE OLD BRIDGE

Guests are offered tea and home-made scones on arrival at this ivy-covered 18th-century town house hotel on the banks of the River Ouse. Its owner, John Hoskins, a Master of Wine, runs an award-winning wine shop on the premises. 'Excellent room, good bathroom; superb food, friendly staff,' said one visitor. Smart, modern bedrooms are styled by John Hoskins's wife, Julia; many have views of the river or garden. Some large doubles have a sofa bed; handsome four-poster rooms are full of character. All rooms are equipped with up-to-date technology (flat-screen TV, DVD-player, iPod dock) and a choice of a wool or a silk duvet. In the bright, conservatory-style *Terrace* restaurant, chef Jack Woolner's contemporary menu might have cured rainbow trout, pea and radish salad; whole Dover sole, clams in parsley butter, ratte potatoes. The international wine list has more than 30 wines by the glass. Meals may also be taken in the lounge or bar, or outside on the patio in summer. The building is hedged by a busy traffic system: bedrooms have triple glazing and air conditioning. (*RL*)

1 High Street
Huntingdon PE29 3TQ

T: 01480-424300
F: 01480-411017
E: office@huntsbridge.co.uk
W: www.huntsbridge.com

BEDROOMS: 24, 2 on ground floor.
OPEN: all year.
FACILITIES: ramps, lounge, bar, restaurant, private dining room, wine shop, business centre, civil wedding licence, free Wi-Fi, 1-acre grounds (terrace, garden), river (fishing, jetty, boat trips), unsuitable for &.
BACKGROUND MUSIC: none.
LOCATION: 500 yds from centre, parking, station 10 mins' walk.
CHILDREN: all ages welcomed.
DOGS: not allowed in restaurant.
CREDIT CARDS: MasterCard, Visa.
PRICES: per room B&B single £89.50–£150, double £160–£230, D,B&B £199–£260. Set menu £17–£21 (not on Sat eve), à la carte £33.

IREBY Cumbria

♘OVERWATER HALL

César award: dog-friendly hotel of the year
'The perfect antidote to the hustle and bustle of
modern life', this small country hotel has been
run for more than 20 years by the owners,
Stephen Bore and Angela and Adrian Hyde. In
the quieter northern Lake District, the Grade II
listed castellated Georgian mansion stands in
large grounds with formal gardens and
woodland. The welcome is warm and personal.
'Angela couldn't have done more to help us,' say
visitors whose arrival was delayed. The boldly
decorated public rooms have 'comfortable
furnishings, books, games'; a log fire burns in
the high-ceilinged sitting room. Dogs, who are
'genuinely welcomed', are allowed to sit in one
of the lounges; they also have the freedom of the
grounds. The bedrooms are 'well provisioned':
fruit and flowers, fresh milk with the tea tray;
mineral water. A ground-floor room has a
terrace leading to the garden; unusual turret
rooms, with their curved walls and huge
windows, are full of character. In the dining
room, Adrian Hyde uses Cumbrian suppliers for
his modern dishes like Solway fish soup, rouille;
trio of lamb, dauphinoise potatoes. (*Martin and
Anna Smith, Susan Chait*)

25% DISCOUNT VOUCHERS

Overwater, nr Ireby
CA7 1HH

T: 017687-76566
F: 017687-76921
E: welcome@overwaterhall.co.uk
W: www.overwaterhall.co.uk

BEDROOMS: 11, 1 on ground floor.
OPEN: all year.
FACILITIES: drawing room, lounge,
bar area, restaurant, free Wi-Fi,
civil wedding licence, 18-acre
grounds, Overwater tarn 1 mile.
BACKGROUND MUSIC: light jazz in
restaurant.
LOCATION: 2 miles NE of
Bassenthwaite Lake.
CHILDREN: all ages welcomed, not
under 5 in restaurant (high tea at
5.30 pm).
DOGS: allowed except in 1 lounge,
restaurant.
CREDIT CARDS: MasterCard, Visa.
PRICES: [2014] per person B&B
£80–£125. Set dinner £45. 1-night
bookings refused Sat.

KIRKBY LONSDALE Cumbria

Map 4: inset C2

SUN INN

In a 'delightful little town with interesting shops and galleries', Lucy and Mark Fuller's 17th-century inn is 'top notch in all departments', says a regular *Guide* correspondent this year. 'The owners were away but the inn ran like clockwork; the staff were warm and friendly. It has become a favourite place to stay.' Arriving guests are given complimentary tea and biscuits in the bar, which has stone walls, wooden floors. The bedrooms are individually designed: 'My second-floor room has exposed beams, fine furniture; the modern bathroom was well equipped and sparkling clean.' A short seasonal menu is served in the restaurant: 'The local roast lamb was so good, I had it both evenings. A sizeable baby Camembert was a delicious starter; puddings were light and scrumptious; the service was faultless. House wines were excellent value by the glass.' Breakfast is 'superb'; freshly squeezed orange juice is served at table; fruit, yogurts and cereal are on a buffet table. 'Eggs, bacon and sausage, all from local suppliers, were beautifully cooked and served.' Residents are given free permits for the town's car parks. (*Trevor Lockwood*)

6 Market Street
Kirkby Lonsdale LA6 2AU

T: 015242-71965
F: 015242-72485
E: email@sun-inn.info
W: www.sun-inn.info

BEDROOMS: 11.
OPEN: all year, bar and restaurant closed Mon lunch.
FACILITIES: bar, restaurant, free Wi-Fi.
BACKGROUND MUSIC: in bar.
LOCATION: town centre.
CHILDREN: all ages welcomed.
DOGS: allowed in 8 bedrooms, bar.
CREDIT CARDS: MasterCard, Visa.
PRICES: [2014] per room B&B £99–£168, D,B&B £143–£226. Set dinner £29.95. 1-night bookings refused Sat.

KIRKBY STEPHEN Cumbria

Map 4:C3

AUGILL CASTLE

'This is no ordinary hotel,' say Simon and Wendy Bennett, who welcome guests in an 'easy-going manner' to their home, an eccentric neo-Gothic Victorian folly in the upper Eden valley. Visitors enjoy the 'laid-back' atmosphere and the feeling of being 'family friends'. A fifteenth bedroom was added in 2014: the Gatehouse is described as a 'hideaway for a couple'. The Brackenber Room in the centre of the castle has been renovated; it has a four-poster bed, a wardrobe in a turret, and south-facing views. Many of the bedrooms are big enough for a family; some are interconnected. Children are warmly welcomed ('my two-year-old daughter said she loved her castle'). There are cats and dogs, a playground, a fort in the forest, a tree house, toys. Early suppers, baby monitors and cots are available, and there is a children's cookery school. Dinner, which must be booked in advance, is a communal affair at a large oak table; the set menu of British seasonal dishes might include smoked brown trout, avocado cream; pork loin stuffed with peaches and garden herbs. (*MS, CF*)

25% DISCOUNT VOUCHERS

South Stainmore
nr Kirkby Stephen CA17 4DE

T: 01768-341937
E: enquiries@stayinacastle.com
W: www.stayinacastle.com

BEDROOMS: 15, 2 on ground floor, 4 in *Stable House*, 2 in *Orangery*.
OPEN: all year, dinner by arrangement, lunch for groups by arrangement.
FACILITIES: hall, cinema, drawing room, library (honesty bar), music (sitting) room, dining room, free Wi-Fi, civil wedding licence, 20-acre grounds (landscaped garden, tennis).
BACKGROUND MUSIC: none.
LOCATION: 3 miles NE of Kirkby Stephen.
CHILDREN: all ages welcomed.
DOGS: allowed by arrangement in designated rooms, not in public rooms.
CREDIT CARDS: Amex, MasterCard, Visa.
PRICES: [2014] per room B&B £140–£280, D,B&B £200–£340. Set dinner £30. 2-night bookings preferred weekends.

LANGAR Nottinghamshire

Map 2:A3

LANGAR HALL

César award in 2000

In the Vale of Belvoir, this honey-stone Georgian mansion has been owned by Imogen Skirving's family since 1860. She runs it as a small hotel in very personal style ('quintessentially English,' she says); the *Guide* award was for 'utterly enjoyable mild eccentricity'. It has many fans among *Guide* readers, cricket commentators reporting from Trent Bridge, and barristers attending Nottingham crown court. 'It feels like staying with friends in the country, except that the food is better,' was a recent comment. The drawing room has a club fender, photographs of the Bloomsbury group; the bar has prints associated with the designer Paul Smith (another regular). 'We could see that a lot of care went into the rooms; ours, Brownlow, was lovely, and housekeeping was superb,' say visitors this year. The themed rooms are named after people associated with the house. Cartland (the author often stayed) is large and light: 'Certainly not pink, though it is romantic.' In the restaurant, chefs Gary Booth and Ross Jeffrey serve seasonal dishes, perhaps chargrilled venison, cauliflower, bitter chocolate, pear and Beauvale blue.

25% DISCOUNT VOUCHERS

Church Lane
Langar NG13 9HG

T: 01949-860559
F: 01949-861045
E: info@langarhall.co.uk
W: www.langarhall.com

BEDROOMS: 12, 1 on ground floor, 1 in garden chalet.
OPEN: all year.
FACILITIES: ramps, sitting room, study, library, bar, garden room, restaurant, free Wi-Fi, civil wedding licence, 30-acre grounds (gardens, children's play area), unsuitable for &.
BACKGROUND MUSIC: none.
LOCATION: 12 miles SE of Nottingham.
CHILDREN: all ages welcomed by arrangement.
DOGS: small dogs on a lead allowed by arrangement, not unaccompanied.
CREDIT CARDS: MasterCard, Visa.
PRICES: [2014] per room B&B single £100–£140, double £130–£199. D,B&B (Sun and Mon) £30 added per person, set dinner (not on Sat) £25, à la carte £35–£45.

LASTINGHAM North Yorkshire

Map 4:C4

LASTINGHAM GRANGE

♥*César award in 1991*

'The hands-on owners make all the difference' at this 'special' hotel, in a creeper-covered 17th-century farmhouse on the edge of the North York Moors. Bertie Wood, his mother, Jane, and brother, Tom, are the 'most welcoming' hosts; 'the service is outstanding'. The traditional hotel is set in 'beautiful' grounds with 'spectacular' views across the moors; inside, there is an open fire in the 'well-furnished' lounge overlooking the terrace and 'delightful' rose garden. Bedrooms are 'small and old-fashioned but spotlessly clean and comfortable'. The whole is 'like being in an Agatha Christie novel'. In the dining room, chefs Paul Cattaneo and Sandra Thurlow cook 'first-class' traditional English dishes using meat from local farms and game from the moors, perhaps roast Lastingham grouse, apple and gale jelly, bread sauce, game chips; 'melt-in-the-mouth' roast beef. Afternoon tea is served every day, with home-made cakes and scones, generous portions of cream and jam. Children have an adventure playground and special meals. 'Superb walking on the moors from the door; a truly charming hotel, unusual in this day and age.' (*Michael and Jenifer Price*)

25% DISCOUNT VOUCHERS

Lastingham YO62 6TH

T: 01751-417345
F: 01751-417358
E: reservations@lastinghamgrange.com
W: www.lastinghamgrange.com

BEDROOMS: 11, plus cottage in village.
OPEN: Mar–mid-Nov.
FACILITIES: ramps, hall, lounge, dining room, laundry facilities, free Wi-Fi in public areas, 12-acre grounds (terrace, garden, adventure playground, croquet, boules), unsuitable for &.
BACKGROUND MUSIC: none.
LOCATION: 5 miles NE of Kirkbymoorside.
CHILDREN: all ages welcomed.
DOGS: not allowed in public rooms.
CREDIT CARDS: Amex, MasterCard, Visa.
PRICES: [2014] per room B&B £140–£199, D,B&B £180–£265. Set dinner £39.75, à la carte £30. 1-night bookings occasionally refused.

LAVENHAM Suffolk

Map 2:C5

THE GREAT HOUSE

🏆 *César award in 2009*

An 'atmosphere of bonhomie' was appreciated by a *Guide* inspector at Régis and Martine Crépy's restaurant-with-rooms, a 'magnificent' Georgian house on the market square of a pretty medieval wool town. The public rooms have been renovated with contemporary flourishes; a courtyard dining room has stainless steel, opaque glass and a retractable canopy. The 15th-century bedrooms, up uneven stairs, are handsomely furnished with 'modern knick-knacks', and have 'ancient beams'. 'Our beamed room was spacious, with a sizeable sitting area.' Fresh fruit, a decanter of sherry and a choice of 'excellent' pillows are among the thoughtful touches: there is 'an aura of great comfort'. In the elegant restaurant, chef Enrique Bilbault's cooking is 'of a high standard'; his daily-changing seasonal menus might include Suffolk pork belly confit, foie gras, port jelly; Devon turbot, glazed salsify, lemon and tomato butter. 'Everything is served by smart, and friendly staff.' Breakfast has French bread, 'good' conserves, stewed fruits, a wide range of cold meats; 'good coffee – and plenty of it'. (*Bryan and Mary Blaxall, and others*)

Market Place
Lavenham CO10 9QZ

T: 01787-247431
F: 01787-248007
E: info@greathouse.co.uk
W: www.greathouse.co.uk

BEDROOMS: 5.
OPEN: Feb–Dec, restaurant closed Sun night, Mon, Tues midday.
FACILITIES: lounge/bar, restaurant, free Wi-Fi, patio dining area, ½-acre garden, unsuitable for ♿.
BACKGROUND MUSIC: 'easy listening' in restaurant.
LOCATION: by Market Cross, near Guildhall, public car park.
CHILDREN: all ages welcomed.
DOGS: not allowed.
CREDIT CARDS: MasterCard, Visa.
PRICES: [2014] per room B&B £119–£249, D,B&B £189–£286. Set dinner £33.50, à la carte £55. 1-night bookings sometimes refused Sat.

SEE ALSO SHORTLIST

LEAMINGTON SPA Warwickshire

Map 2:B2

EIGHT CLARENDON CRESCENT

The 'generous Regency proportions' have been
retained at Christine and David Lawson's
upmarket B&B, a Grade II listed house in a
quiet crescent in the north end of the spa town.
The house is 'immaculately presented and has
some glorious features', according to a regular
Guide correspondent. The 'spacious' drawing
room overlooks the south-facing garden which
leads to a private dell. There are 'many fine
antiques'; fresh flowers are 'beautifully
arranged'. The bedrooms are individually
decorated in neutral colours; three have en suite
facilities, the other has a private bathroom across
the corridor. 'My room was warm, large and
gently scented. It was far superior to many hotel
rooms that have cost four times as much.' The
peaceful aspect is much liked: 'The only sounds
you hear are the chimes of the grandfather
clock.' Breakfast is served communally at a large
circular table. Prepared by Christine Lawson, it
was 'excellent, from the fresh fruit and yogurts
to the home-made bread and perfectly cooked
bacon and eggs'. Tea and coffee are served in
silver pots. No evening meals, but the hosts will
recommend local restaurants. (*TL*)

8 Clarendon Crescent
Leamington Spa CV32 5NR

T: 01926-429840
F: 01926-424641
E: lawson@lawson71.fsnet.co.uk
W: www.eightclarendoncrescent.
co.uk

BEDROOMS: 4.
OPEN: all year except Christmas,
New Year, Easter, occasional
holidays.
FACILITIES: drawing room, dining
room, free Wi-Fi, garden, 1-acre
with private dell, unsuitable for &.
BACKGROUND MUSIC: none.
LOCATION: close to centre.
CHILDREN: all ages welcomed.
DOGS: not allowed.
CREDIT CARDS: none.
PRICES: per room B&B single £50,
double £80.

LEDBURY Herefordshire

Map 3:D5

THE FEATHERS

On the high street of a medieval market town, this black-and-white-timbered 16th-century former coaching inn is today a 'great' town hotel 'with many locals passing through'. It is owned by David Elliston. The 'lovely old building' retains much of its long history in beamed rooms, antique furnishings and original features such as a 'quirky' old staircase. In the oldest part, 'comfortable, clean' bedrooms have exposed beams and original 17th-century wall paintings; high-ceilinged rooms in what was once a grand ballroom are more modern. All rooms have tea- and coffee-making facilities, dressing gowns and slippers. The 'busy' *Fuggles* brasserie has 'a good atmosphere'; in the *Quills* restaurant, chef Suzie Isaacs's modern dishes are served under chandeliers. Typical dishes: twice-baked Gruyère soufflé; wild sea bass fillet, pistachio mortadella croquettes, buttered sprout flowers. Light meals and afternoon tea are available in the bar and lounge; drinks may be taken in the walled garden in warm weather. A visitor who stopped in for morning refreshment reported an 'excellent experience: log fires, helpful staff, good coffee'. (*David Haigh, and others*)

25% DISCOUNT VOUCHERS

High Street
Ledbury HR8 1DS

T: 01531-635266
F: 01531-638955
E: enquiries@feathers-ledbury.
    co.uk
W: www.feathers-ledbury.co.uk

BEDROOMS: 22, 1 suite in cottage, also self-catering apartments.
OPEN: all year.
FACILITIES: lounge, bar, brasserie, restaurant, free Wi-Fi, function/conference/wedding facilities, spa (swimming pool, 11 by 6 metres, whirlpool, gym), civil wedding licence, courtyard garden (fountain, alfresco eating), unsuitable for &.
BACKGROUND MUSIC: none.
LOCATION: town centre, parking.
CHILDREN: all ages welcomed.
DOGS: allowed, only guide dogs in restaurant and brasserie.
CREDIT CARDS: Amex, MasterCard, Visa.
PRICES: [2014] per room B&B £145–£235, D,B&B £165–£195. Set menu (Sun–Thurs) £18.95–£22, à la carte £32.50. 1-night bookings occasionally refused weekends.

LEDBURY Herefordshire

Map 3:D5

THE NOVERINGS

Close to Ledbury and the Malverns, this 'substantial' Edwardian country house stands in extensive grounds with wild-flower meadows and gardens. It is run as a B&B by Peter and Heather Clark, who have 'put a huge amount of thought and effort into their business, and it shows', says a visitor. Decorated in period style, bedrooms have fresh flowers and a sitting area (there is no residents' lounge). The Venetian room was 'palatial, the biggest we have ever been given'; on a cold night, 'it was warm'; the dressing room was 'large enough to be a bedroom in its own right'; a roll-top bath and a separate walk-in shower in the bathroom. In the morning, guests place their orders for a 'simple and delicious' two-course home-cooked supper, perhaps pork braised in local stout, creamed potatoes, seasonal vegetables; frangipane tart. No licence – visitors are encouraged to bring their own wine. An 'excellent' breakfast has fresh fruit, and juice in glass carafes; cooked dishes include American-style pancakes with home-grown blueberries in season. 'You could walk from the house for miles over the fields and hills.' (*AF*)

Brook Lane, Bosbury
Ledbury HR8 1QD

T: 01531-641785
E: info@thenoverings.co.uk
W: www.thenoverings.co.uk

BEDROOMS: 3.
OPEN: Apr–Oct, no meals on Wed.
FACILITIES: dining room, billiard room, free Wi-Fi, 1-acre garden in 17 acres of woodland, unsuitable for &.
BACKGROUND MUSIC: at meal times in dining room.
LOCATION: 5 miles N of Ledbury.
CHILDREN: not welcomed.
DOGS: not allowed.
CREDIT CARDS: MasterCard, Visa (*4% surcharge for credit cards*).
PRICES: [2014] per room B&B £90–£120. Set menu £20. 1-night bookings refused at weekends.

LICHFIELD Staffordshire

Map 2:A2

NETHERSTOWE HOUSE

The welcome is 'friendly, almost overpowering', says a visitor this year to Ben Heathcote's small hotel in an interesting cathedral city. Earlier guests were greeted 'as if we were visiting notables'. A conversion of a 19th-century mill, the Grade II listed half-timbered building is surrounded by modern housing but is well hidden and quiet, entered through a tree-lined drive. Visitors who were 'looking particularly bedraggled after being soaked through on our boat' were 'offered every possible assistance with a friendly smile'. The 'Edwardian-plus' sitting room has 'big, squishy sofas'. Ben Heathcote tells us that following adverse comments in the *Guide* about background music in the public areas, 'new playlists have been created for our guests to enjoy'. The bedrooms in the main house are 'feminine', some with a king-size bed and retro roll-top bath; eight apartments are in a 'sympathetic' modern wing. In the dining room, chef Stephen Garland gives the food miles for the ingredients in his dishes, which might include five-spiced pork belly, glazed cheek, pickled vegetables (six miles). Less formal dining is available in a cellar steakhouse. (*Michael Wace, and others*)

25% DISCOUNT VOUCHERS

Netherstowe Lane
Lichfield WS13 6AY

T: 01543-254270
F: 01543-419998
E: info@netherstowehouse.com
W: www.netherstowehouse.com

BEDROOMS: 9, plus 8 serviced apartments in annexe.
OPEN: all year.
FACILITIES: 2 lounges, bar, 3 dining rooms, free Wi-Fi, cellar, gymnasium, 2-acre grounds, unsuitable for &.
BACKGROUND MUSIC: in public rooms.
LOCATION: 2 miles N of city centre.
CHILDREN: over 12 in hotel, all ages welcomed in apartments.
DOGS: guide dogs only allowed.
CREDIT CARDS: MasterCard, Visa.
PRICES: [2014] per room B&B £105–£195, D,B&B £185–£215. Set dinner £29–£35, à la carte £35.

THE ARUNDELL ARMS

🦢 *César award in 2006*

'A very nice hotel.' Close to the border between Devon and Cornwall, this family-run country hotel is 'an excellent combination of relatively simple accommodation and outstanding cooking'. It is owned by Adam Fox-Edwards, who is 'much in evidence'. The hotel has 20 miles of rights on the River Tamar and its tributaries; fly-fishing is a 'major feature'. (Non-fishing guests were 'made very welcome'.) Decorated in country house style, the 'unfussy' bedrooms have fine antiques; some have views over the terraced garden and its 300-year-old circular cockpit. The 'convivial' bar, popular with locals, has mementoes and paintings of country pursuits, a log fire in winter. The 'comfortable' residents' lounge has books and sofas. Steve Pidgeon is the chef in the main dining room (once the village assembly room); his menus are 'just right'. 'My haddock fillets were perfect: a good batter, no skin or bones. Thin chips were a nice change.' 'Breakfast shared the freshness and elegance of dinner.' Fishing courses are taught by long-serving instructors. (*Peter Anderson, and others*)

Fore Street
Lifton PL16 0AA

T: 01566-784666
F: 01566-784494
E: reservations@arundellarms.com
W: www.arundellarms.com

BEDROOMS: 26, 4 on ground floor.
OPEN: all year, except Christmas (food only).
FACILITIES: ramp, lounge, cocktail bar, public bar, 2 dining rooms, conference/meeting rooms, games room, free Wi-Fi, skittle alley, civil wedding licence, ½-acre garden, 20 miles fishing rights on River Tamar and tributaries, fishing school, secure bicycle storage.
BACKGROUND MUSIC: varied in restaurant and bar.
LOCATION: 3 miles E of Launceston.
CHILDREN: all ages welcomed.
DOGS: not allowed in restaurant.
CREDIT CARDS: MasterCard, Visa.
PRICES: [2014] per person B&B from £90, D,B&B from £130. Set dinner £45.

LODSWORTH West Sussex

THE HALFWAY BRIDGE

There is a 'friendly' atmosphere at Sam and Janet Bakose's refurbished 17th-century country inn between the historic market towns of Petworth and Midhurst. 'The service is exemplary, the bedrooms are stylish,' *Guide* inspectors said. The pub is popular with locals and families; the 'intimate' dining areas have brick walls and wood-burning stoves. The terrace and sheltered garden allow alfresco dining in good weather. Daily specials are written on the blackboard menu: 'We enjoyed upmarket pub food.' The menu might include devilled lamb kidneys; roasted cod in Serrano ham, seaweed tagliatelle, wild mushroom and fish cream sauce. Decorated in modern country style, the bedrooms are in the former stable yard behind the main building, overlooking a sunny lawn at the front and woods at the back. A spacious, beamed room had 'good-quality mahogany furniture and a large, comfortable bed'; full-length windows with wooden shutters. 'Housekeeping was of the highest standard.' Breakfast, served until 10.30 am, has 'a wide range of delicious cooked dishes'; a healthy option has muesli and fruit yogurts. Popular with walkers on the South Downs.

Lodsworth
Petworth GU28 9BP

T: 01798-861281
E: enquiries@halfwaybridge.co.uk
W: www.halfwaybridge.co.uk

BEDROOMS: 7, in converted barns.
OPEN: all year.
FACILITIES: bar, restaurant, free Wi-Fi, terrace, unsuitable for &.
BACKGROUND MUSIC: light jazz in bar and restaurant.
LOCATION: 3 miles W of Petworth.
CHILDREN: all ages welcomed.
DOGS: allowed in bar, not in bedrooms.
CREDIT CARDS: Amex, MasterCard, Visa.
PRICES: [2014] per room B&B single from £85 (Sun–Thurs), double £140–£230. À la carte £35. 1-night bookings refused weekends.

LONGHORSLEY Northumberland

Map 4:B3

THISTLEYHAUGH FARM

César award in 2011

On the banks of the River Coquet in the Cheviot hills, *Thistleyhaugh* 'is a beautiful house', says a visitor this year. But 'what makes it so special' is the hostess, Enid Nelless, because of her 'friendliness and easy conversation'. The Georgian farmhouse, on a 720-acre organic sheep and cattle farm, is 'full of nooks and crannies, lovely furniture and ornaments'. The bedrooms are priced by size. 'Our room was very large and well equipped, with lots of storage, exquisite bedlinen; fresh milk in the fridge, and home-made biscuits. The splendid roll-top bath had a powerful shower over it.' Guests are invited to 'help yourself to a glass of sherry' in the garden room before dinner. The meal cooked by Enid Nelless and her daughter-in-law, Zoë, is taken communally in the dining room ('which usually sparks lively conversation'). 'The meals were, as always, delicious, especially the roast lamb and accompanying vegetables.' Breakfast is 'very good and set us up for a day's walking'. 'Recommended to anyone willing to face a twisty road; we were sorry when the time came to hug Mrs Nelless in farewell.' (*Mary Hewson*)

Longhorsley, nr Morpeth
NE65 8RG

T/F: 01665-570629
E: thistleyhaugh@hotmail.com
W: www.thistleyhaugh.co.uk

BEDROOMS: 5.
OPEN: all year except Jan, dining room closed Sat eve.
FACILITIES: 2 lounges, dining room, free Wi-Fi, 720-acre farm, 1-acre garden (summer house), fishing, shooting, golf, riding nearby, unsuitable for &.
BACKGROUND MUSIC: none.
LOCATION: 10 miles N of Morpeth, W of A697.
CHILDREN: all ages welcomed.
DOGS: not allowed (kennels nearby).
CREDIT CARDS: MasterCard, Visa.
PRICES: per room B&B single £70, double £100. Set dinner £25.

LOOE Cornwall

THE BEACH HOUSE

'We were spoilt,' say visitors this year to Rosie and David Reeve's B&B in an 'ideal position, overlooking the sea just outside Looe'. The greeting is warm (tea and home-made cake will be offered). Three of the five 'clean and spotless' bedrooms face the sea. Fistral has floor-to-ceiling windows with sea views, and a balcony. Two bedrooms at the back of the house have access to a sitting room across the hall, which overlooks the sea. All have a fridge and tea/coffee-making facilities, 'regularly replenished'. Breakfast ('a delight') is ordered the evening before and served at an agreed time in a bright dining room. It has an extensive buffet (fresh fruit salad, home-made muffins, fruit juices, cereals, etc). Hot dishes, cooked to order, include a choice of eggs any way; full English; French toast, scrambled eggs with a smoked salmon muffin. The hosts provide details of local restaurants. 'We were looked after superbly and will definitely return.' The South West Coastal Path runs past the front gate. The private car park is an asset. (*Christopher Maycock, and others*)

Marine Drive, Hannafore
Looe PL13 2DH

T: 01503-262598
F: 01503-262298
E: enquiries@
    thebeachhouselooe.co.uk
W: www.thebeachhouselooe.co.uk

BEDROOMS: 5.
OPEN: all year except Christmas.
FACILITIES: garden room, breakfast room, free Wi-Fi, terrace, ⅓-acre garden, beach opposite, unsuitable for &.
BACKGROUND MUSIC: classical in dining room.
LOCATION: ½ mile from centre.
CHILDREN: children over 16 welcomed.
DOGS: not allowed.
CREDIT CARDS: MasterCard, Visa.
PRICES: [2014] per room B&B £80–£130. 1-night bookings refused weekends, high season.

SEE ALSO SHORTLIST

LORTON Cumbria

Map 4: inset C2

NEW HOUSE FARM

'Beauty, peace and solitude in abundance' were enjoyed by a reader who chose Hazel Thompson's unpretentious guest house in the Lake District for her wedding this year. The 'beautifully decorated' Grade II listed 17th-century farmhouse has stone floors, beamed ceilings and open fires. The 'wonderful' gardens, which have a hot tub, lead to woods, streams and open fields 'surrounded by fells'. Bedrooms are individually decorated: The Old Dairy, on the ground floor of a converted barn next to the main house, has a queen-size solid oak four-poster bed; a Victorian bathroom with a slipper bath. Whiteside, on the first floor of the main house, has a king-size brass bed. Swinside has a window seat facing the Fell. In the dining room, which has a beamed ceiling and an open fire, Mrs Thompson serves traditional English dishes (eg, liver pâté with port jelly; pheasant casserole; spotted dick with custard). Lunches and teas are served in an adjacent converted byre, which is decorated with farming, shooting and fishing artefacts. Breakfast has fruit, porridge, croissants 'straight from the Aga' and cooked dishes. (*Donna Parker, and others*)

Lorton
nr Cockermouth CA13 9UU

T: 07841-159818
E: hazel@newhouse-farm.co.uk
W: www.newhouse-farm.com

BEDROOMS: 5, 1 in stable, 1 in Old Dairy.
OPEN: all year except 25/26 Dec.
FACILITIES: 3 lounges, dining room, free Wi-Fi, civil wedding licence, 17-acre grounds (garden, hot tub, streams, woods, field, lake and river, safe bathing 2 miles), unsuitable for &.
BACKGROUND MUSIC: none.
LOCATION: 2 miles S of Lorton.
CHILDREN: not under 6.
DOGS: allowed in bedrooms by arrangement, not in public rooms.
CREDIT CARDS: MasterCard, Visa.
PRICES: per person B&B £50–£90, D,B&B £34 added. Set dinner £34.

LOUTH Lincolnshire

THE OLD RECTORY AT STEWTON

On the edge of the Lincolnshire Wolds, 'relaxed and charming' hosts Alan and Linda Palmer run their 'delightfully quirky' B&B in an early Victorian former rectory. Down a quiet lane, the B&B is set in large grounds with lawns and mature trees, ideal for the finches, pheasants, squirrels and spring hares that come to visit. Inside, guests have use of a conservatory and a large sitting room with books, fresh flowers, leather sofas, a wood fire in winter. The bedrooms have 'nooks and crannies'; one has a 'cosy little lounge hidden away'. The beds are 'comfortable'; 'the linen is top quality'. There is art and various artefacts throughout. Children are welcomed: family suites have a separate sitting room and convertible sofa bed, and the Palmers have 'an easy rapport' with younger guests. Breakfast, served at flexible times 'within reason', has smoked fish, and eggs from local free-range hens. *The Old Rectory* is in a hamlet close to the historic Georgian market town of Louth; well situated for walks and bicycle rides in the chalk hills of the Wolds. (*WC-W*)

Stewton
Louth LN11 8SF

T: 01507-328063
E: ajp100@postmaster.co.uk
W: www.louthbedandbreakfast.co.uk

BEDROOMS: 4, 1 with private bathroom.
OPEN: all year except Christmas/New Year.
FACILITIES: sitting room, breakfast room, free Wi-Fi, 3-acre garden, unsuitable for &.
BACKGROUND MUSIC: none.
LOCATION: in hamlet 2½ miles SE of Louth.
CHILDREN: all ages welcomed.
DOGS: allowed (£5 charge per visit), in public rooms 'depending on other guests'.
CREDIT CARDS: MasterCard, Visa.
PRICES: [2014] per room B&B single £45, double £65–£80. 1-night bookings refused over August bank holiday.

LOWER BOCKHAMPTON Dorset

Map 1:D6

♛ YALBURY COTTAGE

César award: small hotel of the year

In a hamlet in an 'unspoilt part of England', this small hotel/restaurant, a conversion of a row of 350-year-old thatched cottages, is run by Ariane and Jamie Jones. A family party celebrating a watershed birthday in 2014 commented on 'perfect service from start to finish'. Another comment: 'Ariane is a friendly, helpful host.' The bedrooms, reached by a mishmash of corridors, have views of gardens or fields. They are decorated in simple, rural style; a large room had 'pastel colours, pictures on three sides'. Housekeeping is 'immaculate'. Jamie Jones, the chef, serves a 'superb' dinner in the oak-beamed restaurant in the oldest part of the building. 'He produced delicious meals using local ingredients; pork tenderloin with Blue Vinny sauce, and duck liver parfait were memorable.' 'The food was fresh and beautifully cooked.' An 'imaginative' breakfast has 'porridge made to your liking'; apricots in honey and cinnamon; three types of fish, free-range eggs cooked any way; black and white pudding with the full cooked. *Yalbury Cottage* is close to Thomas Hardy's birthplace and his old schoolhouse. (*Geoffrey Bignell, Tim Moorey, Sara Price*)

25% DISCOUNT VOUCHERS

Lower Bockhampton
nr Dorchester DT2 8PZ

T: 01305-262382
E: enquiries@yalburycottage.com
W: www.yalburycottage.com

BEDROOMS: 8, 6 on ground floor.
OPEN: all year except Christmas/New Year.
FACILITIES: lounge, restaurant, free Wi-Fi, unsuitable for &.
BACKGROUND MUSIC: 'easy listening' in lounge at dinner time.
LOCATION: 2 miles E of Dorchester.
CHILDREN: all ages welcomed, but not in restaurant after 8 pm.
DOGS: allowed in bedrooms, lounge.
CREDIT CARDS: MasterCard, Visa.
PRICES: [2014] per room B&B single £70–£85, double £95–£120, D,B&B single £99–£115, double £160–£180. Set dinner £32.50–£37.50.

LOWER SLAUGHTER Gloucestershire

Map 3:D6

THE SLAUGHTERS COUNTRY INN

'Friendly, welcoming staff; good food and drink; reasonable prices – we will happily return.' On the banks of the River Eye, this 17th-century honey-stone building is run as an 'informal' country inn. It is owned by Andrew and Christina Brownsword; Stuart Hodges is the manager. The 'comfortable' bar, 'extremely popular' with locals and guests, has large sofas, leather armchairs, local brews, and plenty of books and magazines; drinks and bar meals may be taken on the terrace in good weather. Bedrooms are in the main house and cottages in the courtyard. 'Our upstairs room was very nice: sloping ceilings and beams; windows overlooking rooftops on one side, the river and gardens on the other. There was a large, comfortable bed; two armchairs and a coffee table with a good information book; poor reading lights, alas.' Chef Chris Fryer serves a seasonal menu in the newly refurbished restaurant ('good garden views'), perhaps roast chump of Cornish lamb, wild garlic pearl barley. Breakfast has 'a wide choice of cooked dishes, from kippers to salmon, mixed grills to eggs Florentine'. (*P and JT*)

Lower Slaughter GL54 2HS

T: 01451-822143
F: 01451-821045
E: info@theslaughtersinn.co.uk
W: www.theslaughtersinn.co.uk

BEDROOMS: 30, 11 in annexe, 3 on ground floor, 1 suitable for &.
OPEN: all year.
FACILITIES: bar, restaurant, function rooms, free Wi-Fi, civil wedding licence, terrace, 4-acre gardens.
BACKGROUND MUSIC: modern light pop/jazz in public areas.
LOCATION: in village, 3 miles SW of Stow-on-the-Wold.
CHILDREN: all ages welcomed.
DOGS: allowed in some bedrooms, not allowed in restaurant.
CREDIT CARDS: Amex, MasterCard, Visa.
PRICES: per room B&B £85–£160, D,B&B £155–£230. À la carte £35. 1-night bookings refused Sat in peak season.

LUDLOW Shropshire

Map 3:C4

MR UNDERHILL'S

⚜ *César award in 2000*

The sharp-eyed might spot a kingfisher on the River Teme over breakfast at Chris and Judy Bradley's restaurant-with-rooms in a conservation area below the castle ramparts. Dinner is an occasion: Judy Bradley presides over the small restaurant with what has been described as 'approachable formality'. Chris Bradley is the self-taught chef who has long held a *Michelin* star for his 'inventive' eight-course market menu. There is no choice until dessert, which is followed by coffee and chocolates. The style is not to all tastes: fans love the 'playful' food combinations in dishes like white fish velouté, marmalade ice cream; duck liver custard, Ludlow quince cream. One visitor this year found the food 'excessively sweet towards the end'. The accommodation is in suites. The timber-framed Shed in the garden has armchairs by French windows which overlook the river; 'a luxurious bathroom'. The other three have a separate sitting room; one has a garden decor in greens and stone, with maple and walnut wood; another has two bathrooms. Breakfast has 'irresistible' dishes: 'wonderfully light' black pudding and fried bread. (*Philip and Anne Carlisle, and others*)

Dinham Weir
Ludlow SY8 1EH

T: 01584-874431
W: www.mr-underhills.co.uk

BEDROOMS: 4, 1 in annexe.
OPEN: all year except Christmas/New Year, 2 weeks June, 1 week Oct, restaurant closed Mon/Tues.
FACILITIES: small lounge, restaurant, function facilities, free Wi-Fi, ½-acre courtyard, riverside garden (fishing, swimming), unsuitable for ♿.
BACKGROUND MUSIC: none.
LOCATION: below castle, on River Teme, station ½ mile, parking.
CHILDREN: not 2–8.
DOGS: not allowed.
CREDIT CARDS: MasterCard, Visa.
PRICES: per room B&B £235–£365. Set menus £67.50–£75. 1-night bookings sometimes refused Sat.

SEE ALSO SHORTLIST

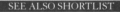

LYMINGTON Hampshire

Map 2:E2

BRITANNIA HOUSE

'We arrived to a warm reception from owner Tobias Feilke,' say visitors to this unusual B&B, which is formed of two houses opposite each other. The 'enthusiastic, amiable' host has created 'a warm and homely environment'; the house is 'spotless' throughout. 'After a friendly chat, we were given house keys and local information.' The first-floor sitting room, in the older building (which dates from 1865), is decorated in blue and yellow, and has wide views of the harbour and marina. There are large sofas, good lighting, plenty of books and magazines. A ground-floor bedroom was 'lavishly decorated in neo-classical style; wooden hangers in a large painted wardrobe; a plump duvet on the comfortable bed'. In the modern three-storey building opposite, rooms are plainer, and have pine furnishings. All rooms have anti-allergic duvet and pillows, and a flat-screen TV. Mr Feilke's breakfasts, served at a 'convivial' communal table in the country-style kitchen, has 'hearty' cooked dishes of eggs and 'delicious' local bacon. *Britannia House*, a short stroll from the marina, cobbled streets and smart shops, is a 'good base' for exploring the seaside town.

Station Street
Lymington SO41 3BA

T: 01590-672091
E: enquiries@britannia-house.com
W: www.britannia-house.com

BEDROOMS: 5, 2 on ground floor.
OPEN: all year.
FACILITIES: lounge, kitchen/breakfast room, free Wi-Fi, courtyard garden, unsuitable for &.
BACKGROUND MUSIC: none.
LOCATION: 2 mins' walk from High Street/quayside, parking.
CHILDREN: not under 8.
DOGS: not allowed.
CREDIT CARDS: MasterCard, Visa.
PRICES: [2014] per room B&B £85–£95. 1-night bookings refused weekends.

LYNDHURST Hampshire

Map 2:E2

LIME WOOD

In ancient heath and moorland, where wild ponies and donkeys roam free, this 'relaxed', family-friendly country house hotel occupies a 'stunning' Regency manor house and several 'beautifully designed' buildings in the extensive grounds. Part of the small Lime Wood group owned by Jim Ratcliffe, and run under the guidance of Hotel du Vin co-founder Robin Hutson, the hotel attracts 'a mixed crowd of families with small children, young couples and more mature guests'. 'We liked the lack of airs and graces,' said one visitor. 'Entrancing, inviting' public rooms are 'styled with flair, wit and humour'; individually designed bedrooms range from 'cosy' rooms to forest suites with a wood-burner and private terrace. 'Our small room, the cheapest, was well appointed, with a lovely bathroom.' Angela Hartnett and Luke Holder are the chefs in the 'vibrant, buzzy' restaurant, *Hartnett Holder & Co.*; the kitchen turns out British dishes with a strong Italian influence, including large sharing plates (perhaps whole monkfish, flageolet beans, celery, pancetta). Breakfast in the *Scullery* has 'an excellent buffet and a delightful atmosphere'. (*BW, Alan Kelly*)

Beaulieu Road
Lyndhurst SO43 7FZ

T: 02380-287177
F: 02380-287199
E: info@limewood.co.uk
W: www.limewoodhotel.co.uk

BEDROOMS: 32, 5 on ground floor, 2 suitable for &, 16 in pavilions and cottages in the grounds.
OPEN: all year.
FACILITIES: lifts, ramps, 2 bars, 3 lounges, 2 restaurants, private dining rooms, civil wedding licence, free Wi-Fi, spa (16-metre swimming pool), 14-acre gardens (outdoor hot pool).
BACKGROUND MUSIC: in some communal areas.
LOCATION: in New Forest, 12 miles SW of Southampton.
CHILDREN: all ages welcomed.
DOGS: allowed in some bedrooms, not in public rooms.
CREDIT CARDS: Amex, MasterCard, Visa.
PRICES: [2014] room £255–£950. Breakfast £13.50 or £18.50, à la carte £55. 1-night bookings refused most weekends, bank holidays.

MARAZION Cornwall

Map 1:E1

MOUNT HAVEN HOTEL & RESTAURANT

'A lovely hotel, just as described in the *Guide*.' A visitor this year was 'more than satisfied' at Mike and Orange Trevillion's small hotel on the edge of a village overlooking St Michael's Mount. 'The owners and staff were all friendly, and the prices are reasonable.' Reached via a car park below road level, it might have a 'slightly boxy' exterior. 'Inside, all is immaculate, long, wood-lined and carpeted corridors, original paintings; a Buddha over the front door and the smell of incense in public areas.' There are leather sofas, bucket chairs, large floral decorations in the lounge/bar, which has glass doors opening on to a decked terrace with tables and chairs for outdoor eating. On a level below (with access to similar decking) is the restaurant. Nathan Williams is now the chef, serving modern dishes like pan-roasted scallops, celeriac and apple purée, black pudding bonbons; Cornish duck breast, caramelised peach, galette potato. Most of the bedrooms have a balcony overlooking the sea. A 'Healing Room' provides treatments for 'rejuvenation and relaxation'. (*JH Bell, and others*)

Turnpike Road
Marazion TR17 0DQ

T: 01736-710249
F: 01736-711618
E: reception@mounthaven.co.uk
W: www.mounthaven.co.uk

BEDROOMS: 18, some on ground floor.
OPEN: all year.
FACILITIES: lounge/bar, restaurant, free Wi-Fi in all public areas and some bedrooms, healing room (holistic treatments), sun terrace, ½-acre grounds (rock/sand beaches 100 yds), unsuitable for &.
BACKGROUND MUSIC: bar, restaurant all day.
LOCATION: 4 miles E of Penzance, car park.
CHILDREN: all ages welcomed.
DOGS: allowed in public rooms only.
CREDIT CARDS: MasterCard, Visa.
PRICES: [2014] per room B&B £130–£240, D,B&B £190–£300. À la carte £30–£35. Min. 2 nights on bank holidays.

MARTINHOE Devon

Map 1:B4

THE OLD RECTORY HOTEL

César award in 2014

Beside the 11th-century church in a hamlet near the coast, this 'beautiful old stone building' is run as a small hotel by Huw Rees and Sam Prosser. 'They are attentive hosts, who give a warm welcome and take trouble to advise where to go locally,' say visitors this year. A stream runs through the 'generously planted' garden, which has a raised deck and seating areas. The part Georgian, part Victorian house has been discreetly extended; the public areas are 'nicely furnished in a mixed modern/classical style with unusual touches'. Tables are well spaced in the dining room where Huw Rees serves a short four-course menu of dishes using local produce, perhaps Ilfracombe crab, lime and avocado cocktail; fillet of Devon Red Ruby beef, chateaubriand sauce. Two of the bedrooms are in an adjacent coach house: 'Ours was furnished in traditional style; it had a good bed, excellent lighting, two easy chairs; plenty of hangers in the large wardrobe; a shower over the bath in the big bathroom.' Breakfast has 'very good local apple juice; every sort of cooked choice'. (*Bob and Sue Olive*)

Martinhoe EX31 4QT

T: 01598-763368
E: info@oldrectoryhotel.co.uk
W: www.oldrectoryhotel.co.uk

BEDROOMS: 11, 2 on ground floor, 2 in coach house.
OPEN: late Mar–Nov.
FACILITIES: 2 lounges, conservatory, dining room, free Wi-Fi, 3-acre grounds.
BACKGROUND MUSIC: in dining room.
LOCATION: 4 miles SW of Lynton.
CHILDREN: not under 14.
DOGS: not allowed.
CREDIT CARDS: Amex, MasterCard, Visa.
PRICES: [2014] per room B&B £160–£185, D,B&B £215–£260. 1-night bookings refused high season and weekends.

MASHAM North Yorkshire

Map 4:D4

SWINTON PARK

César award in 2011

In a 'superb' setting on a huge estate (with parkland, a lake and a walled garden), this 19th-century Gothic castle is the family home of Mark and Felicity Cunliffe-Lister. 'Personal and unfussy', it is run in a relaxed style. 'You can tell they have children,' said a visitor; family needs are anticipated in the bedrooms, which are equipped with nappies, wipes and baby powders. A new family suite has a large bedroom for the parents and a seating area connecting to a twin room for the youngsters. Many of the bedrooms are large (though one visitor was disappointed with a smaller room this year). A larger one was liked: it had a king-size bed, a walk-in wardrobe; a large bath reached by two steps and a separate shower in the bathroom. Tables are 'properly laid' in the dining room, where the cooking is 'superb' and the staff are 'delightful'. Chef Simon Crannage serves modern dishes, perhaps cured trout, pickled vegetables; braised belly and roast rib of fell lamb, broad bean purée. There are many activities in the grounds. (*K and ME, and others*)

25% DISCOUNT VOUCHERS

Masham, nr Ripon
HG4 4JH

T: 01765-680900
F: 01765-680901
E: reservations@swintonpark.com
W: www.swintonpark.com

BEDROOMS: 31, 4 suitable for &.
OPEN: all year, restaurant closed midday Mon.
FACILITIES: lift, ramps, 3 lounges, library, bar, restaurant, free Wi-Fi, banqueting hall, spa, games rooms, civil wedding licence, 200-acre grounds (many activities).
BACKGROUND MUSIC: in bar and dining room.
LOCATION: 1 mile SW of Masham.
CHILDREN: all ages welcomed.
DOGS: not allowed in public rooms, unattended in bedrooms.
CREDIT CARDS: MasterCard, Visa.
PRICES: [2014] per person B&B £78–£230, D,B&B (Tues–Thurs mid-Nov–mid-Feb, excluding Christmas) £106–£260. Set dinner £55–£65. 1-night bookings sometimes refused Sat.

BEDRUTHAN HOTEL AND SPA

❦ *César award in 2012*

In a 'fantastic' location on the north Cornish coast, this 'delightful' family-friendly hotel is owned and managed by sisters Emma Stratton, Deborah Wakefield and Rebecca Whittington. 'What really makes the stay is the easy manner in which the staff ensure that you have everything you could want.' Public rooms are 'airy and spacious, with magnificent views'. Bedrooms – some recently refurbished, many with sea views – have much colour. Chefs Darren Milgate and Ben Harmer cook 'exceptional' food (although one self-confessed fussy eater wished for more choice at dinner); modern dishes in the 'sophisticated' *Herring* restaurant might include fillet of locally reared pork, bean purée, spiced hispi cabbage. Lighter meals are available in the *Wild Café*. Children have 'a wonderful array of entertainment': swimming pools, playgrounds, a jungle gym; kites, nets, buckets, spades and binoculars are available to borrow. Visitors without children had 'a lovely adult experience; the hotel managed to keep contact with children to a minimum'. 'Fantastic breakfasts.' *The Scarlet* (see next entry) is a child-free sister hotel. (*Sharon Stell, and others*)

Mawgan Porth
TR8 4BU

T: 01637-860860
F: 01637-860714
E: stay@bedruthan.com
W: www.bedruthan.com

BEDROOMS: 101, 1 suitable for ♿.
OPEN: all year except 21–27 Dec, 3–29 Jan, restaurant open Thurs–Sun eve only.
FACILITIES: lift, 2 lounges, 2 bars, *Herring* restaurant, *Wild Café*, free Wi-Fi, poolside snack bar, ballroom, 4 children's clubs, spa (indoor swimming pool), civil wedding licence, 5-acre grounds (heated swimming pools, tennis, playing field).
BACKGROUND MUSIC: 'easy listening'.
LOCATION: 4 miles NE of Newquay.
CHILDREN: all ages welcomed.
DOGS: allowed in some bedrooms, public areas.
CREDIT CARDS: MasterCard, Visa.
PRICES: [2014] per room B&B £65 (single)–£470 (double), D,B&B £85 (single)–£510 (double). À la carte £30. 7-night bookings required in school holidays.

MAWGAN PORTH Cornwall

Map 1:D2

THE SCARLET

Down the hillside from its sister hotel, *Bedruthan Hotel and Spa* (see previous entry), this design hotel has strong green credentials and a 'youthful appeal'. Owned by sisters Emma Stratton, Deborah Wakefield and Rebecca Whittington, it has solar panels, sea thrift-planted roofs, rainwater harvesting and a biomass boiler. All the bedrooms have an outside space. 'Our lovely, well-organised room (No. 2) had a large balcony; a comfortable sofa in front of the floor-to-ceiling window gave wonderful views of the beach,' said a visitor this year. In the restaurant, chef Tom Hunter cooks 'tasty' modern dishes, perhaps rump of Cornish hogget, anchovy and potato fritters, root vegetable purée. 'We enjoyed a delicious scallop starter, but, given our seaside location, I expected more shellfish on the menu.' Light meals are available all day. 'The "anytime" menu was brilliant when we got back from a coastal trek after lunch. We had an excellent meal on our balcony (no room-service charge).' The 'sumptuous' Ayurvedic spa has a 'soothing, otherworldly' atmosphere. Breakfast, served at table with a carafe of fruit juice, is 'very good'. (*Barbara Watkinson, and others*)

25% DISCOUNT VOUCHERS

Tredragon Road
Mawgan Porth TR8 4DQ

T: 01637-861800
F: 01637-861801
E: stay@scarlethotel.co.uk
W: www.scarlethotel.co.uk

BEDROOMS: 37, 2 suitable for &.
OPEN: all year except Jan.
FACILITIES: lift, lobby, bar, lounge, library, restaurant, free Wi-Fi, civil wedding licence, spa (indoor swimming pool, 4 by 13 metres, steam room, hammam, treatment room), natural outdoor swimming pool (40 sq metres), seaweed baths.
BACKGROUND MUSIC: all day in bar and restaurant.
LOCATION: 4 miles NE of Newquay.
CHILDREN: normally not under 16.
DOGS: not allowed in restaurant or bar, some bedrooms.
CREDIT CARDS: MasterCard, Visa.
PRICES: [2014] per room B&B £195–£465, D,B&B £260–£530. Set dinner £42.50. 1-night bookings refused Fri/Sat.

MAWNAN SMITH Cornwall

Map 1:E2

BUDOCK VEAN

On the banks of the Helford river, this 'excellent, well-managed' hotel stands in extensive grounds with gardens, terraced ponds, waterfalls and its own nine-hole golf course. 'It remains a super family-run place, with the Barlow family much in evidence,' a returning visitor said. Regular guests welcome the 'old-fashioned' atmosphere, 'reminiscent of the 1940s'; those who prefer to dress up for dinner appreciate the requirement for men to wear a jacket and tie. 'Delightful' public rooms include a cocktail bar, and a snooker room with leather chesterfields; drinks may be taken in the sun lounge on the foreshore. 'Well-appointed' bedrooms have bathrobes and slippers, a tea tray; superior rooms overlook the gardens and golf course. A pianist provides live entertainment during and after dinner in the formal restaurant, where chef Darren Kelly serves a 'first-class' daily-changing menu that might include fried Cornish squid, sweet chilli; fillet of West Country veal, savoy cabbage, horseradish mash. Light lunches are taken in the conservatory and lounges. There is much to do without leaving the grounds; the hotel's river boat meanders up the many creeks.

Helford Passage, Mawnan Smith
nr Falmouth TR11 5LG

T: 01326-252100
F: 01326-250892
E: relax@budockvean.co.uk
W: www.budockvean.co.uk

BEDROOMS: 57, 4 self-catering cottages.
OPEN: all year except 3–22 Jan.
FACILITIES: lift, ramps, 3 lounges, conservatory, 2 bars, restaurant, *Country Club*, snooker room, free Wi-Fi, civil wedding licence, 65-acre grounds (covered heated swimming pool, 15 by 8 metres), spa, 9-hole golf course, tennis.
BACKGROUND MUSIC: live in restaurant.
LOCATION: 6 miles SW of Falmouth.
CHILDREN: no under-7s in dining room after 7 pm.
DOGS: allowed in some bedrooms, not in public rooms.
CREDIT CARDS: Amex, MasterCard, Visa.
PRICES: [2014] per person B&B £73–£133, D,B&B £88–£146. Set dinner £41, à la carte £37. 1-night bookings refused some weekends.

MELLS Somerset

Map 2:D1

♛ THE TALBOT INN   NEW

César award: pub-with-rooms of the year

In a 'fascinating' Domesday village, this former coaching inn 'has a pleasing ambience, cheerful and helpful young staff, and good food'. *Guide* inspectors 'greatly enjoyed the informality' in 2014, earning the *Talbot Inn* an upgrade to a full entry. It has been remodelled 'with feeling and flair' by the owners, Charlie Luxton, Dan Brod and Matt Greenlees (the manager), who also have the *Beckford Arms*, Tisbury (see entry). 'The helpful barman grabbed a key and carried our bag to our front room, reached by steep stairs. It was decorated in simple, modern style; local art on the walls (for sale); it had a high ceiling, a window seat, an immensely comfortable bed; a walk-in wardrobe. The splendid bathroom had a comprehensive emergency kit "in case you forget something".' Narrow corridors link 'intimate' dining areas, where 'decent local produce is nicely cooked' by the chef, Pravin Nayar. At weekends, fish and meats are grilled on an open fire in the *Coach House Grill Room* and served at long shared tables. There are tables and chairs in a courtyard and walled garden.

Selwood Street, Mells
nr Frome BA11 3PN

T: 01373 812254
E: info@talbotinn.com
W: www.talbotinn.com

BEDROOMS: 8, 1 on ground floor.
OPEN: all year, except 25 Dec.
FACILITIES: bar, restaurant, snug, map room, sitting room, dining room, grill, free Wi-Fi, courtyard, garden, unsuitable for ♿.
BACKGROUND MUSIC: in public areas.
LOCATION: in village.
CHILDREN: all ages welcomed.
DOGS: allowed in 1 bedroom.
CREDIT CARDS: MasterCard, Visa.
PRICES: [2014] per room B&B £95–£150. À la carte £45.

MILTON ABBOT Devon

Map 1:D3

HOTEL ENDSLEIGH

'A glorious place, run with a generous spirit,' say *Guide* inspectors this year of Olga Polizzi's luxury hotel, which stands in a 'beautiful estate' on the banks of the River Tamar. The 19th-century fishing lodge has been 'restored with charm and taste appropriate to the building'; it is run by 'friendly but never over-attentive staff, who quickly know you by name'. Adam Cornish joined as manager in 2014. 'There are lots of decent sitting areas inside and out; a library full of real books, a lounge, smaller sitting rooms; no background music, wonderful.' At night, small candles burn in the dimly lit public areas ('but you can find a light to read by'). In the panelled dining room, chef Christopher Dyke serves a short modern menu: 'The food is good, if not exceptional, in the modern manner; delicious sea bream.' One of the smaller bedrooms 'was fine; charmingly done in white and yellow; a wide bed, old wooden chest of drawers. A second armchair was brought when we asked. A neat little bathroom.' Guests have unlimited access to the grounds, which are of 'historic interest'.

Milton Abbot
nr Tavistock PL19 0PQ

T: 01822-870000
F: 01822-870578
E: mail@hotelendsleigh.com
W: www.hotelendsleigh.com

BEDROOMS: 16, 1 on ground floor, also 1 in lodge (1 mile from main house).
OPEN: all year except 18–28 Jan.
FACILITIES: drawing room, library, card room, bar, 2 dining rooms, free Wi-Fi, civil wedding licence, terraces, 108-acre estate (fishing, ghillie available).
BACKGROUND MUSIC: none.
LOCATION: 7 miles NW of Tavistock, train/plane Plymouth.
CHILDREN: all ages welcomed.
DOGS: not allowed in restaurant, or 'near afternoon tea table'.
CREDIT CARDS: all major cards.
PRICES: [2014] per room B&B £190–£390. Set dinner £40. 1-night bookings refused weekends.

MORECAMBE Lancashire

THE MIDLAND

In a 'superb position on the marine parade looking out over the bay', this 'Art Deco wonder' has been restored to its former glory by the small English Lakes group. A *Guide* inspector was 'warmly received; all the staff were friendly and helpful'. Every table has a sea view through floor-to-ceiling windows in the *Sun Terrace* restaurant, which follows the curve of the building. There is 'plenty of choice' on the modern menu: 'We had fried scallops with thin strips of local bacon; sirloin steak with roasted tomatoes, mushrooms, chunky chips. The flavours and textures complemented each other.' Lighter meals can be taken in the 'laid-back' *Rotunda* terrace bar and café. A small lift, and an 'astonishing' spiral staircase, provide access to the bedrooms which are off either side of a 'lovely' curved corridor. Rooms are 'small, but have everything you need; the layout is a model of efficiency'. Some face the sea and have a balcony. The decor is 'plain, flat colours with very little artwork on the walls'. Breakfast (in the restaurant) has a large buffet; hot dishes (including kippers) are cooked to order.

Marine Road West
Morecambe LA4 4BU

T: 01524-424000
F: 01524-424054
E: themidland@englishlakes.co.uk
W: www.englishlakes.co.uk

BEDROOMS: 44, 2 suitable for &.
OPEN: all year.
FACILITIES: lift, lounge, bar/café, restaurant, free Wi-Fi, function rooms, civil wedding licence.
BACKGROUND MUSIC: 1930s/1950s music in bar, restaurant.
LOCATION: on seafront.
CHILDREN: all ages welcomed.
DOGS: not allowed in restaurant.
CREDIT CARDS: Amex, MasterCard, Visa.
PRICES: [2014] per room B&B £148–£402. D,B&B £27 added per person. À la carte £33.

MORETON-IN-MARSH Gloucestershire

Map 3:D6

THE MANOR HOUSE

In a medieval market town, this 'welcoming' hotel in a 16th-century mellow stone building wins praise this year for the 'good service and ambience'. It is 'well managed' by Simon Stanbrook for the small Cotswold Inns and Hotels group (see entry for *The Lamb Inn*, Burford); the staff are 'unfailingly polite and helpful'. The bedrooms, 'thoughtfully furnished and well equipped', vary in style and aspect: smaller double rooms overlook the high street or the garden; a room with a four-poster bed has original arch windows and a window seat with views of the grounds. Adrian Court is the chef in the *Mulberry* restaurant overlooking the garden; his modern four-course menus might be 'too nouvelle' for some tastes. Typical dishes: Stinking Bishop mousse, poached pear, toasted hazelnuts; Cornish sole, nero tagliatelle, curly kale, king prawns. Informal meals and snacks are taken in the *Beagle* bar and brasserie. The extensive breakfast buffet has home-baked bread, home-made preserves, cereals, honeycomb. Hot dishes, including Scotch pancakes served with banana maple syrup, are cooked to order. Stratford-upon-Avon is a half-hour's drive away. (*JR Osborne*)

High Street
Moreton-in-Marsh
GL56 0LJ

T: 01608-650501
F: 01608-651481
E: info@manorhousehotel.info
W: www.cotswold-inns-hotels.
co.uk/manor

BEDROOMS: 35, 1 in cottage, 1 on ground floor suitable for &.
OPEN: all year.
FACILITIES: library, lounge, bar, brasserie, restaurant, function rooms, free Wi-Fi, civil wedding licence, ½-acre garden.
BACKGROUND MUSIC: in bar.
LOCATION: on edge of market town.
CHILDREN: all ages welcomed.
DOGS: 'well-behaved dogs' allowed in allocated bedrooms, 'on leads' in public rooms.
CREDIT CARDS: all major cards.
PRICES: [2014] per person B&B £99–£198, D,B&B £163–£262. Set dinner £39 or £55. 1-night bookings sometimes refused Sat.

SEE ALSO SHORTLIST

MORETON-IN-MARSH Gloucestershire   Map 3:D6

THE REDESDALE ARMS

At his centuries-old coaching inn on the main street of a Cotswold town, Robert Smith is a 'hands-on' owner/manager, whose welcome is 'warm'. The 'terrific service from the staff' is also praised. The bars and restaurant have old passages, original oak beams; leather seating and an open fire in the residents' lounge. The best bedrooms are in a converted stable block at the back, a short walk outdoors (umbrellas are provided). These rooms have a contemporary feel: 'Ours was very comfortable, with close attention to detail throughout, especially the lighting.' A visitor in a wheelchair found a ground-floor room 'easily accessible'. Rooms in the main building have a more traditional style; those at the front are double glazed. The chef, Daniel Ciobotiaru, cooks in the modern British style; his 'excellent' dinner menu has dishes like River Exe mussels, white wine, Cotswold cream and garlic; slow-braised sirloin of beef, creamed horseradish mash, roasted root vegetables. Meals may be taken on the garden terrace in fine weather. There's a wide choice at breakfast, 'to suit every taste'. (*JF, and others*)

High Street
Moreton-in-Marsh
GL56 0AW

T: 01608-650308
F: 01608-654055
E: info@redesdalearms.com
W: www.redesdalearms.com

BEDROOMS: 32, 25 in annexe across courtyard, 1 suitable for &.
OPEN: all year.
FACILITIES: 3 lounge bars, 2 restaurants, heated open dining area, free Wi-Fi.
BACKGROUND MUSIC: in all public areas.
LOCATION: town centre.
CHILDREN: all ages welcomed.
DOGS: allowed on lead in bar, not in bedrooms or restaurant.
CREDIT CARDS: MasterCard, Visa.
PRICES: [2014] per room B&B £79–£180, D,B&B £130–£200. À la carte £30. 1-night bookings refused Sat Apr–Oct.

SEE ALSO SHORTLIST

MORPETH Northumberland

Map 4:B4

ESHOTT HALL

A 'profound country house experience' was enjoyed by a visitor to this 'superb period house' on a large estate with an arboretum and formal gardens. The owners, Robert and Gina Parker, have 'tastefully' renovated the 17th-century crenellated house bringing it up to date while retaining some fine period features. A rare William Morris stained-glass window illuminates a magnificent flying staircase leading from the hall. There are original fireplaces in the light lounge and in the library, which is styled like a gentlemen's club. 'Huge emphasis' is placed on food, which is 'beyond expectation': in the yellow-walled dining room, chef Chris Wood creates innovative dishes from seasonal produce, perhaps pork belly wonton, apple jelly, crackling; guineafowl breast, saffron potatoes, thyme-roasted winter roots. Desserts are 'really interesting'. Each of the eleven bedrooms has been individually designed and furnished 'in traditional style with modern facilities'. Collingwood has muted tones, a four-poster bed and a freestanding roll-top bath in front of the window; the Italian Bedroom has window seats overlooking the garden. Children are welcomed. (*KM, and others*)

Morpeth NE65 9EN

T: 01670-787454
F: 01670-786011
E: info@eshotthall.co.uk
W: www.eshotthall.co.uk

BEDROOMS: 11, plus 5 in *Eshott Grange* annexe.
OPEN: all year.
FACILITIES: drawing room, library, 2 dining rooms, free Wi-Fi in library, civil wedding licence, 35-acre estate, tennis, unsuitable for &.
BACKGROUND MUSIC: classical in dining rooms.
LOCATION: 6 miles N of Morpeth.
CHILDREN: all ages welcomed.
DOGS: allowed in 2 bedrooms, not in public rooms.
CREDIT CARDS: Amex, MasterCard, Visa.
PRICES: [per room] B&B £120–£200, D,B&B £170–£270. À la carte £35.

MORSTON Norfolk

Map 2:A5

MORSTON HALL

César award in 2010

In a stirring landscape of sandbanks and salt marshes on the north Norfolk coast, Tracy and Galton (the chef) Blackiston's acclaimed restaurant-with-rooms is a Jacobean flint-and-brick mansion. There is an air of anticipation as guests gather at 7.30 pm for aperitifs and canapés in two lounges with log fires and candles. Dinner is served in a single sitting in the dining room and conservatory. There is no choice on the seven-course daily-changing menu until dessert or cheese (dietary requirements are discussed and 'dislikes easily dealt with'). The 'high quality' of the cooking is praised. 'The food is always a joy, both for the eyes and for the palate.' One dish stood out for a trusted correspondent: 'When I read it (egg yolk, with vegetables and truffles) I thought how dull; when I ate it I thought how extraordinary.' The bedrooms are divided between the main house and a pavilion in the well-maintained grounds. A room in the house was 'airy, spacious and well equipped'. The pavilion suites have a more modern decor. (*Wolfgang Stroebe, and others*)

Morston, Holt
NR25 7AA

T: 01263-741041
F: 01263-740419
E: reception@morstonhall.com
W: www.morstonhall.com

BEDROOMS: 13, 6 in garden pavilion on ground floor.
OPEN: all year except Christmas, Jan, restaurant closed midday except Sun.
FACILITIES: hall, lounge, sunroom, conservatory, restaurant, free Wi-Fi, 3½-acre garden (pond, croquet).
BACKGROUND MUSIC: none.
LOCATION: 2 miles W of Blakeney.
CHILDREN: all ages welcomed.
DOGS: not allowed in public rooms.
CREDIT CARDS: Amex, MasterCard, Visa.
PRICES: per person D,B&B £180–£195. Set dinner £67. 1-night bookings sometimes refused Sat.

MOUSEHOLE Cornwall

Map 1:E1

THE OLD COASTGUARD

On the edge of a fishing village, this small hotel and restaurant faces the sea across subtropical gardens. Owned by brothers Charles and Edmund Inkin, it is run in 'relaxed' style by a 'welcoming' young staff. The Inkins have continued renovation this year, adapting the bedrooms in the simple style that will be familiar to visitors to their other inns: *The Felin Fach Griffin*, Felin Fach in Wales, and *The Gurnard's Head*, Zennor (see entries). Rooms have a panelled headboard with built-in shelving; a Roberts radio rather than television; 'proper coffee and Cornish tea' on the hospitality tray; books to read. Several rooms have a balcony; one has a bath with a sea view. A lower lounge, which runs the length of the building, has leather sofas and chairs, separate seating areas. There are mismatched wooden tables and chairs in the open-plan bar and dining area, where chef Tom Symons serves a menu of dishes like gazpacho, crab, basil; skate fillet, mussels and saffron risotto. Breakfast has Cornish apple juice; home-made muesli; home-baked soda bread, 'proper pats of butter'; a choice of cooked dishes.

Mousehole
Penzance TR19 6PR

T: 01736-731222
E: enquiries@oldcoastguardhotel.co.uk
W: www.oldcoastguardhotel.co.uk

BEDROOMS: 14.
OPEN: all year except 4 days in Jan, 24/25 Dec.
FACILITIES: bar, sun terrace, dining room, free Wi-Fi in bar and most bedrooms, small garden.
BACKGROUND MUSIC: Radio 4 at breakfast, selected music during meals.
LOCATION: edge of village, 2 miles S of Newlyn.
CHILDREN: all ages welcomed.
DOGS: not allowed in dining room.
CREDIT CARDS: MasterCard, Visa.
PRICES: [2014] per person B&B £60–£100, D,B&B £82.50–£122.50. À la carte £25. 1-night bookings sometimes refused Sat.

MULLION COVE Cornwall

Map 1:E2

MULLION COVE HOTEL

In a prominent position above Mullion Cove, this 'rescued and revived' former railway hotel has 'wonderful views', 'good dinners' and 'unfailingly friendly' staff. It is owned by the 'hands-on' Grose family; 'Matthew Grose takes a keen interest in the hotel, and is determined to see it flourish.' Most of the renovated bedrooms face the sea. 'Our smart, clean room had a bowl of fruit and delicious home-made chocolate brownies; binoculars for taking in the great views. From the bath, we could see out to the cliffs above Mullion Cove.' In the *Atlantic View* restaurant, chef Fiona Were's four-course, daily changing menu has some 'very good' dishes, perhaps line-caught wild bass, cassoulet, squash, cavolo nero. Some guests prefer the Art Deco-inspired *Glenbervie* bar, which serves a simple, all-day menu – 'ideal when we were out walking longer than expected'. A hot breakfast, including local hog's pudding, is cooked to order. 'I asked for a Scotch woodcock and they obliged (the waitress was quite excited at the prospect of a challenge).' A dissenter was less impressed with the cooked dishes in the morning. (*Carie Roots, John Barnes*)

25% DISCOUNT VOUCHERS

Mullion
Helston TR12 7EP

T: 01326-240328
F: 01326-240998
E: enquiries@mullion-cove.co.uk
W: www.mullion-cove.co.uk

BEDROOMS: 30, some on ground floor.
OPEN: all year.
FACILITIES: lift, 3 lounges, bar, restaurant, free Wi-Fi, 3-acre garden, heated outdoor swimming pool (11 by 5.5 metres).
BACKGROUND MUSIC: 'easy listening' in bar.
LOCATION: on edge of village.
CHILDREN: all ages welcomed.
DOGS: allowed in some bedrooms, 1 lounge.
CREDIT CARDS: Amex, MasterCard, Visa.
PRICES: [2014] per room B&B £90–£330, D,B&B £146–£386. Set dinner £36.

NEAR SAWREY Cumbria

EES WYKE COUNTRY HOUSE

'Superb, as usual,' say visitors returning in 2014 to Richard and Margaret Lee's small country hotel above the still waters of Esthwaite in the Lake District. Set in pretty gardens, the Georgian house was once the holiday home of Beatrix Potter. Five of the bedrooms have been refurbished 'to a very high standard' this year. They have new carpets; their bathrooms have been refitted. Dressing gowns are provided in two rooms which have a private bathroom across the landing. The two 'nicely decorated' lounges have 'comfortable' sofas, good pictures and a log fire in winter. Dinner is served in a 'lovely room with super views'. Richard Lee is the chef: he cooks French/English dishes for his 'highly recommended' daily-changing five-course menu, which might include fresh figs, pancetta and goat's cheese on puff pastry; pan-fried prime rib-eye of local beef, red wine and shallot sauce. Breakfast has home-baked bread and croissants, fresh fruit, yogurts, cereals, porridge; a wide range of cooked dishes with sausages and dry-cured bacon from an award-winning butcher. (*E and G Talbot*)

Near Sawrey
Ambleside LA22 0JZ

T: 015394-36393
E: mail@eeswyke.co.uk
W: www.eeswyke.co.uk

BEDROOMS: 8, 1 on ground floor.
OPEN: all year, except 25/26 Dec.
FACILITIES: 2 lounges, restaurant, free Wi-Fi, veranda, 1-acre garden, unsuitable for &.
BACKGROUND MUSIC: none.
LOCATION: edge of village 2½ miles SE of Hawkshead on B5286.
CHILDREN: not under 12.
DOGS: not allowed.
CREDIT CARDS: MasterCard, Visa.
PRICES: per room B&B £99–£155. Set dinner £39.50. 1-night bookings sometimes refused.

NETHER WESTCOTE Oxfordshire

Map 3:D6

THE FEATHERED NEST

♀ *César award in 2013*

There is a 'timeless, country pub feel' at Tony and Amanda Timmer's rural inn. It occupies a 300-year-old former malthouse with views of the verdant Evenlode valley. 'We were made very welcome; our wonderful room was thoughtfully equipped,' say visitors in 2014. Extra touches include 'not just the coffee machine, flowers, fruit and chocolates – there were also books and current magazines, plenty of decent hangers; excellent lighting'. A kitchen garden supplies many herbs and vegetables for chef Kuba Winkowski's 'excellent' modern dishes, perhaps beetroot, sheep's milk curd, black garlic; guineafowl, buckwheat, spring white truffle, cabbage. Informal meals may be taken in the popular bar or, in warm weather, on the terrace, in the shade of a sycamore tree. Breakfast has home-made compotes and preserves, 'chunky toast – bread obviously baked in the kitchen', 'the tastiest smoked bacon and sausage'. DVDs and board games are available to borrow. 'Rustic benches in private corners' of the extensive lawn allow for alfresco lounging. *(Malcolm and Kate MacMaster, and others)*

Nether Westcote
Chipping Norton OX7 6SD

T: 01993-833030
F: 01993-833031
E: info@thefeatherednestinn.co.uk
W: www.thefeatherednestinn.co.uk

BEDROOMS: 4.
OPEN: all year except 25 Dec, restaurant closed Mon except bank holidays.
FACILITIES: bar, dining room, garden room, free Wi-Fi, civil wedding licence, unsuitable for &.
BACKGROUND MUSIC: soft in public areas.
LOCATION: in village.
CHILDREN: all ages welcomed.
DOGS: allowed in bar, not in bedrooms.
CREDIT CARDS: Amex, MasterCard, Visa.
PRICES: [2014] per room B&B single £150–£200, double £180–£230. À la carte £50. 1-night bookings refused weekends.

NETLEY MARSH Hampshire

Map 2:E2

HOTEL TERRAVINA

César award in 2009

In a New Forest village, this 'special' hotel is run in pro-active style by the owners, Gérard and Nina Basset. The welcome they and their staff give 'uplifts the spirits', said one visitor. The red brick Victorian building is 'open, modern, everything tastefully done, with top-quality fittings, glass panels, natural wood or slate flooring'. In the bedrooms, which have a sometimes quirky, contemporary decor, 'a lot of care has been taken in the furnishing'. They are generously equipped (a flat-screen TV with integral DVD and CD, iPod docking station, espresso coffee machine, fresh milk, air conditioning); a deluge rain shower in the bathroom. The chef, George Blogg, forages in the forest for his modern dishes, which have a Californian twist. His menus might include ham hock, goose liver, sourdough, apple and hazelnut crumb; turbot, creamed pearl barley, chestnut mushroom duxelles. A visitor with a dairy intolerance was 'impressed' that soya milk was 'waiting in the room; meals were cheerfully adapted'. Gérard Basset wins international recognition as a sommelier; 'it pays to follow his recommendations'. (*JB, and others*)

174 Woodlands Road
Netley Marsh
nr Southampton SO40 7GL

T: 02380-293784
F: 02380-293627
E: info@hotelterravina.co.uk
W: www.hotelterravina.co.uk

BEDROOMS: 11, some on ground floor, 1 suitable for &.
OPEN: all year.
FACILITIES: ramp, lounge, bar, restaurant, private dining room, free Wi-Fi, civil wedding licence, 1-acre grounds (heated outdoor swimming pool).
BACKGROUND MUSIC: none.
LOCATION: NW of Southampton, 2 miles W of Totton.
CHILDREN: all ages welcomed.
DOGS: not allowed.
CREDIT CARDS: Amex, MasterCard, Visa.
PRICES: [2014] per room B&B £165–£265, D,B&B £205–£245. À la carte £45, tasting menus £65–£85. 2-night bookings preferred at weekends (check with hotel).

NEW MILTON Hampshire

Map 2:E2

CHEWTON GLEN

On the edge of the New Forest, and within easy reach of the sea, this country house hotel (Relais & Châteaux) continues to impress. 'Our room and the facilities were top drawer, but that should be expected at the best hotels. It is the staff and the sheer attention to detail that make *Chewton Glen* stand out,' says a visitor this year. Bedrooms in the main house have antiques, modern fabrics; most have a terrace, balcony or private garden. In a secluded wooded valley on the estate, 12 circular tree-house suites, accessed via a stylish gangplank, are 'great fun'. Each has a wood-burning stove, a whirlpool tub on a wrap-around terrace, and woodland views from a freestanding bathtub; a continental breakfast hamper is delivered to the door. Some guests may prefer to make the trip to the main house for breakfast – 'there's only so much pastry a family can eat'. There is 'a lighter, less fussy ambience' now in the 'much-improved' *Vetiver* restaurant. Chef Luke Matthews's 'eclectic' dishes might include salt beef salad, crisp duck egg; roast rabbit, home-made basil pappardelle. 'Absolutely delightful.' (*Michael Duffy, David Soanes*)

Christchurch Road
New Milton BH25 6QS

T: 01425-275341
F: 01425-272310
E: reservations@chewtonglen.com
W: www.chewtonglen.com

BEDROOMS: 70, 14 on ground floor, 12 tree-house suites in grounds, 1 suitable for &.
OPEN: all year.
FACILITIES: 3 lounges, bar, restaurant, function rooms, free Wi-Fi, civil wedding licence, spa, indoor 17-metre swimming pool, 130-acre grounds, outdoor 15-metre heated swimming pool, tennis centre, par-3 golf course.
BACKGROUND MUSIC: in public areas.
LOCATION: on S edge of New Forest national park.
CHILDREN: all ages welcomed.
DOGS: allowed in tree-house suites only, not in public rooms.
CREDIT CARDS: all major cards.
PRICES: [to Mar 2015] room £325–£695. Breakfast £26, set dinner £60, à la carte £55. 1-night bookings refused weekends.

NEW ROMNEY Kent

Map 2:E5

ROMNEY BAY HOUSE

César award in 2012

In a 'stunning' setting by a links golf course on the Kent coast, Clinton and Lisa Lovell's small hotel 'exceeded our expectations again', say *Guide* readers on their third visit. An earlier comment: 'The chairs, books and artefacts made us feel at home; the Lovells are professional and friendly hosts.' The unusual house was designed by Sir Clough Williams-Ellis for American actress and journalist Hedda Hopper. The bedrooms have many thoughtful touches: bathrobes and mineral water, a sewing kit and binoculars. Two have a four-poster bed, two are twin-bedded. In the conservatory dining room, Clinton Lovell serves a set four-course no-choice dinner on four evenings a week, with dishes like rosette of Romney Marsh lamb stuffed with apricots. The attention to detail shows in a 'beautifully but unpretentiously presented' breakfast. 'The mushrooms were perfectly seasoned and grilled; my wife's bowl of porridge and her boiled egg and soldiers were delicious.' The large main lounge has a log fire; you might catch a view of France (at least with the help of the telescope) from the first-floor lounge. (*Matthew Caminer, and others*)

25% DISCOUNT VOUCHERS

Coast Road, Littlestone
New Romney TN28 8QY

T: 01797-364747
E: romneybayhouse@aol.co.uk
W: www.romneybayhousehotel.co.uk

BEDROOMS: 10.
OPEN: all year except 1 week Christmas, 1 week early Jan (but open for New Year), dining room closed midday, Sun/Mon/Thurs evenings.
FACILITIES: 2 lounges, bar, conservatory, dining room, free Wi-Fi, small function facilities, 1-acre garden, unsuitable for &.
BACKGROUND MUSIC: none.
LOCATION: 1½ miles from New Romney.
CHILDREN: not under 14.
DOGS: not allowed.
CREDIT CARDS: Amex, MasterCard, Visa.
PRICES: [2014] per room B&B single £75–£95, double £95–£164. Set dinner £45. 1-night advance bookings refused weekends.

NEWBIGGIN-ON-LUNE Cumbria

Map 4:C3

BROWNBER HALL

'Arriving on a wet and stormy winter evening', visitors this year to Hilary Reid's B&B in a mid-19th-century country house were impressed by the welcome. 'She greeted us, offered assistance with our luggage and showed us to a spacious double room facing open fields. A wood-burning stove in the lounge and efficient central heating kept us warm.' There is an honesty bar, 'a good selection' of books, guides and maps, a folder of up-to-date local information. Bedrooms, on the first floor, are reached by a lift or a 'fine staircase with wooden and rope banisters'. A south-facing room has shutters and richly coloured full-length curtains; green-striped wallpaper; 'a small bed with a comfortable mattress; a spotless bathroom'. Fresh milk is provided for the tea/coffee tray and a bowl for visiting dogs who are given an edible treat on arrival (canines are 'genuinely' welcomed but numbers may be limited). Breakfast, 'promptly served by Hilary', has 'unpackaged butter and marmalade, good toast'; local ingredients in the hot dishes. *The Black Swan*, Ravenstonedale (see entry), is 'a good choice for an evening meal'. (*Neil Phillips, and others*)

Newbiggin-on-Lune
CA17 4NX

T/F: 015396-23208
E: enquiries@brownberhall.co.uk
W: www.brownberhall.co.uk

BEDROOMS: 10.
OPEN: all year except Christmas.
FACILITIES: lounge, dining room, free Wi-Fi, terrace, garden, unsuitable for &.
BACKGROUND MUSIC: none.
LOCATION: outside village, 5 miles SW of Kirkby Stephen.
CHILDREN: not under 10.
DOGS: welcomed (numbers are limited).
CREDIT CARDS: MasterCard, Visa.
PRICES: [2014] per room B&B single £35–£55, double £70–£90. 1-night bookings refused bank holiday weekends.

NEWCASTLE UPON TYNE Tyne and Wear   Map 4:B4

JESMOND DENE HOUSE

César award in 2013

'A huge success: the staff were welcoming and treated us like VIPs; the food was good.' Praise from regular *Guide* correspondents this year for Peter Candler's 'very good' hotel, an Arts and Crafts mansion at the head of a forested valley close to the city centre. The bedrooms, which vary in size and view, are decorated in muted shades with bursts of colour. They are generously equipped: fruit and mineral water, a minibar, bathrobes and slippers, magazines. 'Our suite was comfortable and quiet, a place to relax.' The furnishing of the public rooms reflects the building's 19th-century heritage: original oak panelling, fine fireplaces, and stained glass alongside striking contemporary artworks. In the restaurant, the inventive cooking of Michael Penaluna is much praised. His menus have dishes like clam risotto, Laphroaig; spring lamb, asparagus, onion, goat's cheese. There are two tasting menus (one for vegetarians). Breakfast has a large buffet with freshly squeezed juices, smoked salmon, cold meats and cheeses. The cooked choices include haggis and duck egg, salse verde. (*Suzanne and Jerome Lyons, and others*)

Jesmond Dene Road
Newcastle upon Tyne
NE2 2EY

T: 0191-212 3000
F: 0191-212 3001
E: info@jesmonddenehouse.co.uk
W: www.jesmonddenehouse.co.uk

BEDROOMS: 40, 8 in adjacent annexe, 2 suitable for ♿.
OPEN: all year.
FACILITIES: lift, 2 lounges, cocktail bar, restaurant, conference/function facilities, free Wi-Fi, civil wedding licence, 2-acre garden.
BACKGROUND MUSIC: in public areas.
LOCATION: 5 mins' drive from centre via A167.
CHILDREN: all ages welcomed.
DOGS: only guide dogs allowed.
CREDIT CARDS: all major cards.
PRICES: [2014] per room B&B £120–£400. À la carte £50, tasting menu £75.

SEE ALSO SHORTLIST

NEWLANDS Cumbria

Map 4: inset C2

SWINSIDE LODGE

'Pastoral sounds' (birds and newborn lambs) 'greet the day' at this small Georgian house, which stands at the foot of Cat Bells, surrounded by Lake District peaks. The owners, Mike and Kath Bilton, have 'the personal touch', says a fan. 'They wanted us to have a great weekend.' The two sitting rooms have fresh flowers, books, local maps; DVDs for viewing in the bedroom are available at the reception desk. The cooking of the long-serving chef, Clive Imber, attracts non-residents to the candlelit dining room. His daily-changing menu of British/French dishes might include seared tuna, prawns, sesame pepper and cucumber salad; loin of venison, leaf spinach, caramelised apple. There are three styles of room. A superior room at the top has 'thrilling' mountain views; smaller rooms are 'well thought-out, pristine'. 'Nice touches' include 'Lake District guides, a sewing kit, tea/coffee tray with home-made biscuits, mineral water'. Beds are turned down in the evening. Breakfast is 'excellent'; options include local ham with poached eggs, smoked salmon with scrambled eggs. The Biltons 'took endless trouble to explain the most rewarding walks in the area'. (*JG, and others*)

Grange Road
Newlands
nr Keswick CA12 5UE

T: 017687-72948
F: 017687-73312
E: info@swinsidelodge-hotel.co.uk
W: www.swinsidelodge-hotel.co.uk

BEDROOMS: 7.
OPEN: all year except Dec, Jan.
FACILITIES: 2 lounges, dining room, free Wi-Fi, ½-acre garden, unsuitable for &.
BACKGROUND MUSIC: in Reception.
LOCATION: 2 miles SW of Keswick.
CHILDREN: not under 12.
DOGS: not allowed in house (dry store available).
CREDIT CARDS: MasterCard, Visa.
PRICES: [2014] per person B&B £73–£127, D,B&B £98–£152. À la carte £45.

HEASLEY HOUSE

In early 2014, this white-painted Grade II Georgian dower house by a meadow that runs down to the River Mole was bought by Mandy and Miles Platt. A 'friendly and enthusiastic couple who try hard to please guests', they have refurbished the exterior and public rooms. 'We were welcomed with handshakes and on first-name terms,' say returning visitors (regular correspondents). 'We were pleased to find the fire lit in the lounge each afternoon. When we asked if there were any scones at afternoon tea, they were made the next day.' There are fresh flowers in the lounge and dining room, which have original features. Miles Platt is the self-taught cook, serving a set menu (preferences discussed when booking). 'A delicious salad had fresh leaves and figs, nicely dressed; we enjoyed a lovely rack of lamb with beautifully cooked savoy cabbage, beetroot jus and dauphinoise potatoes. Vegetarian guests were well catered for.' The bedrooms are individually styled: 'Our quiet room had a separate sitting area.' Breakfast 'passes the scrambled eggs test'. The Platts, who have a 'well-behaved' dog, welcome visiting canines. (*Jill and Mike Bennett*)

Heasley Mill
North Molton EX36 3LE

T: 01598-740213
E: enquiries@heasley-house.co.uk
W: www.heasley-house.co.uk

BEDROOMS: 8.
OPEN: Easter–end Aug, shooting parties only Sept–Jan.
FACILITIES: lounge, bar, restaurant, free Wi-Fi, ¼-acre garden, unsuitable for &.
BACKGROUND MUSIC: none.
LOCATION: N of N Molton.
CHILDREN: all ages welcomed.
DOGS: welcomed (£10 a day).
CREDIT CARDS: MasterCard, Visa.
PRICES: per room B&B single £110, double £150–£170. Set dinner £26–£32.

NORTH WALSHAM Norfolk

Map 2:A6

BEECHWOOD HOTEL

'A welcoming establishment that runs like clockwork and is excellent value for money.' Lindsay Spalding and Don Birch are 'exemplary hosts' at their small hotel, a creeper-clad Georgian house in a market town near the north Norfolk coast. 'Everything is pristine' in the public areas and the bedrooms. The rooms in a new wing are 'particularly spacious; they have under-floor heating, a slipper bath and a walk-in shower in the large bathroom'. The evening turn-down service is 'impressive'. In the 'well-laid-out' restaurant, head chef Steven Norgate prepares a 'Ten-Mile Dinner' where he aims to source all ingredients as close as possible to the hotel (Cromer crab, Morston mussels, Sheringham lamb). The suppliers are named in the menu which might include beetroot and carrot salad, horseradish ice cream; loin of lamb, dauphinoise potatoes, rosemary jus. 'Lovely food with attentive service,' is this year's comment. Agatha Christie was a frequent visitor when the house was in private hands (she wrote in a summer house). A complete set of her books is kept and guests can read her correspondence. (*Roderic Rennison, and others*)

25% DISCOUNT VOUCHERS

20 Cromer Road
North Walsham
NR28 0HD

T: 01692-403231
F: 01692-407284
E: info@beechwood-hotel.co.uk
W: www.beechwood-hotel.co.uk

BEDROOMS: 17, some on ground floor, 1 suitable for ♿.
OPEN: all year, except Christmas, restaurant closed midday Mon–Sat.
FACILITIES: 2 lounges, bar, restaurant, free Wi-Fi, 1-acre garden (croquet).
BACKGROUND MUSIC: none.
LOCATION: near town centre.
CHILDREN: not under 10.
DOGS: allowed (3 'dog' bedrooms).
CREDIT CARDS: MasterCard, Visa.
PRICES: [2014] per room B&B single £88, double £100–£160. Set dinner £39. 1-night bookings sometimes refused Sat.

NORTHLEACH Gloucestershire

Map 3:D6

THE WHEATSHEAF NEW

On the main street of a Cotswold wool town, this former coaching inn has been imaginatively updated by the owners, Sam and Georgie Pearman. It returns to the *Guide* thanks to an enthusiastic report by a regular correspondent, who liked the 'youthful buzz about the place' and the 'cool staff who seem to enjoy themselves'. The bar has flagstone floors, a log fire, 'a good selection of beers'; locals dropping in for a drink. To either side are dining areas with mismatched wooden tables and chairs. 'Lots of snugs and cubbyholes make it special.' There is striking artwork throughout including a portrait of Kate Moss by Sebastian Kruger. James Parn is now the manager; Owen Kaagman is the chef. 'The food is simple, tasty and fresh; the artichoke soup and devilled kidneys were excellent examples of good grub.' The bedrooms come in three sizes (the inn's website has 'helpful floor plans and pictures'). Not all rooms have a wardrobe or a chest of drawers: hooks and hangers are provided instead. There are 'useful extras' in a 'have-you-forgotten' pack. (*David Soanes*)

West End
Northleach GL54 3EZ

T: 01451-860244
E: reservations@
   cotswoldswheatsheaf.com
W: www.cotswoldswheatsheaf.com

BEDROOMS: 14, 3 on ground floor, 2 in annexe.
OPEN: all year.
FACILITIES: sitting room, 2 bars, dining room, 2 private dining rooms, free Wi-Fi, garden.
BACKGROUND MUSIC: in public areas.
LOCATION: town centre.
CHILDREN: all ages welcomed.
DOGS: allowed.
CREDIT CARDS: Amex, MasterCard, Visa.
PRICES: [2014] B&B per room (continental) £140–£230. Cooked breakfast £5, à la carte £35.

NORWICH Norfolk

Map 2:B5

THE OLD RECTORY

In a leafy conservation area close to the city centre, Chris and Sally Entwistle run their Grade II listed, creeper-clad Georgian rectory as a small hotel. 'It remains consistent – near enough to perfect,' say returning visitors this year. 'The staff are well trained and so friendly.' The hotel stands in mature gardens overlooking the River Yare; in warm weather, afternoon tea may be taken on the pool terrace. In the main house and adjoining Victorian coach house, traditionally furnished bedrooms vary in size and aspect: those in the main building are the more spacious, some with a fireplace; those in the quiet coach house have sloping beams. All have books, a hospitality tray, a modern bathroom, bathrobes. Pre-dinner drinks may be taken in front of the log fire in the well-appointed drawing room. In the panelled dining room, chef James Perry's daily-changing menus might include local pork and wild pheasant terrine, gooseberry chutney; Attleborough beef medallions, horseradish mashed potatoes, local cabbage. Breakfast has home-made fruit compotes, local honey; hot dishes are individually cooked. (*JS and F Waters*)

103 Yarmouth Road
Thorpe St Andrew
Norwich NR7 0HF

T: 01603-700772
F: 01603-300772
E: enquiries@oldrectorynorwich.com
W: www.oldrectorynorwich.com

BEDROOMS: 8, 3 in coach house.
OPEN: all year except Christmas/New Year, restaurant closed Sun and bank holiday Mon.
FACILITIES: drawing room, conservatory, dining room, free Wi-Fi, 1-acre garden, unheated swimming pool (9 by 3 metres, spring/summer only), unsuitable for &.
BACKGROUND MUSIC: classical/jazz.
LOCATION: 2 miles E of Norwich.
CHILDREN: all ages welcomed.
DOGS: only guide dogs allowed.
CREDIT CARDS: all major cards.
PRICES: [2014] per room B&B single £90–£170, double £125–£170, D,B&B (min. 2 nights) £160–£220. Set dinner £30. 1-night bookings refused weekends (spring and summer).

SEE ALSO SHORTLIST

NORWICH Norfolk

Map 2:B5

38 ST GILES

'A fine house, stylishly furnished', this restored Grade II listed Georgian building is reached via a discreet entrance on a street of independent shops. It is owned by Jan and William Cheeseman, who run it as an upmarket B&B. Individually designed, the modern bedrooms are up a 'magnificent central staircase'; a suite with a sofa bed in its sitting room is ideal for a family. A top-floor bedroom, which runs the length of the house, overlooks rooftops, trees and gardens. It has 'quality silk curtains, a lovely Chinese cabinet as a wardrobe', a stylish bathroom had a walnut panelled bath, 'nice toiletries'. A smaller room, which overlooks handsome Georgian houses, has a 'spotless' shower room. On the tea tray was a plate of 'divine home-made chocolate brownies with a Cape gooseberry'. Breakfast, served on delicate handmade crockery, is 'a cut above'. There's a choice of yogurt with poached plums, porridge with caramelised rhubarb, home-made granola or muesli. The cooked dishes include poached eggs with hollandaise sauce, wilted spinach, bacon or smoked salmon. 'We had extra toast at the end as we couldn't resist the home-made jams.'

38 St Giles Street
Norwich NR2 1LL

T: 01603-662944
E: 38stgiles@gmail.com
W: www.38stgiles.co.uk

BEDROOMS: 6, 1 on ground floor.
OPEN: all year.
FACILITIES: breakfast room, free Wi-Fi, private parking.
BACKGROUND MUSIC: Radio 3 at breakfast.
LOCATION: central.
CHILDREN: all ages welcomed.
DOGS: allowed by arrangement, not in public rooms.
CREDIT CARDS: MasterCard, Visa.
PRICES: per room B&B single £90, double £130–£160. 2-night bookings 'encouraged' at weekends.

SEE ALSO SHORTLIST

NOTTINGHAM Nottinghamshire

Map 2:A3

HART'S HOTEL

César award in 2007

'We have stayed very happily here,' say returning
visitors this year to this modern, purpose-built
hotel. Close to the castle, it has a secluded garden
and courtyard. It is owned by Tim Hart (see also
Hambleton Hall, Hambleton). In a 'great position'
overlooking the city, it is a short stroll to the
centre. The contemporary bedrooms are 'small
but well equipped', with a work area, flat-screen
TV with DVD-player, and fresh milk in the
fridge; garden rooms have French doors leading
to a terrace with outdoor seating. There is no air
conditioning in the rooms, 'but a system of
louvred shutters works very well'. In the busy
Hart's restaurant, chef Dan Burridge's daily-
changing menus might include dishes like lamb
rump, gnocchi, courgette caponata. Informal
meals and afternoon tea are served in the *Park
Bar* (which also provides 24-hour room service).
Breakfast, served in the bedroom or the bar, has
fresh fruit and juice, locally produced yogurt,
Melton Mowbray sausages and bacon, and breads
from Tim Hart's Hambleton Bakery in nearby
Rutland. (*Gareth and Ros Gunning, and others*)

25% DISCOUNT VOUCHERS

Standard Hill, Park Row
Nottingham NG1 6GN

T: 0115-988 1900
F: 0115-947 7600
E: reception@hartshotel.co.uk
W: www.hartsnottingham.co.uk

BEDROOMS: 32, 2 suitable for ♿.
OPEN: all year.
FACILITIES: lift, ramps,
reception/lobby, bar, restaurant
(30 yds), free Wi-Fi, conference/
banqueting facilities, small exercise
room, civil wedding licence, small
garden, private car park with
CCTV.
BACKGROUND MUSIC: light jazz in
bar.
LOCATION: city centre.
CHILDREN: all ages welcomed.
DOGS: not allowed in public rooms,
or unattended in bedrooms.
CREDIT CARDS: Amex, MasterCard,
Visa.
PRICES: [2014] room £125–£265.
Breakfast £9–£14 per person, set
dinner £24, à la carte £33.75.

OBORNE Dorset

Map 1:C6

THE GRANGE AT OBORNE

'In an excellent position, with quiet and beautiful countryside around', this 200-year-old former farmhouse is owned by Karenza and Ken Mathews, and managed by their daughter, Jennifer, and her husband, Jonathan Fletcher. The family is 'much in evidence', says a visitor this year. 'The staff were extremely helpful when I took my father, who needs disabled facilities. It was good to find people who don't regard the disabled guest as an imposition.' Another comment: 'Pleasant and comfortable; a genial proprietor and helpful staff.' Built of stone from the Purbeck hills, the *Grange* is on the edge of a small country village close to Sherborne. The bedrooms vary in style; several have a balcony, others a French window opening on to the garden. Pre-dinner drinks are taken in the traditionally furnished lounge. In the candlelit dining room, Simon Clewlow is now the chef: he serves a seasonal menu (with daily specials) of dishes like home-cured wild sea trout with teriyaki glaze; roasted breast of guineafowl, ratatouille niçoise, new potatoes. Breakfast has a wide-ranging buffet; cooked dishes include *scrambled eggs with smoked salmon. (Peter Govier, and others)*

Oborne, nr Sherborne
DT9 4LA

T: 01935-813463
F: 01935-817464
E: reception@thegrange.co.uk
W: www.thegrangeatoborne.co.uk

BEDROOMS: 18, 1 suitable for &.
OPEN: all year.
FACILITIES: lounge, bar, restaurant, 2 function rooms, free Wi-Fi, civil wedding licence, ¾-acre garden.
BACKGROUND MUSIC: 'easy listening' all day, in public rooms.
LOCATION: 2 miles NE of Sherborne by A30.
CHILDREN: all ages welcomed.
DOGS: only guide dogs allowed.
CREDIT CARDS: Amex, MasterCard, Visa.
PRICES: [2014] per room B&B single £88–£139, double £99–£169, D,B&B single £113–£164, double £149–£219. Set dinner £28–£35. 1-night bookings sometimes refused Sat in summer.

OLDSTEAD North Yorkshire

Map 4:D4

THE BLACK SWAN AT OLDSTEAD

César award in 2014

'It is a delight to stay at a place where a family puts its life and soul into hospitality.' Praise in 2014 for this restaurant-with-rooms, which is owned and run by the 'welcoming' Banks family. Tom and Ann Banks keep a close eye on the business; their eldest son, James, is the manager; his brother, Tommy, the chef, has a *Michelin* star for his 'fantastic' modern cooking. 'Peaceful' bedrooms overlooking the countryside are 'tastefully decorated, comfortable and well equipped'; each has home-made cake and biscuits, and a private terrace with outdoor seating. Drinks are taken in the 'atmospheric' bar, with a log fire and sunset views; dinner, in the candlelit restaurant, is 'wonderful'. Tommy Banks's menu has dishes with a simple description, perhaps coley, mussel, samphire and quail's egg; saddle and sausage of venison, celeriac, hazelnut and blackberry. Breakfast has 'proper' orange juice, local yogurts, home-made jam and good cafetière coffee; 'generous' servings of eggs on toast. (*Francine and Ian Walsh, and others*)

Oldstead
York YO61 4BL

T: 01347-868387
E: enquiries@blackswanoldstead.co.uk
W: www.blackswanoldstead.co.uk

BEDROOMS: 4, on ground floor in annexe.
OPEN: all year except 1 week Jan, restaurant closed lunch Mon–Wed.
FACILITIES: bar, restaurant, private dining room, free Wi-Fi, small garden.
BACKGROUND MUSIC: in bar and restaurant.
LOCATION: in village 7 miles E of Thirsk.
CHILDREN: not under 10.
DOGS: not allowed.
CREDIT CARDS: MasterCard, Visa.
PRICES: [2014] per room D,B&B £195–£390. Set meals £28–£75, à la carte £45.

ORFORD Suffolk

Map 2:C6

THE CROWN AND CASTLE

César award in 2013

'We were beautifully looked after; two days here felt like a week's rest.' Continuing praise this year for this 'blissfully comfortable' hotel in a peaceful Suffolk village. It is owned by Ruth Watson, her husband, David, and Tim Sunderland, the partner/manager, and run with 'unfailingly cheerful and helpful' staff. 'The atmosphere was less formal than I had feared; every guest was put at ease.' 'Tasteful' bedrooms are divided between the main building and the garden. 'Our large terrace room, down a well-lit path from the main house, was immaculate. The comfortable bed had plenty of pillows; Anglepoise lights were excellent for reading in bed. A pair of double doors opened on to a patio area; the spacious, sensible bathroom had the best shower I have seen.' In the 'cosy, modern' restaurant, chef Charlene Gavazzi's 'superb' Italian-inflected menu has a 'memorable' risotto. Breakfast, with 'good, thick' yogurt and a 'first-class' full English, is served at table. 'We were asked when we wanted the toast, which meant that it was still warm when we ate it.' 'A lovely stay.' (*Susan Chait, Andrew and Moira Kleissner, Robert Gower*)

Orford, nr Woodbridge
IP12 2LJ

T: 01394-450205
E: info@crownandcastle.co.uk
W: www.crownandcastle.co.uk

BEDROOMS: 21, 10 (all on ground floor) in garden, 3 (on ground floor) in terrace.
OPEN: all year.
FACILITIES: lounge/bar, restaurant, private dining room, gallery (with Wi-Fi), 1-acre garden.
BACKGROUND MUSIC: none.
LOCATION: market square.
CHILDREN: not under 8 in hotel and *Trinity* restaurant (any age at lunch).
DOGS: allowed in bar, 5 garden rooms.
CREDIT CARDS: MasterCard, Visa.
PRICES: per room B&B £130–£245, D,B&B £199–£315. À la carte £32. 1-night bookings refused Fri/Sat.

OSWESTRY Shropshire

Map 3:B4

PEN-Y-DYFFRYN

César award in 2003

'The setting could not be better' at this silver-stone building with views of 'beautiful countryside' and the Welsh mountains. Once a Georgian rectory, the small country hotel, on a hillside 100 yards from the Welsh border, is owned by Miles and Audrey Hunter. 'The young, local staff are very helpful without being over-attentive,' says a visitor this year. There are fresh flowers in the public rooms, and a log fire on cold days; in good weather, tea and cake may be taken on the terrace. Most of the 'delightful' bedrooms – 'spotless' and simply decorated – have the views; those in the coach house have a private stone-walled patio with outdoor seating (ideal for dog owners). 'Our coach house room had a smart bathroom with a pleasant spa bath.' The restaurant has white linens, huge, south-facing sash windows. Long-serving chef David Morris's 'very good' daily-changing four-course menus have 'succulent, well-cooked' local lamb and beef. Special diets can be catered for. Breakfast has a generous buffet with pastries, meats, cheeses, fresh fruit; a 'perfectly poached' smoked haddock. 'Excellent local walks.' (*Guy Dehn*)

25% DISCOUNT VOUCHERS

Rhydycroesau
Oswestry SY10 7JD

T: 01691-653700
E: stay@peny.co.uk
W: www.peny.co.uk

BEDROOMS: 12, 4, each with patio, in coach house, 1 on ground floor.
OPEN: all year except Christmas.
FACILITIES: 2 lounges, bar, restaurant, free Wi-Fi, 5-acre grounds (summer house, dog-walking area), unsuitable for &.
BACKGROUND MUSIC: light classical in evening.
LOCATION: 3 miles W of Oswestry.
CHILDREN: not under 3.
DOGS: allowed in some bedrooms, not in public rooms after 6 pm.
CREDIT CARDS: MasterCard, Visa.
PRICES: [2014] per person B&B £65–£95, D,B&B £90–£130. Set dinner £39. 1-night bookings occasionally refused Sat.

OXFORD Oxfordshire

Map 2:C2

OLD BANK

♲ *César award in 2011*

'They do what they do very well,' says a visitor in 2014 to Jeremy Mogford's modern hotel, a conversion of three old stone buildings (one a former bank) on the High Street opposite All Souls College. 'We were very well looked after; our room was compact and serviceable, with a delightful view of the High.' A room in the oldest part of the building had 'beams, a comfortable settee, decent lighting and heating; a small bath and separate shower in the marble bathroom'. Mr Mogford's extensive art collection is on display throughout: large canvases in the 'always busy' bar/brasserie, *Quod*, which occupies the former banking hall; Stanley Spencer pencil drawings and modern works in the corridors and bedrooms. The menu has pizzas, hamburgers and steaks from the grill, and dishes of the day. Breakfast has 'an extensive choice of cooked food and a small buffet; my eggs Benedict were perfect'. The car park 'is a bonus' in a city where parking is expensive. The *Old Parsonage* (see next entry) is under the same ownership. (*David Grant, Lynn Wildgoose*)

92–94 High Street
Oxford OX1 4BJ

T: 01865-799599
E: reservations@oldbank-hotel.
co.uk
W: www.oldbank-hotel.co.uk

BEDROOMS: 42, 1 suitable for &.
OPEN: all year.
FACILITIES: lift, residents' library/
bar, bar/grill, dining terrace,
2 meeting/private dining rooms,
free Wi-Fi, small garden.
BACKGROUND MUSIC: jazz in
library/Reception in evenings.
LOCATION: central, car park.
CHILDREN: all ages welcomed.
DOGS: not allowed.
CREDIT CARDS: Amex, MasterCard,
Visa.
PRICES: [2014] per room B&B
£175–£315, D,B&B from £200. Set
lunch/early supper menu (Mon–Fri)
£12.95–£16.90, à la carte £26.70
(*discretionary service charge 12%
added*). 1-night bookings often
refused Sat.

SEE ALSO SHORTLIST

OXFORD Oxfordshire

Map 2:C2

OLD PARSONAGE

In spring 2014, Jeremy Mogford's luxury hotel, in a 17th-century building behind high walls in St Giles, reopened after a make-over. The *Guide* sent inspectors to report on the changes: 'Traditionalists will be pleased that the public areas have retained their club-like atmosphere,' they said. 'The dark painted walls are enlivened by prints and paintings from the owner's extensive art collection.' In contrast, a new library (built on a roof terrace), is 'a lovely, light room well stocked with decent books and good settle-style seating'. The grey theme (with hard and soft furnishings in plum, deep red and purple) is continued in the corridors (carpeted in herringbone grey) and the bedrooms. Five rooms have been added on the third floor: 'Ours had a huge bed, fitted wardrobes; lovely linen gowns in the marble bathroom; good soundproofing and air conditioning.' Steve Smith, the new chef, serves a 'nicely balanced' menu of classic dishes with modern touches: 'We enjoyed pink and spicy devilled lamb kidneys; tender rack of lamb with Jersey royals. At every turn, we were impressed by the good feeling generated by the quality of the service.'

1 Banbury Road
Oxford OX2 6NN

T: 01865-310210
F: 01865-311262
E: reservations@oldparsonage-hotel.co.uk
W: www.oldparsonage-hotel.co.uk

BEDROOMS: 35, 10 on ground floor, 1 suitable for &.
OPEN: all year.
FACILITIES: lounge, library, bar/restaurant, free Wi-Fi, civil wedding licence, terrace, 2 small gardens.
BACKGROUND MUSIC: 'quiet' jazz.
LOCATION: NE end of St Giles, small car park.
CHILDREN: all ages welcomed.
DOGS: allowed in designated bedrooms, Reception area.
CREDIT CARDS: Amex, MasterCard, Visa.
PRICES: [2014] per room B&B from £226, D,B&B from £310. Set early supper (Mon–Thurs) £15–£18, à la carte £30 (*12½% discretionary service charge added*). 1-night bookings sometimes refused Sat.

SEE ALSO SHORTLIST

PENSFORD Somerset

Map 2:D1

THE PIG NEAR BATH   NEW

In 'glorious' grounds on the edge of the Mendip hills, this honey-stone building has been turned 'with bags of style' into a 'dynamic' reinvention of the country house hotel by Robin and Judy Hutson and their partner, David Elton. A 'grander' sister to *The Pig*, Brockenhurst (see entry), it 'debunks the tradition of formality', and is 'fresh and appealing', say *Guide* inspectors. In the public areas, the floors have been sanded and stained, or replaced with stone flags covered by an occasional rug; there are potted herbs instead of fresh flowers. The bedrooms come in four sizes. A 'spacious' room in a side wing, accessed by an open courtyard (umbrellas provided), had 'three grey walls, a feature wallpaper of brown oak-leaf pattern, bare floorboards, a topless four-poster bed dressed in white; furnishings were shabby chic or distressed'. Loud contemporary music plays in the rustic dining room (with a conservatory), where all ingredients are sourced within 25 miles. 'We enjoyed the robust flavours of venison and pork faggots; a main course of deep-fried sweetbreads disappointed; a replacement was offered. Service was uninhibited and friendly.'

Hunstrete House
Pensford BS39 4NS

T: 01761-490490
E: reservations@thepighotel.com
W: www.thepighotel.com

BEDROOMS: 29, 5 in gardens, some on ground floor, 1 suitable for &.
OPEN: all year.
FACILITIES: lounge, bar, library, restaurant, private dining room, billiard room, free Wi-Fi, treatment rooms, kitchen garden, deer park.
BACKGROUND MUSIC: 'relaxed contemporary' in public areas.
LOCATION: 7 miles SW of Bath.
CHILDREN: all ages welcomed.
DOGS: allowed in 1 bedroom, lounge and bar.
CREDIT CARDS: all major cards.
PRICES: [2014] room B&B £139–£250. Breakfast £10–£15, à la carte £35. 1-night bookings refused weekends, Christmas/New Year.

PENZANCE Cornwall

THE ABBEY HOTEL

🏵 *César award in 1985*

'An amazing place', Jean Shrimpton's Georgian town house is 'run with panache and easy generosity' by her son, Thaddeus Cox. Painted a 'striking sky blue', the house, which dates to 1660, is on a narrow street leading to the harbour. The interiors are decorated in equally bold colours. A fellow *Guide* hotelier was impressed: 'The wood-floored corridors may creak as you walk along, but that is part of the magic. Each of the bedrooms is old-fashioned in the best meaning of the term: sheets and blankets instead of a duvet; all kinds of trinkets to examine and admire.' Afternoon tea and drinks can be taken in a 'wonderful' drawing room with 'a wealth of artworks and books; floor-to-ceiling windows. In fine weather, you can sit on the lawn buried in a book or sip pre-prandial drinks just admiring the view and the peace.' The enclosed gardens are 'a feast for lovers of rare flora and fauna'. In the oak-panelled breakfast room, there is 'freshly squeezed orange juice, local preserves and yogurt, first-class ingredients from Cornish suppliers'. (*John Rowlands*)

Abbey Street
Penzance TR18 4AR

T: 01736-366906
E: hotel@theabbeyonline.co.uk
W: www.theabbeyonline.co.uk

BEDROOMS: 6, also 2 apartments in adjoining building.
OPEN: Mar–Jan, except Christmas.
FACILITIES: drawing room, dining room, free Wi-Fi, garden, unsuitable for ♿.
BACKGROUND MUSIC: none.
LOCATION: 300 yds from centre, parking.
CHILDREN: all ages welcomed.
DOGS: not allowed in dining room.
CREDIT CARDS: Amex, MasterCard, Visa.
PRICES: [2014] per room B&B single £75–£120, double £100–£200. 1-night bookings refused bank holidays.

SEE ALSO SHORTLIST

PENZANCE Cornwall

Map 1:E1

HOTEL PENZANCE

In a quiet residential area on a hill above the harbour, this 'comfortable' small hotel is a conversion of two Edwardian merchants' houses. Standing in Mediterranean-style gardens a short stroll from the town, it is owned by Stephen and Yvonne Hill. 'The welcome was warm; throughout my stay I was treated like a friend,' said a recent visitor. Guests are offered complimentary tea and cake every afternoon. Many of the simply decorated bedrooms have sea views; four have a Juliet balcony. All have fresh coffee and a selection of teas. 'Everything was spotless in our room (No. 17), which had wonderful views of St Michael's Mount on one side and the harbour on the other.' Full-length windows let in the sea views at the *Bay* restaurant, where chef Steven Mesher's seasonal menu might have seared Cornish mackerel, pickled vegetables; maple-glazed duck, fondant potato, sour cabbage. A vegan menu is available. Breakfast, served until 11 am, has home-made bread, fresh fruit and a 'fine grill'. Easy access to the Coastal Path; Land's End, Cape Cornwall and St Ives are within a half-hour drive.

25% DISCOUNT VOUCHERS

Britons Hill
Penzance TR18 3AE

T: 01736-363117
F: 01736-361127
E: reception@hotelpenzance.com
W: www.hotelpenzance.com

BEDROOMS: 25, 2 on ground floor.
OPEN: all year.
FACILITIES: ramps, 3 lounges, bar/restaurant, free Wi-Fi, civil wedding licence, ½-acre garden, terrace, 15-metre swimming pool, rock beach.
BACKGROUND MUSIC: in restaurant.
LOCATION: on hill, ½ mile from centre.
CHILDREN: all ages welcomed.
DOGS: not allowed in restaurant or unattended in bedrooms (£10 per night charge).
CREDIT CARDS: Amex (2½% *surcharge*), MasterCard, Visa.
PRICES: [2014] per room B&B single £89–£94, double £145–£205. D,B&B £20 per person added, set dinner from £25, à la carte £36.

SEE ALSO SHORTLIST

PETERSFIELD Hampshire

Map 2:E3

JSW

'Our day was perfect,' say a couple who held their wedding reception at Jake Watkins's restaurant-with-rooms in this prosperous Hampshire town. 'The staff were extremely helpful and the food was delicious.' Originally a coaching inn on the route from London to Portsmouth, *JSW* (it takes its name from the owner's initials) has a spacious beamed restaurant with well-spaced tables, a cellar with 900 wines, and a secluded rear courtyard for alfresco eating. The owner/chef, who has a *Michelin* star for his 'accomplished' modern cooking, believes in 'simplicity on the plate'. He uses mainly British seasonal ingredients (Solent fish, Cumbrian lamb); the exception is chicken, guineafowl and duck for which he turns to France. Typical dishes: cured salmon, miso vinaigrette; chicken with crispy hen's egg yolk, smoked bacon and sweetcorn. 'Delicious' home-made chocolate truffles are served with coffee. The bedrooms, on the first floor, are simply decorated; they have a widescreen TV, a 'stylish' bathroom. A continental breakfast ('fresh and appetising') is delivered to the room. It has muesli, home-made brown toast and preserves, pastries from Rungis market in Paris.

20 Dragon Street
Petersfield GU31 4JJ

T: 01730-262030
E: jsw.restaurant@btconnect.com
W: www.jswrestaurant.com

BEDROOMS: 4.
OPEN: all year except 31 Dec/1 Jan, Sun night, Mon, Tues, 2 weeks April.
FACILITIES: restaurant, free Wi-Fi, courtyard, unsuitable for &.
BACKGROUND MUSIC: none.
LOCATION: town centre.
CHILDREN: over-5s welcomed as long as well behaved, not allowed at dinner Fri/Sat.
DOGS: not allowed.
CREDIT CARDS: Amex, MasterCard, Visa.
PRICES: [2014] per room B&B single £80–£105, double £90–£130, D,B&B £185–£255. Set menus £27.50–£49.50, à la carte £49.50. 1-night bookings sometimes refused.

PETWORTH West Sussex

Map 2:E3

THE OLD RAILWAY STATION

The train on the platform may not be going anywhere but it provides 'a unique and nostalgic experience' that more than 'lives up to expectation'. On a disused railway line, a renovated Victorian station building and four vintage Pullman carriages make up this unusual B&B. 'We were given a warm welcome by the owner; the Pullman car was very comfortable,' says a visitor in 2014. The owners, Gudmund Olafsson and Catherine Stormont, are happy to talk about the history of the building and the carriages. Guests check in at the original ticket office window. Most of the bedrooms are in the carriages, each of which is divided into two rooms with a separate entrance. 'Although somewhat narrow, they are comfortable and well furnished. Our bathroom was surprisingly spacious, and had a proper bath.' Two bedrooms are in the main building and are reached by a spiral staircase. The old waiting room, where tea and coffee are served, is furnished with leather-buttoned sofas and chairs and a 'modest, but intriguing amount of railwayana'. Breakfast can be taken here or in the carriages. The station is licensed; in fine weather drinks are served at tables on the platform. (*John Bell*)

Petworth GU28 0JF

T: 01798-342346
F: 01798-343033
E: info@old-station.co.uk
W: www.old-station.co.uk

BEDROOMS: 10, 8 in Pullman carriages, 1 suitable for &.
OPEN: all year except 24–26 Dec.
FACILITIES: lounge/bar/breakfast room, free Wi-Fi, platform/terrace, 2-acre garden.
BACKGROUND MUSIC: soft 1920s–1940s in waiting room at breakfast time.
LOCATION: 1½ miles S of Petworth.
CHILDREN: not under 10.
DOGS: not allowed.
CREDIT CARDS: Amex, MasterCard, Visa.
PRICES: [2014] per room B&B £75–£230. 1-night bookings refused weekends and during Goodwood events.

PICKHILL North Yorkshire

Map 4:C4

THE NAG'S HEAD

'As good as ever', this old coaching inn in a village just off the A1 near Thirsk has been run by the Boynton family for more than 40 years. 'It is everything a country inn should be thanks to hard-working Janet and Edward Boynton who set high standards,' says a returning visitor this year. Meals can be taken in the tap room (where 'Edward is proud of his well-kept Yorkshire ales'), the lounge bar or the 'lovely' dining room, which has a library theme (a huge bookcase crammed with books, large mirrors). Vegetarians 'need not settle for second best', say the proprietors whose long, varied menu might include twice-baked Gruyère and blue cheese soufflé, apple and pickled walnut salad; pan-fried loin of North Sea cod, lime and shrimp butter, herb mash, buttered kale. The bedrooms are 'simple, not luxurious but perfectly adequate'; housekeeping is 'very good'. A 'peaceful sleep is guaranteed' in a suite in an adjacent building that has a sitting area through an archway. The Boyntons plan to turn two rooms into a family and executive suite. (*Ian Malone, and others*)

Pickhill, nr Thirsk
YO7 4JG

T: 01845-567391
F: 01845-567212
E: enquiries@nagsheadpickhill.co.uk
W: www.nagsheadpickhill.co.uk

BEDROOMS: 12, 6 in annexe, 3 on ground floor.
OPEN: all year except 25 Dec.
FACILITIES: ramps, lounge, bar, restaurant, free Wi-Fi, meeting facilities, lawn (croquet).
BACKGROUND MUSIC: in lounge, bar and restaurant.
LOCATION: 5 miles SE of Leeming.
CHILDREN: all ages welcomed.
DOGS: allowed in some bedrooms.
CREDIT CARDS: Amex, MasterCard, Visa.
PRICES: [2014] per room B&B single £60–£75, double £80–£95. À la carte £28.

PORLOCK Somerset

Map 1:B5

THE OAKS

'First class in all aspects', Tim and Anne Riley's small traditional hotel is a gabled Edwardian house which stands above Porlock Bay, within the Exmoor national park. 'Standards are high and the hosts are most courteous and helpful,' is another comment this year. The pretty gardens have wide lawns and oak trees. Cases are carried, and tea, coffee and shortbread are served to arriving guests. The entrance hall has polished parquet flooring; the house is brimming with antiques, pictures and flowers. The main lounge has an open fire, chintzes, oil paintings, prints and coastal views. The bedrooms are individually decorated; they have fresh fruit and flowers, tea-making facilities and flat-screen TV. Most have a walk-in power shower. In the *Oaks* dining room, large windows give wrap-around views of the village, the Exmoor hills and Porlock Bay. Anne Riley's daily-changing four-course menu of classic dishes might include escalope of Exmoor rosé veal, mushrooms and dry vermouth. Everything from the marmalade at breakfast to the chocolates after dinner is made in the kitchen. 'Excellent meals and perfect hosts.' (*Michael and Jenifer Price, PW Taylor*)

Porlock TA24 8ES

T: 01643-862265
F: 01643-863131
E: info@oakshotel.co.uk
W: www.oakshotel.co.uk

BEDROOMS: 7.
OPEN: Apr–Nov.
FACILITIES: 2 lounges, bar, restaurant, free Wi-Fi, 2-acre garden, pebble beach 1 mile, unsuitable for &.
BACKGROUND MUSIC: classical during dinner.
LOCATION: edge of village.
CHILDREN: not under 8.
DOGS: not allowed.
CREDIT CARDS: MasterCard, Visa.
PRICES: [2014] per room D,B&B £230–£250. Set dinner £37.50.

PORTSCATHO Cornwall

Map 1:E2

DRIFTWOOD HOTEL

🐾 *César award in 2010*

'A charming place in a wonderful situation; the sea seems to stretch for ever. From the dreamily comfortable bed, to the blissful private beach, we had a glorious time here.' A trusted correspondent fell for the 'air of calm' at Paul and Fiona Robinson's seaside hotel in 'beautifully landscaped' gardens which have 'lots of seating hidden in nooks and behind hedges, like secrets waiting to be found'. A small games room is stocked with books, magazines and board games. Bedrooms are simply decorated in shades of sand and sky; most are sea-facing, some have a decked terrace. 'Our spacious family room under the eaves had a separate room for the children in which two cots had been prepared together with a selection of children's books.' Dinners 'were very special'; chef Chris Eden holds a *Michelin* star for his modern European cooking. 'There are clever combinations (perfectly done brill with curry); and each evening we were given surprising amuse-bouche and pre-desserts.' The wine list 'held fine discoveries, such as Camel Valley sparkling wine'. 'Plentiful' breakfasts have 'an inviting buffet'. (*M Astella Saw*)

Rosevine
nr Portscatho TR2 5EW

T: 01872-580644
F: 01872-580801
E: info@driftwoodhotel.co.uk
W: www.driftwoodhotel.co.uk

BEDROOMS: 15, 4 in courtyard, also 2 in cabin (2 mins' walk).

OPEN: 3 Feb–9 Dec.

FACILITIES: 2 lounges, bar, restaurant, children's games room, free Wi-Fi, 7-acre grounds (terraced gardens, private beach, safe bathing), unsuitable for &.

BACKGROUND MUSIC: jazz in restaurant and bar.

LOCATION: N side of Portscatho.

CHILDREN: all ages welcomed, early supper for children, no very young children in restaurant in evenings.

DOGS: not allowed.

CREDIT CARDS: Amex, MasterCard, Visa.

PRICES: per room B&B £185–£280, D,B&B £230–£300. Set dinner £55. 1-night bookings refused weekends.

PURTON Wiltshire

Map 3:E5

⚜ THE PEAR TREE AT PURTON

César award: country hotel of the year

'A well-run, well-maintained hotel, with excellent service and good food.' *Guide* inspectors found much to like this year at the Young family's small hotel in a 'charming' Cotswold stone building. It is run by Anne Young (her husband, Francis, has retired); their daughter Alix is the manager, assisted by her husband, Tim. The 16th-century former vicarage has been 'sympathetically' extended. 'Inside, it is light, with corridors leading off pretty galleries. The rear garden has lovely herbaceous borders, space for alfresco drinks, and a large wild-flower meadow.' Some of the traditionally decorated bedrooms have a balcony or terrace; all have home-made biscuits. 'Our spacious, comfortable room faced the meadow; it was well equipped and not at all designerish.' Chef Alan Postill's 'superb' dishes are served in the 'peaceful' dining room, spread across two conservatories. 'Delectable amuse-bouche, a delicious tart with pimentos and crème fraîche, excellent hake with breadcrumbs.' Breakfast has 'very good' scrambled eggs, honey from the hotel's bees and 'a good kipper'. (*Gwyn Morgan, and others*)

25% DISCOUNT VOUCHERS

Church End
Purton, nr Swindon SN5 4ED

T: 01793-772100
F: 01793-772369
E: stay@peartreepurton.co.uk
W: www.peartreepurton.co.uk

BEDROOMS: 17, some on ground floor.
OPEN: all year except 25 Dec evening and 26 Dec.
FACILITIES: ramps, lounge/bar, library, restaurant, free Wi-Fi, function/conference facilities, civil wedding licence, 7½-acre grounds (vineyard, croquet, pond, jogging route).
BACKGROUND MUSIC: none.
LOCATION: 5 miles NW of Swindon.
CHILDREN: all ages welcomed.
DOGS: not unattended in bedrooms.
CREDIT CARDS: Amex, MasterCard, Visa.
PRICES: [2014] per room B&B £109–£149, D,B&B £175–£210. À la carte £30–£35.

RAMSGILL-IN-NIDDERDALE N. Yorkshire   Map 4:D3

THE YORKE ARMS

🐾 *César award in 2000*

In a 'beautiful' setting, by the green in a village below the moors, Bill and Frances Atkins's restaurant-with-rooms (a 17th-century former shooting lodge) has long been popular with gourmet visitors. He is the 'caring' host encouraging a 'companionship between guests' in the flagstoned bar, which has old beams, log fires, wooden tables and settles. Frances Atkins, the chef, has a *Michelin* star for her inventive recipes based on 'really good local ingredients', which are presented in 'exciting but well-balanced combinations'. Her 'surprise' eight-course tasting menu (which must be taken by the entire table) might include autumn truffle risotto, Nidderdale mutton; Yorkshire grouse, heather-scented jus. The service is 'professional but friendly; people seem to care'. The 'well-furnished' bedrooms have high-tech fittings. The best rooms are spacious two-storey suites in a courtyard building: they have a ground-floor sitting room. A two-bedroom cottage (200 yards from the inn) has a private garden and terrace. A smaller room in the main house was 'comfortable; the bathroom was modern and well equipped'. (*RB, and others*)

Ramsgill-in-Nidderdale
nr Harrogate HG3 5RL

T: 01423-755243
F: 01423-755330
E: enquiries@yorke-arms.co.uk
W: www.yorke-arms.co.uk

BEDROOMS: 16, 4 in courtyard, 2 in *Ghyll Cottage*.
OPEN: all year, Sun dinner for residents only.
FACILITIES: ramp, lounge, bar, 2 dining rooms, free Wi-Fi, function facilities, 2-acre grounds, unsuitable for ♿.
BACKGROUND MUSIC: classical in dining rooms.
LOCATION: centre of village, train from Harrogate.
CHILDREN: not under 12.
DOGS: allowed by arrangement in 1 bedroom, bar area.
CREDIT CARDS: Diners, MasterCard, Visa.
PRICES: [2014] per room D,B&B £345–£430. Tasting menu £85, à la carte £70.

RAVENSTONEDALE Cumbria

Map 4:C3

THE BLACK SWAN

César award in 2013

'Unstuffy, not over-sophisticated but thoroughly dependable, it maintains its warm welcome, its feeling of cosiness and its remarkable value for money.' Praise this year from a returning guest to Alan and Louise Dinnes's village inn; Selina Procter is the new manager. The popular bar and wood-panelled lounge are 'inviting'; 'the long-serving staff are efficient and friendly'. Some of the bedrooms have views of the garden; ground-floor rooms near the bar might have some noise. 'Our large bedroom had a king-size bed with extra blankets and pillows; a comfortable armchair and sofa; a modern work table and wardrobe.' Chef Kev Hillyer's comfort foods – perhaps chicken, haggis and cured-bacon pie, carrot and swede purée – may be taken in the dining rooms or the bar. 'Everything is made on the premises and is nicely presented, delicious and served in generous portions.' 'Hearty' breakfasts, with 'well-prepared' eggs and 'first-rate' black pudding, 'equip you for a day on the fells'. Less active guests can 'sit happily in the streamside garden, tucked away with the morning paper'. (*Trevor Lockwood, Peter Anderson*)

25% DISCOUNT VOUCHERS

Ravenstonedale
Kirkby Stephen CA17 4NG

T/F: 015396-23204
E: enquiries@blackswanhotel.com
W: www.blackswanhotel.com

BEDROOMS: 15, 5 in annexe, 2 on ground floor suitable for &.
OPEN: all year.
FACILITIES: bar, lounge, 2 dining rooms, free Wi-Fi, beer garden, tennis and golf in village.
BACKGROUND MUSIC: optional 'easy listening' in bar, restaurant.
LOCATION: in village 5 miles SW of Kirkby Stephen.
CHILDREN: all ages welcomed.
DOGS: allowed in 3 ground-floor bedrooms, not in restaurant.
CREDIT CARDS: all major cards.
PRICES: [2014] per room B&B single £65, double £80–£130. À la carte £22. 1-night bookings refused over Christmas and New Year.

REETH North Yorkshire

Map 4:C3

THE BURGOYNE

At the top of the green in a pretty village in Swaledale, this Georgian Grade II listed country house is run as a small hotel by the owners, Mo and Julia Usman. She is the 'hands-on hostess', leading a 'well-trained, attentive' staff. All but one of the bedrooms are at the front of the house with fine views over the dale. They are furnished in traditional style, well lit, and provided with a 'generous' hospitality tray, books and magazines. A new front-facing room has been added this year. A ground-floor room has French windows opening on to a paved area in the garden. Housekeeping is 'good'; there's a turn-down service in the evening. There are fresh flowers in the two 'well-furnished' lounges, which have original features ('fancy' cornices, carved stone ceilings, fine joinery). In the dining room, chef Paul Salonga cooks English dishes 'with a modern twist', perhaps grilled aubergine, sautéed mixed peppers, goat's cheese; salmon, steamed samphire, garlic, ginger, chilli and brown shrimps. Breakfast is served 'promptly and well cooked'. There is good walking ('to suit all') from the front door (packed lunches available).

On the Green, Reeth
nr Richmond DL11 6SN

T/F: 01748-884292
E: enquiries@theburgoyne.co.uk
W: www.theburgoyne.co.uk

BEDROOMS: 10, 1 on ground floor suitable for &.
OPEN: all year.
FACILITIES: ramp, 2 lounges, dining room, free Wi-Fi, ½-acre garden.
BACKGROUND MUSIC: 'quiet', unobtrusive during meals.
LOCATION: village centre.
CHILDREN: all ages welcomed.
DOGS: allowed.
CREDIT CARDS: MasterCard, Visa.
PRICES: [2014] per room B&B £100–£220, D,B&B £180–£300. Set dinner £40.

RICHMOND North Yorkshire

Map 4:C3

MILLGATE HOUSE

César award in 2011

Off the town's cobbled square, Austin Lynch
and Tim Culkin run this personable B&B in
their early Georgian home. 'From the
magnificent lounge, dining room and gardens
to the welcoming conversations throughout,
we had a marvellous stay.' The town house and
its grounds are 'full of interest': the elegant
drawing room is filled with antiques, fine silver
and china, souvenirs and paintings; the award-
winning sheltered gardens, thick with roses,
snowdrops, hellebores and ferns, extend towards
the River Swale. 'Excellent' bedrooms host 'a
continuation of the owners' eclectic collections',
with books, prints and 'comfy' chairs. In the
oldest part of the house, a characterful room has
18th-century shutters and an original fireplace.
A 'stupendous' breakfast is served in a bright
room with floor-to-ceiling sash windows; the
buffet has croissants, fresh fruit and cereals; hot
dishes are cooked to order. The owners are
'eager' to share their extensive knowledge of the
area, 'usually at leisure over tea'. From April to
October, the gardens are open to the public. A
set dinner is available for groups of 16 or more.
(*MB, JJ*)

Richmond DL10 4JN

T: 01748-823571
E: oztim@
    millgatehouse.demon.co.uk
W: www.millgatehouse.com

BEDROOMS: 3, also self-catering
facilities for 12.
OPEN: all year.
FACILITIES: hall, drawing room,
dining room, free Wi-Fi, ½-acre
garden, unsuitable for ⅙.
BACKGROUND MUSIC: occasional
classical.
LOCATION: town centre.
CHILDREN: all ages welcomed,
'depending on the children'.
DOGS: not in public rooms, or
unattended in bedrooms.
CREDIT CARDS: none.
PRICES: per room B&B £110–£145.

RICHMOND-UPON-THAMES Surrey   Map 2:D3

BINGHAM

There is a 'lovely outlook' – over lawns and flowerbeds to the Thames – from Samantha Trinder's smart hotel/restaurant in two renovated Grade II listed Georgian houses. The 'opulent' public rooms facing the river 'make the most of a wonderful setting'. The bedrooms are named after the works of Katherine Bradley and Edith Cooper, poets and lovers who lived at the property in the early 1900s. They have Art Deco-inspired furnishings; the best have river views. 'We heard no road noise; a new bedside light was produced when we protested that the lighting was appalling.' In the bright dining room, chef Mark Jarvis serves modern dishes, perhaps beef, yeast purée, parsley root, bone marrow. 'Very fine food, though portions might not be suitable for rugby players,' said a visitor in 2014. French doors open on to a covered balcony for alfresco meals in warm weather. Breakfast, with home-made fruit smoothies, home-baked bread and a good variety of cooked dishes, 'lived up to the standard of dinner'. Richmond Park is a ten-minute walk away; bikes and cycle maps are available to borrow. (*JS and F Waters, and others*)

61–63 Petersham Road
Richmond-upon-Thames TW10 6UT

T: 020-8940 0902
E: info@thebingham.co.uk
W: www.thebingham.co.uk

BEDROOMS: 15.
OPEN: all year, restaurant closed Sun evening.
FACILITIES: bar, restaurant, function room, free Wi-Fi, civil wedding licence, terrace, garden, unsuitable for ♿.
BACKGROUND MUSIC: 'relaxed, elegant' or 'upbeat' in restaurant.
LOCATION: ½ mile S of centre, underground Richmond.
CHILDREN: all ages welcomed.
DOGS: not allowed.
CREDIT CARDS: all major cards.
PRICES: [2014] per room B&B £210–£365. D,B&B £157.50–£205 per person, set dinner £45–£65, à la carte £45 (*plus 12½% discretionary service charge*).

ROCK Cornwall

Map 1:D2

ST ENODOC

Above the Camel estuary in a resort opposite
Padstow, this seaside hotel was a 'pleasant
surprise' to a visitor initially attracted by the
cooking of the celebrated chef, Nathan Outlaw.
'The hotel and staff are worth a star rating on
their own; they all care.' Kate Simms is the
manager. The public areas have a bright
Mediterranean mood, enhanced by original
paintings. There are two eating places:
Restaurant Nathan Outlaw has two *Michelin* stars
for its seven-course seafood tasting menu (dishes
like soused red mullet, carrots and horseradish;
steamed bass, Jerusalem artichoke, lime). All-
day dining is in the more casual *Outlaw's*, which
is 'worth a detour'. Many of the bedrooms have
a sea view. 'The decoration was simple but done
really well in my well-equipped room; the
bathroom had plenty of space for my things, and
decent lighting. It was the sort of room you
could spend a few days in.' Children are
'welcome guests'; special meals are provided and
there is a games room for rainy days. Breakfast
has daily specials like duck eggs; devilled
kidneys. (*DH*)

Rock
nr Wadebridge PL27 6LA

T: 01208-863394
F: 01208-863970
E: info@enodoc-hotel.co.uk
W: www.enodoc-hotel.co.uk

BEDROOMS: 20.
OPEN: all year except Jan, *Restaurant Nathan Outlaw* closed Sun/Mon.
FACILITIES: lounge, library, billiard room, 2 restaurants, free Wi-Fi, spa, heated outdoor swimming pool (May–Sept, 9 by 4.5 metres), terrace, garden, only restaurants suitable for &.
BACKGROUND MUSIC: radio in lounge.
LOCATION: outskirts of village.
CHILDREN: all ages welcomed.
DOGS: not allowed.
CREDIT CARDS: Amex, MasterCard, Visa.
PRICES: [2014] per room B&B £175–£425, D,B&B (not high season) from £240. Tasting menu (*Restaurant*) £99, à la carte (*Outlaw's*) £45.

ROMALDKIRK Co. Durham

Map 4:C3

THE ROSE AND CROWN

'The welcome was friendly, the housekeeping good; everything was polished and gleaming.' *Guide* inspectors had an 'enjoyable' stay at Thomas and Cheryl Robinson's 18th-century coaching inn opposite the village green. The Robinsons have farmed locally for generations; they also own *Headlam Hall*, Darlington (see Shortlist). The bar has been newly extended and refurbished with colourful wool fabrics, antique Windsor chairs and oak settles; an open fire burns in cool weather. Chef Henny Crosland's seasonal menus can be taken in the bar or the oak-panelled restaurant; her 'excellent' dishes, using much local produce, might include pressed pork belly, black pudding, crispy egg; supreme of chicken, truffled sausage, potato purée, leeks. Modern country-style bedrooms in the main house have beamed ceilings or exposed stone walls; those in the courtyard have a sheltered outdoor seating area. The converted 17th-century *Monk's Cottage*, around the corner from the main building, has a residents' lounge with honesty bar, and a suite with a sofa bed (ideal for a family). Breakfast has fresh fruit, local cheese, 'good' scrambled eggs. Walks from the door.

Romaldkirk
nr Barnard Castle DL12 9EB

T: 01833-650213
E: hotel@rose-and-crown.co.uk
W: www.rose-and-crown.co.uk

BEDROOMS: 14, 2 in *Monk's Cottage*, 5 in rear courtyard, some on ground floor.

OPEN: all year except 23–27 Dec.

FACILITIES: residents' lounge, lounge bar, *Crown Room* (bar meals), restaurant, free Wi-Fi, boot room, fishing (grouse shooting, birdwatching) nearby.

BACKGROUND MUSIC: classical/piano in restaurant.

LOCATION: village centre.

CHILDREN: all ages welcomed.

DOGS: allowed in bar, not unattended in bedrooms.

CREDIT CARDS: Amex, MasterCard, Visa.

PRICES: [2014] per person B&B £57.50–£67.50, D,B&B £87.50–£97.50. À la carte £30.

ROSS-ON-WYE Herefordshire

Map 3:D5

WILTON COURT

'A wonderful stay; the staff are friendly and efficient, the food is good.' Praise this year from a *Guide* hotelier for Helen and Roger Wynn's restaurant-with-rooms on the banks of the River Wye. The part-Elizabethan house was once a magistrates' court – from a cellar a passageway led to the jail across the road. In the public rooms are ancient beams, leaded windows, a huge fireplace with its original iron gate; many curios and objets d'art acquired by the owners from time spent in the Far East. The bedrooms, which overlook the river or the gardens, have patterned carpets and bold printed wallpaper; some have exposed beams and an original fireplace. A family suite on the second floor has a twin and a double bedroom. All rooms are provided with kimonos, mineral water and flat-screen TV/DVD. 'Our comfortable room had lovely views.' Service is 'silky smooth' in the light and airy conservatory restaurant, where chef Martyn Williams cooks modern British dishes, perhaps fillet of Herefordshire beef, champ potatoes, slow-roasted mushrooms. At breakfast, 'my Manx kipper was as tasty as it gets'. (*Annabel Thomas, Sarah and Tony Thomas*)

Wilton Lane, Ross-on-Wye
HR9 6AQ

T: 01989-562569
F: 01989-768460
E: info@wiltoncourthotel.com
W: www.wiltoncourthotel.com

BEDROOMS: 10.
OPEN: all year except first 2 weeks Jan.
FACILITIES: sitting room, bar, restaurant, private dining room, free Wi-Fi, civil wedding licence, 1-acre grounds, only restaurant suitable for &.
BACKGROUND MUSIC: classical at mealtimes in restaurant/bar.
LOCATION: ½ mile from centre.
CHILDREN: all ages welcomed.
DOGS: not allowed in restaurant.
CREDIT CARDS: Amex, MasterCard, Visa.
PRICES: [2014] per person B&B single £100–£155, double £67.50–£92.50, D,B&B £87.50–£175. Set dinner £29.50–£32.50, à la carte £40–£45. 1-night bookings refused weekends Apr–Oct.

SEE ALSO SHORTLIST

RUSHLAKE GREEN East Sussex

Map 2:E4

STONE HOUSE

Through old stone gates and up a winding driveway, this 15th-century manor house is run as a country hotel by Jane and Peter Dunn. 'Well cared for and on good form', the home (Tudor with Georgian additions) has been in the family's hands for more than five centuries; original features and period-style furnishings give it much atmosphere. 'Not for those who favour minimalism', it has beautiful antique furniture, decorative china, family portraits, lovely fabrics. 'Perfection.' In the grand Georgian section and the older Tudor wing, 'every bedroom is comfortable and different'. 'We loved the extra space to lounge around in our suite.' Jane Dunn cooks 'top-notch' dinners using garden and orchard produce, and game and wild mushrooms from the estate. Typical dishes: carpaccio of *Stone House* fallow venison fillet, baby Adam's figs, Parmesan; lamb chump, rosemary, ratatouille. The extensive grounds have parkland, a farm, two lakes and a 'truly wonderful' walled fruit and vegetable garden; private footpaths wind through woods and fields. Peter Dunn, an 'attentive' host, is happy to prepare itineraries for guests; picnic hampers can be delivered to Glyndebourne. (*AB, ZE*)

Rushlake Green
Heathfield TN21 9QJ

T: 01435-830553
F: 01435-830726
W: www.stonehousesussex.co.uk

BEDROOMS: 7, plus 2 in coach house.
OPEN: all year except 22 Dec–3 Jan, 15 Feb–13 Mar.
FACILITIES: hall, drawing room, library, dining room, billiard room, free Wi-Fi, 1,000-acre estate (5½-acre garden, farm, woodland, croquet, shooting, pheasant/clay-pigeon shooting, 2 lakes, rowing, fishing), unsuitable for &.
BACKGROUND MUSIC: none.
LOCATION: 4 miles SE of Heathfield, by village green.
CHILDREN: not under 9.
DOGS: not allowed in public rooms.
CREDIT CARDS: MasterCard, Visa.
PRICES: [2014] per room B&B single £112.50–£140, double £148–£280. Set dinner from £32. 1-night bookings refused weekends 16 May–1 Sept.

RYE East Sussex

Map 2:E5

JEAKE'S HOUSE

César award in 1992

On a cobbled street in the old town, Jenny Hadfield's B&B is a conversion of a 17th-century wool store and neighbouring buildings. 'The staff are charming and helpful,' says a visitor in 2014. 'They carried our bags to the room, provided fresh milk for the tea tray, suggested places to eat and gave ideas for what to do.' Bedrooms are named after artistic visitors who came when the house was owned by the poet Conrad Aitken. 'Our comfortable room, Elizabeth Fry, was light and airy; but we have never before slept in such a small bed.' There is a fire in the oak-beamed parlour, which has a cellar dating back to the wool store era, and a historic square piano; the honesty bar is 'well priced'. Breakfast, served in a galleried hall, is 'excellent'; a buffet or cereals, fruit and yogurt; 'delicious eggs served in different ways; smoked fish and kidneys; we were thanked by other guests when we asked that the background music be turned down'. Parking is limited in Rye; guests have access to a private car park for a small charge. (*SP, and others*)

Mermaid Street
Rye TN31 7ET

T: 01797-222828
E: stay@jeakeshouse.com
W: www.jeakeshouse.com

BEDROOMS: 11.
OPEN: all year.
FACILITIES: parlour, bar/library, breakfast room, free Wi-Fi, unsuitable for &.
BACKGROUND MUSIC: classical in breakfast room.
LOCATION: central, car park (£3 per 24 hours, advance booking needed).
CHILDREN: not under 8.
DOGS: allowed, on leads 'and always supervised', not in breakfast room.
CREDIT CARDS: MasterCard, Visa.
PRICES: per person B&B £45–£75. 1-night bookings occasionally refused weekends.

SEE ALSO SHORTLIST

ST AGNES Cornwall

Map 1:D2

ROSE IN VALE

There is a 'comfortable country house' feel at James and Sara Evans's 'traditional, charming' hotel, an elegant, extended Georgian manor house in a peaceful wooded valley. 'We were impressed,' a regular *Guide* correspondent said this year. 'The hotel is well run by the hard-working Sara, who seems to do everything from Reception to the laundry, and the affable James, who serves in the bar.' Guests have use of a drawing room with 'deep chairs and sofas, an open fire'; there are woodland walks, 'beautifully kept' large gardens and a heated outdoor pool and hot tub in the extensive grounds. In the 'bright and spacious' *Valley* restaurant, chef Mark Firth serves a 'very good' daily-changing menu using local produce, perhaps ham hock terrine, home-made piccalilli; duo of lamb, dauphinoise potatoes. Individually decorated bedrooms vary in size; a large bedroom in the extension had 'a superb bed; a well-appointed tea tray with a teapot (bliss); two good armchairs and glossy magazines'. Breakfast has fresh fruit and fruit compote, 'lots of lovely toast'; scrambled eggs and smoked salmon. The Coastal Path is nearby.

25% DISCOUNT VOUCHERS

Mithian
St Agnes TR5 0QD

T: 01872-552202
F: 01872-552700
E: reception@roseinvalehotel.co.uk
W: www.roseinvalehotel.co.uk

BEDROOMS: 23, 7 on ground floor, 2 suitable for &, 3 in garden annexes.
OPEN: all year except Jan.
FACILITIES: lift, bar, drawing room, restaurant, free Wi-Fi, civil wedding licence, 10-acre grounds, swimming pool (10 by 20 metres), plenty of private parking.
BACKGROUND MUSIC: classical in restaurant.
LOCATION: 2 miles E of St Agnes.
CHILDREN: not under 12.
DOGS: allowed in some bedrooms, bar, not in restaurant.
CREDIT CARDS: MasterCard, Visa.
PRICES: [2014] per room B&B £120–£290, D,B&B £150–£350. Set menu £25, à la carte £20–£40.

ST IVES Cornwall

Map 1:D1

BOSKERRIS HOTEL

From above Carbis Bay, the views from the decked terrace at Jonathan and Marianne Bassett's 'relaxed' small hotel stretch from Godrevy Lighthouse to the harbour at St Ives. Inside, there are 'immaculate', newly redecorated open-plan spaces with white-painted floors; sofas, chairs, books and magazines; much natural light. 'There is a good feeling at the *Boskerris*: a refreshing attitude of "what can we do to help?"' *Guide* inspectors said. Most of the bedrooms have sea views; the best has a sunken bath by a window overlooking the bay. Simple suppers – perhaps a Cornish fish platter of smoked mackerel and roast salmon – are served in the dining room or bar, or on the terrace. A guest whose partner declined dinner was 'made to feel very comfortable' eating on his own. Breakfast has 'wonderful' home-made muesli and 'delicious' cooked dishes. A map of local information is updated regularly, with suggestions for lunch and news on gallery openings. Easy access to the Coastal Path; a short walk down a steep hill leads to the station for the regular train to St Ives. (*TB, and others*)

Boskerris Road
Carbis Bay
St Ives TR26 2NQ

T: 01736-795295
E: reservations@boskerrishotel.co.uk
W: www.boskerrishotel.co.uk

BEDROOMS: 15, 1 on ground floor.
OPEN: Mar–Nov, restaurant closed Sat/Sun.
FACILITIES: lounge, bar, restaurant, private dining/meeting room, free Wi-Fi, decked terrace, 1½-acre garden.
BACKGROUND MUSIC: jazz/Latin.
LOCATION: 1½ miles from centre (5 mins by local train), car park.
CHILDREN: not under 7.
DOGS: not allowed.
CREDIT CARDS: Amex (5% *surcharge*), MasterCard, Visa.
PRICES: [2014] per room B&B £130–£265. À la carte £27.50. 1-night bookings refused bank holidays, sometimes in high season.

SEE ALSO SHORTLIST

ST IVES Cornwall

Map 1:D1

THE TIDE HOUSE

'Very well run and most enjoyable.' On a lane on a hill leading down to the harbour, this 16th-century building has been thoroughly modernised by David and Suzy Fairfield, who run it as a small B&B hotel. He is the 'friendly' host; she was 'the artistic influence' creating interiors which, said a *Guide* inspector, are 'totally gorgeous'. They have a New England feel: 'All pale blues and greys, light, airy and open; big vases of fragrant lilies in both sitting areas and the hall.' There are large, 'comfy' modern sofas around a wood-burning stove in the living room; a children's area has toys, books and a PlayStation. The bedrooms, each named after a lighthouse, have a 'superb comfortable bed', a Nespresso machine and a jar of flapjacks. Godrevy, on the top floor, has a sitting area and a balcony with views of the harbour. Trevose Head, with windows on three sides, 'was the best room I've stayed in for ages'. Breakfast has 'very good ingredients'. No evening meals: there are 'lots of nice little eateries in St Ives, even in winter'. Parking is available ('exceptional').

Skidden Hill
St Ives TR26 2DU

T: 01736-791803
E: enquiries@thetidehouse.co.uk
W: www.thetidehouse.co.uk

BEDROOMS: 6, 1 on ground floor.
OPEN: all year except 23–26 Dec, 2 Jan–10 Feb.
FACILITIES: sitting room, snug/library, breakfast room, children's den, free Wi-Fi, small terrace, unsuitable for &.
BACKGROUND MUSIC: 'low volume' in sitting room.
LOCATION: central.
CHILDREN: all ages welcomed.
DOGS: not allowed.
CREDIT CARDS: MasterCard, Visa.
PRICES: [2014] per room B&B £140–£295. 1-night bookings refused weekends.

SEE ALSO SHORTLIST

ST LEONARDS-ON-SEA East Sussex

Map 2:E4

HASTINGS HOUSE

Off the promenade of this South Coast town, this white stuccoed four-storey Victorian house is run as an upmarket B&B by Seng and Elizabeth Loy. It is commended by a recent visitor. 'The owner arranged secure overnight parking, and greeted us with a welcoming drink.' The house, which faces a garden square, has been given a bold, modern look. A ground-floor lounge has a marble-topped bar and a widescreen TV with a selection of DVDs. The bedrooms, individually decorated in bright colours, have a large bed, flat-screen TV, minibar and a hospitality tray with tea- and coffee-making facilities. Three have a bay window with a sea view; on a clear day you can see the French coast. Room 6 has a deep freestanding tub ('practically big enough for two'); Room 1 has an open-plan layout and a power shower. Breakfast includes muesli topped with fresh fruit, croissants or pains au chocolat, pancakes, or a 'fabulous' full English. Freshly baked bread comes from a local bakery. A picnic hamper can be made up for guests heading to the beach; an evening meal can be provided if requested in advance.

25% DISCOUNT VOUCHERS

9 Warrior Square
St Leonards-on-Sea TN37 6BA

T: 01424-422709
F: 01424-420592
E: sengloy@hastingshouse.co.uk
W: www.hastingshouse.co.uk

BEDROOMS: 8.
OPEN: all year.
FACILITIES: bar/lounge, dining room, free Wi-Fi, small terrace, unsuitable for &.
BACKGROUND MUSIC: jazz in bar/lounge.
LOCATION: seafront, 1 mile from town centre.
CHILDREN: all ages welcomed.
DOGS: allowed in public areas only.
CREDIT CARDS: Amex, MasterCard, Visa.
PRICES: per room B&B single £80–£110, double £95–£145. 1-night bookings refused weekends and bank holidays.

ST LEONARDS-ON-SEA East Sussex

Map 2:E4

ZANZIBAR INTERNATIONAL HOTEL

At the 'posh' end of Hastings, Max O'Rourke has renovated his five-storey Victorian town house with a touch of 'South Coast boho'. Inspired by his own travels, he has given the house an international leitmotif 'without overdoing the theming'. The bedrooms have been styled after the countries and continents he visited: India, on the third floor (there is no lift), has modern Indian wooden bedside tables, framed silver necklaces and an antique mirror; Japan is a 'calm, quiet room', with floor-to-ceiling windows which overlook a 'zen'-style garden; South America has unbroken sea views; a bath big enough for two in a large, open bathroom. Some rooms can accommodate up to three people. Public areas are 'smartly turned out'. In the pretty restaurant, *Pier Nine*, chef Ben Krikorian cooks 'contemporary British' dishes, perhaps spinach and goat's cheese tartlet; pan-fried salmon, Mediterranean vegetables, sautéed potatoes. Breakfast, ordered the night before, has a generous selection of cereals, granola, 'tasty porridge', good granary bread; either large or small full English. 'Coffee was Italian, served in individual cafetières, good and strong.'

9 Eversfield Place
St Leonards-on-Sea
TN37 6BY

T: 01424-460109
E: info@zanzibarhotel.co.uk
W: www.zanzibarhotel.co.uk

BEDROOMS: 8, 1 on ground floor.
OPEN: all year.
FACILITIES: lounge, bar, restaurant, free Wi-Fi, garden, beach across road, unsuitable for &.
BACKGROUND MUSIC: 'easy listening' in bar, restaurant.
LOCATION: seafront, 650 yds W of Hastings pier, free parking vouchers issued.
CHILDREN: not under 5.
DOGS: not allowed.
CREDIT CARDS: Amex, MasterCard, Visa.
PRICES: per person B&B £49.50–£123, D,B&B £89.50–£137.50. À la carte £30–£35. 1-night bookings often refused Sat.

STAR CASTLE

🏆 *César award in 2009*

'Highly recommended' by a visitor this year, the Francis family's hotel is a star-shaped fortress built in 1593 on the commanding heights of Garrison Hill above Hugh Town. James Francis runs the front-of-house; Billy Littlejohn has been promoted to head chef. A visitor in 2014 who arrived 'in a howling gale' quickly 'thawed out in spirit over a fantastic dinner; the service was excellent; all we could hope for'. In the beamed *Castle* dining room, once the officers' mess, there are modern dishes like cauliflower velouté, ribbons of smoked salmon; assiette of lamb, savoy cabbage, smoked pancetta, rosemary jus. It is 'warm and welcoming', with log fires, formal white cloths, silver napkin rings and candles. In the summer, guests can dine under a magnificent vine in the airy *Conservatory*, where seafood is the speciality. The bedrooms are in the castle and single-storey buildings in gardens outside the walls (a short open-air walk away). 'Interesting' main-building rooms, which fit around the star shape, have dark furniture and deep colours. The garden rooms, which are more modern in style, have 'wonderful views'. (*Richard Bright*)

25% DISCOUNT VOUCHERS

The Garrison, St Mary's
Isles of Scilly
Cornwall TR21 0JA

T: 01720-422317
F: 01720-422343
E: info@star-castle.co.uk
W: www.star-castle.co.uk

BEDROOMS: 38, 27 in 2 garden wings.
OPEN: all year.
FACILITIES: lounge, bar, 2 restaurants, free Wi-Fi, civil wedding licence, 3-acre grounds (covered swimming pool, 12 by 3 metres, tennis), beach nearby, unsuitable for ♿.
BACKGROUND MUSIC: none.
LOCATION: ¼ mile from town centre, boat (2¾ hours)/air links.
CHILDREN: not under 5 in restaurants.
DOGS: not allowed in restaurants.
CREDIT CARDS: Amex, MasterCard, Visa.
PRICES: [2014] per person B&B £82–£147, D,B&B £92–£157. Set dinner £38.50–£42.50.

ST MAWES Cornwall

Map 1:E2

IDLE ROCKS `NEW`

On the harbour front, this 100-year-old hotel was given a thorough make-over in 2013 by new owners David and Karen Richards. It briefly closed again after winter storm damage but reopened in April 2014. 'It is the real deal, a well-run hotel,' say *Guide* inspectors. 'Tim House, the director, is exceptional, polite and respectful (though we were addressed by our first names in the welcome letter).' Guests are met at the door, valet parking is provided and luggage taken to the bedrooms. 'The decor throughout has been well chosen: the logo of reef knots sets the nautical style – bright colours (lots of blue), big, vibrant paintings, huge planters full of orchids.' Mark Apsey, the chef, serves a daily-changing market menu in the dining room, which 'is cleverly laid out in three tiers so everyone gets the sea view'. His style is modern (portions are small): 'I loved my lady's size helping of pork tenderloin with chicory and mustard; puddings are super.' There is a turn-down service during dinner. 'Our room was exquisitely furnished; raspberry pink was the dominant colour, which was delightful not horrid.'

Harbourside
St Mawes TR2 5AN

T: 01326-270270
E: info@idlerocks.com
W: www.idlerocks.com

BEDROOMS: 20.
OPEN: all year, except 5–29 Jan.
FACILITIES: lounge, bar, free Wi-Fi, civil wedding licence, terrace, unsuitable for ♿.
BACKGROUND MUSIC: 'mixed' in public areas.
LOCATION: by the harbour.
CHILDREN: all ages welcomed.
DOGS: allowed in 2 bedrooms, not in public rooms.
CREDIT CARDS: Amex, MasterCard, Visa.
PRICES: [2014] per room B&B £150–£350, D,B&B (low season only) £225–£280. À la carte £45.

ST MAWES Cornwall

Map 1:E2

TRESANTON

🏅*César award in 2009*

'Immaculate yet relaxed; you feel unobtrusively well looked after.' In a cluster of houses on a hillside overlooking the sea, Olga Polizzi's 'superb' luxury hotel continues to win praise. 'There is a sense of very good management in the background, and calm, pleasant staff to bring it all together.' Public rooms have fresh flowers, 'original paintings and objects'; 'evident care in all things'. Bedrooms are spread over five buildings; some are reached via stairs (sometimes 'quite a climb') through 'well-planted' gardens. Individually decorated, they have nautical stripes, antiques and Cornish art. 'Even our small room had bags of charm: interesting pictures, good furnishings, a huge bath; views of the sea.' In the mosaic-floored restaurant, chef Paul Wadham's modern, Mediterranean-influenced cooking focuses on 'fresh ingredients, simply done', perhaps cod, lentils, leeks, parsley. Children have much to do: there are indoor and outdoor play areas, a kids' club during the holidays, crabbing from the harbour wall. 'Expensive, but absolutely worth it.' Olga Polizzi also owns *Hotel Endsleigh*, Milton Abbot (see entry). (*Caroline Roots, Penny Simpson*)

27 Lower Castle Road
St Mawes TR2 5DR

T: 01326-270055
F: 01326-270053
E: info@tresanton.com
W: www.tresanton.com

BEDROOMS: 30, in 5 houses.
OPEN: all year.
FACILITIES: 2 lounges, bar, restaurant, cinema, playroom, conference facilities, free Wi-Fi, civil wedding licence, terrace, ¼-acre garden (playhouse), by sea.
BACKGROUND MUSIC: none.
LOCATION: on seafront, valet parking (car park up 'mighty steep and long' steps).
CHILDREN: all ages welcomed, no under-6s in restaurant in evening.
DOGS: allowed in some bedrooms, not in public rooms.
CREDIT CARDS: Amex, MasterCard, Visa.
PRICES: [2014] per room B&B £200–£560, D,B&B from £260. Set lunch £22–£26, à la carte £42. 1-night bookings refused weekends in high season.

SEAHOUSES Northumberland

Map 4:A4

ST CUTHBERT'S HOUSE   **NEW**

Musicians Jill and Jeff Sutheran have transformed a former Presbyterian church (built in 1810) into a 'welcoming and attractive' B&B. It gains a main entry after a positive report by a regular contributor. The Sutherans 'lovingly' restored the building (they live in the former manse next door), working with local craftsmen to preserve original features. The pulpit has been retained as a balcony viewing area above the high-ceilinged main chapel, now the main lounge and dining room. The communion table, pillars and panelling have been preserved; the old floorboards have been reintegrated into the restored building. There are books and DVDs to borrow; an honesty bar. Two of the 'roomy' bedrooms are on the ground floor (one is equipped for visitors with mobility problems); four first-floor rooms are reached by an elegant staircase. An 'excellent' breakfast has a buffet with cereals, fruit juices, fresh fruit, berries (in season). The bread comes fresh daily from the village bakery; the honey from the hosts' own hives. Local fish is a feature of the cooked choices: kipper pâté, kipper fillets and smoked haddock kedgeree. (*Sue Pethen*)

192 Main Street
Seahouses NE68 7UB

T: 01665-720456
E: stay@stcuthbertshouse.com
W: www.stcuthbertshouse.com

BEDROOMS: 6, 2 on ground floor, 1 suitable for &.
OPEN: all year, except Christmas/New Year, occasionally in winter.
FACILITIES: lounge/breakfast room, free Wi-Fi, small garden.
BACKGROUND MUSIC: occasionally in breakfast room.
LOCATION: 1 mile from harbour.
CHILDREN: not under 12.
DOGS: not allowed.
CREDIT CARDS: MasterCard, Visa.
PRICES: [2014] per room B&B £95–£110.

SHAFTESBURY Dorset

Map 2:D1

LA FLEUR DE LYS

'The food is well worth a (long) detour,' says a visitor in 2014 to this restaurant-with-rooms in a Dorset hilltop town that is 'steeped in history'. A former girls' boarding school, the ivy-clad stone building is run in 'hands-on' style by the 'personable' owners David and Mary Griffin-Shepherd and Marc Preston. 'They are very friendly people, a key feature of our visit,' says a guest in 2014. After exploring the interesting town ('individual shops, friendly people'), guests 'enjoyed reading the menu over a glass of wine' in the lounge/bar. In summer, drinks can be taken alfresco in a courtyard. In the 'lovely' restaurant, David Griffin-Shepherd and Marc Preston are the chefs, serving 'unfussy, well-presented' dishes, perhaps loin of local lamb, dark rosemary sauce. A visitor, who 'yearned for a savoury dessert', asked if he could have Scotch Woodcock (scrambled egg with anchovies): 'The chef rose to the challenge and it was perfect.' Bedrooms are 'immaculate': larger rooms have a sofa and a laptop computer. Fresh milk and home-made biscuits are provided with the tea tray. Breakfast is 'excellent'; kedgeree was 'a real treat'. (*Christopher Smith, Carol Burton, Kay and Peter Rogers, John Barnes*)

Bleke Street
Shaftesbury SP7 8AW

T: 01747-853717
E: info@lafleurdelys.co.uk
W: www.lafleurdelys.co.uk

BEDROOMS: 8, 1 on ground floor.
OPEN: all year, restaurant closed Sun night, midday Mon and Tues.
FACILITIES: lounge, bar, dining room, conference room, free Wi-Fi, small courtyard.
BACKGROUND MUSIC: none.
LOCATION: edge of centre, car park.
CHILDREN: all ages welcomed.
DOGS: not allowed.
CREDIT CARDS: Amex, MasterCard, Visa.
PRICES: [2014] per room B&B single £85–£110, double £110–£170. Set meals £27–£34, à la carte £35.

SOAR MILL COVE Devon

SOAR MILL COVE HOTEL

From the home-made cream tea on arrival to the draw-on-me blackboard walls in the café, there is a 'welcoming' atmosphere at Keith Makepeace's child-friendly, family-run hotel. it stands above a secluded, sandy cove on the south Devon coast. Well-equipped bedrooms have French doors opening on to a private patio; some have views of the coast (binoculars, ideal for spotting dolphins, are available on request). Family suites have a separate bedroom for children, and plenty of storybooks to borrow. Dinners are 'a delight' in the bright restaurant, decorated in cool blues: there are 'high-quality and varied' menus; the fish – perhaps pan-roasted monkfish, Black Forest ham, wild mushrooms – is 'always excellent'. There is much to do in and around the hotel: the heated indoor saltwater pool (strikingly decorated with a wall-length panorama of Salcombe fishing boats) is a recent addition; the sun lounge has a good selection of books, magazines and board games; coasteering, sailing and surfing expeditions can be arranged. The dog-friendly beach is a stroll away; picnics are available for Coastal Path walks – crab sandwiches optional. (*JT, MHB*)

Soar Mill Cove
nr Salcombe TQ7 3DS

T: 01548-561566
F: 01548-561223
E: info@soarmillcove.co.uk
W: www.soarmillcove.co.uk

BEDROOMS: 22, all on ground floor.
OPEN: all year, except Jan, 1–13 Feb.
FACILITIES: lounge, 2 bars, restaurant (pianist), coffee shop, free Wi-Fi, indoor swimming pool (10 by 7 metres), treatment room (hairdressing, reflexology, aromatherapy, etc), civil wedding licence, 10-acre grounds (tennis, children's play area), sandy beach, 600 yds.
BACKGROUND MUSIC: in restaurant and bar.
LOCATION: 3 miles SW of Salcombe.
CHILDREN: all ages welcomed (children's tea, baby-listening service, free cots and baby meals).
DOGS: well-behaved small dogs allowed, but not in public rooms other than coffee shop.
CREDIT CARDS: MasterCard, Visa.
PRICES: [2014] per room B&B £159–£249, D,B&B £209–£309.

SOMERTON Somerset

Map 1:C6

THE LYNCH COUNTRY HOUSE

The 'attention to detail' is praised at this 'beautiful' Georgian country house. It is run as a B&B by Mike and Chris McKenzie ('lovely hosts') for the owner, former jazz musician Roy Copeland. On the edge of the market town, the ancient capital of Wessex, it stands in secluded gardens (with a topiary, a rill and a lake with black swans) above the River Cary. A 'sun bonnet' lantern at the top of the house floods light on to its central core; guests have access to an observation deck which has wide-reaching views. Although the house has classical proportions, it retains an intimate feel; it is furnished with antiques, family photographs and jazz memorabilia. The bedrooms are in the main building and on the ground floor of a coach house in the grounds, which has its own entrance. Somerton, on the first floor of the main house, is high-ceilinged, and has double-aspect windows; Edington has large sash windows looking over a quiet courtyard. A 'superb' breakfast is served in an orangery. Advice is given about local eating places. 'Delightful and faultless.' (*Lydia Molyneux, and others*)

4 Behind Berry
Somerton TA11 7PD

T: 01458-272316
F: 01458-272590
E: enquiries@
   thelynchcountryhouse.co.uk
W: www.thelynchcountryhouse.co.uk

BEDROOMS: 9, 4, in coach house, on ground floor.
OPEN: all year (limited opening at Christmas/New Year).
FACILITIES: breakfast room, small sitting area, free Wi-Fi, 2½-acre grounds (lake), unsuitable for &.
BACKGROUND MUSIC: none.
LOCATION: N edge of village.
CHILDREN: all ages welcomed.
DOGS: allowed in coach house, not in public rooms.
CREDIT CARDS: Amex, MasterCard, Visa.
PRICES: [2014] per room B&B single £70–£95, double £80–£115.

SEE ALSO SHORTLIST

SOUTHAMPTON Hampshire

Map 2:E2

THE PIG IN THE WALL

On the 'stylish side of shabby chic', this 'charming' white-painted building is set into the ancient city walls close to shops, medieval buildings and museums. It has been turned into a B&B hotel, with a bar and a deli counter, by Robin Hutson and his wife, Judy, who was the designer. The bedrooms come in three sizes. A 'Snug' room, reached by its own staircase, is in the eaves; it has original beams, slanted ceilings and a walk-in monsoon shower. 'Comfy' rooms are larger; 'Spacious' rooms have a super-king-size bed and a stand-alone roll-top bath (some within the bedroom). 'Everything is modern and well thought out'; each room has a larder with snacks, drinks, a kettle (with a wide selection of teas) and a Nespresso machine. The deli counter on the ground floor, open from noon to 7 pm, has 'Piggy bits' (perhaps a savory and garlic sausage roll). For dinner, a free shuttle service takes guests to the sister hotel, *The Pig*, Brockenhurst (see entry), which is 'magical at night'. Breakfast (not included in the room rate) is a help-yourself continental buffet.

8 Western Esplanade
Southampton SO14 2AZ

T: 02380-636900
E: reservations@thepiginthewall.com
W: www.thepighotel.com

BEDROOMS: 12, 2 on ground floor.
OPEN: all year.
FACILITIES: lounge, bar, deli counter, free Wi-Fi.
BACKGROUND MUSIC: in public areas.
LOCATION: central.
CHILDREN: all ages welcomed.
DOGS: not allowed.
CREDIT CARDS: all major cards.
PRICES: [to 31 Mar 2015] room £129–£185. Breakfast £10.

SOUTHWOLD Suffolk
Map 2:B6

THE SWAN NEW

Overlooking the market square, this 'surprisingly vibrant town centre hotel' is managed by Martin Edwards for Adnams Brewery. 'Some of the decor could do with a refresh, but they get so many other things absolutely right. Chief among these is the attention to service,' says a regular *Guide* correspondent, whose report earns *The Swan* an upgrade to a full entry. The bedrooms in the main house are traditionally furnished; Lighthouse rooms in the garden (family-friendly and good for dog owners) are more modern. 'Our large garden room had the biggest bed I have ever seen; our exemplary bathroom had an oval bath and a walk-in shower.' Some of these ground-floor rooms have a patio. Meals can be taken in the bar and in the restaurant. The chef, Rory Whelan, 'knows what he is doing and is in touch with modern tastes; we had crab, fillet steak and ice cream, all made with local ingredients and having interesting combinations'. Breakfast 'deserves a special mention'. Holistic treatments are available. It is a short stroll to 'one of the most delightful beaches in Britain'. (*David Berry*)

Market Place
Southwold IP18 6EG

T: 01502-722186
F: 01502-724800
E: reception@adnams.co.uk
W: www.adnams.co.uk

BEDROOMS: 42, 17 in garden annexe on ground floor, 1 suitable for ♿.
OPEN: all year.
FACILITIES: Lift, drawing room, bar, reading room, restaurant, private dining room, free Wi-Fi (in public areas only), civil wedding licence, garden, function facilities, treatment room.
BACKGROUND MUSIC: none.
LOCATION: central.
CHILDREN: all ages welcomed.
DOGS: allowed in Lighthouse rooms (£10 charge), Reception.
CREDIT CARDS: MasterCard, Visa.
PRICES: [2014] per room B&B single £115–£125, double £185–£255, D,B&B single £145–£155, double £235–£305. Set dinner (restaurant) £35, à la carte (bar) £25.

STAMFORD Lincolnshire

Map 2:B3

THE GEORGE

Travellers on the old Great North Road used to wait for their stagecoaches in the panelled rooms of this 16th-century coaching inn. Today's guests await the cake trolley at afternoon tea. The historic building has 'a nice, old-fashioned atmosphere (nothing old-fashioned about the facilities, though)'. 'A very comfortable, very well-organised hotel', it is owned by Lawrence Hoskins. Visitors this year praise the 'excellent service' and the 'cheerful, friendly and helpful' staff. 'They parcelled up the shoes and sweater my husband had left behind, and sent them to us with no charge.' Bedrooms vary in size; some overlook the cobbled courtyard. 'Our small room was well planned, with good storage and perfectly placed bedside lights.' A classic menu of 'good food, well presented' is served in the oak-panelled *George* restaurant: beef sirloin is carved at the table; a sweets trolley appears at dessert. Informal meals and a cold buffet are available in the *Garden Room* or the ivy-clad courtyard. There is a 'very good' choice at breakfast, including 'excellent' scrambled eggs and 'lovely local yogurt'. 'I have booked my return.' (*Helen Ann Davies, Rosemary Wright*)

71 St Martins
Stamford
PE9 2LB

T: 01780-750750
F: 01780-750701
E: reservations@
    georgehotelofstamford.com
W: www.georgehotelofstamford.com

BEDROOMS: 47.
OPEN: all year.
FACILITIES: ramps, 2 lounges, 2 bars, 2 restaurants, 4 private dining rooms, business centre, free Wi-Fi, civil wedding licence, 2-acre grounds (courtyard, gardens), only public areas suitable for ♿.
BACKGROUND MUSIC: none.
LOCATION: ½ mile from centre.
CHILDREN: all ages welcomed.
DOGS: allowed, but not unattended in bedrooms, only guide dogs in restaurants.
CREDIT CARDS: all major cards.
PRICES: [2014] per room B&B single £95–£155, double £165–£290. À la carte £47. 1-night bookings sometimes refused Sat.

SEE ALSO SHORTLIST

STANTON WICK Somerset

Map 1:B6

THE CARPENTER'S ARMS

In a 'great location' in the rural Chew valley, this stone-built inn is well placed for travel to Bath or Bristol: it is 20 minutes from the airport. 'It is more like a small hotel than a cosy pub,' says a visitor in 2014. Converted from a row of miners' cottages, it has log fires, tartan rugs and leather armchairs. Bedrooms are simply decorated in a modern style; all have tea- and coffee-making facilities with fresh milk. A small room was 'clean and comfortable, well equipped and designed to maximise the space'. 'Our bathroom had lots of storage.' At night it is quiet enough to sleep with the windows open. 'Generous portions' of 'unfussy' food are served in the two dining areas. 'We enjoyed excellent duck and walnut salad with maple syrup; perfect sea bass with risotto.' Special diets are catered for, by arrangement. There is a good variety at breakfast, with hot toast and good coffee; a fruit platter; 'the poached eggs deserve a special mention'. Packed lunches can be provided. 'Ridiculously good value.'
(*Peter Anderson, and others*)

Stanton Wick, nr Pensford
BS39 4BX

T: 01761-490202
F: 01761-490763
E: carpenters@buccaneer.co.uk
W: www.the-carpenters-arms.co.uk

BEDROOMS: 12.
OPEN: all year except evenings 25/26 Dec, 1 Jan.
FACILITIES: bar, 2 restaurants, function room, free Wi-Fi, patio, secure parking, unsuitable for &.
BACKGROUND MUSIC: none.
LOCATION: 8 miles S of Bristol, 8 miles W of Bath.
CHILDREN: all ages welcomed.
DOGS: allowed in bar only.
CREDIT CARDS: Amex, MasterCard, Visa.
PRICES: [2014] per room B&B single £72.50, double £105, D,B&B single £90, double £137.50. À la carte £27.85.

STRATFORD-UPON-AVON Warwickshire   Map 3:D6

THE ARDEN   NEW

'I cannot think of a better place to stay when seeing a play at the superbly rebuilt Royal Shakespeare Theatre.' A good report by a regular correspondent brings an entry for this 'lovely' hotel across a 'traffic-restricted' road from the theatre. Owned by Sir Peter Rigby's small Eden Hotel Collection, and managed by Josefine Blomqvist, *The Arden* has been 'tastefully' refurbished. 'The style is modern but not designer. They have got it just right with contemporary bathrooms and air conditioning throughout; it is professionally run and very comfortable.' Meals can be taken in the brasserie restaurant and, in warmer weather, on a terrace; late suppers are available in the lounge. 'They are geared up for theatre-goers with early and late dinners on offer.' The chef, Abhijeet Dasalkar, serves a modern menu of dishes like pork and drunken prune terrine; cod saltimbocca, chorizo, Puy lentils, crispy cod cheek. The breakfast has a 'good traditional English, served efficiently and courteously by well-trained staff'. 'A real bonus' is the secure parking in the centre of the town. (*Allan Kelly*)

Waterside
Stratford-upon-Avon
CV37 9DB

T: 01789-298682
F: 01789-206989
E: enquiries@
   theardenhotelstratford.com
W: www.theardenhotelstratford.com

BEDROOMS: 45, 1 on ground floor suitable for &.
OPEN: all year.
FACILITIES: lounge, restaurant, bar, free Wi-Fi, civil wedding licence, terrace, small knot garden.
BACKGROUND MUSIC: mixed in public areas.
LOCATION: opposite theatre.
CHILDREN: all ages welcomed.
DOGS: only guide dogs allowed.
CREDIT CARDS: Diners, MasterCard, Visa.
PRICES: [2014] per room B&B £145–£405, D,B&B £195–£455. Set meals £24, à la carte £32. 1-night bookings sometimes refused Sat.

SEE ALSO SHORTLIST

STRATFORD-UPON-AVON Warwickshire   Map 3:D6

CHERRY TREES

On the south side of the River Avon, close to a footbridge, Tony Godel and Royd Laidlow's B&B 'could not be in a better position for the theatre'. The 'helpful and knowledgeable hosts' make the modern house a 'B&B of choice in Stratford' for several *Guide* readers. 'We knew things would go well when Royd brought us a large pot of leaf tea and home-made marmalade cake,' says a visitor in 2014. 'Our room had a comfortable bed, a television in a separate area, fresh milk in the fridge, an umbrella in the porch; we had our own front-door key; good Wi-Fi.' The large Garden room, which has its own conservatory, has been refurbished this year. The Tiffany suite, which has an Art Nouveau theme, has a fireplace, sitting room and a round stained-glass window. Breakfast, taken in a 'sunny dining area' on the first floor, is 'beautifully cooked': 'Freshly ground coffee and Drambuie-soaked raisins in the porridge set us up for the day.' The parking space is an asset in a busy town. (*Tessa Stuart, Anne and Howard Thornthwaite, and others*)

Swan's Nest Lane
Stratford-upon-Avon CV37 7LS

T: 01789-292989
E: cherrytreesstratforduponavon@
  gmail.com
W: www.cherrytrees-stratford.co.uk

BEDROOMS: 3, all on ground floor.
OPEN: all year except 23 Nov–19 Dec, 3 Jan–13 Feb.
FACILITIES: breakfast room, free Wi-Fi, garden.
BACKGROUND MUSIC: none.
LOCATION: central, near river.
CHILDREN: not under 12.
DOGS: not allowed.
CREDIT CARDS: MasterCard, Visa.
PRICES: [2014] per room B&B £110–£135. 1-night bookings sometimes refused.

SEE ALSO SHORTLIST

STUCKTON Hampshire

Map 2:E2

THE THREE LIONS

Once a farmhouse, this restaurant-with-rooms is run in informal style by the 'experienced' owners, Jayne and Mike Womersley. 'We enjoyed a relaxing dinner, bed and breakfast; Jayne is an excellent host,' said a visitor this year. It is reached by a rural lane on the northern edge of the New Forest. The decor in the public areas is 'old-fashioned in the best possible sense'; there are patterned carpets, flowers on the wooden tables in the 'cosy' dining room. Mike Womersley cooks classic British/French dishes, promising 'no molecular squiggles, foams or smears on the plate'. The menu (on a portable blackboard) might include galette of smoked haddock; parsley-roasted partridge, Muscat grapes. A house speciality is wild mushrooms: 'We enjoyed mushrooms picked that day, served with a delicious velvety cream sauce which we mopped up with the superb bread made by Jayne, a qualified pastry chef.' Bedrooms have a 'country-living' decor; four are in a single-storey building with direct access to the garden, which has a hot tub. Children are 'warmly welcomed'; cots can be provided. Breakfast is 'beautifully arranged'. (*Jean Taylor, and others*)

25% DISCOUNT VOUCHERS

Stuckton, nr Fordingbridge
SP6 2HF

T: 01425-652489
F: 01425-656144
E: the3lions@btinternet.com
W: www.thethreelionsrestaurant.co.uk

BEDROOMS: 7, 4 in courtyard block on ground floor.
OPEN: all year except last 2 weeks Feb, restaurant closed Sun night/Mon.
FACILITIES: ramps, conservatory, meeting/sitting room, public bar, restaurant, free Wi-Fi, 2½-acre garden (sauna, whirlpool).
BACKGROUND MUSIC: on request, in bar.
LOCATION: 1 mile E of Fordingbridge.
CHILDREN: all ages welcomed.
DOGS: allowed in bedrooms, conservatory (£10 charge for up to two dogs).
CREDIT CARDS: MasterCard, Visa.
PRICES: [2014] per room B&B single £79, double £125. À la carte £42.

STURMINSTER NEWTON Dorset

Map 2:E1

PLUMBER MANOR

César award in 1987

One of the oldest families in Dorset, the Prideaux-Brunes, has lived in this manor house since it was built in the early 17th century. For 40 years, it has been run 'with evident enjoyment' as a restaurant-with-rooms by Richard Prideaux-Brune (who promises 'to provide a laugh') and his wife, Alison; his brother, Brian, is the chef. The bedrooms in the main house are reached by a gallery of portraits, including one of Charles II that the King presented to a mistress (possibly a family member). These rooms have views of the gardens. Other rooms, in a converted barn, have window seats overlooking the river that runs through the grounds. Dogs are allowed in four of these rooms (which have direct access to the car park) but not in the main house. In the elegant three-roomed restaurant, Brian Prideaux-Brune serves a daily-changing menu of English dishes 'with French overtones', perhaps crab mousseline, light curry sauce; confit of duck, apricot and chorizo cassoulet. 'The food was extremely good, the vegetables in particular were excellent,' is a recent comment. Public footpaths lead from the door.

Sturminster Newton DT10 2AF

T: 01258-472507
F: 01258-473370
E: book@plumbermanor.com
W: www.plumbermanor.com

BEDROOMS: 16, 10 on ground floor in courtyard.
OPEN: all year except Feb.
FACILITIES: lounge, bar, 3 dining rooms, gallery, free Wi-Fi, 1-acre grounds (garden, tennis, croquet, stream).
BACKGROUND MUSIC: none.
LOCATION: 2 miles SW of Sturminster Newton.
CHILDREN: all ages welcomed, by prior arrangement.
DOGS: allowed in 4 bedrooms, not in public rooms.
CREDIT CARDS: all major cards.
PRICES: [2014] per room B&B single £115–£150, double £150–£230. Set dinner £29–£36.

SWAFFHAM Norfolk

Map 2:B5

STRATTONS

♥ *César award in 2003*

In neatly planted gardens off the town square, Les and Vanessa Scott's restored Grade II listed Palladian villa 'has a pleasant feel'. It is run on sustainable lines by the Scotts' daughter, Hannah, and her husband, Dominic Hughes, with a team of 'friendly, helpful' staff. 'It is the antithesis of a "standard" chain hotel,' says a visitor this year. The 'imaginatively designed' rooms are filled with 'varied and unusual ornaments and decorations'. In the main house and other converted buildings in the grounds, each bedroom is 'a work of art'. Opium has a bed flanked with Doric columns; Stalls replicates the feel of the old horse block it once was; Boudoir has Parisian touches. In the restaurants, chef Julia Hetherton's menus might include whole roasted plaice, new potatoes, chilli and cashew broccoli. They use the 'seasonal produce on our doorstep'. Children are welcomed: family rooms and special meals are available; young guests may feed the free-range chickens and collect an egg for their 'very good' breakfast. (*Jane and Martin Bailey, and others*)

4 Ash Close
Swaffham PE37 7NH

T: 01760-723845
E: enquiries@strattonshotel.com
W: www.strattonshotel.com

BEDROOMS: 14, 6 in annexes, 1 on ground floor.
OPEN: all year except 1 week self-catering at Christmas.
FACILITIES: drawing room, reading room, restaurant, free Wi-Fi, terrace, café/deli, 1½-acre garden.
BACKGROUND MUSIC: 'chill-out/jazz' in lounges, restaurant.
LOCATION: central, parking.
CHILDREN: all ages welcomed.
DOGS: allowed in some bedrooms, lounges.
CREDIT CARDS: Amex, MasterCard, Visa.
PRICES: [2014] per room B&B £99–£155, D,B&B £153–£209. À la carte £29. 1-night bookings refused weekends and bank holidays.

TALLAND-BY-LOOE Cornwall

Map 1:D3

TALLAND BAY HOTEL

In a 'magical setting overlooking a secluded bay viewed through old Scots pines', this 400-year-old white-painted manor house stands in large subtropical gardens with a collection of sculptures and stone ornaments. Vanessa Rees is the owner. 'The decoration is eccentric, with much modern art and furniture; some ornaments may be rather kitsch but are in the spirit of amusement,' said a recent visitor. The Reeses have two dogs and two cats; visiting dogs are gladly welcomed (£10 per night charge) with a blanket and biscuits in the room, and chicken at dinner. Bedrooms are individually decorated (nautical stripes here, a country-style brass bed there); many have views of the sea. Three cottages in the grounds are ideal for a family. 'Our room was comfortable and spotless.' In the candlelit, panelled restaurant overlooking the bay, chef Nick Hawke serves 'imaginative' daily-changing menus that might include pork belly confit, parsnip, apple; haddock fillet, squid, saffron new potatoes, fish broth. Lunch and informal meals are taken in the bar/brasserie. Easy access to coastal walks; the hosts are happy to advise on dog-friendly beaches.

Porthallow, nr Looe
PL13 2JB

T: 01503-272667
F: 01503-272940
E: info@tallandbayhotel.co.uk
W: www.tallandbayhotel.co.uk

BEDROOMS: 22, 3 in cottages, 6 on ground floor.
OPEN: all year, restaurant closed for lunch Mon–Sat.
FACILITIES: lounge, bar, restaurant, conservatory, free Wi-Fi, civil wedding licence, patio, 2-acre garden.
BACKGROUND MUSIC: 'easy listening'.
LOCATION: 2½ miles SW of Looe.
CHILDREN: all ages welcomed.
DOGS: not allowed in restaurant.
CREDIT CARDS: MasterCard, Visa.
PRICES: [2014] per room B&B £100–£245, D,B&B £176–£321. Set dinner £36–£42, à la carte £35. 1-night bookings sometimes refused Sat, high season.

TAPLOW Berkshire

Map 2:D3

CLIVEDEN HOUSE   NEW

'The definitive country house', this renowned stately home stands above the Thames in 'beautiful' National Trust grounds. In the same private ownership as *Chewton Glen*, New Milton (see entry), it returns to a full entry after an enthusiastic report in 2014 by *Guide* hoteliers. 'Eccentric and fabulous at the same time; Sue Williams, the manager, and her team are very much present to maintain spot-on attention to detail.' An earlier comment: 'A well-run, professional and happy place.' Royalty and politicians have been among *Cliveden*'s many illustrious visitors; it was also the venue for John Profumo's first meeting with Christine Keeler. 'Profumo affair' breaks and a Profumo treasure hunt in the grounds are available. The spectacular public rooms have oak panelling, rich tapestries, fine paintings. In the 'lovely' restaurant, which has been given a facelift, André Garrett is the chef: 'The cuisine is exquisite.' The bedrooms are furnished with antiques: nine rooms in the east wing have been refurbished this year. 'Our suite had an old-fashioned but wonderful bathroom.' Children are welcomed, as are dogs (special packages). (*Richard Morgan-Price and Huw Thomas*)

Taplow SL6 0JF

T: 01628-668561
F: 01628-661837
E: info@clivedenhouse.co.uk
W: www.clivedenhouse.co.uk

BEDROOMS: 39, some on ground floor, plus Spring Cottage.
OPEN: all year.
FACILITIES: Lift, Great Hall, library, boudoir, restaurant, private dining rooms, snooker room, free Wi-Fi, spa, indoor and (heated) outdoor swimming pools, terrace, tennis, 376-acre National Trust gardens.
BACKGROUND MUSIC: classical in restaurant, pianist sometimes in Great Hall.
LOCATION: 10 miles NW of Windsor.
CHILDREN: all ages welcomed.
DOGS: welcomed but not in restaurant.
CREDIT CARDS: all major cards.
PRICES: [2014] per room B&B £252–£1,572, D,B&B £382–£1,702. Set dinner £65, tasting menu £95. 1-night bookings occasionally refused Sat.

TARRANT LAUNCESTON Dorset

Map 2:E1

LAUNCESTON FARM

In the 'quiet and peaceful' Tarrant valley, Sarah
Worrall has stylishly renovated the Grade II
listed Georgian farmhouse on her family's
organic beef farm. 'It is a lovely old house in
attractive gardens,' says a visitor this year, who
enjoyed 'a very pleasant stay'. 'We were given a
pot of tea and home-made cake when we
arrived, even though it was late.' A cast iron
spiral staircase leads to the bedrooms, which are
individually styled. 'Our spacious room had a
comfortable bed, window shutters not curtains,
reasonable bedside lighting; wooden hangers in
the wardrobe. There was a roll-top bath in the
bedroom; shelf space was limited in the en suite
shower room.' Sarah Worrall, a Cordon Bleu-
trained cook, serves an evening meal on a
Monday or a Friday by arrangement. It is taken
communally as is breakfast (ordered the
previous evening). 'It had good juice, stewed
apple and cinnamon (no fresh fruit); a choice of
cereals, various cooked options.' Sarah Worrall's
son, Jimi, leads tours of the farm; meat, eggs and
jam are for sale. Nearby pubs serve 'good
evening meals'. (*Margaret Crick*)

25% DISCOUNT VOUCHERS

Tarrant Launceston
nr Blandford Forum DT11 8BY

T: 01258-830528
E: info@launcestonfarm.co.uk
W: www.launcestonfarm.co.uk

BEDROOMS: 6.
OPEN: all year.
FACILITIES: 2 lounges, dining room,
breakfast room, free Wi-Fi, terrace,
1-acre walled garden, unsuitable
for &.
BACKGROUND MUSIC: classical
during breakfast.
LOCATION: 5 miles NE of Blandford
Forum.
CHILDREN: not under 12.
DOGS: allowed in a purpose-built
Dog House, not in house.
CREDIT CARDS: MasterCard, Visa.
PRICES: per room B&B single
£70–£125, double £100–£125. Set
dinner £30.

TAUNTON Somerset

Map 1:C5

THE CASTLE AT TAUNTON

🎉 *César award in 1987*

In the centre of Taunton, this 'venerable' hotel has welcomed travellers since the 12th century. 'It is an excellent town hotel which fulfils its function well,' say *Guide* inspectors in 2014. Marc MacCloskey is the manager for the Chapman family (Kit and Louise, and their sons, Nicholas and Dominic). The bedrooms, reached by a fine wrought iron staircase, were designed by Louise Chapman. 'Our spacious room had the feel of a guest bedroom in a smart country house: it had curved walls, masses of storage, china ornaments on shelves.' There are two dining options. Meals are served from breakfast until the evening in *BRAZZ*, a 'light-hearted' café and brasserie. 'Lunch was excellent, and breakfast was good also: a massive buffet; chunky toast and lovely marmalade; delicious poached egg on smoked haddock.' From Wednesday to Saturday evenings, chef Liam Finnegan serves a modern menu in the *Castle Bow* restaurant (renamed this year), a 'charming' Art Deco room. 'We greatly enjoyed a salad of thinly sliced tomatoes; turbot in a delicate sauce. The only downside in the restaurants was the low-level muzak.'

Castle Green
Taunton TA1 1NF

T: 01823-272671
F: 01823-336066
E: reception@the-castle-hotel.com
W: www.the-castle-hotel.com

BEDROOMS: 44.
OPEN: all year, *Castle Bow* closed Sun/Mon/Tues.
FACILITIES: lift, ramps, lounge/bar, *BRAZZ*, *Castle Bow* restaurant (Wed–Sat evenings), private dining/meeting rooms, free Wi-Fi, civil wedding licence, 1-acre garden.
BACKGROUND MUSIC: in lounge and brasserie.
LOCATION: central.
CHILDREN: all ages welcomed.
DOGS: not allowed in public rooms.
CREDIT CARDS: all major cards.
PRICES: [2014] per room B&B £99–£200, D,B&B £115–£300. Set menu (*Castle Bow*) £27–£34, à la carte (*Castle Bow*) £39, (*BRAZZ*) £24.50.

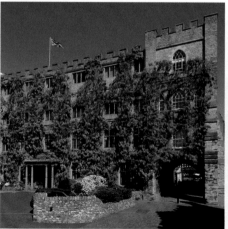

TEFFONT EVIAS Wiltshire

Map 2:D1

HOWARD'S HOUSE

♔ *César award in 2010*

Close to the church in this 'pretty' Nadder valley
village, this 'beautiful' mellow stone dower
house is run as a small hotel by a partnership
that includes the chef, Nick Wentworth. His
mother-in-law, Noële Thompson, and Simon
Greenwood are the managers. 'A lovely
experience,' says a visitor this year. 'Dinner was
excellent and we had a very comfortable time.'
Drinks and canapés are served in the lounge,
'where there was a blazing fire and comfy sofas'.
In the newly refurbished dining room, Nick
Wentworth's modern dishes focus on seasonal
produce, much of it from the hotel's potager.
'The bread sauce was the best I remember
outside home cooking; service was slick without
feeling rushed; we lingered over coffee and
petits fours.' Typical dishes on the 'varied' menu:
home-smoked goose breast salad, onion
marmalade; wild Cornish turbot, crispy chilli
squid, fondant potato. 'Our large bedroom was
on two levels. Lighting was good; the spacious
bathroom had plenty of towels and useful
goodies.' Most rooms overlook the 'charming'
gardens or countryside. Breakfast has 'delicious
local eggs'. (*Sara Price, and others*)

25% DISCOUNT VOUCHERS

Teffont Evias
nr Salisbury SP3 5RJ

T: 01722-716392
E: enq@howardshousehotel.co.uk
W: www.howardshousehotel.co.uk

BEDROOMS: 9.
OPEN: all year except 25/26 Dec
(available for exclusive use).
FACILITIES: lounge, snug, restaurant,
free Wi-Fi, 2-acre grounds (garden
terrace, croquet), river, fishing
nearby, only restaurant suitable
for &.
BACKGROUND MUSIC: light jazz
during meals.
LOCATION: 10 miles W of Salisbury.
CHILDREN: all ages welcomed.
DOGS: allowed (£11 surcharge in
rooms), not allowed in restaurant.
CREDIT CARDS: Amex, MasterCard,
Visa.
PRICES: [2014] per room B&B single
£120, double £190–£210. Set menu
from £29.50, à la carte £45.

TEMPLE SOWERBY Cumbria

Map 4: inset C3

TEMPLE SOWERBY HOUSE

At their small hotel, a Grade II listed red brick mansion in a conservation village in the Eden valley, Paul and Julie Evans 'could not be more helpful or hospitable'. A visitor in 2014, celebrating a significant birthday, found 'standards were as high as ever'. Another comment this year: 'This is one of those rare places to which one can return time and time again and not be disappointed.' 'Comfortable', characterful bedrooms in the restored 18th-century house vary in size and style, from smaller doubles with antique beams to spacious, high-ceilinged rooms facing the village green and the fells beyond. In warm weather, drinks are taken on the terrace overlooking the croquet lawn; a log fire in the lounge provides warmth on colder days. Chef Ashley Whittaker's 'exquisite cooking' features much local produce, including lamb from the fells, and beef and pork from nearby farms. 'It is a seasonal menu and game featured strongly when we stayed. The venison in a blackcurrant sauce and the partridge were both very good.' No buffet at breakfast, which is served entirely at table. 'We thoroughly recommend.' (*Anne and Howard Thornthwaite, Peter Anderson*)

25% DISCOUNT VOUCHERS

Temple Sowerby
Penrith CA10 1RZ

T: 017683-61578
F: 017683-61958
E: stay@templesowerby.com
W: www.templesowerby.com

BEDROOMS: 12, 2 on ground floor, 4 in coach house (20 yds).
OPEN: all year except 25/26 Dec.
FACILITIES: 2 lounges, bar, restaurant, conference/function facilities, free Wi-Fi, civil wedding licence, 2-acre garden (croquet).
BACKGROUND MUSIC: in restaurant at night.
LOCATION: village centre.
CHILDREN: not under 12.
DOGS: by prior arrangement in 2 bedrooms, not allowed in public rooms.
CREDIT CARDS: Amex, MasterCard, Visa.
PRICES: [2014] per room B&B £140–£170, D,B&B £190–£240. Set dinner £33–£43.

TETBURY Gloucestershire

Map 3:E5

CALCOT MANOR

♀ *César award in 2001*

In 'admirable' gardens in the Cotswold countryside, this luxury hotel, part of Michael Stone's small Calcot Hotels group, has extensive facilities for adults and children. The hotel occupies a converted 14th-century farmhouse and a collection of medieval stone barns and stables around a courtyard of lime trees. Young guests have much to occupy them: the littlest ones have an Ofsted-registered *Playzone*; older children gather at the *Mez*, with its game consoles, computers and 12-seat cinema. 'Extremely comfortable' bedrooms have soothing colours; ten are designated for a family. 'We lacked for nothing.' In the bright *Conservatory* restaurant, chef Michael Benjamin's modern dishes might include Calcot Estate organic beef, horseradish melt, fondant potato. The informal *Gumstool Inn* 'is popular with people of all ages'. 'Over three nights we dined in both restaurants and enjoyed everything we were given.' Breakfast 'is top class in quality and the range of dishes offered'. *Barnsley House*, Barnsley (see entry), is under the same ownership. (*J and JS, and others*)

nr Tetbury GL8 8YJ

T: 01666-890391
F: 01666-891244
E: frontdesk@calcotmanor.co.uk
W: www.calcotmanor.co.uk

BEDROOMS: 35, 10 (family) in cottage, 11 around courtyard, on ground floor.
OPEN: all year.
FACILITIES: ramps, lounge, 2 bars, 2 restaurants, cinema, crèche, free Wi-Fi, civil wedding licence, 250-acre grounds (tennis, heated outdoor 8-metre swimming pool, children's play area, spa with 16-metre swimming pool).
BACKGROUND MUSIC: in restaurants.
LOCATION: 3 miles W of Tetbury.
CHILDREN: all ages welcomed.
DOGS: allowed in courtyard bedrooms.
CREDIT CARDS: Amex, MasterCard, Visa.
PRICES: [2014] per room B&B from £280, D,B&B from £360. À la carte £40. 1-night bookings refused weekends.

SEE ALSO SHORTLIST

TILLINGTON West Sussex

Map 2:E3

THE HORSE GUARDS INN

'If only all village pubs were like this,' said *Guide* inspectors who found much to like at Sam Beard and Michaela Hofirkova's 'unpretentious, warm and welcoming' inn. In a conservation village on a hill with a view over the South Downs, the 350-year-old inn took its name in the 1840s when the household cavalry would rest their horses at nearby Petworth House. In winter, guests can roast chestnuts on the open fire in the bar, which has wooden tables, leather sofas, stripped floorboards. Two bedrooms above the bar are reached by steep stairs ('we were not disturbed by noise from a convivial party of farmers below'). 'Our room, in shades of white and taupe, had a good wardrobe; when we asked for sheets and blankets rather than a duvet, they were readily provided.' A third room is in a cottage next door. In the dining room, chef Mark Robinson uses vegetables from his own patch for his short seasonal menus. Typical dishes: potato and pine nut croquettes; lemon sole, sauté potatoes, salsa romesco. 'The food and drink were excellent.'

Upperton Road, Tillington
Petworth GU28 9AF

T: 01798-342332
E: info@thehorseguardsinn.co.uk
W: www.thehorseguardsinn.co.uk

BEDROOMS: 3, 1 in adjacent cottage.
OPEN: all year except 25 Dec.
FACILITIES: bar, dining room, free Wi-Fi, 1-acre garden, unsuitable for &.
BACKGROUND MUSIC: jazz/blues in pub.
LOCATION: 1 mile W of Petworth.
CHILDREN: all ages welcomed.
DOGS: allowed in 1 bedroom, public rooms.
CREDIT CARDS: MasterCard, Visa.
PRICES: [2014] per room B&B from £95. À la carte £27.

TISBURY Wiltshire

Map 2:D1

THE BECKFORD ARMS   NEW

On the edge of the Fonthill estate, this ivy-covered pub is run in informal style by the owners, Dan Brod and Charlie Luxton, and their 'friendly' young staff. *Guide* inspectors in 2014 thought it 'a special place'. The building has 'an airy, modern feel with large windows, a light-filled conservatory dining room which opens on to a charming garden. There are log fires, a cosy bar, wooden floors and comfy sofas in a pretty sitting room.' In the restaurant, 'the cooking is seriously good: we enjoyed the delicate flavours of smoked trout rillettes with herby crème fraîche; guineafowl, chestnut and sage mash, cider and mustard cream'. The bedrooms in the main building are 'elegant, though some are small; there might be noise at weekends as it's a deservedly popular pub'. Two rooms are in a lodge, five minutes' walk down a lane: 'Ours was luxurious, decorated in a mix of country chic and metropolitan loft style: a mezzanine bedroom and bathroom overlooking a double-height living room; a small kitchen had a fridge packed with breakfast goodies.' Excellent walking on the estate.

Fonthill Gifford
Tisbury SP3 6PX

T: 01747-870385
E: info@beckfordarms.com
W: www.beckfordarms.com

BEDROOMS: 10, 2 in lodge nearby.
OPEN: all year except 25 Dec.
FACILITIES: sitting room, bar, restaurant, private dining room, free Wi-Fi, function facilities, 1-acre garden.
BACKGROUND MUSIC: light background jazz in public areas.
LOCATION: in village 1 mile N of Tisbury.
CHILDREN: all ages welcomed.
DOGS: allowed in 1 bedroom, public areas.
CREDIT CARDS: MasterCard, Visa.
PRICES: [2014] per room B&B £95–£175. À la carte £30.

SEE ALSO SHORTLIST

25% DISCOUNT VOUCHER

THE GOOD HOTEL GUIDE 2015

Use this voucher to claim a 25% discount off the normal price for bed and breakfast at hotels with a `25% DISCOUNT VOUCHERS` sign at the end of the entry. **You must request a voucher discount at the time of booking and present this voucher on arrival. Further details and conditions overleaf.** Valid to 5th October 2015.

25% DISCOUNT VOUCHER

THE GOOD HOTEL GUIDE 2015

Use this voucher to claim a 25% discount off the normal price for bed and breakfast at hotels with a `25% DISCOUNT VOUCHERS` sign at the end of the entry. **You must request a voucher discount at the time of booking and present this voucher on arrival. Further details and conditions overleaf.** Valid to 5th October 2015.

25% DISCOUNT VOUCHER

THE GOOD HOTEL GUIDE 2015

Use this voucher to claim a 25% discount off the normal price for bed and breakfast at hotels with a `25% DISCOUNT VOUCHERS` sign at the end of the entry. **You must request a voucher discount at the time of booking and present this voucher on arrival. Further details and conditions overleaf.** Valid to 5th October 2015.

25% DISCOUNT VOUCHER

THE GOOD HOTEL GUIDE 2015

Use this voucher to claim a 25% discount off the normal price for bed and breakfast at hotels with a `25% DISCOUNT VOUCHERS` sign at the end of the entry. **You must request a voucher discount at the time of booking and present this voucher on arrival. Further details and conditions overleaf.** Valid to 5th October 2015.

25% DISCOUNT VOUCHER

THE GOOD HOTEL GUIDE 2015

Use this voucher to claim a 25% discount off the normal price for bed and breakfast at hotels with a `25% DISCOUNT VOUCHERS` sign at the end of the entry. **You must request a voucher discount at the time of booking and present this voucher on arrival. Further details and conditions overleaf.** Valid to 5th October 2015.

25% DISCOUNT

THE GOOD HOTEL GUIDE 2015

Use this voucher to claim a 25% discount off the normal price for bed and breakfast at hotels with a `25% DISCOUNT VOUCHERS` sign at the end of the entry. **You must request a voucher discount at the time of booking and present this voucher on arrival. Further details and conditions overleaf.**

CONDITIONS

1. Hotels with a **25% DISCOUNT VOUCHERS** sign have agreed to give readers a discount of 25% off their normal bed-and-breakfast rate.
2. One voucher is good for the first night's stay only, at the discounted rate for yourself alone or for you and a partner sharing a double room.
3. Hotels may decline to accept a voucher reservation if they expect to be fully booked at the full room price.

✂ -

CONDITIONS

1. Hotels with a **25% DISCOUNT VOUCHERS** sign have agreed to give readers a discount of 25% off their normal bed-and-breakfast rate.
2. One voucher is good for the first night's stay only, at the discounted rate for yourself alone or for you and a partner sharing a double room.
3. Hotels may decline to accept a voucher reservation if they expect to be fully booked at the full room price.

✂ -

CONDITIONS

1. Hotels with a **25% DISCOUNT VOUCHERS** sign have agreed to give readers a discount of 25% off their normal bed-and-breakfast rate.
2. One voucher is good for the first night's stay only, at the discounted rate for yourself alone or for you and a partner sharing a double room.
3. Hotels may decline to accept a voucher reservation if they expect to be fully booked at the full room price.

✂ -

CONDITIONS

1. Hotels with a **25% DISCOUNT VOUCHERS** sign have agreed to give readers a discount of 25% off their normal bed-and-breakfast rate.
2. One voucher is good for the first night's stay only, at the discounted rate for yourself alone or for you and a partner sharing a double room.
3. Hotels may decline to accept a voucher reservation if they expect to be fully booked at the full room price.

✂ -

CONDITIONS

1. Hotels with a **25% DISCOUNT VOUCHERS** sign have agreed to give readers a discount of 25% off their normal bed-and-breakfast rate.
2. One voucher is good for the first night's stay only, at the discounted rate for yourself alone or for you and a partner sharing a double room.
3. Hotels may decline to accept a voucher reservation if they expect to be fully booked at the full room price.

✂ -

CONDITIONS

1. Hotels with a **25% DISCOUNT VOUCHERS** sign have agreed to give readers a discount of 25% off their normal bed-and-breakfast rate.
2. One voucher is good for the first night's stay only, at the discounted rate for yourself alone or for you and a partner sharing a double room.
3. Hotels may decline to accept a voucher reservation if they expect to be fully booked at the full room price.

TITCHWELL Norfolk

Map 2:A5

TITCHWELL MANOR

Originally a Victorian farmhouse, Ian and Margaret Snaith's hotel/restaurant on the coastal road near the RSPB Titchwell Nature Reserve is popular with walkers and birdwatchers. Their son, Eric, is the chef. 'The outside might look a bit stern,' says a visitor this year, 'but the bar and restaurant are very pleasant.' The public areas have mosaic tiled floors, potted plants and Lloyd Loom furniture. The bedrooms vary in style: eight traditionally furnished rooms are in the main house. Others are in outbuildings: 12 rooms, with a contemporary style, are in a single-storey building around a pretty garden square with lavender and herbs. The Potting Shed, which stands apart, has private decking. A visitor this year complained of maintenance problems. There are two restaurants: the informal *Eating Rooms*, with a seaview terrace, which has simple dishes such as soup, fish and chips, barbecued meats. In the 'fine dining' *Conservatory Restaurant*, there are 'plenty of choices (good food)', perhaps warm smoked salmon with beetroot; chicken, fennel and girolles. At breakfast, 'wild mushrooms on toast were excellent'. (*Clare Roskill, Peter Anderson, and others*)

Titchwell, nr Brancaster
PE31 8BB

T: 01485-210221
E: info@titchwellmanor.com
W: www.titchwellmanor.com

BEDROOMS: 27, 12 in herb garden, 4 in converted farm building, 1 in Potting Shed, 2 suitable for ＆.
OPEN: all year.
FACILITIES: 2 lounges, bar, 2 restaurants, free Wi-Fi, civil wedding licence, ¼-acre garden.
BACKGROUND MUSIC: in public rooms.
LOCATION: on coast road, 6 miles E of Hunstanton.
CHILDREN: all ages welcomed.
DOGS: not allowed in main restaurant.
CREDIT CARDS: Amex, MasterCard, Visa.
PRICES: [2014] per room B&B £95–£275, D,B&B (min. 2 nights) £70–£150 per person, set menus £55–£65, à la carte £35. 1-night bookings sometimes refused weekends.

SEE ALSO SHORTLIST

TITLEY Herefordshire

Map 3:C4

THE STAGG INN

🌸 *César award in 2013*

'The service can't be beaten,' says a visitor this year to this 'unpretentious' village inn. It is liked for its 'friendly welcome', 'fine food' and 'reasonable prices'. It is owned by Steve and Nicola Reynolds. The best bedrooms – with a high ceiling and original fireplace – are in a part-Georgian, part-Victorian former vicarage set in 'beautifully kept' gardens 300 yards down the road (transport can be provided); other rooms are in the pub. 'We stayed in a dog-friendly, self-contained unit with a comfortable bed; real coffee on the hospitality tray; bedside lighting as good as it gets. Our dog was happy to find a dish there just for her.' Popular with locals, the rustic pub has a *Michelin* star for Steve Reynolds's modern cooking, which uses much local produce, and wild garlic, nettles and mushrooms foraged by the chefs. Dishes might include spiced lamb shoulder, apricot, lemon. A good vegetarian menu is available (perhaps fig, walnut and blue cheese tart). There are home-made sausages and bacon at breakfast; 'I ate a kipper and was glad to see Marmite alongside the home-made jams and marmalades.' (*Tony Thomas*)

25% DISCOUNT VOUCHERS

Titley, nr Kington
HR5 3RL

T: 01544-230221
F: 01544-231390
E: reservations@thestagg.co.uk
W: www.thestagg.co.uk

BEDROOMS: 6, 3 at Old Vicarage (300 yds).
OPEN: all year except Mon/Tues, 25–27 Dec, 1 Jan, 1 week in Feb, 2 weeks in Nov.
FACILITIES: (*Old Vicarage*) sitting room, free Wi-Fi, 1½-acre garden, (*Stagg Inn*) bar, restaurant areas, free Wi-Fi, small garden, unsuitable for ♿, 'ample parking'.
BACKGROUND MUSIC: none.
LOCATION: on B4355 between Kington (3½ miles) and Presteigne.
CHILDREN: all ages welcomed.
DOGS: only allowed in pub, some pub bedrooms.
CREDIT CARDS: Amex, MasterCard, Visa.
PRICES: per room B&B £100–£150. À la carte £35. 1-night bookings sometimes refused.

TUDDENHAM Suffolk

TUDDENHAM MILL

The millrace, wheel mechanism and grinding stones have been retained in the restoration of this Grade II listed 18th-century mill, which is owned by Agellus Hotels (a small East Anglian group). The original building has been 'thoughtfully' renovated, with extra bedrooms added in two wood-clad buildings. Check-in is at the mill; on the first floor, the restaurant overlooks the millpond. Lee Bye, who was appointed chef in 2014, uses regional produce for his seasonal menus of 'hearty' dishes, perhaps white onion and cider soup, Norfolk crab toast; Dingley Dell pork chop, crispy pig's head, clapshot potato, Madeira wine. Three bedrooms in the mill have original beams, Italian furniture; a stone bath 'big enough for three', a separate walk-in shower. A room in one of the new buildings was 'light and modern'; large French windows opened on to a deck with a table and chairs. All rooms are well equipped (dressing gowns; a fridge with orange juice, water and fresh milk; a 'superior' tea-making tray; a useful information folder). Breakfast has freshly squeezed juice, 'real butter and chunky toast'; 'delicious' cooked dishes. (*CJ*)

High Street, Tuddenham
nr Newmarket IP28 6SQ

T: 01638-713552
E: info@tuddenhammill.co.uk
W: www.tuddenhammill.co.uk

BEDROOMS: 15, 12 in 2 separate buildings, 8 on ground floor, 1 suitable for &.
OPEN: all year.
FACILITIES: bar, restaurant, 2 function rooms, free Wi-Fi, 12-acre grounds.
BACKGROUND MUSIC: 'modern' in bar and restaurant.
LOCATION: in village, 8 miles NE of Newmarket.
CHILDREN: all ages welcomed.
DOGS: welcomed in some bedrooms (£15 a night).
CREDIT CARDS: MasterCard, Visa.
PRICES: [2014] per room B&B £185–£395. À la carte £38, early dining menu (Sun–Fri) £19.50, tasting menu £38.50. 1-night bookings refused weekends.

TWO BRIDGES Devon

Map 1:D4

PRINCE HALL

In a 'dramatic' situation on Dartmoor, this 'relaxed, welcoming' hotel is 'an excellent place for visiting dogs – and their owners', said *Guide* inspectors this year. 'There is a lively atmosphere, with dogs ever-present in the entrance hall (a bowl of dog biscuits on the reception desk, I nearly nibbled one by mistake).' The high-ceilinged lounge and bar have a 'relaxed' 'lived-in feel' and 'wonderful' moor views. 'We were given complimentary tea and biscuits when we arrived; the house Labrador politely offered to share them.' A 'good-sized' room had a view of an ancient packhorse bridge and the West Dart valley; a 'large, comfortable bed; mismatched furnishings. It was wonderfully quiet at night.' In the intimate restaurant, chef Richard Greenway's daily-changing menus are 'outstanding'. 'We had mouth-watering canapés of rare beef wrapped around tiny chips; a rack of pink lamb, dauphinoise potatoes, minted peas. A nicely chosen wine list had many organic wines.' The young staff were 'especially friendly and efficient'. Breakfast, with freshly squeezed juice, home-baked bread and 'tasty' home-made preserves, is served at table. 'There is a good feel overall.'

Two Bridges
Dartmoor PL20 6SA

T: 01822-890403
E: info@princehall.co.uk
W: www.princehall.co.uk

BEDROOMS: 8, plus Shepherd's Hut in grounds.
OPEN: all year.
FACILITIES: 2 lounges, dining room, free Wi-Fi in bar/lounge, terrace, 5-acre grounds, only ground floor suitable for &.
BACKGROUND MUSIC: classical in early evening.
LOCATION: 1 mile E of Two Bridges.
CHILDREN: not under 10.
DOGS: welcomed (treats; facilities for food storage and dog washing; pet-friendly garden and grounds), not in restaurant.
CREDIT CARDS: MasterCard, Visa.
PRICES: [2014] per person B&B £60–£95, D,B&B £95–£135. Set dinner £42.50.

ULLSWATER Cumbria

HOWTOWN HOTEL

❦César award in 1991

For more than a century, the Baldry family has 'shared their family home with visitors who believe in the same values and have the same passion for this unspoilt part of the Lake District'. *Guide* readers have long praised the hospitality shown by Jacquie Baldry and her son, David, at their stone house set back from Lake Ullswater. It appeals to those who prefer conversation to surfing the Internet: there is no Wi-Fi and a mobile phone signal is not guaranteed. Guests must phone to book, and must confirm it in writing. The simple bedrooms have no phone, TV or radio (there is a television room). They do have good storage, sheets and blankets on the bed; lots of hot water (four rooms have a private bathroom across the corridor). A gong calls guests to meals; a four-course dinner, which is served at 7 pm, might include favourites like potted shrimps; grilled lamb's liver and bacon. There is a set lunch; a cold supper is served on Sunday. Packed lunches are available; superb walking from the door.

Ullswater, nr Penrith CA10 2ND

T: 01768-486514
W: www.howtown-hotel.com

BEDROOMS: 13, 4 in annexe, 4 self-catering cottages for weekly rent.
OPEN: Mar–1 Nov.
FACILITIES: 3 lounges, TV room, 2 bars, dining room, no Wi-Fi, 2-acre grounds, 200 yds from lake (private foreshore, fishing), walking, sailing, climbing, riding, golf nearby, unsuitable for ⑁.
BACKGROUND MUSIC: none.
LOCATION: 4 miles S of Pooley Bridge, bus from Penrith station 9 miles.
CHILDREN: all ages welcomed (no special facilities).
DOGS: not allowed in public rooms.
CREDIT CARDS: none.
PRICES: [2014] per person D,B&B £89. Set dinner £25. 1-night bookings sometimes refused.

SEE ALSO SHORTLIST

ULVERSTON Cumbria

THE BAY HORSE

César award in 2009

In a 'serene setting' on the edge of the Leven estuary, Robert Lyons and Lesley Wheeler's 'excellently kept' 17th-century former coaching inn is 'always reliable and a real treat', say regular visitors. They come for the 'beautiful position, super food and warm welcome'. On a cold weekend, 'there was an open fire in the bar, the heating on full blast and lashings of hot water; it was difficult to venture out when it was so pleasant inside'. The well-equipped, traditionally furnished bedrooms are 'small, but have wonderful views over Morecambe Bay'; six have French windows opening on to a terrace with seating. 'Sleep with the windows open and all you hear are the seabirds.' Dinner is served at 8 pm in the conservatory restaurant, where 'watching the tide as you dine is such fun'; Robert Lyons is the chef. 'We had a very good duck breast in a sweet and sour sauce, and a tasty and tender lamb shank, accompanied by vegetables that differed from night to night.' Lunches and simpler meals are taken in the bar and lounge. Breakfast is 'terrific'. (*LW, and others*)

Canal Foot
Ulverston
LA12 9EL

T: 01229-583972
F: 01229-580502
E: reservations@
  thebayhorsehotel.co.uk
W: www.thebayhorsehotel.co.uk

BEDROOMS: 9.
OPEN: all year, restaurant closed Mon midday (light bar meals available).
FACILITIES: bar lounge, restaurant, free Wi-Fi, picnic area, unsuitable for &.
BACKGROUND MUSIC: mixed 'easy listening'.
LOCATION: 8 miles NE of Barrow-in-Furness.
CHILDREN: not under 12.
DOGS: not allowed in restaurant.
CREDIT CARDS: all major cards.
PRICES: [2014] per room B&B £95–£120, D,B&B (min. 2 nights Fri–Sat or Sat–Sun) £155–£180. À la carte £36–£40. 1-night bookings refused bank holidays.

UPPER SLAUGHTER Gloucestershire

Map 3:D6

♔ LORDS OF THE MANOR NEW

César award: country house hotel of the year
In an 'idyllic' setting, amid 'superb gardens' on
the edge of a Cotswold village, this 17th-century
former rectory is a 'superlative' country house
hotel, 'classy without ostentation'. Paul
Thompson is the manager for the owners, the
Munir family. 'We were immediately made to
feel at home by the friendly porter who greeted
us in the drive, and the charming receptionist,'
said *Guide* inspectors in 2014. 'The interiors are
impeccable: smart, tasteful, furnished with
antiques and elegant modern furniture.' The
bedrooms are reached by corridors overlooking
internal courtyards. 'Our room was spacious yet
cosy; a huge bed enlivened by a sumptuous
Tudor-style woven bedspread; the bathroom was
warm and well lit. In the formal dining room
(white tablecloths, classic silverware and china),
chef Richard Edwards has a *Michelin* star for his
cooking: 'Everything was perfectly cooked and
presented in elegant, well-judged portions: we
had a delicious ravioli of smoked haddock and
quail egg yolk; poached and roast breast of
pigeon. The service was pleasant, courteous.'
Breakfast, 'equally satisfying', has the 'lightest
ever' croissants and petits pains au chocolat.

Upper Slaughter GL54 2JD

T: 01451-820243
F: 01451-820696
E: reservations@lordsofthemanor.com
W: www.lordsofthemanor.com

BEDROOMS: 26, 1 on ground floor.
OPEN: all year.
FACILITIES: 3 lounges, bar,
restaurant, free Wi-Fi, civil
wedding licence, terrace, 8-acre
grounds, unsuitable for ♿.
BACKGROUND MUSIC: none.
LOCATION: edge of village, 3 miles
SW of Stow-on-the-Wold.
CHILDREN: all ages welcomed, no
under-7s in restaurant in evening
(high tea served).
DOGS: 'on request'.
CREDIT CARDS: all major cards.
PRICES: [2014] per room B&B
£199–£495, D,B&B £329–£625. Set
menus £69–£75.

UPPINGHAM Rutland

Map 2:B3

LAKE ISLE HOTEL & RESTAURANT

'An immaculate hotel in a lovely town', Richard and Janine Burton's hotel/restaurant is 'excellent value', say correspondents this year. The Grade II listed building, which dates from the mid-17th century, is in the oldest part of the town. 'Parking is a squeeze but the helpful staff gave us tickets for a nearby public car park, then came out early the next day to put another ticket on at no charge.' Some of the bedrooms in the main house, which are individually designed, have a whirlpool bath. 'We were in one of the two small cottages in the courtyard; it was comfortable and quiet.' All rooms have tea- and coffee-making facilities, complimentary sherry. Everything is 'immaculate and beautifully presented'. In the restaurant, chef Stuart Mead cooks modern English dishes 'without fuss or over-elaboration', perhaps butternut steak, peppered goat's cheese butter glaze, wilted spinach, chunky chips. 'Dinner was excellent and breakfast likewise, including a kipper. Although only six miles from Rutland Water, the hotel takes its name from the WB Yeats poem ('for its sentiments of peace, relaxation and tranquillity'). (*Val and Alan Green*)

16 High Street East
Uppingham LE15 9PZ

T: 01572-822951
F: 01572-824400
E: info@lakeisle.co.uk
W: www.lakeisle.co.uk

BEDROOMS: 12, 2 in cottages.
OPEN: all year except bank holiday Mon, 1–3 Jan, restaurant closed Sun night, Mon lunch.
FACILITIES: lounge, bar, restaurant, free Wi-Fi, unsuitable for &.
BACKGROUND MUSIC: in restaurant.
LOCATION: town centre.
CHILDREN: all ages welcomed.
DOGS: allowed in bedrooms by arrangement, not in public areas.
CREDIT CARDS: MasterCard, Visa.
PRICES: [2014] per room B&B single £59.50–£69.50, double £85–£105, D,B&B single £89.50–£99.50, double £145–£165. À la carte £30–£35.

VENTNOR Isle of Wight

Map 2:E2

HILLSIDE

On St Boniface Down, overlooking the Victorian seaside town, this small hotel in a thatched mellow stone villa has 'superb views across the sea'. Gert Bach, the 'hands-on' owner, is 'a most charming host'. 'Throughout our stay, he and his staff were helpful and efficient,' says a visitor in 2014. The Grade II listed Georgian house has been given a 'modern, fresh, Scandinavian decor'; public rooms have bold contemporary art. 'Spotless' bedrooms have minimalist furnishings, original art and plenty of natural light. 'Our room was pleasant, comfortable.' Chefs Matt Allen and Gerald Frutier serve 'excellent' French-influenced menus using 'much local produce' and home-grown vegetables; meals (ordered in advance) might include locally reared pork, Medjool date purée, potato croquette. After dinner, coffee is served in the conservatory; 'the staff offered soft Welsh wool shawls in the cooling evening'. A short walk away in Ventnor, the *Hillside Bistro*, under the same ownership, has 'similar standards'. Breakfast has home-made yogurt and marmalade, island-roasted coffee; cooked dishes have home-made sausages. (*Michael and Marigold Wace, and others*)

25% DISCOUNT VOUCHERS

151 Mitchell Avenue
Ventnor PO38 1DR

T: 01983-852271
E: mail@hillsideventnor.co.uk
W: www.hillsideventnor.co.uk

BEDROOMS: 12, plus 2 self-catering apartments.
OPEN: all year, restaurant closed Sun, Bistro open all week.
FACILITIES: bar, lounge, restaurant, conservatory, free Wi-Fi, civil wedding licence, terrace, 5-acre garden, unsuitable for &.
BACKGROUND MUSIC: 'quiet background music' in public areas (turned off on request).
LOCATION: top of town, at foot of St Boniface Down.
CHILDREN: not under 12.
DOGS: not allowed.
CREDIT CARDS: MasterCard, Visa.
PRICES: [2014] per room B&B single £65–£110, double £140–£160. D,B&B £99 per person, set menus £25–£30. Min. 2-night bookings preferred.

SEE ALSO SHORTLIST

VERYAN-IN-ROSELAND Cornwall

THE NARE

César award in 2003

'In tiptop form: when I arrived I was greeted by name.' Praise in 2014 for Toby Ashworth's luxury hotel where 'the guest really does come first'. A *Guide* inspector commented that the 'default attitude of the staff is "of course, we're here for you"'. Many of the guests are repeat visitors, who appreciate touches that 'resonate from a bygone era': a 'scrumptious' complimentary cream tea, evening turn-down, 'proper' shoe cleaning, a hot-water bottle in winter; the dress code of jacket and tie for men in the main dining room. Public rooms have 'masses of current magazines', fresh flowers and the family's collection of modern prints and pictures, many by Cornish artists. Bedrooms have books and 'lovely' antique furniture. Chef Richard James serves a 'superb' daily-changing table d'hôte menu in the dining room (perhaps whole lemon sole, brown shrimps, caper nut-brown butter); informal dinners and children's teas are taken in the *Quarterdeck*. Breakfast can be served in the bedroom at no extra charge. The hotel's yacht, skippered by Toby Ashworth, is available for a half- or full day's sailing. (*Peter Govier, and others*)

Carne Beach
Veryan-in-Roseland
nr Truro TR2 5PF

T: 01872-501111
F: 01872-501856
E: stay@narehotel.co.uk
W: www.narehotel.co.uk

BEDROOMS: 37, some on ground floor, 1 in adjoining cottage, 5 suitable for &.
OPEN: all year.
FACILITIES: lift, ramps, lounge, drawing room, sun lounge, gallery, study, bar, billiard room, light lunch/supper room, 2 restaurants, conservatory, free Wi-Fi, indoor 10-metre swimming pool, gym, 2-acre grounds (heated 15-metre swimming pool, tennis, safe sandy beach), concessionary golf at Truro golf club.
BACKGROUND MUSIC: none.
LOCATION: S of Veryan, on coast.
CHILDREN: all ages welcomed.
DOGS: not allowed in public rooms.
CREDIT CARDS: Amex, MasterCard, Visa.
PRICES: [2014] per room B&B £276–£791. Set dinner £50, à la carte £60.

WADDESDON Buckinghamshire

Map 2:C3

THE FIVE ARROWS

Named after the family emblem (a shield with five arrows representing each of the Rothschild brothers who founded banks across Europe), this small hotel/restaurant is run by the Rothschild family trust for the National Trust. The elaborate half-timbered building (on the site of an old coaching inn) stands at the gates of Waddesdon Manor, the family's magnificent country retreat styled like a Loire château. Alex McEwen is the manager; Karl Penny is the chef. The bedrooms in the main house have a traditional decor; five spacious rooms have been added in a converted coach house in the grounds. They have high ceilings, beams, soothing colours. Fixed soap dispensers in the bathroom are 'a minor irritant'; rooms at the front might suffer from traffic noise. There is no guest lounge; a small bar has tables which might be taken for dinner. Everyone praises the cooking in the 'immaculate' dining room; the weekly-changing menu has modern European dishes like wild mushroom and thyme soup, truffle foam; pork loin medallions, confit potatoes, black pudding, pear, apple and cider jus. Hotel guests receive complimentary garden tickets to visit the manor.

High Street
Waddesdon HP18 0JE

T: 01296-651727
F: 01296-658596
E: five.arrows@nationaltrust.org.uk
W: www.thefivearrows.co.uk

BEDROOMS: 16, 5 in *Old Coach House*, 3, in courtyard, on ground floor.
OPEN: all year.
FACILITIES: bar, restaurant, free Wi-Fi, civil wedding licence, 1-acre garden.
BACKGROUND MUSIC: none.
LOCATION: in village.
CHILDREN: all ages welcomed.
DOGS: allowed in 1 bedroom, not in public rooms.
CREDIT CARDS: Amex, MasterCard, Visa.
PRICES: [2014] per room B&B single £75–£100, double £105–£235, D,B&B single £105, double £185–£240. À la carte £35.

WAREHAM Dorset

Map 2:E1

THE PRIORY

♥César award in 1996

'The river views are stunning' from this 'well-run, friendly and relaxed' country hotel on the banks of the Frome, in an ancient market town whose Saxon walls date back to the 9th century. In 'superb, well-kept gardens', the hotel occupies a former 16th-century priory; it is owned by Anne Turner and her brother-in-law, Stuart. The public rooms are 'full of antique (but comfortable) furniture'; the gardens have 'many delightful corners' in which you can sit in good weather. In the main house and the riverside boathouse, bedrooms have books, magazines and fresh fruit; 'housekeeping is of a high standard'. In the *Abbot's Cellar* restaurant, chef Stephan Guinebault's 'very good' French-influenced dishes might include beef fillet, foie gras, wild mushroom and potato rösti, seasonal vegetables. 'We had, variously, duck, halibut, crab salad and pork, and each was cooked very well.' 'Splendid' breakfasts: 'Every egg was cooked to perfection.' There is much to see and do nearby: 'We greatly enjoyed visiting the Isle of Purbeck and several wonderful Dorset villages.' (*David Grant, Richard and Jan Barrett*)

Church Green
Wareham
BH20 4ND

T: 01929-551666
F: 01929-554519
E: reservations@theprioryhotel.co.uk
W: www.theprioryhotel.co.uk

BEDROOMS: 18, some on ground floor (in courtyard), 4 suites in boathouse.
OPEN: all year.
FACILITIES: ramps, lounge, drawing room, bar, 2 dining rooms, free Wi-Fi, 4-acre gardens (croquet, river frontage, moorings, fishing), unsuitable for &.
BACKGROUND MUSIC: pianist in drawing room Sat night.
LOCATION: town centre.
CHILDREN: not under 14.
DOGS: not allowed.
CREDIT CARDS: all major cards.
PRICES: [2014] per room B&B £215–£375, D,B&B £265–£425. Set dinner £46.50. 1-night bookings sometimes refused.

WELLS Somerset

Map 2:D1

STOBERRY HOUSE

'The hospitality is outstanding' at Frances and Tim Young's elegant B&B standing in parkland with grazing sheep and a 'beautifully laid-out' garden. 'We were delighted,' returning guests said this year. The converted 18th-century coach house is on the outskirts of the 'lovely' medieval city; 'entered through a private park, the house has a magnificent outlook over the Vale of Avon, with Glastonbury Tor on the horizon. Finer views are hard to find.' Charming sitting rooms have fresh flowers, books and board games; guests staying in the main house have access to a pantry for light snacks. 'On a fine day, several hours could be spent idly exploring the grounds, with surprises around every corner: water features, sculptures; a delightful sunken garden; wildlife.' In the main building and a studio a short stroll away, the accommodation is 'of the highest standard'. 'Comfortable, well-appointed rooms contain every luxury and many interesting knick-knacks.' 'The biggest treat is breakfast: the extensive choice ranges from a very full English to the fabulous continental option; much is home cooked by Frances using fresh local produce, often from her own potager.' (*Ron Greenman*)

Stoberry Park
Wells BA5 3LD

T: 01749-672906
F: 01749-674175
E: stay@stoberry-park.co.uk
W: www.stoberry-park.co.uk

BEDROOMS: 5, 1 in studio cottage.
OPEN: all year except 15 Dec–5 Jan.
FACILITIES: sitting room, breakfast room, free Wi-Fi, 6½-acre grounds, unsuitable for &.
BACKGROUND MUSIC: none.
LOCATION: outskirts of Wells.
CHILDREN: not welcomed.
DOGS: not allowed.
CREDIT CARDS: Amex (*3% surcharge*), MasterCard, Visa.
PRICES: [2014] per room B&B (continental) £75–£145. Cooked breakfast £5.50.

WEST HOATHLY West Sussex

Map 2:E4

THE CAT INN

🔔 *César award in 2014*

'A modern take on the traditional pub', Andrew
Russell's 16th-century inn is in a village on a
spur of the Weald. It is a 'friendly, warm place',
say visitors this year. He is a hands-on host,
greeting guests, carrying their bags to the room,
waiting at table. 'The service was upfront and
good in his absence.' In the two dining areas
there are oak beams, inglenook fireplaces,
wooden tables on wooden floors ('a wonderful
posy of flowers on each table'). The cooking of
the chef, Max Leonard, is much admired. 'Cod
and prawn fishcakes were properly fishy and
beautifully presented; a delicious home-made
Scotch egg was served with piccalilli salad.' The
extensive wine list has several Sussex wines,
appropriate in a village where the church is set
in a former medieval vineyard. The bedrooms
are 'simply but pleasantly furnished'; they vary
in size but all have a 'good king-size bed; an oak
chest, bedside tables with reading lamps; a
proper mirror'. The 'excellent' breakfast has
'lovely' bacon and 'particularly good' coffee.
There is good walking in the area.

North Lane
West Hoathly RH19 4PP

T: 01342-810369
E: thecatinn@googlemail.com
W: www.catinn.co.uk

BEDROOMS: 4.
OPEN: all year, restaurant closed
25 Dec and Sun evening.
FACILITIES: bar, 2 dining areas, free
Wi-Fi, small terrace.
BACKGROUND MUSIC: none.
LOCATION: in village.
CHILDREN: not under 7.
DOGS: not allowed in dining room.
CREDIT CARDS: MasterCard, Visa.
PRICES: per room B&B single
£80–£130, double £110–£160.
À la carte £26–£35.

WHASHTON North Yorkshire

Map 4:C3

THE HACK & SPADE

'An interesting, unpretentious place', this restaurant-with-rooms occupies a renovated 19th-century pub on a quiet street in a peaceful hilltop village with views of the valley and rolling hills. Jane and Andy Ratcliffe are the 'hospitable and enthusiastic' hosts. She is the chef in the candlelit restaurant decorated with prints of country pursuits. Her blackboard menu of traditional dishes might include warm salad of Victorian sausage, bacon and Stilton; pork tenderloin, cider, caramelised apples. Portions are 'generous'; the main course comes with 'a large side helping of vegetables'. Smart, 'uncluttered' bedrooms overlook the countryside or the village green. A table on the landing has a help-yourself decanter of sherry, and sweets. A large room had a 'cool, contemporary feel'; an enormous bed with an upholstered headboard; a cushioned window seat with rural views; ample storage and free-range hangers in an oak wardrobe. The bathroom 'added the wow factor'. No menu at breakfast, just a question: 'What would you like?' 'When we ordered scrambled eggs, we were asked if we would like the toast buttered before the eggs were put on, an important but rarely asked question.'

Whashton
Richmond DL11 7JL

T: 01748-823721
E: info@hackandspade.com
W: www.hackandspade.com

BEDROOMS: 5.
OPEN: all year except last week Jan, first week Feb.
FACILITIES: lounge, restaurant, free Wi-Fi, only restaurant suitable for &.
BACKGROUND MUSIC: none.
LOCATION: 4 miles NW of Richmond.
CHILDREN: not under 7.
DOGS: not allowed.
CREDIT CARDS: MasterCard, Visa.
PRICES: [2014] per room B&B £120–£130. À la carte £25.

WHITEWELL Lancashire

Map 4:D3

THE INN AT WHITEWELL

Conversation hums in the busy bar of Charles Bowman's cheerful rural inn on the banks of the River Hodder. The bar's many rooms occupy most of the ground floor. They have 'nice old tables', chairs of many sizes and shapes, sofas, sporting and fashion prints on the walls; 'all great fun'. There is no background music, just 'people talking to each other'. The 14th-century manor house has views down the valley into the Forest of Bowland. Individually styled bedrooms have antiques, rich fabrics, prints and pictures; many have an open fire. 'Our bedroom was huge and long; there were blankets and sheets on the good-sized bed; free-range hangers in an old-fashioned wardrobe; a chest of drawers and a table in the bay window which looked over the river, binoculars provided.' In the 'calm' dining room, long-serving chef Jamie Cadman uses local ingredients for his modern dishes, perhaps confit of Goosnargh duck, potato rösti, tomato concassé; roast loin of Cumbrian venison, mushroom pithivier, parsnip purée. Breakfast has a 'perfectly cooked' full English. Plenty of marked walks from the door. 'The inn is as good as ever; so peaceful,' says a returning visitor in 2014. (*Michael Crick, and others*)

Whitewell, Forest of Bowland
nr Clitheroe BB7 3AT

T: 01200-448222
F: 01200-448298
E: reception@innatwhitewell.com
W: www.innatwhitewell.com

BEDROOMS: 23, 4 (2 on ground floor) in coach house, 150 yds.
OPEN: all year.
FACILITIES: 3 bars, restaurant, boardroom, private dining room, free Wi-Fi, civil wedding licence, 5-acre garden, 7 miles fishing (ghillie available), unsuitable for &.
BACKGROUND MUSIC: none.
LOCATION: 6 miles NW of Clitheroe.
CHILDREN: all ages welcomed.
DOGS: not allowed in dining room.
CREDIT CARDS: MasterCard, Visa.
PRICES: [2014] per room B&B £125–£248. À la carte £36–£50.

WILMINGTON East Sussex

Map 2:E4

CROSSWAYS HOTEL

'A real treat. The two-night Glyndebourne break (one night opera, one night dinner) is very good value.' A regular visitor received the 'usual warm welcome' this year at Clive James and David Stott's restaurant-with-rooms at the foot of the South Downs national park. The smart, white-painted Georgian house is surrounded by large, 'delightful' grounds; in warm weather, a gazebo provides a place to lounge alfresco. Individually styled bedrooms have many thoughtful touches: a clothes brush, earplugs, a selection of Penguin classics; fresh milk in the fridge. The 'badinage' over dinner 'fits in with the place'. 'David recites the menu which evolves slowly from year to year and seems even lighter and tastier than previous (good) experiences. I enjoyed smoked duck and pears; my guest had a grilled peach with cheese which was much better than it sounded; delicious sea bass with a vermouth cream sauce; runner beans from the garden. There was a superb carrot, orange and tomato soup in between – and good puddings.' Breakfast has home-made marmalade, and eggs laid just down the road. With easy access to Glyndebourne, *Crossways* is popular during the opera season. (*Richard Parish*)

Lewes Road
Wilmington
BN26 5SG

T: 01323-482455
F: 01323-487811
E: stay@crosswayshotel.co.uk
W: www.crosswayshotel.co.uk

BEDROOMS: 7, also self-catering cottage.
OPEN: all year except 24 Dec–24 Jan, restaurant closed Sun/Mon.
FACILITIES: breakfast room, restaurant, free Wi-Fi, 2-acre grounds (duck pond), unsuitable for &.
BACKGROUND MUSIC: quiet classical in restaurant.
LOCATION: 2 miles W of Polegate on A27.
CHILDREN: not under 12.
DOGS: not allowed.
CREDIT CARDS: Amex, MasterCard, Visa.
PRICES: per room B&B £145–£180. D,B&B £110–£132 per person, set dinner £42.50.

THE LION INN

Restored in Scandinavian style with subdued
colours, and given a mix of retro and vintage
furnishings by the owner, Annie Fox-Hamilton,
this 15th-century Cotswold inn is a popular
local gathering place. Managed by Andrew
Newsham, it has a 'relaxed, modern air' (says an
inspector). Guests collect their room key from
the bar. The bedrooms vary in size and style; one
is a converted hayloft, two are reached by an
external stone staircase. A high-ceilinged room,
in shades of grey, had a painted chest of drawers,
a huge vase of flowers and a built-in wardrobe.
The rooms have Scrabble and playing cards but
no television; 'we hope guests will join us in the
bar and restaurant,' says the owner. There are
newspapers, magazines and board games in a
'delightful, white-washed, beamed snug', which
has distressed leather chairs. Meals can be taken
in the bar or at wooden tables in the restaurant.
Alex Dumitrache is now the chef, cooking
artisan dishes like warm poached and pickled
trout with brown bread; rolled slow-cooked
pork belly, leek fondue, cider sauce. Breakfast
can be taken from 8 to 11 am.

37 North Street
Winchcombe GL54 5PS

T: 01242-603300
E: reception@thelionwinchcombe.co.uk
W: www.thelionwinchcombe.co.uk

BEDROOMS: 7, 2 accessed by external staircase.
OPEN: all year.
FACILITIES: club room, bar, restaurant, free Wi-Fi, courtyard garden, unsuitable for &.
BACKGROUND MUSIC: in bar and restaurant.
LOCATION: town centre.
CHILDREN: all ages welcomed.
DOGS: allowed in bedrooms (£15), not in restaurant.
CREDIT CARDS: MasterCard, Visa.
PRICES: [2014] per room B&B £100–£200, D,B&B £170–£270. À la carte £35.

WINDERMERE Cumbria

GILPIN HOTEL AND LAKE HOUSE

♥César award in 2000

'A gold standard for small luxury hotels: the type of place where you do not feel you need to wear a tie.' In extensive grounds with cultivated gardens and woodland, this 'friendly, family-run' country house hotel (Relais & Châteaux) has 'delightful, efficient' staff who 'seem to enjoy what they are doing'. It is run by Barney and Zoë Cunliffe, and his parents, John and Christine. The Reception area has been refreshed this year, and a lounge and dining room have been refurbished. 'We were welcomed and shown to our large and airy room, which had French windows leading to a private patio overlooking the garden and pond. There was a super bed, and plenty of wardrobe and drawer space; the silent fridge, with fresh milk, was replenished twice daily.' In the candlelit dining rooms, 'our table was reserved for us for the whole of our stay'. Head chef Lee Clarkson's modern menus use much Lake District produce, perhaps hickory-smoked bone marrow, crispy kale, cèpe purée; Cumbrian hogget, black garlic, rosemary. Breakfast is 'a feast'. (*Wolfgang Stroebe*)

Crook Road
nr Windermere LA23 3NE

T: 015394-88818
F: 015394-88058
E: hotel@gilpinlodge.co.uk
W: www.gilpinlodge.co.uk

BEDROOMS: 26, 6 in orchard wing, 6 in *Lake House* (½ mile from main house).
OPEN: all year.
FACILITIES: ramps, bar, 2 lounges, 4 dining rooms, free Wi-Fi, 22-acre grounds (ponds, croquet), free access to nearby country club, golf course opposite, unsuitable for &.
BACKGROUND MUSIC: none.
LOCATION: on B5284, 2 miles SE of Windermere.
CHILDREN: not under 7.
DOGS: not allowed (kennels at nearby farm).
CREDIT CARDS: all major cards.
PRICES: [2014] per room B&B £255–£525, D,B&B £335–£605. Set dinner £65, à la carte £36–£125. 1-night bookings refused Sat.

SEE ALSO SHORTLIST

WINDERMERE Cumbria

Map 4: inset C2

HOLBECK GHYLL

Built as a hunting lodge for Lord Lonsdale, this ivy-covered Arts and Crafts house stands in extensive grounds that slope down to Lake Windermere. It is managed by Andrew McPherson for the owners, Stephen and Lisa Leahy. 'Highly recommended' by a regular correspondent this year, it is liked for the 'tastefully decorated' rooms, *Michelin*-starred cooking and 'genuinely friendly' staff. The bedrooms are divided between the main house, a lodge and cottages in the grounds. 'Our room in the lodge, which had access to a shared terrace, was spacious; the bathroom equally so.' Rooms are 'well appointed and well equipped': they have 'ample tea and coffee facilities, a decanter of damson gin; in the bathroom, good toiletries were replenished regularly'. The interiors in the main house have wood carvings and fine stained glass. In the oak-panelled restaurant, chef David McLaughlin's modern menu might include honey-glazed Gloucestershire Old Spot pork belly, spiced carrot, sautéed Scottish langoustine, pea foam. 'Breakfast was relaxed and beautifully served'; there are freshly baked pastries, fresh fruit; many local ingredients in the cooked dishes. (*David Haigh, and others*)

Holbeck Lane
Windermere LA23 1LU

T: 015394-32375
F: 015394-34743
E: stay@holbeckghyll.com
W: www.holbeckghyll.com

BEDROOMS: 25, 1 suitable for &, 6 in lodge, 5 in cottages, 2 suites.
OPEN: all year except first two weeks Jan.
FACILITIES: ramp, 2 lounges, bar, restaurant, free Wi-Fi, function facilities, civil wedding licence, small spa, 17-acre grounds (tennis).
BACKGROUND MUSIC: piano in lounges.
LOCATION: 4 miles N of Windermere.
CHILDREN: not under 8 in restaurant.
DOGS: allowed in lodge rooms.
CREDIT CARDS: Amex, MasterCard, Visa (*charge for credit card use*).
PRICES: [2014] per room B&B £150–£390, D,B&B £250–£490. Set dinner £68–£88 per person. 1-night bookings sometimes refused Sat.

SEE ALSO SHORTLIST

WOLD NEWTON East Yorkshire

Map 4:D5

THE WOLD COTTAGE

Once a gentleman's retreat, Katrina and Derek Gray's red brick Georgian country house stands in landscaped grounds with the views to the Yorkshire Wolds (the landscape that inspired David Hockney's *A Bigger Picture*). 'Excellent hosts', they welcome visitors on a B&B basis, serving evening meals by arrangement. 'It is a heavenly home from home with an atmosphere of calm,' says a returning visitor this year. Four spacious bedrooms in the main house are furnished in keeping with the building; two have a four-poster bed. The Miss Davey Suite has 'adjustable' twin beds, each with memory-foam mattresses. Two 'light and airy' rooms are in a barn extension. All rooms are well equipped: biscuits, chocolates and cake on the hospitality tray; mineral water; bathrobes. Katrina Gray cooks the evening meal which is served by her husband in the red-walled dining room. All the produce is locally sourced ('you can tell by the taste'). At breakfast a buffet has fresh fruit, home-made compotes, cereals; bread is home baked, preserves are prepared in the kitchen. The heating and hot water are supplied by a straw-burner. (*Derrick Priestley*)

Wold Newton, nr Driffield
YO25 3HL

T/F: 01262-470696
E: katrina@woldcottage.com
W: www.woldcottage.com

BEDROOMS: 6, 2 in converted barn, 1 on ground floor.
OPEN: all year.
FACILITIES: lounge, dining room, free Wi-Fi in public areas, 3-acre grounds (croquet) in 300-acre farmland.
BACKGROUND MUSIC: at mealtimes, contemporary.
LOCATION: just outside village.
CHILDREN: all ages welcomed.
DOGS: not allowed.
CREDIT CARDS: MasterCard, Visa.
PRICES: [2014] per person B&B £50–£75. Set dinner £28.

WOLTERTON Norfolk

THE SARACEN'S HEAD

'Lost in lanes' amid fields in rural Norfolk ('the loudest noise is the rookery opposite'), Tim and Janie Elwes's country inn is liked for the 'honest-to-goodness food and accommodation'. The owners, who used to run a small hotel in the French Alps, are 'relaxed, informal, friendly'; he 'willingly carried the bags to our room'. The bedrooms, decorated in modern style, have a flat-screen television, tea- and coffee-making facilities; plug-in Internet access ('as we are in the middle of nowhere, it is going to be slower than you are used to'). The family room has a double bed and two singles. There are guidebooks and maps in a small upstairs sitting room. 'Local, fresh and seasonal' are the watchwords in the kitchen ('we may venture over the border to Lincolnshire to source our potatoes'). The chef, Mark Sayers, cooks a seasonal menu of dishes like Cromer crab, pink grapefruit salad; slow-cooked shoulder of Barningham Green lamb, crushed new potatoes, Italian green sauce. Meals may be taken in the 'cosy bar'. History doesn't record why the house was built in 1806 in the style of a Tuscan farmhouse.

Wall Road
Wolterton, nr Erpingham
NR11 7LZ

T: 01263-768909
F: 01263-768993
E: info@saracenshead-norfolk.co.uk
W: www.saracenshead-norfolk.co.uk

BEDROOMS: 6.
OPEN: all year except Christmas, restaurant closed Mon, Tues lunchtime except summer.
FACILITIES: lounge, bar, restaurant, free Wi-Fi, courtyard, 1-acre garden, accommodation unsuitable for &.
BACKGROUND MUSIC: 'when suitable' in bar and dining rooms.
LOCATION: 5 miles N of Aylsham.
CHILDREN: all ages welcomed.
DOGS: not allowed in restaurant.
CREDIT CARDS: MasterCard, Visa.
PRICES: [2014] per room B&B single £70, double £100. D,B&B £30 added per person, à la carte £32.

WOOLACOMBE Devon

Map 1:B4

WATERSMEET

'An excellent hotel: well managed, well run, with a relaxed atmosphere and first-class staff.' Praise in 2014 from a visitor who regretted an 'all-too-short' stay at Amanda James's traditional hotel, originally an Edwardian gentleman's retreat, above Woolacombe Bay. It has a 'stunning setting' above a quiet, sandy beach, the public rooms have 'impressive' Atlantic views across the bay to Lundy Island. 'The loveliness of the views is matched by the graciousness of the accommodation.' All but three bedrooms look out to sea; some have a wooden balcony or a garden terrace. A spacious room had a seating area with a view of the cove; a 'comfortable bed, responsive heating; a beautiful, well-equipped bathroom'. In the restaurant overlooking the bay – with 'sunsets to die for' – John Prince is the chef; his classic dishes might include fennel-cured sea trout, curried crab, fennel toast; loin and belly of pork, hog's pudding, parsnip purée, confit leeks. Simpler meals 'for all ages' are taken in the *Bistro*; in good weather, afternoon tea and snacks may be served on the terrace or the lawn. (*Richard and Pam James, SH*)

Mortehoe
Woolacombe EX34 7EB

T: 01271-870333
F: 01271-870890
E: info@watersmeethotel.co.uk
W: www.watersmeethotel.co.uk

BEDROOMS: 29, 3 on ground floor, 1 suitable for &.
OPEN: all year.
FACILITIES: lift, lounge, bar, restaurant, *Bistro*, function room, free Wi-Fi, civil wedding licence, terrace, ½-acre gardens, heated indoor and outdoor swimming pools, sandy beach below.
BACKGROUND MUSIC: 'easy listening' in restaurant in evening.
LOCATION: by the sea, 4 miles SW of Ilfracombe.
CHILDREN: all ages welcomed, no under-8s in restaurant in evening.
DOGS: not allowed.
CREDIT CARDS: MasterCard, Visa (*3% surcharge on credit cards*).
PRICES: [2014] per person B&B £70–£145, D,B&B £100–£175. Set dinner £42, à la carte (*Bistro*) £30. 1-night bookings refused in high season.

YARM North Yorkshire

Map 4:C4

JUDGES

'Lovely to be back at *Judges*,' says a regular *Guide* correspondent, returning this year to this restored Victorian mansion, once a residence for circuit court judges. 'We were hoping that standards were as high as ever and we were not disappointed; they have never let us down.' Tim Howard is the 'charming' manager. The house stands in extensive grounds with waterfalls, ornate bridges, well-tended lawns and pathways with shady seats in natural woodland. There is a panelled bar and a lounge filled with antiques. 'The food and service in the conservatory dining room was excellent; the quality and presentation of the dishes was of a high standard.' Chef John Schwarz promises 'no garnishing for garnishing's sake' in his modern menus, which might include dishes like game mosaic, quince, pistachio biscotti; cod loin, creamed potato, shellfish ragout. Bedrooms are individually decorated and furnished; some rooms have a four-poster bed. 'Our room overlooked the entrance and was very spacious yet had a cosy, comfortable feeling. Complimentary brandy and biscuits made our stay extra special.' The 'delicious' breakfast is 'served promptly'. (*William Wood, and others*)

25% DISCOUNT VOUCHERS

Kirklevington Hall
Yarm TS15 9LW

T: 01642-789000
F: 01642-782878
W: www.judgeshotel.co.uk

BEDROOMS: 21, some on ground floor.
OPEN: all year.
FACILITIES: ramps, lounge, bar, restaurant, private dining room, free Wi-Fi, function facilities, business centre, civil wedding licence, 36-acre grounds (paths, running routes), access to local spa and sports club.
BACKGROUND MUSIC: none.
LOCATION: 1½ miles S of centre.
CHILDREN: all ages welcomed.
DOGS: only guide dogs allowed.
CREDIT CARDS: all major cards.
PRICES: [2014] per room B&B £140–£230, D,B&B £215–£315. Set dinner £39.50, à la carte £58.50.

YORK North Yorkshire

MIDDLETHORPE HALL & SPA

In 'beautiful gardens with a splendid walk to the river', this 'striking' William and Mary country mansion on the outskirts of York is owned by the National Trust. Once the home of diarist Lady Mary Wortley Montagu, it was sympathetically restored by Historic House Hotels, who donated it to the Trust. Lionel Chatard is the manager. 'Like its sister, *Hartwell House* [Aylesbury, see entry], it is very special; we cannot fault it,' wrote one visitor. 'Stylish without being staid', the public rooms have original antiques, 'beautiful furnishings', gilded mirrors and paintings. The service is 'attentive, discreet; we were recognised from an earlier visit'. The best bedrooms, in the main house, have a sitting room and gas coal fire. Other rooms are in a coach house and the garden. Some rooms interconnect to create family accommodation. In the panelled dining rooms, which overlook the gardens, chef Nicholas Evans serves a modern British menu which might include roast beetroot and fennel risotto; roast fillet of Scottish salmon, brassicas, horseradish. The many specimen trees in the grounds partially shield the noise of the busy ring road. (*JB*)

Bishopthorpe Road
York YO23 2GB

T: 01904-641241
F: 01904-620176
E: info@middlethorpe.com
W: www.middlethorpe.com

BEDROOMS: 29, 17 in courtyard, 2 in garden, 1 suitable for ♿.
OPEN: all year.
FACILITIES: drawing room, sitting rooms, library, bar, restaurant, free Wi-Fi, civil wedding licence, 20-acre grounds, spa (indoor swimming pool, 10 by 5 metres).
BACKGROUND MUSIC: none.
LOCATION: 1½ miles S of centre.
CHILDREN: not under 6.
DOGS: only in garden suites, only guide dogs in public rooms.
CREDIT CARDS: Amex, MasterCard, Visa.
PRICES: [2014] per room B&B single £139–£179, double £199–£499. D,B&B from £129 per person, set dinner £43–£69, à la carte £55. 1-night bookings refused weekends in summer.

SEE ALSO SHORTLIST

ZENNOR Cornwall

Map 1:D1

THE GURNARD'S HEAD

🐾 *César award in 2009*

'A place where children and pets are welcomed with open arms', Charles and Edmund Inkin's old yellow-painted inn is liked for 'the food and good, friendly service'. 'The staff treat you like a human being, not a "guest" to make a fuss of.' The simple bedrooms are 'far from luxurious, but are cosy and warm, and lack nothing'. 'We particularly liked the library of paperbacks in the rooms, the romantic view of the moors (and the cows walking up the road in the morning),' said a visitor this year. Downstairs, 'there is plenty to keep one occupied, newspapers and reading materials' in the bar and a newly created snug. 'There are lovely Cornish beers and gulpable wines.' Matt Smith is now the chef. His menu, which can be taken in the bar or the dining room, has 'above-average' dishes like beef rump, parsley risotto, radish, wild mushrooms, shallot. Breakfast has Cornish apple juice, home-baked soda bread as well as a large farmhouse loaf; porridge on request; hog's pudding in the full English. The Inkin brothers also run *The Old Coastguard* in Mousehole and *The Felin Fach Griffin* in Felin Fach, Wales (see entries). (*SA Mathieson, and others*)

Treen, nr Zennor
St Ives TR26 3DE

T: 01736-796928
E: enquiries@gurnardshead.co.uk
W: www.gurnardshead.co.uk

BEDROOMS: 7.
OPEN: all year except 24/25 Dec, 4 days in Dec.
FACILITIES: bar area (with free Wi-Fi), small connecting room with sofas, dining room, ½-acre garden, unsuitable for &.
BACKGROUND MUSIC: Radio 4 at breakfast, selected music at other times.
LOCATION: 6½ miles SW of St Ives, on B3306.
CHILDREN: all ages welcomed.
DOGS: not allowed in dining room.
CREDIT CARDS: MasterCard, Visa.
PRICES: [2014] per person B&B £52.50–£85, D,B&B £77.50–£110. À la carte £36. 1-night bookings occasionally refused on Sat.

SCOTLAND

Loch Carron in the Scottish Highland

LOCH MELFORT HOTEL

The owners, Calum and Rachel Ross, are 'very much present' at their country hotel in 'beautiful surroundings' on the Argyll coast. Sheltered by woodland, it stands on Asknish Bay and has 'wonderful views' over the Sound of Jura. In the dining room, chef Peter Carr serves modern Scottish dishes, perhaps roast salmon, lemon gratin potato, sauce vierge. In the summer, family-friendly meals can be taken in the *Chartroom II* bistro (which has showers for yachting visitors taking advantage of free berthing). An all-day menu is now available in the bistro and can be taken on the balcony of a bedroom. The five bedrooms in the main house vary in size; 20 others ('light, with plenty of storage and a good-sized bathroom') are in a wood-framed extension attached to the main house by a partly open walkway. Children are warmly welcomed: there is a play park with swings and slides and they can feed the three Highland cattle, Campbell, McDonald and Dougal; extra beds, toys, books and games can be provided in some bedrooms. Dogs are allowed in six rooms, which have direct access to the grounds.

Arduaine
by Oban PA34 4XG

T: 01852-200233
F: 01852-200214
E: reception@lochmelfort.co.uk
W: www.lochmelfort.co.uk

BEDROOMS: 25, 20 in *Cedar Wing* annexe, 10 on ground floor.
OPEN: Feb–Nov, last 2 weeks Dec, closed Mon–Wed Nov–Mar.
FACILITIES: sitting room, library, bar/bistro, restaurant, wedding facilities, free Wi-Fi in public rooms and main house bedrooms, 17-acre grounds (including National Trust for Scotland's Arduaine Garden).
BACKGROUND MUSIC: modern Scottish in public areas.
LOCATION: 19 miles S of Oban.
CHILDREN: all ages welcomed, under-2s free.
DOGS: allowed in 6 bedrooms, not in public rooms.
CREDIT CARDS: MasterCard, Visa.
PRICES: [2014] per person B&B £74–£134, D,B&B £105–£153, £30 single supplement. Set menu £39.50, à la carte £42.

BALCARY BAY HOTEL

Taking its name from the bay on which it stands, Graeme Lamb's white-painted hotel has 'an instantly relaxing atmosphere'. Elaine Ness, the manager, 'provides a warm welcome'; the staff are 'local, interested in their guests' satisfaction and comfort', says a visitor this year. A log fire burns in the lounge, which has been renovated. In the dining room, which overlooks the tidal bay, the cooking of the chef, Craig McWilliam, 'is as delicious as ever'. Typical dishes on his dinner menu: saffron and vegetable linguine, pea velouté, truffle oil; seared venison loin, red cabbage, wild mushrooms, juniper berry jus. The head waiter is 'attentive'. The bedrooms vary in size and aspect. 'My room had been redecorated and the bathroom refurbished in modern but tasteful style. Excellent lighting over the bed, and a teapot on the tea tray; chocolates and fresh fruit – with a knife and plate.' Steps to some of the upper rooms might be steep. Many bedrooms overlook the bay, others face the mature gardens. Breakfast has a good buffet; 'eggs with a deep orange yolk'. (*Dr M Tannahill, and others*)

Shore Road
Auchencairn
Castle Douglas DG7 1QZ

T: 01556-640217
F: 01556-640272
E: reservations@balcary-bay-hotel.co.uk
W: www.balcary-bay-hotel.co.uk

BEDROOMS: 20, 3 on ground floor.
OPEN: Feb–Nov.
FACILITIES: 2 lounges, bar, conservatory, restaurant, free Wi-Fi, 3½-acre grounds.
BACKGROUND MUSIC: none.
LOCATION: on shore, 2 miles SW of village.
CHILDREN: all ages welcomed.
DOGS: allowed.
CREDIT CARDS: MasterCard, Visa.
PRICES: per person B&B £75–£93, D,B&B £89–£117. Set meals £34–£50. 1-night bookings usually refused weekends.

BOATH HOUSE

César award in 2013

One of the finest Regency houses in Scotland, this once-endangered mansion has been restored by Wendy and Don Matheson, who run it as a 'wonderful' small hotel. Their son, Sam, is the manager. The house, which has a marble hall and circular staircase, is filled with a collection of contemporary Scottish art and pottery (which guests may purchase). Pre-dinner drinks and canapés are taken in a candlelit drawing room. In the dining room, which has floor-to-ceiling windows, chef Charlie Lockley has a *Michelin* star for his modern Scottish cooking. An 'avid follower' of the Slow Food Movement, he serves a daily-changing dinner menu of simply described dishes like hake, leek, celeriac, chickweed; duck, orange, carrot, anise. 'Memorable, delicious and not too fussy,' is a typical comment. The bedrooms are individually styled. 'Our lovely, large room had a very comfortable four-poster bed, a day bed at the window, and a view of the lake.' Breakfast is 'another wonderful meal', served at table ('just the right amount of food'). The house stands in extensive grounds, which have a productive walled garden, a lake, woodland and streams.

Auldearn
Nairn
IV12 5TE

T: 01667-454896
F: 01667-455469
E: info@boath-house.com
W: www.boath-house.com

BEDROOMS: 8, 1, in cottage (50 yds), suitable for &.
OPEN: all year.
FACILITIES: 2 lounges, library, orangery, restaurant, health/beauty spa, free Wi-Fi, wedding facilities, 20-acre grounds (woods, gardens, meadow, streams, trout lake).
BACKGROUND MUSIC: none.
LOCATION: 1½ miles E of Nairn.
CHILDREN: all ages welcomed.
DOGS: not in public rooms.
CREDIT CARDS: MasterCard, Visa.
PRICES: per room B&B single £190–£260, double £260–£365, D,B&B £345–£450. Set dinner £45–£70.

COSSES COUNTRY HOUSE

In 'colourful' gardens and woodland in a secluded valley, this pretty, low, white building is run as a guest house by Susan and Robin Crosthwaite, 'charming hosts'. The house has been 'lovingly furnished'; the Crosthwaites have 'clearly done much work on the picturesque estate', said *Guide* inspectors. Two of the bedrooms are in converted byres and stables across a courtyard; a smaller (and cheaper) room is in the main house. The rooms are decorated in traditional style with floral patterns. Each of the larger ones has a private sitting room with 'lots of local information, usefully displayed'. There are 'all kinds of pretty extras'. The 'multi-talented' Susan Crosthwaite cooks a seasonal no-choice dinner of Ayrshire-sourced produce (vegetables from the garden). Her menu might include seared scallops, Dalduff black pudding; Crailoch pheasant, whisky, cream, bay and thyme. The 'delicious' meal is taken communally. 'Crossing the courtyard to our room after dinner, we had a magnificent view of the night sky.' Breakfast, in the kitchen, 'was lovely and informal, we chatted to Susan as she cooked. The table was prettily laid and anything you could want was on offer.'

Ballantrae
KA26 0LR

T: 01465-831363
F: 01465-831598
E: staying@cossescountryhouse.com
W: www.cossescountryhouse.com

BEDROOMS: 3, on ground floor, 2 across courtyard.
OPEN: all year except 21 May–9 June, Christmas/New Year.
FACILITIES: drawing room, dining room, games room (table tennis, darts), free Wi-Fi, 12-acre grounds.
BACKGROUND MUSIC: none.
LOCATION: 2 miles E of Ballantrae.
CHILDREN: not under 12.
DOGS: allowed by arrangement in 1 suite, not in public rooms.
CREDIT CARDS: MasterCard, Visa.
PRICES: [2014] per room B&B £100–£120. D,B&B £85–£95 per person, set dinner £35.

GLENAPP CASTLE

Designed by the doyen of Victorian castle architects, David Bryce, this baronial castle was in a state of disrepair when it was bought by the McMillan family. It was restored by Graham and Fay (née McMillan) Cowan, who run it as a luxury country house hotel (Relais & Châteaux). John Orr is their manager. They have furnished the house 'beautifully' with antiques collected during the restoration. There is intricate plasterwork, an Austrian oak-panelled entrance and staircase, a parquet-floored library. The massive main drawing room feels 'cosy' thanks to its squashy sofas. In the dining room, Tyron Ellul has been promoted to head chef: he uses garden and foraged produce for his modern dishes like Ballantrae-landed lobster ravioli, shellfish consommé, leek fondue; red wine-braised feather blade of beef, wild mushrooms. The bedrooms are spacious; they have a wide bed, an open fire, books, 'everything for your comfort'. A ground-floor room has a seating area; a claw-footed bath and a separate shower in the bathroom. Guests may wander in the wooded grounds, which have a lake, a walled garden, and a magnificent Victorian glasshouse.

25% DISCOUNT VOUCHERS

Ballantrae
KA26 0NZ

T: 01465-831212
F: 01465-831000
E: info@glenappcastle.com
W: www.glenappcastle.com

BEDROOMS: 17, 7 on ground floor.
OPEN: 27 Mar–3 Jan, except Christmas.
FACILITIES: ramp, lift, drawing room, library, 2 dining rooms, wedding facilities, free Wi-Fi, 36-acre gardens (tennis, croquet), fishing, golf nearby, access to spa.
BACKGROUND MUSIC: none.
LOCATION: 2 miles S of Ballantrae.
CHILDREN: no under-5s in dining room after 7 pm.
DOGS: allowed in certain bedrooms, not in public rooms, no charge.
CREDIT CARDS: Amex, MasterCard, Visa.
PRICES: [2013] per room B&B £370–£575, D,B&B £430–£635. Set dinner £65. 1-night bookings refused at bank holidays, New Year.

NO 45

Formerly known as the *Deeside Hotel*, this 'excellent' small guest house has been renamed *No 45*. The owners, Gordon Waddell and Penella Price, tells us that the restaurant will only be open to resident diners on five nights a week, closing on Monday and Tuesday. Two bedrooms on the ground floor have been combined to create a larger garden room with a triple aspect, French windows and a wet room with a bath, a separate shower and under-floor heating. Gordon Waddell's modern cooking is consistently praised. He now serves a short set menu (two choices for each of three courses), which must be pre-booked. Typical dishes: lamb cooked two ways (roast leg and slow-cooked shoulder), minted new potatoes, aubergine purée. 'Excellent food; Penella is ever-present and always pleasant.' The Victorian house, which sits back from the road on the edge of the town, has log fires in the library and lounge. The bedrooms, with a king-size bed, vary in size and have good storage; the hospitality trays have Deeside mineral water, herbal teas and Fairtrade hot chocolate. Breakfast is thought 'delicious'. (*Carol Jackson, Alan and Edwina Williams*)

45 Braemar Road
Ballater AB35 5RQ

T: 013397-55420
F: 0871 989 5933
E: mail@no45.co.uk
W: www.no45.co.uk

BEDROOMS: 8, 1 on ground floor.
OPEN: Mar–Dec, closed Christmas/New Year, restaurant closed Mon/Tues.
FACILITIES: ramp, library, lounge, restaurant, free Wi-Fi in public areas, 1-acre garden.
BACKGROUND MUSIC: classical in bar and restaurant.
LOCATION: village outskirts.
CHILDREN: all ages welcomed.
DOGS: not allowed.
CREDIT CARDS: MasterCard, Visa (debit cards only).
PRICES: [2014] per room B&B £100–£120, D,B&B £150–£170. Set dinner £25. 1-night bookings sometimes refused Sat in season.

KINLOCH HOUSE

In 'lovely' gardens with fine views of hills and fields, the Allen family's traditional country house hotel (Relais & Châteaux) is managed by Paul Knott. There is 'lots of space' in the public rooms, which have antiques, 'wonderfully comfortable' sofas, rich fabrics (damask and chintz). Log fires make them 'a bolt-hole in harsh weather'. The bedrooms are also decorated in traditional style: some have a four-poster bed with an elaborate canopy; there are brass lamps on antique dressing tables; beds are made with sheets and blankets; fresh flowers; 'everything is spotlessly clean'. A single traveller was impressed with a spacious room, 'nicely decorated'; a stand-alone bath and a small shower cubicle in the huge bathroom. In the formal dining room, chef Steve MacCallum serves a short menu of modern country house dishes, perhaps smooth terrine of chicken livers, date chutney, Cumberland sauce; Hebridean salmon and smoked salmon fishcake, sea spinach, tomato and lemon butter sauce. 'Outstanding: beautifully cooked and seasoned, well presented,' is a recent comment. Breakfast has freshly squeezed orange juice, 'good freshly baked bread, and cooked dishes'. (*JG*)

Dunkeld Road
by Blairgowrie PH10 6SG

T: 01250-884237
F: 01250-884333
E: reception@kinlochhouse.com
W: www.kinlochhouse.com

BEDROOMS: 15, 4 on ground floor.
OPEN: all year except 12–29 Dec.
FACILITIES: ramp, bar, 2 lounges, conservatory, dining room, private dining room, free Wi-Fi (in most areas), wedding facilities, 25-acre grounds.
BACKGROUND MUSIC: none.
LOCATION: 3 miles W of Blairgowrie.
CHILDREN: no under-6s in dining room at night.
DOGS: allowed by arrangement only.
CREDIT CARDS: MasterCard, Visa.
PRICES: [2014] per room B&B £215–£325. D,B&B £145–£215 per person, set dinner £53. 1-night bookings refused at busy periods, New Year.

TIGH AN DOCHAIS

'A lovely place; glorious views, comfortable rooms and great breakfasts.' New praise this year for this stunning modern building designed by award-winning architects to make the most of the situation above Broadford Bay. Neil Hope and Lesley Unwin, the 'friendly' owners, run the house as a B&B that 'shines out' on Skye. It is entered by a bridge to the upper floor, where the guest lounge and dining room have full-length picture windows. There is solid oak flooring throughout; contemporary art; a wood-burning stove, sofas, many books in the lounge. The bedrooms, 'well equipped and of a good size', are on the floor below and also have the views. Neil Hope, a 'keen and accomplished cook', will prepare a 'delicious meal', discussing likes and dislikes in advance. It will highlight local produce and might depend on what fish has been landed on the day. Breakfast, taken at a communal table ('a bonus thanks to the interesting other guests'), has fresh fruit salad, house yogurt, home-made muffins; locally smoked haddock and kippers are often among the cooked choices. 'Good value.' (*Caroline Rand, and others*)

13 Harrapool, Broadford
Isle of Skye IV49 9AQ

T: 01471-820022
E: hopeskye@btinternet.com
W: www.skyebedbreakfast.co.uk

BEDROOMS: 3, all on ground floor.
OPEN: Apr–Nov.
FACILITIES: lounge, dining area, free Wi-Fi, ½-acre garden, unsuitable for &.
BACKGROUND MUSIC: Celtic at breakfast.
LOCATION: 1 mile E of Broadford.
CHILDREN: all ages welcomed.
DOGS: not allowed.
CREDIT CARDS: Diners, MasterCard, Visa.
PRICES: per room B&B £90. Set dinner £25.

KILMICHAEL COUNTRY HOUSE

In extensive grounds with 'beautiful gardens' on the largest island in the Firth of Clyde, this intimate period mansion is run in personal style as a small hotel by the owners, Geoffrey Botterill and Antony Butterworth. Said to be the oldest house on the island, *Kilmichael* has the feel of a private home; the well-travelled owners have filled it with their collection of pictures and artefacts. Antony Butterworth cooks a daily-changing no-choice menu (allergies discussed in advance), which is taken in the conservatory dining room (fine silver and crystal on the tables). Herbs, fruit, vegetables and salad leaves come from the potager; bread, ice cream and sorbets are home made. Vegetarian options are provided 'as a matter of course'. Pre-dinner drinks and canapés, and coffee and petits fours after the meals are served in one of the two lounges. Five of the bedrooms are in the main house; three are in converted stables in the grounds. They are 'thoughtfully' equipped: a bone china tea set, Ordnance Survey map, history of the island. There are many outdoor pursuits on the island, which has a mountainous interior and pretty coastal villages. Good golfing on the island.

Glen Cloy, by Brodick
Isle of Arran KA27 8BY

T: 01770-302219
F: 01770-302068
E: enquiries@kilmichael.com
W: www.kilmichael.com

BEDROOMS: 8, 3 in converted stables (20 yds), 7 on ground floor, 4 self-catering cottages.
OPEN: Easter–Oct, restaurant closed Mon and Tues.
FACILITIES: 2 drawing rooms, dining room, free Wi-Fi (in Yellow drawing room), 4½-acre grounds (burn).
BACKGROUND MUSIC: light classical during meals.
LOCATION: 1 mile SW of village.
CHILDREN: not under 12.
DOGS: not allowed in public rooms.
CREDIT CARDS: MasterCard, Visa.
PRICES: [2014] per room B&B single £78–£98, double £130–£205. Set dinner £45. 1-night bookings sometimes refused Sat.

SEE ALSO SHORTLIST

POPPIES HOTEL AND RESTAURANT

NEW

In a small resort town within the Loch Lomond and The Trossachs national park, this small hotel is run in an 'unhurried but efficient fashion' by the owners, John and Susan Martin. 'They are around all the time, concerned and warm without ever being intrusive,' said a *Guide* inspector this year, who found *Poppies* 'a well-run hotel with an excellent restaurant'. The white-painted Victorian mansion faces west towards the River Teith and distant hills. It is set back from the main road ('efficient double glazing means we hardly noticed what traffic there is'). In the 'nicely decorated' dining room, chef Jim O'Reilly serves a 'tempting' menu of contemporary dishes. 'The food and presentation were first class: we enjoyed smoked haddock fishcakes; appetising main courses of pheasant and venison, well-dressed plates, just the right amount of food; plenty of vegetables.' A spacious first-floor bedroom was 'clean and warm; we slept well in an extremely comfortable bed; we enjoyed the view from two armchairs in front of the big bay window; a spotless modern bathroom'. One bedroom is on the ground floor. An 'excellent' breakfast is cooked to order.

25% DISCOUNT VOUCHERS

Leny Road
Callander FK17 8AL

T/F: 01877-330329
E: info@poppieshotel.com
W: www.poppieshotel.com

BEDROOMS: 9, 1 on ground floor.
OPEN: 20 Jan–23 Dec.
FACILITIES: Reception, bar, restaurant, free Wi-Fi, small front garden.
BACKGROUND MUSIC: in bar and restaurant.
LOCATION: ½ mile W of town centre.
CHILDREN: all ages welcomed.
DOGS: allowed in bedrooms, not in public rooms.
CREDIT CARDS: Amex, MasterCard, Visa.
PRICES: [2014] per room B&B single £50–£75, double £75–£115. D,B&B £20 added per person. Early evening menu £13.95–£17.95, à la carte £27.

DUNVALANREE IN CARRADALE

With 'breathtaking' views across Kilbrannan Sound to the Isle of Arran, this 'homely' hotel/restaurant stands 'at the end of the road' in a small fishing village on the Mull of Kintyre. It is run in a 'laid-back' manner by the owners, Alan and Alyson Milstead, whose 'endeavour to please their guests' is praised by readers. The simple bedrooms are individually done in neutral colours: a ground-floor room (fully equipped for disabled visitors) has French doors leading to a patio with a table and chairs. Two rooms share a bathroom. A large room at the front of the house has been decorated in Charles Rennie Mackintosh style. Alyson Milstead (the chef) is a founder member of the Scottish Seafood Trail (which suggests a West Coast culinary journey). Her modern table d'hôte menu might include crispy crab cakes, avocado and spring onion salsa; Kintyre sea bass in a parcel with fennel, dill and lime. Alan Milstead chats to guests while serving. Breakfast has freshly squeezed orange juice; 'thick toast'; eggs from the hotel's chickens.

Port Righ, Carradale
PA28 6SE

T: 01583-431226
E: book@dunvalanree.com
W: www.dunvalanree.com

BEDROOMS: 7, 1 on ground floor suitable for &.
OPEN: all year except Christmas.
FACILITIES: lounge, dining room, free Wi-Fi, ½-acre garden.
BACKGROUND MUSIC: jazz in dining room.
LOCATION: on edge of village 15 miles N of Campbeltown.
CHILDREN: all ages welcomed.
DOGS: allowed in bedrooms only.
CREDIT CARDS: MasterCard, Visa.
PRICES: per person B&B £53–£68, D,B&B £75–£90. Set menu £29.50.

CHIRNSIDE HALL

Built as a holiday retreat by an Edinburgh businessman, this late Georgian mansion in the Borders is run as a small hotel by the hands-on owners, Tessa and Christian Korsten. A 'natural front-of-house', Tessa Korsten provides a 'warm welcome' and creates a 'relaxing' atmosphere. 'This laid-back hotel is definitely run for the benefit of the resident,' says a returning visitor this year. 'She showed us to a large bedroom, with a fantastic view across to the Cheviot hills. To our joy, there was a house martins' nest in the corner of the window, with chicks and feeding parents.' Each of the bedrooms has a hospitality tray; a modern tiled bathroom. The public rooms have bold colours, rich fabrics. 'Renovation continues: the sofas (and there are a lot of them) were being re-covered when we stayed.' In the dining room, the modern cooking of the chef, Tim Holmes, is 'mouth-wateringly good; over three days, we were treated to line-caught cod and mackerel; rose deer and new season grouse'. Local produce is to the fore at breakfast, perhaps Eyemouth kippers. Christian Korsten organises shooting parties with 'good-humoured' beaters. (*GC*)

Chirnside, nr Duns
TD11 3LD

T: 01890-818219
F: 01890-818231
E: reception@chirnsidehallhotel.com
W: www.chirnsidehallhotel.com

BEDROOMS: 10.
OPEN: all year except Mar.
FACILITIES: 2 lounges, dining room, private dining room, free Wi-Fi, billiard room, fitness room, library/conference rooms, wedding facilities, 5-acre grounds, unsuitable for &.
BACKGROUND MUSIC: 'easy listening' and classical.
LOCATION: 1½ miles E of village, NE of Duns.
CHILDREN: all ages welcomed.
DOGS: not allowed in public rooms, unattended in bedrooms.
CREDIT CARDS: Amex, MasterCard, Visa.
PRICES: [2014] per person B&B single £100, double £90, D,B&B single £130, double £115.

THE COLONSAY

On a 'magical' island reached by ferry from Oban, this white-painted inn was built in 1750 on a hillside above the harbour to serve the locals and 'the rare visitor'. Renovated by the owners, Jane and Alex Howard, it is run in a 'relaxed, unpretentious' style that is 'just right for the setting'. The spacious public rooms are 'light and airy'; there are open fires, painted floorboards, deep sofas, books and games; the bar is the hub of island life and is popular with yachting visitors. In the dining room, which has a wood-burning stove, chef Robert Smyth uses vegetables and herbs from the garden for his 'simple but delicious' dishes on a menu that might have Colonsay oysters; Argyll lamb shank, red wine, cannellini beans. Children have their own menu. The bedrooms, which vary in size and outlook, are simply furnished, and have interesting fabrics. Pigs Paradise (named after cliffs on the western side of the island) is good for a family: a double room, an interconnecting bedroom/sitting room, and a bathroom. There are beaches, a golf course 'shared with the sheep'.

Isle of Colonsay
PA61 7YP

T: 01951-200316
F: 01951-200353
E: hotel@colonsayestate.co.uk
W: www.colonsayestate.co.uk

BEDROOMS: 9.
OPEN: Mar–Oct, Christmas, New Year, no check-in Mon and Sat.
FACILITIES: conservatory lounge, log room, bar, restaurant, free Wi-Fi, wedding facilities, accommodation unsuitable for &.
BACKGROUND MUSIC: 'easy listening' occasionally in bar.
LOCATION: 400 yds W of harbour.
CHILDREN: all ages welcomed.
DOGS: allowed in 2 bedrooms.
CREDIT CARDS: MasterCard, Visa.
PRICES: [2014] per room B&B £70–£145. D,B&B £30 added per person.

COUL HOUSE

'Good-humoured and enthusiastic', Susannah and Stuart Macpherson are the hands-on owners of this Georgian hunting lodge in woodland outside a small Highland village. Their manager, Chris McLeod, and the staff are 'friendly and professional'. It is a 'wonderful place to stay'. Refurbishment is 'a journey, not a destination', say the Macphersons, who have reinstated original features in the 'beautifully proportioned' public rooms. There's an open fire in the large hall/sitting room; the lounge has a fine Regency fireplace. In a splendid octagonal dining room, chef Garry Kenley serves 'outstanding' meals. Typical dishes on his contemporary Scottish menu might be noisettes of smoked chicken, savoury apple crumble; hickory-smoked salmon, red pesto pasta, shellfish tomato saffron broth. He cures and smokes meat and fish using traditional Highland methods; bread is home baked. The bedrooms vary in size and shape. The owners concede that some bathrooms are dated; this year a master bedroom has been given a modern bathroom. Breakfast has 'generous' cooked dishes. Children are welcomed, and *Coul House* is dog-friendly. (*VF, and others*)

Contin
by Strathpeffer
IV14 9ES

T: 01997-421487
F: 01997-421945
E: stay@coulhouse.com
W: www.coulhouse.com

BEDROOMS: 21, 4 on ground floor.
OPEN: all year except 22–26 Dec.
FACILITIES: ramp, bar, lounge, restaurant, conference/wedding facilities, 8-acre garden (children's play area, 9-hole pitch and putt).
BACKGROUND MUSIC: mixed in bar, classical in restaurant.
LOCATION: 17 miles NW of Inverness.
CHILDREN: all ages welcomed, discounts up to age 15.
DOGS: allowed (£5 per day).
CREDIT CARDS: Amex, MasterCard, Visa.
PRICES: per room B&B £100–£295. À la carte £32.50.

CRINAN HOTEL

In a 'sensational setting' overlooking the Crinan
Canal basin and the Sound of Mull, this white-
painted hotel has been run for 45 years by Nick
and Frances Ryan. The building is filled with
contemporary art. Frances Ryan (the painter
Frances Macdonald) displays her own work
(and that of her son, Ross Ryan) throughout; she
leads painting holidays (by arrangement) and
has started a 'sleep with art' project. Some
bedrooms, each of which is named after an
artist, have a display of appropriate original
work. All bedrooms have the view. While some
visitors find the decor in the public areas 'tired',
others like the informal atmosphere and the
friendly welcome. There are linen cloths and
fresh flowers in the ground-floor *Westward*
restaurant, where the chef, Gregor Bara, uses
fish landed on the quay in front of the hotel for
his 'excellent dishes, perhaps whole langoustines,
garlic mayonnaise. *Loch 16*, a rooftop restaurant,
opens with the same menu on Friday and
Saturday evenings from June to September. The
Seafood Bar, popular with the yachting
fraternity, has a carte (with some meat dishes).

25% DISCOUNT VOUCHERS

Crinan
by Lochgilphead
PA31 8SR

T: 01546-830261
F: 01546-830292
E: reservations@crinanhotel.com
W: www.crinanhotel.com

BEDROOMS: 20.
OPEN: all year except Christmas.
FACILITIES: lift, ramps, 2 lounges,
gallery bar, seafood bar, 2
restaurants, coffee shop, free Wi-Fi
in public areas, treatment room
(health and beauty), wedding
facilities, patio, ¼-acre garden.
BACKGROUND MUSIC: none.
LOCATION: village centre,
waterfront.
CHILDREN: all ages welcomed.
DOGS: not allowed in restaurants.
CREDIT CARDS: MasterCard, Visa.
PRICES: [2014] per room B&B
£190–£260, D,B&B £260–£320. Set
dinner (restaurant and *Loch 16*) £35,
à la carte (*Seafood Bar*) £21.

THE THREE CHIMNEYS AND THE HOUSE OVER-BY

César award in 2001

'Our menu is our story,' say Shirley and Eddie Spear. Their acclaimed restaurant-with-rooms attracts food lovers to this remote setting by Loch Dunvegan in the north-west of Skye. Their chef/director, Michael Smith, works in 'collaboration' with island producers for his 'outstanding' cooking – on a three-course dinner menu and an Isle of Skye showcase (to be taken by the whole table). The menu, punctuated by small dishes ('today's wee taste' and 'another wee taste'), might include Talisker-glazed Boer goat, Cairnsmore pastilla, spiced couscous; half Moonen Bay lobster and squid, Anna potatoes, tarragon butter. Visitors enjoy the lack of pretension and the absence of rules: 'Staff are considerate, friendly and consistently knowledgeable, up for a "chat" whenever we wanted, but discreet and thoughtful when we simply wanted peaceful contemplation of the amazing food and location.' The spacious bedrooms, in *The House Over-By* (next door), were refurbished this year as were the public areas. They have a tea/coffee tray with fresh milk, home-made tablet and shortbread. (*HV*)

Colbost, Dunvegan
Isle of Skye IV55 8ZT

T: 01470-511258
F: 01470-511358
E: eatandstay@threechimneys.co.uk
W: www.threechimneys.co.uk

BEDROOMS: 6, all on ground floor in separate building, 1 suitable for &.
OPEN: all year except 1 Dec–22 Jan, restaurant closed for lunch Nov–Feb and Sun Oct–May.
FACILITIES: ramps, 3 public rooms, free Wi-Fi, garden on loch.
BACKGROUND MUSIC: in lounge in evenings.
LOCATION: 4 miles W of Dunvegan.
CHILDREN: no under-5s at lunch, no under-8s at dinner, tea at 5 pm.
DOGS: only guide dogs allowed.
CREDIT CARDS: Amex, MasterCard, Visa.
PRICES: [2014] per room B&B £345, D,B&B (27 Oct–30 Nov) £385. Set lunch £28.50–£37, set dinner £60–£90.

BEALACH HOUSE

🏆*César award in 2009*

The only dwelling in Salachan Glen, this former farmhouse is reached by a 'challenging' mile and a half of forestry track. Porsche owners might struggle but *Guide* readers love the 'fabulous' setting and appreciate the 'warm welcome' from the owners, Jim and Hilary McFadyen. Guests can sit by a wood-burning stove in the lounge, take in the views from the conservatory, study the guides and maps of the area, or finish the jigsaw puzzle on a table. Dinner is taken communally in the small dining room ('we were entertained by our fellow guests'). Hilary McFadyen, 'an excellent cook', serves a short daily-changing menu of modern dishes like baked haggis, creamy whisky and onion sauce; carrot and pecan nut pasty, mildy curried apple sauce (there is always a vegetarian option). The bedrooms are not large but are well equipped (a tea and coffee tray, fresh chilled milk on the landing, a decanter of whisky). Bathrooms have a power shower (one also has a bath). Visitors are encouraged to walk in the grounds where they might spot a deer or a golden eagle.

Salachan Glen
Duror PA38 4BW

T: 01631-740298
E: enquiries@bealachhouse.co.uk
W: www.bealachhouse.co.uk

BEDROOMS: 3.
OPEN: Feb–Nov, dining room closed Mon evening.
FACILITIES: lounge, conservatory, dining room, free Wi-Fi, 8-acre grounds, unsuitable for ♿.
BACKGROUND MUSIC: none.
LOCATION: 2 miles S of Duror, off A828.
CHILDREN: not under 14.
DOGS: not allowed.
CREDIT CARDS: MasterCard, Visa.
PRICES: per room [2014] B&B £90–£110. Set dinner £30.

EDINBURGH

Map 5:D2

ARDMOR HOUSE

In a quiet street opposite Pilrig Park, this 'immaculate' B&B is 'mainly looked after' by the owner, Robin Jack, 'with a little help from my partner, Barry, and our lovely team'. 'We were very warmly welcomed by Robin,' said a visitor, who thought *Ardmor House* a 'good and well-placed find' in Edinburgh. The house has been restored throughout and 'tastefully' decorated in modern style. The high-ceilinged bedrooms have a neutral background livened by bold colours. They are well equipped: chocolate bars with the tea tray; a flat-screen television and a digital radio with an iPod dock; extras can be provided. An 'excellent' breakfast has a help-yourself buffet with yogurt, fresh fruit and juices, cereals, home-made oatcakes; 'limitless' bread for do-it-yourself toasting. The owners 'go to some lengths to source local produce' for the cooked choices, which include smoked bacon, potato waffles and maple syrup ('popular with our American guests'). The free street parking is appreciated: buses to Princes Street run from the front door or you can walk in about 20 minutes. The resident miniature schnauzer/poodle, Vera, may greet visitors. (*ID*)

74 Pilrig Street
Edinburgh EH6 5AS

T/F: 0131-554 4944
E: info@ardmorhouse.com
W: www.ardmorhouse.com

BEDROOMS: 5, 1 on ground floor.
OPEN: all year.
FACILITIES: breakfast room, free Wi-Fi.
BACKGROUND MUSIC: classical in breakfast room.
LOCATION: Leith, 1 mile NE of city centre.
CHILDREN: all ages welcomed.
DOGS: allowed by arrangement.
CREDIT CARDS: Diners, MasterCard, Visa.
PRICES: per room B&B £85–£170. 1-night bookings may be refused at weekends in peak season.

SEE ALSO SHORTLIST

THE BONHAM

In a quiet square near the West End, this conversion of three Victorian town houses is 'perfectly placed for the city, just five minutes' walk from Princes Street'. It is managed by David Barkley for Peter Taylor's Town House Collection. 'The staff are kind, friendly and helpful; the bedrooms are luxurious and well priced,' says a returning visitor this year. The buildings, which once housed a medical clinic and later became a university hall of residence, have 'interesting architectural details'; a permanent collection of modern Scottish art is displayed throughout. In the dining room, which has a minimalist decor ('to help you focus on the food'), the chef, Maciej Szymik, serves seasonal menus of modern dishes like rare beef bavette, pickled onions; North Sea cod, garam masala, aubergine purée, brandade. The well-equipped bedrooms have bright colours, textured fabrics. Some rooms have a bay window with views across to the Firth of Forth. One has a freestanding Edwardian copper bath. Breakfast is 'generous'. The (free) secure car park is 'a bonus'. Children are welcomed (cots and high chairs provided). (*Christian Bartoschek*)

35 Drumsheugh Gardens
Edinburgh EH3 7RN

T: 0131-226 6050
F: 0131-226 6080
E: reception@thebonham.com
W: www.thebonham.com

BEDROOMS: 49, 1 suitable for ♿.
OPEN: all year.
FACILITIES: reception lounge, bar, restaurant, free Wi-Fi, wedding facilities.
BACKGROUND MUSIC: in public areas all day.
LOCATION: central, free parking.
CHILDREN: all ages welcomed.
DOGS: not allowed in public rooms, additional charge in bedrooms.
CREDIT CARDS: all major cards.
PRICES: [2014] per room B&B £100–£400. D,B&B £25 added per person, à la carte £30. 1-night bookings sometimes refused Sat, Christmas/New Year.

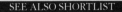

SEE ALSO SHORTLIST

THE HOWARD

'We were pampered,' say visitors to this luxury hotel (part of the Edinburgh Collection), which lays on a comprehensive butler service. Butlers 'will take care of everything' (says the hotel), from car parking, unpacking (taking items a way for pressing 'if they think it is needed'), to in-room dining. The service is 'thoughtful and attentive'. Small enough to feel like 'your own Georgian town house' (according to a recent visitor), the *Howard* is furnished in period style, with rich fabrics, oil paintings. 'Our room was spacious and well appointed; a most comfortable bed; particularly good lighting in the bathroom.' There is 'no tray of do-it-yourself sachets' in the room: instead, a butler will bring leaf tea (chosen from an extensive menu) and 'home-baked shortbread' on request. In the *Atholl* restaurant, which has seating for only 14 people ('don't forget to book'), William Poncelet serves a menu of sophisticated dishes like woodland pigeon, beetroot and orange relish; steamed turbot, cauliflower beignet, Mayan gold potato mash. Breakfast has a wide choice of cooked dishes. Private whisky tastings can be arranged. (*RO, and others*)

34 Great King Street
Edinburgh EH3 6QH

T: 0131-557 3500
F: 0131-557 6515
E: reserve@thehoward.com
W: www.thehoward.com

BEDROOMS: 18.
OPEN: all year.
FACILITIES: drawing room, restaurant, free Wi-Fi, wedding facilities, small garden.
BACKGROUND MUSIC: 'minimal' classical in drawing room, restaurant.
LOCATION: central.
CHILDREN: all ages welcomed.
DOGS: only guide dogs allowed.
CREDIT CARDS: all major cards.
PRICES: [2014] per room B&B from £134. Tasting menu £55, à la carte £40. 1-night bookings refused weekends.

SEE ALSO SHORTLIST

MILLERS64

On a 'relatively quiet' street off Leith Walk, this Victorian town house has been given a 'stylish' make-over by sisters Shona and Louise Clelland. They run it 'with warmth and humour' as an upmarket B&B. 'The decor, light grey and beige with bold black furniture and flamboyant splashes of bright colour, gives it a chic but never cold feel.' A front-facing bedroom had 'high ceilings, stunning Victorian cornices, a big bay window; a dramatic black ceiling lamp above a plush king-size bed; lots of storage; a sofa by the bay window'. Rooms are well equipped: home-made fudge and shortbread biscuits with the tea tray ('replenished daily'); an iPod docking station; bathrobes. Breakfast is taken at a communal table in a room with sofas, newspapers and magazines. 'Louise baked something new every morning (gingerbread or scones)'; porridge with fruit compote; miniature pots of fruit and cereal; jams and marmalade are home made; a wide choice of cooked dishes. The city centre is a 20-minute walk (there's a bus stop outside the door). Guests are sent a selection of favourite cafés and restaurants 'we like to frequent'.

64 Pilrig Street
Edinburgh EH6 5AS

T/F: 0131-454 3666
E: louise@millers64.com
W: www.millers64.com

BEDROOMS: 3.
OPEN: all year.
FACILITIES: dining room, patio, free Wi-Fi, unsuitable for &.
BACKGROUND MUSIC: none.
LOCATION: Leith.
CHILDREN: not under 12.
DOGS: not allowed.
CREDIT CARDS: none.
PRICES: per room B&B £95–£150. 1-night bookings refused weekends, min. 3-night stay Christmas/New Year, during Festival.

SEE ALSO SHORTLIST

23 MAYFIELD

A short walk from the city centre, Ross Birnie's detached Victorian house has 'an immediately welcoming, well-cared-for appearance'. The 'sympathetic' host has restored the house 'with meticulous attention to detail', said *Guide* inspectors. 'Although some of the colours might appear sombre, great care has been taken to match the original Victorian shades and textures; similarly, the furniture might seem old-fashioned, but it is of good quality and well suited to the house. Skill and empathy have guided the refurbishment.' A spacious club room has original cornicing, dark panelling; leather sofas and chairs; a library of rare books (and popular paperbacks). There's an honesty bar, a Georgian chessboard, a guest computer. The bedrooms have panelled walls, hand-carved mahogany furniture; two rooms have a four-poster bed; another room can accommodate a family. A ground-floor room has 'a large bed; a tea tray hidden in the capacious wardrobe where we found bathrobes, extra blankets; an excellent walk-in power shower in the small bathroom'. In a well-proportioned dining room, breakfast has 'outstanding' dishes of the day. The smoked herring was particularly enjoyed this year.

23 Mayfield Gardens
Edinburgh EH9 2BX

T: 0131-667 5806
E: info@23mayfield.co.uk
W: www.23mayfield.co.uk

BEDROOMS: 8, 1 on ground floor.
OPEN: all year except Christmas.
FACILITIES: club room, dining room, free Wi-Fi, ½-acre garden, patio (hot tub), unsuitable for &.
BACKGROUND MUSIC: 'chill-out' in club room, dining room.
LOCATION: 1 mile S of city centre.
CHILDREN: all ages welcomed.
DOGS: not allowed.
CREDIT CARDS: MasterCard, Visa.
PRICES: per room B&B £80–£180. 1-night bookings usually refused weekends.

SEE ALSO SHORTLIST

EDENWATER HOUSE

With lovely views over the pretty garden to the Eden Water, this old stone manse in a hamlet near Kelso is run as a rural retreat by the owners, Jacqui and Jeff Kelly. 'It is like staying with friends in their comfortable country house,' said a recent visitor. Jeff Kelly manages the front-of-house ('happy to chat or not as you wish'); his wife cooks a 'superb' four-course meal, served on three nights a week in the candlelit dining room. Typical dishes: chicken consommée with manzanilla; paupiettes of sole, smoked salmon mousseline; roast breast of duck, duck liver crouton. From June to August, food- and wine-tasting nights are held in the *Wine Cellar*; d'Vine weekends are organised monthly with one dinner in each room. Two of the 'elegant, spacious' bedrooms have a 'wonderful outlook', facing the river which winds through fields to the Cheviots. The Church Room has a king-size bed and a shower room; the Cheviot Room has a bath and shower. The West Room, which has twin beds, faces the setting sun. In the morning, a 'substantial and varied breakfast' is served.

Ednam, nr Kelso
TD5 7QL

T: 01573-224070
E: winendine@
edenwaterhouse.co.uk
W: www.edenwaterhouse.co.uk

BEDROOMS: 3, plus a self-catering apartment.
OPEN: Mar–Nov, dining room closed Sun–Wed.
FACILITIES: drawing room, TV room, study, dining room, wine-tasting room, free Wi-Fi, 5-acre grounds, unsuitable for &.
BACKGROUND MUSIC: none.
LOCATION: 2 miles N of Kelso on B6461.
CHILDREN: not under 10.
DOGS: not allowed.
CREDIT CARDS: MasterCard, Visa.
PRICES: [2014] per person B&B £60–£85, D,B&B £85–£105. Set dinner £40.

ISLE OF ERISKA HOTEL, SPA AND ISLAND

César award in 2007

As much a resort as a luxury hotel (Relais & Châteaux), the Buchanan-Smith family's baronial mansion stands on a private island at the mouth of Loch Creran. Reached by a rattling bridge, the island has a nine-hole golf course and a driving range, a sports hall with badminton and table tennis and indoor putting, and a spa with a swimming pool. Beppo Buchanan-Smith is the flamboyant host, welcoming guests, serving drinks. In the formal dining room, chef Ross Stovold uses West Coast produce (with vegetables and herbs from the island's redeveloped gardens) for his 'superb' daily-changing menus of dishes like Mallaig-landed halibut, seaweed-braised potatoes, samphire mayonnaise. Lighter meals can be taken on a veranda. The largest bedrooms are spa suites in the grounds; each has a private terrace with a hot tub, and a lounge or conservatory. 'Comfortable' main-house rooms have an 'elegant bathroom'. Two self-catering Hilltop Reserves were being completed on a bluff above the main house as the *Guide* went to press. (*Susan Chait*)

Benderloch, Eriska
by Oban PA37 1SD

T: 01631-720371
F: 01631-720531
E: office@eriska-hotel.co.uk
W: www.eriska-hotel.co.uk

BEDROOMS: 25, including 5 spa suites, 2 garden cottages, 2 Hilltop Reserves, some on ground floor.
OPEN: all year except 3–30 Jan.
FACILITIES: ramp, 5 public rooms, free Wi-Fi, leisure centre, swimming pool (17 by 6 metres), gym, sauna, treatments, wedding facilities, tennis, 350-acre grounds, 9-hole golf course.
BACKGROUND MUSIC: none.
LOCATION: 12 miles N of Oban.
CHILDREN: all ages welcomed, but no under-5s in leisure centre, and special evening meal arrangements.
DOGS: not allowed in public rooms or in spa suites.
CREDIT CARDS: Amex, MasterCard, Visa.
PRICES: [2014] per person B&B £175, D,B&B £185–£225. Set dinner £50. 2-night min. stay. 1-night bookings sometimes refused.

THE GRANGE

Within walking distance from the town centre, this 'gracious' white-painted Victorian Gothic house is run as a B&B by the owners, Joan and John Campbell. It stands in a 'delightful' garden with lawns and well-maintained borders; lovely views across Loch Linnhe. Joan Campbell is 'charming and helpful', happy to assist with restaurant bookings and to suggest walks. Visitors are given a 'warm' greeting over tea and home-made shortbread in the lounge, which has a log fire, antiques, flowers from the garden. The three bedrooms are lavishly equipped: a decanter of sherry, apples, binoculars, an iron and ironing board; towels wrapped in white ribbon. The Turret Room has a window seat with garden and loch views and a Louis XV king-size bed. Rob Roy has a colonial-style bed, 'plenty of drawer and wardrobe space'; a bath and a large walk-in shower. A garden room has a sleeping area and, through an arch, a sitting room with chaise longue and armchairs; a pedestal bath and walk-in shower. Breakfast, ordered the evening before, has an 'excellent' fresh fruit platter; 'interesting' dishes like Scotch pancakes with bacon and maple syrup.

Grange Road
Fort William PH33 6JF

T: 01397-705516
E: info@thegrange-scotland.co.uk
W: www.grangefortwilliam.com

BEDROOMS: 3.
OPEN: Mar–Nov.
FACILITIES: lounge, breakfast room, free Wi-Fi, 1-acre garden, unsuitable for &.
BACKGROUND MUSIC: none.
LOCATION: edge of town.
CHILDREN: not under 16.
DOGS: not allowed.
CREDIT CARDS: MasterCard, Visa (only to hold room).
PRICES: [2014] per person B&B £65–£70. 1-night bookings sometimes refused.

SEE ALSO SHORTLIST

INVERLOCHY CASTLE

In a splendid setting in the foothills of Ben Nevis, this baronial mansion (built on the site of a 13th-century castle) is now a luxury hotel (Relais & Châteaux), part of the small ICMI group. The building is 'impressive'; a huge hall/lounge has enormous chandeliers and a 'stunning' painted ceiling. Jane Watson is the 'charming' manager; visitors consistently praise the 'courteous and efficient service'; guests are met at the door, cars unpacked; there is no lift but bags are carried to the bedroom. 'Comfortable and spacious', the rooms are individually designed; they are generously equipped and have mountain views. A dress code (jacket and tie for men) is required in the three formal dining rooms at dinner. The chef, Philip Carnegie, has a *Michelin* star for his 'creative' cooking; his dinner menu might include caramelised scallops, onion confit, Puy lentils; stuffed saddle of French-farmed rabbit, savoy cabbage, white beans. Children are welcomed (though the youngest are not allowed in public rooms after 6 pm); there is a games room and many outdoor activities. High teas and babysitting can be arranged.

Torlundy
Fort William PH33 6SN

T: 01397-702177
F: 01397-702953
E: info@inverlochy.co.uk
W: www.inverlochycastlehotel.com

BEDROOMS: 17, plus 2 in Gate Lodge.
OPEN: all year.
FACILITIES: Great Hall, drawing room, dining room, wedding facilities, free Wi-Fi, 600-acre estate (tennis), only restaurant suitable for &.
BACKGROUND MUSIC: pianist or harpist in Great Hall in evening.
LOCATION: 4 miles NE of Fort William.
CHILDREN: all ages welcomed, young children not allowed in public areas after 6 pm.
DOGS: not in public rooms.
CREDIT CARDS: Amex, MasterCard, Visa.
PRICES: per room B&B £335–£620, D,B&B £480–£660. Set dinner £67, tasting menu £85.

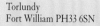

SEE ALSO SHORTLIST

GRASSHOPPERS

It will not be everybody's idea of a *Guide* hotel, but Barry Munn's modern city space appealed to inspectors who liked the 'spare and comfortable style' and the 'incredible value'. Beside the city's Central Station, it is a conversion of the sixth floor of the former Caledonian Railway head office. The entry might be 'less than salubrious' (a lift accessed between two shops) but you step out into a smart contemporary area with oak flooring and purpose-built furniture. The bedrooms, in different shapes and sizes, are styled on clean Scandinavian lines, with bright colours. A small room was 'not oppressive thanks to the high ceiling'; it had big Victorian windows (which can be opened – some traffic hum); 'a small but well-designed shower room'. Arriving guests are offered complimentary tea and coffee with cakes (and other treats). A light supper is served from Monday to Thursday in *The Kitchen*, an 'internal but surprisingly cheerful space' with a mix of small and large (shared) wooden tables. A 'good' breakfast has a buffet; eggs cooked to order. Meals can be taken in the bedroom.

6th floor Caledonian Chambers
87 Union Street
Glasgow G1 3TA

T: 0141-222 2666
F: 0141-248 3641
E: info@grasshoppersglasgow.com
W: www.grasshoppersglasgow.com

BEDROOMS: 29.
OPEN: all year, restaurant closed Fri–Sun.
FACILITIES: breakfast/supper room, free Wi-Fi, unsuitable for &.
BACKGROUND MUSIC: none.
LOCATION: by Central Station.
CHILDREN: all ages welcomed.
DOGS: allowed.
CREDIT CARDS: all major cards.
PRICES: per room B&B £70–£125. Set menus £13.50–£16.50.

SEE ALSO SHORTLIST

GLENFINNAN Highland

GLENFINNAN HOUSE HOTEL

In an 'idyllic' setting on the shore of Loch Shiel, the MacFarlane family's Victorian mansion is run as a 'lovely traditional hotel' by the 'pleasant' managers, Manja and Duncan Gibson. Guests 'arrive to the sound of a tumbling stream and the scent of a log fire'. 'As returning guests, we were welcomed with a box of chocolates and a hand-written note,' say visitors in 2014. There are fresh flowers in the hall and the drawing room. Many of the paintings in the panelled rooms have a Jacobite theme including an impressive portrayal of the 1745 rising at Glenfinnan (a monument to Bonnie Prince Charlie stands across the loch). Traditional music is often played in the bar, where meals can be taken off the same menu as in the more formal dining room. Duncan Gibson is the chef: there is 'plenty of choice' on his 'very good' menus. 'A venison-tasting platter was especially good.' 'We were well looked after in a modest but friendly Highland way.' No key to the 'comfortably furnished' bedrooms ('we think of this as a Highland home'). Packed lunches can be provided for the many walks in the area. (*Alan and Edwina Williams*)

25% DISCOUNT VOUCHERS

Glenfinnan
by Fort William PH37 4LT

T: 01397-722235
F: 01397-722249
E: availability@glenfinnanhouse.com
W: www.glenfinnanhouse.com

BEDROOMS: 14.
OPEN: 20 Mar–1 Nov.
FACILITIES: ramps, drawing room, playroom, bar, restaurant, wedding facilities, free Wi-Fi, 1-acre grounds, playground, unsuitable for &.
BACKGROUND MUSIC: Scottish in bar and restaurant.
LOCATION: 15 miles NW of Fort William.
CHILDREN: all ages welcomed.
DOGS: not in restaurant.
CREDIT CARDS: Amex, MasterCard, Visa.
PRICES: [2014] per room B& double £135–£230. À la carte £24–£44.

THE PRINCE'S HOUSE

At the head of Loch Shiel ('one of the most remote and beautiful areas in the Western Highlands'), this white-painted former coaching inn is managed in hands-on style by owners Kieron and Ina Kelly. 'She is welcoming and attentive,' say regular correspondents in 2014. In the oldest part of the building, with wood panelling and original works by Scottish and French artists, Kieron Kelly serves a seasonal four-course dinner menu. This must be booked in advance. Typical dishes: hot smoked breast of goose, candied shallot; West Coast scallop, chorizo, potato pancake. There's a blackboard menu with much choice in the 'spacious' bar, which has a vaulted pine ceiling, antlers on the walls; a view of the burn that runs alongside. 'We cure our herring, bake our own bread and make our own ice cream,' say the hosts. The best of the traditionally furnished bedrooms are at the front: the largest, which has a Jacobean four-poster bed, is equipped with bathrobes, a decanter of sherry. 'Our excellent room had a very comfortable double bed, lots of storage space and a good bathroom.'

25% DISCOUNT VOUCHERS

Glenfinnan
by Fort William PH37 4LT

T: 01397-722246
E: princeshouse@glenfinnan.co.uk
W: www.glenfinnan.co.uk

BEDROOMS: 9.
OPEN: Mar–Oct, New Year, restaurant open Easter–end Sept.
FACILITIES: lounge/bar, bar, dining room, free Wi-Fi in public areas, small front lawn, only bar suitable for &.
BACKGROUND MUSIC: classical in restaurant, contemporary in bar.
LOCATION: 15 miles NW of Fort William.
CHILDREN: all ages welcomed.
DOGS: allowed in bar.
CREDIT CARDS: Amex, MasterCard, Visa.
PRICES: [2014] per person B&B £60–£80, D,B&B £100–£120. Set menu £43.50.

GRANTOWN-ON-SPEY Highland Map 5:C2

CULDEARN HOUSE

Set back from the road beside woodland on the edge of this Speyside town, this 'four square Scottish dwelling house' is run as a small hotel by William and Sonia Marshall. 'It is clear that they take tremendous pride in their hotel/home,' says a visitor this year. 'They deserve congratulations for the standard of cleanliness and tidiness.' Guests gather in the lounge for pre-dinner drinks ('a nice opportunity to chat'). Sonia Marshall cooks a four-course dinner on a daily-changing menu which might include tower of mango and melon, raspberry coulis; roast breast of duck, Grand Marnier glaze. 'Good if not fine dining; plain potatoes, unadorned steamed vegetables.' For a post-dinner drink, William Marshall can suggest a suitable local whisky (he has more than 50 on offer). 'Our bedroom at the side of the house was immaculate; beautiful wallpaper and wall hangings; a pristine bathroom.' Breakfast has 'excellent' poached haddock and kippers. The Marshalls are ever-present: 'This must be a labour of love; it is a well-run and caring operation.' There are forest walks and distilleries to visit. (*David Birnie*)

Woodlands Terrace
Grantown-on-Spey PH26 3JU

T: 01479-872106
F: 01479-873641
E: enquiries@culdearn.com
W: www.culdearn.com

BEDROOMS: 6, 1 on ground floor.
OPEN: all year.
FACILITIES: lounge, dining room, free Wi-Fi, ¾-acre garden.
BACKGROUND MUSIC: pre-dinner classical in lounge.
LOCATION: edge of town.
CHILDREN: not under 10.
DOGS: only guide dogs allowed.
CREDIT CARDS: Diners, MasterCard, Visa.
PRICES: [2014] per person B&B £70–£82, D,B&B £100–£145. À la carte £43.

SEE ALSO SHORTLIST

GORDON'S   `NEW`

In a village near the North Sea coast, this smartly painted terrace house (dating to the 1800s) is run as a restaurant-with-rooms by Gordon and Maria Watson and their son, Garry. A trusted correspondent, who enjoyed a 'truly memorable meal', was impressed by a 'hugely successful' renovation which was completed in early 2014. The restaurant has been redecorated in sage and grape colours, with 'wonderfully tasteful' lamps and central chandeliers; 'the small lounge has a purple tone which is continued in the bedrooms'. Garry Watson is increasingly taking over the cooking mantle from his father (his mother runs front-of-house). 'We enjoyed lightly curried celeriac soup with Arbroath smokie; moreish home-baked bread; saddle of venison had exquisite colour and tenderness. This is dining to rival the best.' The bedrooms have contemporary furnishings, bold wallpaper, a monsoon shower in the bathroom. The largest room has thistle-patterned wallpaper, a high ceiling with decorative corcining; a 'beautifully tiled' bathroom with a roll-top bath and a separate shower. A room in the courtyard has a king-size bed, decor in terracotta and stone. (*Robert Gower*)

Main Street
Inverkeilor DD11 5RN

T: 01241-830364
E: gordonsrest@aol.com
W: www.gordonsrestaurant.co.uk

BEDROOMS: 5, 1 on ground floor.
OPEN: all year except Jan, restaurant open to residents only on Mon.
FACILITIES: lounge, restaurant, free Wi-Fi, small garden.
BACKGROUND MUSIC: none.
LOCATION: in village.
CHILDREN: not under 12.
DOGS: not allowed.
CREDIT CARDS: MasterCard, Visa.
PRICES: [2014] per room B&B £110–£150. Set dinner £55.

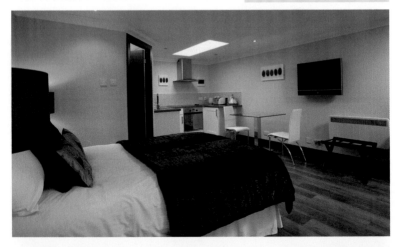

KILBERRY INN

♀ *César award in 2010*

'A very relaxing place', this small red-roofed restaurant-with-rooms is reached by a single-track road through 'wild and magical' scenery. It is run by David Wilson (the 'witty' host, 'who welcomed us like old friends') and Clare Johnson, 'who still cooks a mean feast'. He dispenses a cocktail of the day and supervises the 'attentive' service in the beamed bar/dining room (there is a small second dining room). She has a *Michelin* Bib Gourmand for her short seasonal menu: 'We enjoyed mussels with chorizo; hake with tomato and pepper sauce; ice cream and chocolate brownie sundae.' Each of the 'simple but comfortable' bedrooms, around the back in 'individual little cottages', has its own hall. 'Our room, Arran, usually given to dog owners, has a sitting room and a shower room.' Rooms contain 'an interesting selection of books'. There is 'a Mediterranean courtyard-style garden, with raised beds containing thyme, seasonal flowers and outdoor seating'. Breakfast has a choice of three fruit juices; toast and soda bread with home-made preserves; Sleepy Hollow smoked salmon with scrambled eggs; a tattie scone with the full cooked. (*GC*)

Kilberry, by Tarbert
PA29 6YD

T: 01880-770223
E: relax@kilberryinn.com
W: www.kilberryinn.com

BEDROOMS: 5, all on ground floor.
OPEN: Tues–Sun 14 Mar–1 Nov, weekends only Nov and Dec, New Year.
FACILITIES: bar/dining room, smaller dining room, no Wi-Fi (Kilberry is in a 'not spot').
BACKGROUND MUSIC: in larger dining room, lunch and dinner.
LOCATION: 16 miles NW of Tarbert, on B8024.
CHILDREN: no under-12s.
DOGS: only in one bedroom, not in public rooms.
CREDIT CARDS: MasterCard, Visa.
PRICES: [2014] per room D,B&B £210. 1-night bookings 'not often' refused.

ARDANAISEIG

In a remote setting on Loch Awe, reached by miles of twisting, single-track road, this late Georgian manor was built by William Burn, the founder of the Scottish baronial style of architecture. The High Victorian decor has been heightened by the furnishing provided by the owner, antique dealer Bennie Gray. Marcel Wassen is the manager; Cornel Uys is now the chef. They have changed the style of dining, introducing an à la carte menu in the candlelit dining room (with a nine-course tasting menu also available). Vegetables, herbs and fruit come from the kitchen garden, and wild food is foraged from the forest for modern dishes like risotto of cèpe, herbs and Parmesan; charred sirloin of Aberdeen beef, potato purée, wild mushrooms. As the *Guide* went to press, a new bistro was due to open in the cellar, serving a simpler all-day menu. Open fires burn in the long drawing room, which has panelled walls painted in mottled gold, and in the more intimate library bar. The bedrooms have bold colours, opulent furnishings. Kedgeree is among the dishes in an 'excellent' breakfast.

Kilchrenan
by Taynuilt PA35 1HE

T: 01866-833333
F: 01866-833222
E: hello@ardanaiseig.com
W: www.ardanaiseig.com

BEDROOMS: 18, some on ground floor, 1 in boatshed, 1 self-catering cottage.
OPEN: all year.
FACILITIES: drawing room, library/bar, games room, restaurant, free Wi-Fi, wedding facilities, 360-acre grounds on loch (open-air theatre, tennis, bathing, fishing).
BACKGROUND MUSIC: none.
LOCATION: 4 miles E of Kilchrenan.
CHILDREN: all ages welcomed, but no under-10s at dinner.
DOGS: allowed in bedrooms (£20 charge) and drawing room, not in bar or dining room.
CREDIT CARDS: all major cards.
PRICES: [2014] room £185–£330. Breakfast £16.50, à la carte £40, tasting menu £60.

KILLIECRANKIE Perth and Kinross

Map 5:D2

KILLIECRANKIE HOTEL

♀*César award in 2011*

In expansive wooded grounds at the entrance to the Pass of Killiecrankie, this white dower house is run as a small hotel by the 'engaging' owner Henrietta Fergusson. 'Wonderful: the quality of the accommodation, the food and Henrietta's highly efficient management style make this our favourite Scottish venue,' say returning visitors this year. The long-serving chef, Mark Easton, cooks 'exceptional' modern dishes on his table d'hôte menu, perhaps warm salad of wild mushrooms and walnuts, crumbled Stilton; crispy-skinned sea bream, pea and shallot tortellini. The service, by a young tartan-clad staff, is 'elegant without being too formal'. Light suppers can be taken in the conservatory bar. This year, the sitting room has been extended and several bedrooms have been refurbished. The rooms, each of which has its own character, are decorated in rich colours and fabrics; they have fresh flowers, good coffee and shortbread on the hospitality tray; a hot-water bottle is placed in the bed at evening turn-down. Breakfast, served on tables with fine linen and crockery, has freshly squeezed juice, porridge, 'good hot dishes'. (*Alan and Edwina Williams*)

Killiecrankie
by Pitlochry PH16 5LG

T: 01796-473220
F: 01796-472451
E: enquiries@killiecrankiehotel.co.uk
W: www.killiecrankiehotel.co.uk

BEDROOMS: 10, 2 on ground floor.
OPEN: 12 Mar–3 Jan.
FACILITIES: ramp, sitting room, bar with conservatory, dining room, breakfast conservatory, free Wi-Fi, 4½-acre grounds.
BACKGROUND MUSIC: none.
LOCATION: hamlet 3 miles W of Pitlochry.
CHILDREN: all ages welcomed.
DOGS: not allowed in eating areas, some bedrooms.
CREDIT CARDS: MasterCard, Visa.
PRICES: [2014] per person D,B&B £110–£145. Set dinner £42. 1-night bookings sometimes refused weekends.

KINGUSSIE Highland

Map 5:C2

THE CROSS AT KINGUSSIE

In a town within the Cairngorms national park, Derek and Celia Kitchingman ('open and friendly') run this 'interesting' former tweed mill as a restaurant-with-rooms. The award-winning modern cooking of their young chef, Ross Sutherland, is praised by readers and a *Guide* inspector alike. In the white-walled dining room his 'beautifully presented' dishes can be taken off a short three-course set menu or a six-course tasting menu. Typical dishes: beetroot, walnuts, goat's cheese snow; fillet of beef, oxtail ravioli, cèpes, smoked mushroom tea. Larger bedrooms face the rushing Gynack burn (one has a small balcony); a room overlooking woods where roe deer and red squirrels can be seen was 'warm, comfortable, and had a modern shower room'. Two lounges have books and games; a south-facing terrace overlooking the burn has seating and tables where pre-dinner drinks and breakfast can be taken in warmer weather. Breakfast has a 'full buffet selection of fruit, cereals, yogurt and juice' and 'good choices' of cooked dishes. 'They gave me breakfast (for free) when I got off the overnight sleeper, and drove me to the station on the last morning,' says a skiing visitor in 2014.

Tweed Mill Brae, Ardbroilach Road
Kingussie PH21 1LB

T: 01540-661166
E: relax@thecross.co.uk
W: www.thecross.co.uk

BEDROOMS: 8.
OPEN: early Feb–early Jan except Christmas.
FACILITIES: 2 lounges, restaurant, free Wi-Fi in some areas, 4-acre grounds, only restaurant suitable for &.
BACKGROUND MUSIC: none.
LOCATION: 440 yds from village centre.
CHILDREN: all ages welcomed.
DOGS: allowed by arrangement, not in public rooms.
CREDIT CARDS: Amex, MasterCard, Visa.
PRICES: [2014] per room B&B £100–£180, D,B&B £210–£270. Set dinner £55, tasting menu £58.

KIRKBEAN Dumfries and Galloway

Map 5:E2

CAVENS

'The atmosphere is restful' at the Fordyce family's white-painted manor house near Dumfries, which they run as a small hotel. 'The staff were smiling and the service was exemplary,' says a regular *Guide* correspondent on a first visit. The lounge ('lovely and light') has 'comfortable' chairs and sofas, books, magazines and guidebooks; 'the (quiet) background music seemed unnecessary'. The bedrooms, which face the garden or the countryside, vary in size. 'Our large room had a big bed (lovely bedlinen) and plenty of storage space; we also had a large sunroom, with a wall of windows, a big sofa to lounge on and look at the view, and an antique desk. The well-equipped bathroom had a large bath. Pleasing touches included heavy floor-length curtains which matched the bedhead and the cushions.' Angus Fordyce, who is manager and chef, serves a daily-changing no-choice market menu (perhaps roast fennel salad, pine nuts; corn-fed chicken, cream and tarragon sauce; rhubarb tartlet) or a short carte. Breakfasts are 'particularly good, with plenty of choice and well-presented cooked dishes'. (*Mary Hewson, and others*)

25% DISCOUNT VOUCHERS

Kirkbean
by Dumfries DG2 8AA

T: 01387-880234
F: 01387-880467
E: enquiries@cavens.com
W: www.cavens.com

BEDROOMS: 6, 1 on ground floor.
OPEN: Mar–Nov, exclusive use only at New Year.
FACILITIES: sitting room, dining room, meeting facilities, free Wi-Fi, 20-acre grounds, unsuitable for &.
BACKGROUND MUSIC: light classical in sitting room, dining room.
LOCATION: 13 miles S of Dumfries.
CHILDREN: all ages welcomed.
DOGS: allowed by arrangement, not in public rooms.
CREDIT CARDS: MasterCard, Visa.
PRICES: per room B&B £100–£200. Set dinner £25, à la carte £35. 1-night bookings refused Easter, bank holidays.

GLENHOLME COUNTRY HOUSE

'Welcoming, comfortable, relaxed and homely', this 'deceptively large' Victorian mansion is run as an upmarket guest house by retired diplomat Laurence Bristow-Smith and his artist wife, Jennifer. 'I am uncertain whether this house (and its owner) is idiosyncratic, characterful, tasteful or cosmopolitan,' said a visitor this year. 'Probably all four, in a most interesting and charming way. There was a relaxed view about arrival times; we were greeted warmly and offered tea and biscuits in the library.' Each bedroom is named after a Victorian politician. 'The Curzon room had a spectacular view and was comfortable and quiet. It had a four-poster bed, a radio (no TV) and a good en suite with a shower.' Lansdowne is a 'charming room in white and pale grey, with good reading lights'. Laurence Bristow-Smith cooks a short no-choice menu by arrangement (dislikes discussed when booking). 'A feta and spinach roll was accompanied by baby asparagus tips and salad leaves from the garden; poached chicken breast wrapped in Parma ham came with potatoes and leeks.' Breakfast 'is also very good; lots of fresh fruit'; 'all manner of cooked dishes'.

Tongland Road
Kirkcudbright DG6 4UU

T: 01557-339422
E: info@
glenholmecountryhouse.com
W: www.glenholmecountryhouse.
com

BEDROOMS: 4.
OPEN: all year.
FACILITIES: library, dining room, free Wi-Fi, 1½-acre garden, unsuitable for &.
BACKGROUND MUSIC: music system in library and dining room at guests' discretion.
LOCATION: 1 mile N of town.
CHILDREN: not under 12.
DOGS: not allowed.
CREDIT CARDS: MasterCard, Visa.
PRICES: [2014] per room B&B single £80–£95, double £95–£120. 1-night bookings sometimes refused weekends in high season.

KYLESKU HOTEL

♀ *César award in 2014*

In a 'most beautiful situation' by a sea loch, this white-painted inn is run as a small hotel by Tanja Lister and Sonia Virechauveix. 'They are three steps ahead of everything,' say trusted correspondents this year. '*Kylesku* cannot be faulted for consideration to residents, comfort and cleanliness; good food for which locals travel many miles. The staff are young, intelligent and well trained.' The lounge has a 'roaring fire', plenty of reading material; 'most of the time, there is complete silence'. The bedrooms are not large but all have been renovated. 'Our room had magnificent views of the ever-changing mountains and the activity on the slip.' Sonia Virechauveix oversees the kitchen: her menus, which can be taken in the bar or the restaurant, 'reflect her French background'. The daily specials might include West Coast shore clams, garlic butter and herbs; Kinlochbervie lemon sole, caper beurre noisette. 'Nowhere else have we experienced such fresh fish. Tanja keeps a high profile at breakfast, when almost every guest can enjoy the view. Full of enthusiasm, she helps guests plan their daily forays.' (*Janet and Dennis Allom*)

Kylesku
IV27 4HW

T: 01971-502231
E: info@kyleskuhotel.co.uk
W: www.kyleskuhotel.co.uk

BEDROOMS: 8, 1 in annexe.
OPEN: 1 Mar–3 Nov.
FACILITIES: lounge, bar, restaurant, free Wi-Fi in bar and lounge, small garden (tables for outside eating), unsuitable for ♿.
BACKGROUND MUSIC: in bar.
LOCATION: 10 miles S of Scourie, 30 miles north of Ullapool.
CHILDREN: all ages welcomed.
DOGS: allowed.
CREDIT CARDS: MasterCard, Visa.
PRICES: [2014] per room B&B £97–£160. À la carte £28.

LANGASS LODGE

In 'splendid isolation' above a stone circle by a sea loch, Niall and Amanda Leveson Gower run this 'elegant' small hotel in a sympathetically extended former hunting lodge. The bedrooms, which vary in quality and price, are split between the main house (simpler, cheaper) and a newer hillside wing. These rooms are spacious and have plenty of storage, wooden floors with rugs, and a king-size bed. Four have a door opening on to the garden where, on a clear day, you might catch a glimpse of Skye. There are two eating options: fine dining in a split-level conservatory restaurant and simpler meals in the bar. The chef, John Buchannan, uses game from the island and seafood (often gathered from the hotel's pots) for his menus. In the restaurant you might choose game terrine with onion chutney; hand-dived Uist scallops, Stornoway black pudding. Children are welcomed (a special menu, high chairs, a family room). There is much to do on the island: fishing and shooting (with the necessary support) can be arranged; there are prehistoric sites to visit and white-sand beaches to explore. More reports, please.

Locheport
Isle of North Uist
Western Isles HS6 5HA

T: 01876-580285
F: 01876-580385
E: langasslodge@btconnect.com
W: www.langasslodge.co.uk

BEDROOMS: 11, 1 suitable for ♿.
OPEN: all year except Christmas.
FACILITIES: lounge, bar, restaurant, free Wi-Fi, wedding facilities, 11-acre garden in 200-acre grounds.
BACKGROUND MUSIC: in bar.
LOCATION: 7½ miles S of Lochmaddy.
CHILDREN: all ages welcomed.
DOGS: allowed, £5 charge.
CREDIT CARDS: MasterCard, Visa.
PRICES: [2014] per room B&B single £75–£80, double £95–£145. Set dinner £30–£36, à la carte (bar) £38.

THE ALBANNACH

High above Lochinver's working harbour ('lovely views over the village, sea and mountains'), this Victorian house is run as a restaurant-with-rooms by Lesley Crosfield and Colin Craig. The self-taught chef/proprietors, who share the cooking, have a *Michelin* star for their 'exquisite' meals ('as good as it gets,' is a recent comment). They 'construct' the five-course (no-choice) menu daily, using herbs and vegetables 'grown organically to order' and local produce. Taken in a wood-panelled restaurant, it might include langoustine with ginger; Jerusalem artichoke risotto; roast hill-fed Highland lamb, red wine and blackcurrant sauce. The Penthouse suite is 'so large, we often lost one another'; it has under-floor heating; a bath 'big enough for two' and a separate shower in the spacious bathroom. The Byre suite has a terrace with a hot tub. Pre-dinner drinks and afternoon tea are taken in a conservatory ('a good place to lounge around with a book') or a snug. The hosts also cook the 'excellent' breakfast. They tell us they have bought a bar in the village, the *Caberfeidh*, which they are turning into a dining pub. (*J and MB*)

Baddidarroch
Lochinver
Sutherland IV27 4LP

T: 01571-844407
E: info@thealbannach.co.uk
W: www.thealbannach.co.uk

BEDROOMS: 5, 1 in byre.
OPEN: mid-Mar–early Jan, closed Mon, 'possibly' at Christmas.
FACILITIES: ramp, snug, conservatory, dining room, free Wi-Fi, ½-acre garden, unsuitable for &.
BACKGROUND MUSIC: none.
LOCATION: ½ mile from village.
CHILDREN: not under 12.
DOGS: not allowed.
CREDIT CARDS: MasterCard, Visa.
PRICES: [2014] per person D,B&B from £150. Set dinner £65. 1-night bookings generally refused Sat.

SEE ALSO SHORTLIST

THE DOWER HOUSE

❧ *César award in 2008*

The 'home from home' atmosphere at Robyn and Mena Aitchison's small guest house, a single-storey Georgian cottage-orné, has long been liked by readers. It stands in mature well-tended grounds (which have a miniature orchard and a large goldfish pond), bordered by the rivers Beauly and Conon. They have given their home a lived-in feel; it is filled to the brim with antiques, precious rugs and vases; there are well-stocked bookshelves and potted plants. Mena Aitchison is the 'friendly' front-of-house. Guests can sample one of the range of malts from a self-service cupboard, in front of a wood-burning stove in the lounge; play a board game or watch television in the snug. Robyn Aitchison cooks a 'gutsy' modern no-choice menu of dishes like bruschetta of figs and Parma ham; monkfish and langoustine, saffron sauce. His puddings are 'magnificent', perhaps hot pineapple, rum and chocolate sauce. There is home-made tablet with the coffee. All the 'cosy' bedrooms face the garden; they have a large bed; the suite has a sitting room. Breakfast has free-range eggs from hens in the garden, proper porridge. Children are welcomed.

Highfield
Muir of Ord IV6 7XN

T/F: 01463-870090
E: info@thedowerhouse.co.uk
W: www.thedowerhouse.co.uk

BEDROOMS: 4, all on ground floor.
OPEN: April–Oct.
FACILITIES: lounge, dining room, TV room, free Wi-Fi, wedding facilities, 4½-acre grounds, unsuitable for &.
BACKGROUND MUSIC: none.
LOCATION: 14 miles NW of Inverness.
CHILDREN: no under-5s at dinner (high tea at 5).
DOGS: not allowed in public rooms.
CREDIT CARDS: MasterCard, Visa.
PRICES: [2014] per room B&B £140–£160. Set dinner £38.

BARLEY BREE

The Auld Alliance between Scotland and France is flourishing at this former coaching inn in a conservation village. It is run as a restaurant-with-rooms by French chef Fabrice Bouteloup and his Scottish wife, Alison. The cooking style – seasonal Scottish with a French twist – secured for *Barley Bree* the Scottish Restaurant of the Year award in 2013. A returning *Guide* correspondent found 'the overall experience fine' this year. In the candlelit restaurant, 'busy on both evenings of our visit', Fabrice Bouteloup's menu might include confit rabbit, caper and grain mustard terrine, pomegranate and pickled beetroot; wild sea bass, swede and saffron purée, curried roasted cauliflower. Alison Bouteloup supervises a wine list that has 'a good selection by the glass and a mini-carafe, which helps prevent overindulgence'. Service is by a 'well-trained young staff'. The bedrooms are decorated in 'classic contemporary' style. A corner room has windows on two sides and is 'light and airy'. Children are welcomed (they have their own menu, and a travel cot is available). Breakfast has freshly baked croissants, pains au chocolat as well as 'delicious' porridge. (*William Wood*)

6 Willoughby Street
Muthill PH5 2AB

T: 01764-681451
F: 01764-910055
E: info@barleybree.com
W: www.barleybree.com

BEDROOMS: 6.
OPEN: all year except Christmas, occasional periods shown on website.
FACILITIES: lounge, restaurant, free Wi-Fi in certain parts of building, small terrace, unsuitable for &.
BACKGROUND MUSIC: jazz in lounge.
LOCATION: village centre.
CHILDREN: all ages welcomed.
DOGS: only guide dogs allowed.
CREDIT CARDS: MasterCard, Visa.
PRICES: [2014] per room B&B £110–£150. À la carte £35–£43.

KIRROUGHTREE HOUSE

🏵 *César award in 2003*

In February 2014, the ownership of this country hotel transferred from the McMillan group to a privately owned company, which promised a 'seamless change, with management and staff remaining in place'. Readers have often praised the long-serving manager, Jim Stirling, who 'creates a jolly atmosphere with the warmth of his personality'. The bow-windowed part-Georgian, part-Victorian mansion stands in 'superb' gardens in 'wild, breathtaking countryside' within Galloway forest park. Arriving guests appreciate being met in the car park by a porter and given afternoon tea with silver service in one of the elegant public rooms. The baronial-style hall and drawing room have rich oak panelling, opulent drapes; the restaurant is a high-ceilinged room. Chef Matt McWhir sources ingredients from within Dumfries and Galloway for his daily-changing menus, which might include Scottish salmon, herb-mashed potatoes, white wine and dill sauce. Each of the traditionally decorated bedrooms has a separate sitting area, a decanter of sherry, fruit, biscuits, a 'well-lit dressing table'. More reports, please.

Newton Stewart DG8 6AN

T: 01671-402141
F: 01671-402425
E: info@kirroughtreehouse.co.uk
W: www.kirroughtreehouse.co.uk

BEDROOMS: 17.
OPEN: 14 Feb–2 Jan.
FACILITIES: lift, 2 lounges, 2 dining rooms, free Wi-Fi, 8-acre grounds (gardens, tennis, croquet, pitch and putt).
BACKGROUND MUSIC: none.
LOCATION: 1½ miles NE of Newton Stewart.
CHILDREN: not under 10.
DOGS: allowed in lower ground-floor bedrooms only, not in public rooms.
CREDIT CARDS: Amex, MasterCard, Visa.
PRICES: [2014] per person B&B £68–£100, D,B&B £88–£135. Set dinner £35. 1-night bookings refused Christmas/New Year.

THE MANOR HOUSE

In an 'ideal situation near the ferry terminal but completely quiet', Leslie and Margaret Crane's Georgian villa (built in 1780 for the Duke of Argyll) has 'fantastic views towards the harbour'. A regular *Guide* correspondent, who had 'an excellent experience' in 2014, praised the 'charming' staff. The public rooms are 'stylishly' furnished: an entrance hall with a tiled mosaic floor leads to the lounge, which has an open fire, books, newspapers and magazines, 'interesting' artwork. A 'wee lounge' is a quieter space. Dinner orders are taken in *Nelson's* bar, where guests might watch the sun set over Mull. The tables are well spaced in the dining room, which is 'obviously the posh place to eat in Oban'. The cooking of the long-serving chef, Shaun Squire, is widely praised: his dinner menu might include Inverawe smoked trout, West Coast scallops, lemon salad; roast loin of lamb, shepherd's pie, honey-roast root vegetables. Five of the bedrooms have sea views; there are sheets and blankets on the beds. Because the building is listed, some rooms are 'cosy'. All are equipped with mineral water, a hospitality tray, fruit and biscuits. (*Christian Bartoschek*)

Gallanach Road
Oban PA34 4LS

T: 01631-562087
F: 01631-563053
E: info@manorhouseoban.com
W: www.manorhouseoban.com

BEDROOMS: 11, 1 on ground floor.
OPEN: all year except Christmas.
FACILITIES: 2 lounges, bar, restaurant, free Wi-Fi, wedding facilities, 1½-acre grounds, unsuitable for &.
BACKGROUND MUSIC: traditional in bar and dining room.
LOCATION: ½ mile from centre.
CHILDREN: not under 12.
DOGS: by arrangement, not allowed in public rooms.
CREDIT CARDS: all major cards.
PRICES: [2014] per room B&B £115–£235, D,B&B £190–£310. Set dinner £42.

SEE ALSO SHORTLIST

CRAIGATIN HOUSE AND COURTYARD

In wooded grounds with off-street parking close to the town centre, this Victorian house has been given a bright, modern interior by the owners, Martin and Andrea Anderson. 'We were made to feel welcome from the moment we arrived,' is a recent comment. Light floods into the guest lounge and dining room, a 'fabulous' Scandinavian-style extension with beams on a vaulted ceiling, a freestanding wood-burning stove, and rugs on a wooden floor. Breakfast is a generous affair: on a buffet is a seasonal fruit salad, home-made muesli and other cereals, fruit juices and grapefruit segments. The cooked offerings include the usual fry-up (with potato scones), a choice of omelettes, perhaps Arnold Bennett (smoked haddock and cheese). Vegetarians can choose from apple pancake with banana, sultanas and honey; French toast with mixed fruits. Seven of the 'spotless' bedrooms are in the main house; the others are in converted courtyard stables behind. They are individually decorated with feature wallpapers and accented colours. One of the ground-floor rooms has a walk-in wet room adapted for a wheelchair-user. (*JS*)

25% DISCOUNT VOUCHERS

165 Atholl Road
Pitlochry PH16 5QL

T: 01796-472478
E: enquiries@craigatinhouse.co.uk
W: www.craigatinhouse.co.uk

BEDROOMS: 14, 7 in courtyard, 2 on ground floor, 1 suitable for &.
OPEN: Mar–Dec, New Year but not Christmas.
FACILITIES: lounge, 2 dining rooms, free Wi-Fi, 2-acre garden.
BACKGROUND MUSIC: light jazz.
LOCATION: central.
CHILDREN: not under 13.
DOGS: not allowed.
CREDIT CARDS: Diners, MasterCard, Visa.
PRICES: [2014] per room B&B £80–£117 (single prices by arrangement). 1-night bookings refused Sat.

SEE ALSO SHORTLIST

PITLOCHRY Perth and Kinross

DALSHIAN HOUSE

'Excellent in every way; a lovely house and gardens, warm, very comfortable and friendly.' Praise this year for this listed 18th-century country house on the outskirts of the Victorian resort town. It is run 'with lots of fine touches' by Martin and Heather Walls, who used to be part of the management team of a now-closed country house hotel. The house stands in quiet surroundings – woodland and well-tended gardens (with seating areas). The spacious bedrooms are decorated in individual style, with a mix of traditional furnishings, and more contemporary colours. Children are welcomed: there are two family rooms on the top floor. The lounge is 'comfortable in small country house style'; it has sofas, armchairs, books and magazines, a wood-burning stove. The breakfast, served at well-spaced tables, is 'outstanding'. A help-yourself buffet has imaginative choices like compote of berries, cinnamon and vanilla; honey and ginger apricots with almonds; porridge can come with a nip of Edradour whisky; Stornoway black pudding Benedict in addition to the usual cooked dishes. The theatre and restaurants are a short drive away. (*Janet and Dennis Allom*)

Old Perth Road
Pitlochry PH16 5TD

T: 01796-472173
E: dalshian@btconnect.com
W: www.dalshian.co.uk

BEDROOMS: 7.
OPEN: all year except Christmas.
FACILITIES: lounge, dining room, free Wi-Fi, 1-acre garden, unsuitable for ♿.
BACKGROUND MUSIC: none.
LOCATION: 1 mile S of centre.
CHILDREN: all ages welcomed.
DOGS: allowed by arrangement, not in public rooms.
CREDIT CARDS: MasterCard, Visa.
PRICES: [2014] per person B&B £35–£40.

SEE ALSO SHORTLIST

PITLOCHRY Perth and Kinross

Map 5:D2

⚜ THE GREEN PARK

César award: Scottish hotel of the year

'Our initial impressions were that this wasn't a typical *Guide* hotel; it seemed vast, with a great many guests, mostly elderly, and many of them regular visitors. After a two-day stay, we have to endorse the comments on the incredibly personal service offered to guests, and the awesome attention to detail.' Praise comes from regular correspondents this year for the McMenemie family's traditional hotel on the banks of the River Tummel. Another comment: 'We certainly join in the enthusiasm: the staff are helpful, sometimes without even being asked.' There are two lifts and 16 ground-floor bedrooms (one has a fully equipped disabled bathroom). 'Our room was large and very comfortable; the bathroom was excellent.' The 'choicest' tables in the large dining room are in 'great demand'. 'The food is superb.' Chef Chris Tamblin's daily-changing menu might include seafood salad of poached salmon, mackerel, prawns, and anchovies. A complimentary buffet of tea, coffee, biscuits and cakes is laid out on the dining room sideboard from 11 am to 5 pm. 'A surprising and impressive hotel.' (*Alan and Edwina Williams, JFM and M West*)

25% DISCOUNT VOUCHERS

Clunie Bridge Road
Pitlochry PH16 5JY

T: 01796-473248
F: 01796-473520
E: bookings@thegreenpark.co.uk
W: www.thegreenpark.co.uk

BEDROOMS: 51, 16 on ground floor, 1 suitable for ♿.
OPEN: all year except Christmas.
FACILITIES: 2 lifts, 3 lounges, library, bar, restaurant, free Wi-Fi, 3-acre garden.
BACKGROUND MUSIC: none.
LOCATION: western edge of town.
CHILDREN: all ages welcomed.
DOGS: allowed, not in public rooms.
CREDIT CARDS: MasterCard, Visa.
PRICES: [2014] per person B&B £75–£86, D,B&B £87–£111. À la carte £25–£27.

SEE ALSO SHORTLIST

THE AIRDS HOTEL

'Small and personal', this luxury hotel (Relais & Châteaux) has a 'beautiful setting' facing Lismore Island with views over Loch Linnhe. It is run with 'great attention to detail' by the owners, Shaun and Jenny McKivragan, and a 'professional and charming' staff, say visitors this year. Ayrshire-born Jordan Annabi is now the chef; he cooks 'faultless' modern British dishes ('with a hint of France') like seared scallops, apple and ginger purée, apple caramel; loin of Highland venison, braised suet pudding, spiced red cabbage, blackberry jus. The restaurant is now 'less formal and more relaxed', Shaun McKivragan tells us. The style of the bedrooms (some are small) varies from country house to more modern; Whisky Mac and a jug of iced water are supplied. 'Nice touches' include complimentary tea and juice delivered to the room in the morning with a newspaper. Breakfast is served at the table. Each of the two lounges has an open fire, a well-stocked bookcase; there are fine views from a conservatory. There is much to do in the area; bicycles can be hired to explore Lismore Island. (*Ian and Barbara Dewey*)

Port Appin PA38 4DF

T: 01631-730236
F: 01631-730535
E: airds@airds-hotel.com
W: www.airds-hotel.com

BEDROOMS: 11, 2 on ground floor, also self-catering cottage.
OPEN: all year except 2 days a week Nov, Dec, Jan.
FACILITIES: 2 lounges, conservatory, snug bar, restaurant, wedding facilities, free Wi-Fi, ¾-acre garden (croquet, putting), unsuitable for &.
BACKGROUND MUSIC: none.
LOCATION: 25 miles N of Oban.
CHILDREN: all ages welcomed, but no under-9s in dining room after 7.30 (high tea at 6.30).
DOGS: allowed by prior agreement, not in public rooms.
CREDIT CARDS: Amex, MasterCard, Visa.
PRICES: [2014] per room D,B&B £290–£495.

SEE ALSO SHORTLIST

KNOCKINAAM LODGE

Shielded by cliffs and wooded hills, this grey
stone 19th-century hunting lodge stands in
extensive grounds close to a private beach. It is
run in country house style by the owners, Sian
and David Ibbotson. There are stags' heads in
the bar, a log fire and comfy sofas in the lounge
('no background music'). The bedrooms vary in
size and aspect. Whin has a triple aspect; it has
a roll-top bath and a walk-in shower in the
bathroom; Hannay, on the second floor, has a
separate lounge area with panoramic views of
the sea. It can be linked to an adjacent twin-
bedded room to create a family suite. Children
are welcomed: high teas are available for the
under-12s at 6 pm, and families can take an
early dinner together by arrangement. In the
dining room chef Tony Pierce has a *Michelin* star
for his modern Scottish tasting menus with
dishes like fillet of salted cod, chive hollandaise;
roast canon of Galloway lamb, herb, brioche and
pine nut crust. In fine weather there are tea,
drinks and barbecues on the lawn. There is good
walking from the grounds.

25% DISCOUNT VOUCHERS

Portpatrick
DG9 9AD

T: 01776-810471
F: 01776-810435
E: reservations@
knockinaamlodge.com
W: www.knockinaamlodge.com

BEDROOMS: 10.
OPEN: all year.
FACILITIES: 2 lounges, 1 bar,
restaurant, free Wi-Fi, wedding
facilities, 30-acre grounds, only
restaurant suitable for &.
BACKGROUND MUSIC: classical in
restaurant.
LOCATION: 3 miles S of Portpatrick.
CHILDREN: no under-12s in dining
room after 7 pm (high tea at 6).
DOGS: allowed in some bedrooms,
not in public rooms.
CREDIT CARDS: Amex, MasterCard,
Visa.
PRICES: [2014] per room D,B&B
£190–£420. Set dinner £65. 1-night
bookings sometimes refused.

VIEWFIELD HOUSE

❦César award in 1993

In large wooded grounds on the outskirts of Skye's main town, this 200-year-old country house is run as a quirky guest house by Hugh Macdonald. A hands-on owner with a personable style, he is helped by 'charming' assistants. Visitors like the 'attentive' service and informal style. Mr Macdonald's great-great-grandfather transformed what was a modest Georgian house into a baronial fantasy. It is furnished with hunting trophies, fading family portraits and mementos of ancestral colonial service (an elephant's foot umbrella stand, Benares brass and other relics of the Raj). An open fire burns in the elegant sitting room; there is no bar, but the house is licensed, and drinks are available on request. No television in the bedrooms (addicts will find a set in the morning room) but the Wi-Fi system has been upgraded this year. Most of the rooms are large (as are some bathrooms); they have a view of the bay or the woodland. A short daily-changing supper menu is available by arrangement (soup, lemon-roasted chicken, etc). Breakfast is generous. (*WT*)

25% DISCOUNT VOUCHERS

Viewfield Road
Portree
Isle of Skye IV51 9EU

T: 01478-612217
F: 01478-613517
E: info@viewfieldhouse.com
W: www.viewfieldhouse.com

BEDROOMS: 11, 1, on ground floor, suitable for ♿.
OPEN: Easter–mid-Oct.
FACILITIES: ramp, drawing room, morning/TV room, dining room, free Wi-Fi, 20-acre grounds (croquet, swings).
BACKGROUND MUSIC: none.
LOCATION: S side of Portree.
CHILDREN: all ages welcomed.
DOGS: not allowed in public rooms except with permission of other guests (except guide dogs).
CREDIT CARDS: MasterCard, Visa.
PRICES: per person B&B £67–£77. Set dinner £25.

⚜ MOOR OF RANNOCH HOTEL   **NEW**

César award: newcomer of the year

In a 'spectacular' position on the edge of one of Europe's last wildernesses, this 19th-century hotel stands close to a station on the West Highland line. It has been renovated by new owners, Scott Meikle and Stephanie Graham, who are 'extremely friendly, full of information about walks, local Munros, train times, etc'. *Guide* inspectors were impressed: 'This is a place to get away from it all: no TV, no radio, no Wi-Fi and poor mobile reception; you just have to go for a walk.' The interiors are 'cosy and light'; in a 'comfortable' bedroom, 'our bed was on a raised platform so we could gaze out at the magnificent scenery'. The views are equally striking from the dining room (popular with non-residents): 'Dinner is very good; the appetising menu has three choices for each course of well-balanced dishes, beautifully prepared. We enjoyed perfectly poached duck egg, white pudding and bacon; cumin and coriander lamb cutlets, date and almond bulgur wheat.' In the gloaming, 'a deer family came close to the house; we watched the light of a train approaching across the moor'.

Rannoch Station PH17 2QA

T: 01882-633238
E: info@moorofrannoch.co.uk
W: www.moorofrannoch.co.uk

BEDROOMS: 5.
OPEN: 10 Feb–end Oct.
FACILITIES: lounge, bar, dining room, no Wi-Fi, unsuitable for &.
BACKGROUND MUSIC: none.
LOCATION: end of road, 36 miles W of Pitlochry.
CHILDREN: all ages welcomed.
DOGS: welcomed.
CREDIT CARDS: MasterCard, Visa.
PRICES: [2014] per room B&B single £80, double £114. Set meals £23–£29.

FOVERAN

'Thoughtful' owner/chef Paul Doull runs this
unassuming single-storey building on the shores
of Scapa Flow as a restaurant-with-rooms.
There are 'wonderful views out to sea' from
the 'pleasant' dining room, which 'showcases
Orkney produce' in dishes like scallops with
strawberry, reduced balsamic and tempura
samphire; Orkney fillet steak in puff pastry,
caramelised mushrooms, haggis, creamy whisky
sauce. 'Paul offered to vary some of the dishes
to give us more choice,' said visitors staying
over five nights this year. 'We can thoroughly
recommend the fillet steak, which was served
precisely as we wished. The staff were all
friendly and delighted in helping us celebrate
a significant birthday. The restaurant was
unsurprisingly busy with locals who clearly rate
it highly.' A lounge, where pre-dinner drinks
are taken, has 'plenty of seating, including the
traditional Orkney chair which is more
comfortable than it looks'. The bedrooms vary
in size and aspect (not all have sea views); they
are well equipped with tea-making facilities.
Breakfast has a good buffet. Children are
welcomed; smaller portions are made available
on request. (*Jill and Mike Bennett*)

St Ola
Kirkwall KW15 1SF

T: 01856-872389
F: 01856-876430
E: info@thefoveran.com
W: www.thefoveran.com

BEDROOMS: 8, all on ground floor.
OPEN: mid-Apr–early Oct, by
arrangement at other times, only
restaurant Christmas/New Year,
restaurant closed Sun evening end
Sept–early June.
FACILITIES: lounge, restaurant, free
Wi-Fi, 12-acre grounds (private
rock beach).
BACKGROUND MUSIC: Scottish, in
evening, in restaurant.
LOCATION: 3 miles SW of Kirkwall.
CHILDREN: all ages welcomed.
DOGS: not allowed.
CREDIT CARDS: MasterCard, Visa.
PRICES: [2014] per person B&B
£55–£78, D,B&B £80–£103.
À la carte £27. 1-night bookings
sometimes refused.

SCARISTA HOUSE

🍃 *César award in 2012*

With perhaps the remotest setting of any hotel in the *Guide*, this white-painted Georgian manse is run by the owners, Tim and Patricia Martin, who are 'hard working and delightful'. On the Isle of Harris, it is 'a beautiful place; the peacefulness is remarkable', say visitors this year. *Scarista* has many fans who like 'the wonderfully laid-back but professional service, the character, simplicity and most of all the fantastic food'. 'There is something special about it,' said *Guide* inspectors. Detractors find it 'expensive'; the owners point to the short season and the high costs of island life. The house has rugs on wooden floors, comfortable sofas, open fires, 'a wealth of books and good art' in a downstairs library and a first-floor drawing room. The bedrooms are in the main house and in a converted outbuilding. 'Dinner is delicious; mainly fish as you might expect but also delectable lamb one evening; an extensive cheeseboard of interest and quality.' Breakfast has 'excellent freshly squeezed orange juice, decent strong coffee and superb cooked dishes of any variety'. (*Nigel Mackintosh, and others*)

Scarista
Isle of Harris HS3 3HX

T: 01859-550238
E: stay@scaristahouse.com
W: www.scaristahouse.com

BEDROOMS: 6, 3 in annexe.
OPEN: 2 Mar–23 Oct.
FACILITIES: drawing room, library, dining room, free Wi-Fi, 1-acre garden, unsuitable for ♿.
BACKGROUND MUSIC: none.
LOCATION: 15 miles SW of Tarbert.
CHILDREN: all ages welcomed.
DOGS: by arrangement in bedrooms, library.
CREDIT CARDS: Amex, MasterCard, Visa.
PRICES: [2014] per room B&B £210–£235. Set meals £43.50. 1-night bookings 'might be refused' in high season.

SKIRLING HOUSE

♀*César award in 2004*

In a 'superb setting' by a tranquil village green, this 'fascinating' house was built in the Arts and Crafts style as a summer retreat for the art collector Sir Thomas Gibson-Carmichael. It has differently shaped roofs sweeping over eaves with square windows, much decorative ironwork. It is run as a guest house by Isobel and Bob Hunter, whose hospitality has long been liked by *Guide* readers. The sunny drawing room (the outstanding feature of the house) has a 16th-century carved Florentine ceiling; Isobel Hunter's collection of contemporary, largely Scottish art is 'worth examination'. Dinner is a carefully paced affair, taken at separate tables in a conservatory overlooking the garden, or in winter by a log fire in the dining room. Bob Hunter cooks a no-choice four-course menu (preferences discussed in advance) of classic dishes, perhaps fillet of salmon, saffron sauce; breast of Barbary duck, rowanberry sauce; there are regional farmhouse cheeses and a dessert. The bedrooms are 'beautifully fitted with every conceivable extra'; carpets are custom designed. A smaller room was less liked this year. Breakfast is an 'event'.

25% DISCOUNT VOUCHERS

Skirling, by Biggar ML12 6HD

T: 01899-860274
F: 01899-860255
E: enquiry@skirlinghouse.com
W: www.skirlinghouse.com

BEDROOMS: 5, plus 1 single available if let with a double, 1 on ground floor suitable for &.
OPEN: Mar–Dec except Christmas, closed occasionally and 1 week in Nov/Dec.
FACILITIES: ramps, 4 public rooms, free Wi-Fi (available as stone walls allow), 5-acre garden (tennis, croquet) in 100-acre estate with woodland.
BACKGROUND MUSIC: none.
LOCATION: 2 miles E of Biggar, by village green.
CHILDREN: all ages welcomed.
DOGS: allowed by arrangement, not in public rooms or unattended in bedrooms.
CREDIT CARDS: MasterCard, Visa.
PRICES: [2014] per person B&B £65–£95. Set dinner £35.

SLEAT Highland

TORAVAIG HOUSE

In a glorious setting above the coast road, this handsome white-painted house is run as a small hotel by the owners, Anne Gracie and Kenneth Gunn. They have renovated the building giving it a 'smart' interior. The bedrooms, some small, have rich fabrics and wallpapers; hillside or sea views. They are colour-themed and named after Hebridean islands. Colonsay, in nutmeg and copper, has a sea-facing sitting/dining area. Eriskay, in olive and gold, has a wooden sleigh bed, dark oak furnishings. The 'lovely' drawing room has a marble fireplace, log fire, baby grand piano, 'comfy sofas'. In the contemporary dining room, Joel Kirby has been promoted to head chef this year; his short dinner menu might include braised Lochaber pork cheek; West Coast cod, wild garlic gnocchi, butternut squash, gingerbread. Breakfast, served at table, has 'the best' porridge; traditional cooked offerings; fish dishes include smoked haddock, Mallaig kippers and Skye smoked salmon. Kenneth Gunn, a master mariner, organises day-trips on his 50-foot luxury yacht; guests can get married on it. *Duisdale House* (see Shortlist) nearby is under the same ownership.

Knock Bay, Sleat
Isle of Skye
IV44 8RE

T: 01471-820200
F: 01471-833404
E: info@skyehotel.co.uk
W: www.skyehotel.co.uk

BEDROOMS: 9.
OPEN: all year.
FACILITIES: lounge, dining room, free Wi-Fi, wedding facilities, 2-acre grounds, unsuitable for ⅃.
BACKGROUND MUSIC: gentle classical all day.
LOCATION: 7 miles S of Broadford.
CHILDREN: not under 5.
DOGS: not allowed.
CREDIT CARDS: MasterCard, Visa.
PRICES: [2014] per person B&B £79–£130, D,B&B £106–£175. Set dinner £48.

SEE ALSO SHORTLIST

CREAGAN HOUSE

In a sheltered valley at the head of Loch Lubnaig, this 17th-century farmhouse is run as a restaurant-with-rooms by Gordon Gunn ('the chef par excellence') and his wife, Cherry ('a warm and genuine hostess'). 'They are experienced hoteliers and they bring that to bear in every aspect of their hospitality,' reports a regular correspondent this year. A fan 'thoroughly enjoyed another wonderful visit'. Cherry Gunn 'is perfection personified as front-of-house'. In the mock-baronial vaulted dining hall ('a wonderful room with enormous tables'), the 'superb' menus might include Spanish-style pork cheek braised in Pedro Ximénez sherry; wild turbot on Moroccan couscous en papillote. 'The canapés were unusual and very tasty.' The 'comfortable' bedrooms are furnished with antiques, fine fabrics; one room has a four-poster bed 'in hand-embroidered satin'. Fresh milk with the tea tray is appreciated, as are 'unusually good reading lights'. Strathyre is known as 'the first village in the Highlands' – there might be some road noise – and is within the Loch Lomond and The Trossachs national park. (*Wendy Montague, William Wood*)

25% DISCOUNT VOUCHERS

Strathyre FK18 8ND

T: 01877-384638
F: 01877-384319
E: eatandstay@creaganhouse.co.uk
W: www.creaganhouse.co.uk

BEDROOMS: 5, 1 on ground floor.
OPEN: 27 Mar–28 Oct, closed Wed/Thurs.
FACILITIES: lounge, restaurant, private dining room, free Wi-Fi, 1-acre grounds.
BACKGROUND MUSIC: none.
LOCATION: ¼ mile N of village.
CHILDREN: all ages welcomed.
DOGS: not allowed in public rooms.
CREDIT CARDS: MasterCard, Visa.
PRICES: per person B&B £65–£75, D,B&B single £125–£135, double £100–£110. Set dinner £35.

SEE ALSO SHORTLIST

STRONTIAN Highland

KILCAMB LODGE

One of the oldest stone houses in Scotland (with two Victorian wings), this luxury hotel has an isolated setting on the shore of Loch Sunart. It is run by the owners, Sally and David Ruthven-Fox. There are log fires in the 'warm and homely' public rooms, which have a 'tasteful' decor; 'lovely pictures throughout'. All the bedrooms have a view of the loch. A suite with a separate sitting room occupies the second floor; a first-floor room was decorated 'in relaxed blue and yellow with a large bed in white linen'. A new double room has been added this year, and several rooms have been refurbished. There is a choice of dining options. Service is 'exemplary' in the main dining room, which has 'fresh roses on the table, good napery and china'. The chef, Gary Phillips, serves modern European and Scottish dishes, perhaps roasted turnip and horseradish soup, crispy chilli beef; pan-fried sea bass, tomato and olive tart. Light lunches and evening meals can be taken in the *Driftwood Brasserie*. Spike, the resident dog, welcomes canine visitors; there are four dog-friendly rooms.

25% DISCOUNT VOUCHERS

Strontian
PH36 4HY

T: 01967-402257
F: 01967-402041
E: enquiries@kilcamblodge.co.uk
W: www.kilcamblodge.co.uk

BEDROOMS: 11.
OPEN: All year, except Jan.
FACILITIES: drawing room, lounge bar, dining room, brasserie, free Wi-Fi, wedding facilities, 22-acre grounds, unsuitable for &.
BACKGROUND MUSIC: jazz/classical/guitar in dining room.
LOCATION: edge of village.
CHILDREN: not under 10.
DOGS: allowed in 4 bedrooms, not in public rooms.
CREDIT CARDS: MasterCard, Visa.
PRICES: [2014] per person B&B £80–£110, D,B&B £100–£200. Set dinner (restaurant) £52–£65, à la carte (*Driftwood Brasserie*) £35.

TRIGONY HOUSE

In a lovely setting of garden and woodland in the Nithsdale valley, this 'handsome' former shooting lodge is run in 'friendly' style as a small hotel by the owners, Adam and Jan Moore. He is the chef (following the 'timeless tradition of Scottish, English and continental peasant cooking'); she is the 'chatty and helpful' hostess. The hallway has impressive Japanese oak panelling and an Art Deco window above the staircase. There is a 'cosy' sitting room with a stove, a light wooden-floored dining room which, like the bar, has an open fire and views over the 'pretty' garden. Adam Moore uses vegetables from the kitchen garden, and organic produce when possible, for his menus, which might include field mushroom and tarragon tart; thyme breast of chicken, braised wild garlic, chorizo, pancetta and Parmesan sauce. Traditionally furnished bedrooms vary in size; some have lovely views. A large room 'had a conservatory sitting room, big bed, well-equipped bathroom (power shower'). Dogs are 'not just allowed but welcomed'; there are good walks in the grounds, and doggie treats are available.

25% DISCOUNT VOUCHERS

Closeburn
Thornhill DG3 5EZ

T: 01848-331211
F: 01848-331303
E: info@trigonyhotel.co.uk
W: www.
    countryhousehotelsscotland.com

BEDROOMS: 9, 1 on ground floor.
OPEN: all year except 24–26 and 31 Dec.
FACILITIES: lounge, bar, dining room, free Wi-Fi, wedding facilities, 4-acre grounds.
BACKGROUND MUSIC: jazz in bar in evening.
LOCATION: 1 mile S of Thornhill.
CHILDREN: all ages welcomed.
DOGS: not allowed in dining room.
CREDIT CARDS: all major cards.
PRICES: per room B&B £90–£155, D,B&B £140–£225. Set dinner £35. 1-night bookings 'very occasionally' refused Sat.

FORSS HOUSE

Built by a Victorian adventurer (Major Radclyffe) in 1810 by a waterfall near Thurso, Scotland's most northerly town, this listed Georgian house is run as a small hotel by Ian and Sabine Richards. It has long been managed in very personal style by Anne Mackenzie, who 'looks after all of us – staff and guests'. In the whisky bar, she will supervise a tasting of the house's collection of 300 malts. Traces of the previous ownership have been preserved during sympathetic renovation. An 'odd-looking' entrance hall, built as a trophy room, has a wood-burning stove, seating, newspapers and a tally of recent catches on the River Forss. There are pictures of the major's exploits in his smoking room, now a private dining room; Radclyffe family portraits hang in the restaurant where the chef, Paul Ruttledge, serves modern Scottish dishes, perhaps caramelised Scrabster scallops, crispy halloumi cheese; roasted Mey beef fillet, cheek terrine, confit potato. The two biggest bedrooms, with Georgian proportions and views of the river, are in the main house. Other rooms are divided between the main house, the *River House* and the *Fishing Lodge*.

Forss
by Thurso KW14 7XY

T: 01847-861201
E: relax@forsshousehotel.co.uk
W: www.forsshousehotel.co.uk

BEDROOMS: 14, 3 in main house on ground floor, 4 in *River House*, 2 in *Fishing Lodge*.
OPEN: all year except 23 Dec–4 Jan.
FACILITIES: entrance lounge, bar, dining room, private dining room, free Wi-Fi, wedding facilities, 20-acre grounds.
BACKGROUND MUSIC: classical in dining room.
LOCATION: 5 miles W of Thurso.
CHILDREN: all ages welcomed.
DOGS: not allowed in main building.
CREDIT CARDS: all major cards.
PRICES: [2014] per room B&B single £99–£135, double £135–£185, D,B&B single £137–£170, double £205–£260. À la carte £31.50–£38.

TIRORAN HOUSE

At their white-painted Victorian hunting lodge on the shores of Loch Scridain, near Mull's highest mountain, Laurence and Katie Mackay create a house party atmosphere. 'It makes it a place to return to; you always meet great people,' says an enthusiast this year. 'The staff are a delight.' Guests are encouraged to gather for pre-dinner drinks, canapés and conversation in one of the two sitting rooms. Craig Ferguson, the chef, serves a short daily-changing menu of modern dishes (perhaps lamb's kidney, tomato, tarragon and wholegrain mustard sauce; Isle of Gigha halibut, parsley root purée). 'The food, always excellent and locally grown, is now even better, a delightful culinary experience with surprises on every plate; no repeats in a week.' The 'relaxing' bedrooms vary in size and style. They have 'crisp bedlinen'; a hospitality tray with island bakery biscuits. Dogs are welcomed in four rooms in an annexe ('same standard as main house'). Breakfast has full Scottish options with free-range eggs, home-made muesli, breads, marmalade and preserves. A burn tumbles past the house; the garden leads to a private beach. (*Gillian Todd, and others*)

25% DISCOUNT VOUCHERS

Tiroran, Isle of Mull
PA69 6ES

T: 01681-705232
E: info@tiroran.com
W: www.tiroran.com

BEDROOMS: 10, 2 on ground floor, 4 in annexes.
OPEN: all year, except Christmas/New Year.
FACILITIES: 2 sitting rooms, dining room, conservatory, free Wi-Fi, 17½-acre grounds, beach with mooring.
BACKGROUND MUSIC: none.
LOCATION: N side of Loch Scridain.
CHILDREN: all ages welcomed.
DOGS: allowed in 4 bedrooms, not in public rooms.
CREDIT CARDS: MasterCard, Visa.
PRICES: [2014] per room B&B £185–£220. D,B&B £48 added per person (£36 for Sun supper), à la carte £48. 1-night bookings 'seldom' refused.

HIGHLAND COTTAGE

On a hill in the main village of the Island of Mull, David and Josephine Currie have been running this purpose-built small hotel for 17 years. 'It is a comfortable and friendly place with a high standard of attention to what you want,' says a visitor this year. 'The star attraction, aside from the view over the water and town, is the food; not cheap but well worth it from the amuse-bouche to the amazing desserts.' Josephine Currie uses island produce (with much local fish) for her three-course menus. Typical dishes: Croig crab cakes, chilli caper sauce; roast monkfish, herb mash, mussel cream sauce. There's an honesty bar in the upper sitting room ('they will make you any cocktail you want'); pre-dinner drinks can also be taken in a conservatory with sofas and chairs. Background music in the public areas was less liked. The bedrooms vary in size. There is a four-poster bed in two 'light' sea-facing rooms; a room on the ground floor has level access to the street; bathrooms are 'well appointed'. David Currie will help guests book boat trips. (*Yorick Wilks*)

25% DISCOUNT VOUCHERS

Bredalbane Street
Tobermory
Isle of Mull PA75 6PD

T: 01688-302030
E: davidandjo@highlandcottage.co.uk
W: www.highlandcottage.co.uk

BEDROOMS: 6, 1 on ground floor.
OPEN: Apr–16 Oct.
FACILITIES: 2 lounges, restaurant, free Wi-Fi.
BACKGROUND MUSIC: in 1 lounge, restaurant.
LOCATION: village centre.
CHILDREN: not under 10.
DOGS: not allowed in restaurant.
CREDIT CARDS: MasterCard, Visa.
PRICES: [2014] per room B&B £125–£165. Set dinner £39.50. 1-night bookings refused weekends.

SEE ALSO SHORTLIST

THE CEILIDH PLACE

'Friendly and informal', Jean Urquhart's small hotel is an institution in this Highland fishing village. Founded by her late husband, the actor Robert Urquhart, as 'a place for eating, meeting, talking and singing', it is a local hub encompassing an all-day bar and café, an 'excellent' bookshop and an arts centre with much live entertainment. The public area is a warren of rooms. 'A bonus is the gorgeous, rambling, enormous guests' lounge and the little kitchen where you can help yourself to tea and coffee,' said *Guide* inspectors. 'If the weather defeated you (which has been known to happen in these parts), you could spend happy days here, especially if you like to read.' The simple bedrooms are decorated in rustic country style; each room has a selection of books chosen by a Scottish author ('they take literature seriously'). In the 'lively' main dining room, the chef, Scott Morrison, serves 'robust and flavourful' dishes like West Coast mussels steamed with Indian spices; Ross-shire beef and best ale casserole, spring onion and mustard mash. Breakfast has a 'very good' Scottish fry-up.

25% DISCOUNT VOUCHERS

12–14 West Argyle Street
Ullapool IV26 2TY

T: 01854-612103
F: 01854-613773
E: stay@theceilidhplace.com
W: www.theceilidhplace.com

BEDROOMS: 13, 10 with facilities en suite, plus 11 in *Clubhouse* across road.
OPEN: all year except Jan.
FACILITIES: bar, parlour, café/bistro, restaurant, bookshop, conference/function/wedding facilities, free Wi-Fi, 2-acre garden, only public areas suitable for &.
BACKGROUND MUSIC: 'variable' in public areas.
LOCATION: village centre, large car park.
CHILDREN: all ages welcomed.
DOGS: not allowed in public rooms.
CREDIT CARDS: MasterCard, Visa.
PRICES: [2014] per person B&B £53–£82. À la carte £26.

SEE ALSO SHORTLIST

WINDLESTRAW LODGE

'A beautiful house and very welcoming hosts.' Praise this year for Alan and Julie Reid's small hotel, an Edwardian mansion in the Tweed Valley forest park. They have restored the original features of the house, which was built by a mill owner for his Austrian bride. They uncovered a fireplace with gilt-edged carvings and reinstated oak floorboards that had been covered by carpets. The open-plan public areas, which have Austrian decorative wood panelling and a two-foot-deep plaster frieze, are arranged to provide six separate seating areas. The 'sublime cooking' of Alan Reid is an 'outstanding feature': he serves a daily-changing menu of local ingredients in the elegant dining room. 'Alan starts with a small cup of soup, which was always delicious. Picking out special dishes from the menu is difficult because the overall quality is so good; that said, pan-roasted sea trout with prawn and lobster risotto did stand out.' The 'smart' bedrooms are 'big and comfortable'. This year the Peddie Room has been refurbished. Breakfast has an extensive menu: 'Don't miss the smoked haddock and poached egg.' (*Peter Anderson, and others*)

Galashiels Road
Tweed Valley
Walkerburn EH43 6AA

T: 01896-870636
E: reception@windlestraw.co.uk
W: www.windlestraw.co.uk

BEDROOMS: 6, all on first floor.
OPEN: all year except 1 week Feb, 1 week May, 1 week June, Christmas/New Year.
FACILITIES: bar lounge, sun lounge, drawing room, dining room, free Wi-Fi, 2-acre grounds, unsuitable for &.
BACKGROUND MUSIC: none.
LOCATION: outskirts of village, 2 miles E of Innerleithen.
CHILDREN: not under 12 at dinner (high tea 5–6 pm).
DOGS: not allowed in public rooms.
CREDIT CARDS: MasterCard, Visa.
PRICES: [2014] per person B&B £85–£105. Set dinner £55.

BURRASTOW HOUSE

'Staying at *Burrastow* is like being in someone's home rather than a hotel,' says Pierre Dupont, the Flemish owner of this 18th-century 'Haa' house originally built for the local laird. It stands in a sheltered bay on a promontory facing the island of Vaila in the west of Mainland (the name of Shetland's largest island). Guests have use of the house, a 'maze of stairs and corridors', at all times: 'A call at the kitchen door produces a coffee on demand,' a visitor said, 'and the well-stocked library would be enough to while away months of inclement weather.' Pierre Dupont, who does the cooking, asks guests in the morning if they would like dinner and prepares a three-course menu based on what is fresh and available locally on the day: it might be fish or heather-fed lamb from the hills, he says. Vegetarian options are available. There is a wood-burning stove in a 'cosy' lounge. 'A silent night' is guaranteed in the bedrooms; three are in an extension. Breakfast has 'proper oatmeal porridge', home-baked croissants; black pudding, kippers and locally smoked fish. (*IM*)

Walls
Shetland ZE2 9PD

T: 01595-809307
E: info@burrastowhouse.co.uk
W: www.burrastowhouse.co.uk

BEDROOMS: 7, 3 in extension, 2 on ground floor.
OPEN: Apr–Oct.
FACILITIES: sitting room, library, dining room, free Wi-Fi, wedding facilities, unsuitable for ♿.
BACKGROUND MUSIC: none.
LOCATION: 27 miles NW of Lerwick.
CHILDREN: all ages welcomed.
DOGS: small dogs allowed by arrangement, in ground-floor rooms only.
CREDIT CARDS: MasterCard, Visa.
PRICES: [2014] per person B&B £55, D,B&B £90.

WALES

Snowdonia

HARBOURMASTER HOTEL

🏆 *César award in 2005*

'A wonderful place to stay', Glyn and Menna Heulyn's small hotel is a conversion of three characterful buildings on the quayside of an appealing small town. 'What makes it so special is that all the staff seem motivated, cheerful and happy,' says a returning visitor this year. 'Many are local, which means they can tell you about places to visit. We like the newsletter on the breakfast table which gives suggestions for the day.' The bedrooms are in the original building, a converted grain store next door, and a historic cottage. 'We liked our room, Aeron Queen, which had excellent soundproofing from the bar below; large windows and a balcony had panoramic views of the harbour.' Gwalia, on the first floor, has muted sea colours spiced with scarlet Welsh blankets ('no cushions, no knick-knacks, no frills'). Separate menus are served in the bar and the restaurant, where chef Ludovic Dieumegard's menu might include Welsh goat's cheese, pistachio-stuffed peppers; fillet of cod, pesto bean fricassée. 'The food is good, especially at breakfast which is freshly prepared using good local ingredients.' (*Lynn Wildgoose, SA Mathieson*)

Pen Cei, Aberaeron
SA46 0BT

T: 01545-570755
F: 01545-570762
E: info@harbour-master.com
W: www.harbour-master.com

BEDROOMS: 13, 2 in cottage, 1 suitable for &.
OPEN: all year except 25 Dec.
FACILITIES: bar, restaurant, free Wi-Fi, pebble beach (safe bathing nearby).
BACKGROUND MUSIC: 'not loud' in bar.
LOCATION: central, on harbour.
CHILDREN: under-5s in cottage only.
DOGS: not allowed.
CREDIT CARDS: Amex, MasterCard, Visa.
PRICES: [2014] per room B&B £110–£250, D,B&B £140–£300. Set dinner £25–£30, à la carte £30. 1-night bookings refused weekends.

TREFEDDIAN HOTEL

'I cannot think of anywhere nicer to spend a week recharging batteries; the staff are wonderful, remembering us on each visit.' Praise this year from one of many repeat visitors to the Cave family's 'pleasing' traditional hotel on a bluff with glorious views across Cardigan Bay. Out of season, *Trefeddian* is popular with older visitors who enjoy the low rates, the sociable public areas (including an adult-only lounge and a library with a card table) and the traditional values (like the dress code for dinner – 'gentlemen are required to wear a jacket or tie' – which 'invokes a sense of style'). When school is out, the mood changes: children are warmly welcomed and have much to do. There is an indoor swimming pool (refurbished this year), a games room, a family-friendly lounge and sand dunes to explore. The bedrooms have clean lines, fitted pale wood furnishings. Children have a dedicated menu (taken at 5.15 pm). In the formal dining room, the English/French cooking of chef Tracy Sheen is much admired. Breakfast has 'real marmalade'. Wheelchair-users regularly praise the facilities. (*Peter Rogers, and others*)

Tywyn Road
Aberdyfi LL35 0SB

T: 01654-767213
F: 01654-767777
E: info@trefwales.com
W: www.trefwales.com

BEDROOMS: 59.
OPEN: Jan–Nov.
FACILITIES: lift, 3 lounges, bar lounge, restaurant, free Wi-Fi, fitness centre, indoor swimming pool (6 by 12 metres), beauty salon, 15-acre grounds (tennis, putting green).
BACKGROUND MUSIC: none.
LOCATION: ½ mile N of village.
CHILDREN: all ages welcomed.
DOGS: allowed in 1 lounge, some bedrooms.
CREDIT CARDS: MasterCard, Visa.
PRICES: [2014] per person B&B £45–£65, D,B&B £65–£133. Set dinner £29.50. 1-night bookings sometimes refused.

THE ANGEL HOTEL

The Griffiths family have been much involved in the regeneration of this small market town surrounded by seven hills between the Welsh/English border and the Brecon Beacons. This former coaching inn on the main street of the town is owned by Alun Griffiths, a builder, his wife Pauline (who also runs an adjacent gallery/art shop) and their son, William, who manages the hotel. The public areas are popular with locals ('this is very much a town hotel and all the better for it,' says a *Guide* inspector). An in-house baker prepares the award-winning afternoon tea served in a 'pretty' lounge. Meals may be taken in the often busy *Foxhunter Bar*, which has leather sofas, wooden tables and vintage settles, or in the more formal *Oak Room*. Standard rooms are 'comfortable if old-fashioned'; renovated rooms have a modern decor (cream walls, good furniture, an updated bathroom). Two bedrooms are in a converted stable block. The Griffiths family also co-own with Shaun Hill the nearby *Michelin*-starred *Walnut Tree* restaurant. A 'Foodies Delight' package includes dinner at the restaurant and a champagne afternoon tea at the *Angel*.

15 Cross Street
Abergavenny NP7 5EN

T: 01873-857121
F: 01873-858059
E: mail@angelabergavenny.com
W: www.angelabergavenny.com

BEDROOMS: 35, 2 in adjacent mews, plus 2 cottages.
OPEN: all year except 25 Dec.
FACILITIES: ramps, lift, lounge, bar, restaurant, private function rooms, free Wi-Fi, civil wedding licence, courtyard.
BACKGROUND MUSIC: live piano at weekend in restaurant.
LOCATION: town centre.
CHILDREN: all ages welcomed.
DOGS: allowed in bedrooms (£10 charge), bar, not in restaurant.
CREDIT CARDS: Amex, MasterCard, Visa.
PRICES: [2014] per room B&B £101–£168, D,B&B from £80.50 per person, set dinner £25, à la carte £30.

PORTH TOCYN HOTEL

César award in 1984

In a magnificent position above Cardigan Bay,
this conversion of three old miners' cottages has
been run as an unstuffy child-friendly hotel by
the Fletcher-Brewer family for 65 years. It is
recommended this year by regular *Guide*
correspondents on a first visit. 'A warm welcome
from the staff; excellent dinner and breakfast.
Our spacious room had views over the sea to
Snowdonia.' Younger visitors have an 'area to
escape' with television, books and a games room.
There is an outdoor heated swimming pool and
a 'makeshift' football pitch; many other activities
are available nearby. In the restaurant, Louise
Fletcher-Brewer and Martin Williams serve a
modern menu of dishes like grilled sea bass,
caramelised fennel and baby leeks, chorizo
linguini. An alternative light supper menu (fish
pie, bangers and mash, etc) is available for those
'who do not want fine dining night after night'.
Younger children are given high tea at 5.30 pm;
those aged over six may dine with their parents.
The public areas have been recarpeted and
'freshened' this year and bedrooms are being
given a more modern decor. (*AD and J Lloyd*)

Bwlch Tocyn
Abersoch LL53 7BU

T: 01758-713303
F: 01758-713538
E: bookings@porthtocyn.fsnet.co.uk
W: www.porthtocynhotel.co.uk

BEDROOMS: 17, 3 on ground floor.
OPEN: week before Easter–early
Nov.
FACILITIES: ramp, sitting rooms,
children's rooms, cocktail bar,
dining room, free Wi-Fi, 25-acre
grounds (swimming pool, 10 by
6 metres, heated May–end Sept,
tennis), telephone to discuss disabled
access.
BACKGROUND MUSIC: none.
LOCATION: 2 miles outside village.
CHILDREN: high tea for under-5s; no
babies or young children at dinner.
DOGS: by arrangement, not allowed
in public rooms.
CREDIT CARDS: MasterCard, Visa.
PRICES: [2014] per room B&B single
£77.50–£92.50, double £105–£185.
Set dinner £38.50–£45.50. 1-night
bookings occasionally refused.

GWESTY CYMRU

The name translates as 'Welsh hotel' and a sense of national identity is strong at Huw and Beth Roberts's stylish restaurant-with-rooms on the Victorian seafront promenade. Using Welsh materials (handcrafted oak furnishings inlaid with slate), they have given their Grade II listed Georgian terrace house a sleek look. In the restaurant (modern furnishings on a grey slate floor), the chef, Pawel Banaszynski, uses local ingredients for his bilingual menu of dishes like venison terrine; cod fillet with a mango and mint crust. The Polish chef ('with a Welsh soul') might include Szarlotka (Polish apple cake) among the desserts. The bedrooms have a bold decor chosen to echo the colours of the surrounding landscape: terracotta, fired earth and bronze; the sepia tones of the beach; the red sky at night; the deep blue of the sea. Two rooms at the front have a bathtub in a bay window. A large attic room connects with an adjacent single to form a family suite. There is no residents' lounge; guests may sit in the cellar bar or in the restaurant's sea-facing terrace, which also provides outdoor dining. More reports, please.

19 Marine Terrace
Aberystwyth SY23 2AZ

T: 01970-612252
F: 01970-623348
E: info@gwestycymru.co.uk
W: www.gwestycymru.co.uk

BEDROOMS: 8, 2 on ground floor.
OPEN: all year except 23–31 Dec, restaurant closed for lunch Tues.
FACILITIES: bar, restaurant, terrace, free Wi-Fi, secure parking (book in advance), unsuitable for &.
BACKGROUND MUSIC: in Reception and restaurant.
LOCATION: central, on seafront.
CHILDREN: all ages welcomed at lunch, no under-5s to stay or in restaurant in evenings.
DOGS: not allowed.
CREDIT CARDS: MasterCard, Visa.
PRICES: [2014] per room B&B single £67–£80, double £87–£160, £10 supplement for twin beds, D,B&B (Nov–Mar, Sun–Thurs, excluding half-term) single £85–£110, double £150. À la carte £30.

BRYNIAU GOLAU

🪶 *César award in 2014*

In an elevated position overlooking Lake Bala, this renovated Victorian mansion is run as a small guest house by the owners, Katrina Le Saux and Peter Cottee. 'They are delightful hosts, who make their guests feel like friends,' said one visitor. There is 'plenty of space' for guests in the sitting room, which has a log fire and an honesty bar. In good weather, visitors will be 'tempted outside' to the terrace and gardens, which have 'lots of little corners for relaxation'. Two of the 'spotless' bedrooms have a four-poster bed and a spa bath in the bathroom. A third room has a king-size bed which can be split into twin beds; in the bathroom is a large bath overlooking the lake. 'An excellent cook', Peter Cottee will prepare a three-course dinner by arrangement: dishes might include watercress soup; chicken in a creamy tarragon and cider sauce, sautéed potatoes, braised shallots. Breakfast, taken at a long table in a room with a grand piano, has home-made breads and preserves, award-winning marmalade; a hearty traditional cooked dish. (*LF, and others*)

25% DISCOUNT VOUCHERS

Llangower, Bala
LL23 7BT

T: 01678-521782
E: katrinalesaux@hotmail.co.uk
W: www.bryniau-golau.co.uk

BEDROOMS: 3.
OPEN: Mar–end Oct.
FACILITIES: sitting room, dining room, free Wi-Fi, ½-acre garden, unsuitable for ♿.
BACKGROUND MUSIC: none.
LOCATION: 2 miles SE of Bala.
CHILDREN: not under 12.
DOGS: not allowed.
CREDIT CARDS: MasterCard, Visa.
PRICES: [2014] per room B&B single £75, double £100–£110. Set dinner £27.50. 1-night bookings refused weekends and peak times.

LLWYNDU FARMHOUSE

'Peace and tranquillity' prevail at this Grade II listed 16th-century farmhouse, which stands on a hillside above Barmouth overlooking Cardigan Bay. It is run as a small hotel/restaurant by Peter and Paula Thompson, whose 'engaging' service creates an atmosphere that is 'like being wrapped in a warm blanket' (according to a visitor). Peter Thompson's 'skilful, locally sourced, home-cooked food' is praised by readers. In the candlelit dining room he serves a regularly changing ('sometimes daily') short menu of modern dishes with international influences. It might include chicken liver and grapes in butter and sherry; crab and cockle noodles, spicy Thai sauce. The 'fantastic food always includes a vegetarian choice'. The bedrooms in the old house have quirky features reflecting the age of the building, like a sink fitted to a door. Four rooms in a converted granary, which have direct access to the garden, have high ceilings, exposed timbers. These are good for a family (*Llwyndu Farmhouse* is 'very child friendly'); dogs can also be accommodated in these rooms. Breakfast has a wide-ranging menu with naturally smoked kippers and haddock; free-range eggs any way.

25% DISCOUNT VOUCHERS

Llanaber
Barmouth LL42 1RR

T: 01341-280144
F: 01341 281236
E: intouch@
    llwyndu-farmhouse.co.uk
W: www.llwyndu-farmhouse.co.uk

BEDROOMS: 7, 4 in granary, 1 on ground floor.
OPEN: all year except 24–26 Dec, restaurant closed Sun evening.
FACILITIES: lounge, restaurant, free Wi-Fi, 4-acre garden, unsuitable for &.
BACKGROUND MUSIC: occasionally 'but not at breakfast'.
LOCATION: 2 miles N of Barmouth.
CHILDREN: all ages welcomed.
DOGS: allowed in 4 outside bedrooms (£6 charge), not in public rooms.
CREDIT CARDS: MasterCard, Visa.
PRICES: [2014] per person B&B £50–£65, D,B&B £85–£99. Set dinner £24.50–£29.50, à la carte £35–£45. 1-night bookings refused peak weekends.

YE OLDE BULLS HEAD

For more than 500 years, this ancient inn has been welcoming travellers to the likeable little ferry port. First-time visitors in 2014 (regular *Guide* correspondents) were 'impressed by the welcoming staff'. The owners, David Robertson (the manager) and Keith Rothwell, have renovated the inn and added accommodation in an updated 16th-century building 100 yards away. 'Our room in the main building was superb, spacious and comfortable, with a king-size bed; a freestanding cast iron bath and multiple lighting options in the lavish bathroom. The tea tray had fresh milk in a flask, and home-made shortbread biscuits. We can confirm that there is much in the way of creaking and plumbing noises through the night.' Rooms in *The Townhouse*, which has a lift, have a contemporary decor. There are two dining options. Chef Hefin Roberts serves a fine-dining menu in the *Loft* restaurant from Tuesday to Saturday (dishes like roast loin and rump of Anglesey lamb, wild mushroom and tongue risotto). The menu is 'modern and imaginative' in the 'bright and cheerful' brasserie in converted stables. Breakfast is 'excellent'. (*Alan and Edwina Williams*)

Castle Street
Beaumaris, Isle of Anglesey
LL58 8AP

T: 01248-810329
F: 01248-811294
E: info@bullsheadinn.co.uk
W: www.bullsheadinn.co.uk

BEDROOMS: 26, 2 on ground floor, 1 in courtyard, 13 in *Townhouse* adjacent, 1 suitable for &.
OPEN: all year, except 25/26 Dec, *Loft* restaurant closed lunch, Sun/Mon nights.
FACILITIES: lift (in *Townhouse*), lounge, bar, brasserie, restaurant, free Wi-Fi, sea 200 yds, only brasserie and *Townhouse* suitable for &.
BACKGROUND MUSIC: 'chill-out' in brasserie.
LOCATION: central.
CHILDREN: not in Bull suites, no under-7s in restaurant.
DOGS: allowed in 3 bedrooms, bar.
CREDIT CARDS: Amex, MasterCard, Visa.
PRICES: [2014] per room B&B single £82.50–£89.50, double £105–£150. Set dinner (restaurant) £45, à la carte (brasserie) £25.

TŶ MAWR

25% DISCOUNT VOUCHERS

♀ *César award in 2011*

In a peaceful position beside a stream on the edge of the Brechfa forest, Annabel and Stephen Thomas's country hotel is a 16th-century farmhouse (later a school). It offers a 'very warm welcome' and the 'outstanding' value. The public areas have thick exposed stone walls, fireplaces and beams. In warm weather, pre-dinner drinks can be taken on the 'manicured' lawn of the large garden. Stephen Thomas uses Carmarthenshire produce for his daily-changing menu: 'Dinner was divine,' says a visitor this year (a fellow hotelier). 'We had perfectly prepared lobster and a gorgeous fillet of beef with oxtail; dessert was pear and almond sponge with honey ice cream.' The bedrooms are simply decorated: 'Our immaculate room was like a suite; it had a large bed, good sitting area; a well-appointed bathroom and all the amenities you might expect.' Breakfast, in a sunny room, is 'leisurely and civilised'. A well-stocked buffet has fresh fruit salad, cereals, organic Welsh yogurts and home-baked bread. The cooked breakfast has home-cured bacon, black pudding, free-range eggs; honey and preserves from a nearby farm. (*Richard Morgan-Price, AD and J Lloyd*)

Brechfa SA32 7RA

T: 01267-202332
E: info@wales-country-hotel.co.uk
W: www.wales-country-hotel.co.uk

BEDROOMS: 6, 2 on ground floor.
OPEN: all year.
FACILITIES: sitting room, bar, breakfast room, restaurant, free Wi-Fi, 1-acre grounds, unsuitable for &.
BACKGROUND MUSIC: classical in restaurant.
LOCATION: village centre.
CHILDREN: not under 12.
DOGS: by arrangement (no charge), not allowed in breakfast room, restaurant.
CREDIT CARDS: Amex, MasterCard, Visa.
PRICES: [2014] per room B&B double £115–£130, D,B&B £160–£175. Set dinner £25–£30 per person, à la carte £30.

GLANGRWYNEY COURT

In extensive parkland with 'splendid' walled gardens stocked with mature magnolias, acers and rhododendrons, this Grade II listed Palladian house is run as an upmarket B&B by the owners, Christina and Warwick Jackson. 'We could find no fault with anything; it lived up to its reputation,' said a recent visitor. Guests are invited to spend time in the public rooms, which have been decorated with period antiques and classic furnishings and fabrics. There are floor-to-ceiling windows and large sofas in front of a log-burner in the lounge; the library has an honesty bar and a grand piano ('feel free to tinkle away'). A cantilevered staircase 'of significant architectural interest' leads to the main-house bedrooms. 'Beautifully furnished', they have antiques, fine fabrics; several have a coronet over the bed. One room has a Victorian roll-top bath in the en suite bathroom, while another, the largest, has a bay window overlooking the lily pond. There is a ground-floor room in a courtyard building 20 yards from the house. Breakfast, served at separate tables in the dining room, has bacon and sausage from nearby farms; locally pressed apple juice. (*TB*)

Glangrwyney, Crickhowell
NP8 1ES

T: 01873-811288
F: 01873-810317
E: info@glancourt.co.uk
W: www.glancourt.co.uk

BEDROOMS: 9, 1, on ground floor, in courtyard, 4 cottages in grounds.
OPEN: all year.
FACILITIES: sitting room, library/honesty bar, dining room, free Wi-Fi, civil wedding licence, 4-acre garden (croquet, boules, tennis) in 33-acre parkland, unsuitable for &.
BACKGROUND MUSIC: on request.
LOCATION: 2 miles SE of Crickhowell, off A40.
CHILDREN: all ages welcomed.
DOGS: allowed in cottages only.
CREDIT CARDS: MasterCard, Visa.
PRICES: [2014] per room B&B £95–£140. 1-night bookings sometimes refused weekends.

SEE ALSO SHORTLIST

GLIFFAES

❇ *César award in 2009*

The River Usk runs through the grounds of this 19th-century Italianate building. A smart sporting hotel, it is run by Susie and James Suter (the third generation of the family owners). 'A very nice hotel with an efficient and friendly staff,' says a visitor this year. Another comment from a returning guest: 'Just as I remembered it, with an unspoiled charm and comfort.' Dinner is 'excellent and well served'. The chef, Karl Cheetham, subscribes to the Slow Food Movement, sourcing ingredients from as close as possible to the hotel. Typical dishes in his daily-changing menu: marinated sesame beef; lemon sole, seaweed purée, sage and Welsh beer sauce. Most of the 'immaculate' bedrooms are large; the best have a balcony overlooking the river. There are attractive indoor sitting areas, particularly the conservatory with a view down the valley. The hotel has a private stretch of the trout- and salmon-laden river: 'I enjoyed a productive evening fishing.' A packed lunch with Spanish tortilla was 'a welcome change'. 'We were given unstinting and accurate advice about the locality.' (*Peter Anderson, David Walton*)

25% DISCOUNT VOUCHERS

Crickhowell
NP8 1RH

T: 01874-730371
F: 01874-730463
E: calls@gliffaeshotel.com
W: www.gliffaeshotel.com

BEDROOMS: 23, 4 in annexe, 1 on ground floor.
OPEN: all year except Jan.
FACILITIES: ramp, 2 sitting rooms, conservatory, bar, dining room, free Wi-Fi, civil wedding licence, 33-acre garden (tennis, croquet, fishing).
BACKGROUND MUSIC: in bar in evening.
LOCATION: 3 miles W of Crickhowell.
CHILDREN: all ages welcomed, £23 B&B on a camp bed in parents' room.
DOGS: not allowed indoors.
CREDIT CARDS: Amex, MasterCard, Visa.
PRICES: per room B&B £89–£275, D,B&B £177–£363. Set dinner £36–£44. 1-night bookings refused high season weekends.

SEE ALSO SHORTLIST

THE OLD VICARAGE

In the hills of the Welsh Marches, this red brick Victorian vicarage on the main road to Newtown is run as a small guest house by the 'charming, helpful' owners, Helen and Tim Withers. 'We were warmly greeted and given tea and Welsh cakes,' says a visitor this year. The 'comfortable' bedrooms 'lack nothing'. Teme, decorated in calm greens, has a southerly view; a deep roll-top bath in the bathroom. Ithon, a smaller room, has Indian summer printed wallpaper; a westerly aspect facing fields. Mule (named after a river) is decorated in Chinese Ming blue toile. 'One small grouse: the light was poor for reading.' In the dining room, Tim Withers serves an Aga-cooked dinner: 'It is no-nonsense cooking which does not bow to fashion,' says one visitor (a fellow *Guide* hotelier). Typical dishes on the short menu: leek and potato soup; pot-roast Welsh lamb, orange and laver bread sauce, new potatoes. The Witherses, who have a green philosophy, emphasise the low food miles involved in their breakfast. A discount is given to guests arriving by public transport; bicycles can be hired. (*Kate MacMaster, JR*)

25% DISCOUNT VOUCHERS

Dolfor, nr Newtown
SY16 4BN

T: 01686-629051
F: 01686-207629
E: tim@theoldvicaragedolfor.co.uk
W: www.theoldvicaragedolfor.co.uk

BEDROOMS: 4.
OPEN: all year except Christmas/ New Year, Sun.
FACILITIES: drawing room, dining room, free Wi-Fi, 2-acre garden, unsuitable for &.
BACKGROUND MUSIC: none.
LOCATION: 3 miles S of Newtown.
CHILDREN: all ages welcomed.
DOGS: not allowed.
CREDIT CARDS: Amex, MasterCard, Visa.
PRICES: per room B&B single £70–£90, double £95–£120, D,B&B single £98–£125, double £151–£190. Set dinner £28–£35, à la carte £35. 1-night bookings sometimes refused.

BRYN MAIR HOUSE

In walled gardens at the foot of Cadair Idris stands this Georgian townhouse. A Grade II listed former rectory, it has been furnished 'simply and elegantly' by Jan and Peter Ashley, the 'welcoming' owners. It stands on an incline on the outskirts of a market town within the Snowdonia national park. Two of the bedrooms are double aspect with views of the town and the mountains. A spacious room in cream and grey has a king-size double bed, which can be converted to twin beds; it has a private bathroom across the landing, with a roll-top bath and a separate shower. One bedroom has an en suite wet room ; a smaller room is decorated in cream. All rooms are equipped with satellite television, an iPod docking system, and a tea/coffee tray and shortbread biscuits. On the landing is a small fridge with fresh milk and bottled water. At breakfast, a sideboard buffet has home-made granola, yogurt, fruit juices; a wide choice of cooked dishes (the eggs are 'wonderfully yellow'). There are books in the dining room for guests to read; a telescope in the sitting room. (*LL*)

Love Lane, Dolgellau
LL40 1SR

T: 01341-422640
E: jan@janashley.wanadoo.co.uk
W: www.brynmairbedandbreakfast.co.uk

BEDROOMS: 3.
OPEN: 14 Feb–20 Dec.
FACILITIES: lounge, dining room, free Wi-Fi, 1-acre garden, unsuitable for &.
BACKGROUND MUSIC: none.
LOCATION: central.
CHILDREN: not under 14.
DOGS: not allowed.
CREDIT CARDS: MasterCard, Visa.
PRICES: [2014] per room B&B single £75–£85, double £95–£105. 1-night bookings refused Easter–Oct.

SEE ALSO SHORTLIST

Y GOEDEN EIRIN

❦ César award in 2008

'Welsh is spoken by everyone here,' say Eluned and John Rowlands, who run this informal guest house in a hamlet on the edge of the Snowdonia national park. 'But guests are welcomed from all over the world.' The bilingual couple (retired academics) are 'seriously green, but not in an oppressive way'. Environmental policies encompass solar panels, recycling and composting, water conservation, Fairtrade tea and coffee; a charging point has been installed for electric cars. The renovated farm buildings (local granite, slates, beams) have a mix of traditional and modern furnishings, 'beautiful' objets d'art and fine pictures. The bedrooms are well equipped, showing 'care and attention to the needs of the guest'. Dinner is served by arrangement. The host does most of the cooking on an Aga, using organic ingredients from the garden or sourced locally for his no-choice menus (guests are consulted beforehand). Dishes might include Tuscan-style bean soup; pork with pears, cider and honey. Breakfasts have freshly squeezed orange juice; porridge or muesli; home-made bread and preserves; a choice of cooked dishes.

25% DISCOUNT VOUCHERS

Dolydd, Caernarfon
LL54 7EF

T: 01286-830942
E: john_rowlands@tiscali.co.uk
W: www.ygoedeneirin.co.uk

BEDROOMS: 3, 2 in annexe.
OPEN: all year except Christmas/New Year, dining room occasionally closed.
FACILITIES: dining room (occasional live piano music), lounge by arrangement, free Wi-Fi, 20-acre pastureland, unsuitable for ₷.
BACKGROUND MUSIC: none.
LOCATION: 3 miles S of Caernarfon.
CHILDREN: not under 12.
DOGS: not allowed.
CREDIT CARDS: none, cash or cheque payment requested on arrival.
PRICES: [2014] per room B&B single £60, double £80–£90. Set dinner £28. 1-night bookings sometimes refused weekends.

YNYSHIR HALL

Once Queen Victoria's country retreat, this 'pretty' manor house is run as a luxury hotel/restaurant (Relais & Châteaux) by Joan and Rob Reen, who own it with John and Jenny Talbot. The Reens celebrated their 25th year at *Ynyshir* in 2014. 'It is good to see them around even at quiet times; the staff are very helpful,' said a visitor. Rob Reen is a noted artist: his bold canvases can be seen throughout the hotel. In the formal restaurant, which has picture windows with views of the Cambrian Mountains, chef Gareth Ward prepares eight- and eleven-course tasting menus. His elaborate dishes might include leeks (BBQ, purée, fermented); roe deer, mushroom, wild garlic, pine. There has been much recent renovation: two therapy rooms have been opened, offering holistic treatments. The bedrooms, named after famous artists, have bright colours, an 'opulent' feel. Two are in garden suites: Chagall has a living room and an outdoor seating area; Miró, which has a private balcony, is suitable for wheelchair-users. *Ynyshir* stands in 'lovely' grounds backed by ancient trees alongside a 'rewarding' RSPB reserve.

25% DISCOUNT VOUCHERS

Eglwysfach
nr Machynlleth SY20 8TA

T: 01654-781209
F: 01654-781366
E: info@ynyshirhall.co.uk
W: www.ynyshirhall.co.uk

BEDROOMS: 10, 2 garden suites, 1 in studio annexe, 3 on ground floor, 1 suitable for ♿.
OPEN: all year except 4–31 Jan.
FACILITIES: drawing room, bar lounge, breakfast room, restaurant, free Wi-Fi, civil wedding licence, 14-acre gardens in 1,000-acre bird reserve.
BACKGROUND MUSIC: classical/jazz in bar, restaurant.
LOCATION: 6 miles SW of Machynlleth.
CHILDREN: not under 9 in evening in restaurant.
DOGS: allowed in some bedrooms by arrangement, not in public rooms.
CREDIT CARDS: Amex, MasterCard, Visa.
PRICES: [2014] per room B&B £230–£750, D,B&B £375–£895. Set dinner £72.50–£90. 1-night bookings refused on busy weekends.

EGLWYSWRW Pembrokeshire

Map 3:D2

AEL Y BRYN

In farmland near the Pembrokeshire coast,
Robert Smith and Arwel Hughes have
converted a former prisoner-of-war camp into
an unusual B&B. They are 'kind and considerate
hosts'. 'When we arrived, we were welcomed
with delicious baked delights,' said a Dutch
visitor in 2014. 'Our room was spacious, clean
and beautifully furnished, with a huge bed –
quality bedding included a top sheet which is
sadly missing at most B&Bs/hotels. It looked
over the garden to the hills beyond; we watched
the sunset each evening. The bathroom had a
bath and large shower.' The public rooms have
'interesting objects', an antique glass collection.
A 'stunning' music room has a grand piano, an
organ and a 'superb' fireplace. There are exotic
plants, a telescope in the conservatory. A
baronial-style hall has a 'spectacular' chandelier.
Tables are 'well dressed' for dinner. The
vegetables, served in oven dishes, are
'outstanding'. 'A beautiful lemon posset was one
of the best desserts I've ever tasted.' A
'wonderful' breakfast has a 'magnificent' fruit
salad, home-made jams. 'Lots of choice' of
cooked dishes. (*Adelheid Smitt*)

25% DISCOUNT VOUCHERS

Crymych SA41 3UL

T: 01239-891411
E: stay@aelybrynpembrokeshire.
co.uk
W: www.aelybrynpembrokeshire.
co.uk

BEDROOMS: 4, all on ground floor.
OPEN: all year except Christmas/
New Year.
FACILITIES: library, music room,
dining room, conservatory, free
Wi-Fi, courtyard, garden (wildlife
pond, stream, bowls court).
BACKGROUND MUSIC: 'easy
listening'/classical.
LOCATION: ½ mile N of village.
CHILDREN: not under 14.
DOGS: not allowed.
CREDIT CARDS: MasterCard, Visa.
PRICES: [2014] per room B&B
£96–£120. Set dinner £24–£28.

THE FELIN FACH GRIFFIN

♀ *César award in 2013*

Between the Brecon Beacons and the Black Mountains, this roadside inn has been owned by brothers Charles and Edmund Inkin, whose childhood home is nearby, for 14 years. It is here that they created the relaxed style ('a modern version of a traditional inn,' they say) that is much liked by *Guide* readers. There are books and a Roberts radio (not a television) in the bedrooms; mobile phone signals are restricted, though satellite broadband is being installed for those who insist on them. There are leather sofas, wooden floors, open fires, wooden tables and chairs in the linked rooms in the bar and dining areas. Dogs are welcomed 'as much as their owners', and are allowed to sit under the table in the tack room. Head gardener Joe Hand provides vegetables, fresh fruit and rhubarb from the kitchen garden in the grounds for the menus of chef Ross Bruce. Typical dishes: cured salmon, pea and broad bean Caesar salad; shin of Welsh beef, cèpe risotto, asparagus and wet garlic. The brothers run *The Gurnard's Head*, Zennor, and *The Old Coastguard*, Mousehole (see entries), in similar style.

Felin Fach, nr Brecon
LD3 0UB

T: 01874-620111
E: enquiries@felinfachgriffin.co.uk
W: www.felinfachgriffin.co.uk

BEDROOMS: 7.
OPEN: all year except 24/25 Dec.
FACILITIES: bar area, dining room, breakfast room, private dining room, free Wi-Fi, 1-acre garden (stream, kitchen garden), only bar/dining room suitable for &.
BACKGROUND MUSIC: Radio 4 at breakfast, 'carefully considered music at other times'.
LOCATION: 4½ miles NE of Brecon, in village on A470.
CHILDREN: all ages welcomed.
DOGS: allowed in bedrooms, at some tables in bar.
CREDIT CARDS: MasterCard, Visa.
PRICES: [2014] per room B&B £117.50–£185, D,B&B £170–£217.50. Set menus £23–£28.50, à la carte £38.50. 1-night bookings occasionally refused.

THE MANOR TOWN HOUSE

Near the town square of the ferry port (with 'wonderful' views of the lower town harbour), this Grade II listed Georgian house is run as a B&B by Helen and Chris Sheldon. In warm weather, guests can take cream teas with home-baked cakes on a sea-facing terrace; these are served in the lounge on less clement days. Many of the bedrooms have an original fireplace; all have a mix of antique furniture; one room has an ornate mirror and an Edwardian theme; another has walnut Art Deco-style furniture. All are equipped with a welcome tray (spring water, Fairtrade tea and coffee); dressing gowns are provided. Children are welcomed: a travel cot and a fold-out single bed are available. Breakfast has free-range ingredients from a local butcher; special diets are catered for (by arrangement). Fresh fruit and Greek yogurt are a lighter option. There is good walking from the door; the Pembrokeshire Coastal Path can be joined in the wooded valley below or walkers can use the excellent local bus services to tackle stretches further afield. Bespoke tours of the area can be arranged in the summer months.

11 Main Street
Fishguard SA65 9HG

T: 01348-873260
E: enquiries@manortownhouse.com
W: www.manortownhouse.com

BEDROOMS: 6.
OPEN: all year except Christmas.
FACILITIES: 2 lounges, breakfast room, free Wi-Fi, small walled garden, unsuitable for &.
BACKGROUND MUSIC: classical at breakfast.
LOCATION: central.
CHILDREN: all ages welcomed.
DOGS: not allowed.
CREDIT CARDS: MasterCard, Visa.
PRICES: [2014] per room B&B single £65–£85, double £85–£110. 1-night bookings sometimes refused peak weekends.

PENBONTBREN

❧César award in 2012

'Everything is of a high standard' at this luxury B&B, a conversion of an old farmhouse hotel in extensive grounds near National Trust beaches. The owners, Richard Morgan-Price and Huw Thomas, were 'very welcoming to us and our dog', says a visitor this year. 'I cannot think of anything they had not supplied that we might have needed.' The accommodation is in five spacious suites in converted farm buildings (a former stable, a granary, an old mill and a threshing barn). Each has a sitting room and a private terrace; three are on the ground floor; two reach their terrace by covered steps. The furnishings and fittings are 'faultless'. One suite, with a separate bedroom and a wet room, is suitable for a family and a visitor in a wheelchair. The owners will recommend eating places nearby. Breakfast is taken in another converted barn which has 'pretty wallpaper, wooden blinds and crisp white linen'. There is a buffet with juices, cereals, prunes stewed in Earl Grey and Triple Sec. A dish of local cockles, bacon and laver bread is among the cooked choices. (*Annabel Thomas, and others*)

25% DISCOUNT VOUCHERS

Glynarthen
Llandysul SA44 6PE

T: 01239-810248
F: 01239-811129
E: contact@penbontbren.com
W: www.penbontbren.com

BEDROOMS: 5 in annexe, 3 on ground floor, 1 suitable for &.
OPEN: all year except Christmas.
FACILITIES: breakfast room, free Wi-Fi, 32-acre grounds.
BACKGROUND MUSIC: none.
LOCATION: 5 miles N of Newcastle Emlyn.
CHILDREN: all ages welcomed.
DOGS: not allowed in breakfast room, most bedrooms.
CREDIT CARDS: MasterCard, Visa.
PRICES: per room B&B £99–£110. 1-night bookings sometimes refused weekends.

HARLECH Gwynedd

CASTLE COTTAGE

Chef/proprietor Glyn Roberts and his wife, Jacqueline, have run this former coaching inn as a restaurant-with-rooms for 25 years. It stands on a steep slope above the river estuary near the castle ('an amazing setting with wonderful views'). This year they have restructured the menu: guests can choose between two or three courses (pre-dinner canapés taken in the bar, and home-made bread are included). A five-course tasting menu ('portions are smaller') can be taken by an entire table. In the contemporary restaurant (linen on Welsh oak tables, leather chairs), Mr Roberts serves 'delicious' dishes with 'imaginative' combinations, perhaps smoked haddock kedgeree, poached egg, light curry sauce; cod with vanilla salt, saffron potatoes, white wine and prawn jus. The bedrooms, in the main building and a Grade II listed stone cottage next door, have a modern decor, with splashes of colour on headboards and curtains. 'My large room had high-quality fittings, a seven-foot bed; a bath and wet room; superb,' said a visitor this year. There is limited parking by the restaurant; guidance will be given on where best to go. (*Ian Malone, and others*)

25% DISCOUNT VOUCHERS

Y Llech, Harlech
LL46 2YL

T: 01766-780479
E: glyn@castlecottageharlech.co.uk
W: www.castlecottageharlech.co.uk

BEDROOMS: 7, 4 in annexe, 2 on ground floor.
OPEN: all year except Christmas and 3 weeks Nov.
FACILITIES: bar/lounge, restaurant, free Wi-Fi.
BACKGROUND MUSIC: 'discreet' in bar, restaurant.
LOCATION: town centre.
CHILDREN: all ages welcomed.
DOGS: not allowed.
CREDIT CARDS: MasterCard, Visa.
PRICES: [2014] per room B&B £130–£175. Set menu £35–£50. 1-night bookings sometimes refused bank holidays.

KNIGHTON Powys

❧ MILEBROOK HOUSE

César award: Welsh hotel of the year

The 'settled and reassuring feel' at Beryl and
Rodney Marsden's small country hotel in the
Teme valley was liked by returning visitors this
year. Three generations of the family are now
involved in running the stone dower house.
Beryl Marsden is 'endlessly on duty; at breakfast
she is in the kitchen; in the afternoon she is in
the bar talking to guests; when I got back late,
she was the one to open the door'. Her daughter,
Joanne, helps her in the office and front-of-
house; her 27-year-old granddaughter, Katie, is
the chef. The 'well-varied' seasonal menu of
modern dishes might include coarse duck and
pistachio terrine, red onion confit; slow-roast
pork belly, bubble and squeak. A separate menu
can be taken in the 'intimate' bar. The house
wine is recommended. The quietest bedrooms
are at the rear. 'Yes, the road at the front is busy,
but not at night; anyway you face a hill with
sheep and woodland; only a fussy person could
complain.' A bedroom overlooking the garden
was well equipped; 'the bathroom was
beautifully clean'. (*Richard Creed, John Bell*)

25% DISCOUNT VOUCHERS

Milebrook
Knighton, Powys LD7 1LT

T: 01547-528632
E: hotel@milebrookhouse.co.uk
W: www.milebrookhouse.co.uk

BEDROOMS: 10, 2 on ground floor.
OPEN: all year, restaurant closed
Sun/Mon Nov–Feb.
FACILITIES: lounge, bar, 2 dining
rooms, free Wi-Fi, 4-acre grounds
on river (terraces, pond, croquet,
fishing).
BACKGROUND MUSIC: classical in bar
and restaurant.
LOCATION: on A4113, 2 miles E of
Knighton.
CHILDREN: not under 8.
DOGS: not allowed.
CREDIT CARDS: MasterCard, Visa.
PRICES: [2014] per room B&B £144,
D,B&B £195. À la carte £32.

LAMPETER Ceredigion

THE FALCONDALE

'Run with good traditional taste and without pretension', this Italianate hotel stands in landscaped gardens above the Teifi valley. It is owned by Chris and Lisa Hutton: 'The staff and proprietors are helpful, down-to-earth people whose pride in what they are doing is reflected in high standards,' said a visitor. *Guide* inspectors 'really enjoyed' their stay. The public areas are 'roomy and well decorated'; there's a grand piano in the lounge; leather bucket chairs in an enclosed veranda; an 'elegant, formal' dining room. The 'excellent' cooking of chef Mike Green is much admired. His menu might include dishes like seared escalope of smoked salmon, potato pancake; loin of Welsh lamb, honey-roasted vegetables. 'He created a special menu for me,' said a visitor on a dairy-free diet, 'and explained how he made his lovely sorbets.' Each of the 'charming' bedrooms 'has its own character, with individually chosen ornaments, wallpaper, curtain and bedspread'. An 'enormous' room had classical furnishings, a separate sitting area. Dogs are welcomed: 'Bowls and treats are left in the room and there is plenty of space to walk in the grounds.' (*Francis Kearney, and others*)

25% DISCOUNT VOUCHERS

Falcondale Drive
Lampeter SA48 7RX

T: 01570-422910
E: info@thefalcondale.co.uk
W: www.thefalcondale.co.uk

BEDROOMS: 18.
OPEN: all year.
FACILITIES: lift, bar, lounge, conservatory, restaurant, free Wi-Fi, civil wedding licence, terrace, 14-acre gardens.
BACKGROUND MUSIC: classical in public areas.
LOCATION: 1 mile N of Lampeter.
CHILDREN: all ages welcomed.
DOGS: welcomed.
CREDIT CARDS: MasterCard, Visa.
PRICES: [2014] per room B&B £140–£190. Set dinner £40.

LLANARTHNE Carmarthenshire

Map 3:D2

LLWYN HELYG `NEW`

In countryside near the National Botanic Garden of Wales, Caron and Fiona Jones welcome B&B guests to their lavishly finished, newly built stone house. 'It has an unexpected wow factor, particularly for the rural setting,' said *Guide* inspectors, who had a 'memorable' visit. 'The house has been done in granite, marble and limestone. An impressive oak staircase leads to the bedrooms: ours had lovely rugs on the brown granite floor; a fine bed with four barley twist posts, plump pillows and a black Italianate bedcover; large Etruscan table lamps; decent hangers in a good-quality wardrobe; a huge, luxurious bathroom had his and hers basins, a whirlpool bath and a separate walk-in shower. One could easily have been in a five-star hotel in Italy.' There are 'lots of sitting areas' in the hallways and the more intimate lounges. The Listening Room, which has squashy sofas, a high raftered ceiling, has 'the best sound system we have heard outside the Albert Hall'. Breakfast, 'fresh and of good quality', is taken at separate tables in a 'bright' room facing a courtyard with a water feature.

Llanarthne SA32 8HJ

T: 01558-668778
E: caron.jones1@btopenworld.com
W: www.llwynhelygcountryhouse.co.uk

BEDROOMS: 3.
OPEN: all year, except Christmas.
FACILITIES: 5 lounges, breakfast room, free Wi-Fi, 3-acre garden, unsuitable for &.
BACKGROUND MUSIC: radio at breakfast 'if requested'.
LOCATION: 8 miles E of Carmarthen.
CHILDREN: not under 16.
DOGS: not allowed.
CREDIT CARDS: Amex, MasterCard, Visa.
PRICES: [2014] per room B&B £125–£150.

TYDDYN LLAN

❦César award in 2006

Once a shooting lodge, Bryan and Susan Webb's restaurant-with-rooms is 'a truly lovely place', say trusted reporters this year. The pretty Georgian house stands in well-maintained lawns and gardens facing the Berwyn Mountains. Susan Webb runs the front-of-house 'with allure and dynamism; she is enchanting in the way she approaches guests'. Bryan Webb, the *Michelin*-starred chef, is 'a generous man, and the portions served, often minute in such restaurants, are equally generous'. He dismisses the trend for foams and jellies in his presentation of dishes like dressed crab, avocado salsa; Goosnargh duck breast, potato pancake, apples and cider. Everything about the house, 'the style, the comfort, the housekeeping, shows meticulous attention to detail'. The bedrooms are individually styled: some have an antique bed, one has a Victorian roll-top bath. 'Their sangfroid during a power cut at breakfast has to be commended. They produced perfect scrambled eggs on a camping stove, boiled water in an outbuilding, and even managed to provide toast; a tour de force.' (*Francine and Ian Walsh, and others*)

25% DISCOUNT VOUCHERS

Llandrillo
nr Corwen LL21 0ST

T: 01490-440264
F: 01490-440414
E: info@tyddynllan.co.uk
W: www.tyddynllan.co.uk

BEDROOMS: 13, 1, on ground floor, suitable for ♿.
OPEN: all year.
FACILITIES: ramp, 2 lounges, bar, 2 dining rooms, free Wi-Fi, civil wedding licence, 3-acre garden.
BACKGROUND MUSIC: none.
LOCATION: 5 miles SW of Corwen.
CHILDREN: all ages welcomed.
DOGS: allowed in some bedrooms (£10 per night), not in public rooms.
CREDIT CARDS: MasterCard, Visa.
PRICES: [2014] per room B&B £195–£300, D,B&B £270–£410. Set dinner £45–£55, tasting menus £70–£85.

BODYSGALLEN HALL AND SPA

❦César award in 1988

'Impressive and hospitable', this Grade I listed
17th-century mansion is owned by the National
Trust and run by Historic House Hotels. 'A
place for a quiet luxury break', it stands in a
park with woodland walks, a knot garden and
follies; views of Snowdonia and Conwy Castle.
The 'beautiful' house and gardens have been
'well maintained', say visitors. In the oldest part
of the building, the large entrance hall and the
first-floor drawing room have oak panelling and
stone mullioned windows, antique furniture,
fine pictures. The bedrooms in the main
building, large and elegant, have chintz, floral
patterns, heavy drapes; sheets and blankets on
the bed. Cottage suites cater for families
(children must be over six); some have a private
garden. Smart casual dress is required in the
main dining room where the chef, Michael
Cheetham, serves imaginative modern dishes,
perhaps Aberdaron crab, parsnip brittle, truffle
powder, chestnut purée; honey-glazed duck
breast, confit leg roll, stewed cucumber.
Simpler meals are served in the bistro. Various
treatments are offered in the spa, which has a
large swimming pool, sauna and gym.

Llandudno LL30 1RS

T: 01492-584466
F: 01492-582519
E: info@bodysgallen.com
W: www.bodysgallen.com

BEDROOMS: 31, 16 in cottages,
1 suitable for ♿.
OPEN: all year, restaurant closed Mon.
FACILITIES: hall, drawing room,
library, bar, dining room, bistro, free
Wi-Fi, civil wedding licence, 220-acre
park (gardens, tennis, croquet), spa
(16-metre swimming pool).
BACKGROUND MUSIC: none.
LOCATION: 2 miles S of Llandudno.
CHILDREN: no children under 6 in
hotel, under 8 in spa.
DOGS: allowed in some cottages, not
in bedrooms.
CREDIT CARDS: Amex, MasterCard,
Visa.
PRICES: [2014] per room B&B single
£159–£195, double £179–£265.
Dinner (main dining room) £32–£49,
(bistro) £19.50–£27.50. 1-night
bookings sometimes refused.

SEE ALSO SHORTLIST

OSBORNE HOUSE

On the 'elegant' promenade of the seaside resort, this small hotel 'takes a lot of beating', says a returning visitor this year. Sister to the larger *Empire Hotel*, 200 yards away, it is managed by Elyse Waddy; Michael Waddy is the chef. Accommodation is in six suites, each with a separate sitting room. An 'atmospheric' first-floor room was 'beautifully furnished with antiques. It had wooden floors with rugs throughout, a sitting room with a large bay window overlooking the promenade, a real flame-effect gas fire and a large squishy sofa in front of a square coffee table; table lamps everywhere.' An archway leads to a bedroom. A pantry has a fridge, china, cafetière and kettle; the bathroom has a roll-top bath and separate rain shower. Suites on the second and third floors (no lift) have views of 'the beautiful bay and cliffs'. There is a bar and a café on the ground floor, which serves a bistro-style menu all day, 'far better than many hotel restaurants'. A continental breakfast is brought to the bedroom (a cooked option can be taken at the *Empire*). (*Barbara Watkinson*)

17 North Parade
Llandudno, LL30 2LP

T: 01492-860330
F: 01492-860791
E: sales@osbornehouse.co.uk
W: www.osbornehouse.co.uk

BEDROOMS: 6.
OPEN: all year, except Christmas.
FACILITIES: sitting room, bar, café/bistro, free Wi-Fi, unsuitable for &.
BACKGROUND MUSIC: 'varied' in café/bistro.
LOCATION: on promenade.
CHILDREN: not under 14.
DOGS: not allowed.
CREDIT CARDS: all major cards.
PRICES: per room B&B £140–£180, D,B&B £160–£215. Set menu £22.50. 1-night bookings refused Sat.

SEE ALSO SHORTLIST

ST TUDNO HOTEL

❦ *César award in 1987*

On the seafront of the Victorian resort, this traditional hotel has been owned and managed in hands-on style by owner Martin Bland for more than 40 years. 'He is still very much involved,' said a returning visitor in 2014. 'He greeted and helped us on arrival and when we departed. The staff are pleasant, professional; the hotel feels like a big family.' The 'well-maintained' public rooms have patterned wallpaper, swagged drapery; an award-winning afternoon tea can be taken in the bar/lounge facing the bay. Everyone admires the 'consistently excellent' cooking of chef Andrew Foster, served in the Italianate dining room. His seasonal menu might include baked haddock, Conwy Bay mussel chowder, Anglesey scallops, white wine and kale. A rare dissenter complained of 'lack of value for money' and a cramped car park. The brightly decorated bedrooms have a hospitality tray bearing home-made biscuits, and fresh milk in the fridge; the best rooms have a sea view. Breakfast, served entirely at table, is 'especially good; the cooked dishes have kidneys as part of the grill, a rare treat'. (*Stephen and Pauline Glover, and others*)

North Parade, Promenade
Llandudno LL30 2LP

T: 01492-874411
F: 01492-860407
E: sttudnohotel@btinternet.com
W: www.st-tudno.co.uk

BEDROOMS: 18.
OPEN: all year.
FACILITIES: lift, three lounges, restaurant, free Wi-Fi, indoor heated swimming pool (8 by 4 metres), civil wedding licence, patio, 'secret garden', unsuitable for &.
BACKGROUND MUSIC: when quiet.
LOCATION: on promenade, parking.
CHILDREN: all ages welcomed, under-5s have early supper.
DOGS: by arrangement (£10 per night), only in coffee lounge, not unattended in bedrooms.
CREDIT CARDS: all major cards.
PRICES: [2014] per person B&B single £80–£95, double £49–£155, D,B&B single £113–£128, double £82–£188. Set menus £22.50–£27.50, à la carte £35.

SEE ALSO SHORTLIST

LLANGAMMARCH WELLS Powys

Map 3:D3

THE LAKE

César award in 1992

In a 'beautiful' rural setting by a lake on the River Irfon, Jean-Pierre Mifsud's country house hotel has a traditional ambience. Built as a sporting lodge, the half-timbered building became the only barium spa resort outside Germany. Kaiser Wilhelm II visited in 1912 (his signature is in the visitors' book). The owner is often found greeting guests in the evening; 'the staff are always welcoming,' said one visitor. Bedrooms in the main house are decorated in country house style with rich patterned fabrics; twelve suites in a new wing, each with an open-plan sitting area, have a more modern look; a room for wheelchair-users has been 'thoughtfully designed'. The three large lounges have plenty of seating, and are furnished with antiques, a grand piano, log fires, fresh floral decorations. In the formal restaurant, Darren Tattersall is now the chef; he serves a four-course dinner menu of modern dishes which might include Jerusalem artichoke bavarois; pork fillet, smoked belly, black pudding, creamed cabbage. A variety of treatments is available in the spa, which has a swimming pool and an outdoor hot tub.

Llangammarch Wells
LD4 4BS

T: 01591-620202
F: 01591-620457
E: info@lakecountryhouse.co.uk
W: www.lakecountryhouse.co.uk

BEDROOMS: 31, 12 suites in adjacent lodge, 7 on ground floor, 1 suitable for &.

OPEN: all year.

FACILITIES: ramps, 3 lounges, orangery, restaurant, free Wi-Fi, spa (15-metre swimming pool), civil wedding licence, 50-acre grounds (tennis).

BACKGROUND MUSIC: none.

LOCATION: 8 miles SW of Builth Wells.

CHILDREN: all ages welcomed.

DOGS: allowed (£10 charge), not in public rooms.

CREDIT CARDS: Amex, MasterCard, Visa.

PRICES: per room B&B £125–£260, D,B&B £195–£310. Set dinner £45. 1-night bookings sometimes refused.

LLOYDS

In an unassuming building in a small market town in the Cambrian Mountains, this 'modest' guest house is liked for the 'quirky and personal' style of the owners, Tom Lines and Roy Hayter. They tell us that they plan to put the house on the market in August 2015 and offer B&B only thereafter until it is sold. *Guide* readers (and 'regular guests who have become friends') will still be able to book the highly regarded dinners which are 'quite an occasion'. Spring cleaning has carried on regardless and the stairs and one bedroom have been given new carpets this year. The bedrooms are 'nicely decorated, well equipped and designed'. They are reached by a steep narrow staircase – the owners will help with luggage. Tom Lines 'meets and greets guests in a pleasant and natural manner'; when dinner has been ordered, he 'presents' the four-course menu. Roy Hayter uses ingredients from local farmers and suppliers for his 'imaginative' dishes, perhaps oriental chicken salad, roast romano peppers; pancetta-wrapped roast sirloin of beef, mushroom and shallot stuffing. Breakfast is 'of equal quality'. (*S and PG*)

25% DISCOUNT VOUCHERS

6 Cambrian Place
Llanidloes SY18 6BX

T: 01686-412284
E: lloyds@dircon.co.uk
W: www.lloydshotel.co.uk

BEDROOMS: 7.
OPEN: mid-Mar–end Dec, closed Christmas, occasionally at other times.
FACILITIES: sitting room, breakfast room, restaurant, free Wi-Fi, unsuitable for &.
BACKGROUND MUSIC: none.
LOCATION: near the town centre.
CHILDREN: all ages welcomed.
DOGS: not allowed.
CREDIT CARDS: MasterCard, Visa.
PRICES: [2014] per person B&B single £52–£71, double £43–£49, D,B&B single £87–£106, double £88–£94. Set dinner £35.

CARLTON RIVERSIDE

♥ *César award in 1998*

In a small mid-Wales spa town, Mary Ann and Alan Gilchrist give a 'warm welcome' to their restaurant-with-rooms by a bridge over the River Irfon. 'The food is very good at both dinner and breakfast,' say visitors this year. 'Alan Gilchrist is a good host in the bar before dinner and at table.' In the small, modern restaurant, Mary Ann Gilchrist's cooking is much admired. She is passionate about finding local and organic ingredients for her modern dishes, perhaps scallop and crab lasagne, cauliflower cream; roast rump of Welsh lamb, Madeira jus, crushed new potatoes. Her husband has assembled an extensive wine list which has more than 20 half bottles. There is no dress code: 'We just want you to be comfortable.' Home-made pizzas are served in the *Riverside* bar on the lower ground floor, which is open from Thursday to Sunday evenings. The bedrooms vary in size: the 'spacious' Oriental Room has a large sofa and antique oriental furnishings. Road noise 'might be a problem'. The Chapel Room has a king-size bed; a compact bathroom. (*AD and J Lloyd*)

25% DISCOUNT VOUCHERS

Irfon Crescent
Llanwrtyd Wells LD5 4SP

T: 01591-610248
E: carltonriverside@hotmail.co.uk
W: www.carltonriverside.com

BEDROOMS: 5.
OPEN: all year except 22–30 Dec, restaurant closed Sun.
FACILITIES: Reception, bar/lounge, restaurant, free Wi-Fi, unsuitable for &.
BACKGROUND MUSIC: classical piano in lounge.
LOCATION: town centre, no private parking.
CHILDREN: all ages welcomed.
DOGS: not allowed in public rooms.
CREDIT CARDS: MasterCard, Visa.
PRICES: [2014] per room B&B single £50, double £65–£100, D,B&B £70–£140. À la carte £35. 1-night bookings sometimes refused.

SEE ALSO SHORTLIST

LLANGOED HALL

'The changes are immense and everything is lovely,' says a visitor, returning to this Jacobean mansion, now a country house hotel once owned by the late Sir Bernard Ashley. More than £3 million has been spent on refurbishment by a private owner, who has restored Calum Milne as the manager. There may be new furnishings and carpets, but much has been preserved: Sir Bernard's collection of mainly 20th-century art is displayed throughout (two Laura Ashley wallpapers remain in the renovated rooms). Fine bone china in exclusive patterns has been introduced: 'It might be posh but in no way does it feel over the top; just exclusive and a treat.' In the formal dining room, the chef, Nick Brodie, combines fruit and vegetables from the garden with local ingredients for his modern dishes, eg, tartare of Welsh Black beef, wild mushrooms, pine tree powder. The bedrooms, which have views of the Wye valley, have fine pictures and ornaments, antiques; sheets and blankets; a decanter of sherry and fresh flowers; a modern bathroom. 'The staff, all local, were most helpful; a fabulous place.' (*Richard Morgan-Price, Sue Winter*)

Llyswen
Brecon LD3 0YP

T: 01874-754525
F: 01874-754545
E: enquiries@llangoedhall.com
W: www.llangoedhall.co.uk

BEDROOMS: 23.
OPEN: all year.
FACILITIES: morning room, drawing room, billiard room, function rooms, free Wi-Fi, 17-acre gardens and parklands.
BACKGROUND MUSIC: pianist in morning room at weekends.
LOCATION: 1 mile N of Llyswen.
CHILDREN: all ages welcomed, over-5s only in restaurant.
DOGS: allowed in grounds, not in restaurant or bedrooms (heated kennels).
CREDIT CARDS: MasterCard, Visa.
PRICES: [2014] per room B&B £150–£400. À la carte £70.

PEN-Y-GWRYD HOTEL

♦ *César award in 1995*

Time has stood still at this historic climbing hotel which has been owned by the Pullee family for three generations. It remains 'eccentric and old-fashioned in style', say visitors this year, who remained enthusiastic despite having to ask to change from a 'cramped' double bedroom to a 'more spacious' room. 'Would we recommend it? Yes. Would we go again? Yes.' An earlier visitor was reminded of 'the best facets of hostels we visited in our youth'. There is neither TV nor radio in the simple bedrooms ('what a blessing'); nor are there locks on the doors. Only five rooms have an en suite bathroom. A 'hot soak in a Victorian tub awaits in the genuine Victorian bathrooms'. Nick and Rupert Pullee are the self-effacing hosts; the service is 'cheerful, friendly and informed'. The bar, which has memorabilia of the 1953 ascent of Everest (*Pen-y-Gwryd* was the training base), has 'excellent local draught beer'. A gong announces dinner, taken at separate tables: 'The food was good and plentiful; no fancy gourmet cooking.' Most guests come for the climbing or walking. (*AD and J Lloyd, and others*)

Nant Gwynant
LL55 4NT

T: 01286-870211
E: escape@pyg.co.uk
W: www.pyg.co.uk

BEDROOMS: 16, 1 on ground floor, garden suite in annexe.
OPEN: Mar–Nov, New Year, weekends Jan/Feb.
FACILITIES: lounge, bar, games room, dining room, Wi-Fi (£2 charge), chapel, 1-acre grounds (natural unheated 60-metre swimming pool, sauna).
BACKGROUND MUSIC: none.
LOCATION: between Beddgelert and Capel Curig.
CHILDREN: all ages welcomed.
DOGS: allowed (£2 charge), not in some public rooms.
CREDIT CARDS: Amex, MasterCard, Visa.
PRICES: [2014] per person B&B £42–£52. Set dinner £25–£30. 1-night bookings often refused weekends.

THE GROVE

Close to a village of 'surprisingly interesting shops' facing the Preseli hills, this 'imposing' building is run as a small hotel by the owners Neil Kedward and Zoë Agar. 'Relaxed' hosts, they have rescued the 18th-century mansion from dereliction, adding bedrooms in a recently built wing, a coach house and a 15th-century longhouse in the grounds. They have restored Arts and Crafts features added during a Victorian renovation, including some fine ceramic fireplaces in the lounges and library and first-floor bedrooms. The public areas have work by leading Welsh artists (some of which are for sale). A 'capacious' main-house bedroom was liked: it overlooks the 'beautifully designed' formal gardens. A suite in the coach house has oak beams, exposed masonry walls, an inglenook fireplace. Well-proportioned rooms in the longhouse have considerable character. Produce from the kitchen garden supplies chef Duncan Barham's 'delicious' modern menus of dishes like bresaola, pea and pepper délice, goat's curd; spiced monkfish, lentil dhal, mango and cucumber. Breakfast, in a light garden room with a terrace, has 'wonderful softly smoked kippers and grilled, full-flavoured tomatoes'.

Molleston
Narberth SA67 8BX

T: 01834-860915
F: 01834-861000
E: info@thegrove-narberth.co.uk
W: www.thegrove-narberth.co.uk

BEDROOMS: 20, 2 in coach house (1 on ground floor), 4 in longhouse, plus 4 self-catering cottages.
OPEN: all year.
FACILITIES: 4 lounges, library, restaurant, breakfast room, free Wi-Fi, civil wedding licence, 26-acre grounds.
BACKGROUND MUSIC: jazz, 'easy listening' in public areas.
LOCATION: 1 mile S of village.
CHILDREN: all ages welcomed.
DOGS: allowed in public areas.
CREDIT CARDS: Amex, MasterCard, Visa.
PRICES: [2014] per room B&B £150–£320, D,B&B £248–£418. Tasting menus £79, à la carte £54.

SEE ALSO SHORTLIST

CNAPAN

The Cooper family, 'lovely, caring people', have been running this listed Georgian town house in the centre of a small coastal town as a restaurant-with-rooms for 30 years. Judith Cooper is in charge of the kitchen ('I'm a cook, not a chef,' she says); her husband, Michael, and their son, Oliver, are active front-of-house. The public areas of the pink-painted house have a 'lived-in and loved' interior, filled with family treasures and photographs (it is also the Coopers' home). The sitting room has a wood-burning stove; around the house are maps, books, magazines and games. In the restaurant, which has linen cloths on wooden tables and a Welsh dresser, Judith Cooper uses local ingredients for her 'high-quality' meals, with dishes like smoked salmon and crab tart, zesty laver bread, caper mayonnaise; roasted guineafowl breast, red onion, thyme and leek ragout. The pretty bedrooms are light and bright; each has a shower; guests who would prefer a 'relaxing soak' have access to a shared bathroom. Two bedrooms were renovated this year. Breakfasts have home-made muesli and preserves; fresh farm eggs, kippers and local bacon.

East Street, Newport
nr Fishguard SA42 0SY

T: 01239-820575
F: 01239-820878
E: enquiry@cnapan.co.uk
W: www.cnapan.co.uk

BEDROOMS: 5, plus a self-catering cottage.
OPEN: 21 Mar–2 Jan, closed Christmas, B&B only at New Year, restaurant closed Tues.
FACILITIES: lounge, bar, restaurant, free Wi-Fi, small garden, only restaurant suitable for &.
BACKGROUND MUSIC: jazz/Latin in evenings in dining room.
LOCATION: town centre.
CHILDREN: all ages welcomed.
DOGS: only guide dogs allowed.
CREDIT CARDS: MasterCard, Visa.
PRICES: per person B&B single £62.50, double £95. D,B&B £77.50 per person, à la carte £30. 1-night bookings sometimes refused during peak season and some Saturdays.

SEE ALSO SHORTLIST

LLYS MEDDYG

Once a coaching inn, then a doctor's house (the name translates as Doctor's Court), this Grade II listed Georgian building has been given a smart make-over by Ed and Lou Sykes. They run it as a restaurant-with-rooms. There is a guest sitting room, a spacious dining room, and an informal cellar bar. The chef, Patrick Szenasi, looks locally for the ingredients for his modern menus with dishes like brown crab brûlée, white crab meat, pickled cucumber; beef fillet and ox cheek, horseradish pommes, artichoke purée. The menu can be taken in the flagstoned bar on the lower ground floor (where dogs are welcomed) and, in summer, in the 'lovely' enclosed kitchen garden at the rear. Children are welcomed: meals can be tailored for younger tastes; there are beanbags and giant garden games to play. The bedrooms have a contemporary decor. A 'spacious' room had a king-size bed; 'a fridge with fresh milk; a dressing room with curtained wardrobe, mirror and chair'. An attic room has light oak furniture, cream-painted panelling, a bright red-and-white-striped bedspread. Three rooms have a sofa bed for children. More reports, please.

25% DISCOUNT VOUCHERS

East Street, Newport
nr Fishguard SA42 0SY

T: 01239-820008
E: info@llysmeddyg.com
W: www.llysmeddyg.com

BEDROOMS: 8, 1 on ground floor, 3 in annexe, plus a cottage.
OPEN: all year, except 2 weeks Jan, 2 weeks Nov.
FACILITIES: bar, restaurant, sitting room, free Wi-Fi, civil wedding licence, garden.
BACKGROUND MUSIC: in bar and restaurant.
LOCATION: central.
CHILDREN: all ages welcomed.
DOGS: allowed in 3 bedrooms, cellar bar.
CREDIT CARDS: MasterCard, Visa.
PRICES: per person B&B £50–£90, D,B&B £80–£120. Set dinner £29.50–£35, à la carte £40. 1-night bookings sometimes refused weekends.

SEE ALSO SHORTLIST

PORTMEIRION Gwynedd

HOTEL PORTMEIRION

César award in 1990

'One of the best tourist attractions in Wales', this eccentric resort was built on a wooded peninsula by the architect Sir Clough Williams-Ellis to demonstrate that it was possible to develop a beautiful site without spoiling it. His belief that 'architectural good manners could be good business' is upheld by the 250,000 annual visits (most for the day). The juxtaposition of styles and structures 'would be hideous anywhere else but look as though they belong here', said a recent visitor. Overnight guests are accommodated in the main hotel, which was opened in 1926, in *Castell Deudraeth*, a renovated Victorian castellated mansion, and in rooms, suites and cottages dotted around the Italianate village. There are various eating options in the village during the day. In the evening, guests can eat at the hotel's Art Deco dining room, redesigned by Sir Terence Conran in 2005, where the chef, Mark Threadgill, serves modern dishes like torched mackerel, apple, beetroot gazpacho; black truffle-roasted chicken breast, confit potatoes. *Castell Deudraeth* has an informal contemporary brasserie. There is much to see and do in the village.

25% DISCOUNT VOUCHERS

Minffordd
Penrhyndeudraeth LL48 6ER

T: 01766-770000
F: 01766-770300
E: stay@portmeirion-village.com
W: www.portmeirion-village.com

BEDROOMS: 55, 14 in hotel, some on ground floor, 1 suitable for &; 11 in *Castell Deudraeth*, 30 in village.
OPEN: all year.
FACILITIES: hall, lift, 3 lounges, bar, restaurant, brasserie in *Castell*, children's supper room, function room, beauty salon, free Wi-Fi, civil wedding licence, 170-acre grounds (garden), heated swimming pool (8 by 15 metres, May–Sept).
BACKGROUND MUSIC: none.
LOCATION: 2 miles SE of Porthmadog.
CHILDREN: all ages welcomed.
DOGS: only guide dogs allowed.
CREDIT CARDS: MasterCard, Visa.
PRICES: per room B&B £119–£209, D,B&B £169–£259. Set meals £38, à la carte £50. 1-night bookings sometimes refused.

THE OLD RECTORY

Near the church on the 'beautiful' Lleyn peninsula, this handsome Georgian rectory is run as a B&B by Gary and Lindsay Ashcroft, who are 'wonderfully welcoming'. 'They clearly love this place and love what they are doing,' said a *Guide* inspector on an earlier visit. The 'light-filled' bedrooms are 'thoughtfully' furnished; they have special touches like complimentary sherry or sloe gin and chocolates. A small twin room had a built-in cupboard, a dressing table and stool and an armchair. Housekeeping is 'excellent': the linen is 'pristine', and the bathrooms are 'immaculate'. The 'delicious' breakfast can be 'a stimulating affair' as guests sit around a large table and help themselves to juices, cereals and yogurts. The 'creamy' porridge is recommended as are the cooked dishes which include bacon cured by a local butcher. There are no evening meals but a long list of nearby possibilities is given and recommendations are made. 'The fire was lit on our return in the evening so we could sit there before going to bed.' A kennel is provided in the stable ('our dog was perfectly happy'). (*David Lipsey, Wendy and Ken Edmond*)

Boduan
nr Pwllheli LL53 6DT

T: 01758-721519
E: theashcrofts@theoldrectory.net
W: www.theoldrectory.net

BEDROOMS: 3, also self-catering cottage.
OPEN: all year except Christmas.
FACILITIES: drawing room, dining room, free Wi-Fi, 3½-acre grounds, walking, riding, sailing.
BACKGROUND MUSIC: none.
LOCATION: 4 miles NW of Pwllheli.
CHILDREN: all ages welcomed.
DOGS: not allowed in house (kennel and run available).
CREDIT CARDS: MasterCard, Visa.
PRICES: per room B&B single £85–£90, double £100–£105. 1-night bookings sometimes refused high season and bank holidays.

PLAS BODEGROES

♥*César award in 1992*

The first sight of this white Georgian manor house in wooded grounds on the remote Lleyn peninsula 'raises expectations' that are invariably met by visitors to Chris and Gunna Chown's popular restaurant-with-rooms. The ambience is 'relaxing'; a fire burning in the lounge before dinner creates 'an atmospheric mood' enhanced by the 'absence of piped music (how nice)'. The 'excellent' cooking of Chris Chown and Hugh Bracegirdle is an 'outstanding feature'. In the L-shaped dining room (decorated with modern Welsh paintings), their 'imaginative' menu might include dishes like smoked salmon and halibut terrazzo, wood sorrel, horseradish cream; roast loin of Welsh Mountain lamb, devilled kidneys, onion cake, rosemary sauce. The service is 'mature, self-assured, friendly'. The bedrooms, which overlook the tranquil gardens, are decorated in grey, blue and fawn. Two rooms in a cottage in the garden face a courtyard. Home-made biscuits and mineral water are provided; early-morning tea is delivered. One room has been redecorated this year; also new is an acer and azalea garden. (*Max Lickfold, and others*)

Nefyn Road
Efailnewydd
Pwllheli LL53 5TH

T: 01758-612363
F: 01758-701247
E: gunna@bodegroes.co.uk
W: www.bodegroes.co.uk

BEDROOMS: 10, 2 in courtyard cottage.
OPEN: Mar–Nov, closed Sun and Mon except bank holidays.
FACILITIES: lounge, bar, breakfast room, restaurant, free Wi-Fi, 5-acre grounds, unsuitable for ♿.
BACKGROUND MUSIC: none.
LOCATION: 1 mile W of Pwllheli.
CHILDREN: all ages welcomed, but no under-5s in restaurant.
DOGS: not allowed in public rooms, 1 bedroom.
CREDIT CARDS: MasterCard, Visa.
PRICES: per room B&B £130–£195. D,B&B (2 nights) £170–£235 per person, set dinner £45. 1-night bookings sometimes refused.

FAIRYHILL

'Our favourite hotel anywhere', Andrew Hetherington and Paul Davies's small country hotel stands in 'wonderful' grounds with lawns, woodland, a stream and a lake. There are log fires in the public rooms of this creeper-covered 18th-century Georgian mansion. The 'comfortable and cosy' bedrooms have a modern decor and are well equipped with the latest technology. Fruit bowls are replenished daily, and beds turned down in the evening. In warm weather, 'the patio is a perfect place for a pre-dinner drink'; the restaurant is 'relaxed and the food is excellent'. David Whitecross, the chef, has a modern cooking style on a menu that has seven choices for each of three courses. Typical dishes: seared ballottine of salmon and herbs, Puy lentils; loin of Welsh lamb, lamb rissole, aubergine, thyme jus. The service by smartly dressed young staff is 'exemplary'. Breakfast has a comprehensive buffet; 'proper bread' with a toaster; 'excellent' hot dishes. Swansea is 30 minutes' drive away; the magnificent beaches of the Gower peninsula, an area of outstanding natural beauty, are nearby. (*Helen Crookston*)

Reynoldston, Gower
nr Swansea SA3 1BS

T: 01792-390139
F: 01792-391358
E: postbox@fairyhill.net
W: www.fairyhill.net

BEDROOMS: 8.
OPEN: all year except 26 Dec, 3 weeks in Jan.
FACILITIES: lounge, bar, 3 dining rooms, meeting room, free Wi-Fi, civil wedding licence, spa treatment room, 24-acre grounds, unsuitable for &.
BACKGROUND MUSIC: jazz/classical/pop in lounge, bar, dining room at mealtimes.
LOCATION: 11 miles W of Swansea.
CHILDREN: not under 8.
DOGS: 'well-behaved' dogs allowed in bedrooms, none in public rooms.
CREDIT CARDS: MasterCard, Visa.
PRICES: [2014] per room B&B £190–£290, D,B&B £280–£380. Set dinner £35–£45. 1-night bookings refused Sat.

CRUG-GLAS

In countryside close to St David's, Britain's smallest city, this Georgian farmhouse has been modernised by Perkin and Janet Evans to provide accommodation and a restaurant on their working farm. 'They are a busy couple,' say inspectors in 2014. 'He was mowing the lawn when we arrived; later he served us dinner. She took us to our room and cooked the meal.' The bedrooms are in the house and a converted milking parlour and coach house. A 'charming' suite in the converted building had 'rugs, a tiled floor, new wooden furniture, leather seating; a large, comfortable bed with good bedlinen; the modern bathroom had a whirlpool bath and a wet room shower'. Guests gather in a traditional lounge (with 'interesting' furniture, antiques and pottery) to take pre-dinner drinks from an honesty bar. In the dining room (draped curtains, an 'austere' fireplace), the 'highlight at dinner was tasty canon of lamb, reduced redcurrant jus; mixed vegetables came in individual portions'. An 'excellent' breakfast has a 'superb selection of fresh fruit, nicely laid out on a buffet table; wonderfully creamy yogurt; good-quality cooked dishes'.

nr Abereiddy, St David's
Haverfordwest SA62 6XX

T: 01348-831302
E: janet@crugglas.plus.com
W: www.crug-glas.co.uk

BEDROOMS: 7, 2 in outbuildings, 1 on ground floor.
OPEN: all year except 22–28 Dec.
FACILITIES: drawing room, dining room, free Wi-Fi, civil wedding licence, 1-acre garden on 600-acre farm.
BACKGROUND MUSIC: classical in restaurant.
LOCATION: 3½ miles NE of St David's.
CHILDREN: not under 12.
DOGS: allowed in one suite only, not in public rooms.
CREDIT CARDS: Amex, MasterCard, Visa.
PRICES: [2014] per room B&B £115–£170. À la carte £32.

THE OLD RECTORY ON THE LAKE

NEW

On the shore of Lake Tal-y-llyn beneath Cadair Idris in southern Snowdonia, this peaceful stone-built house has lake views from every window. 'Wonderful: our visit is an annual highlight,' says a regular correspondent, whose commendation brings a full entry for *The Old Rectory*. The house is run in personal style by the owners, John Caine, 'a welcoming and chatty host', and Ricky Francis, who cooks the 'very good' evening meals. There are two double bedrooms on the first floor; one has a free-standing bath and a separate walk-in shower in the bathroom. A smaller (and cheaper) room is on the ground floor. A self-contained ground-floor apartment, *The Rectory Retreat*, is equipped for visitors with mobility issues. It can be booked on a B&B basis; dogs are allowed to share this room with their owners. There is no mobile phone signal but free Wi-Fi is available. In the *Orangery* dining room, Ricky Francis uses Welsh produce for his four-course dinners. Typical dishes: locally smoked trout salad; slow-roasted Welsh lamb shank; banoffee pie. There is good walking, mountain biking and fishing. (*David Lipsey*)

25% DISCOUNT VOUCHERS

Tal-y-llyn LL36 9AJ

T: 01654-782225
E: enquiries@rectoryonthelake.co.uk
W: www.rectoryonthelake.co.uk

BEDROOMS: 3, 1 on ground floor, plus *Rectory Retreat*, a self-catering apartment on ground floor suitable for &. (also available for B&B).
OPEN: all year except Jan, dining room closed Wed.
FACILITIES: lounge, *Orangery* dining room, free Wi-Fi, 1½-acre grounds, outdoor hot tub.
BACKGROUND MUSIC: none.
LOCATION: on lake 9½ miles E of Tywyn.
CHILDREN: not under 18.
DOGS: allowed in Rectory Retreat only.
CREDIT CARDS: MasterCard, Visa.
PRICES: [2014] per room B&B single £60–£90, double £90–£120. Set dinner £30. Only 2-night bookings accepted at weekends.

DOLFFANOG FAWR

The absence of house rules (except for meal times) and the 'near perfect' service appealed to the nominators (trusted correspondents) of this small guest house at the head of Lake Tal-y-llyn. It is run by the owners, Alex Yorke and Lorraine Hinkins, who once managed a ski chalet. 'They are friendly and professional, and pay attention to detail in every way.' The bedrooms are 'well appointed, with comfortable beds, good lighting and storage'. Some have views of the lake; one room has views of Cadair Idris, the mountain that 'virtually rises from the back garden'; all are 'quiet'. Redecoration this year includes the renovation of a bathroom. There is 'plenty of reading matter, guidebooks and maps' in the lounge, which has a log fire, leather sofas and oak furniture. 'Alex likes to chat before dinner, giving advice on walking and climbing routes.' On five nights a week, Lorraine Hinkins cooks a seasonal menu of dishes like twice-baked goat's cheese soufflé; roasted rack of lamb. The meal is generally taken communally: 'should this not be to your taste a separate table is available'. Breakfast is 'extremely generous'.

Tal-y-llyn
Tywyn LL36 9AJ

T: 01654-761247
E: info@dolffanogfawr.co.uk
W: www.dolffanogfawr.co.uk

BEDROOMS: 4.
OPEN: mid-Mar–Oct, dining room closed Sun/Mon except bank holidays.
FACILITIES: lounge, dining room, free Wi-Fi, 1-acre garden, unsuitable for &.
BACKGROUND MUSIC: varied.
LOCATION: by lake 10 miles E of Tywyn.
CHILDREN: not under 7.
DOGS: allowed in bedrooms and lounge.
CREDIT CARDS: MasterCard, Visa.
PRICES: [2014] per person B&B £50. Set menu £25. 1-night bookings sometimes refused.

CHANNEL ISLANDS

Bouley Bay, Jersey

THE WHITE HOUSE

César award in 1987

Three miles from Guernsey, car-free Herm has a little harbour, several shops, pastel-coloured self-catering cottages, a campsite, and this hotel, which opens seasonally. The island cultivates peace and quiet, as does *The White House*: there is no television, iPod docking station, clock or telephone in the bedrooms ('somehow they don't seem appropriate on Herm'). There is no background music in the interconnected lounges, which have board games and 'sofas and chairs arranged to encourage guests to chat'. Karl Ginniver is the new chef this year. In the formal conservatory restaurant, he serves dishes like chicken breast, garlic and thyme polenta, root vegetable crush, brandy cream. A simpler menu can be taken in the informal *Ship Inn* brasserie. Young children are given high tea at 5.15 pm. The bedrooms are divided between the main building and cottages (one is about 100 yards away). Many have sea views; all the bathrooms have been updated for the 2014 season. Tea can be taken by a solar-heated pool in the garden; there is tennis and croquet. On the north of the island are six white-sand beaches. (*N and JJ*)

Herm, via Guernsey GY1 3HR

T: 01481-750075
F: 01481-710066
E: hotel@herm.com
W: www.herm.com

BEDROOMS: 40, 18 in cottages, some on ground floor.
OPEN: Apr–Sept.
FACILITIES: 3 lounges, 2 bars, 2 restaurants, conference room, wedding facilities, free Wi-Fi, 1-acre garden (tennis, croquet, 7-metre solar-heated swimming pool), beach 200 yds, Herm unsuitable for &.
BACKGROUND MUSIC: none.
LOCATION: by harbour, air/sea to Guernsey, then ferry from Guernsey (20 mins).
CHILDREN: all ages welcomed.
DOGS: allowed in 1 bedroom, not allowed in main lounge.
CREDIT CARDS: MasterCard, Visa.
PRICES: [2014] per person B&B £69–£109, D,B&B £98–£150. Set dinner £30. 1-night bookings refused Sat.

THE ATLANTIC HOTEL

In extensive landscaped grounds, this luxury hotel has a prominent headland position overlooking Jersey's premier wildlife site and the five-mile beach at St Ouen's Bay. It has been owned and managed by the Burke family since it was built in 1970 by Henry Burke. His son, Patrick, has expanded and remodelled the white-painted building, softening the 1960s facade to give it an Art Deco look. In the *Ocean* restaurant, head chef Mark Jordan has a *Michelin* star for his sophisticated cooking: he uses local ingredients for dishes like oak-smoked haddock, Jersey royal pavé, curry emulsion; assiette of Jersey beef, lobster ravioli; consommé. Lighter meals can be taken in the lounge or on the terrace. The decor is understated throughout. The public areas have tiled floors, exposed brick, water features. The 'beautiful' bedrooms are 'very comfortable, and well equipped'. Some have full-length, sliding windows and a terrace or a Juliet balcony facing the sea. This year they have been given a new television system (with more than 300 channels) concealed in a hand-made mahogany cabinet, which also houses a fridge and a cocktail cabinet. More reports, please.

Le Mont de la Pulente
St Brelade JE3 8HE

T: 01534-744101
F: 01534-744102
E: info@theatlantichotel.com
W: www.theatlantichotel.com

BEDROOMS: 50, some on ground floor.
OPEN: 7 Feb–2 Jan.
FACILITIES: lift, lounge, library, cocktail bar, restaurant, private dining room, fitness centre (swimming pool, sauna, mini-gym), free Wi-Fi, wedding facilities, 6-acre garden (tennis, indoor and outdoor heated swimming pools, 10 by 5 metres), unsuitable for &.
BACKGROUND MUSIC: in restaurant.
LOCATION: 5 miles W of St Helier.
CHILDREN: all ages welcomed.
DOGS: not allowed.
CREDIT CARDS: all major cards.
PRICES: [2014] per room B&B £150–£350, D,B&B £250–£450. Set dinner £55, à la carte £65.

LONGUEVILLE MANOR

In 'immaculate gardens' inland from St Helier, this extended 14th-century manor house is Jersey's most sumptuous hotel (Relais & Châteaux). 'Certainly luxurious but friendly and welcoming', it has been run by three generations of the Lewis family. Today's custodians are Malcolm Lewis, his wife, Patricia, and her brother-in-law, Pedro Bento. The dress code is 'casual chic' in the evening for dinner, which is served in the *Oak Room*, with its dark panelling from ships of the Spanish Armada, or in the less formal *Garden Room*. The chef, Andrew Baird, emphasises simplicity and flavour in the dishes for his modern menus, which might include local deep-water crab, sweet pickled cucumber, melon, avocado; 'traditional' coq au vin, creamed potato, mushrooms and bacon. The spacious bedrooms, each named after a rose, are traditionally furnished and have fresh flowers, a bowl of fruit, home-made biscuits. Families are welcomed: an extra bed can be put in the parents' room; there are special menus, board games, activities during the holidays. New this year are a mini-gym, a treatment room and a 'quiet garden'.

Longueville Road
St Saviour JE2 7WF

T: 01534-725501
F: 01534-731613
E: info@longuevillemanor.com
W: www.longuevillemanor.com

BEDROOMS: 31, 8 on ground floor, 2 in cottage.
OPEN: all year.
FACILITIES: lift, ramp, 2 lounges, cocktail bar, 2 dining rooms, free Wi-Fi, function/conference/wedding facilities, 15-acre grounds (croquet, tennis, heated swimming pool, woodland), sea 1 mile.
BACKGROUND MUSIC: in bar and restaurant.
LOCATION: 1½ miles E of St Helier.
CHILDREN: all ages welcomed.
DOGS: not allowed in public rooms.
CREDIT CARDS: all major cards.
PRICES: [2014] per room B&B £175–£575, D,B&B £255–£655. Set dinner £40–£80, à la carte £60.

SARK

LA SABLONNERIE

A pony and trap transports visitors from the ferry to this 'unusual small hotel' on a charming, car-free island noted for its abundant flora and fauna. Elizabeth Perrée is the 'welcoming' host, aided by 'friendly, attentive' staff. 'It was superb – like stepping back into the past, with no television and no Wi-Fi,' said a visitor this year. The whitewashed building, a long, low farmhouse dating back to the 16th century, is surrounded by secluded cottage gardens with a croquet lawn; the flowerbeds are bright with lupins, hollyhocks and hydrangea in season. 'Eating lunch in the garden is the nearest thing I know to paradise.' The simple, rustic bedrooms are individually decorated; a self-contained cottage a short stroll from the main house is ideal for a family. 'Our favourite room, over the bar, has lovely views; we have never found it noisy.' Freshly caught fish and Sark lobster are specialities in the dining room, where chef Colin Day's 'excellent' daily-changing menus (perhaps ravioli of scallops, poached halibut, hollandaise) use butter, cream, meat, fruit and vegetables from the hotel's own farm and gardens. (*David Lundie, and others*)

Little Sark
Sark, via Guernsey GY10 1SD

T: 01481-832061
F: 01481-832408
E: reservations@sablonneriesark.com
W: www.sablonneriesark.com

BEDROOMS: 22, also accommodation in nearby cottages.
OPEN: Easter–Oct.
FACILITIES: 3 lounges, 2 bars, restaurant, Wi-Fi not available, wedding facilities, 1-acre garden (tea garden/bar, croquet), Sark unsuitable for &.
BACKGROUND MUSIC: classical/piano in bar.
LOCATION: S part of island, boat from Guernsey (hotel will meet).
CHILDREN: all ages welcomed.
DOGS: allowed at hotel's discretion, but not in public rooms.
CREDIT CARDS: MasterCard, Visa.
PRICES: per person B&B £40–£107.50, D,B&B £69.50–£175. Set menu £29.50, à la carte £49.50 (*excluding 10% service charge*).

IRELAND

The Claddagh, Galway

LORUM OLD RECTORY

César award in 2014

In large grounds in rolling land at the foot of Mount Leinster, Bobbie Smith welcomes guests to her family home, a mid-Victorian rectory which she runs as a small guest house. 'Bobbie and her daughter, Rebecca, treated us like royalty,' says a visitor this year. Earlier praise: 'A wonderful host and a most pleasant atmosphere.' The house is furnished with 'obvious passion for detail'. A grandfather clock stands in a corner of the high-ceilinged hallway, a vase of flowers on the hallstand. A turf or log fire burns in the marble fireplace of the drawing room, which has three large sofas, books, family curios and photographs. Pre-dinner drinks are taken here before Bobbie Smith's 'magnificent' five-course dinner of home-cooked food. It is a communal affair around a large mahogany table in the red dining room. A typical menu: melon and avocado; celeriac soup; elderflower sorbet; butterflied lamb; brioche bread and butter pudding. The 'spacious' bedrooms have large bed, 'good linen and bathroom items'. All have views across fields where horses graze, to the Blackstairs Mountains. (*Helen Macevilly, and others*)

25% DISCOUNT VOUCHERS

Kilgreaney, Bagenalstown

T: 00 353 59-977 5282
F: 00 353 59-977 5455
E: bobbie@lorum.com
W: www.lorum.com

BEDROOMS: 4.
OPEN: Feb–Nov.
FACILITIES: drawing room, study, dining room, free Wi-Fi, wedding facilities, 1-acre garden (croquet), 17-acre grounds, unsuitable for &.
BACKGROUND MUSIC: none.
LOCATION: 4 miles S of Bagenalstown.
CHILDREN: all ages welcomed by arrangement.
DOGS: allowed by arrangement.
CREDIT CARDS: Diners, MasterCard, Visa.
PRICES: per person B&B €75. Set dinner €45.

THE MUSTARD SEED AT ECHO LODGE

'A wonderful place', Daniel Mullane's restaurant-with-rooms is a 'beautifully decorated country house' in fine gardens in one of Ireland's prettiest villages. A returning visitor in 2014 was 'welcomed like an old friend'. In the restaurant, which is often busy with locals, the cooking of chef Angel Pirev has evolved 'to reflect prevailing trends'. His dinner menu might include modern dishes like Cooleeney cheese, salt-baked beetroot, pistachio soil; guineafowl, burnt carrots, butternut froth, dill oil. 'Service is attentive, but never overbearing.' The well-equipped bedrooms are decorated in a mix of period and contemporary styles; dark wood antiques, modern fabrics and wallpapers. 'Our room was spacious yet cosy, with beautiful furniture, and a lovely corner bath in the en suite.' The largest rooms have dual-aspect windows. The house has been filled with objets d'art, prints and photographs; there are 'interesting books and magazines' to enjoy in the library. Breakfast, 'as delicious as dinner', has rhubarb from the garden, home-baked brown bread, eggs from hens that roam the grounds. (*Sheila Robinson*)

Ballingarry

T: 00 353 69-68508
F: 00 353 69-68511
E: mustard@indigo.ie
W: www.mustardseed.ie

BEDROOMS: 15, 1, on ground floor, suitable for ♿.
OPEN: all year except 15 Jan–14 Feb, closed Christmas.
FACILITIES: lounge, library, dining room, free Wi-Fi (in public areas, some bedrooms), wedding facilities, 12-acre grounds.
BACKGROUND MUSIC: in restaurant.
LOCATION: in village, 18 miles SW of Limerick.
CHILDREN: all ages welcomed.
DOGS: not allowed in public rooms.
CREDIT CARDS: Amex, MasterCard, Visa.
PRICES: [2014] per person B&B €65–€160, D,B&B €125–€220. Set menus €45–€60.

SEAVIEW HOUSE

'You might not always see me, but I am never far away,' Kathleen O'Sullivan tells visitors to her extended, white, bay-windowed Victorian house overlooking Bantry Bay. She runs a hotel that is 'warmly welcoming and admirably efficient'. The decor is traditional: 'It would take months to make an inventory of the house contents,' said a recent visitor. The public rooms, bedrooms, landings and corridors 'are full of mostly Victorian furniture, much of it of good quality. The collection of paintings, ornaments and miscellaneous objects is vast.' The large, mature garden (trees block some of the sea view) is 'immaculately tended'. Locals chat with visitors in the small bar (no background music is a bonus). Dinner is served in an 'attractive', light-filled conservatory restaurant, which is open to non-residents. The chef, Eleanor O'Donovan, serves country house dishes on a daily-changing menu; 'not exactly cutting edge', but 'good'. Typical dishes: seafood platter, Marie Rose sauce; roast stuffed duckling, port and orange sauce. All the bedrooms, in the main house and an extension, are large (the family rooms are vast), and have 'ample storage'.

25% DISCOUNT VOUCHERS

Ballylickey, Bantry Bay

T: 00 353 27-50073
F: 00 353 27-51555
E: info@seaviewhousehotel.com
W: www.seaviewhousehotel.com

BEDROOMS: 25, 2, on ground floor, suitable for &.
OPEN: 15 Mar–15 Nov.
FACILITIES: bar, library, 2 lounges, restaurant/conservatory, free Wi-Fi, wedding facilities, 3-acre grounds on waterfront (fishing, boating), riding, golf nearby.
BACKGROUND MUSIC: none.
LOCATION: 3 miles N of Bantry.
CHILDREN: all ages welcomed, special menus and babysitting available.
DOGS: not allowed in public rooms.
CREDIT CARDS: Amex, MasterCard, Visa.
PRICES: [2014] per room B&B €120–€165. D,B&B €95–€110 per person, set dinner €35–€45.

TEMPLE HOUSE

'We're not a hotel, this is our family home,' say Roderick and Helena Perceval, who welcome guests with a handshake to their Georgian mansion. It stands on a large estate with parkland, a boating lake and ancient woods. Waterproofs and wellington boots are set aside for guests in the porch; in the entrance hall are antiques and family portraits. The bedrooms, off an L-shaped corridor in a wing of the house, are spacious with high ceilings; each has a dressing table, heavy curtains and shutters; free-range hangers in a wardrobe. Beds are turned down during dinner. Guests gather for pre-dinner drinks taken from an honesty bar in a drawing room with French windows facing terraced gardens and a croquet lawn. The communal meal, at a large mahogany table, has a no-choice menu (likes and dislikes discussed in advance) of country house dishes with an Irish twist. It might include lamb from the estate and home-grown vegetables. Breakfast, a leisurely affair, has cereals, fruit compotes ('delicious stewed rhubarb'), home-made bread and marmalade. 'Excellent' local produce is cooked to order by the hosts.

Ballinacarrow
nr Ballymote

T: 00 353 71-918 3329
E: stay@templehouse.ie
W: www.templehouse.ie

BEDROOMS: 7.
OPEN: Apr–Nov, dining room closed Sun eve.
FACILITIES: drawing room, snooker room, dining room, free Wi-Fi, wedding facilities, 1½-acre garden, 1,000-acre estate, unsuitable for &.
BACKGROUND MUSIC: none.
LOCATION: 12 miles S of Sligo.
CHILDREN: all ages welcomed.
DOGS: not allowed in house.
CREDIT CARDS: Diners, MasterCard, Visa.
PRICES: per person B&B €80–€95. Set dinner €47.

CAIRN BAY LODGE

In a seaside town overlooking Ballyholme Bay, this 'impressive' Edwardian villa is run as a B&B by Chris and Jenny Mullen, 'whose commitment to making your stay enjoyable would be hard to match'. A visitor this year 'appreciated how they made my daughters, aged seven and five, feel very welcome'. The children were given sweets and crisps on arrival and enjoyed access to a DVD library. The public areas have oak panelling, Dutch fireplaces and stained-glass windows; two lounges at the front have sofas and chairs, books and magazines; large bay windows facing the sea. The bedrooms have 'lots of character'. All rooms contain DVDs, books, free Wi-Fi. There is an 'imaginative' tea tray; a jug of fresh milk and home-made cake are left in the landing. A family suite at the top of the house (two bedrooms, two bathrooms and a lounge) has been added this year. Breakfast is a substantial affair. There is a help-yourself selection of juices, cereals, etc; slow-baked organic porridge; potato and soda bread with the Ulster grill; other choices include poached eggs, chilli, rocket and bacon on toasted crumpets.

278 Seacliff Road
Ballyholme, Bangor
BT20 5HS

T: 028-9146 7636
F: 028-9145 7728
E: info@cairnbaylodge.com
W: www.cairnbaylodge.com

BEDROOMS: 8.
OPEN: all year.
FACILITIES: 2 lounges, dining room, free Wi-Fi, beauty salon, small shop, ½-acre garden, unsuitable for &.
BACKGROUND MUSIC: in dining room during breakfast.
LOCATION: ¼ mile E of centre.
CHILDREN: all ages welcomed.
DOGS: not allowed.
CREDIT CARDS: MasterCard, Visa.
PRICES: per person B&B £40–£50. 1-night bookings sometimes refused.

CAPPOQUIN Co. Waterford

RICHMOND HOUSE

The 'relaxed style' and 'pleasantly old-fashioned feel' are liked by visitors to Paul and Claire Deevy's small hotel and restaurant on the outskirts of an 'appealing, old-fashioned' town. Guests are invariably greeted by a family member; the long-serving staff are all local. Approached through parkland (illuminated at night), the house was built for the Earl of Cork in 1704. There's a stove in the high-ceilinged hall, log fires in the drawing room and dining room ('a succession of small spaces with an intimate feel'). Claire Deevy supervises the meal service with 'charm and efficiency'. Paul Deevy, the award-winning chef, serves generous portions of modern dishes, perhaps rillette of duck, Cumberland sauce; roast hake, sautéed courgettes, pesto dressing. An early bird menu, served until 7.30 pm from Tuesday to Friday, is good value; vegetarians have their own menu. The bedrooms, which vary in size, are decorated in country house style. A spacious second-floor room had a large bed, plenty of storage; 'housekeeping was meticulous'. Breakfast might have fresh fruit from the garden in season; 'better-than-average toast and coffee'.

Cappoquin

T: 00 353 58-54278
F: 00 353 58-54988
E: info@richmondhouse.net
W: www.richmondhouse.net

BEDROOMS: 10.
OPEN: 15 Jan–23 Dec, restaurant normally closed Sun/Mon except July and Aug.
FACILITIES: lounge, restaurant, free Wi-Fi, 12-acre grounds, fishing, golf, pony trekking nearby, unsuitable for &.
BACKGROUND MUSIC: 'easy listening' in restaurant.
LOCATION: ½ mile E of Cappoquin.
CHILDREN: all ages welcomed.
DOGS: not allowed.
CREDIT CARDS: all major cards.
PRICES: [2014] per person B&B €60–€70. Early bird dinner €28–€33, set dinner €55.

CARRIG COUNTRY HOUSE

In wooded grounds on the shores of a lake facing Macgillycuddy's Reeks (a mountain range with the highest peaks in Ireland), this country hotel was built as a hunting and fishing lodge for English aristocrats. Frank and Mary Slattery, the first Irish owners, have restored and extended the house, which they run in personal style. Turf fires warm the 'pleasant' public rooms: a drawing room where 'soft' background music might play, and several smaller, quieter areas (a snug and a library). The restaurant has polished wooden floors, linen cloths, William Morris green-leaf wallpaper, and picture windows with views of the lake. The chef, Patricia Teahan, cooks modern Irish and international dishes on a four-course dinner menu (and a carte), perhaps duo of Dingle Bay prawns; Irish sirloin steak, Gruyère cheese croquette, crispy shallot rings, smoked bacon jus. The best bedrooms overlook the lake; standard rooms face the 'lovely' gardens. All rooms are furnished in period style. A presidential suite has a huge canopied Indian bed with footstools to provide access; a sitting room with a panoramic outlook; his and hers dressing rooms.

Caragh Lake
Killorglin

T: 00 353 66-976 9100
E: info@carrighouse.com
W: www.carrighouse.com

BEDROOMS: 17, some on ground floor.
OPEN: Mar–Nov, restaurant open only at weekends Mar/Apr.
FACILITIES: 2 lounges, snug, library, TV room, dining room, free Wi-Fi, wedding facilities, 4-acre garden on lake.
BACKGROUND MUSIC: classical in lounge and restaurant.
LOCATION: 22 miles W of Killarney.
CHILDREN: not under 8 (except infants under 12 months).
DOGS: not allowed in house (kennel available).
CREDIT CARDS: MasterCard, Visa.
PRICES: [2014] per person B&B €75–€175, D,B&B €99–€145. Set dinner €47.50, à la carte €45.

CASTLEHILL Co. Mayo

ENNISCOE HOUSE

On an estate that has been in the same family since the 1650s (an ancestor came over with Cromwell), this classic mansion was built in the 1790s. It is run as a private hotel ('the sort the *Guide* is all about') by the thirteenth and fourteenth generations of the family, Susan Kellett and her son, DJ. 'It is a lovely house; they are welcoming hosts who serve fine food,' said a trusted reporter. There are two vast sitting rooms (one contains DJ's grandmother's giant doll's house). The 'lived-in' one has rugs on polished floors, fine 18th-century plasterwork), big sofas in front of an open fire; other more intimate seating areas. There are vases of wild flowers on the 'lovely' old wooden tables in the dining room where the short menu (two choices for each course) has an Irish country house style with French influences. Dishes might include globe artichoke with spiced butter; herb-roasted rack of lamb, green beans. The grandest bedrooms are at the front of the house; they are traditionally furnished. Pets are welcomed and can stay with their owners for no charge. (*EC*)

25% DISCOUNT VOUCHERS

Castlehill, Ballina

T: 00 353 96-31112
F: 00 353 96-31773
E: mail@enniscoe.com
W: www.enniscoe.com

BEDROOMS: 6, plus self-catering units behind house.
OPEN: Apr–Oct, groups only at New Year.
FACILITIES: 2 sitting rooms, dining room, free Wi-Fi, wedding facilities, 150-acre estate (garden, tea room, farm, heritage centre, conference centre, forge, fishing), unsuitable for &.
BACKGROUND MUSIC: none.
LOCATION: 2 miles S of Crossmolina.
CHILDREN: all ages welcomed.
DOGS: not allowed in public rooms, some bedrooms.
CREDIT CARDS: MasterCard, Visa.
PRICES: [2014] per person B&B €80–€120, D,B&B €130–€170. Set menus €30–€50.

BALLYVOLANE HOUSE

César award in 2009

In extensive grounds, this grand country house (built in 1728 for a Lord Chief Justice of Ireland) has been the home of the Green family for more than 60 years. It is run in relaxed style by Justin and Jenny Green, professional hoteliers who welcome guests 'in a laid-back Irish way'. Visitors are greeted on first-name terms and shown around the house, which is furnished with antiques and family curios but has been given more modern colour schemes. There are no keys to the bedrooms, which are off a corridor that runs the length of the house; there are big beds, a radio as well as television, a hospitality tray. 'Our bathroom had a stag's head above the claw-footed bath.' In the summer, adventurous guests can choose 'glamping' – sleeping in bell tents with proper beds; 'luxurious loos' are in a wash house. Dinner is a sociable affair around an enormous mahogany table. A leisurely breakfast is cooked by Justin Green; afterwards he will round up visiting children for a tractor ride. There are three trout lakes in the grounds; six miles of fishing on the River Blackwater.

Castlelyons, Fermoy

T: 00 353 25-36349
F: 00 353 25-36781
E: info@ballyvolanehouse.ie
W: www.ballyvolanehouse.ie

BEDROOMS: 6.
OPEN: all year except Christmas/ New Year, closed Sun/Mon except bank holiday weekends.
FACILITIES: hall, drawing room, honesty bar, dining room, free Wi-Fi, wedding facilities, 80-acre grounds (15-acre garden, croquet, 3 trout lakes), unsuitable for &.
BACKGROUND MUSIC: none.
LOCATION: 22 miles NE of Cork.
CHILDREN: all ages welcomed.
DOGS: allowed.
CREDIT CARDS: MasterCard, Visa.
PRICES: per person B&B main house €95–€120. Glamping per tent €150–€240. Set dinner €55.

THE QUAY HOUSE

🍃 *César award in 2003*

On the small harbour below the town, this cluster of buildings, originally the harbourmaster's house, later a monastery, is run as a B&B by Paddy and Julia Foyle. It has long been liked by readers for the quirky but kindly hospitality that combines a genuine interest in guests with professionalism. Peat fires burn in the two large sitting rooms, which have sofas, books, board games, curios, Irish paintings. Tea and drinks can be taken here. The bedrooms in the main house have a garden or bay view; most are spacious, but the ones at the top are small. The newest section contains studios with a balcony overlooking the water (six have a kitchenette). Several rooms have a quirky theme: the Napoleon Bonaparte Room has appropriate mementos; the Mirror Room a huge gilded mirror. Two ground-floor rooms are equipped for visitors with a disability; a third ground-floor room has been added this year. Breakfast, served in a leafy conservatory, has a 'splendid' menu; it might include oysters with smoked salmon or devilled kidneys. Orange juice is freshly squeezed. More reports, please.

Beach Road
Clifden

T: 00 353 95-21369
F: 00 353 95-21608
E: thequay@iol.ie
W: www.thequayhouse.com

BEDROOMS: 15, 3 on ground floor, 1 suitable for &, 7 studios (6 with kitchenette) in annexe.
OPEN: late Mar–end Oct.
FACILITIES: 2 sitting rooms, breakfast conservatory, free Wi-Fi (in downstairs sitting room), ½-acre garden, fishing, sailing, golf, riding nearby.
BACKGROUND MUSIC: none.
LOCATION: harbour, 8 mins' walk from centre.
CHILDREN: all ages welcomed.
DOGS: not allowed.
CREDIT CARDS: MasterCard, Visa.
PRICES: per room B&B €135–€150. 1-night bookings refused bank holiday weekends.

SEA MIST HOUSE

A fierce storm in 1998, which lifted the roof from this 1820s town house, initiated the renovation that led to its opening as a B&B. Sheila Griffin, whose grandfather bought the house in 1920, supervised the renovation to add modern 'environmentally conscious' conveniences. Solar panels and a wood-pellet stove provide much of the hot water and heating. 'It is beautifully maintained and good value,' said the nominator. The bedrooms vary in size (and are priced accordingly). A 'light and airy' room was 'decorated in relaxing colours, with patterns in the heavy curtains, matching bedhead and window-seat cushion; plenty of lighting; a table with a tea tray and a bottle of drinking water; everything worked in the bathroom'. There is no TV in the bedrooms but there is free Wi-Fi throughout. A mini-library on a landing has a large sofa and a wide selection of books. There are pictures everywhere ('something to appeal to everyone'). Breakfast, taken in a conservatory, has a buffet of cereals and granolas, fresh fruit salad and a fruit compote, natural yogurts, home-made brown bread; an extensive selection of hot dishes. More reports, please.

Seaview
Clifden

T: 00 353 95-21441
E: sheila@seamisthouse.com
W: www.seamisthouse.com

BEDROOMS: 4.
OPEN: Mar–Nov.
FACILITIES: 2 sitting rooms, conservatory dining room, free Wi-Fi, ¾-acre garden, unsuitable for &.
BACKGROUND MUSIC: none.
LOCATION: central.
CHILDREN: not under 4.
DOGS: not allowed.
CREDIT CARDS: Amex, MasterCard, Visa.
PRICES: per person B&B €40–€60.

HILTON PARK

The Madden family entertain guests in house-party style at the imposing Italianate mansion which has been their home since it was built in 1704. Today it is run by Fred and Joanna Madden (of the ninth generation); his parents, Johnny and Lucy, 'lend their experience and love of hospitality'. The house is filled with paintings and family memorabilia. Large windows ('that a Ruritanian monarch would be proud of') throw light on to the grand public rooms. A 'beguiling' drawing room has 'lots of lived-in sofas and chairs, all comfy'. A 'huge golden pelmet' runs the length of the dining room, where guests can choose to dine communally or at separate tables. 'Lucy and Fred, who share the cooking duties, produce tasty fresh meals'; their no-choice menu might include warm salad of wood pigeon and hazelnuts; slow-roasted leg of lamb, wild garlic and anchovies. 'The home-made bread was nutty and delicious.' The spacious bedrooms are individually decorated; they are furnished with antiques; baths are claw-footed. There are books everywhere; one bedroom has a library. The generous breakfast is taken in a vaulted former servants' hall.

Clones

T: 00 353 47-56007
F: 00 353 47-56033
E: mail@hiltonpark.ie
W: www.hiltonpark.ie

BEDROOMS: 4.
OPEN: Apr–Oct, groups only Nov–Mar.
FACILITIES: drawing room, sitting room, TV room, breakfast room, dining room, free Wi-Fi, 400-acre grounds (3 lakes, golf course, croquet), unsuitable for &.
BACKGROUND MUSIC: none.
LOCATION: 3 miles S of Clones.
CHILDREN: not under 8.
DOGS: not allowed in bedrooms, public areas.
CREDIT CARDS: MasterCard, Visa.
PRICES: [2014] per person B&B €85–€135. Set dinner €55.

BALLYWARREN HOUSE

Owners David and Diane Skelton moved from Hayling Island to build their family home in farmland close to the Atlantic coast. They welcome visitors 'warmly' on a B&B basis; she will cook an evening meal by arrangement. Purpose-built in Georgian style, the house has high ceilings and appropriate antique furnishings. There are magazines, chocolates and sherry in the 'thoughtfully equipped' bedrooms. Lavender has 'curtains in green, white and purple, posies of fresh lavender'. No television (guests can ask for one) or tea-making kit; Mrs Skelton brings a tray of fresh tea at 8 am ahead of breakfast which is taken at 9.30 am. It has a large buffet, home-made bread, cakes and scones, and a choice of cooked dishes. The informal dinner is from a no-choice menu (allergies are established in advance) of slow-cooked dishes, perhaps Irish seafood chowder; venison braised in red wine with herbs, vegetables and orange rind. Coffee is taken by an open fire in the drawing room. In warm weather, guests can sit in the garden; indoors, there are board games and books for rainy days.

25% DISCOUNT VOUCHERS

Cross, Cong

T/F: 00 353 9495-46989
E: ballywarrenhouse@gmail.com
W: www.ballywarrenhouse.com

BEDROOMS: 3.
OPEN: all year.
FACILITIES: reception hall, sitting room, 2 dining rooms, free Wi-Fi, 1-acre garden in 6-acre grounds (lake, fishing nearby), unsuitable for &.
BACKGROUND MUSIC: none.
LOCATION: 2 miles E of Cong.
CHILDREN: not under 14, except babies.
DOGS: not allowed in house.
CREDIT CARDS: MasterCard, Visa.
PRICES: [2014] per person B&B €68–€80. Set dinner €45. 1-night bookings occasionally refused.

RATHSALLAGH HOUSE

In extensive parkland (with a golf course and a walled garden), the O'Flynn family's hotel is a 'low-key' yet 'totally spoiling' country house. There are sofas and armchairs in the traditional drawing rooms, which have turf fires. Tables are laid with linen cloths in the dining room, which has rugs on wooden flooring. Here the chef, Nico Krumbholz, serves a daily-changing menu of modern dishes, perhaps home-spiced beef, pickled vegetables; butter confit cod, Pernod-flavoured saffron broth, mussels, potato gnocchi, roasted fennel. Game in season and fresh fish are specialities. Fish is home smoked; all preserves are made in the kitchen. The older part of the house is a conversion of Queen Anne stables. Some spacious bedrooms here have country views. Simpler rooms are in the stable yard. Rooms in a more recent addition are large, and have a luxurious bathroom. The award-winning breakfast has a generous buffet with home-baked bread, Irish cheeses, ham on the bone; cooked dishes might include eggs Benedict, kedgeree and devilled kidneys. For non-golfers, there is good walking in the Wicklow Mountains. (*DG*)

25% DISCOUNT VOUCHERS

Dunlavin

T: 00 353 45-403112
F: 00 353 45-403343
E: info@rathsallagh.com
W: www.rathsallagh.com

BEDROOMS: 32, 20 in courtyard, 3 in gate lodge.
OPEN: all year except 23–27 Dec, specified dates in winter.
FACILITIES: 2 drawing rooms, bar, dining room, snooker room, free Wi-Fi, wedding facilities, 500-acre grounds (golf course, tennis).
BACKGROUND MUSIC: in dining room.
LOCATION: 2 miles SW of village.
CHILDREN: not under 6.
DOGS: allowed (heated kennels).
CREDIT CARDS: all major cards.
PRICES: per room B&B €119–€200, D,B&B €199–€299. À la carte €45.

BALLINKEELE HOUSE

♀ *César award in 2012*

In parkland, with three lakes, woods, lawns and gardens, this 'magnificent' Georgian mansion was built for the Maher family in 1840. It remains their 'welcoming family home', these days under the stewardship of Val Maher of the sixth generation, and his wife, Laura. The family has retained the period glamour of the Italianate house: the entrance has porticoes of Wicklow granite; the hall has two impressive Corinthian columns; a floating staircase leads to the first-floor bedrooms. Much of the original furniture remains (like the four-poster bed in the largest room); beautiful pictures and china, period details. All rooms have a view of the parkland and the well-maintained gardens through large windows. Visitors are welcomed on first-name terms. Pre-dinner drinks in one of the two drawing rooms, which have fine decorated ceilings, huge fireplaces, is a sociable occasion. Dinner is generally taken communally at the family's huge table (a separate table will be laid for those who prefer privacy). Game comes from the estate, vegetables and herbs from the recently restored walled garden, for the no-choice meal of country house dishes.

Ballymurn
Enniscorthy

T: 00 353 53-913 8105
E: info@ballinkeele.ie
W: www.ballinkeele.ie

BEDROOMS: 5.
OPEN: Feb–Nov.
FACILITIES: 2 drawing rooms, dining room, free Wi-Fi (available in 'most areas'), 6-acre gardens in 350-acre estate, lakes, ponds, unsuitable for ♿.
BACKGROUND MUSIC: none.
LOCATION: 6 miles SE of Enniscorthy.
CHILDREN: all ages welcomed.
DOGS: allowed in owner's car only.
CREDIT CARDS: Amex, MasterCard, Visa.
PRICES: [2014] per person B&B €75–€105. Set dinner €35.

SALVILLE HOUSE

♀*César award in 2013*

In large wooded grounds on a quiet hilltop, Gordon and Jane Parker's Victorian country house was found 'as good as ever' by a regular correspondent this year. 'We enjoyed a house-party atmosphere with delightful fellow guests attending the Wexford opera festival.' The handsome house has the 'feel of a real home': in the drawing room, the interesting artwork, Malaysian memorabilia and family photographs 'suggest a lifetime of memories'. There are 'comfortable' sofas and chairs around the fireplace. In the dining room, Gordon Parker's food is 'as ambrosial as ever': he uses organic produce from the garden for his dishes, perhaps prawn tempura, aubergine and mango salad; beef fillet, beetroot gel, garden salad, preserved lemon dressing. There is no drinks licence; guests are encouraged to bring their own bottle (a corkscrew is provided but there is no corkage charge). The three spacious bedrooms in the main house have views over the River Slaney. The furnishings are in keeping with the house. Breakfast has leaf tea; home-made bread (perhaps sourdough) and jams; 'excellent' cooked dishes. (*Catherine Fraher, and others*)

Salville
Enniscorthy

T/F: 00 353 53-923 5252
E: info@salvillehouse.com
W: www.salvillehouse.com

BEDROOMS: 5, 2 in apartment at rear.
OPEN: all year except Christmas.
FACILITIES: drawing room, dining room, free Wi-Fi, 5-acre grounds ('rough' tennis, badminton, croquet), golf nearby, beach, bird sanctuary 10 miles, unsuitable for &.
BACKGROUND MUSIC: none.
LOCATION: 2 miles S of town.
CHILDREN: all ages welcomed.
DOGS: allowed by arrangement.
CREDIT CARDS: none.
PRICES: per person B&B €55. Set dinner €40.

MARLFIELD HOUSE

Antiques, chandeliers and fine pictures add to the charm of this fine Regency mansion which has been run as a luxury country house hotel (Relais & Châteaux) by the Bowe family since 1978. Mary and Ray Bowe have retired nearby; their daughters, Margaret and Laura, maintain the family management. Once the Irish residence of the earls of Courtown, the house stands in extensive grounds with woodlands, a wildfowl reserve, a lake with ducks, geese and black swans. Inside is a grand marble hall, a lounge with an open fire, spectacular flower displays. Many of the bedrooms overlook the gardens or the lake; they are sumptuously furnished in traditional style with rich fabrics, period pieces; a marble bathroom. The largest, 'state' rooms have a sitting area. In the 'glorious' dining room, which has a domed conservatory with hanging baskets, flowers and statues, chef Ruadhan Furlong serves a seasonal menu using produce from the kitchen garden. Typical dishes: roast carrot and cumin soup, julienne of smoked duck and herb oil; braised beef cheek, Madeira jus. Children are welcomed and have their own menu.

Courtown Road
Gorey

T: 00 353 53-942 1124
F: 00 353 53-942 1572
E: info@marlfieldhouse.ie
W: www.marlfieldhouse.com

BEDROOMS: 19, 8 on ground floor.
OPEN: Mar–Dec except Christmas, restaurant closed Mon/Tues in Mar/Apr, Oct–Dec.
FACILITIES: reception hall, drawing room, library/bar, restaurant with conservatory, free Wi-Fi, wedding facilities, 36-acre grounds (gardens, tennis, croquet, wildfowl reserve, lake).
BACKGROUND MUSIC: classical in library.
LOCATION: 1 mile E of Gorey.
CHILDREN: no under-8s at dinner, high tea provided, babysitting available.
DOGS: not allowed in public rooms.
CREDIT CARDS: all major cards.
PRICES: per person B&B €80–€300, D,B&B €145–€360. Set dinner €64. 1-night bookings sometimes refused Sat.

RAYANNE HOUSE

Second-generation family owners, Conor and
Bernadette McClelland, have created an
'individualistic place' at their Victorian merchant's
mansion in large gardens in a small dormitory
town near Belfast. The 'lovely' building has been
furnished in Art Deco style; it has wide landings,
a sweeping staircase, display cabinets filled with
fine ornamentation. There are spectacular views
across the Belfast Lough from many of the
bedrooms, which are equipped with 'everything
extra you can think of'. A room with a golf
theme (the house is close to Holywood golf club,
home of the local golfing hero, Rory McIlroy) has
'grass tiles' in the bathroom. Conor McClelland,
an acclaimed chef, prepares dinner by
arrangement for small groups: his nine-course
Titanic menu recreates the final meal served in
the first-class dining room of the ill-fated liner.
His breakfast menu has an extensive selection of
dishes: guests choose the evening before from
seven starters and a dozen main courses. An
inspector 'loved the hot Rayanne baked cereal
with fresh fruit, honey and cream'; County Down
kippers were 'perfectly grilled'. 'Exactly the sort
of establishment *Guide* readers are looking for.'

60 Demesne Road
Holywood BT18 9EX

T/F: 028-9042 5859
E: info@rayannehouse.com
W: www.rayannehouse.com

BEDROOMS: 10, 1, on ground floor,
suitable for &.
OPEN: all year, 'limited service'
24–26 Dec.
FACILITIES: 2 lounges, dining room,
free Wi-Fi, conference facilities,
1-acre grounds.
BACKGROUND MUSIC: light jazz in
dining room.
LOCATION: ½ mile from town
centre, 6 miles E of Belfast.
CHILDREN: all ages welcomed.
DOGS: not allowed.
CREDIT CARDS: MasterCard, Visa.
PRICES: [2014] per room B&B single
£75–£82, double £117–£137. Set
menus £35–£69, à la carte £49.

SHELBURNE LODGE

Set back from the road in spacious grounds on the eastern edge of the town, this 1740s house has been run as a B&B by the Foley family for 20 years. Their 'cheery, helpful charm' is much admired. Arriving guests are invariably greeted by a family member ('everyone becomes a friend'), and given tea and home-made cake in an elegant drawing room, which has an open fire, books for visitors to read. Filled with 'the personality of the owners', the house has bold colour schemes, fresh flowers and plants, interesting artwork. The spacious bedrooms are traditionally furnished; two simpler rooms in a coach house at the back, which has a separate lounge, are suitable for a family. Tom Foley is in charge at breakfast, which is taken in a large, airy room. It has a choice of fruit, freshly squeezed orange juice; bread and preserves are home made. The highlight is the fish dish, which changes daily depending on what has been landed locally. A short walk leads to the town where *Packie's* restaurant is owned by the family.

Cork Road
Kenmare

T: 00 353 64-664 1013
F: 00 353 64-664 2135
E: shelburnekenmare@eircom.net
W: www.shelburnelodge.com

BEDROOMS: 8, plus 2 in coach house.
OPEN: mid-Mar–mid-Nov.
FACILITIES: drawing room, library, lounge in annexe, breakfast room, free Wi-Fi, 3-acre garden (tennis), golf adjacent, unsuitable for &.
BACKGROUND MUSIC: none.
LOCATION: ⅛ mile E of centre.
CHILDREN: all ages welcomed.
DOGS: not allowed.
CREDIT CARDS: MasterCard, Visa.
PRICES: per person B&B €50–€95.

SEE ALSO SHORTLIST

VIRGINIA'S GUESTHOUSE

At the head of Kenmare Bay, this little town is popular with tourists exploring the Ring of Kerry and the Ring of Beara. Above a restaurant in its busy centre is this unpretentious guest house, run by Neil and Noreen Harrington, who are much liked for their easy charm. Once a shoemaker in the family business on the same site, he is the 'information man', dispensing advice on what to see and where to go as he serves the generous breakfast. She generally cooks the food, which is ordered the evening before and served at an agreed time. It has a choice of freshly squeezed juices, perhaps his 'zingy' juice cocktail of orange, cranberry and ginger; home-made muesli, rhubarb and rosemary compote or creamy porridge; the house speciality is blue cheese, pears and bacon; or you can choose from a wide range of other cooked dishes. The bedrooms are simple but 'spotless'; earplugs are provided for sleepers who might be disturbed as visitors leave the town's bars and restaurants. Tea and coffee are available in the sitting room.

36 Henry Street
Kenmare

T: 00 353 86-372 0625
E: virginias.guesthouse@gmail.com
W: www.virginias-kenmare.com

BEDROOMS: 8.
OPEN: all year except 20–27 Dec.
FACILITIES: library, breakfast room, free Wi-Fi, unsuitable for ♿.
BACKGROUND MUSIC: none.
LOCATION: central.
CHILDREN: not under 12.
DOGS: not allowed.
CREDIT CARDS: MasterCard, Visa.
PRICES: per person B&B single €45–€60, double €35–€47.50. 1-night bookings refused bank holidays.

SEE ALSO SHORTLIST

ROSLEAGUE MANOR

César award in 2010

Looking across a sea lough, this Georgian manor house, owned by Mark Foyle and his father, Edmund, has many fans among regular *Guide* reporters. This year's praise: 'We are in love with it: the setting, the good taste, the tranquillity, the sense that whatever you want to do is no problem'; 'Efficient and discreet service, no unnecessary fussing.' Mark Foyle, the hands-on manager, is 'the key – he has easy-going hospitality in his DNA'. There are large flower arrangements, turf fires, lots of comfortable sitting places in the lounges. The cooking style of the chef, Emmanuel Neu, is 'refreshing and unfussy: fillet of beef with a traditional shallot and peppercorn stuffing; breast of duck came with spiced plums'. Visitors whose 'dietary requirements put the kitchen to the test' were delighted with the flexibility shown. Bedrooms range from 'large to enormous'. 'Saying our ground-floor suite was large barely does it justice; we liked the warm tones of the decor. Not everything is perfect, eg, bedroom lighting, but we'll be going again.' Breakfast has 'plenty of everything'. (*Andrew Wardrop, Jeanette Bloor*)

Letterfrack

T: 00 353 95-41101
F: 00 353 95-41168
E: info@rosleague.com
W: www.rosleague.com

BEDROOMS: 20, 2 on ground floor.
OPEN: Easter–Halloween bank holiday.
FACILITIES: 2 drawing rooms, conservatory/bar, dining room, wedding facilities, 25-acre grounds (tennis), unsuitable for &.
BACKGROUND MUSIC: none.
LOCATION: 7 miles NE of Clifden.
CHILDREN: all ages welcomed.
DOGS: 'well-behaved dogs' allowed in conservatory/bar, with own bedding in 2 bedrooms.
CREDIT CARDS: MasterCard, Visa.
PRICES: [2014] per person B&B €75–€105, D,B&B €95–€135. Set dinner €32–€46. 1-night bookings refused bank holiday Sat.

NO. 1 PERY SQUARE

In a city at the head of the Shannon estuary, Patricia Roberts's small hotel is a conversion of two town houses in a terrace regarded as a fine example of late Georgian architecture. 'One of the nicest places in Ireland; the food is streets ahead of most,' was the comment of a fellow *Guide* hotelier. In *Brasserie One*, the chef, Christian Baldenecker, uses Irish artisan produce for his dishes, which have 'strong French influences', perhaps crispy octopus, pan-fried prawns, lemon and coriander; seared O'Loughlin's rib-eye steak, rosemary-infused Béarnaise. 'Innovative and served with genuine care.' *Brasserie One* won an award for 'the best wine experience' in the 2014 Irish restaurant awards. The four most spacious bedrooms and a suite are on the top floors, overlooking the People's Park; other rooms are more compact: 'Ours was small but well furnished, with an enormous bed; the bathroom was almost as big as the bedroom; no tea-making facilities but the lads who greeted us were quick to bring complimentary tea.' Afternoon tea can be taken in an elegant drawing room with an original marble fireplace. (*VD, and others*)

Georgian Quarter
1 Pery Square
Limerick

T: 00 353 61-402402
F: 00 353 61-313060
E: info@oneperysquare.com
W: www.oneperysquare.com

BEDROOMS: 20, 2 suitable for &.
OPEN: all year except 24–27 Dec, restaurant closed Mon.
FACILITIES: lounge, drawing room, bar, restaurant, private dining room, free Wi-Fi, wedding facilities, terrace, basement spa.
BACKGROUND MUSIC: classical in public areas.
LOCATION: central.
CHILDREN: all ages welcomed.
DOGS: only guide dogs allowed.
CREDIT CARDS: Amex, MasterCard, Visa.
PRICES: per room B&B €135–€195, D,B&B €225–€285. Set menus €25–€29, à la carte €45.

SHEEDY'S

For eleven months a year, Lisdoonvarna is a 'typical small Irish country town well placed for exploring the Burren and the Cliffs of Moher'; in September it is transformed during the annual matchmaking festival into a 'seething mass of people'. John and Martina Sheedy's small hotel/restaurant manages to 'remain a haven of tranquillity', says a regular correspondent. 'The welcome from Martina is warm and genuine; a pot of tea with biscuits materialises in no time.' The bedrooms have a traditional decor: 'Our room was pleasant apart from the net curtains and poor lighting; in contrast the bathroom was bright and had excellent towels.' Pre-dinner drinks can be taken in a 'cosy' bar or the lounge, or in the light reception area. John Sheedy is the chef: 'He trained in Paris and London and it shows: his lamb and monkfish were the real deal; so, too, a goat's cheese salad that redefines a ubiquitous dish. Quite pricey but completely satisfying.' Breakfast also has 'the little touches that set the standard: linen napkins, leaf tea with a strainer; excellent home-made muesli and proper conserves and butter'. (*Esler Crawford*)

Lisdoonvarna

T: 00 353 65-707 4026
F: 00 353 65-707 4555
E: info@sheedys.com
W: www.sheedys.com

BEDROOMS: 11, some on ground floor, 1 suitable for &.
OPEN: 28 Mar–6 Oct, may close 1 day a week in April.
FACILITIES: ramp, sitting room/library, sun lounge, bar, restaurant, free Wi-Fi, ¼-acre garden (rose garden).
BACKGROUND MUSIC: light jazz at dinner.
LOCATION: 20 miles SW of Galway.
CHILDREN: all ages welcomed.
DOGS: not allowed.
CREDIT CARDS: MasterCard, Visa.
PRICES: [2014] per room B&B €109–€160. D,B&B €100–€120 per person, à la carte €45. 1-night bookings refused Sept.

❧NEWFORGE HOUSE

César award: Irish guest house of the year
Midway between Belfast and Armagh (which has two cathedrals), this Georgian country house is well placed for touring Northern Ireland or for visitors venturing further south. It is run by John and Louise Mathers (his family has owned the house for six generations) in hands-on fashion. Ten years ago they sympathetically renovated the house (built in 1785) to run it as an upmarket guest house. The 'most helpful host' greets visitors, serving tea and cake, and cooking meals of the 'highest order' in the evening. There are fresh flowers, original antique furniture in the hall; fine paintings, good-quality fabrics, books and magazines in the drawing room. On the daily-changing menu, 'simple Irish country house' dishes might include butternut squash risotto; roast saddle of venison, port and juniper jus. A first-floor bedroom had 'good storage, fruit and flowers; its impressive bathroom had a freestanding bath, a separate shower'. The award-winning breakfast has home-baked bread and pastries, home-made preserves; apple juice from nearby Armagh orchards; black and white puddings and potato bread with the full cooked dish.

58 Newforge Road
Magheralin
Craigavon BT67 0QL

T: 028-9261 1255
F: 028-9261 2823
E: enquiries@newforgehouse.com
W: www.newforgehouse.com

BEDROOMS: 6.
OPEN: all year except 21 Dec–30 Jan.
FACILITIES: drawing room, dining room, free Wi-Fi, civil wedding licence, 4-acre gardens (vegetable garden, orchard), unsuitable for ♿.
BACKGROUND MUSIC: mixed in dining room.
LOCATION: edge of village, 3 miles E of Craigavon.
CHILDREN: not under 10 (except for under-1s).
DOGS: not allowed.
CREDIT CARDS: Diners, MasterCard, Visa.
PRICES: [2014] per person B&B £60–£90. Set dinner £40.

ROUNDWOOD HOUSE

🦆 *César award in 1990*

In pastures and woods in the rural Irish Midlands, this fine Palladian villa is the family home of Paddy and Hannah Flynn. The restoration of the house has been a labour of love for the family for many years. 'They continue to make improvements,' says a returning visitor this year. 'Our bedroom had been repainted (the same lovely green and white); the walls and floor of the bathroom had been tiled.' The spacious bedrooms in the main house have high ceiling, original features; four smaller rooms in the Yellow House (an older building) face a walled garden. Rooms are 'spotlessly clean and comfortable'. Paddy Flynn cooks an 'excellent' five-course dinner on five evenings a week, using 'simple and honest' ingredients for dishes like tempura salmon, ginger and sesame; sirloin of beef, Irish whiskey and peppercorn sauce, warm sweet potato salad. Orange juice is freshly squeezed for breakfast, which has home-baked bread and scones. Theatre performances are held. 'A one-act play by Shaw was followed by readings of ghost stories by candlelight. An unusual and entertaining evening.' (*Jeanette Bloor*)

Mountrath

T: 00 353 57-873 2120
F: 00 353 57-873 2711
E: info@roundwoodhouse.com
W: www.roundwoodhouse.com

BEDROOMS: 10, 4 in garden building.
OPEN: all year except Christmas.
FACILITIES: drawing room, study/library, dining room, playroom, table tennis room, free Wi-Fi, wedding facilities, 20-acre grounds (garden, woodland), golf, walking, river fishing nearby, unsuitable for &.
BACKGROUND MUSIC: none.
LOCATION: 3 miles N of village.
CHILDREN: all ages welcomed.
DOGS: not allowed indoors.
CREDIT CARDS: all major cards.
PRICES: [2014] per person B&B €75–€90. Supper €40 (Sun/Mon), set dinner (Tues–Sat) €50.

MULTYFARNHAM Co. Westmeath

Map 6:C5

MORNINGTON HOUSE

The rural tranquillity is broken only by the dawn chorus at this old country house, which stands in parkland with walled gardens near Lough Derravaragh. Visitors are entertained on house-party lines by 'excellent hosts' Warwick and Anne O'Hara – his family has owned the house for 150 years, and he is happy to share stories about its history. The 17th-century house was remodelled in 1896 on a town-house design giving the rooms an 'intimacy not always found in a country house'. The large hallway has a pot-bellied stove, polished wood floors, old prints. The elegant drawing room has golden-yellow flock wallpaper and slate-blue velvet curtains, 'lots of light' from large windows; sofas, armchairs and occasional tables on three sides of a fireplace. Guests gather here for pre-dinner drinks served by the host, who then seats them for dinner around a big table with two candelabras. Many of the ingredients (vegetables, fruit and herbs) come from the walled garden for Anne O'Hara's 'tasty' country house meals. Her husband cooks the breakfast (hot dishes to order). The 'idiosyncratic' bedrooms vary in size; bathrooms are 'cleverly fitted out'.

25% DISCOUNT VOUCHERS

Multyfarnham

T: 00 353 44-937 2191
F: 00 353 44-937 2338
E: stay@mornington.ie
W: www.mornington.ie

BEDROOMS: 4.
OPEN: Apr–Oct.
FACILITIES: drawing room, dining room, 1-acre garden, 50-acre grounds (croquet, bicycle hire), unsuitable for &.
BACKGROUND MUSIC: none.
LOCATION: 9 miles NW of Mullingar.
CHILDREN: all ages welcomed.
DOGS: not allowed in house.
CREDIT CARDS: all major cards.
PRICES: [2014] per person B&B €75, D,B&B €120. Set dinner €45.

CURRAREVAGH HOUSE

♀César award in 1992

In beautiful parkland and woodland on Lough
Corrib, this early Victorian manor house has
been run as a hotel by the Hodgson family since
1890. Henry Hodgson is assisted by his mother,
June; his wife, Lucy, is the chef. It is run 'along
the lines of a private country house rather than
an impersonal hotel'. 'They make you feel
comfortable in their family home,' said a recent
guest. A long-time visitor reports this year: 'I
love coming here; not much changes though the
decor has been spruced up.' The bedrooms have
large beds with sheets and blankets, spring
water and fresh flowers; views of Lough Corrib
or Benlevy Mountain. They do not have a
television – or a key. Lucy Hodgson cooks a
four-course dinner (no choice but 'you can ask
for a change') of modern dishes, perhaps cured
Corrib wild brown trout, fennel, citrus and
spring herbs. 'The risk of too much food is
obviated by taking a small main course followed
by second helpings.' Breakfast has an Edwardian
buffet. Fishing on the lake 'is a major dimension'.
(*Richard Parish, and others*)

Oughterard

T: 00 353 91-552312
F: 00 353 91-552731
E: info@currarevagh.com
W: www.currarevagh.com

BEDROOMS: 12.
OPEN: 1 Apr–2 Nov.
FACILITIES: sitting room/hall,
drawing room, library/bar with TV,
dining room, free Wi-Fi, 180-acre
grounds (lake, fishing, ghillies
available, boating, swimming,
tennis, croquet), golf, riding nearby,
unsuitable for ઠ.
BACKGROUND MUSIC: none.
LOCATION: 4 miles NW of
Oughterard.
CHILDREN: all ages welcomed.
DOGS: allowed.
CREDIT CARDS: all major cards.
PRICES: per person B&B €70–€90,
D,B&B €105–€135. Set dinner €47.50.
1-night bookings occasionally
refused.

RATHMULLAN Co. Donegal

RATHMULLAN HOUSE

In 'wild and wonderful Donegal', this much-extended Georgian mansion has been owned by the Wheeler family for more than 50 years; Mark Wheeler is the manager. The spacious public rooms have high ceilings, chandeliers, antiques, marble fireplaces, log fires, oil paintings, lots of books. In the *Weeping Elm* restaurant, Micheál Harley is now the chef: his dinner menu is 'influenced by garden produce and local suppliers' for dishes like warm chorizo salad, pickled carrots, shaved fennel; assiette of Greencastle fish, velouté of leeks. Main-house bedrooms are traditionally furnished; extension rooms have a contemporary look. 'Our spacious bedroom in an extension had a sitting area in front of windows that opened on to the terrace; a modern bathroom had a deep bath and a separate shower.' Breakfast has 'an unusually extensive buffet; stewed fruits and compotes were from the garden; an unusual range of home-made breads. We were less sure about the single toaster with its counter-intuitive controls (toast rage awaits).' To walk from the 'interesting gardens' on to the sandy shore of Lough Swilly is 'an exhilarating treat'. (*AW*)

Rathmullan

T: 00 353 74-915 8188
F: 00 353 74-915 8200
E: info@rathmullanhouse.com
W: www.rathmullanhouse.com

BEDROOMS: 34, some on ground floor, 2 suitable for &.
OPEN: mid-Feb–6 Jan, closed midweek Nov/Dec, Christmas.
FACILITIES: ramps, 4 sitting rooms, library, TV room, cellar bar/bistro, restaurant, free Wi-Fi in lounges, 15-metre indoor swimming pool, wedding facilities, 7-acre grounds (tennis, croquet).
BACKGROUND MUSIC: none.
LOCATION: ½ mile N of village.
CHILDREN: all ages welcomed.
DOGS: allowed in 1 bedroom, but not in public rooms.
CREDIT CARDS: Amex, MasterCard, Visa.
PRICES: [2014] per person B&B €75–€125, D,B&B €115–€170. Set dinner €45/€55. 1-night bookings refused bank holiday Sat.

COOPERSHILL

🌢 *César award in 1987*

On a large estate on the River Arrow, with a sizeable deer farm and woodland, this Palladian mansion has been home to the O'Hara family since it was built in 1774. Visitors are welcomed as house guests by Simon O'Hara and his partner, Christina McCauley. A *Guide* inspector enjoyed 'a wonderful, unforgettable experience'; a reader thought it 'very special; back to bygone times'. A magnificent high-ceilinged staircase, which is lined with stags' heads and swords, leads to the bedrooms which are furnished with antiques (the largest has two original four-poster beds). 'We only provide keys on request because this is a family home,' says Simon O'Hara. Christina McCauley is the *Ballymaloe*-trained cook, picking vegetables, herbs and fruit from the garden for each evening's no-choice four-course menu. Typical dishes: spinach and rosemary soup; Coopershill venison medallions, juniper sauce. When venison is on the menu, 'the distance from farm to plate' for most ingredients is 200 yards. The meal is taken at separate (well-spaced) tables but 'you will get more from your stay if you are willing to mix' in the 'elegant and beautiful' lounge.

Riverstown

T: 00 353 71-916 5108
E: ohara@coopershill.com
W: www.coopershill.com

BEDROOMS: 8.
OPEN: Apr–Oct, off-season house parties by arrangement.
FACILITIES: 2 halls, drawing room, dining room, snooker room, free Wi-Fi, wedding facilities, 500-acre estate (garden, tennis, croquet, woods, farmland, river with trout fishing), unsuitable for ♿.
BACKGROUND MUSIC: none.
LOCATION: 11 miles SE of Sligo.
CHILDREN: by arrangement.
DOGS: by arrangement.
CREDIT CARDS: MasterCard, Visa.
PRICES: per person B&B €99–€122. Set dinner €54.

SCHULL Co. Cork

GROVE HOUSE

Overlooking the harbour in a village popular with yachting folk, this restored period house has a long association with the arts; George Bernard Shaw and Edith Somerville were on the guest list when it opened as a hotel in 1880. Today, its Swedish owner, Katarina Runske, maintains the artistic connections; she teaches the piano (there's a baby grand in the sitting room) and hosts regular musical gigs, art exhibitions and events. She runs *Grove House* as an informal guest house with her son, Nico, who is the chef. The house has a lived-in feel ('a fair share of clutter, but it is charming and comfortable'). Period features have been retained in the nicely proportioned rooms; spacious bedrooms have a pitch pine floor, work by local artists, books to read; the Carbery Room has a record player and vinyl LPs. In the dining room, which has a conservatory extension, Nico Runske uses local produce for his menus in dishes like moules marinière; there is an occasional Swedish twist (herring three ways; meatballs). 'Great pride' is taken in the wine list. 'Excellent value.'

25% DISCOUNT VOUCHERS

Colla Road
Schull

T: 00 353 28-28067
F: 00 353 28-28069
E: info@grovehouseschull.com
W: www.grovehouseschull.com

BEDROOMS: 5.
OPEN: Mar–Nov, Christmas/New Year.
FACILITIES: bar, sitting room, dining room, free Wi-Fi, wedding facilities, terrace, 1-acre garden, only dining room suitable for &.
BACKGROUND MUSIC: classical in dining room.
LOCATION: outskirts of village.
CHILDREN: all ages welcomed.
DOGS: allowed.
CREDIT CARDS: Amex, MasterCard, Visa.
PRICES: per person B&B single €50, double €40. Set dinner €30.

SHANAGARRY Co. Cork

BALLYMALOE HOUSE

🏆 *César award in 1984*

In 2014, the Allen family's renowned hotel/restaurant celebrated its 50th anniversary. Myrtle Allen had been farming on the estate with her late husband, Ivan, for 16 years when she first opened a restaurant. The relationship of the farm to the table still underpins the hospitality at *Ballymaloe*; Myrtle remains a presence alongside her daughters-in law, Hazel, who manages the hotel/restaurant, and Darina, who runs the famous cookery school. Dinner, in a series of 'cheerful' rooms with green walls, is 'totally unpretentious, very good'. Head chefs Jason Fahey and Gillian Hegarty use 'wonderful local ingredients' for their menus. The 'civilised' atmosphere is enjoyed: 'books are scattered around, interesting paintings and sculptures everywhere; no muzak, no little notes, but a ban on mobiles in public rooms.' Log fires are lit on wet days in summer in the drawing room; in the 'charming' conservatory, 'we ate delicious scones with our tea (leaf tea, of course)'. The biggest bedrooms are in the main house; 'Our room was cosy, like a spare room in a friend's house.' The 'lovely' grounds have woodland walks, ancient trees, ponds.

25% DISCOUNT VOUCHERS

Shanagarry

T: 00 353 21-465 2531
F: 00 353 21-465 2021
E: res@ballymaloe.ie
W: www.ballymaloe.ie

BEDROOMS: 29, 7 in adjacent building, 4 on ground floor, 5 self-catering cottages suitable for ♿.
OPEN: all year except 3 weeks in Jan.
FACILITIES: drawing room, 2 small sitting rooms, conservatory, 7 dining rooms, free Wi-Fi, wedding and conference facilities, 6-acre gardens, 400-acre grounds (tennis, swimming pool, 10 by 4 metres), cookery school nearby.
BACKGROUND MUSIC: none.
LOCATION: 20 miles E of Cork.
CHILDREN: all ages welcomed.
DOGS: allowed in courtyard rooms, not in house.
CREDIT CARDS: all major cards.
PRICES: [to April 2015] per person B&B €95–€140. Set dinner €70.

SHORTLIST

The Shortlist complements our main section by including potential but untested new entries and appropriate places in areas where we have limited choice. It also has some hotels that have been full entries in the *Guide*, but have not attracted feedback from our readers.

Greywalls, Gullane

Map 2:D4

THE ALMA, 499 Old York Road, SW18 1TF. Tel 020-8870 2537, www.almawandsworth.com. Down a cobbled alley, this modern inn, a former metal works, has a popular local bar and comfortable bedrooms. Managed by Sean Young, it is run on green lines: solar panels provide energy for hot water and electricity; lights and electrical appliances are programmed to work only when guests are indoors. The Victorian pub (Young & Co's Brewery) has cask ales and beers from local breweries; chef Imants Erbreiders serves gastropub classics in the modern dining room at the back of the busy bar. Spacious bedrooms have bold wallpaper, a king-size bed and bespoke furniture; a garden suite has a private terrace with outdoor seating. Breakfast is served until 11 am on weekends. Bar, restaurant, function room. Free Wi-Fi. Background music. Civil wedding licence. Use of Virgin spa and gym nearby. Children welcomed (cots). 23 bedrooms (2 on ground floor suitable for &). Per person B&B £109–£275. Dinner £30. (Opposite Wandsworth Town railway station; 15 mins to Waterloo)

THE AMPERSAND, 10 Harrington Road, SW7 3ER. Tel 020-7589 5895, www.ampersandhotel.com. In a renovated Victorian building, this eclectic South Kensington hotel takes inspiration from its learned neighbours: rooms and suites are decorated in themes (botany, geometry, ornithology, astronomy, music) borrowed from nearby museums and the Royal Albert Hall. Staff are 'laid back'. Modern bedrooms (some small; 16 allow smoking) have a high ceiling, an oversized bedhead and velvet fabrics; there are free soft drinks in the minibar. Chef Chris Golding cooks Mediterranean dishes in the white-tiled basement restaurant, *Apero*; light meals and afternoon tea are taken in the *Drawing Rooms*. Bar, restaurant, drawing room, business centre; private dining room. Games room (table tennis), gym; running maps and information on activities in Hyde Park (horse riding, inline skating) available. Free Wi-Fi. Contemporary background music. Lift. Children (cots), and dogs welcomed. Public parking nearby (reservation required). 111 bedrooms and suites. Room only £234–£248. À la carte breakfast £14. Dinner £30. (Underground: South Kensington)

B+B BELGRAVIA, 64–66 Ebury Street, SW1W 9QD. Tel 020-7259 8570, www.bb-belgravia.com. 'A great place.' A short walk from Victoria station, this 'modern' B&B occupies an elegant Grade II listed Georgian town house. Some rooms have views over the garden; those at the top are quietest; larger studios are well equipped for eating in. Complimentary tea, coffee, hot chocolate and biscuits are served all day in the lounge; extras such as an alarm clock, laptop cable, adaptor, extra heater or fan are available to borrow. Breakfast has locally baked pastries, cereals, toast, fruit and yogurt; 'bacon and eggs so good I had them twice'. Lounge (fireplace, guest laptop, newspapers, DVDs, books), open-plan kitchen/breakfast room (organic breakfasts). Free Wi-Fi and bicycles. No background music. Small garden.

Children (cots, high chairs) and dogs welcomed. 17 bedrooms (2 family; 1 suitable for &), plus 9 studios close by. Per room B&B £135–£209. (Underground: Victoria)

BERMONDSEY SQUARE HOTEL,

Bermondsey Square, Tower Bridge Road, SE1 3UN. Tel 020-7378 2450, www.bermondseysquarehotel.co.uk. In a 'fabulously modish' area – a branch of the White Cube gallery is a few minutes' walk away – this modern hotel has 'reasonably sized' rooms with a wet room, and a 'comfortable bed with plenty of pillows and cushions'. *GB Grill & Bar* serves a small menu of 'uncomplicated' British food all day, perhaps 'very good' smoked salmon; 'rich fish pie, with meaty scallops and prawns'; the continental breakfast has yogurts, 'reasonable' coffee, 'good' fruit salad. City bike hire adjacent; well placed for Borough Market and walks across Tower Bridge. Business facilities. Lift. Free Wi-Fi. Background music. Children and dogs welcomed (boutique dog beds). 80 bedrooms (5 suites; some suitable for &). Room only from £94. Continental breakfast £9.95. (Underground: Bermondsey, Tower Hill)

CHARLOTTE STREET HOTEL, 15–17

Charlotte Street, W1T 1RJ. Tel 020-7806 2000, www.charlottestreethotel. com. On a lively street north of Soho, this stylish hotel, part of Tim and Kit Kemp's Firmdale group, is boldly decorated with vivid colours, and much original art by Bloomsbury artists. A small cinema in the basement screens current films and classics on Sunday evenings. Bedrooms are exuberantly styled in cheery prints and fabrics; each

has a writing desk, and a handsome bathroom in granite and oak. Service is 'attentive, pleasant and helpful' in the 'bright' restaurant; a room-service menu is available all day. Within walking distance of the West End theatres. Drawing room, library, *Oscar* bar, open-plan restaurant (chef Robin Read). 3 private dining/meeting rooms; 75-seat screening room; gym. Free Wi-Fi. No background music. Children welcomed (cots; babysitting). 52 bedrooms. Room only from £300. Breakfast £18–£30. (Underground: Goodge Street, Tottenham Court Road)

CITIZENM, 20 Lavington Street,

SE1 0NZ. Tel 020-3519 1680, www.citizenm.com. 'Excellent value for money.' A trusted *Guide* correspondent was 'impressed' by this contemporary hotel close to the Tate Modern museum. It is part of an international chain of stylish budget hotels catering for 'mobile citizens'. Service is minimalist: guests check themselves in and show themselves to their room, but staff, when needed, are 'friendly and helpful'. 'Spotlessly clean' modular bedrooms have a large bed against a floor-to-ceiling window, a television (free movies on demand), a fridge, a shower room; lighting, room temperature, window blinds and the TV are controlled via a touch-screen tablet. The vast lobby and open-plan bar and canteen have modern art, Vitra furniture, iMacs; accessible 24 hours a day, they serve as working and lounging space. Breakfast has 'divine' freshly squeezed clementine juice and 'probably the best breakfast coffee I can remember'. Open-plan lobby/bar/deli/seating areas. Meeting rooms. Lift. Free Wi-Fi. 192 bedrooms (some suitable for &). Room only £99–£219. Breakfast from £11.95. (Underground: London Bridge, Southwark)

COUNTY HALL PREMIER INN, Belvedere Road, SE1 7PB. Tel 0871-527 8648, www.premierinn.com. Minutes away from the London Eye, this good-value hotel occupies the historic Portland stone County Hall building on the banks of the Thames. The simply furnished bedrooms have a desk, tea- and coffee-making facilities, a basic bathroom; double glazing minimises street noise. The Sea Life London Aquarium and the London Dungeon are in the same building; the attractions of the South Bank are five minutes' walk away. Busy at breakfast. Self-service check-in. Lobby, bar, *Thyme* restaurant; lift. Conference facilities. Wi-Fi (first half-hour free; subsequently £3 per 24 hours or £10 per 7 days). Background music. Children welcomed. 314 bedrooms (some suitable for &). Room only from £169. Meal deal (dinner and breakfast) £22.99 per person. (Underground: Waterloo)

COVENT GARDEN HOTEL, 10 Monmouth Street, WC2H 9HB. Tel 020-7806 1000, www.firmdalehotels.com. 'Distinctively decorated' in vivid patterns and bright colours, this small hotel, part of Tim and Kit Kemp's Firmdale group, is liked for its 'superb comfort and fantastic service'. Bedrooms are individually designed with striking fabrics and an oversized bedhead; many have views of London's rooftops. Connecting rooms are available for families and larger parties. Wood-panelled sitting rooms have fresh flowers and a stone fireplace; a basement

screening room hosts Saturday movie nights. The 'excellent' meals in *Brasserie Max* are available for room service; breakfasts (extra charge) have a vast choice. Drawing room, library (honesty bar), restaurant. Meeting room; screening room; gym. Free Wi-Fi. No background music. Children welcomed. 58 bedrooms. Room only £350–£2,210. Breakfast £20–£34. (Underground: Covent Garden, Leicester Square)

DORSET SQUARE HOTEL, 39–40 Dorset Square, Marylebone, NW1 6QN. Tel 020-7723 7874, www.firmdalehotels. com. In a Regency town house overlooking a quiet garden square (the original site of Thomas Lord's first cricket ground), this small hotel is part of the Firmdale group owned by Tim and Kit Kemp. Eva Mount is the manager. The interior is decorated in the Kemps' signature lively mix of colours, patterns and textiles. Many of the individually styled bedrooms have views of the leafy square; some can be small. English brasserie dishes are served in *The Potting Shed*, a popular basement bar and restaurant, which is open all day. Children have their own menu and toiletries; dogs are welcomed, by arrangement. Drawing room (fireplace, honesty bar), brasserie. Free Wi-Fi. No background music. Room service. DVD library. 38 bedrooms. Room only from £198. Continental breakfast buffet £10.50. (Underground: Marylebone)

FLEET RIVER ROOMS, 71 Lincoln's Inn Fields, WC2A 3JF. Tel 020-7691 1457, www.fleetriverbakery.com. There is much people-watching to be done from the large sash windows of the modern studio apartments at this B&B on a bustling square. The high-ceilinged rooms are above a popular bakery and café; they have polished floors, a sitting area and a smartly outfitted kitchen (fridge, oven, microwave, washing machine). Some rooms have a sofa bed for an extra guest (£15 per night charge for over-5s); baby cots are available on request. No dinner is served; many restaurants are within walking distance. Generous portions of scrambled eggs, sourdough toast and fruit salad at breakfast. Free Wi-Fi. Children welcomed. 4 bedrooms. Per room B&B £88–£120. (Underground: Holborn)

41, 41 Buckingham Palace Road, SW1W 0PS. Tel 020-7300 0041, www.41hotel.com. With a champagne trolley wheeled out at check-in, guests receive a royal welcome at this luxury hotel close to Buckingham Palace. Part of the Red Carnation group, the hotel occupies the fifth floor of a historic building that is also home to sister hotel *The Rubens at the Palace*. Public rooms have mahogany panelling and polished brass; decorated in a black-and-white theme, modern bedrooms have a selection of magazines and books, and season-appropriate bathrobes. Complimentary afternoon tea and canapés are taken in the lounge; guests are invited to 'plunder the pantry' and help themselves to light meals and snacks each evening until late. An extensive breakfast is served until 1 pm on Sundays. Room, and butler service. Free Wi-Fi. Background music. Business facilities. Complimentary pass to nearby fitness club (swimming pool, sauna, spa). Children and dogs welcomed. 30 bedrooms and suites.

Room only £443–£467. Breakfast £19.50–£25. (Underground: Victoria)

GREAT NORTHERN HOTEL, King's Cross St Pancras Station, Pancras Road, N1C 4TB. Tel 020-3388 0800, www.gnhlondon.com. The luxurious refurbishment of this grand Victorian railway hotel has been 'very well done'. Designed in 1851 by master builder Lewis Cubitt (famous for King's Cross railway station), the dramatic, curving brick building has 'spacious', elegant bedrooms reminiscent of railway carriage sleepers; each has a high ceiling, bespoke furniture and good soundproofing. Guests help themselves to coffee, tea, biscuits, sweets and home-made cake in a pantry on each floor; there are also books, newspapers and magazines to borrow. Open all day, the lively *Plum + Spilt Milk* restaurant has 'excellent' food and service; the Art Deco bar has light bites and cocktails. The hotel opens directly onto the Western concourse of King's Cross station; the Eurostar terminal at St Pancras International is a few yards from the front door. Bar, restaurant, *Kiosk* food stall. Free Wi-Fi. 91 bedrooms. Per room B&B from £209. (Underground: King's Cross St Pancras)

THE HALKIN BY COMO, 5 Halkin Street, SW1X 7DJ. Tel 020-7333 1000, www.comohotels.com/thehalkin. Guests are offered a welcome drink at this contemporary hotel in an elegant neighbourhood of embassies and grand Georgian-style residences. Part of the COMO group, the hotel is managed by Simon Wakefield. Bedrooms have large windows (some overlooking the garden) and a marble bathroom; residents control temperature and lighting, and access guest services, via a touch-screen console. Daughter-and-father team Elena and Juan Mari Arzak have a *Michelin* star for their modern Basque cooking in the restaurant, *Ametsa with Arzak Instruction*; light lunches and afternoon tea are taken in the informal *Halkin Bar*. Guests have access to the Shambhala Urban Escape spa in sister hotel *Metropolitan* on Park Lane. Bar, restaurant (background music). Gym (trainer and yoga teacher available). Garden. Free Wi-Fi. Children welcomed. 41 bedrooms. Room only from £288. (Underground: Hyde Park Corner)

HAYMARKET HOTEL, 1 Suffolk Place, SW1Y 4HX. Tel 020-7470 4000, www.haymarkethotel.com. In the theatre district, this 'beautifully furnished' hotel (Firmdale Hotels) occupies three John Nash-designed buildings. It is managed by Lisa Brooklyn, with 'the nicest and most helpful staff'. Public rooms and bedrooms have striking sculptures and contemporary art, spirited prints, and co-owner Kit Kemp's distinctive mix of antique and modern furnishings; a 'stunning' heated indoor swimming pool has dramatic lighting and a pewter poolside bar. Lift. Conservatory, library, bar, *Brumus* restaurant. Indoor swimming pool, gym. Free Wi-Fi. Background music. Civil wedding licence. 50 bedrooms (2 suites; 5-bedroom town house). Room only from £324. Breakfast £18–£28. (Underground: Green Park, Piccadilly)

THE HOXTON, 81 Great Eastern Street, EC2A 3HU. Tel 020-7550 1000, www. hoxtonhotels.com. 'Urban industrial design meets chic comfort' at this 'intensely stylish' hotel in a lively part of town. The 'enormous' lobby has exposed brick walls, stone fireplaces, leather armchairs; upstairs, 'well-equipped' bedrooms have a 'decent' large bed, 'proper' hangers, 'good lighting'; a 'splendid' bathroom. The 'excellent' *Hoxton Grill* serves an American-influenced menu all day; meals may be taken in the 'huge' brasserie or covered garden courtyard. The 'buzzy' bar, popular with locals, is open till late. The room rate includes a breakfast bag (yogurt, granola, banana, orange juice) delivered to the room each morning. Weekly music and art events. Bicycles available to borrow. Lounge (background music) and outdoor space (interior courtyard). Lift. Meeting rooms; shop. Free Wi-Fi. Children welcomed. 208 rooms. Per room B&B £69–£269. (Underground: Old Street)

H10 LONDON WATERLOO, 284–302 Waterloo Road, SE1 8RQ. Tel 020-7928 4062, www.hotelh10 londonwaterloo.com. Guests are offered a glass of cava on arrival at this good-value Spanish chain hotel, in a modern, purpose-built block on busy Waterloo Road. Public rooms are decorated in sleek, contemporary style, with striking photographic murals; they have a 'good selection' of newspapers and magazines. There are large windows in the bright, sometimes compact bedrooms ('good' double glazing makes traffic noise 'bearable'); top-floor city-view rooms have the best, panoramic views. Service is 'prompt and friendly' in the restaurant, where 'outstanding' modern Spanish dishes are served. 'A breakfast buffet of considerable size'; 'excellent' cooked dishes. The South Bank is 15 minutes' walk away. Lounge, bar, *Three O Two* restaurant. Leisure centre (gym, sauna, hydromassage shower; treatments); meeting rooms. Free Wi-Fi. 177 bedrooms. Per room B&B £169–£239. Dinner £30. (Underground: Waterloo)

INDIGO, 16 London Street, W2 1HL. Tel 020-7706 4444, www.ihg.com/hotelindigo. In a converted town house opposite a small garden square, this modern hotel (part of the InterContinental Hotels Group) is conveniently located for Paddington station and the express trains to Heathrow. Decorated in contemporary style with photographic murals of nearby Hyde Park and Little Venice, bedrooms (some small) have an espresso machine, complimentary soft drinks; a spa-inspired shower. Street-facing rooms may have some noise (earplugs provided). Lounge/lobby, bar, brasserie; terrace. Fitness studio. Free Wi-Fi. Background music. Children welcomed. 64 bedrooms (some with private balcony or terrace; 2 suitable for &). Per room B&B £189–£299. (Underground: Paddington)

KNIGHTSBRIDGE HOTEL, 10 Beaufort Gardens, SW3 1PT. Tel 020-7584 6300, www.knightsbridgehotel.com. On a quiet, tree-lined street minutes from Hyde Park, this handsome town house hotel is part of Tim and Kit Kemp's Firmdale group. The cosy sitting areas are filled with contemporary art and sculpture; bright, colourful bedrooms are individually designed. Most rooms have views of Beaufort Gardens or across Harrods and the city skyline.

There is no restaurant; cocktails and a room-service menu are available all day in the sitting rooms or bedroom. Families are welcomed; the children's afternoon tea menu has jellies and milkshakes. In-room massages and beauty treatments can be arranged. Drawing room, library, bar. Free Wi-Fi. Room service. No background music. Children welcomed. 44 bedrooms. Room only from £294. À la carte breakfast £3.50–£14.50. (Underground: Knightsbridge)

THE MAIN HOUSE, 6 Colville Road, Notting Hill, W11 2BP. Tel 020-7221 9691, www.themainhouse.co.uk. Loved for its location and gracious decoration, this 'elegant home from home' is in a Victorian house on a quiet street off Portobello Road. Each suite of the B&B occupies an entire floor and has period features, antique furnishings, modern technology and an airy, uncluttered look. A complimentary newspaper and morning coffee or tea are brought to the room or served on the balcony; an organic continental or full English breakfast is also available. Guests receive special day rates at the nearby BodyWorksWest health club, and discounts at several smart delis and an artisan baker nearby. Roof terrace. Free Wi-Fi. No background music. Mobile phones available to borrow; DVD library. Children welcomed. Reasonable rates for chauffeur service to airports. 4 bedrooms. Room only from £110 (min. 3-night stay). (Underground: Notting Hill Gate)

THE MONTAGUE ON THE GARDENS, 15 Montague Street, WC1B 5BJ. Tel 020-7637 1001, www.montaguehotel.com.

Across the street from the British Museum, this 'well-run' town house hotel occupies an 'attractive' Georgian terrace overlooking peaceful gardens. It is managed by Dirk Crokaert, with 'enthusiastic' staff, for the Red Carnation group. Public rooms are lavishly decorated with draped curtains, crystal chandeliers, graphic floral prints; with gilded mirrors and hand-crafted furniture, the 'generously equipped' bedrooms can be equally flamboyant. Children are welcomed with games, DVDs, their own slippers and bathrobe. In the informal *Blue Door* bistro, chef Martin Halls serves a seasonal menu; in the summer, alfresco meals are taken on the terrace in the *Garden Grill*. Classic contemporary background music in public areas; pianist in *Terrace* bar in evening except Sun. Lounge, bar, 2 conservatories; terrace. Fitness suite. Designated outdoor smoking area. Civil wedding licence. Free Wi-Fi. Children, and dogs (special treats) welcomed. 100 rooms (1 suitable for &). Per room B&B single from £226, double from £248. (Underground: Russell Square)

THE NADLER, 25 Courtfield Gardens, SW5 0PG. Tel 020-7244 2255, www.thenadler.com. Formerly known as *base2stay*, this modern hotel near the museums and Kensington Gardens aims to provide no-frills 'affordable luxury'. It is part of the Nadler Hotels group (see also the Nadler Liverpool). It occupies a white stucco town house in a leafy residential square; inside, there are simply furnished bedrooms – including many good-value single rooms – each with a mini-kitchen (microwave, fridge, sink, cutlery). Larger rooms with a sofa bed are suitable for families. There is no restaurant or bar, but guests receive discounts at local eating spots; a continental breakfast (£8.50) may be delivered to the room, by arrangement. City bike hire nearby; helmets available to borrow. Reception lobby (background music). Music library, games. Free Wi-Fi. Children welcomed. 65 bedrooms (some with bunk beds; 1 suitable for &). Room only from £107. (Underground: Earls Court, Gloucester Road)

THE ORANGE, 37 Pimlico Road, SW1W 8NE. Tel 020-7881 9844, www.theorange.co.uk. Occupying an impressive white-painted building dating back to 1846, this smart pub-with-rooms has been renovated in a chic rustic style. It is part of the Cubitt House group (see also *The Grazing Goat*, Marble Arch, London, main entry). The lively ground-floor pub is popular with well-heeled locals; modern European menus are served in the restaurant on the first floor (wood-fired pizzas are 'a highlight'). Up the narrow stairs, the bedrooms are 'well designed, simple, yet very smart and comfortable'; they have limewashed walls, a king-size bed, a marble bathroom. Bar, restaurant. Private functions. Free Wi-Fi. Background music (soul, jazz). Children welcomed (cots). 4 bedrooms. Room only £205–£240. Full English breakfast £12.50. Dinner £35. (Underground: Sloane Square, Victoria)

THE PORTOBELLO, 22 Stanley Gardens, W11 2NG. Tel 020-7727 2777, www.portobellohotel.com. On an 'elegant' Notting Hill street, this 'discreet' hotel, in two grand white stucco houses, is under new ownership (A Curious Group of Hotels). Some 'light' refurbishment has recently been completed. The quirky bedrooms vary considerably in size and style: 'Good' rooms feature a wall mural depicting an exotic scene; flamboyantly decorated 'Exceptional' rooms have a sitting area and a large bathroom. Some rooms overlook the garden; all have a minibar and Nespresso coffee machine. A continental breakfast (juice, tea/coffee, croissants, toast) is included in the room rate; additional charge for cooked breakfast. Light bites, sandwiches and drinks are available throughout the day. Lounge. Lift. Free Wi-Fi. No background music. Children welcomed. 21 bedrooms. Per room B&B (continental) £125–£385. Closed Christmas. (Underground: Notting Hill Gate)

QBIC HOTEL, 42 Adler Street, E1 1EE. Tel 020-3021 3300, london.qbichotels. com. Close to Brick Lane, in a lively neighbourhood known for its curry houses and young creatives, this new Dutch chain hotel has stylish, no-frills rooms and a hip, buzzy atmosphere. The enormous lobby/seating area, open to non-residents, has mismatched furnishings and plenty of space to work or socialise; complimentary teas and coffees are available here all day. Pod-like, pre-fabricated rooms have a large bed with an organic wool mattress, a Skype-ready television, mood lighting, British and European plug sockets; a shower room, with sliding doors and a power shower, is efficiently tucked behind the headboard. There is no restaurant or bar; a row of vending machines has drinks, snacks and easy meals (vacuum-packed stews, organic crisps, locally brewed beers). Breakfast

'grab bags' (juice, fruit, cereal bar) are included in the room rate. Self-service check-in. Lifts. Children welcomed (connecting rooms, baby cots). 171 rooms (some suitable for &). Room only £59–£199. Breakfast buffet £7.50. Free Wi-Fi. (Underground: Aldgate East, Whitechapel)

ST JAMES'S HOTEL AND CLUB, 7–8 Park Place, SW1A 1LS. Tel 020-7316 1600, www.stjameshotelandclub.com. In a quiet cul-de-sac, this opulent town house hotel (Althoff Hotels) has marble pillars, Murano glass chandeliers, rich fabrics, and original artwork including a collection of portraits from the 1920s to the 1940s. Henrik Muehle is the manager. The restful bedrooms have a glamorous bathroom; some rooms have their own balcony. In the dramatically designed restaurant (striking wallpaper, bold mixes of patterns and colours), chef William Drabble has a *Michelin* star for his modern French cooking. Traditional afternoon tea is served in the elegant lounge or bistro. Lounge, bar, *William's* bar and bistro, *Seven Park Place* (closed Sun, Mon). 4 private dining rooms. Free Wi-Fi. Background music. Children welcomed (dedicated kids' concierge). 60 bedrooms (10 suites; 2 on ground floor). Room only £405–£3,000. Breakfast £24. Dinner £61. (Underground: Green Park)

SANCTUARY HOUSE HOTEL, 33 Tothill Street, SW1H 9LA. Tel 020-7799 4044, www.sanctuaryhousehotel.co.uk. Above a traditional pub serving home-made pies, there are good-value modern rooms at this updated Victorian ale-and-pie house (part of Fuller's Hotels and Inns). The 'very comfortable' bedrooms (some can be snug) have a desk, and tea- and coffee-making facilities; superior rooms also have bathrobes and take-home slippers. Minutes from Westminster Abbey, the Houses of Parliament and St James's Park. Bar, restaurant. Lift. Room service. Free Wi-Fi. Background music. Children welcomed. 34 bedrooms (some suitable for &). Room only £120–£270. Breakfast £10.25–£12.95. (Underground: St James's Park)

SLOANE SQUARE HOTEL, 7–12 Sloane Square, SW1W 8EG. Tel 020-7896 9988, www.sloanesquarehotel.co.uk. On a fashionable square, this 'very pleasant' hotel is well located for the shops and restaurants of Chelsea and Knightsbridge. Some of the 'smart' bedrooms overlook the lively square; quieter rooms at the rear of the building have views of a historic church. 'Our modern room was very small but brilliantly fitted out, with an extremely comfortable bed, desk/dressing table with Nespresso coffee machine; minibar filled with things you might actually want.' Breakfast has 'good cooked dishes'. Cadogan Hall and the Royal Court Theatre are nearby. *Côte* brasserie (background music), bar. Meeting rooms. Lift. Free Wi-Fi, and local and national phone calls. Parking (charge). Children welcomed. 102 bedrooms. Room only £185–£330. Full English breakfast £9.95. (Underground: Sloane Square)

THE SOHO HOTEL, 4 Richmond Mews, off Dean Street, W1D 3DH. Tel 020-7559 3000, www.sohohotel.com. There is much character in this glamorous hotel (part of Tim and Kit Kemp's Firmdale collection), from the massive Botero bronze cat in the lobby to the imaginative melange of prints, colours and patterns throughout. Public rooms have fresh flowers and modern art; the elegant bedrooms have floor-to-ceiling windows and a luxurious bathroom. A small cinema hosts regular Sunday afternoon film events including lunch, tea or dinner. Drawing room, library, bar, *Refuel* restaurant; 4 private dining rooms. Lift. Gym; beauty treatment rooms. 2 screening rooms; DVD library. Free Wi-Fi. Background music. Civil wedding licence. 91 bedrooms and suites (some suitable for &). Also 4 apartments. Room only £295–£4,140. Breakfast £19.50–£32. Set dinner £21–£24. (Underground: Leicester Square)

SOUTH PLACE HOTEL, 3 South Place, EC2M 2AF. Tel 020-3503 0000, www.southplacehotel.com. Filled with contemporary art, this modern hotel has a sophisticated and lively atmosphere. It is owned by restaurant group D&D London. The 'excellent' top-floor *Angler* restaurant (closed Sat lunch, and Sun) has a *Michelin* star for its British seafood dishes; bistro food is available all day at *3 South Place* bar and grill (DJ most nights). Bedrooms have artwork by London artists, a minibar with British treats; ample storage space, floor-to-ceiling windows, electric blackout blinds; mood lighting controlled by a touch panel. The extensive breakfast selection, served until 11 am, has healthy options, a butty menu, porridge served with London honey. 3 bars, 2 restaurants, *Le Chiffre* residents' lounge and games room (books, magazines, games, turntable, cocktails); roof terrace; 'secret' garden. Gym;

treatment room. Private dining, meeting rooms. Free Wi-Fi. Background music. Children welcomed (cots; interconnecting rooms). 80 bedrooms, studios and suites (4 suitable for &). Room only £185–£480. Full English breakfast £16.50. (Underground: Moorgate, Liverpool Street)

SYDNEY HOUSE CHELSEA, 9–11 Sydney Street, SW3 6PU. Tel 020-7376 7711, www.sydneyhousechelsea.com. In a peaceful residential street just minutes from the King's Road, this Georgian town house is part of Brownsword Hotels' aBode collection. Vojin Mandic is the manager. The compact, modern bedrooms vary in size; all have quality linens and Scottish lambswool throws. One has a balcony with views over the Chelsea rooftops; another, the Room at the Top, has a private roof garden with terracotta pots and teak chairs. Drawing room, bar, restaurant (open to non-residents for breakfast), 24-hour room service (light snacks); boardroom. Free Wi-Fi. Background music in lobby. Children welcomed (cots). 21 bedrooms. Room only £125–£255. À la carte breakfast £5.95–£18.95. Dinner £20. Closed Christmas. (Underground: South Kensington)

TEN MANCHESTER STREET, 10 Manchester Street, W1U 4DG. Tel 020-7317 5900, www.tenmanchesterstreet hotel.com. In a red brick Edwardian town house just off fashionable Marylebone High Street, this discreet hotel (City and Country Hotels) has 'comfortable', individually designed bedrooms; four open on to a private terrace with seating, music and heaters. Modern Italian menus are served in

Dieci restaurant; snacks are available all day in the cosy, L-shaped bar. Cigar smokers are well provided for with a new cigar-tasting room with a walk-in humidor, and an all-weather smoking terrace. Regent's Park is 10 minutes' walk away. Lounge/bar (background music). Free Wi-Fi. Children welcomed. 24-hour room service; chauffeur service. 44 bedrooms (9 suites). Per room B&B £165–£365, D,B&B £225–£425. (Underground: Bond Street)

THREADNEEDLES, 5 Threadneedle Street, EC2R 8AY. Tel 020-7657 8080, www.hotelthreadneedles.co.uk. 'The staff could not have done more to help us and our wedding party; they formed a guard of honour when the bride left for the ceremony.' A conversion of a Victorian banking hall, this luxury hotel, close to the Bank of England, is part of Marriott's Autograph Collection. There are marble floors, walnut panelling, ornate pillars; a hand-painted stained-glass dome hangs over the reception area. Porters help guests unload cars. 'The bedrooms have every amenity and are beautifully decorated.' Bar, *Bonds* restaurant (modern British cuisine, closed at weekends). Lift. 3 meeting rooms; conference facilities. Free Wi-Fi. Background music. 74 bedrooms (1 suitable for &). Room only £259–£525. Breakfast £15.

TOWN HALL HOTEL & APARTMENTS, Patriot Square, E2 9NF. Tel 020-7871 0460, www.townhallhotel.com. Occupying a sympathetically refurbished Grade II listed Edwardian building, this modern hotel, once Bethnal Green town hall, is liked for its stylish rooms and 'friendly, helpful staff'. The ornate moulded ceilings, stately staircases and marble pillars have been restored; spacious, individually styled bedrooms have vintage furniture and sheepskin rugs. 'Our large, airy apartment had an excellent kitchen; a modern bathroom with lots of storage space; large, opening windows.' The well-regarded *Corner Room* restaurant serves a short menu of modern dishes; a room-service menu is available 24 hours a day. A new restaurant, *Typing Room*, is run under the direction of chef Lee Westcott. Free shuttle bus to Liverpool Street and Bank on weekday mornings. Parking can be difficult. Bar, 2 restaurants. 'Gorgeous' indoor pool, gym (open 6 am to midnight). Lift. Free Wi-Fi. Background music. Civil wedding licence/function facilities. Children welcomed. 98 bedrooms and studios (with kitchen). Room only from £172. Breakfast from £15. (Underground: Bethnal Green)

Z HOTEL, 17 Moor Street, W1D 5AP. Tel 020-3551 3700, www.thezhotels. com/soho. In the heart of the West End, this contemporary hotel occupies 12 Georgian town houses gathered around a central courtyard. The compact, simply furnished bedrooms have a glass-fronted wet room; inside rooms have no window. A buffet breakfast, available until 11.30 am on weekends, includes unlimited tea, filter coffee and chilled fruit juices; a good selection of pastries and cooked items. Complimentary cheese and wine are served every evening in the café. Free Wi-Fi. 85 bedrooms (5 suitable for &). Per room B&B £212.50–£275. (Underground: Leicester Square)

ENGLAND

ALDEBURGH Suffolk
Map 2:C6
DUNAN HOUSE, 41 Park Road, IP15 5EN. Tel 01728-452486, www.dunanhouse.co.uk. Simon Farr (an artist) and Ann Lee (a potter) have filled their attractive Victorian home with much colour and many interesting artworks. B&B guests have a spacious bedroom with garden or river views; a family room on the top floor has a smaller connecting room with a single bed. A communal breakfast (served on Ann Lee's own pottery) has freshly laid eggs from resident hens. On a wooded private road; the beach and high street are less than ten minutes' walk away; a footpath beyond the front gate leads to the marshes and the river. ½-acre garden. Free Wi-Fi. No background music. Parking. Children welcomed. 3 bedrooms (1 family room). Per room B&B from £85. 2-night min. stay preferred. Closed Christmas.

ALFRISTON East Sussex
Map 2:E4
WINGROVE HOUSE, High Street, BN26 5TD. Tel 01323-870276, www.wingrovehousealfriston.com. In a 19th-century colonial-style house fronted by an elegant veranda, this 'comfortable', 'relaxed' restaurant-with-rooms is owned by Nick Denyer. 'Top-quality' dinners have 'lots of good choices', perhaps locally caught sea bream and gurnard, pea and broad bean bouillon, crispy chorizo. The stylish bedrooms are 'perfection'; all have views of the village and surrounding countryside. Breakfast has fruit salad, croissants, home-made jams; hot dishes

are cooked to order. Lounge/bar (extensive gin menu), restaurant (closed Mon–Fri lunchtime). Free Wi-Fi. Background music. Children welcomed. 5 bedrooms (2 with access to balcony). Per room B&B £100–£175. Dinner £30.

ALKHAM Kent
Map 2:D5
THE MARQUIS AT ALKHAM, Alkham Valley Road, CT15 7DF. Tel 01304-873410, www.themarquisatalkham.co.uk. Close to Dover and the Channel Tunnel, this 200-year-old inn (managed by Bespoke Hotels) stands above a sloping cricket pitch in a pretty village at the southern end of the Kent Downs. The modern interior has exposed brickwork, wooden floors, up-to-date fabrics and furnishings; bedrooms have a large pocket-sprung bed, under-floor heating, a TV and DVD-player, and views of the Alkham valley. Michael Fowler is now the chef. His Kentish menus make use of locally sourced produce and foraged food. Breakfast has an extensive buffet with seasonal fruits, cured meats, fish and cheese; hot dishes are cooked to order. The building is on a busy road; rooms at the back are quietest. Lounge/bar, restaurant (closed Mon lunch); small garden. Free Wi-Fi. Background music. Civil wedding licence. Children welcomed (no under-8s in restaurant after 6 pm). 10 bedrooms (3 in 2 cottages, 3 mins' drive away). Per room B&B £99–£229. Dinner £30–£55.
25% DISCOUNT VOUCHERS

AMBLESIDE Cumbria
Map 4: inset C2
NANNY BROW, Clappersgate, LA22 9NF. Tel 015394-33232, www.nannybrow. co.uk. Up a steep drive, Sue and Peter Robinson's white-painted guest house sits in a prominent position with a 'most attractive' view of the River Brathay below and the fells beyond. Mark Jones is manager. The Robinsons have devoted 'a lot of thought' to the restoration of their Arts and Crafts house; eco-efficient improvements include a biomass boiler, insulation and thermal blackout blinds. The large bedrooms are individually decorated with antiques and modern fabrics; some have an original tiled fireplace. Three new garden suites were added in 2014. Breakfast in the spacious dining room has home-made drop scones, locally cured salmon and freshly baked butter croissants. Good walks to Loughrigg and Grasmere. Lounge, bar, dining room. Free Wi-Fi. 'Easy listening' background music. Civil wedding licence. 6 acres of formal garden and woodlands; 1½ miles W of town. Resident dog and cat. Parking. 13 bedrooms (2 in an adjacent annexe). Per room B&B £130–£280. 2-night min. stay at weekends.
25% DISCOUNT VOUCHERS

APPLEDORE Devon
Map 1:B4
THE SEAGATE, The Quay, EX39 1QS. Tel 01237-472589, www.theseagate.co.uk. 'Muddy boots and dogs' are welcomed at this white-painted 17th-century inn, in a small fishing village overlooking the Torridge estuary. It has been extensively refurbished by new owners Phil and Jan Hills. Simply furnished bedrooms (some beamed) have tea- and coffee-making facilities, a modern bathroom; a family room has bunk beds for children. (Rooms above the busy pub may have some noise.) Chef Patryk Sala cooks

daily fish specials at dinner; weekend barbecues are held throughout the summer months. Breakfast has local yogurts, home-made granola, a good selection of cooked dishes. Bar (wood-burner, local ales), restaurant. 2 terraces, walled garden. 'Easy listening' background music. Free Wi-Fi. Parking. Children and dogs welcomed. 10 bedrooms. Per room B&B single £50, double £72–£95. 2-night min. stay at weekends preferred. Dinner £24.

ARMSCOTE Warwickshire
Map 3:D6
THE FUZZY DUCK, Ilmington Road, CV37 8DD. Tel 01608-682635, www.fuzzyduckarmscote.com. In a small village eight miles south of Stratford-upon-Avon, this former 18th-century coaching inn (previously *The Fox and Goose*) has been stylishly refurbished by new owners Tania Fossey and Adrian Slater, the sister-and-brother team behind beauty products company Baylis and Harding. Distinctive flagstone floors, exposed beams and original fireplaces have been retained; bedrooms have luxury linens, woollen bed throws, complimentary goodies. A large room with an extra loft bed above the bathroom is suitable for a family. A double-aspect fireplace separates the main restaurant from a cosy private dining area; in both spaces, traditional pub favourites are given a contemporary twist by chef Joe Adams. Bar, restaurant (closed Mon in winter). Free Wi-Fi. Jazz, 'easy listening' background music. 1-acre garden. Children (dressing-up box) and dogs (doggy welcome pack; home-made dog biscuits and snacks in the bar) welcomed. Hunter boots and maps

available to borrow. 4 bedrooms. Per room B&B £110–£160. Dinner £30–£45.

ARNSIDE Cumbria
Map 4: inset C2
NUMBER 43, The Promenade, LA5 0AA. Tel 01524-762761, www.no43.org.uk. There are exceptional views across the Kent estuary and surrounding fells from this modern B&B, in a row of Victorian hillside villas on the promenade. Lesley Hornsby is the owner. Alfresco drinks and breakfasts may be taken on terraces at the front and back; the elegant, spacious lounge has window seats, sofas, books, magazines, an honesty bar. The bedrooms have plenty of pillows and cushions, ample storage space, a hospitality tray with freshly ground coffee and home-made biscuits; two suites overlooking the South Lakes landscape have binoculars for watching wildlife. There are home-made compotes, home-roasted maple syrup granola, locally caught and smoked haddock at breakfast; milk and eggs come from a farm less than 20 miles away. Light suppers (meat, cheese and smoked fish platters) available; summer barbecue packs by arrangement. Lounge, dining room (honesty bar); garden; front and rear terraces. Free Wi-Fi. Children over 5 welcomed. 6 bedrooms (some with estuary views). Per room B&B £100–£185.

BAINBRIDGE North Yorkshire
Map 4:C3
YOREBRIDGE HOUSE, Leyburn, DL8 3EE. Tel 01969-652060, www.yorebridgehouse.co.uk. By the River Ure, with stunning views over the Dales, Charlotte and David Reilly's small hotel and restaurant occupy a

Victorian stone-built school; the former schoolmaster's house stands opposite the courtyard. Individually styled bedrooms have been designed with the owners' favourite places in mind: Mougins, the French room, is decorated in creams, whites and golds, with chandeliers and carved furniture; Greenwich is a New York–style loft suite with a large leather settee and two freestanding baths. Six rooms have a private terrace with an outdoor hot tub. In the candlelit restaurant, chef Dan Shotton's modern menus use many local suppliers. Lounge, bar, restaurant (open to non-residents). Free Wi-Fi (in public areas). Background music. Civil wedding licence. Children, and dogs (in 2 rooms) welcomed. 2-acre grounds. 13 bedrooms (4 in schoolhouse; 2 in village; ground-floor rooms suitable for &). Per room B&B £200–£285, D,B&B £290–£345.

BARNSLEY Gloucestershire
Map 3:E6
THE VILLAGE PUB, Barnsley, GL7 5EF. Tel 01285-740421, www.thevillagepub.co.uk. In a pretty Cotswold village, four miles from Cirencester, this restaurant-with-rooms is under the same ownership as *Calcot Manor*, Tetbury, and *Barnsley House*, up the street (see main entries); pub guests have free access to the late horticulturalist Rosemary Verey's famous gardens at *Barnsley House*. Bedrooms have a separate entrance from the pub; some have exposed beams, others a four-poster bed. (Some rooms face the road and may have traffic noise.) The welcoming dining room ('quite upmarket for a pub') serves contemporary pub food using much locally sourced produce, and fruit and

vegetables from *Barnsley House*'s kitchen garden. Daniel Craythorne is the new chef. English farmhouse breakfasts; home-made jams and home-baked bread (background radio). Free Wi-Fi. Dogs welcomed. 6 bedrooms. Per room B&B £140–£170.

BATH Somerset
Map 2:D1
ABBEY HOTEL, 1 North Parade, BA1 1LF. Tel 01225-461603, www.abbeyhotelbath.co.uk. Close to the Abbey, this handsome stone building has been transformed by hands-on owners Christa and Ian Taylor into a stylish hotel and popular venue. It has an all-day restaurant, a lively cocktail bar, and a terrace on the wide pavement for lunches, afternoon teas and light snacks. It is colourfully furnished, with contemporary art on the walls. Bedrooms range from small doubles to large rooms suitable for a family; all have good storage. In *Allium Brasserie* (oak flooring, plush purple seating), chef Chris Staines blends European and Asian flavours in his modern dishes; bread is home made. Lounge, bar, restaurant. Lift. Free Wi-Fi. Background music. Civil wedding licence. Children, and dogs (£10 per day charge) welcomed. 60 bedrooms (some on ground floor; 7 family rooms). Per person B&B from £99. Dinner £50.

AQUAE SULIS, 174–176 Newbridge Road, BA1 3LE. Tel 01225-420061, www.aquaesulishotel.co.uk. A pleasant 30-minute stroll along the river, or a short bus ride, leads guests from the town centre to David and Jane Carnegie's traditional guest house, in an Edwardian building in the suburbs;

there is easy parking for those arriving by car. The simply furnished, well-equipped bedrooms (hospitality tray, iPod docking station) are named after personalities associated with Bath, and have a modern bathroom. French and Spanish are spoken. Lounge bar, dining room (evening snack menu), computer lounge; patio/garden. Free Wi-Fi. Background music. Courtesy car to and from Bath Spa railway and bus station. Private parking, and unrestricted parking on street. Children welcomed. 14 bedrooms (2 on ground floor). Per room B&B single £59–£99, double £69–£135. 2-night min. stay at weekends. Closed 21–28 Dec.

25% DISCOUNT VOUCHERS

BRINDLEYS, 14 Pulteney Gardens, BA2 4HG. Tel 01225-310444, www.brindleys bath.co.uk. In an 'ideal' location within walking distance of the city centre, this 'attractive' Victorian villa filled with white-painted furniture, pretty fabrics and fresh flowers has a contemporary French ambience. It is owned by Michael and Sarah Jones, and run with great enthusiasm by James Grundy and his wife, Anel. The 'very smart and bright' breakfast room overlooks the 'well-kept' front garden; it has comfortable chairs and is decorated with interesting culinary ornaments and pictures. Breakfast choices are listed on a blackboard menu. Lounge, breakfast room (soft background music); small garden. Free Wi-Fi. Complimentary on-street parking permits. 6 bedrooms (some are small). Per room B&B £110–£190. 2-night min. stay at weekends preferred.

DORIAN HOUSE, 1 Upper Oldfield Park, BA2 3JX. Tel 01225-426336,

www.dorianhouse.co.uk. In a Victorian stone house with 'fabulous' views over the Royal Crescent, cellist Tim Hugh and his wife, Kathryn, have imbued their stylish B&B with a musical atmosphere. Robert and Lize Briers are the managers. Public rooms are decorated with modern art, sculptures and intriguing artefacts; the tasteful bedrooms, named after composers (Gershwin, Grieg, Ellington, etc), have a marble bathroom. Breakfast has freshly baked croissants, fruit and a cooked option. Ten minutes' walk from the centre. Lounge (open fire), conservatory breakfast room/music library; classical background music. Free Wi-Fi. 'Immaculate, vertiginous' small garden. Parking. Children welcomed. 13 bedrooms (1 on ground floor). Per room B&B single £65–£78, double £80–£165.

GRAYS, 9 Upper Oldfield Park, BA2 3JX. Tel 01225-403020, www.graysbath.co.uk. On the southern slopes of the city, this charming B&B – under the same ownership as *Brindleys* (above) – has good views over Bath, and convenient on-site parking. The large Victorian villa is in a peaceful residential location, and has a calm interior to match. Light, bright rooms are painted in soft colours, with French-style furniture; some in the attic may be snug. The breakfast bar has cereals, yogurts, fruit, compotes and preserves; hot dishes (vegetarian option available) are cooked to order. A 15-minute downhill walk to the centre. Lounge, breakfast room; small garden. Free Wi-Fi. No background music. Parking. 12 bedrooms. Per room B&B £120–£195. 2-night min. stay at weekends preferred.

HARINGTON'S HOTEL, 8–10 Queen Street, BA1 1HE. Tel 01225-461728, www.haringtonshotel.co.uk. Close to Bath's attractions, Melissa and Peter O'Sullivan's small, modern hotel is formed from three Georgian town houses on a picturesque, cobbled side street. It is managed by Julian Mather. Individually decorated bedrooms vary in size; all have oversized towels, and tea- and coffee-making facilities. Guests have use of a bar and lounge with magazines and guide books; drinks can be taken in the outdoor hot tub. Chef Steph Box serves light meals and snacks in the café/bar until 9 pm; staff are happy to recommend local restaurants. Breakfasts are cooked to order; gluten-free meals available. Lounge, breakfast room, café/bar ('easy listening' background music); small conference room. Free Wi-Fi. Small courtyard; hot tub (£7.50 per hour). Secure reserved parking nearby (£11 for 24 hrs). Children welcomed (cots, toy box). 13 bedrooms, plus 2 self-catering apartments. Per room B&B £89–£193. 2-night min. stay on some weekends. Closed New Year. **25% DISCOUNT VOUCHERS**

THE KENNARD, 11 Henrietta Street, BA2 6LL. Tel 01225-310472, www.kennard.co.uk. 'We were impressed.' Conveniently situated just over Pulteney Bridge, Mary and Giovanni Baiano's 'attractively decorated' 18th-century town house B&B has an Italianate air. There are Venetian chandeliers and elegant seating in the entrance hall and public rooms; some superior bedrooms have a high ceiling, fine plasterwork and a canopied bed. (The bedrooms are gradually being refurbished in a plainer, more modern

style.) In the original Georgian kitchen, lavish breakfasts, cooked by Giovanni Baiano, are served on tables set with fine linen and china. The 'well-kept, carefully designed' small garden is inspired by Jane Austen. 2 sitting areas, breakfast room; courtyard. Free Wi-Fi. No background music. Children over 8 welcomed. Drivers are given a free parking permit. 12 bedrooms (2 on ground floor; 2 share a bathroom; 6 flights of stairs). Per person B&B £55–£80. 2-night min. stay at weekends preferred. Closed Christmas.

THREE ABBEY GREEN, 3 Abbey Green, BA1 1NW. Tel 01225-428558, www.threeabbeygreen.com. Mother-and-daughter team Sue Wright and Nici Jones run their 'very comfortable' B&B in a Grade II listed town house on a quiet square in the centre of Bath. Handsome bedrooms retain original features such as wood panelling and a fireplace; they are furnished with antiques. 'Our room had a good bed; a lovely big bath.' There is a wide choice at breakfast, 'all freshly cooked and served promptly'. Friendly and efficient, the hosts offer visitors plenty of helpful information about the city. Close to the Abbey, Roman Baths and Pump Rooms. Dining room (background radio). Free Wi-Fi (computer available). Children welcomed. 10 bedrooms (3 in adjoining building; 2 on ground floor suitable for ♿; plus 1-bedroom apartment). Per room B&B £90–£180. 2-night min. stay at weekends. Closed Christmas.

BELPER Derbyshire
Map 2:A2
DANNAH FARM, Bowmans Lane, Shottle, DE56 2DR. Tel 01773-550273,

www.dannah.co.uk. On a working farm, Joan and Martin Slack's country B&B lies on a ridge in the Derbyshire Dales, surrounded by extensive gardens and beautiful countryside. Many of the bedrooms have an indulgent bathroom with a roll-top or spa bath. A spa cabin (available for exclusive use) houses a Finnish sauna and a double steam shower; an outdoor hot tub sits on a large secluded terrace. Cooked farmhouse breakfasts include award-winning black pudding, locally made sausages and eggs from free-range hens; supper platters with home-baked bread and home-made puddings are available. Vegetarians catered for. 2 sitting rooms, dining room; meeting room. Free Wi-Fi. Licensed. No background music. Large walled garden; arbour; medieval moat. Parking. Children welcomed. 8 bedrooms (4 in courtyard; 3 on ground floor). Per room B&B £175–£295. Supper platter £16.95. 2-night min. stay on Fri, Sat. Closed Christmas.

BERWICK East Sussex
Map 2:E4
GREEN OAK BARN, The English Wine Centre, Alfriston Road, BN26 5QS. Tel 01323-870164, www.englishwine.co.uk. More than 140 varieties of English wine are available at Christine and Colin Munday's English Wine Centre on the South Downs; there are also 'smart and comfortable' bedrooms in a modern barn set in landscaped gardens. Guests have use of a large communal space on the ground floor of the barn, with sofas, a bar and a baby grand piano. In the thatched *Flint Barn* next door, unusual English wines can be sampled by the glass to accompany the 'short, interesting' seasonal menus devised by

Austen Gould and Tony Rutland; alfresco dining in the courtyard in summer. Bar/lounge, restaurant (no background music; closed Mon); wedding/function facilities in 17th-century country barn (civil wedding licence). Free Wi-Fi. Lift; ramps. Garden with water features. Wine shop; tutored wine tastings. Children welcomed. 5 bedrooms (1 suitable for &). Per room B&B single £75, double £120–£175, D,B&B £176–£230. Closed Christmas and New Year.
25% DISCOUNT VOUCHERS

BEXHILL-ON-SEA East Sussex
Map 2:E4
COAST, 58 Sea Road, TN40 1JP. Tel 01424-225260, www.coastbexhill.co.uk. In a 'peaceful' location close to the seafront, this 'well-kept' B&B is in an elegant Edwardian villa with 'bright, modern' decor. Linda and Chris Wain are the 'pleasant' hosts. Simply furnished bedrooms have tea- and coffee-making facilities, bottled water and biscuits. Breakfast is taken in a front room overlooking the street; a good variety of hot dishes includes vegetarian options. Convenient for shops, restaurants and the station. Breakfast room. Free Wi-Fi. No background music. Children over 5 welcomed. 3 bedrooms. Per room B&B £75–£95.

BIBURY Gloucestershire
Map 3:E6
BIBURY COURT, GL7 5NT. Tel 01285-740337, www.biburycourt.com. In a 'magical' setting by the River Coln, this 'serene and beautiful' Grade I listed Jacobean mansion has high-ceilinged rooms, 'striking' chandeliers, flagstone

floors and open fireplaces; a sweeping staircase leads to the bedrooms upstairs. Individually decorated, all rooms have views across the grounds; some have a four-poster bed, others a window seat, yet others a freestanding bath. A dark single room up 'awkward' steps was not liked. In the restaurant overlooking the front lawn, chef James Graham's modern menus feature local produce and wild and foraged ingredients. 'We liked the Art Deco bar', with its 1920s panelling and curved wooden fire surround. Staff are 'attentive' and 'polite'. 'Generous' portions of smoked salmon and scrambled eggs at breakfast. Good walking on public footpaths from the garden. Drawing room, bar (light bites), *Origin* restaurant; study, billiard room. Conservatory, riverside terrace; 'secret' garden. In-room treatments. Free Wi-Fi (second-floor bedrooms have a weak signal). Background music. Civil wedding licence. Children (£25 charge), and dogs (in some rooms; £15 charge) welcomed. 7 miles from Cirencester. 18 bedrooms (some on ground floor). Per room B&B £145–£345.

THE SWAN, GL7 5NW. Tel 01285-740695, www.cotswold-inns-hotels.co.uk. In a 'lovely' setting on the banks of the River Coln, this 17th-century former coaching inn (Cotswold Inns and Hotels) has been refurbished in English country house style by owners Pamela and Michael Horton. It is managed by Quentin Fisher. Most bedrooms overlook the river; one superior room has a four-poster bed and a large dressing area. Modern European cuisine is served in the brasserie, which is decorated with oil paintings, a highly patterned floor and a log wall; in summer months, doors open on to a courtyard for alfresco dining. Breakfasts are 'very good'. Lift. Lounge, bar (wood-burning stove), brasserie. Free Wi-Fi. Background music. ½-acre garden. Civil wedding licence; function facilities. Children, and dogs (in some bedrooms) welcomed. Trout fishing can be arranged. 22 bedrooms (4 in garden cottages, 1 with hot tub). Per person B&B £85–£185. Dinner £29.50–£35. **25% DISCOUNT VOUCHERS**

BISHOP'S TACHBROOK
Warwickshire
Map 2:B2

MALLORY COURT, Harbury Lane, CV33 9QB. Tel 01926-330214, www.mallory.co.uk. 'Beautifully situated', this 'elegant' manor house (Relais & Châteaux) in 'extensive' gardens has 'comfortable' bedrooms and 'pleasant, attentive' staff. Sarah Baker is the long-serving manager. Individually decorated bedrooms are in the main house and adjacent Knights Suite; the best have views over the grounds. 'I was very pleased to have a bed made with sheets and blankets rather than an unmanageable duvet.' The 'beautiful' garden, arranged in six distinct areas, has manicured lawns, mature trees and shrubs; a formal Old English rose garden; a pond garden with original stone paths; and a kitchen garden growing herbs, vegetables and soft fruits for use in the restaurant. Paul Foster was appointed chef in 2014; his modern menus are served in the oak-panelled dining room. The informal *Brasserie* has an Art Deco-inspired interior, and walled gardens for alfresco dining. 2 lounges, brasserie, restaurant. Background music. Free Wi-Fi. Terrace (alfresco snacks). Outdoor swimming pool, tennis court, croquet. Civil wedding licence; function facilities. 31 bedrooms (11 in new wing, 2 suitable for &). Per room B&B £165–£455. Set dinner £47.50, tasting menu £85.

BLACKBURN Lancashire
Map 4:D3
MILLSTONE AT MELLOR, Church Lane, Mellor, BB2 7JR. Tel 01254-813333, www.millstonehotel.co.uk. Chef/patron Anson Bolton cooks award-winning seasonal Lancashire dishes in the 'pleasant' wood-panelled restaurant at this stone-built former coaching inn (Thwaites Inns of Character) in the Ribble valley. 'We enjoyed a very good lunch.' Comfortable, country-style bedrooms vary in size and style; each has fluffy bathrobes, fresh milk and home-made biscuits. Breakfasts are hearty. Residents' lounge (log fire), bar, restaurant (open to non-residents); terrace (alfresco dining). Free Wi-Fi in public areas. Background radio at breakfast. Parking. Children welcomed. 23 bedrooms (6 in courtyard; 2 suitable for &). Per room B&B £90–£180, D,B&B £140–£230.

BLACKPOOL Lancashire
Map 4:D2
NUMBER ONE ST LUKE'S, 1 St Luke's Road, South Shore, FY4 2EL. Tel 01253-343901, www.numberoneblackpool.com. Mark and Claire Smith's stylish B&B is in a detached 1930s Art Deco house in the residential South Shore area. Well-equipped rooms are imaginatively decorated and have a king-size bed; up-to-date gadgetry includes a large plasma TV, a DVD- and CD-player, a whirlpool bath and remote-controlled

lighting. Conservatory; garden (hot tub), water feature; putting green. Free Wi-Fi. Background music. Parking. Children over 3 welcomed. 3 bedrooms. Per person B&B £50–£110.

NUMBER ONE SOUTH BEACH, 4 Harrowside West, FY4 1NW. Tel 01253-343900, www.numberonesouth beach.com. 'We could not have stayed at a better establishment.' With sea views over South Beach Promenade, this 'very comfortable', low-carbon-footprint hotel has a welcoming atmosphere and a lively modern interior. It is owned by Janet and Graham Oxley, with Claire and Mark Smith (see *Number One St Luke's*, above); all are 'excellent hosts, and very informative as to what was going on in their town'. The colourful bedrooms are 'well equipped' with 'lovely beds and bedlinens'; some have a four-poster bed, balcony and whirlpool bath. Lift. Lounge, bar, restaurant; background music; pool table; meeting/conference facilities. Free Wi-Fi. Garden with putting green. Parking. 14 bedrooms (disabled facilities). Per room B&B single £78–£130, double £120–£150. Dinner £30. 2-night min. stay at weekends in high season.

RAFFLES HOTEL & TEA ROOM, 73–77 Hornby Road, FY1 4QJ. Tel 01253-294713, www.raffleshotelblackpool. co.uk. Graham Poole and Ian Balmforth run their immaculate small hotel and traditional English tea room in a flower-bedecked, bay-fronted house close to the Winter Gardens and Promenade. Home-made cakes and light snacks are served at teatime; home-cooked, good-value three-course set dinners are available in the evenings. Homely, traditionally furnished rooms have a TV and hospitality tray. Extensive choice at breakfast. Lounge, bar, breakfast room, tea room (closed in winter, and on Mon). Free Wi-Fi. Classical background music. Parking. Children welcomed; dogs by arrangement. 17 bedrooms, plus 4 apartment suites. Per person B&B £38–£40. Dinner (set menu) from £9.95.

BORROWDALE Cumbria
Map 4: inset C2
LEATHES HEAD HOTEL, CA12 5UY. Tel 017687-77247, www.leatheshead.co.uk. In a 'stunning' lakeside setting, this country hotel in an Edwardian house has good walks from the front door, and easy access to Keswick. 'Enthusiastic, helpful, caring' service is maintained by managers Jamie Adamson and Jane Cleary. Bedrooms are a blend of old-style elegance and modern comforts; some bathrooms have a whirlpool spa bath and walk-in monsoon shower; all have 'magnificent' views overlooking Derwentwater or the surrounding countryside. Long-serving chef David Jackson's monthly menus feature seasonal ingredients in his Aga-cooked British dishes; daily specials might include roast Herdwick lamb, slow-braised hogget shoulder, Keswick brewery ale. Lounge, bar; conservatory. 3-acre grounds. Free Wi-Fi. Background music. Dogs allowed in 2 rooms (£7.50 per day). 4 miles from Keswick. 11 bedrooms (1 on ground floor). Per room B&B £110–£200, D,B&B £165–£243. Closed Dec–Feb.

BOURNEMOUTH Dorset
Map 2:E2
THE GREEN HOUSE, 4 Grove Road, BH1 3AX, www.thegreenhousehotel.com.

Just a few minutes' walk from the seafront and the town centre, this cream-painted hotel is in its own grounds with palm trees. It has been renovated with a commitment to sustainability: there are bee hives on the roof, an ecological energy system; natural and organic materials, eco paints, and furniture made from storm-felled wood have been used in the chic, modern interior. The smartly decorated bedrooms have a stylish bathroom with a natural stone basin and walk-in shower; some can be small. In the informal *Arbor* restaurant, chef Andy Hilton serves unfussy modern menus using much local and organic produce. Bar, restaurant. Background music. Children welcomed. Free Wi-Fi. Lift. Civil wedding licence. Parking. 32 bedrooms (1 suitable for &). Per room B&B £99–£220. Dinner £28–£30. 2-night min. stay at weekends.

URBAN BEACH, 23 Argyll Road, BH5 1EB. Tel 01202-301509, www.urbanbeachhotel.co.uk. There is a laid-back atmosphere at this small, contemporary hotel, a short walk from Boscombe beach. It is owned by Mark Cribb, who runs it with manager Helen McCombie and friendly staff. Individually decorated rooms have luxury bedding and toiletries, a plasma TV and DVD player. The bar has a large cocktail list; the buzzy bistro serves local, seasonal produce and home-baked bread. Packed lunches available. Hotel guests have priority booking at *Urban Reef*, the sister restaurant on the beach. Bar, bistro; covered seating deck. DVD, iTunes library. Free Wi-Fi. Background music. Wellies, umbrellas provided. Complimentary use of local gym. Children welcomed (special menu). 12 bedrooms. Per room B&B single £72, double £97–£180. Dinner from £28. 2-night min. stay at weekends.

BOWNESS-ON-WINDERMERE
Cumbria
Map 4: inset C2

LINDETH HOWE, Lindeth Drive, Longtail Hill, LA23 3JF. Tel 015394-45759, www.lindeth-howe.co.uk. Overlooking Lake Windermere, this Victorian country house, once a summer home for a wealthy industrialist, stands in large mature gardens with sloping lawns and woodland. It was once owned by Beatrix Potter, who spent family holidays and wrote some of her books here. 'Well-appointed' bedrooms have views of the garden or the lake and fells; larger rooms can accommodate a family. Chef Rob Taylor's modern menus are served in the candlelit dining room; vegetarians are well catered for. Afternoon tea is popular. Lounge, library, bar, restaurant (pianist on alternate Sat evenings). Free Wi-Fi. Background music. Sun terrace; indoor swimming pool, sauna, fitness room. 6-acre grounds. Electric bikes for hire. Children welcomed (no under-7s in the restaurant at night; children's high tea, babysitting available). 34 bedrooms (some on ground floor suitable for &.). Per person B&B £79–£149. Set dinner £46.50.

BRANSCOMBE Devon
Map 1:C5

THE MASON'S ARMS, EX12 3DJ. Tel 01297-680300, www.masonsarms.co.uk. 'A very good example of the all-too-rare village inn.' In a 'delightful' village, this creeper-covered 14th-century pub-with-rooms has 'pleasant and willing' staff.

'Comfortably furnished' bedrooms are in the main building and in thatched cottages on the hillside, with views over the valley or out to sea. 'A good bed; I could happily have taken home the curtains from my room.' The traditional bar (slate floors, stone walls, log fireplace, real ales) is popular with locals. In the restaurant, chef Lee Villiers serves 'excellent, freshly cooked and nicely served' dishes featuring much local produce. 'The fish was outstanding.' Ten minutes down a field path to the sea. 'Well placed for visiting other south coast resorts.' Bar, restaurant; garden with outdoor seating. Free Wi-Fi (in main bar only). No background music. Children, and dogs (in some cottages) welcomed. 21 bedrooms (14 in cottages). Per room B&B £80–£190. Dinner £35.

BRIDPORT Dorset
Map 1:C6

THE BULL HOTEL, 34 East Street, DT6 3LF. Tel 01308-422878, www. thebullhotel.co.uk. In the centre of a busy market town, this family-friendly hotel occupies a Grade II listed former coaching inn with a handsome blue facade. It is owned by Nikki and Richard Cooper, who run it in relaxed fashion, with 'young, very friendly and helpful' staff. 'Quirky, spacious' bedrooms have striking wallpaper and imaginatively mismatched furniture; some have a bay window, others a vintage roll-top bath or four-poster bed. Chef George Marsh serves rustic, locally sourced food in the restaurant; the *Stable* has cider and pizzas (special diets catered for). 2 bars (background music), lounge, restaurant; ballroom; private dining room. Free Wi-Fi. Civil wedding licence; function facilities. Sunny courtyard. Children welcomed (cots, toys, DVDs, organic nappies; babysitting; children's tea by arrangement). 19 bedrooms (3 accessed via courtyard). Per room B&B £100–£210, D,B&B £170–£280.

BRIGHTON East Sussex
Map 2:E4

DRAKES, 43–44 Marine Parade, BN2 1PE. Tel 01273-696934, www.drakesofbrighton.com. 'Standards are high' at this modern seafront hotel formed from two white stucco Regency town houses. It is owned by Andy Shearer, and managed by Richard Hayes with 'courteous, helpful' staff. Some sea-facing bedrooms have a freestanding bath by a window overlooking the pier; many have a wet room. One room features 'Brighton's biggest bed', and triple-aspect floor-to-ceiling windows with stunning views. Chef Andrew MacKenzie serves 'some seriously good cooking' in the basement restaurant; breakfast is 'also excellent'. Lounge/bar, restaurant. Free Wi-Fi. Light background music. Children welcomed (cots; £25 per room). 20 bedrooms. Room only £115–£345. Breakfast £6–£12.50, dinner £39.95.

FIVE, 5 New Steine, BN2 1PB. Tel 01273-686547, www.fivehotel.com. On a Georgian square close to the beach and pier, and within easy reach of shops and restaurants, this homely B&B is owned by Caroline and Simon Heath. Rooms are decorated with local artwork and photography; many of the well-equipped modern bedrooms (some can be snug) face the sea. A continental breakfast basket with pastries, muffins,

cereals, yogurts, fruit and juice is delivered to the room at a time to suit guests. The friendly hosts have much local knowledge to share. Good-value (compact) single room. 2 public rooms. Free Wi-Fi. No background music. DVD library. Bike storage. Children over 5 welcomed. 9 bedrooms (some with sea views). Per room B&B single £45–£75, double £70–£130. 2-night min. stay at weekends.

PASKINS, 18–19 Charlotte Street, BN2 1AG. Tel 01273-601203, www.paskins. co.uk. Susan and Roger Marlowe's environmentally friendly B&B occupies two Grade II listed 19th-century houses near the seafront in Kemp Town. Bedrooms are immaculate and 'comfortable', though small. 'Delicious' organic breakfasts 'with unusual options' are served in the Art Deco breakfast room; vegetarian and vegan guests are well catered for with home-made meat-free sausages and fritters. Lounge, dining room. Free Wi-Fi. No background music. Children and dogs welcomed. 19 bedrooms (some with sea views). Per person B&B £45–£75.

A ROOM WITH A VIEW, 41 Marine Parade, BN2 1PE. Tel 01273-682885, www.aroomwithaviewbrighton.com. With wonderful views over the seafront and the Brighton Wheel, this stylish new Kemp Town guest house is in a Grade II listed building close to all of Brighton's attractions. It is owned by Stephen Bull. Modern bedrooms have wooden flooring and soft neutral tones; a room at the top has a staircase leading to a roof terrace with panoramic views of the ocean. Some rooms have a stylish bathroom with a roll-top bath, others have a walk-in power-shower wet room; bathrobes are provided. Complimentary refreshments. Breakfast is served until 10.30 am at the weekend; special diets are catered for. Some steep stairs. Lounge (gentle background music), breakfast room. Free Wi-Fi. Parking (for 8 cars). 9 bedrooms. Per room B&B £80–£190.

BRUTON Somerset
Map 2:D1
AT THE CHAPEL, High Street, BA10 0AE. Tel 01749-814070, www.atthechapel.co.uk. Drawing a modish congregation, this 19th-century chapel has been converted with great style by Catherine Butler and her husband, Ahmed Sidki, into a multi-use space hosting bedrooms, a café/bar, a bakery and a wine shop. The minimalist, yet warm, interior has soaring ceilings and scuffed floorboards; white walls hung with contemporary art; arched, leaded windows with views over a 12th-century church. Tastefully decorated bedrooms, all with a large bed, vary in size and aspect; an attic suite has a sitting room with a sofa bed, ideal for a family. Freshly baked croissants are delivered each morning to the room. The café has newspapers, backgammon and chess; pizzas, available to take away, are cooked in a floor-to-ceiling wood-fired oven. Bar, café. Free Wi-Fi. No background music. Parking. Children welcomed. 8 bedrooms. Per room B&B (continental) £100–£250.

BUCKFASTLEIGH Devon
Map 1:D4
KILBURY MANOR, Colston Road, TQ11 0LN. Tel 01364-644079, www. kilburymanor.co.uk. 'Outstandingly kind' hosts Julia and Martin Blundell run their 'tastefully furnished' B&B in a renovated 17th-century longhouse. In impressive four-acre grounds overlooking the River Dart, the garden and courtyard are peaceful places in which to sit; a private island is a short walk down the fields. Comfortable and spacious rooms are thoughtfully equipped; two, in the converted barn, have their own entrance. Extensive breakfasts include Julia Blundell's home-made compotes, marmalade and conserves (special dietary needs catered for). Helpful advice is given on local eating places. One mile from town; the South Devon Railway is close by. Breakfast room (wood-burning stove). Free Wi-Fi. No background music. Bicycle and canoe storage. Children over 6 welcomed. Resident dogs, Dillon and Buster. 4 bedrooms (2 in converted stone barn; plus one 1-bedroom cottage). Per room B&B £79–£89.

BUDLEIGH SALTERTON Devon
Map 1:D5
ROSEHILL ROOMS AND COOKERY, 30 West Hill, EX9 6BU. Tel 01395-444031, www.rosehillroomsandcookery.co.uk. In peaceful gardens, Willi and Sharon Rehbock's immaculate B&B is in a Grade II listed Victorian house close to the beach, the Coast Path and the centre of town. Spacious bedrooms have large windows, a sofa, home-made cakes or biscuits. Communal breakfasts are plentiful. A large veranda overlooks the garden, with distant views to the sea. In winter months, Willi Rehbock, a professional chef, hosts cookery classes and demonstrations on bread-making, seafood, Mediterranean cuisine, etc. Dining room. Free Wi-Fi. No

background music. 4 bedrooms. Per room B&B £100–£130. 2-night min. stay.

BUNGAY Suffolk
Map 2:B6
EARSHAM PARK FARM, Old Railway Road, Earsham, NR35 2AQ. Tel 01986-892180, www.earsham-parkfarm.co.uk. Part of a 600-acre working arable farm with regularly visiting rabbits, house martins and woodpeckers, this quirky, 'good-value' B&B is run by friendly hosts Bobbie and Simon Watchorn. Country-style bedrooms in the Victorian farmhouse overlook the fields and the Waveney valley; all have antique furniture, hot chocolate and biscuits (a fly swatter helps with unwanted intruders). 'Excellent' breakfasts are taken communally at the large farmhouse table, with home-made breads and jam, sausages and bacon from the farm, and eggs from local free-range hens. Special diets are catered for. Guests are welcome to visit the Watchorns' herd of free-range pigs. Lounge, dining room. Free Wi-Fi. No background music. Garden. Farm walks; birdwatching. Parking. 2 miles from Bungay. Children, dogs and horses (by arrangement) welcomed. 4 bedrooms. Per person B&B single £52–£74, double £82–£104. 2-night min. stay at bank holiday weekends.

BURFORD Oxfordshire
Map 2:C2
BAY TREE HOTEL, Sheep Street, OX18 4LW. Tel 01993-822791, www.cotswold-inns-hotels.co.uk. Near the high street, this 'lovely' wisteria-clad, honey-coloured limestone building has been welcoming visitors for more than 400 years. It is part of Michael and Pamela Horton's small Cotswold Inns and Hotels group, which also owns the nearby *Lamb Inn* and *The Broadway Hotel* in Broadway (see main entries). The hotel has a galleried staircase, oak-panelled rooms, an inglenook fireplace, tapestries and flagstone floors; up an oak staircase, bedrooms are individually designed in country style with fine, often antique furniture. Award-winning modern British food is served in the elegant restaurant overlooking the patio and rose garden. Library, *Woolsack* bar (background music), *Bay Tree* restaurant; patio (alfresco dining). Free Wi-Fi. Walled garden; croquet. Civil wedding licence; function facilities. Children and dogs welcomed. 21 bedrooms (2 adjoining garden rooms on ground floor). Per person B&B £90–£135. Dinner £33.
25% DISCOUNT VOUCHERS

BURY ST EDMUNDS Suffolk
Map 2:B5
OAK FARM BARN, Moat Lane, Rougham, IP30 9JU. Tel 01359-270014, www.oakfarmbarn.co.uk. Guests praise the 'warm welcome' and attention to detail at Rachel and Ray Balmer's 'magnificent' restored timber-framed barn down a quiet country lane. There are 'homely', 'well-appointed' bedrooms and plenty of thoughtful extras (books, DVDs, walking maps, slippers and boots to borrow). Country-style rooms have exposed oak beams, a 'luxurious' bed, biscuits, tea- and coffee-making facilities; a hot-water bottle is available. 'Breakfast, cooked to order, was a real treat, with eggs from the hosts' own chickens.' Lounge (honesty bar), seating area overlooking patio. Free Wi-Fi. Background music.

Garden with outdoor seating. Parking. 3 bedrooms (2 on ground floor; 1 suitable for &). Per room B&B single £70, double £80.

OUNCE HOUSE, Northgate Street, IP33 1HP. Tel 01284-761779, www.ouncehouse.co.uk. Within walking distance of the town centre, this traditional B&B, in a spacious Victorian merchant's house, is owned by Jenny and Simon Pott. It is decorated with ornaments, photographs and period furniture; well-equipped bedrooms have fresh flowers, paintings and antiques. Communal breakfasts (cereals, fruit, hams, cheese; hot dishes cooked to order). Drawing room (honesty bar), snug/bar/library, dining room. Free Wi-Fi. No background music. Parking; secure bicycle storage. Children welcomed. 5 bedrooms (quietest 2 face the ⅔-acre walled garden). Per room B&B single £85–£95, double £125–£135.

BUXTON Derbyshire
Map 3:A6
HARTINGTON HALL, Hall Bank, SK17 0AT. Tel 01298-84223, www.yha.org.uk/hostel/hartington. 'Amazing value.' In 'immaculate' grounds, this 17th-century manor house is run as an upmarket youth hostel by the YHA. Period features (mullioned windows, oak panelling, log fires) make a handsome backdrop for basic accommodation in the main house; more rooms are available in the coach house and barn. Walks and cycle routes from the front door; packed lunches available. 2 lounges, bar, restaurant (home-cooked, hearty English fare; local ingredients). Games room; self-catering kitchen; drying room; meeting rooms.

Free Wi-Fi (YHA members, in public rooms only). Background music. Extensive grounds: beer garden, adventure playground, pet area. Civil wedding licence. Children welcomed. 35 bedrooms (19 en suite; 10 in barn annexe, 5 in coach house; 1 suitable for &). Room only from £20. Breakfast £4.99, dinner £11.95.

CAMBRIDGE Cambridgeshire
Map 2:B4
DUKE HOUSE, 1 Victoria Street, CB1 1JP. Tel 01223-314773, www.dukehousecambridge.co.uk. Close to the city's historic colleges, this welcoming B&B is run on sustainable lines, with 'no compromise on comfort'. It is owned by Liz and Rob Cameron, who have decorated the former student home of the Duke of Gloucester with great attention to detail. The Victorian house 'still carries his stamp'; original features such as wooden shutters, brass fittings and a marble surround have been retained. Smartly decorated bedrooms, all with bathrobes and tea- and coffee-making facilities, are named after famous dukes. Breakfast has a buffet of organic muesli and granola, fresh fruit, yogurts and cheeses, and a weekly cooked special. Sitting room, breakfast room; 2 balconies, courtyard with mural. Free Wi-Fi. No background music. Parking, by prior arrangement. 4 bedrooms. Per room B&B £110–£195. 2-night min. stay at weekends.

HOTEL FELIX, Whitehouse Lane, Huntingdon Road, CB3 0LX. Tel 01223-277977, www.hotelfelix.co.uk. In a peaceful setting in extensive landscaped gardens on the edge of the city, this large, privately owned hotel has a sleek interior enlivened with striking contemporary art. Shara Ross is the manager. The late Victorian yellow brick mansion has modern extensions; bedrooms (all with a large bed, and a bathroom with under-floor heating) are divided between the original mansion and the more recently added east and west wings. Chef Ashley Bennett serves Mediterranean-influenced dishes in the restaurant overlooking the terrace and garden; informal meals and afternoon tea are taken in the conservatory, in the bar or on the pretty terrace. Small lounge, bar, *Graffiti* restaurant; conservatory. Free Wi-Fi. Background music. Civil wedding licence; function facilities. 4-acre garden, terrace (alfresco dining), gazebo. Parking. Children (cots) and dogs welcomed. 52 bedrooms (4 suitable for ♿). Per room B&B (continental) single from £175, double £212–£305. Full English breakfast £7.95. Dinner £33.

THE VARSITY HOTEL & SPA,

Thompson's Lane, off Bridge Street, CB5 8AQ. Tel 01223-306030, www.thevarsityhotel.co.uk. In a 'very central' location, overlooking the river near Magdalene Bridge, this modern hotel has 'wonderful' views from its rooftop terrace. Individually designed bedrooms (some small) have floor-to-ceiling windows, feature wallpaper, a modern bathroom with under-floor heating; suites also have books, a Nespresso coffee machine, and access to a Nintendo Wii and iPad. *The River Bar* steakhouse and grill, set on two levels in a restored 17th-century warehouse on the quayside, is next door (background music). There are 'a good buffet and plenty of choice of cooked dishes' at breakfast. Complimentary walking tours every Sat. Roof terrace (in season; open to non-residents); *Glassworks* health club and spa (spa bath overlooking the River Cam); lift; gym. Free Wi-Fi. Civil wedding licence; conference facilities. Valet parking service (parking charge); local car parks. Children welcomed. 48 bedrooms (3 suitable for ♿). Per room B&B (continental) £199–£950. Set dinner £32.95–£38.50.

CANTERBURY Kent
Map 2:D5

MAGNOLIA HOUSE, 36 St Dunstan's Terrace, CT2 8AX. Tel 01227-765121, www.magnoliahousecanterbury.co.uk. On a quiet residential street in the St Dunstan's area close to the centre, this comfortable Georgian guest house is owned by Isobelle Leggett. There are many thoughtful touches: well-equipped bedrooms have complimentary wine, and fresh milk for coffee and tea; books, magazines and board games are available to borrow. Helpful recommendations are given on local restaurants and places of interest. An extensive breakfast, ordered the night before, includes smoked haddock omelette, eggs Benedict or Florentine, kippers and home-made jam and marmalade. Dinner is served by arrangement in winter (Nov–Feb); no licence – bring your own bottle. Cutlery and crockery can be provided for picnics in the walled garden. Sitting room, dining room (background music). Free Wi-Fi. Parking limited. 6 bedrooms (some with a four-poster bed). Per person B&B £50–£70. Dinner £35.

CHADDESLEY CORBETT
Worcestershire
Map 3:C5

BROCKENCOTE HALL, DY10 4PY. Tel 01562-777876, www.brockencotehall. com. 'The whole experience reminds me of a bygone age.' Set in 'lovely' parkland with a 'serene' lake and grazing sheep, this 'elegant' country house hotel (Eden Hotel Collection) has 'pleasantly large' bedrooms, 'terrific' dinners and 'charming' staff. The comfortable bedrooms are traditionally decorated and have a modern bathroom; all have views of the estate. Slippers are laid out at turn-down; in the morning, a newsletter with the day's weather forecast is delivered to the room. Chef Adam Brown serves a selection of modern menus in *Chaddesley* restaurant (open to non-residents); informal meals and afternoon tea are taken in the high-ceilinged bar and lounge. 2 private dining rooms. Free Wi-Fi. Light jazz background music. 70-acre grounds; 3 miles SE of Kidderminster. Children welcomed. 21 bedrooms (some suitable for &). Per room B&B single £115–£345, double £135–£435. D,B&B £130–£205 per person (min. 2-night stay). Set dinners £32.95–£59.95, tasting menu £75.

CHAGFORD Devon
Map 1:C4

MILL END HOTEL, Sandy Park, TQ13 8JN. Tel 01647-432282, www. millendhotel.com. In a 'beautiful' riverbank setting in wooded gardens, Sue and Peter Davies's country hotel occupies a former 15th-century corn mill with an 18-foot working waterwheel. Staff are 'pleasant and helpful'. The well-appointed bedrooms, some with a private patio, have views of the gardens and surrounding countryside; a charming family room has a window seat overlooking the grounds. Chef Chris Billingsley serves seasonally changing menus in the restaurant; on warm days, afternoon tea may be taken in the garden. Within Dartmoor national park, with river path walks to Fingle Bridge and Castle Drogo. Packed lunches available. 3 lounges (log fires), bar, restaurant. Free Wi-Fi. 15-acre grounds: river, fishing, bathing. Background music (classical in the hall, restaurant and one lounge). Children (high teas; under-12s not allowed in restaurant in evening), and dogs welcomed. 15 bedrooms (3 on ground floor). Per room B&B single £75–£195, double £90–£210. Dinner £22–£40.

CHARMOUTH Dorset
Map 1:C6

THE ABBOTS HOUSE, The Street, DT6 6QF. Tel 01297-560339, www. abbotshouse.co.uk. Guests like the home-made treats and 'amazing' attention to detail at Sheila and Nick Gilbey's small, characterful B&B. Dating back to the 16th century, the restored and carefully updated house has oak-panelled walls, an ornate beamed ceiling, flagstone floors and dainty bedrooms; bathrooms have a double-ended bath and flat-screen TV. Sheila Gilbey's breakfasts are 'a delight'; her home-made jams and marmalade, and home-baked bread, are available for purchase. Close to the centre, and a five-minute walk from the beach. Lounge, garden room, garden (model railway). Free Wi-Fi. Background music at breakfast. 4 bedrooms (plus 1-bedroom

self-contained cottage in the garden).
Per room B&B £120–£140 (2-night min.
stay). Closed 16 Dec–10 Jan.

CHATTON Northumberland
Map 4:A3

CHATTON PARK HOUSE, Alnwick,
NE66 5RA. Tel 01668-215507,
www.chattonpark.com. 'It exceeded
our expectations.' On the edge of
Northumberland national park, this
imposing Georgian house is run as a
B&B by 'most welcoming' hosts Paul
and Michelle Mattinson. Spacious, well-
equipped bedrooms are named after
local towns or villages, and furnished in
period style. Breakfasts ('of the highest
quality') are ordered in advance. 'Huge'
sitting room, cosy bar, breakfast room;
no background music. Free Wi-Fi;
weak mobile phone signal. 6-acre
grounds; grass tennis courts (May–Sep).
½ mile from Chatton; Alnwick,
Bamburgh and Holy Island are close
by. 5 bedrooms (plus 2-bedroom self-
catering stone lodge with private
garden). Per room B&B £110–£189.
Closed early Jan.

CHELTENHAM Gloucestershire
Map 3:D5

BEAUMONT HOUSE, 56 Shurdington
Road, GL53 0JE. Tel 01242-223311,
www.bhhotel.co.uk. There is 'excellent'
accommodation at Fan and Alan
Bishop's B&B, in a former Victorian
merchant's home in large gardens. Well-
appointed bedrooms vary considerably
in size; all have a 'comfortable' bed, tea-
and coffee-making facilities and biscuits.
The spacious lounge has an honesty bar
and complimentary hot drinks; a
'limited but changing' menu is available
in the evenings (Mon–Thurs). In the

dining room overlooking the flower
garden, breakfast includes smoked fish,
local sausages and American-style
pancakes; breakfast in bed can be
arranged. The shops and restaurants of
Montpellier Arcade are 25 minutes'
walk away. Lounge, conservatory,
dining room (background music). Free
Wi-Fi. Parking. Children welcomed.
16 bedrooms. Per room B&B single £82–
£260, double £105–£260.

THE BRADLEY, 19 Royal Parade,
Bayshill Road, GL50 3AY. Tel 01242-
519077, www.thebradleyhotel.co.uk.
'Helpful and friendly' hosts Chris
and Sue Light run this 'excellent,
wonderfully quiet' B&B in the
Montpellier district. The elegantly
refurbished town house has been in the
family for more than 100 years; rooms
are filled with antique furniture and
objets d'art. Decorated with paintings
and family heirlooms, bedrooms vary in
style; up-to-date touches include an iPod
dock, flat-screen TV, plenty of electrical
sockets; a modern bathroom with robes
and luxury toiletries. Good choice of
breakfast options; the 'breakfast in a
bag', for guests in a rush, includes a hot
bacon baguette. Lounge, breakfast room
(classical background music); small
garden. Free Wi-Fi. Parking; electric
vehicle charging points. 8 bedrooms
(plus 1-bed apartment). Per room B&B
£88–£145. Closed 1 week at Christmas.

BUTLERS, Western Road, GL50 3RN.
Tel 01242-570771, www.butlers-hotel.
co.uk. In a former gentleman's residence
on a quiet street within walking
distance of the town centre, discreet and
unobtrusive hosts Robert Davies and
Guy Hunter set standards to match

their butler-themed B&B. Bedrooms are named for famous butlers in literature and film (Jeeves, Hudson, Brabinger, etc). Stationery, books, games and newspapers are available in the lounge. Breakfast is taken in a room overlooking the walled garden. Ten minutes' walk to the bus and railway stations. Drawing room, dining room (quiet radio in the mornings); ¼-acre garden. Free Wi-Fi. Parking. Children over 5 welcomed. 8 bedrooms (self-catering rooms available for longer stays). Per room B&B single £60–£75, double £85–£120. 2-night min. stay during Festival weekends.

THE CHELTENHAM TOWNHOUSE, 12–14 Pittville Lawn, GL52 2BD. Tel 01242-221922, www.cheltenhamtownhouse.com. Well located for both town and racecourse, this relaxed B&B, in a renovated Regency building, has a modern atmosphere and calm, airy rooms. It is owned by Adam and Jayne Lillywhite. The comfortable lounge has fresh flowers and newspapers, an open fire in cool weather; drinks may be taken on the sun deck on warmer days. Individually designed bedrooms vary in size, from a compact 'economy' room to studio apartments (some in an annexe) with a kitchen and additional sofa bed. Good breakfasts. Two bicycles and helmets available to borrow. Lounge (honesty bar; help-yourself fruit bowl), breakfast room (background music); sun deck. DVD library. Free Wi-Fi. Lift. Parking. Children welcomed (family rooms). 21 bedrooms (1 with private bathroom), 5 studio apartments (4 in nearby annexe), 1 two-bed suite. Per room B&B single £58–£98, double £68–£108.

HANOVER HOUSE, 65 St George's Road, GL50 3DU. Tel 01242-541297, www.hanoverhouse.org. In the centre of town, this Italianate Grade II listed early Victorian town house is the 'beautiful' home of Veronica and James McIntosh-Ritchie. It is an elegant and homely place: the house is filled with fresh flowers, pictures, 'interesting objects' and a 'splendidly varied selection of books'. B&B guests have a decanter of sherry in their spacious, colourful bedroom; beds have an electric blanket in wintertime. A civilised breakfast, served on blue-and-white china, is taken in the Aga-equipped kitchen or the Victorian dining room overlooking the walled garden; there are home-made bread and preserves, and locally sourced produce. Drawing room (open fire in winter), breakfast room; walled garden. Free Wi-Fi. Classical background music. Parking. 3 bedrooms (1 with private bathroom; robes provided). Per person B&B £50–£70.

CHESTER Cheshire
Map 3:A4

THE CHESTER GROSVENOR, Eastgate, CH1 1LT. Tel 01244-324024, www.chestergrosvenor.com. In a gabled, half-timbered Grade II listed building, this large, luxurious hotel is in the centre of the city, close to the cathedral, the ancient city walls and the Eastgate Clock. Owned by the Duke of Westminster, it has an opulent interior with grand chandeliers and elegant, traditionally styled bedrooms. There are several dining options: the *Michelin*-starred restaurant, *Simon Radley at The Chester Grosvenor*, is 'an experience not to be missed'; the informal *Brasserie* has barbecued meats cooked on a wood-burning grill; afternoon tea and light meals are served in the *Arkle* bar and lounge; bespoke menus are created for private dining in the *Riedel Cellar*. Lift. Ramps. Drawing room. Civil wedding licence; function facilities. Spa (crystal steam room, herb sauna, themed shower, ice fountain; 5 treatment rooms). Free Wi-Fi. Background music. Children welcomed (special menu; interconnecting family rooms). 80 bedrooms and suites (1 suitable for &). B&B £165–£1,522, D,B&B £210–£1,720.

CHEWTON MENDIP Somerset
Map 2:D1

THE POST HOUSE, Bathway, BA3 4NS. Tel 01761-241704, www.theposthousebandb.co.uk. Close to Bath and the cathedral city of Wells, 'excellent hostess' Karen Price offers B&B accommodation in her 'beautifully' renovated Grade II listed former post office and village bakery. The spacious bedrooms are stylishly rustic: there are wild flowers, white-painted furniture, limewashed walls in muted colours; a supply of home-made biscuits is topped up every day. *The Old Bakery* ('a luxurious space') is equipped for self-catering; it has a stone fireplace and its own secluded courtyard. 'Delicious' breakfasts have fresh fruit salad, home-baked bread, locally sourced bacon and sausages. Sitting room, dining room (no background music); Mediterranean-style courtyard; small garden. Free Wi-Fi. Parking. Children welcomed. Resident dog, Monty. 2 bedrooms (plus 1 self-catering cottage). Per room B&B £80–£120. 2-night min. stay at weekends

CHICHESTER West Sussex
Map 2:E3

CROUCHERS, Birdham Road, PO20 7EH. Tel 01243-784995, www.croucherscountryhotel.com. Close to the harbour and West Wittering beach, Lloyd van Rooyen's hotel and restaurant are set in 'refreshing greenery, with lots of patios and grassy areas'. Simply furnished bedrooms are in the main building and the converted coach house, barn and stable; some have a private patio. (On the main road between Chichester and the Witterings; there may be some traffic noise; rear rooms are quietest.) In the oak-beamed restaurant, chef Nick Markey uses much local produce in his 'varied' menus. 3 miles S of the town centre. Lounge, bar, restaurant (classical background music; open to non-residents); courtyard; 2-acre garden. Civil wedding licence; function facilities. Free Wi-Fi. Parking. Children welcomed (family rooms). 26 bedrooms (23 in coach house, barn and stables; 10 with patio; 2 suitable for &). Per room B&B £134–£159, D,B&B £179–£204. Set dinner £25.50.

CHIDDINGFOLD Surrey
Map 2:D3

THE CROWN INN, The Green, Petworth Road, GU8 4TX. Tel 01428-682255, www.thecrownchiddingfold.com. On the edge of the village green, this restored 14th-century inn has stained-glass windows, medieval walls, 'passageways a bit like a rabbit warren'; a warm, old-fashioned atmosphere. Daniel and Hannah Hall are the owners. Characterful bedrooms have ancient oak beams, original sloping floors and handsome antique furnishings; up-to-date technology includes a flat-screen TV and an iPod dock/digital clock radio. Classic pub dishes are served in the 'superb' oak-panelled restaurant (special diets catered for); the bars, popular with locals, have a barbecue and wood-burning pizza oven in the summer. Plenty of choice at breakfast. 2 bars (*Crown* and *Half Crown* with open fire; monthly quiz night), restaurant (background music/radio); small courtyard for alfresco dining; private dining room. Free Wi-Fi. Children welcomed. 8 bedrooms (front ones hear traffic). Per room B&B single £100, double £135–£200. Dinner £25–£30.

CHILGROVE West Sussex
Map 2:E3

THE WHITE HORSE, 1 High Street, PO18 9HX. Tel 01243-519444, www.thewhitehorse.co.uk. Tucked into the foothills of the South Downs, this 'simply lovely' 18th-century staging post inn has been renovated in contemporary rustic style. Niki Burr is the 'charming' manager. It has a 'welcoming' bar and restaurant in the original building; bedrooms in the rear have a modern four-poster bed, steamer trunks, sheepskin rugs and wool throws. All open on to a courtyard with wonderful views of the Downs. Chef Rob Armstrong serves 'good-quality pub food' in the restaurant; stylish dining areas have banquette seating, and cosy booths covered in yak skin. Free Wi-Fi. 'Soft' background music. Bar, restaurant, private dining room; terrace; garden: croquet. Parking. Helipad. Children welcomed. 12 bedrooms (all on ground floor; 2 adjoining, suitable for a family; 2 with private patio and hot tub). Per person B&B £99–£190.

CHRISTCHURCH Dorset
Map 2:E2

THE KINGS ARMS, 18 Castle Street, BH23 1DT. Tel 01202-588933, www.thekings-christchurch.co.uk. Overlooking the manicured bowling green in the centre of town, this 'attractive' hotel, in a restored Georgian building, has smart, elegant rooms and a well-regarded restaurant (*Michelin Bib Gourmand* awarded in 2014). Part of the small Harbour Hotels group, it has a relaxed atmosphere; Gin O'Clock (jazz music, £5 cocktails) strikes every evening in the bar. Spread over three floors, the modern bedrooms are individually decorated; the best have full-length French windows with views of the green and the ruins of an ancient priory. Daily specials are written on the blackboard in the restaurant, where chef Alex Aitken's 15 Mile Menu showcases locally sourced food from Dorset and the New Forest. Lounge, bar, restaurant; sun terrace (alfresco dining). Lift. Civil wedding licence; function facilities. Free Wi-Fi. Background music. Children welcomed. 20 bedrooms. Per room B&B £105–£169. Set dinner £15 (two courses, 6–7 pm), tasting menu £29.50.

CLEY-NEXT-THE-SEA Norfolk
Map 2:A5

CLEY WINDMILL, The Quay, NR25 7RP. Tel 01263-740209, www.cleywindmill. co.uk. Beside a bird sanctuary on the north Norfolk coast, this characterful small B&B is in an ingeniously converted 18th-century grinding mill. Owners Julian and Carolyn Godlee have recently refurbished it throughout; it is managed by Simon Whatling. The circular sitting room at the base of the mill has an open fire and a beamed ceiling; upstairs, the bedrooms and galleries have far-reaching views across the salt marshes and the sea. Accessed via a steep ladder, the top-floor Wheel Room has a four-poster bed and four windows, each with a different panoramic view. Dinner is a convivial affair; chefs Emma Wedderburn and Jimi Cubitt prepare daily changing three-course menus, served in the cosy, candlelit dining room in the original granary. Free Wi-Fi. Sitting room, restaurant (background jazz; open to non-residents); ¼-acre garden. Civil wedding licence. Children welcomed in some rooms (early suppers by arrangement). 9 bedrooms (3 in converted boathouse and granary). Per room B&B £110–£199, D,B&B £168–£257. 2-night min. stay on Fri and Sat nights.

COCKERMOUTH Cumbria
Map 4: inset C2
TROUT HOTEL, Crown Street, CA13 0EJ. Tel 01900-823591, www.trouthotel.co.uk. 'One of the best hotels we have stayed in.' On the banks of the River Derwent, this much-extended 17th-century home has retained many period features: original stone walls, exposed beams, stained-glass windows, reconditioned marble fireplaces. Spacious modern bedrooms are in the main house and converted stables; they are 'attractive, well-equipped, light and welcoming'. Seasonal Lake District dishes are served in the *Derwent* restaurant; the bustling bistro is 'clearly part of the life and soul of Cockermouth'. 'Both are excellent.' Packed lunches. Wordsworth's childhood home (National Trust) is next door. Bar, restaurant, bistro (background music); function facilities. Terrace (alfresco

dining); garden. Room service. Free Wi-Fi. Parking. Children, and dogs by arrangement, welcomed. 49 bedrooms (15 on ground floor; 4 family rooms). Per room B&B £125–£173.

COMBE HAY Somerset
Map 2:D1
THE WHEATSHEAF, BA2 7EG. Tel 01225-833504, www.wheatsheafcombe hay.co.uk. Ian Barton and his son, James, have updated this traditional pub and restaurant in contemporary rustic style. Surrounded by beautiful countryside, the white-painted 18th-century inn is in large gardens overlooking a village, five miles from Bath. At its heart is the restaurant, where chef Eddy Rains cooks with many home-grown and -produced ingredients (honey from the inn's bees, eggs from resident chickens and ducks, vegetables and fruit from the kitchen garden). Menus include a seven-course 'Taste of the West Country'. A wide selection of ales and wines (the Bartons are wine buffs) can be taken beside the fire, or on the terrace. Bedrooms have modern furniture and luxurious extras, such as fine-quality bedlinen and a 'tuck box' of Italian coffee and biscuits; *The Barn Room*, in a riverside building nearby, has soaring beams and vintage decoration. Sitting room, bar, restaurant; terrace. Free Wi-Fi (in main building). Background music. Parking. 'Polite' dogs welcomed; resident dogs, Milo and Brie. 3 bedrooms. Per room B&B £120–£150.

CONSTANTINE BAY Cornwall
Map 1:D2
TREGLOS HOTEL, Padstow, PL28 8JH. Tel 01841-520727, www.tregloshotel.com. 'It was a great pleasure to stay here

again.' Popular with families, this traditional hotel stands in landscaped gardens overlooking the white sandy beach of Constantine Bay. It has been owned by Jim and Rose Barlow for more than 40 years. Many of the 'well-appointed, comfortable' bedrooms have fine sea views; some have a balcony. A daily-changing menu is served in the formal dining room (smart attire is required after 7 pm except during school holidays); Gavin Hill is the new chef. 2 lounges, bar, conservatory, *Quies* restaurant; children's den, snooker room; indoor swimming pool; beauty treatments. 1-acre grounds. Ramps. Free Wi-Fi (variable signal). No background music. Children (special menus), and dogs (in some rooms) welcomed. 42 bedrooms (1 on ground floor; 2 suitable for &.). Per room B&B £129–£220, D,B&B £162–£269. 2-night min. stay in Jul, Aug. Closed mid-Nov–mid-Feb.

CORSE LAWN Gloucestershire
Map 3:D5

CORSE LAWN HOUSE, GL19 4LZ. Tel 01452-780771, www.corselawn.com. Fronted by a large ornamental pond, this Queen Anne Grade II listed building in the Severn valley near Tewkesbury is run as a small hotel and restaurant in personal style by Baba Hine. There are open fires and antiques in the two drawing rooms. The chef, Martin Kinahan, serves French and English dishes in the informal bistro and the more formal dining room. The extensive grounds have well-tended gardens, a croquet lawn and an all-weather tennis court; there is a covered (heated) swimming pool. No background music. Free Wi-Fi. Children and dogs welcomed.

18 bedrooms (decorated in country house style). Per room B&B single £100, double £160–£190. Dinner £33.50.

CORSHAM Wiltshire
Map 2:D1

THE METHUEN ARMS, 2 High Street, SN13 0HB. Tel 01249-717060, www.themethuenarms.com. In an attractive market town eight miles from Bath, Martin and Debbie Still run their restaurant-with-rooms in this handsomely refurbished Georgian inn. It has a modern rustic look inside: intimate dining areas have elm floorboards, ancient beams, exposed stone walls and log fires; tasteful, well-equipped bedrooms, all with thick blankets and a Roberts radio, are individually decorated in heritage shades. A wide variety of eating options is available throughout the day; chef Piero Boi cooks unfussy modern British dishes – 'no foams, towers, swipes or tortured carrots,' the owners say – using seasonal produce. 2 bars (background music; real ales); private dining room; courtyard (alfresco dining); garden. Free Wi-Fi. Parking. Children welcomed. 14 bedrooms. Per room B&B single from £90, double from £140, D,B&B double from £210. 2-night min. stay bank holiday weekends.

COVENTRY Warwickshire
Map 2:B2

BARNACLE HALL, Shilton Lane, Shilton, CV7 9LH. Tel 02476-612629, www.barnaclehall.co.uk. A welcoming refuge in a rural location five miles NE of the city centre, Rose Grindal's small B&B is in a Grade II listed 16th-century farmhouse with an 18th-century limestone facade. Full of nooks and crannies, it has oak beams, polished wood and an inglenook fireplace with a wood-burning stove. Large, comfortable bedrooms are furnished in period style. For guests needing to make an early start, tasty breakfasts are served from 7 am. Sitting room, dining room; garden, patio. Free Wi-Fi (in some rooms). No background music. Children welcomed. 3 bedrooms. Per person B&B single £40–£50, double £70–£80.

COVERACK Cornwall
Map 1:E2
THE BAY HOTEL, North Corner, nr Helston, TR12 6TF. Tel 01326-280464, www.thebayhotel.co.uk. 'Well run in a very personal way' by Ric and Gina House and their daughter, Zoë, this 'comfortable' hotel is in a pretty fishing village. 'Nicely decorated' in coastal shades, the pleasant lounge and many of the bedrooms have panoramic views across the water. In the candlelit restaurant, Ric House uses Cornish produce, and fresh fish landed in the bay for his 'very good' cooking; dinner is ordered the night before. Full Cornish breakfasts. Lounge, bar/restaurant, terrace; garden. Free Wi-Fi in public areas; no mobile phone signal; no telephone in the rooms. Background music (between 7 pm and 9 pm). Parking. Children over 8 welcomed. 15 bedrooms (1 on ground floor suitable for &). Per person D,B&B £60–£145. Closed mid-Nov–mid-Mar, 22–29 Dec, some rooms available on B&B basis (£40–£125 per person) at other times.

CRAYKE North Yorkshire
Map 4:D4
THE DURHAM OX, Westway, YO61 4TE. Tel 01347-821506, www.thedurhamox. com. With exposed beams, carved wood

panelling and an inglenook fireplace, Mike and Sasha Ibbotson's characterful 300-year-old country pub-with-rooms has a traditional feel. Bedrooms are in the main building or in renovated farm cottages; the spacious Studio, over the pub, has sofas, a kitchen, an honesty bar, and a private balcony with views across the Vale of York. Unpretentious food, including Crayke game and charcoal-roasted steaks, is served in three areas: the flagstone-floored dining room, a traditional bar or the *Burns Bar*, an all-weather garden room. Seasonal literary lunches with visiting authors. Walks from the door; maps available. 3 bars, restaurant, private dining room. Function facilities. Free Wi-Fi. Background music. Convenient for Park and Ride into York. Children and dogs welcomed. 6 bedrooms (1 suite, accessed via external stairs; others in converted farm cottages; 2 on ground floor). Per room B&B £120–£150. Dinner £28.

CROSTHWAITE Cumbria
Map 4: inset C2
THE PUNCH BOWL INN, Lyth Valley, Kendal, LA8 8HR. Tel 01539-568237, www.the-punchbowl.co.uk. Next to the parish church, this 300-year-old inn has sweeping views of the unspoilt Lyth valley. It is owned by Richard Rose. 'Comfortable' country-style bedrooms have characterful beams; the largest, Noble, has a chandelier and twin roll-top baths. Morning tea or coffee is 'swiftly' brought to the room on request; tea and scones are offered every afternoon. In the busy traditional bar or 'pleasant' restaurant, meals are 'very nicely presented, without too much fussiness'. 2 bars, restaurant

(background jazz); 2 terraces. Civil wedding licence; conference facilities. Free Wi-Fi (in bar only). Parking. Children welcomed. 9 bedrooms. Per room B&B £105–£305.

DARLINGTON Co. Durham
Map 4:C4

HEADLAM HALL, nr Gainford, DL2 3HA. Tel 01325-730238, www.headlamhall.co.uk. In beautiful walled gardens, surrounded by rolling farmland, the Robinson family's handsome 17th-century country house has a Jacobean hall, stone walls, huge fireplaces and traditional furnishing. Modern British and continental cuisine is served in the intimate, panelled dining room, the airy *Orangery* and the spa brasserie. Private dining is also available. 3 lounges, drawing room, bar, restaurant (classical/jazz background music). Free Wi-Fi. Lift. Wedding/ function facilities. Spa (outdoor hydrotherapy pool, sauna, gym; treatment rooms). Terraces; 4-acre garden: lake, ornamental canal; tennis, 9-hole golf course, croquet. Children and dogs welcomed. 40 bedrooms (6 in mews, 9 in coach house, 7 in spa; 2 suitable for ᴅ). Per person B&B from £62.50, D,B&B from £96.50 (2 people sharing).

DARTMOUTH Devon
Map 1:D4

BROWNS HOTEL, 27–29 Victoria Road, TQ6 9RT. Tel 01803-832572, www.brownshoteldartmouth.co.uk. Owners Clare and James Brown run their informal hotel in a 200-year-old town house on a side street near the centre of town. It has a contemporary interior; brightly decorated bedrooms have space to sit. Food and wine events

(open to the public) are occasionally organised in the sleek, open-plan *Wine Hub* bar and shop; when the bar is closed, guests are offered complimentary pre- and post-dinner drinks. Light, Mediterranean-influenced meals and small plates are available during the day; sharing platters on Friday and Saturday evenings. Lounge, bar (complimentary tapas on Fri eve), restaurant (closed Sun–Thurs). Free Wi-Fi. Modern/jazz background music. Parking permits supplied. Children welcomed. 8 bedrooms. Per room B&B £90–£185. Dinner from £20. 2-night min. stay in peak seasons. Closed Christmas, Jan.

STRETE BARTON HOUSE, Totnes Road, Strete, TQ6 0RU. Tel 01803-770364, www.stretebarton.co.uk. Stuart Litster and Kevin Hooper's 16th-century manor house has panoramic views across the bay, from Start Point lighthouse to the mouth of the River Dart. They have decorated it in artistic contemporary style with an eastern flavour; bedrooms have silks, Buddha carvings and bold prints. Guests enjoy tea and home-made cake beside a roaring fire in winter; on warm days, they sit on the terrace. Seasonal fruit and local farm yogurts are served at breakfast. Close to the South West Coastal Path, 5 miles SW of Dartmouth. Sitting room, breakfast room (classical/ 'easy listening' background music). Garden. Free Wi-Fi. In-room massages/ spa treatments, by arrangement. Children over 8 welcomed. 6 bedrooms (1 in cottage; dogs allowed). Per person B&B £52–£80. 2-night min. stay preferred in peak season.
25% DISCOUNT VOUCHERS

DITTISHAM Devon
Map 1:D4
FINGALS, Old Coombe, Dartmouth, TQ6 0JA. Tel 01803-722398, www.fingals.co.uk. There is a 'wonderful atmosphere' at Richard and Sheila Johnston's 'quirky', family-friendly hotel, in a 'comfortably and artistically' extended old farmhouse near Dartmouth. 'It's like visiting a relaxed country house; the staff looked after everybody extremely well.' Country-style bedrooms are individually designed; public rooms have inglenook fireplaces and oak beams. 'Delicious' dinners are cooked by arrangement; 'superb' breakfasts have local sausages. Many walks from the front door; bicycles available to borrow. Lounge, TV room, 2 dining rooms, honesty bar, library. Free Wi-Fi. Background music in bar. Indoor heated pool with partly removable roof, spa bath, sauna; orangery, summer house; grass tennis court, croquet lawn; games room; art gallery. Children, and dogs (in some rooms) welcomed. Resident dogs. 8 bedrooms (2 in separate buildings beside a stream). Per room B&B £75–£260. Dinner £36. Closed Jan–Mar.

DOUGLAS Isle of Man
Map 4:D1
INGLEWOOD, 26 Palace Terrace, Queens Promenade, IM2 4NF. Tel 01624-674734, www.inglewoodhotel-isleofman.com. 'The extra touches made all the difference.' At this modern guest house on the seafront, obliging hosts Pip and Andy Cross help plan days out, provide picnic lunches, and will book restaurants and taxis. The simply furnished bedrooms have a 'comfortable' bed; those at the front overlook the promenade and sea. The well-stocked bar (evenings only) specialises in gin and malt whisky; a coffee and cake shop serves light snacks home made every day. No dinners; restaurants within walking distance. Bar/lounge, dining room. Free Wi-Fi. No background music; occasional radio at breakfast. Steep stairs. 20 mins' walk from the ferry terminal. 16 bedrooms. Per person B&B from £42.50.

DOVER Kent
Map 2:D5
WALLETT'S COURT, Westcliffe, St Margaret's-at-Cliffe, CT15 6EW. Tel 01304-852424, www.wallettscourt hotelspa.com. In a pretty hamlet, ten minutes' drive from the port, Christopher and Leonora Oakley offer a wide choice of accommodation at their quirky, family-friendly hotel. There are spacious traditional rooms in the white-painted Jacobean manor house; snug stable-block rooms overlooking the gardens and meadows of White Cliffs Country; high-ceilinged Kentish barn suites; and a hut, a woodcutter's cabin, a bathing wagon and luxury tipis, all with outdoor fire pits, spread out in the seven-acre landscaped gardens. Much local, home-grown and foraged produce is used in chef David Hoseason's cooking. Lounge, bar, library, conservatory, restaurant (classical background music; open to non-residents). Free Wi-Fi in main house. 12-metre indoor swimming pool with Endless Pools swim trainer and hydrotherapy massage; sauna, steam room, fitness studio, indoor hot tub, treatment cabins, relaxation room; tennis courts, croquet lawn, boules court; sun terraces. Civil wedding licence; function facilities. Children

welcomed (baby-listening devices; high teas). 17 bedrooms (plus 2 tipis in grounds). Per room B&B £135–£265, D,B&B £215–£345. 2-night min. stay July, Aug.

DULVERTON Somerset
Map 1:B5
THREE ACRES COUNTRY HOUSE, Brushford, TA22 9AR. Tel 01398-323730, www.threeacresexmoor.co.uk. Overlooking a peaceful village on the edge of Exmoor, Julie and Edward Christian's 'peaceful, comfortable, beautifully furnished' B&B is set in mature grounds. 'It was like staying with friends.' It has a stunning hillside view and is ideally placed for country walks. The 1930s house is thoughtfully equipped; bedrooms have a large bed, a fridge, a silent-tick alarm clock. Breakfasts include a daily special, and home-made fruit compotes using berries from the garden. Light suppers (soups, pâtés, sandwiches, puddings) can be arranged. Picnic hampers available. Bar, sitting room (log fire), dining room; sun terrace. Free Wi-Fi. No background music. 2 miles S of Dulverton. Country pursuits arranged. Children welcomed. The house is also available for exclusive use. 6 bedrooms (1 on ground floor). Per person B&B £45–£60 (£15 single person supplement).
25% DISCOUNT VOUCHERS

DUNWICH Suffolk
Map 2:B6
THE SHIP AT DUNWICH, St James Street, IP17 3DT. Tel 01728-648219, www.shipatdunwich.co.uk. Close to the beach, this characterful old inn, part of the small Agellus Hotels group, is surrounded by a nature reserve. It is in a peaceful village that was once the capital of East Anglia, before the sea destroyed the medieval port. Original stone and wood floors have been retained; in cold weather, a wood-burning stove provides a 'welcoming atmosphere'. 'Good' and 'Best' bedrooms are quirky, 'crisp and clean', though 'space can be rather tight'; some are accessed via an outside staircase. Pub favourites and traditional English puddings are served in the bar, conservatory or covered courtyard. At breakfast, cooked options include kippers, omelettes or a full English. Bar (real ales), dining room, breakfast room, conservatory, covered courtyard; large garden. Free Wi-Fi. No background music. Children and dogs welcomed. 15 bedrooms (4 on ground floor in converted stables; 1 suitable for &). Per room B&B £95–£135. Dinner £22.50.
25% DISCOUNT VOUCHERS

DURHAM Co. Durham
Map 4:B4
CATHEDRAL VIEW, 212 Gilesgate, DH1 1QN. Tel 0191-386 9566, www.cathedralview.co.uk. 'Very welcoming' hosts Jim and Karen Garfitt run this B&B out of their refurbished Georgian merchant's house with a view of the cathedral. Well-equipped bedrooms have a good selection of amenities (binoculars, clothes brush, sewing kit, pack of cards); there are magazines, books on local history, and complimentary sherry in the lounge. Breakfast has fresh fruit, muesli, home-made marmalade; toast, from home-baked bread, is brought to the table. Ten-minute downhill walk to the town and to the cathedral. Lounge (communal guests' netbook with access to a printer), breakfast room. Free

Wi-Fi. No background music. Garden, with decking, seating and fish ponds. Near a main road. Parking (permits supplied). 5 bedrooms. Per room B&B single from £70, double from £90.

EASTBOURNE East Sussex
Map 2:E4
GRAND HOTEL, King Edwards Parade, BN21 4EQ. Tel 01323-412345, www.grandeastbourne.com. 'Impeccable.' Regular guests at this 'beautifully run' Victorian hotel on the seafront like its 'old-fashioned' feel and 'wonderful service'. Traditionally furnished rooms are 'sumptuous'; many have sea views. The monthly gathering of the Palm Court quartet at teatime is 'an event worth going to'; live band at weekends. 2 lounges, bar, *Mirabelle* (closed Sun, Mon) and *Garden* restaurants (both with background music); 'nice' terrace. Civil wedding licence; conference/function facilities. Free Wi-Fi. Health spa; 'lovely' heated indoor and outdoor swimming pools; 2-acre garden: putting, etc. Parking. Children welcomed (Junior Crew club, family dining, crèche). 152 bedrooms (1 suitable for &). Per room B&B £230–£380. Dinner £34–£45.

OCKLYNGE MANOR, Mill Road, BN21 2PG. Tel 01323-734121, www.ocklyngemanor.co.uk. In stunning gardens, a short walk from the town centre, Wendy and David Dugdill's small B&B is in a pink Georgian mansion built on a site once occupied by the Knights of St John of Jerusalem; it also bears a blue plaque dedicated to *Peter Pan* illustrator Mabel Lucie Attwell, who lived here in the 1930s. Comfortable, country-style bedrooms have views over the beautiful gardens. The grounds (part of the National Gardens Scheme) include a ¾-acre walled garden, a well, an 18th-century gazebo and a 150-year-old manna ash; plenty of seating. Organic breakfasts (home-made bread and marmalade). Bread-making courses (Nov–Mar). Free Wi-Fi. No background music. DVD-players. 1¼ miles from seafront. Parking. 3 bedrooms. Per person B&B from £50. 2-night min. stay at weekends preferred.

EGGESFORD Devon
Map 1:C4
THE FOX & HOUNDS, Chulmleigh, EX18 7JZ. Tel 01769-580345, www.foxandhoundshotel.co.uk. Within North Devon's Biosphere Reserve (renowned for its conservation and beauty), the Culverhouse family's 'lovely' hotel occupies a former Victorian coaching inn. It is also home to the Devon School of Fly Fishing, and has five miles of the River Taw and two lakes for piscatorial pursuits. Large, country-style bedrooms have antique furniture; most have space for a cot or child's bed. In the informal restaurant, chef Alex Pallet's menus offer 'a good choice' of traditional West Country food; afternoon teas may be taken on the terrace overlooking the garden. Eggesford is on the Tarka Line between Exeter and Barnstaple. Bar (background music), dining room; terrace; health and beauty room (holistic treatments). Free Wi-Fi. Function facilities. Civil wedding licence. 6-acre garden. Children (cots, high chairs, monitors; babysitting; special menus), and well-behaved dogs (by arrangement; £10 per night) welcomed. 20 bedrooms (3 on ground floor; 1 suitable for &); plus

1 luxury self-catering tree house). Per room B&B £58–£195, D,B&B £80–£255.
25% DISCOUNT VOUCHERS

ELTERWATER Cumbria
Map 4:inset C2

THE ELTERMERE INN, Ambleside, LA22 9HY. Tel 015394-37207, www.eltermere.co.uk. In glorious countryside in the Langdale valley, Mark and Ruth Jones's refurbished country hotel with Georgian origins is a family affair: daughter Aimee is manager; son Edward is chef. On arrival, guests are offered complimentary tea and cake, which may be taken on the terrace in fine weather. Bedrooms, many with a window seat for admiring lake or fell views, have an 'attractive' new bathroom. 'A good list' of modern European dishes and daily specials is served in the cosy Venetian bar (beamed ceiling, original slate floor, 'beautiful' fireplace with log fire) or in the smart restaurant with panoramic vistas over Elter Water. Walks from the front door; large gardens have access to the lake with rowing boat and private jetty for fishing. 2 lounges, bar, restaurant; terrace; large garden. Free Wi-Fi (in public areas). Contemporary background music. Complimentary leisure passes for Langdale Spa (pool, hot tub, steam room). Children over 8 welcomed, dogs allowed in some rooms. 12 bedrooms. Per room B&B £140–£250. Dinner £36. Closed Christmas.
25% DISCOUNT VOUCHERS

EVERSHOT Dorset
Map 1:C6

THE ACORN INN, 28 Fore Street, DT2 0JW. Tel 01935-83228, www.acorn-inn.co.uk. 'At once a local pub for faithful regulars and a sophisticated place in which someone from Sloane Square would feel at home.' In a pretty Dorset village (believed to have featured in Thomas Hardy's novels), this homely, 16th-century stone inn is run in a relaxed way by Jack Mackenzie, who is the chef, and his wife, Alexandra, for the Red Carnation Hotel Collection. The inn has beams, oak panelling, stone floors and log fires; the smartly decorated bedrooms have a modern bathroom. Guests may use the spa swimming pool, sauna and gym of sister hotel *Summer Lodge*, opposite (£15 charge). Local, sustainably sourced produce is served in the bars and restaurant. Lounge, 2 bars (skittle alley), restaurant with sitting area; small beer garden. Free Wi-Fi (in public areas). Background music. Children and dogs welcomed. 10 bedrooms. Per room B&B £99–£205, D,B&B £159–£265.

EXETER Devon
Map 1:C5

THE MAGDALEN CHAPTER, Magdalen Street, EX2 4HY. Tel 01392-281000, www.themagdalenchapter.com. Occupying the former West of England Eye Hospital, this eye-catching hotel retains the original marble floors and gold-lettered visitor notices of the iconic building. Fiona Moores is the manager for Chapter Hotels. Quirky, modern bedrooms (single rooms available) have an iPad, Nespresso coffee machine and complimentary minibar; all are decorated with original works of art. The striking circus tent-like restaurant leads to the terrace and garden; in the open kitchen, chef Ben Bulger cooks seasonal, daily-changing menus. Lounge, bar, library, dining room.

Free Wi-Fi. Background music. Walled garden; indoor-outdoor pool with wood-burning stove. Spa; treatments (open to non-residents); gym. Children and dogs welcomed. 59 bedrooms. Per room B&B from £160, D,B&B from £190.

FALMOUTH Cornwall
Map 1:E2
THE ROSEMARY, 22 Gyllyngvase Terrace, TR11 4DL. Tel 01326-314669, www.therosemary.co.uk. Lynda and Malcolm Cook offer guests a 'very friendly' welcome, with tea and home-made cake, at their 'excellent' B&B in a 'beautifully furnished' Edwardian house close to the beach and town centre. The large drawing room and most of the 'well-appointed' bedrooms have 'fantastic' sea views. 'Good' Cornish breakfasts. Bar, lounge, dining room; south-facing garden, sun deck. Free Wi-Fi. No background music. Children and dogs welcomed (the latter not in high season). 8 bedrooms (two 2-bedroom suites, ideal for a family). Per room B&B single £48–£61, double £77–£152. Closed mid-Nov–Feb.

FOLKESTONE Kent
Map 2:E5
ROCKSALT, 4–5 Fish Market, CT19 6AA. Tel 01303-212070, www.rocksaltfolkestone.co.uk. There are comfortable bedrooms, fresh seafood and exceptional sea views at this stylish restaurant-with-rooms in a small port town. In a striking dark-timber-and-glass building cantilevered over Folkestone's fishing harbour, chef Mark Sargeant's well-regarded restaurant has a contemporary interior with limewashed oak flooring, curved banquettes and floor-to-ceiling windows looking out to sea; the lively bar above serves cocktails and light bites. Across a cobbled street, accommodation is in a converted old building on a narrow passageway; snug rooms have exposed brick, an antique bed and a wet room. Continental breakfast hampers are delivered to the room. Bar, restaurant; terrace. Free Wi-Fi. No background music. Children welcomed. On-street parking. 4 bedrooms. Per room B&B £75–£115.

FOWEY Cornwall
Map 1:D3
THE OLD QUAY HOUSE, 28 Fore Street, PL23 1AQ. Tel 01726-833302, www.theoldquayhouse.com. Guests enjoy wonderful views of the estuary from the lounge and terrace of Jane and Roy Carson's waterfront hotel, in this pretty medieval harbour town. Converted from a Victorian seamen's mission, the hotel has stylish, well-equipped bedrooms with a large bed, bathrobes, waterproofs and umbrellas for inclement weather; several rooms have a small balcony. New chef Ben Bass's two- and three-course seasonal menus are served in the modern restaurant; special diets are catered for. Visitors arriving by car are encouraged to drop off their baggage before parking up the hill. Many steep, narrow streets in town. Lounge, bar, restaurant (closed Mon, Tues in Jan, Feb; background music). Civil wedding licence. Free Wi-Fi. 11 bedrooms. Per room B&B £120–£325. Dinner £37.50.

GATWICK West Sussex
Map 2:D4
LANGSHOTT MANOR, Ladbroke Road, Langshott, Horley, RH6 9LN. Tel 01293-786680, www.langshottmanor.com. In

large, well-kept grounds close to Gatwick airport, this 'beautiful' Elizabethan timber-framed manor house (part of the small Alexander Hotels group) has many period features (exposed beams, oak panels and feature fireplaces). Many of the individually styled bedrooms have an antique bathtub or four-poster bed; some superior rooms also have a private patio garden. In the *Mulberry* restaurant, chef Phil Dixon's 'delicious' menus include good vegetarian options. Afternoon tea may be taken in the lounges or on the terrace overlooking the lawns. 2 lounges (background music), bar, restaurant; terrace (alfresco dining). Civil wedding licence; conference facilities. Free Wi-Fi. 3-acre garden; medieval moat. Children welcomed. 22 bedrooms (7 in main house, some with four-poster bed; 15 across garden). Room only £199–£309. Breakfast £12.50–£16.95, dinner £50–£65.

GILSLAND Cumbria
Map 4:B3
HILL ON THE WALL, Brampton, CA8 7DA. Tel 01697-747214, www.hillonthewall.co.uk. Elaine Packer welcomes guests to her 'elegant' B&B with tea and home-made cake in the drawing room of this Grade II listed building, a fortified 'bastle' farmhouse built in 1595. It has an outstanding hilltop location overlooking Hadrian's Wall, with 'stunning' views over the Irthing valley. 'Beautifully furnished' bedrooms are supplied with thoughtful items; locally sourced Northumbrian breakfasts, ordered the night before, are 'delicious'. Walkers and cyclists are welcomed; packed lunches available (£6). Lounge (library, wood-burning stove), breakfast room; terrace; 1-acre garden. Free Wi-Fi. No background music. Parking; secure cycle storage. Near Hadrian's Wall at Birdoswald. 3 bedrooms. Per person B&B £37.50–£42.50. Closed Dec–Mar.

WILLOWFORD FARM, CA8 7AA. Tel 01697-747962, www.willowford.co.uk. On one of the longest unbroken stretches of Hadrian's Wall, with the remains of a bridge and two turrets, this B&B stands on a 100-acre organic farm along the National Trail between Gilsland village and Birdoswald Roman fort. It is owned by Liam McNulty and Lauren Harrison. Accommodation is in the former milking parlour, cart house and grain store, where the homely, energy-efficient bedrooms have exposed wooden beams, slate floors and antique furniture. Bathrooms have under-floor heating and handmade organic soaps. Evening meals can be taken at *The Samson Inn* in the village, under the same management; lamb from the farm appears on chef Barrie Garton's menus. Packed lunches available (£6). Lounge, dining room. Free Wi-Fi (in public areas). No background music. Children welcomed (family rooms); dogs by arrangement. Resident dog. ½ mile W of Gilsland. 5 bedrooms (all on ground floor). Per room B&B £80–£85. Dinner £18. Closed Dec–Feb.

GRAFFHAM West Sussex
Map 2:E3
WILLOW BARNS, nr Petworth, GU28 0NT. Tel 01798-867493, www.willowbarns.co.uk. 'Highly recommended.' On the edge of a village five miles from Petworth, this 'stylish' B&B, built in 2010 using traditional

methods in flint and brick, is in a 'stunning, quiet location'. It is owned by Amanda Godman and Wendy Judd. Pretty bedrooms are set around a serene courtyard; all have fresh flowers, sweet treats, a 'gorgeous' bathroom and wonderful views of the countryside. The owners recently acquired the adjacent pub, where they plan to serve meals throughout the day. Communal breakfasts. Many footpaths and bridleways nearby. Cyclists and riders welcomed; stabling, by arrangement, for visiting horses (or turnout in adjacent field). Clay-pigeon shooting can be organised. Sitting room; courtyard garden. Free Wi-Fi in public areas. No background music. Parking. 6 bedrooms (all on ground floor). Per room B&B £90–£125. 2-night min. stay at peak weekends.
25% DISCOUNT VOUCHERS

GRANGE-OVER-SANDS Cumbria
Map 4: inset C2
CLARE HOUSE, Park Road, LA11 7HQ. Tel 015395-33026, www.clarehousehotel. co.uk. 'Another lovely stay.' 'The very best of the traditional', the Read family's Victorian hotel attracts many regular guests, who like its 'great welcome, comfy – even homely – bedrooms and the excellent food' cooked by Andrew Read. 'Wonderful' views over the garden to Morecambe Bay. Ramps. 2 lounges, dining room (open to non-residents). Free Wi-Fi. No background music. ¾-acre grounds. Mile-long promenade at the bottom of the garden (bowling green, tennis courts, putting green; easy access to ornamental gardens). Parking. Children welcomed. 18 bedrooms (1 on ground floor suitable for ♿). Per person B&B

£71–£75, D,B&B £91–£95. Closed mid-Dec–end Mar.
25% DISCOUNT VOUCHERS

GRASSINGTON North Yorkshire
Map 4:D3
GRASSINGTON HOUSE, 5 The Square, nr Skipton, BD23 5AQ. Tel 01756-752406, www.grassingtonhousehotel.co.uk. Chef/patron John Rudden and his wife, Sue, hold lively weekend events at their small, refurbished hotel in this popular market town. Their limestone Georgian house overlooks the picturesque cobbled square, and has a dramatic, contemporary interior. 'Very enjoyable' classic English food is served by 'friendly, efficient' staff in the smart restaurant or fireside bar, or on the terrace. The Ruddens' rare-breed pigs provide the restaurant with bacon, sausages and pork (with plenty of crackling). Lounge, bar, *No.5* restaurant. Civil wedding licence; function facilities. Free Wi-Fi. Background music. Children welcomed. Cookery master classes. Wild food foraging trips on the Dales Way trail. Parking. 9 bedrooms. Per room B&B £110–£130, D,B&B £175–£220.

GREAT LANGDALE Cumbria
Map 4: inset C2
THE OLD DUNGEON GHYLL, LA22 9JY. Tel 015394-37272, www.odg.co.uk. There are good-value, country-style bedrooms and a wide selection of Scottish malt whiskies at this comfortable, informal inn, which has welcomed fell walkers and climbers for more than 300 years. It is run by Jane and Neil Walmsley for the National Trust. The residents' lounge has home-baked treats with morning coffee and

afternoon tea; the lively *Hikers' Bar*, open to non-residents, has real ales and occasional open-mic nights. No television; mobile reception patchy. Walking routes and packed lunches available. Residents' bar and lounge, dining room, public *Hikers' Bar* (old cow stalls); live music on first Wed of every month. No background music. Free Wi-Fi (in public areas). Drying room. 1-acre garden. 12 bedrooms. Per person B&B £58, D,B&B £78. 2-night min. stay at weekends.

GURNARD Isle of Wight
Map 2:E2

THE LITTLE GLOSTER, 31 Marsh Road, PO31 8JQ. Tel 01983-200299, www. thelittlegloster.com. Decorated in nautical style, with airy, blue-and-white accommodation and a bright, beachy dining room, this charming restaurant-with-rooms sits on the water's edge, on a little bay just west of Cowes. It is run by chef Ben Cooke with his wife, Holly, and support from family members. The well-equipped bedrooms have a Nespresso coffee machine; two, with superb sea views, also have binoculars. Much seafood and Isle of Wight produce is served in the unpretentious restaurant; breakfast, taken until 11 am on weekends, has plenty of choice, including 'super' juices, home-made marmalade, home-cured gravadlax, and eggs all ways. Bar, restaurant (closed Mon, and Tues in winter); function facilities. Free Wi-Fi. Background music. Garden; croquet lawn. Children welcomed. 5 mins' drive from Cowes. 3 bedrooms (in adjoining building). Per room B&B £90–£180. Dinner (Wed–Fri, except in Jul and Aug) £20–£24, à la carte £38. Closed Jan–mid-Feb.

HALIFAX West Yorkshire
Map 4:D3

SHIBDEN MILL INN, Shibden Mill Fold, HX3 7UL. Tel 01422-365840, www.shibdenmillinn.com. Opposite a millstream in the Shibden valley, Simon and Caitlin Heaton's 'very attractive' 17th-century country inn has a 'bustling' oak-beamed bar with an open fire at its heart. Imaginatively styled bedrooms, some with archways and soaring ceilings, are 'great'. Chef Darren Parkinson uses Yorkshire produce for his modern British dishes; the selection of cask ales includes *Shibden Mill*'s own brew. 'The staff really cared.' Glen Pearson is the manager. 2 miles NE of Halifax. Bar, restaurant; private dining room; patio (alfresco dining). DVD library. Small conference facilities. Free Wi-Fi. Background music. Parking. Children welcomed (special menu). 11 bedrooms. Per room B&B single £95–£162, double £117–£192, D,B&B double £177–£243. Closed Chrismas, New Year.

HARROGATE North Yorkshire
Map 4:D4

THE BIJOU, 17 Ripon Road, HG1 2JL. Tel 01423-567974, www.thebijou.co.uk. A five-minute walk from the town centre, Stephen and Gill Watson's good-value B&B is in a Victorian villa, off a main road. It has contemporary furnishing and artwork, original wood and tiled floors, and a wood-burning stove in the sitting room. Modern bedrooms (those at the back are quietest) have up-to-date magazines and a hospitality tray with sweets and biscuits. Some steep stairs; the coach house behind the main building is ideal for a family. Lounge (afternoon teas; honesty bar; computer), breakfast room. Free

Wi-Fi. Background music. Small front garden. Parking. Children welcomed. 10 bedrooms (2 in coach house; 1 on ground floor). Per room B&B single £64–£104, double £84–£114.

HATCH BEAUCHAMP Somerset
Map 1:C6

FARTHINGS, nr Taunton, TA3 6SG. Tel 01823-480664, www.farthingshotel. co.uk. John Seeger runs this small country hotel and restaurant in a white-painted Georgian house with curved bays and shuttered windows. The lounge has crackling log fires in winter; individually decorated bedrooms have antique furniture and views of the gardens. Extensive orchards in the grounds produce figs, cherries, medlars and sweet chestnuts for the kitchen; much home-reared meat features on chef Shaun Barnes's traditional menus, served in the 'intimate' dining rooms. Lounge, bar, 3 dining rooms; 3-acre grounds (orchards, roses; chickens, pigs). Civil wedding licence. Free Wi-Fi. Classical background music in restaurant. 4 miles S of Taunton. Children, and well-behaved dogs (£8 charge) welcomed. Resident dogs. 11 bedrooms (2 on ground floor), plus 1-bed cottage. Per room B&B single £110–£155, double £130–£175.
25% DISCOUNT VOUCHERS

HAWORTH West Yorkshire
Map 4:D3

ASHMOUNT COUNTRY HOUSE, Mytholmes Lane, BD22 8EZ. Tel 01535-645726, www.ashmounthaworth.co.uk. In Brontë country, Ray and Gill Capeling's stone-built guest house is a short stroll from the Brontë Parsonage Museum; it was once the home of Dr Amos Ingham, physician to the Brontë sisters. Wayne and Claire Saud are the managers. Bedrooms are romantic; some have a private patio and hot tub, sauna cabin and whirlpool bath, music and mood lighting. Modern British dishes, cooked by Alastair Bowling, are served in the restaurant overlooking the garden and the countryside beyond; vegetarian menus are available. Yorkshire breakfasts. Lounge, morning room, *The Drawing Room* restaurant (open to non-residents; closed Mon, Tues). Civil wedding licence; function facilities. Free Wi-Fi (in some rooms). 'Easy listening' background music. Mature ¾-acre garden; picnics available. Ample private parking. Children over 10 welcomed. 12 bedrooms (4 in former chauffeur and gardener's cottage, across the street). Per room B&B £85–£225, D,B&B £145–£285. 2-night min. stay at weekends.
25% DISCOUNT VOUCHERS

HAY-ON-WYE Herefordshire
Map 3:D4

THE BEAR, 2 Bear Street, HR3 5AN. Tel 01497-821302, www.thebearhay.com. David Gibbon's B&B is in a former 16th-century coaching inn, steps away from the world-renowned bookshops, galleries and attractions of this small market town. Decorated in a smart, eclectic style, rooms have old beams and vintage furniture offset by quirky artwork and modern accessories. Breakfasts include home-made fruit salads and compotes, and locally baked bread. Lounge, dining room; walled patio. Free Wi-Fi in public rooms. No background music. Children welcomed. Small car park. Credit cards not accepted. 3 bedrooms. Per room B&B

£75–£95 (£25 additional charge during Festival). Closed Christmas/New Year.

TINTO HOUSE, 13 Broad Street, HR3 5DB. Tel 01497-821556, www.tinto-house.co.uk. Close to the castle, John and Karen Clare's 'attractive' B&B has a 'beautiful' garden bounded by the River Wye, with distant views of the hills above Clyro. The listed Georgian house is handsomely furnished and decorated with drawings, sculptures and original paintings (many by John Clare). The garden is also home to regular sculpture installations; the converted stable block contains an art gallery. Breakfast has home-made jams and compotes, and fruit from the garden. Offa's Dyke is close by. Dining room, library. Free Wi-Fi. No background music. 1-acre garden. Children welcomed. 4 bedrooms. Per room B&B single £65, double £90–£100. Closed for 4 weeks over Christmas/New Year.

HEACHAM Norfolk
Map 2:A4
HEACHAM HOUSE, 18 Staithe Road, PE31 7ED. Tel 01485-579529, www.heachamhouse.com. Rebecca and Rob Bradley's beautifully presented three-storey Victorian house overlooks the village duck pond, in an area famed for its miles of sandy beaches, salt marshes and sunset views. B&B guests are welcomed with tea and home-made cake on arrival; walkers and cyclists are provided with drying facilities and secure storage. Immaculate bedrooms have fresh flowers; the varied breakfast menu features home-made bread and preserves, award-winning sausages, and muffins served with crème fraîche and fruit compote. The Bradleys are helpful

with suggestions on restaurants and places of interest. Lounge with log-burner, breakfast room. Free Wi-Fi. No background music. Small front garden overlooking pond. Parking; bicycle storage. 3 bedrooms. Per room B&B single £50–£65, double £75–£90. Closed Christmas, New Year.

HELMSLEY North Yorkshire
Map 4:C4
NO54, 54 Bondgate, YO62 5EZ. Tel 01439-771533, www.no54.co.uk. 'A very good base' for exploring the 'wonderful' surrounding countryside, Lizzie Rohan's welcoming B&B is in a house formed from two cottages in a York stone terrace, half a mile from the market square. Tea and home-baked cake are served on arrival. The main building has flagstone floors and open fires; pretty bedrooms ('quiet and very well equipped') are set around a sunny, flowery courtyard. An 'excellent' breakfast, served at a communal table, includes locally smoked kippers, freshly baked muffins, and eggs from free-range hens just down the road. Sitting room, breakfast room. No background music. Free Wi-Fi. Garden. Resident dog. Near the North York Moors national park; picnics available. 3 bedrooms in courtyard. Per person B&B £50–£65.

HERTFORD Hertfordshire
Map 2:C4
NUMBER ONE PORT HILL, 1 Port Hill, SG14 1PJ. Tel 01992-587350, www.numberoneporthill.co.uk. Annie Rowley's elegant B&B, in a Grade II listed Georgian town house, is well placed for visiting the town. The handsome building is mentioned in the Pevsner architectural guide to

Hertfordshire; inside, there are chandeliers, huge mirrors, vintage glassware, sculptures and fresh flowers. Bedrooms on the top floor have thoughtful touches (bathrobes, Belgian hot chocolate, an 'eclectic' mix of reading material). The drawing room has an original corniced ceiling and roaring fire. An accommodating hostess, Annie Rowley serves a wide breakfast selection, taken at a communal table; home-cooked dinners may be ordered in advance. Drawing room; walled courtyard garden. Free Wi-Fi. No background music. Resident Labrador, Presley. Limited street parking. 3 bedrooms (1 with private bathroom). Per room B&B £105–£130. Dinner £30.

HEXHAM Northumberland
Map 4:B3

BARRASFORD ARMS, Barrasford, NE48 4AA. Tel 01434-681237, www.barrasfordarms.co.uk. In a small village close to Hadrian's Wall, chef/patron Tony Binks's 'very attractive old pub' sits on a 'quiet' road, with 'a pretty garden and wide views'. It has a 'relaxed, pleasant' atmosphere: 'Although the staff were kept busy serving, they were always friendly and happy to help.' The simply decorated bedrooms are clean, though some can be snug; 'good shower'. In the 'stylish' dining rooms, popular with locals, Tony Binks cooks 'delicious' traditional English dishes with a French twist. 'Breakfast was excellent'. Regular quoits tournaments, hunt meets, darts finals and vegetable competitions. Bar, 2 dining rooms; private dining. Background music in bar and restaurant. Free Wi-Fi. Parking. Children welcomed (family rooms).

7 bedrooms. Per room B&B £67–£87. Dinner from £25.

THE HERMITAGE, Swinburne, NE48 4DG. Tel 01434-681248, www.thehermitagebedandbreakfast.co.uk. Approached through a grand arch and up a long drive, Katie and Simon Stewart's 'beautiful' stone-built house is in a 'charming setting'. 'A wonderful refuge', the home is furnished with antiques, and has a 'true country house atmosphere'. A welcoming tea is served in front of a roaring log fire; the hosts are happy to help with restaurant bookings, and advise on circular walks on Hadrian's Wall nearby. Drawing rooms, breakfast room; 4-acre grounds: terrace, tennis. Free Wi-Fi. No background music. Children over 7 welcomed. Resident dogs. 7 miles N of Corbridge (ask for directions). 3 bedrooms. Per room B&B £90. Closed Nov–Mar.

HOARWITHY Herefordshire
Map 3:D4

ASPEN HOUSE, HR2 6QP. Tel 01432-840353, www.aspenhouse.net. Surrounded by farmland in a tranquil Wye valley village, this 18th-century red sandstone farmhouse is run as an environmentally friendly B&B by Sally Dean and Rob Elliott. There are homely, cosy bedrooms, and a guest lounge with a balcony and views over the gardens; organic breakfasts have home-made yogurt and preserves, and locally produced bacon and sausages. The hosts run Real Food Discovery weekends, with much home cooking. Good walks from the front door; maps and drying facilities provided. Lounge (opening on to a decked area overlooking the ½-acre garden). Free Wi-Fi. No background music. 4 miles from Ross-on-Wye. 3 bedrooms (plus self-catering cottage). Per room B&B single £45–£55, double £72–£78. 2-night min. stay on peak weekends.

HOPE Derbyshire
Map 3:A6
LOSEHILL HOUSE, Losehill Lane, Edale Road, S33 6AF. Tel 01433-621219, www. losehillhouse.co.uk. In a 'magnificent setting', Paul and Kathryn Roden's secluded spa hotel is in a white-painted Arts and Crafts house on a hillside, with footpath access to the Peak District national park. Refurbished modern bedrooms are well equipped with bathrobes, slippers, locally produced biscuits; a complimentary newspaper is provided. The outdoor hot tub has 'amazing' views over the Hope valley. In the restaurant overlooking the green countryside, chef Darren Goodwin cooks an extensive menu of 'appetising' modern British food. 'Thoroughly enjoyed.' Drawing room, bar, *Orangery* restaurant. Lift. Civil wedding licence; function/conference facilities; exclusive use. Free Wi-Fi. Background music. 1-acre garden; terrace. Spa: indoor swimming pool; hot tub; treatment rooms (open to non-residents). Children, and dogs (in 2 rooms) welcomed. Parking. 23 bedrooms (4 with external entrance). Per room B&B £180, D,B&B £225. 2-night min. stay on weekends.
25% DISCOUNT VOUCHERS

HUDDERSFIELD West Yorkshire
Map 4:E3
THE THREE ACRES INN & RESTAURANT, Roydhouse, Shelley, HD8 8LR. Tel 01484-602606, www.3acres.com. Set in rolling Pennine countryside, this old roadside drovers' inn has been run by Brian Orme and Neil Truelove for more than 40 years; Neil's son, Tom, is now a partner. Comfortable bedrooms are simply furnished; some may be small. In the restaurant, chef Tom Davies serves English comfort food with international influences; Sunday lunches are popular. 5 miles from the town centre (busy morning traffic); close to the Yorkshire Sculpture Park and National Mining Museum. Bar, restaurant; ramp. Civil wedding licence; small function/ private dining facilities. Free Wi-Fi. Background music. Terraced garden; decked dining terrace. Children, and dogs (in 1 room) welcomed. 17 bedrooms (1 suitable for &; 6 in adjacent cottages). Per room B&B £75–£125. Dinner £50.

ILFRACOMBE Devon
Map 1:B4
THE ELMFIELD, Torrs Park, EX34 8AZ. Tel 01271-863377, www.theelmfield.com. Minutes from Tunnels Beaches and the north Devon coastline, Matt and Zoë Brewer run their very family-friendly B&B in this large Victorian villa. Comfortable bedrooms range in size from 'cosy' to 'glamorous'; a family suite has two bedrooms, each with a bathroom. There is much to occupy guests: a pool complex, a movie lounge, a games room (darts, toys, children's books); the terraced gardens have an outdoor play area, a gazebo, a fire pit, a stream, and peaceful areas in which to sit. Lounge, bar, breakfast room (background music); playroom (fridge, microwave). Indoor 10-metre pool (heated Easter–Oct). Free Wi-Fi in public areas and most rooms. 1-acre

garden. Parking. Licensed for small weddings. Children welcomed (baby listening; babysitters can be arranged). In-room treatments. Picnic hampers. 11 bedrooms. Per room B&B £75–£135. 2-night min. stay in high season. Closed Dec–Mar.

ILMINGTON Warwickshire
Map 3:D6

THE HOWARD ARMS, Lower Green, nr Stratford-upon-Avon, CV36 4LT. Tel 01608-682226, www.howardarms.com. By the green in a picturesque village, this 'fantastic' 400-year-old Cotswold stone inn has arched windows, beamed ceilings, flagstone floors and a mix of old furniture; there are cheering log fires on cold days. Bedrooms vary in size and decor: they may have a country-style painted wood headboard or striking feature wallpaper. The popular restaurant uses produce from local suppliers in the inventive monthly menus. 'A particularly good breakfast.' Good walks from the village. Snug, bar, dining room ('easy listening' background music); patio/garden (alfresco dining). Free Wi-Fi. Parking. Children welcomed. 8 bedrooms (5 through separate door under covered walkway). Per room B&B £96–£150. Dinner £30.

ILSINGTON Devon
Map 1:D4

ILSINGTON COUNTRY HOUSE, nr Newton Abbot, TQ13 9RR. Tel 01364-661452, www.ilsington.co.uk. 'A delightful hotel in a stunning location', the Hassell family's traditionally furnished, white-painted house is perched high in Dartmoor national park, with 'lovely' moorland views all around. Some bedrooms have recently been refurbished. In the dining room, chef Mike O'Donnell's modern European menus focus on local produce; bistro food and snacks are taken in the *Blue Tiger Inn*. The 'excellent' leisure centre (open to non-residents) is in a separate building, and has a 12-metre heated indoor swimming pool, spa, sauna and well-equipped gym. 2 lounges, bar, restaurant, pub, conservatory; croquet. Lift. Ramps. Civil wedding licence; conference facilities. Free Wi-Fi. Background music. 10-acre grounds. Children, and dogs (in ground-floor rooms, conservatory; £8 per night) welcomed. 25 bedrooms (8 on ground floor). Per room B&B £110–£220, D,B&B £170–£280.

IRONBRIDGE Shropshire
Map 2:A1

THE LIBRARY HOUSE, 11 Severn Bank, TF8 7AN. Tel 01952-432299, www.libraryhouse.com. Next to a bridge by the River Severn, this Grade II listed Georgian guest house, once the village library, is well placed for those visiting the town. It was taken over by exemplary hosts Tim and Sarah Davis in 2013. The sitting room has comfortable seating, a wood-burning stove and the original library shelves. Pretty bedrooms, named after writers, are well equipped with a hospitality tray, flat-screen TV and DVD-player, and cotton waffle dressing gowns. Sitting room, dining room. Free Wi-Fi. No background music. Mature garden; courtyard. Parking passes supplied for local car parks. Restaurants nearby. Children by arrangement. Resident dog. 4 bedrooms

(1 with private terrace). Per person B&B £65–£100.
25% DISCOUNT VOUCHERS.

KESWICK Cumbria
Map 4: inset C2
DALEGARTH HOUSE, Portinscale, CA12 5RQ. Tel 017687-72817, www.dalegarth-house.co.uk. Walkers can access the fells straight from the door of this spacious, traditionally furnished Edwardian house high above Derwentwater; easy-going hosts Craig and Clare Dalton provide maps and local information. Bedrooms, most with glorious lake and fell views, are comfortable and modern. Home-cooked dinners – 'a taste of the Lakes' – are served at 7 pm (earlier meals may be arranged for guests attending the Theatre by the Lake). Cumbrian breakfasts. In a village 1 mile from Keswick. Background radio at breakfast; classical/'easy listening' music at dinner. Lounge, bar, dining room. Free Wi-Fi. Garden. Parking. 10 bedrooms (2 in annexe). Per person B&B £45–£55, D,B&B £60–£75. Closed 25 Nov–Mar.

LYZZICK HALL, Underskiddaw, CA12 4PY. Tel 017687-72277, www.lyzzickhall.co.uk. On the lower slopes of Skiddaw, this country hotel, run by the Fernandez and Lake families, lies amid the 'stunning' scenery of the Borrowdale valley and Catbells. Most bedrooms have views towards the Lakeland fells; lounges have comfortable seating and log fires; a spacious, sunny orangery leads directly to the garden. Chef Ian Mackay's traditional and contemporary British cuisine, sourced from local suppliers, is served at elegantly set tables in the dining room; wine is mainly from the Iberian peninsula. An inventive seven-course tasting menu is also available. 2 lounges, orangery, bar, restaurant (open to non-residents). Free Wi-Fi. Background music. Indoor pool; sauna, whirlpool bath. 4-acre landscaped grounds. Children welcomed. 30 bedrooms (1 on ground floor). Per person B&B £77–£123, D,B&B £99–£145. Closed Christmas.

KINGHAM Oxfordshire
Map 3:D6
THE KINGHAM PLOUGH, The Green, nr Chipping Norton, OX7 6YD. Tel 01608-658327, www.thekinghamplough.co.uk. There are exposed beams, flagstone floors and church candles at this family-friendly pub-with-rooms facing the green in a 'charming' Cotswolds village. With head chef Ben Dulley, chef/patronne Emily Watkins serves popular daily-changing menus in the bar and restaurant using local game and produce, and foraged fungi; a good selection of local cheeses is served with home-made quince jelly. Pretty bedrooms (several suitable for a family) have freshly baked biscuits and a DVD library; some are small. 4 miles SW of Chipping Norton. Bar, restaurant (background music); terrace; garden. Free Wi-Fi. Discount at Daylesford Organic Spa, ½ mile away. Children, and dogs (annexe only; £10) welcomed. 7 bedrooms (3 in annexe). Per room B&B £95–£145. À la carte £38.

KING'S LYNN Norfolk
Map 2:A4
CONGHAM HALL, Lynn Road, Grimston, PE32 1AH. Tel 01485-600250, www.conghamhallhotel.co.uk. 'We have nothing but praise for this lovely

country hotel.' On a peaceful 30-acre estate, this fine Georgian house – now remodelled, and with a new spa – is back in the hands of Nicholas Dickinson, who once co-owned it with Nigel Chapman. 'Spacious' bedrooms in the main house are 'pretty, with flowery curtains and nice watercolours'; they face the walled garden and cricket pitch in the front of the house, or lawns and parkland at the rear. In the new garden wing, modern rooms have a private patio. The famous gardens (more than 700 varieties of herbs; open to the public Apr–Sept, 10 am–3 pm) provide fruit, vegetables and herbs for the 'super' food served in the restaurant overlooking glorious parkland. 6 miles E of King's Lynn. Lounge, library, *Orangery* restaurant; terrace. Spa (pool, sauna, steam room, treatments, foot bath, bio-sauna, outside hot tub). Free Wi-Fi in public areas. No background music. Putting, croquet, tennis, trampoline; clay-pigeon shooting. Children (cots), and dogs (in some rooms; £10 per day) welcomed. Resident dog. 26 bedrooms (11 garden rooms; some family rooms). Per room B&B £125–£275. Dinner £41–£48.

KINGSBRIDGE Devon
Map 1:D4

THURLESTONE HOTEL, Thurlestone, TQ7 3NN. Tel 01548-560382, www.thurlestone.co.uk. Standing in extensive subtropical gardens, this large, family-friendly hotel is a five-minute walk to the sea. It has been owned by the Grose family since 1896. 'Staff are first class; housekeeping is of the highest standard.' Diversions are plenty: there are sun terraces, croquet lawns, a spa with a heated outdoor pool, a 16th-century village pub with real ales; cream teas are taken in the garden in fine weather. Children are well provided for, with a games library, a playroom, family badminton courts, and a children's club during the school holidays. Lounges, bar, *Margaret Amelia* restaurant (open to non-residents; Hugh Miller cooks); lift. Outdoor *Rock Pool* eating area (teas, lunches, snacks, dinners); terrace; *The Village Inn* pub. Civil wedding licence; function facilities. Spa (indoor swimming pool, laconium, fitness studio, speciality showers; treatments); outdoor heated swimming pool (May–Sept); tennis, squash, badminton, croquet, 9-hole golf course; children's club in school holidays. Free Wi-Fi. No background music. Children, and dogs (in some rooms only; £8 per night charge) welcomed. 4 miles SW of Kingsbridge. 65 bedrooms (2 suitable for &; some with balcony, sea views). Per room B&B £200–£450, D,B&B £250–£500. 2-night min. stay.

KNUTSFORD Cheshire
Map 4:E3

BELLE EPOQUE, 60 King Street, WA16 6DT. Tel 01565-633060, www.thebelleepoque.com. An air of faded theatrical grandeur prevails at this 'quaint' restaurant-with-rooms in the centre of a delightful town. It has been owned by the Mooney family for more than three decades; Richard Walker is the manager. It is decorated in an eclectic mix of Venetian glass mosaic floors, marble pillars, Art Nouveau fireplaces, dark oak beams and life-size figurines. Overlooking the roof garden and walled courtyard, bedrooms and bathrooms have a contemporary feel. In the restaurant, chef Gareth Chappell uses local produce in his 'good' French-influenced cooking (farmers and suppliers are credited on the menu). Lounge/bar, restaurant (closed Sun), private dining rooms; roof garden (alfresco dining). Free Wi-Fi. Background music. 7 bedrooms. Per room B&B single £95, double £110–£115. Dinner £30.

25% DISCOUNT VOUCHERS

LANCASTER Lancashire
Map 4:D2

THE ASHTON, Well House, Wyresdale Road, LA1 3JJ. Tel 01524-68460, www.theashtonlancaster.com. Near Williamson Park and the university, this elegant, modern B&B stands in its own well-maintained grounds. Personable host James Gray is a former TV and film set designer; his sandstone Georgian house is impeccably styled. Guests praise the attention to detail: a decanter of port in the bedroom; a daily home-baked treat; much local information provided. Simple meals are served on weekday evenings, by arrangement; on weekends, supper platters of meat, fish and cheese with salad, chutneys and home-baked bread can be taken in the dining room or bedroom. Generous breakfasts; eggs from the house's free-range hens. Lounge, dining room (occasional background music); 1-acre garden. Free Wi-Fi. Parking. Children welcomed (no under-8s on Sat eve). 5 bedrooms (1 on ground floor; some overlook the garden and park). Per room B&B single £100–£120, double £130–£180. Dinner £25.

GREENBANK FARMHOUSE, Abbeystead, LA2 9BA. Tel 01524-792063, www.greenbankfarmhouse.co.uk. 'A special find and a haven for birdwatchers', Sally Tait's small B&B is in a Victorian stone-built house on a former cheese-making farm. Smart, rustic bedrooms have a spacious bathroom and 'excellent' views of the fells, greaves and gills from which the rooms take their name; among the birds that have been spotted are curlews, swifts, herons, pheasants and partridges. Breakfast has local produce, eggs from the house's hens, and 'delicious' home-made bread. Dining room; ½-acre garden. Free Wi-Fi. No background music. Parking. Children welcomed. 8 miles from the city. 3 bedrooms (plus 1 ground-floor studio flat). Per person B&B single £35, double £60–£62.

LAVENHAM Suffolk
Map 2:C5

THE SWAN, High Street, CO10 9QA. Tel 01787-247477, www.theswanat lavenham.co.uk. In the centre of a medieval village, this revitalised hotel (part of the small Suffolk-based TA Hotel Collection) is formed from three timber-framed 15th-century buildings. It has a bright, modern brasserie and an impressive medieval dining room with a minstrels' gallery; characterful bedrooms, some with a four-poster bed and inglenook fireplace, are furnished in country house style. A new spa is due to open in Dec 2014. Justin Kett cooks classic British dishes in the *Gallery* restaurant (no children under 10); informal dining is in the brasserie. Afternoon tea. Lounge, *Airmen's* bar, brasserie, restaurant. Courtyard; small garden. Free Wi-Fi. Occasional background music. Civil wedding licence; private dining/function facilities. Children (early suppers), and dogs (in some rooms) welcomed.

45 bedrooms (some suitable for &). Per room B&B from £195, D,B&B from £254.

LEEK Staffordshire
Map 2:A2

THE THREE HORSESHOES, Buxton Road, Blackshaw Moor, ST13 8TW. Tel 01538-300296, www.3shoesinn.co.uk. Beneath the gritstone outcrops of the Roaches, on the edge of the Peak District national park, this old stone inn has low beamed ceilings and candlelit dark oak furnishings. Owned by Mark and Stephen Kirk, it has been extended to provide a range of accommodation and a number of dining options; a spa extension is planned. 'Excellent' bedrooms are variously decorated in country-cottage style or with a smart, modern look; some superior rooms have a four-poster bed. Steve Kirk cooks modern British food with a Thai influence in an open kitchen in the modern brasserie; traditional pub dishes and popular carvery food can be taken in the original part of the inn. Generous breakfasts. Bar, 2 restaurants, 7 dining areas; patio (alfresco dining); garden. Free Wi-Fi. Background music. Lift. Civil wedding licence; conference facilities; themed events in *Kirk's Restaurant*. Beauty treatments. Parking. Children welcomed (outdoor play area). 2 miles N of town. 26 bedrooms. Per room B&B £95–£170, D,B&B £148.50–£216. Closed Christmas, New Year.

LEICESTER Leicestershire
Map 2:B3

THE BELMONT, De Montfort Street, LE1 7GR. Tel 0116-254 4773, www.belmonthotel.co.uk. In a 'brilliant' location on leafy New Walk, within easy reach of the city, this 'quality' town hotel is formed from a row of Victorian residences. It has been owned by the Bowie family for four generations, with continual refurbishments. Bedrooms are 'modernised in an impeccable and stylish way'; the elegant, contemporary bars and restaurant (serving seasonal modern European food) are popular with locals. Lounge/bar, bar/conservatory, *Windows on New Walk* restaurant (closed Sat lunch, Sun eve), conservatory. Free Wi-Fi. Background music. Lift. Civil wedding licence; function facilities. Parking. Children, and dogs (by arrangement) welcomed. 75 bedrooms (3 family rooms; 1 suitable for &). Per room B&B £69–£149. Dinner £28–£35.

HOTEL MAIYANGO, 13–21 St Nicholas Place, LE1 4LD. Tel 0116-251 8898, www.maiyango.com. Aatin Anadkat's 'different', contemporary hotel is in a 150-year-old former shoe factory near the centre. It has been decorated throughout with bespoke wood furnishings and commissioned artwork; its *Glass Bar*, with floor-to-ceiling windows and a wraparound terrace, has fantastic views of the city centre. Spacious bedrooms have a chic bathroom; they are well equipped with organic tea and coffee, fresh milk, a snack tray and a DVD library. In the informal restaurant (lanterns, cushions, curious booths made of uneven wooden slats), new chef Nick Wilson cooks seasonal modern European dishes using locally sourced ingredients. The *Maiyango Kitchen Deli* around the corner serves 'convenience restaurant food', available to take away. Bar, cocktail lounge, restaurant (closed lunchtime Sun–Tues); terrace. Free

Wi-Fi. Lift. Background music in lobby/Reception area. Function facilities. Cooking and cocktail classes. 14 bedrooms. Room only from £79. Breakfast £7.95–£15. Dinner £32.
25% DISCOUNT VOUCHERS

LEWDOWN Devon
Map 1:C3
LEWTRENCHARD MANOR, nr Okehampton, EX20 4PN. Tel 01566-783222, www.lewtrenchard.co.uk. Set in extensive parkland with streams and ponds, fountains and statuary, this small hotel occupies an 'impressive' Jacobean stone manor house that was once the ancestral home of the Reverend Sabine Baring-Gould, who wrote 'Onward, Christian Soldiers'. It is owned by the Murray family. Inside are ornate ceilings, stained-glass windows and ornamental carving; bedrooms have views of the gardens and surrounding countryside. A recently restored walled garden provides fresh produce for chef Matthew Peryer's modern British menus. Lounge, bar, 2 restaurants (open to non-residents; background music), ballroom. Free Wi-Fi. In-room beauty treatments. 12-acre grounds; croquet. Fishing, clay-pigeon shooting; falconry can be arranged. Children (no under-8s at dinner), and dogs welcomed. 14 bedrooms (4 in courtyard annexe; bridal suite in 2-storey folly; 1 suitable for &). Per room B&B £145–£235, D,B&B £235–£325. 2-night min. stay at weekends May–Oct.
25% DISCOUNT VOUCHERS

LINCOLN Lincolnshire
Map 4:E5
THE CASTLE, Westgate, LN1 3AS. Tel 01522-538801, www.castlehotel.net. In a 'splendid' position in the historic Bailgate area, this refurbished Grade II listed house has 'smart', modern bedrooms with views of the castle walls or the cathedral. 'From our room, we heard the church bells chime.' It is built on the site of the old Roman Forum; guests can reach out and touch the second-century Mint Wall – the outer wall of the old basilica. Chef Mark Cheseldine's 'elegantly presented' modern European cooking is served in the 'charming' panelled restaurant; sandwiches and light meals are taken in the bar. 'Excellent' scrambled eggs at breakfast. 2 small lounges, bar (a popular local), *Reform* restaurant (evenings only; background music). Free Wi-Fi. Massage and beauty treatments. Wedding/function facilities. Parking. Children welcomed. 18 bedrooms (some in attic, some in courtyard; 1 suitable for &); plus 1 apartment. Per room B&B £110–£150, D,B&B £170–£220.

LIVERPOOL Merseyside
Map 4:E2
HARD DAYS NIGHT, Central Buildings, North John Street, L2 6RR. Tel 0151-236 1964, www.harddaysnighthotel.com. Close to the Cavern Club, this Beatles-themed hotel occupies a Grade II listed building fronted by marble columns; inside, there are plenty of original artworks and photographs of the famous four. The modern bedrooms are individually designed, with a monsoon shower in the bathroom; some rooms have a private balcony. Michael Dewey is the manager. Lounge (live music on Fri and Sat nights), *Bar Four* cocktail bar, brasserie, *Blakes* restaurant (open to non-residents; closed Sun, Mon; 2- and 3-course menus; Paul Feery is chef);

art gallery. Free Wi-Fi. Background music. Civil wedding licence; function facilities. Beatles tours can be arranged. 110 bedrooms. Room only from £275. Breakfast £15.95, dinner £14.95.

HEYWOOD HOUSE, 11 Fenwick Street, L2 7LS. Tel 0151-224 1444, www. heywoodhousehotel.co.uk. With 'comfortable' bedrooms and a popular, 'absolutely humming' bar and brasserie, this contemporary hotel has 'a most pleasing and relaxing ambience'. There is 'an emphasis on comfort and service': staff are 'courteous and highly efficient'. Well-equipped bedrooms vary in size; the best have a balcony. 'Quality fare at breakfast and supper.' Free Wi-Fi. Lift. Wedding/function facilities. Discounts for nearby parking. Children welcomed. 35 bedrooms. Room only £89–£209.

HOPE STREET HOTEL, 40 Hope Street, L1 9DA. Tel 0151-709 3000, www. hopestreethotel.co.uk. In the cultural quarter, opposite the Philharmonic Hall, this handsome modern hotel, a former 19th-century coach factory, has exposed brick walls, old beams, and minimalist bedrooms, some with 'fantastic' views of the river, the cathedral or the city skyline. 'We could even see the ferry on the Mersey going to Belfast.' *The London Carriage Works* restaurant has 'delicious' modern international dishes; the residents' lounge has cocktails, sandwiches and sharing plates. Tea and coffee are brought to the table at breakfast; a good variety of hot dishes is cooked to order. 'We enjoyed everything enormously.' Lounge, bar, restaurant; lift; gym, treatment rooms. Free Wi-Fi. Background music. 24-hour room service. Civil wedding licence; function

facilities. Limited parking nearby (£10 charge). Children, and dogs (£30 charge) welcomed. 89 bedrooms (some suitable for ♿). Room only £190–£490. Breakfast £16.50, dinner £17.50–£22.50.

THE NADLER LIVERPOOL, 29 Seel Street, L1 4AU. Tel 0151-705 2626, www.thenadler.com. In a converted print works in the lively Rope Walks area, this 'practical and efficient' hotel (sister to *The Nadler*, London – see Shortlist above) has stylish, good-value rooms, ideal for 'a simple, short stay'. 'Surprisingly quiet' modern bedrooms range from large singles to double-height gallery studios; all have a 'well-equipped' mini-kitchen with a microwave, fridge, sink, kettle, crockery and cutlery. There is no bar or dining room, but a continental breakfast can be ordered in advance; discounts at local restaurants, bars and clubs are available. Free local and national landline calls for 30 minutes per day. Free Wi-Fi. Lounge, meeting room. Background music. Lift. Vending machines. Parking discounts. Children welcomed. 106 bedrooms (some suitable for ♿). Room only from £49. Breakfast £6–£8.50.

LOOE Cornwall
Map 1:D3
TRELASKE HOTEL & RESTAURANT, Polperro Road, PL13 2JS. Tel 01503-262159, www.trelaske.co.uk. Guests return time and again to Hazel Billington and Ross Lewin's 'relaxing' hotel, in a peaceful location two miles outside town. There are 'excellent' views over the gardens to moorland beyond; inside, 'spacious and welcoming' modern bedrooms, each with a balcony or patio, have ample

storage and seating space. Hazel Billington is a warm and attentive host; service is 'consistently good'. Ross Lewin's award-winning, daily-changing menus use freshly caught fish, Cornish-reared meat, and fruit, vegetables and herbs from the hotel's polytunnels. Coastal and woodland walks. 2 lounges, bar/conservatory (background music); terrace (summer barbecues). 4-acre grounds. Free Wi-Fi (in main house only). Wedding/function facilities. Children welcomed (no under-4s in restaurant). Dogs allowed in 2 bedrooms (£6.50 per night). 7 bedrooms (4 in building adjacent to main house). Per room B&B £105–£120, D,B&B £149–£180. Closed Christmas, New Year.

LUDLOW Shropshire
Map 3:C4
HOPTON HOUSE, Hopton Heath Road, SY7 0QD. Tel 01547-530885, www.shropshirebreakfast.co.uk. 'A wonderful and welcoming hideaway' in a rural location, this former granary has been transformed into a 'fabulous' B&B with a modern rustic interior. It is owned by Karen Thorne. Spacious, well-equipped bedrooms have a large bed, comfortable seating, double- or triple-aspect windows, and home-made cake and shortbread; the Paddock Room has a balcony. Supper platters of local cheese, smoked salmon and a deli selection are available by arrangement; BYO wine (glasses and corkscrews supplied). Resident hens supply the eggs for the 'phenomenal' breakfasts, ordered the night before. 'We loved our stay.' Lounge, dining room (background music); 1¾-acre garden. Dogs welcomed (in 1 room only), by arrangement; 2 resident dogs. Free Wi-Fi. 10 miles west

of Ludlow. 3 bedrooms (2 in separate building). Per room B&B £115–£125.
25% DISCOUNT VOUCHERS

SHROPSHIRE HILLS, Aston Munslow, SY7 9ER. Tel 01584-841565, www.shropshirehillsbedandbreakfast.co.uk. In a village in an area of outstanding natural beauty between Wenlock Edge and the Brown Clee, Chris and Linda Baker's B&B is well positioned for walkers on the Shropshire Way. The bedrooms in the modern house, which have a separate entrance, have comfortable seating, a silent fridge, home-made cakes, and overlook beautiful countryside or the garden; alpacas graze in the paddock beyond. Breakfast has fresh fruit, home-made jams and compotes made from fruit in the garden, tomatoes from the greenhouse, eggs from the Bakers' own chickens, and local produce. There is a boot room and changing and drying facilities for walkers and cyclists. Lounge/breakfast room; terrace with table and chairs; 2-acre garden. Free Wi-Fi. No background music. 8 miles from Ludlow. 3 bedrooms. Per room B&B single from £85, double £95–£115. Closed Nov–Mar.

LUPTON Cumbria
Map 4: inset C2
THE PLOUGH, Cow Brow, LA6 1PJ. Tel 015395-67700, www.theploughatlupton.co.uk. 'An attractive place to eat and stay', this painstakingly refurbished 18th-century coaching inn is owned by Richard Rose, proprietor of *The Punch Bowl Inn* at Crosthwaite (see Shortlist above). Jon Simmons is the manager. 'The sense of quality is tangible'. Public rooms have oak beams, antique

furniture, comfortable sofas and wood-burning stoves; upstairs, light and airy bedrooms have a large bathroom (some with a roll-top bath). Hutton, a two-bedroom suite, was recently added. British dishes and a selection of sharing platters (Fisherman's, Ploughman's and Gardener's) are served in the restaurant adjoining the bar. Lounge, bar, restaurant; terrace; garden. Free Wi-Fi (signal variable). Background music. Civil wedding licence. Children, and dogs (in 1 room only) welcomed. 6 bedrooms. Per room B&B £115–£195. Dinner £24.

LYNMOUTH Devon
Map 1:B4

SHELLEY'S, 8 Watersmeet Road, E35 6EP. Tel 01598-753219, www.shelleyshotel. co.uk. In the summer of 1812, when this 18th-century house was a humble cottage, Percy Bysshe Shelley came here with his 16-year-old bride, Harriet, for their honeymoon. Today, Jane Becker and Richard Briden offer informal B&B accommodation in pristine bedrooms, some with a private balcony. Praiseworthy breakfasts are taken in the conservatory, which has fine views over Lynmouth Bay. A short walk to the harbour. Lounge, bar, conservatory breakfast room. Free Wi-Fi. No background music. 11 bedrooms (1 on ground floor). Per room B&B £85–£125. Closed Mar/Apr, Nov, Christmas, New Year.

LYNTON Devon
Map 1:B4

LYNTON COTTAGE, North Walk, EX35 6ED. Tel 01598-752342, www. lyntoncottage.com. High on a cliff-top along the North Devon Coastal Path,

this small hotel has breathtaking views over Lynmouth Bay and the Bristol Channel. Bill and Cita Garfield, who took over in 2013, have upgraded the spacious bedrooms (most with sea views). Home-cooked dinners, with an emphasis on fish and game, are served between 6 pm and 7.30 pm; traditional English cream teas and light lunches can be taken on the terrace from Easter till the end of summer (open to non-residents). Lounge, bar, restaurant (background music); terrace; 2-acre garden. Free Wi-Fi. Parking. Children welcomed (in some rooms only). 16 bedrooms. Per room B&B £75–£139. Dinner £27. Closed 8 Dec–8 Jan. 2-night min. stay in peak season.

LYTHAM Lancashire
Map 4:D2

THE ROOMS, 35 Church Road, FY8 5LL. Tel 01253-736000, www. theroomslytham.com. Within close walking distance of shops, restaurants and the sea, Jackie and Andy Baker's modern B&B has 'beautifully fitted' rooms equipped with up-to-date technology (digital radio, iPod docking station, flat-screen TV). Andy Baker is 'a helpful host' with much local knowledge (though some guests have found that he is not always on site). Breakfast, served in the walled garden in good weather, has home-made smoothies, locally baked bread, sausages from the butcher across the street, and 'a large choice' of cooked dishes; Buck's Fizz on weekends. Breakfast room (background TV). Free Wi-Fi. No background music. Children welcomed. 5 bedrooms ('lots of stairs'), plus 2-bed serviced apartment. Per room B&B single £95–£125, double £125–£160.

MALVERN Worcestershire
Map 3:D5

THE OLD RECTORY, Cradley,
WR13 5LQ. Tel 01886-880109,
www.oldrectorycradley.com. At the foot
of the Malvern hills, this fine Georgian
house is run as an elegant B&B by Claire
and John Dawkins. 'A special place; we
were made to feel welcome.' The well-
appointed rooms have antiques, original
art and fresh flowers; the drawing room
has a large chess set and an open fire in
cool weather. A monthly-changing
dinner menu uses much home-grown
produce and ingredients from local
suppliers; breakfast has home-made
jams and marmalade, and locally baked
bread. Good walks from the door; lifts
are offered to and from the Malvern
hills. Packed lunches available. Drawing
room, library, morning room, dining
room. 1-acre garden; croquet, boules.
Free Wi-Fi. No background music.
Parking. Well-behaved children and
dogs welcomed. 4 bedrooms. Per room
B&B single from £100, double from
£130. Dinner £26.50–£37.50.

MANCHESTER
Map 4:E3

DIDSBURY HOUSE, Didsbury Park,
Didsbury Village, M20 5LJ. Tel 0161-
448 2200, www.didsburyhouse.co.uk.
In a leafy suburb within easy reach of
the city centre, this Victorian villa hosts
a 'friendly' contemporary hotel (part of
the Eclectic Hotel Collection; see *Eleven
Didsbury Park*, below). There are deep
armchairs in the lounge overlooking the
lawn; the pretty terrace next to the bar is
ideal for alfresco drinks. Individually
styled, 'comfortable' bedrooms range
from snug Classic rooms to an indulgent
loft suite with exposed beams and twin

cast iron roll-top baths. Reached by a
'quick train' from East Didsbury;
otherwise, 'a cab ride from the centre
late at night'. 'Pleasant walks' in the
botanical gardens, nearby. 2 lounges,
bar, breakfast room; meeting room; spa;
gym; walled terrace with water feature.
Free Wi-Fi. 'Chill-out' background
music. Exclusive use for weddings/
functions. Children welcomed. 27
bedrooms. Room only £144–£264.
Breakfast £13.50–£15.50.

ELEVEN DIDSBURY PARK, 11 Didsbury
Park, Didsbury Village, M20 5LH. Tel
0161-448 7711, www.elevendidsbury
park.com. With loungers, a hammock
and a croquet set in its pretty garden,
there is a laid-back atmosphere at this
stylish modern hotel (Eclectic Hotel
Collection), in a fashionable urban
village near the city centre. The well-
appointed bedrooms (some are compact)
have many thoughtful touches: books,
fresh milk on the butler tray, candles
and matches by the bath; one large room
has a private canopied terrace. Good
breakfasts cooked to order. Convenient
for the airport (ten minutes' drive).
2 lounge/bars (background music);
veranda; large walled garden. Free
Wi-Fi. Gym; treatment room.
Conference facilities. Parking. Children
and dogs welcomed. 20 bedrooms
(1, on ground floor, suitable for &).
Room only £142–£260. Breakfast
£13.50–£15.50.

VELVET, 2 Canal Street, M1 3HE. Tel
0161-236 9003, www.velvetmanchester.
com. In a vibrant neighbourhood with
much nightlife, this modern hotel has
friendly staff, a popular bar and
decadently furnished bedrooms

decorated with artwork and striking wallpaper (some erotic). Bathrooms are well equipped with bathrobes and slippers, steam-free mirrors, automatic lighting; a welcome tray in the bedroom includes fresh fruit and a biscuit barrel. A glass fish tank is set into the stairs leading to the basement restaurant, where a straightforward menu of comfort food, pizzas, salads and sharing plates is served until late. Bar (DJs on Fri and Sat nights; noise may affect some rooms), restaurant (alfresco dining on front terrace; background music). Free Wi-Fi. Lift. Within easy reach of the city centre and railway station. Discounted car park. Children welcomed. 19 bedrooms. Room only £99–£305. Breakfast £9.50–£13.50, dinner £15.95 (two courses, 4 pm–7 pm).

MARCHAM Oxfordshire
Map 2:C2

B&B RAFTERS, Abingdon Road, OX13 6NU. Tel 01865-391298, www. bnb-rafters.co.uk. Sigrid Grawert runs her B&B in a half-timbered house on the edge of a village eight miles south of Oxford. Bedrooms are decorated in muted tones, with feature wallpaper, colourful cushions and double-glazed windows; they have fresh flowers, a DVD-player, a DAB radio and an iPod docking station. A single room has a waterbed. Breakfast, taken at a communal table, has freshly squeezed orange juice, whisky porridge, home-baked bread, and home-made jams and marmalades; other ingredients come from local farms and shops. Vegetarian and special diets catered for. Lounge, breakfast room; garden. Free Wi-Fi. No background music. Parking. 4 bedrooms. Per person B&B £57–£119.

MARGATE Kent
Map 2:D5

THE READING ROOMS, 31 Hawley Square, CT9 1PH. Tel 01843-225166, www.thereadingroomsmargate.co.uk. Owners Louise Oldfield and Liam Nabb have restored their stylish town house with an air of 'dilapidated grandeur'. Intricate plasterwork has been revealed, a mantelpiece or mirror leans artfully; there are distressed walls, wooden floors, original shutters and antiques. Each comfortable, white-painted bedroom takes up an entire floor and has crisp bedlinen on a large bed; bathrooms are 'stunning – the size of a bedroom', with a roll-top bath, walk-in shower, luxury toiletries and bathrobes. Breakfast from an extensive choice is brought to the room and 'beautifully' served: 'As good as any I have eaten.' On a Georgian square; the Turner Contemporary art gallery, the old town and the beach are all nearby. Free Wi-Fi. No background music. 3 bedrooms. Per room B&B £160–£180.

SANDS HOTEL, Marine Drive, CT9 1DH. Tel 01843-228228, www.sandshotelmargate.co.uk. On the seafront, this Victorian hotel was 'smartly renovated' in 2013 by Nick and Karen Conington, in colours inspired by the sea and the sky. Ornate mirrors and glitzy lamps add 'a touch of glamour' to calming bedrooms; many have an ironwork balcony with sweeping views over Margate Sands. 'Pretty good bathrooms, too.' Tina Arnold is the manager. The glass-fronted *Bay* restaurant is 'a fusion of classic and contemporary elements': columns and cornices are cleverly lit; alcoves are enlivened with semi-abstract Turnerish seascapes by artist Paul Bennett. 'We enjoyed it all and wouldn't fault it.' Background music. Free Wi-Fi. Limited parking nearby. Bar, restaurant, terrace (alfresco dining); ice cream parlour. Children welcomed (sofa beds). 20 bedrooms (1 suitable for &). Per room B&B £130–£190. Dinner £32.

MATLOCK Derbyshire
Map 3:A6
MANOR FARM, Dethick, DE4 5GG. Tel 01629-534302, www.manorfarmdethick. co.uk. In a peaceful hamlet with three farms, a church and plenty of winding country lanes, this historic Grade II* listed stone house is 'excellently' run as a B&B by 'welcoming and friendly' hosts Gilly and Simon Groom. It was once the home of Sir Anthony Babington, who in 1586 conspired to assassinate Queen Elizabeth; today, more tranquil activities take place in the cosy sitting rooms and country-style bedrooms, each full of character with beams, old stonework or buttresses and corbels. Organic breakfasts are served on a large refectory table in the original Tudor kitchen; all diets are catered for. On an attractive, 'user-friendly' farm. Sitting rooms (TV, games), breakfast room. Free Wi-Fi. No background music. Drying facilities. Parking; bike/motorcycle storage. Children over 6 welcomed. 2½ miles E of Matlock; collection from railway/bus station can be arranged. 4 bedrooms (1 on ground floor). Per room B&B from £85. 2-night min. stay on Sat, Apr–Oct.

MELTON MOWBRAY Leicestershire
Map 2:A3
SYSONBY KNOLL, Asfordby Road, LE13 0HP. Tel 01664-563563, www.sysonby. com. With 'fine' views of the gardens and the River Eye, this traditional hotel and restaurant, in an extended, brick-built Edwardian house, has been owned and run by the same family since 1965. At the helm today are 'friendly and flexible' hosts Jenny and Gavin Howling; Vicky Wilkin is the manager. Bedrooms vary in size; some are large enough for a family. 'Meals are impeccable, with more-than-generous servings, including the local Stilton cheese.' Sue Meaking is chef. Complimentary fishing for guests (tackle available to borrow). Good walks nearby. Lounge, bar, restaurant. Free Wi-Fi. Background music. 4½-acre gardens and meadow. Parking. Children and dogs welcomed (resident dog). 30 bedrooms (some on ground floor; some in neighbouring annexe; ramp). Per room B&B £81–£135, D,B&B £98.50–£170. Closed Christmas.

MEVAGISSEY Cornwall
Map 1:D2
TREVALSA COURT, School Hill, PL26 6TH. Tel 01726-842468, www.trevalsa-hotel.co.uk. Liked for a lack of 'pretentious attitude', this 'attractive' cliff-top Arts and Crafts house is owned by Susan and John Gladwin, who run it as a small hotel with 'pleasant, helpful' staff. Landscaped subtropical gardens (with a summer house) lead to the Coastal Path; a steep staircase takes guests to a secluded sandy beach. Most of the individually styled bedrooms have 'great' sea views; there are books and games in the sitting room, and a roaring fire in cold weather. Drinks can be taken on a terrace overlooking the sea. Chef Adam Cawood sources local, sustainable produce for menus served in the oak-panelled dining room (light jazz background music). Lounge,

bar, restaurant; 2-acre garden. Free Wi-Fi. Children welcomed, dogs by arrangement. 15 bedrooms (3 on ground floor; family suite accessed from outside). Per room B&B single £60–£105, double £110–£250, D,B&B single £95, double £160–£300. Closed Dec–mid-Feb.
25% DISCOUNT VOUCHERS

MILLOM Cumbria
Map 4: inset C2
BROADGATE HOUSE, Broadgate, Thwaites, LA18 5JZ. Tel 01229-716295, www.broadgate-house.co.uk. Diana Lewthwaite provides peaceful guest house accommodation in her fine Georgian house, which has been in her family for almost 200 years. It is within the Lake District national park, and has panoramic views across the Duddon estuary. The grand public rooms have antique furniture, sumptuous fabrics and an original fireplace; spacious bedrooms have a separate bathroom with a throne loo and freestanding bath. The two-acre grounds are designed as a series of 'garden rooms', with a walled garden, terraces, a croquet lawn and an 'oasis' with a palm tree. Sitting room (wood-burning stove), dining room, breakfast room. Free Wi-Fi. No background music. 3 miles W of Broughton-in-Furness; beaches nearby. 5 bedrooms. Per room B&B single £55, double £90. Dinner (by arrangement) £25. Closed Christmas.

MISTLEY Essex
Map 2:C5
THE MISTLEY THORN, High Street, CO11 1HE. Tel 01206-392821, www.mistleythorn.co.uk. In the centre of an 'interesting' coastal village on the River Stour, this informal restaurant-with-

rooms is run by chef/proprietor Sherri Singleton. The former 18th-century coaching inn has a congenial atmosphere: thoughtfully equipped bedrooms (some with traffic noise) have home-made biscuits. 'Unpretentious' dinners are 'very good'; the restaurant is popular with locals at Sunday lunch. Good base for exploring Constable Country. Sherri Singleton runs cookery workshops at the *Mistley Kitchen*, next door. Small sitting area, bar, restaurant (background music); ramp. Free Wi-Fi. Children, and 'well-mannered' dogs (£5 per night charge) welcomed. 11 bedrooms (3 in annexe). Per room B&B £75–£145, D,B&B £125–£190.

MORETON-IN-MARSH
Gloucestershire
Map 3:D6
THE OLD SCHOOL, Little Compton, GL56 0SL. Tel 01608-674588, www.theoldschoolbedandbreakfast.com. Wendy Veale, a food writer and stylist, has converted this Victorian stone-built schoolhouse to provide homely B&B accommodation and rather a lot of treats. She makes her own cakes, cookies and preserves wherever possible; picnic hampers, supper trays and four-course dinners, made with much locally sourced produce, are available by arrangement. Bedrooms have fresh flowers, fresh milk, bathrobes, a radio, access to a DVD library. Drinks may be taken in the beamed sitting room, a handsome space with a striking church-style window. Vaulted drawing room, dining room (BYO bottle at dinner); boot room. Free Wi-Fi (computer available). No background music. Garden (pergolas, patios, fish pond, orchard; bantam hens; pet rabbits, cat).

4 bedrooms (1 on ground floor). Per person B&B £60–£150. 2-night min. stay at weekends. Dinner £32.

MOULTON Suffolk
Map 2:B4
THE PACKHORSE INN, Bridge Street, CB8 8SP. Tel 01638-751818, www.thepackhorseinn.com. There are country walks from the door of this stylishly revitalised former pub, in a rural location close to Newmarket. It is managed by Hayley Lee and her husband, Chris, the chef, for Philip Turner's Chestnut Inns. Spacious, elegantly furnished bedrooms overlook the terraced gardens or the village green; three have a large bath. A new ground-floor room is planned. Chris Lee cooks traditional pub grub as well as more exotic dishes using local produce, served in the informal restaurant. Bar, restaurant; function room; large courtyard. Free Wi-Fi. Occasional background music. Children (cots, extra beds, £10 per night), and dogs (in some rooms, £10 per night) welcomed. 4 bedrooms. Per room B&B single £85–£100 (Sun–Thurs), double £100–£175. Dinner £35.

MULLION Cornwall
Map 1:E2
POLURRIAN BAY HOTEL, Helston, TR12 7EN. Tel 01326-240421, www.polurrianhotel.com. Perched on a cliff above a sandy bay on the Lizard peninsula, this family-friendly hotel (part of Nigel Chapman's Luxury Family Hotels group) has 'glorious' views of the coastline from a glass-fronted lounge, and from the 'well-appointed, comfortable' bedrooms. There are 'excellent' facilities for all ages: books and board games, cream teas and cocktails, a games room and a cinema. The 12 acres of landscaped gardens have plenty of space and diversions: indoor and (seasonal) outdoor pools, a hot tub, a gym and spa (treatments); tennis courts, a sports field; an adventure playground and more. 6 lounges, dining room (background music), cinema; terrace. The Den (nursery for children 3 months–8 years old); The Blue Room (older children; video games, pool, table football). Free Wi-Fi. Civil wedding licence; function facilities. Children (baby equipment), and dogs (£10 per night) welcomed. 41 bedrooms (some on ground floor). Per room B&B £120–£520, D,B&B £180–£590. 2-night min. stay in peak season.

NEWBY BRIDGE Cumbria
Map 4: inset C2
THE SWAN HOTEL & SPA, LA12 8NB. Tel 015395-31681, www.swanhotel.com. Popular with boating visitors, this whitewashed 17th-century coaching inn stands by a five-arch bridge on the banks of the River Leven, on the southern tip of Lake Windermere. It has been renovated by the Bardsley family, who have complemented its original features with an imaginative modern look. Sarah Gibbs is the manager. Families are welcomed: children have an adventure playground, a nature trail, games and books; there are complimentary milk and biscuits before bedtime. Bedrooms have feature wallpaper, and garden or river views. Sitting room, library, bar, *River Room* restaurant, breakfast room; terrace. Free Wi-Fi. Background music. Spa (treatments), indoor pool, hot tub, sauna, steam room; gym. Civil wedding

licence; function facilities. Parking; mooring. Children welcomed. 51 bedrooms (some interconnecting). Per room B&B £99–£119. 2-night min. stay on bank holiday weekends. Dinner £30.

NEWCASTLE UPON TYNE Tyne and Wear
Map 4:B4
THE TOWNHOUSE, 1 West Avenue, Gosforth, NE3 4ES. Tel 0191-285 6812, www.thetownhousehotel.co.uk. In a quiet residential neighbourhood, Cathy Knox runs her B&B in this elegant Victorian town house, a short metro ride from the centre. Individually designed bedrooms (some may be snug) are decorated 'with flair'; each has a limestone bathroom or wet room. 'Straightforward' home-cooked food is served in the small café; 'generous and varied' breakfasts. Breakfast room (newspapers, morning TV), café (afternoon teas with home-made scones and cakes; open until 6 pm; 4 pm on Sun). Free Wi-Fi. Background music. Parking permits available (£7). Children, and dogs (by arrangement) welcomed. 10 bedrooms. Per room B&B £95–£150.

NEWENT Gloucestershire
Map 3:D5
THREE CHOIRS VINEYARDS, Newent GL18 1LS. Tel 01531-890223, www.three-choirs-vineyards.co.uk. Guests may meander through 70 acres of cultivated vines at this restaurant-with-rooms on an award-winning vineyard (one of the largest in Britain). Guided tours take in the history and processes of wine-making, with opportunities to taste the results. Bedrooms are in a single-storey block

beside the restaurant; each has French doors opening on to a small private patio. Five hundred yards from the main building, three rooms are in lodges among the vines, with views on a string of ponds (continental breakfast hampers are delivered to the room). In the restaurant overlooking the vine-clad valley, chef Siobhan Hartley serves modern European dishes; her seasonal menus feature local produce and British cheeses. Lounge, restaurant (occasional background music), wine shop. Free Wi-Fi (in public areas). 11 bedrooms (all on ground floor, 1 suitable for &). Per room B&B £135–£185, D,B&B £225–£265. Closed 23–26 Dec.

NEWQUAY Cornwall
Map 1:D2
THE HEADLAND HOTEL, Headland Road, TR7 1EW. Tel 01637-872211, www.headlandhotel.co.uk. On a jutting headland, this imposing red brick Victorian hotel has dramatic views over Fistral Bay. Continual improvements have been made by the Armstrong family, who have owned it for three decades: a new wellness area was recently added (spa pool, sauna, Cornish salt steam room, aromatherapy showers), and further spa facilities are planned. Darryl Redburn is the manager. Bedrooms are decorated in a mix of traditional and contemporary styles; many have sea views. Lounges, bar, 2 restaurants; *The Terrace* (background music; alfresco dining; Nick Osborne is chef); veranda. Free Wi-Fi. 10-acre grounds. Table tennis; 2 heated swimming pools (indoor and outdoor); croquet; 3 tennis courts; putting, boules; on-site surf school. Civil wedding licence; conference/event

facilities. Children welcomed (bunk beds; entertainment). Dogs welcomed (£15 per night charge). 96 bedrooms (12 suites; 1 room suitable for ♿; plus 40 self-catering cottages in the grounds). Per room B&B £79–£389, D,B&B £129–£439.

LEWINNICK LODGE, Pentire Headland, TR7 1QD. Tel 01637-878117, www.lewinnicklodge.co.uk. Above a stylish open-plan restaurant and bar, on the edge of a rocky headland, Pete and Jacqui Fair have added ten ultra-modern bedrooms, all with stunning coastline or promontory vistas. Decorated in soothing colours and natural materials (mohair, plush velvet and aged leather), rooms have a large bed, local artwork and home-made biscuits; bathrooms, some with a view, have a power shower and slipper bath. Rich Humphries cooks Cornish produce, fish and seafood in the informal restaurant; floor-to-ceiling windows open on to a large decked terrace jutting over the sea. Good walks from the door; Fistral Beach is nearby. Bar, restaurant; 'gentle' background music. Free Wi-Fi. In-room treatments. Parking. Children, and dogs (in some rooms) by arrangement. 10 bedrooms (1 family suite). Per room B&B £130–£230. Dinner £27.

NEWTON ABBOT Devon
Map 1:D4
THE ROCK INN, Haytor Vale, TQ13 9XP. Tel 01364-661305, www.rock-inn.co.uk. 'We have stayed in many more expensive hotels that were not half so good as this one.' In a hamlet below Haytor Rocks, just inside Dartmoor national park, this 'charming' country

inn has been welcoming travellers since the 18th century. It is run by the Graves family; the staff are 'very attentive and friendly, without being overwhelming'. All of the traditionally furnished bedrooms have views of the gardens or moor. 'Our beautiful room, Sheila's Cottage, had an oak four-poster bed, antique furniture and a delightful sitting area.' 'Seriously good' traditional English fare, with imaginative touches, is served in the bar with a log fire, or in cosy dining areas. Guests can walk straight into the wilderness from the front door. Lounge (DVDs, books), bar, restaurant (open to non-residents). Large garden with tables and seating. Free Wi-Fi in public areas. No background music. Parking. Children, and dogs (in some rooms) welcomed. 9 bedrooms. Per room B&B £95–£160, D,B&B £155–£220.

NORTHALLERTON North Yorkshire
Map 4:C4
CLEVELAND TONTINE, Staddlebridge, DL6 3JB. Tel 01609-882671, www.theclevelandtontine.co.uk. Once a resting place for weary travellers and mail coaches on the Sunderland to London route in the early 1800s, this stone-built Victorian house (formerly named *McCoys at the Tontine*) has since undergone a striking transformation. It is owned by Charles and Angela Tompkins, who undertook the massive renovation; Adam Dyke is the manager. The small hotel is colourfully decorated throughout, with Art Deco flourishes; sophisticated, air-conditioned bedrooms have eye-catching wallpaper, a stylish bed, and a bathroom with underfloor heating, bathrobes and slippers.

Informal dining is in the intimate, candlelit bistro, with its original vaulted ceiling and impressive stone fireplace, or in the airy conservatory, which leads directly to the gardens. Chef James Cooper cooks classic French dishes with local ingredients and an English twist. Yorkshire breakfasts. On the western edge of the North York Moors national park, close to the A19. Lounge, bar, bistro. Free Wi-Fi. Background music. Private dining. Room service. Function facilities. Parking. Children welcomed. 7 bedrooms. Per room B&B single from £115, double £130–£190.

NORWICH Norfolk
Map 2:B5
NORFOLK MEAD, Church Loke, Coltishall, NR12 7DN. Tel 01603-737531, www.norfolkmead.co.uk. Standing in pretty gardens stretching down to the River Bure, this Georgian merchant's house is in a 'near-perfect' position. It is owned by James Holliday and Anna Duttson. The smart, modern bedrooms are individually designed; larger rooms in the cottage and summer house accommodate families and larger parties. In the restaurant overlooking the garden and river, Anna Duttson cooks modern British menus, inspired by locally sourced produce; afternoon tea and aperitifs may be taken in the walled garden in fine weather. Lounge, bar, snug, restaurant; background music; private dining. Free Wi-Fi. Walled garden; fishing lake (swans, geese); off-river mooring. Small conference/wedding facilities. Day boating trips arranged. Children, and dogs (in some rooms; £15 per night charge) welcomed. 7 miles NE of Norwich. 13 bedrooms (some in cottage

and summer house). Per room B&B £130–£185. Dinner £26.50–£32.

OLD HUNSTANTON Norfolk
Map 2:A5
THE NEPTUNE, 85 Old Hunstanton Road, PE36 6HZ. Tel 01485-532122, www.theneptune.co.uk. A short stroll from the sea, this former 18th-century inn has a cosy atmosphere, with low doors and many steps along narrow corridors. It is run as a restaurant-with-rooms by *Michelin*-starred chef/patron Ken Mengeolles and his wife, Jacki, a 'friendly and professional' front-of-house. Light, bright bedrooms are 'nicely done up', seaside style; some bathrooms are small. Pre-dinner drinks and 'delicious' canapés are taken in the bar/lounge area (flagstone floor, wicker seating, subdued lighting). 'Really lovely' food; a 9-course tasting menu is available. 'Exemplary' breakfasts are served at the table. Bar (background jazz), restaurant (closed Mon). Free Wi-Fi. Parking. 5 bedrooms. Per person B&B £60–£75, D,B&B £105–£120. Closed 2 weeks in Nov, 3 weeks in Jan.

OUNDLE Northamptonshire
Map 2:B3
LOWER FARM, Main Street, Barnwell, PE8 5PU. Tel 01832-273220, www.lower-farm.co.uk. On a small arable farm on the edge of a pretty village, this 'excellent' B&B is run along green lines; there are photovoltaic panels, under-floor heating, low-energy lighting and rainwater harvesting. Caroline Marriott is the 'friendly and accommodating hostess'; husband, John, and his brother manage the farm, which has been in the Marriott family since the 1920s. Arranged around a central courtyard,

modern rooms, in converted stables and a former milking parlour, are 'really nice'. Copious farmhouse breakfasts include a steak-and-eggs special. Plenty of footpaths and cycleways in the area. Breakfast room (background radio/CDs); courtyard garden with seating. Free Wi-Fi; no mobile phone signal. Parking. Children, and dogs (in some rooms) welcomed. 3 miles from Oundle. 10 bedrooms (on ground floor; family rooms; 1 suitable for &.). Per person B&B from £45.
25% DISCOUNT VOUCHERS

OXFORD Oxfordshire
Map 2:C2
THE BELL AT HAMPTON POYLE,
11 Oxford Road, Hampton Poyle, OX5 2QD. Tel 01865-376242, www.thebelloxford.co.uk. Dating, in part, from the mid-1700s, George Dailey's welcoming roadside pub is in a small village close to Oxford. It has cosy snugs, flagstone floors, beams, leather seating and a large log fire. Light-filled bedrooms are decorated in soft tones, with pale wood furnishing. Friendly staff serve seafood, locally sourced meats, and pizzas cooked in a wood-burning oven; Nick Anderson is chef. 2 bars (background music), library (for private parties), restaurant; terrace. Free Wi-Fi. Wedding facilities. Parking. Children, and dogs (in 1 bedroom) welcomed. 4 miles N of Oxford. 9 bedrooms (1 on ground floor). Per room B&B (continental) single £96–£135, double £120–£155. Dinner £30.

BURLINGTON HOUSE, 374 Banbury Road, OX2 7PP. Tel 01865-513513, www.burlington-hotel-oxford.co.uk. North of Summertown, this sympathetically modernised Victorian merchant's house is run as a 'cheerfully' decorated B&B. Nes Saini is the 'extremely efficient' manager. In the main house and around the courtyard, snug bedrooms have striking wallpaper, coordinating fabrics and triple-glazed windows. There are home-made yogurt, granola and muesli, and 'excellent' home-baked bread at breakfast. In a suburb 10 minutes outside the city; frequent buses into the centre. Sitting room, breakfast room; small Japanese garden. Free Wi-Fi. No background music. Limited parking. 12 bedrooms (4 on ground floor; 2 in courtyard). Per room B&B £91–£125. Closed Christmas, New Year.

VANBRUGH HOUSE HOTEL, 20–24 St Michael's Street, OX1 2EB. Tel 01865-44622, www.vanbrughhousehotel.co.uk. In the heart of Oxford, this impeccably designed hotel (part of Sojourn Hotels; managed by David Robinson) is on a quiet side street near the Oxford Union. It is formed from two centuries-old buildings. The handsome bedrooms are individually styled along three themes – Georgian, Eclectic, and Arts and Crafts; each has a fireplace, hand-crafted furniture and a media hub. The Vicarage Suite and Nicholas Hawksmoor Room have a private garden and terrace area. Lunch, dinner and pre-theatre brasserie menus are served in *Vanbrugh Vaults*, where remains of the old city walls can be seen; afternoon tea, canapés and aperitifs are taken in the elegant drawing room or on the sunken terrace with its 'secret' garden. Drawing room, bar, restaurant. Free Wi-Fi. No background music. Park and Ride recommended. 22

bedrooms. Per room B&B £135–£205, D,B&B £175–£245. 2-night min. stay at weekend.

PADSTOW Cornwall
Map 1:D2

TREANN HOUSE, 24 Dennis Road, Barton, PL28 8DE. Tel 01841-533855, www.treannhouse.com. Just outside the town, Emma and Paul Caddis have renovated their Edwardian house, and filled it with a mix of antique, vintage and contemporary furnishings. B&B accommodation is in charming rooms well stocked with complimentary wine and nibbles; one has a private balcony for alfresco breakfasts. Guests are offered afternoon tea with home-made cake on arrival; the breakfast menu includes sweet and savoury pancakes, and marmalade and jams made from garden fruits. The comfortable sitting room has books, magazines, games, DVDs and an open fire in cool weather; wonderful views over the Camel Estuary. Sitting room, dining room (background music); small garden. Free Wi-Fi. Parking. Notable restaurants nearby. 3 bedrooms. Per room B&B £100–£130. Closed Dec–Mar (open New Year).

PENRITH Cumbria
Map 4: inset C2

WESTMORLAND HOTEL, nr Orton, CA10 3SB. Tel 01539-624351, www. westmorlandhotel.com. 'Quiet and peaceful, with superb views of the fells', the Dunning family's modern hotel serves as an 'excellent, no-fuss stop-over' for trips to and from Scotland, or as a base for touring that side of the Lakes. It is situated off the M6, between junctions 38 and 39, part of the Tebay Motorway Services site; Ken Kerr is the manager.

Contemporary interiors are mixed with traditional materials; bathrooms have locally made organic toiletries. The restaurant serves 'well-cooked' rustic British dishes, particularly beef and lamb from the family's farm, less than a mile away. An on-site farm shop sells food from local producers. Lounge, bar (log fires), dining room. Free Wi-Fi. 'Unobtrusive' background music. Civil wedding licence; function/conference facilities. Children and dogs welcomed. 51 bedrooms (some family rooms; 1 suitable for &). Per room B&B single £65–£92, double £70–£115. Dinner £27. **25% DISCOUNT VOUCHERS**

PENZANCE Cornwall
Map 1:E1

ARTIST RESIDENCE, 20 Chapel Street, TR18 4AW. Tel 01736-365664, www. artistresidence.co.uk. Lively and bright, the eclectic interior of this Grade II listed 17th-century Georgian house is a visual feast. Justin Salisbury and Charlotte Newey are the owners; Jason Clark manages, with a friendly, helpful team. The bedrooms have been individually designed and decorated by Cornish and British artists: some have a street-art mural, others are painted in pastel seascapes, or have a vintage theme. Varied breakfasts are taken in a cheery room on the ground floor, with mismatched furniture and a vintage radiogram; original artworks, displayed on the walls, are available for purchase. Close to the seafront, town and railway station. Lounge/breakfast room. Small courtyard garden. Occasional background music. Free Wi-Fi. Children (cots), and dogs (in some rooms) welcomed. 13 bedrooms (1 family room). Per room B&B £60–£150.

PICKERING North Yorkshire
Map 4:D4

THE WHITE SWAN, Market Place,
YO18 7AA. Tel 01751-472288,
www.white-swan.co.uk. On the main
street of a 'nice old market town', this
16th-century former coaching inn is a
hub of community life. It is managed
by Catherine Feather for Victor and
Marion Buchanan, who have owned the
inn for 29 years. On the first and second
floors of the main building, bedrooms
are traditionally styled; more modern
rooms are in the *Hideaway*, the converted
stables across the open courtyard. Hotel
guests have use of the *Bothy*, a converted
barn with sofas, a wood-burning stove,
complimentary tea, coffee and biscuits,
newspapers and magazines, and a
television; in the cosy restaurant, long-
serving chef Darren Clemmit serves
'honest food'. Children are well catered
for with special menus, toys, board
games and colouring pens. Yorkshire
breakfasts. Lounge, bar, bothy,
restaurant; private dining rooms. Small
terrace; 1½-acre grounds. Free Wi-Fi.
No background music. Conference/
meeting facilities. Children (early suppers,
cots, baby monitors), and dogs (in some
annexe rooms) welcomed. 21 bedrooms
(9 in annexe, on ground floor). Per room
B&B single £119–£159, double £149–
£189. D,B&B £149–£249 per person.

PRESTON Lancashire
Map 4:D2

BARTON GRANGE HOTEL, 746–768
Garstang Road, Barton, PR3 5AA. Tel
01772-862551, www.bartongrangehotel.
co.uk. Built in 1900 as the country home
of a cotton mill owner, this old manor
house is today a much-expanded,
modernised hotel with a spa. It has been
run by the Topping family for more
than 60 years; Guy Topping is now
in charge. Well-equipped modern
bedrooms, many recently refurbished,
are decorated with lively colours;
executive and superior rooms have a
coffee machine. Chef Paul Jobling cooks
charcoal-grilled steaks and seasonal
dishes in the *Walled Garden* bistro;
drinks are taken in the oak-panelled
lounge, with a cosy fire in winter. Buffet
breakfasts. 2 lounges, bistro/wine bar;
private dining. Free Wi-Fi. Background
music. Leisure centre (indoor pool,
sauna; gym). Pool/bar billiards. Civil
wedding licence; conference facilities.
A few minutes' drive from the M6.
51 bedrooms (8 in cottage in the
grounds; 1 suitable for &). Per room
B&B £87–£142, D,B&B £112–£167.

ROMSEY Hampshire
Map 2:E2

THE WHITE HORSE, Market Place,
SO51 8ZJ. Tel 01794-512431, www.
thewhitehorseromsey.co.uk. 'Slap bang'
in the centre of a popular and prosperous
market town, this refurbished medieval
coaching inn has an equine theme:
there is hunting-scene wallpaper in the
Reception area; bedrooms are named
after well-known racehorses. The
Tudor lounge has exposed timbers
and leather seating, board games and
newspapers, and a cheery stove in the
hearth; it is a 'cosy and appealing'
setting for afternoon tea. Overlooking
the courtyard (ideal for alfresco dining),
the brasserie is 'a lovely place to eat –
restful but interesting'. Chef Chris
Rock's modern British menu is 'very
nicely presented'; 'I could have chosen
more or less anything off it quite
happily.' 2 sitting rooms, *Silks* bar and

brasserie; courtyard. Beauty treatments in the Saddlery. Wedding/function facilities. Free Wi-Fi. Background music. Pay-and-display parking. Children and dogs welcomed. 31 bedrooms (5 in Coach House across the courtyard). Room only £95–£265. Breakfast £7.50–£15. Dinner from £24.

ROSS-ON-WYE Herefordshire
Map 3:D5
THE HILL HOUSE, Howle Hill, HR9 5ST. Tel 01989-562033, www.thehowlinghillhouse.com. Set in four acres of woodland with spectacular views of the Forest of Dean and Wye valley, this rambling 17th-century home is run with great warmth, eccentricity and humour by owners Duncan and Alex Stayton. Guests are invited to sip champagne in the seven-seater outdoor hot tub, relax in the oak-lined bar, and write on the 'Wisdom and Poetry' wall. Rooms are traditional, with Gothic elements; one has a Japanese bathtub for up-to-the-neck bathing. The Staytons cook organic suppers on the Aga; 'wholesome' breakfasts, sourced locally, can be served in bed, at a time to suit guests. Vegetarians are catered for. Packed lunch/evening meal by arrangement. Lounge, morning room, bar (background music: morning Radio 4), restaurant. Free Wi-Fi. Hot tub; sauna (£4–£6); cinema (DVD film library). Garden. Children, and dogs (by arrangement) welcomed. Resident dog, cats, pigs and chickens. 5 bedrooms. Per person B&B £34–£39. Supper £21.

ROWSLEY Derbyshire
Map 3:A6
THE PEACOCK AT ROWSLEY, Bakewell Road, DE4 2EB. Tel 01629-733518, www.thepeacockatrowsley.co.uk. 'We had a very comfortable night here.' On the edge of a Peak District village, this charming old inn, owned by Lord Edward Manners, was built in 1652 as the dower house for Haddon Hall, a seat of the Duke of Rutland. It is managed by Ian and Jenni MacKenzie, with 'very jolly' staff. There are mullioned windows, leaded lights, and log fires in stone fireplaces; soft furnishings in the 'cosy' bar have been updated in apple green and purple velvets. Some bedrooms overlook the gardens that run down to the River Derwent (an ideal spot for fly-fishing); those facing the busy road have double-glazed windows. Dan Smith cooks ambitious modern British dishes ('delicious bread; good, strong, local cheese'). Free Wi-Fi. No background music. Discounts for Haddon Hall and Chatsworth House. Lounge, bar, dining room; conference rooms. Civil wedding licence. ½-acre garden on river (fishing Apr–Oct). Children (no under-10s on Fri or Sat nights), and dogs (£10 per night) welcomed. 15 bedrooms. Per room B&B £170–£350, D,B&B £230–£495.
25% DISCOUNT VOUCHERS

RYE East Sussex
Map 2:E5
THE HOPE ANCHOR, Watchbell Street, TN31 7HA. Tel 01797-222216, www.thehopeanchor.co.uk. At the end of a cobbled street, with good views over the town and adjacent marshes, this white-painted, family-owned hotel dates back to the 18th century, when it was a watering hole for sailors and shipbuilders. More recently, it featured in EF Benson's Mapp and Lucia novels. It is managed by Christopher George;

'all staff are pleasant'. In the spacious, modern dining room, chef Kevin Sawyer serves 'well-cooked' traditional English dishes using fish, meat and produce from Rye and the surrounding area. 'Lovely' country-style bedrooms. Lounge, bar (snack menu), dining room; room service. Free Wi-Fi. Background music. Wedding facilities. Children (cots, baby-listening devices, high chairs) and dogs welcomed. 16 bedrooms (1 in roof annexe; 2 apartments; cottage). Per room B&B £99–£180, D,B&B £112–£210.

THE SHIP INN, The Strand, TN31 7DB. Tel 01797-222233, www.theshipinnrye. co.uk. Once a 16th-century warehouse used to store contraband seized from smugglers, this cosy inn now has neat, simple bedrooms decorated with a seaside theme. It is owned by Karen Northcote; Theo Bekker is the manager. The 'charming hodgepodge of a pub' has uneven wooden floors, exposed beams (some low), mismatched furniture and retro decorations; the menu 'goes well beyond pub grub', with seasonal specials, fish from Rye Bay ('you can taste how fresh the fish is'), and bread from a local artisan baker. Close to Rye Harbour Nature Reserve and Camber Sands. Lounge, bar, restaurant; terrace. Free Wi-Fi. Background music. Pay and display parking. Children and dogs welcomed. 10 bedrooms. Per room B&B from £100. 2-night min. stay on Sat. Dinner £24.

ST IVES Cornwall
Map 1:D1
BLUE HAYES, Trelyon Avenue, TR26 2AD. Tel 01736-797129, www.bluehayes. co.uk. Decorated in chic coastal style, Malcolm Herring's immaculate small hotel is in a 1920s house perched high above Porthminster Point. In good weather, breakfast, cream teas and snacks can be taken on the white balustraded terrace, which has stunning views over the harbour and bay. A gate from the small garden leads directly to the beach (five minutes) or to the harbour (ten minutes). Bedrooms have sea views; some have a balcony, roof terrace or patio. 2 lounges, bar, dining room (light, Mediterranean-style suppers; Nicola Martin is chef; room-service menu); terrace. Free Wi-Fi. No background music. Small function facilities. Parking. Children over 10 welcomed. 6 bedrooms. Per room B&B single £100–£120, double £170–£250. Supper from £12. Closed Nov–Mar.

HEADLAND HOUSE, Headland Road, TR26 2NS. Tel 01736-796647, www. headlandhousehotel.co.uk. Mark and Fenella Thomas's three-storey Edwardian house overlooks the sandy beach and turquoise waters of Carbis Bay. Bright bedrooms, many with stunning panoramic views, are named after local places, and decorated in maritime stripes or colonial hues; Heligan has its own secluded garden with a table and chairs. Guests can relax in the Snug, which has board games, magazines and books, and a fully stocked bar; the decked terrace, hammock and lawn seating allow for alfresco lounging. Breakfast (with organic and local produce) has plenty of options. Complimentary afternoon tea and cake. Lounge, conservatory dining room; large front garden; terrace. Free Wi-Fi. No background music. Parking. Beach 600 yards; 1½ miles from St Ives.

7 bedrooms. Per room B&B £95–£150. Closed Nov–mid-Mar.

No1 St Ives, 1 Fern Glen, TR26 1QP. Tel 01736-799047, www.no1stives.co.uk. In a stone-built house, a short downhill walk from the town and the Tate gallery, this B&B is run with great attention to detail by Anna Bray and Simon Talbot. The modern bedrooms are well equipped, with an iPod docking station, TV with Freeview, a DVD/CD-player, hot drinks and biscuits (replenished daily); two rooms have distant ocean views towards Godrevy Lighthouse. Breakfast, served communally at a large wooden table, has an extensive choice with much local produce. Sitting room, dining room (background jazz); small back garden; terrace. Free Wi-Fi. Parking close by. Children over 7 welcomed. 4 bedrooms. Per room B&B £95–£139.

Primrose Valley Hotel, Porthminster Beach, TR26 2ED. Tel 01736-794939, www.primroseonline. co.uk. Within easy reach of the town, and seconds from the beach and the station, this small hotel occupies an 'attractive' Edwardian seaside villa at the foot of a steep, narrow road. Owners Andrew and Sue Biss run it on environmentally friendly lines. Bedrooms, some with sea views, are snug; one has French doors opening on to a private terrace. Organic breakfasts are taken in the open-plan lounge/breakfast room overlooking the beach. Lounge, café/bar (Cornish platters; cream teas), breakfast room; small terrace overlooking sea. Free Wi-Fi. Background music. Parking. Children over 8 welcomed.

10 bedrooms. Per room B&B £75–£170. 2-night min. stay preferred at weekends and in high season.
25% DISCOUNT VOUCHERS

Trevose Harbour House, 22 The Warren, TR26 2EA. Tel 01736-793267, www.trevosehouse.co.uk. Angela Giannuzzi and Olivier Noverazz, 'a lovely, sophisticated young couple', have brought a retro charm to their 'very chic, beautifully appointed' whitewashed terraced house, in the historic centre between the Porthminster and Harbour beaches. Blue-and-white bedrooms 'echo the colours of surf and sky', and are furnished with vintage pieces and the latest gadgetry; each has a large bed, a hospitality tray and organic toiletries. The cosy Snug has newspapers, books, magazines, an open fire and an honesty bar; the sunny terrace overlooks the pretty streets of The Warren. There are organic yogurts, muesli and granola, and home-made preserves at breakfast; picnic hampers are available. Snug, breakfast room; terrace. In-room treatments on request. Free Wi-Fi. Background music. Limited parking close by. 6 bedrooms (1 in annexe behind the house). Per room B&B £140–£265. Closed mid-Dec–Mar.

SALCOMBE Devon
Map 1:E4

Salcombe Harbour Hotel, Cliff Road, TQ8 8JH. Tel 01548-844444, www.salcombe-harbour-hotel.co.uk. Overlooking the 'wonderful' estuary, the former *Marine Hotel* has emerged 'phoenix-like' after a massive refurbishment; under a new name, it is today a stylish modern hotel with its own cinema and luxury spa. Pared-down bedrooms are decorated in pale blues and maritime stripes, with white wicker furniture; they have a fridge and complimentary sherry and gin. Many have a balcony with panoramic sea views (warm throws and binoculars provided). 'Most attractive', the Alex Aitken-run restaurant takes full advantage of its waterside location: 'The extremely comprehensive menu has excellent choice, and makes good use of the shellfish available at the door.' Tony Hole is head chef. Bar/lounge, *Jetty* restaurant. Spa (indoor pool, spa bath, sauna, steam room, fitness suite, treatment rooms). Free Wi-Fi. Background music. Children, and dogs (in some rooms; dog beds and special canine treats and toys) welcomed. Valet parking. 50 bedrooms (some interconnecting). Per room B&B £210–£340. Dinner £40.

SOUTH SANDS, Bolt Head, TQ8 8LL. Tel 01548-859000, www.southsands.com. 'Relaxed and informal', this family-friendly hotel by the Salcombe ferry is practically on the beach. 'Beautifully designed' interiors have unique fittings and a maritime slant. 'The light wood circular staircase with contracting banded treads was a pleasure to walk up.' Bedrooms, 'all very tasteful, clean and restful', vary in size and aspect: some have large windows with wonderful views of the beach and sea, others have twin roll-top baths. The airy beachside restaurant has painted wicker chairs and a wooden floor (it can be noisy); chef Stuart Downie's modern British cooking focuses on fish and seafood. Lounge, bar, restaurant (background music); terrace. Free

Wi-Fi. Civil wedding licence. Parking. Children, and dogs (in some bedrooms) welcomed. 27 bedrooms (5 beach suites; ground-floor rooms). Per room B&B £160–£450. 2-night min. stay on Fri, Sat. Dinner £35–£40.

SALISBURY Wiltshire
Map 2:D2
LEENA'S GUEST HOUSE, 50 Castle Road, SP1 3RL. Tel 01722-335419, www.leenasguesthouse.co.uk. Leena and Malcolm Street and their son, Gary, are the welcoming hosts at this good-value B&B, in an Edwardian guest house within walking distance of the city centre and cathedral. Good-sized bedrooms are traditionally furnished; a family room sleeps three. 'Excellent' breakfasts have fresh fruit, warm muffins, and hot dishes cooked to order. Fifteen-minute riverside walk to the centre. Lounge, breakfast room; garden. Free Wi-Fi. No background music. Parking. Children welcomed. 6 bedrooms (1 on ground floor). Per room B&B single £39–£45, double £68–£70 (no debit or credit cards).

SPIRE HOUSE, 84 Exeter Street, SP1 2SE. Tel 01722-339213, www.salisbury-bedandbreakfast.com. Lois and John Faulkner's small B&B, in an 18th-century Grade II listed town house, is 'really convenient' for the cathedral, and shops, restaurants and pubs in the city. The owners provide 'a very pleasant welcome' and helpful advice: 'They made our brief stay in Salisbury really good.' The 'nicely decorated' bedrooms ('No chintz!') are 'pleasant to be in'; two overlook the quiet walled garden. 'Tasty' breakfasts have lots of choice. Breakfast room; garden. Free Wi-Fi. No

background music. Parking opposite.
4 bedrooms. Room only £85. Breakfast
£5. Closed late Dec–Mar.

SAWLEY Lancashire
Map 4:D3

THE SPREAD EAGLE INN, nr Clitheroe,
BB7 4NH. Tel 01200-441202, www.
spreadeaglesawley.co.uk. On the banks
of the River Ribble, this refurbished,
stone-built pub-with-rooms (Individual
Inns) has flagstones, oak beams and
'comfortable', smartly furnished
bedrooms. Individually designed, the
rooms vary in size and aspect; some
overlook the river. Light meals, sharing
platters and pub classics are taken in the
informal eating areas; special diets are
catered for. Guided walks (with a bacon
sandwich) are regularly organised. Bar,
dining room. Free Wi-Fi. Background
music. Wedding/function facilities.
Parking. Children welcomed.
7 bedrooms. Per room B&B single £69–
£95, double £85–£140.

SCARBOROUGH North Yorkshire
Map 4:C5

PHOENIX COURT, 8–9 Rutland Terrace,
YO12 7JB. Tel 01723-501150, www.
hotel-phoenix.co.uk. Alison and Bryan
Edwards are the welcoming hosts at this
environmentally friendly guest house, in
two Victorian houses overlooking North
Bay and the beach. Walkers are well
provided for with drying facilities, route
information, and packed lunches with
home-baked rolls and cakes (£6 per
person); theatre-goers may enjoy special
breaks that include tickets for the
Stephen Joseph theatre. Breakfast has
home-made jams and much Yorkshire
produce, such as locally smoked kippers
and sausages from local farms; a

continental breakfast may be taken in
the room. 10 mins' walk from the town
centre. Guided wildlife tours are
planned. Lounge, bar area, dining room
(background music). Free Wi-Fi.
Parking. Children welcomed.
13 bedrooms (9 with sea views; 1 on
ground floor; 2 family rooms). Per room
B&B single £36–£40, double £50–£64.
Closed New Year.
25% DISCOUNT VOUCHERS

SEDLESCOMBE East Sussex
Map 2:E4

KESTER HOUSE, The Street, TN33 0QB.
Tel 01424-870035, www.kesterhouse.
co.uk. Period features and modern
comforts come together at Derek and
Monique Wright's characterful B&B, in
their 16th-century listed home. Guests
can choose the soaring oak beams and
four-poster bed in Armada, or the cosy,
country feel of Brede; Tithe Barn has its
own sitting room and quirky references
to its original use. Varied breakfasts;
packed lunches available. On Sundays,
indulgent afternoon teas are served in
the sitting room by an open fire. 2 sitting
rooms, dining room; small walled
garden. Free Wi-Fi. No background
music. Holistic therapies, massage,
health and beauty treatments can be
booked. Children over 7 welcomed.
6 miles from Rye and Hastings.
3 bedrooms (2 with private bathrooms).
Per room B&B single £50–£85, double
£70–£105. Closed Christmas, New Year.

SHANKLIN Isle of Wight
Map 2:E2

RYLSTONE MANOR, Rylstone Gardens,
Popham Road, PO37 6RG. Tel 01983-
862806, www.rylstone-manor.co.uk.
Mike and Carole Hailston's small,

traditional hotel stands in a public park on a cliff above Sandown Bay. The house was built in 1863 as a gentleman's residence, with Gothic, Tudor and Georgian influences, and has 'wonderful' sea views from the garden. There are heavy fabrics, books and ornaments in the green-walled lounge, basket chairs in a Victorian covered patio. Country house-style bedrooms, each named after an English tree, have antique furniture; they vary in size. In the dining room, with its ornate chandelier and matching wall lights, Mike Hailston serves a short menu of modern European dishes. The secluded private garden is 'a pleasant place to sip wine on a summer afternoon'. Drawing room, bar lounge, dining room; terrace. Free Wi-Fi. No background music. 1-acre garden in 4-acre public gardens; direct access to sand/shingle beach. 9 bedrooms. Per person B&B £67.50–£72.50, D,B&B £96.50–£101.50. 2-night min. stay in peak season.

SHEFFIELD South Yorkshire
Map 4:E4

LEOPOLD HOTEL, 2 Leopold Street, Leopold Square, S1 2GZ. Tel 08450-780067, www.leopoldhotelsheffield.com. Close to the cathedral, on a lively public square with many cafés and restaurants, this modern hotel (part of Small Luxury Hotels of the World) occupies a sympathetically converted Grade II listed building that once housed a boys' grammar school. Arched doorways, school photos and ranks of coat pegs echo the building's history; sleek, modern bedrooms have top-of-the-class technology (iPod docking station, digital radio, flat-screen TV). A small gym was recently added. Breakfast is served until 10.30 am on the weekend; meals and drinks may be taken on the terrace facing bustling Leopold Square. Lounge bar, dining room; terrace. Limited free Wi-Fi (charge for 'greater bandwidth connection'). Background music. 24-hour room service; private dining rooms. Fitness suite. Civil wedding licence; conference/function facilities. Parking discounts in public car park nearby. Children welcomed. 90 bedrooms (6 suitable for &). Room only £65–£175. Breakfast £7.95–£12.95.

SHERBORNE Somerset
Map 2:E1

THE KINGS ARMS, North Street, Charlton Horethorne, DT9 4NL. Tel 01963-220281, www.thekingsarms. co.uk. In the centre of a pretty village on the Somerset/Dorset border, this stately Edwardian building has been transformed by Anthony and Sarah Lethbridge into a modern pub and restaurant, with rooms above. Colourful, individually styled bedrooms have a marble wet room; some have views of the croquet lawn. Downstairs, a log-burning stove separates a cosy seating area from the slate- and wood-floored bar. Chef Sarah Lethbridge uses a Josper (charcoal) oven for some of her British dishes; bread, pasta and ice cream are home made. There are displays of local art and sculpture throughout. Lift. Lounge, snug, bar, restaurant. Free Wi-Fi. No background music. Terrace; garden; croquet. Function/small business facilities; shooting parties. Free use of sports centre in Sherborne (4 miles); discounts at Sherborne Golf Club; clay-pigeon shooting can be arranged. Parking. Children welcomed (special menu). 10 bedrooms (1 suitable for &;

3 accessible by lift). Per room B&B £135, interconnecting family room £220. Dinner £35.

SHREWSBURY Shropshire
Map 3:B4

CHATFORD HOUSE, Bayston Hill, Chatford, SY3 0AY. Tel 01743-718301, www.chatfordhouse.co.uk. Surrounded by organic farmland, this 18th-century Grade II listed farmhouse has comfortable B&B accommodation and Aga-cooked breakfasts. Christine and Rupert Farmer are the friendly hosts, who offer guests tea and home-made cake on arrival. Simple, country cottage-style bedrooms have fresh flowers, magazines and a hospitality tray; they overlook the garden and the Wrekin. The Farmers rear hens, ducks, geese, sheep and cattle on their smallholding; guests are welcome to visit the animals, and explore the pretty garden and orchard. There are eggs from the resident hens, and home-made jams and compotes at breakfast. Close to the Shropshire Way. Five miles south of Shrewsbury; within walking distance of Lyth Hill. Sitting room, breakfast room (open fire; background piano, CDs). Free Wi-Fi. Garden; orchard. Children welcomed. 3 bedrooms. Per room B&B single from £50, double from £70.

GROVE FARM HOUSE, Condover, SY5 7BH. Tel 01743-718544, www.grovefarmhouse.com. Liz Farrow's B&B is in a three-storey Georgian house in a peaceful setting on the edge of a small village, six miles south of Shrewsbury. Modern, country-style bedrooms have a DVD/CD-player, bathrobes, home-made biscuits, and flowers from the garden. Walks can be taken around the farm or through beautiful parkland and wooded areas; local maps and guidebooks are available to borrow. Breakfast has locally produced meat, eggs from home-reared chickens and home-made blueberry muffins. Complimentary tea and cake are offered to guests arriving in the afternoon; a full English tea (scones with cream and jam, and a selection of cakes and biscuits) is available by arrangement (£5.50). Liz Farrow makes recommendations for dinner at local restaurants. Lounge, dining room; ½-acre garden. Free Wi-Fi. No background music. Parking. Children welcomed. 4 bedrooms (plus 2 self-catering suites with log-burner and private courtyard). Per room B&B £85–£90. 2-night min. stay May–Sept.

THE INN AT GRINSHILL, High Street, Grinshill, SY4 3BL. Tel 01939-220410, www.theinnatgrinshill.co.uk. Seven miles north of Shrewsbury, this country inn is in a renovated Grade II listed Georgian building in the lee of Grinshill, a site of special scientific interest and an area of outstanding natural beauty. It is owned and managed by Victoria and Kevin Brazier. Soft-hued bedrooms have a concealed Freeview TV and a stylish bathroom. There are varied dining options: seasonal English provincial fare is served in the restaurant and conservatory; bistro meals are taken in the cosy, wood-panelled bar, which has books, games, comfy sofas and an open fire. A new chef, Paul Maders, has joined the team. 2 bars (*The Elephant and Castle* and *Bubbles*), restaurant (closed Sun eve, Mon and Tues; background music). Free Wi-Fi. Rose garden with fountain. Function facilities. Parking. Children welcomed. 6 bedrooms. Per room B&B single £89.50, double £119.50. D,B&B £79.50 per person (based on 2 people sharing). **25% DISCOUNT VOUCHERS** (Nov–Mar for guests who dine in)

LION AND PHEASANT, 50 Wyle Cop, SY1 1XJ. Tel 01743-770345, www.lionandpheasant.co.uk. By the English Bridge, on one of the oldest streets in town, this former coaching inn has been modernised with 'a simple but sure touch'. It is 'a pleasant place to stay, handy for the town centre'; Jim Littler is the manager. There are a number of dining areas, from the bar (oak floors, wide benches) to the inglenook room (flagstone floors, open fire) to the split-level restaurant (cosy, with bare tables); in all of them, chef Richard Alexander turns out 'well-cooked, confident food'. A warren of smartly styled, beamed corridors leads to the 'well-furnished and -equipped' bedrooms (some snug). 'Our corner room overlooking the bridge had a compact, well-lit, modern bathroom. Earplugs by the bed were a nice touch: we slept well despite the morning traffic noise (also dampened by double glazing).' 3 bars, restaurant, function room. Free Wi-Fi. Background music. Children welcomed. Per room B&B single £79, double £99, D,B&B £150.

THE SILVERTON, 9–10 Frankwell, SY3 8JY. Tel 01743-248000, www.thesilverton.co.uk. Just across the Welsh Bridge, within easy walking distance of the riverside and town centre, this restaurant-with-rooms occupies a former dairy, refurbished with a modern, minimalist interior. It is managed by Tim Moody. Named after

Shropshire hills, the contemporary bedrooms vary in size and aspect; interconnecting rooms can accommodate a family. Chef Michael Jordan uses much produce from local suppliers; 'excellent' breakfasts have sausages and bacon from a farm just two miles up the road. Bar, restaurant; lift; terrace. Free Wi-Fi. Background music. Valet parking. Children welcomed. 7 bedrooms (1 suitable for &). Per room B&B £75–£135. Dinner £30. **25% DISCOUNT VOUCHERS**

SIDLESHAM West Sussex
Map 2:E3
THE CRAB & LOBSTER, Mill Lane, PO20 7NB. Tel 01243-641233, www.crab-lobster.co.uk. 'Better than ever.' Peacefully located on the banks of the Pagham Harbour nature reserve, this 350-year-old inn has been renovated in spare, modern style by structural engineer-turned-hotelier Sam Bakose and his wife, Janet. Sophie Harwood is the manager. The inn is in an area of outstanding natural beauty and special scientific interest; binoculars and a telescope are provided in some bedrooms. New chef Clyde Hollett's menus are strong on fresh local fish, crab, lobster; breakfast has honey from Sidlesham bees. Bar, restaurant (background jazz); terrace; garden. Free Wi-Fi. Children welcomed. 6 bedrooms (2 in adjoining cottage). Per room B&B £155–£195. 2-night min. stay on Fri, Sat. Dinner £50.

SIDMOUTH Devon
Map 1:D5
HOTEL RIVIERA, The Esplanade, EX10 8AY. Tel 01395-515201, www.hotelriviera.co.uk. 'A wonderful experience.' Occupying a fine Regency

terrace, this traditional hotel is on the esplanade overlooking Lyme Bay. 'We had a seafront room, and could hear the waves lapping on the beach.' It has been run by the Wharton family 'with great dedication and charm' for more than 40 years, with 'excellent service from all staff'. 'Outstanding' English dishes with a French influence are served in the smart dining room (also open to non-residents); Matthew Weaver is the long-serving chef. Lounge, cocktail bar (live piano music), restaurant; ballroom; terrace. Free Wi-Fi. Lift; entrance ramp. 2 minutes from the town centre. Golf nearby; pheasant and duck shooting can be arranged. Children and dogs welcomed. 26 bedrooms (some suitable for &; many with sea views). Per person B&B £109–£180, D,B&B £129–£221.

VICTORIA HOTEL, The Esplanade, EX10 8RY. Tel 01395-512651, www. victoriahotel.co.uk. Standing in five acres of landscaped grounds overlooking the bay, this large traditional hotel (part of Brend Hotels) is a 'comfortable, very popular' place for many returning visitors. It has recently been refurbished. Most of the bedrooms are south facing; some have a balcony. Men are asked to wear a jacket and tie at a 'generally good' dinner in the *Jubilee* restaurant, which has live musical accompaniment, and dinner dances on Saturday nights. Room service. Free Wi-Fi. Background music. Sun lounge, lounge bar, restaurant; outdoor and indoor swimming pools; tennis court, snooker, putting. Spa, sauna, treatments. Gift shop. Parking. Children welcomed. 61 bedrooms (3 poolside suites). Room only single

£140–£160, double £185–£370. Breakfast £18. D,B&B £105–£245 per person. 2-night min. stay.

SISSINGHURST Kent
Map 2:D5
THE MILK HOUSE, The Street, TN17 2JG. Tel 01580-720200, www. themilkhouse.co.uk. At the centre of a village renowned for Sissinghurst Castle Gardens, a former pub (*The Bull*) has been modishly restyled by chef/proprietor Dane Allchorne and his wife, Sarah. 'Attractive both inside and out', it has simply decorated contemporary bedrooms (Byre, Buttery, Churn and Dairy), painted in dairy creams and milky whites. Uncomplicated, seasonal pub fare and more adventurous dishes (lime-seared red snapper, pickled cucumber and peashoot salad) are cooked by Dane Allchorne and served in the rustic bar and dining area; open fires in winter. 'A very pleasant meal.' Bar, restaurant ('easy listening' background music, closed Sun eve); private dining. Large garden and sun terrace. Free Wi-Fi. Parking. Children welcomed (special menu). 4 bedrooms (1 family room). Per room B&B £95–£120. 2-night min. stay at weekends.

SISSINGHURST CASTLE FARMHOUSE, nr Cranbrook, TN17 2AB. Tel 01580-720992, www.sissinghurstcastlefarm house.com. There are breathtaking views – of ancient woodland, fields, gardens or the castle's Elizabethan tower – from all the bedrooms in Sue and Frazer Thompson's elegant B&B. The Victorian farmhouse on the Sissinghurst estate was restored by the National Trust; the Thompsons have filled it with pictures, fresh flowers, and a mix of contemporary and period furniture. Tea and home-made cake are served on arrival; breakfasts, with home-made marmalade, and hot dishes cooked to order, are praised. Near the entrance to Sissinghurst Castle Garden; guests have access to the estate grounds. Lift. Sitting room (books, magazines), dining room; meeting room; small functions. Free Wi-Fi. No background music. Resident dog. 7 bedrooms (easy access). Per room B&B £150–£190. 2-night min. stay on Fri, Sat, Easter–Sept. Closed Jan–Mar.

SKIPTON North Yorkshire
Map 4:D3
HELLIFIELD PEEL CASTLE, Peel Green, Hellifield, BD23 4LD. Tel 01729-850248, www.peelcastle.co.uk. 'A complete and utter joy.' The painstaking restoration of Francis and Karen Shaw's ancient, ruined tower house was featured on Channel 4's *Grand Designs* programme. The building, which has parts dating from the 13th century, has now been transformed into a beautifully designed home, 'amazing and completely unique'. B&B guests relax by a wood-burning stove in the cosy, red-painted lounge, or retire to spacious bedrooms that have fresh flowers and lots of thoughtful touches, including home-made chocolates and cakes. Each room is different: the Old Room has a log fire; the modern Attic Apartment has self-catering facilities and a private roof terrace. Karen Shaw cooks 'delicious' breakfasts, with home-baked bread and locally sourced ingredients; vegetarian options are available. In parkland, ½ mile from village. Sitting room, breakfast room; 2-acre garden. Free Wi-Fi. No background music. Parking.

Children over 8 welcomed. 5 bedrooms. Per room B&B single £135–£190, double £165–£220.

SNETTISHAM Norfolk
Map 2:A4
THE ROSE & CROWN, Old Church Road, PE31 7LX. Tel 01485-541382, www.roseandcrownsnettisham.co.uk. Opposite a cricket pitch in the village centre, Jeannette and Anthony Goodrich's quintessential English inn is in a whitewashed 14th-century building with low beams, leaning walls, twisting passages and cosy corners. Modern bedrooms, decorated in seaside tones, are simply furnished. Adjoining the lounge, a newly refurbished garden room has comfortable seating and a large open fire (background music). One disabled visitor recently reported a stay that 'ticked all the boxes; staff were helpful at all times'. Chef Jamie Clarke sources traditional pub favourites from local food suppliers. Lounge, 3 bars, 3 dining areas. Walled garden. Ramps. Beaches nearby. Children (cots £10 per night; play galleon), and dogs welcomed. 16 bedrooms (2 on ground floor; 2 suitable for &.). Per room B&B single £80–£110, double £100–£125. 2-night min. stay Jul, Aug and bank holidays. Dinner £27.

SOMERTON Somerset
Map 1:C6
THE WHITE HART, Market Place, TA11 7LX. Tel 01458-272273, www.whitehartsomerton.com. Beside a church on an attractive market square, this 16th-century pub has been revamped with flair by the Draco Pub Company, owners of *The Swan*, Wedmore (see Shortlist below). It is managed by

Natalie Patrick. Exposed stone walls, wooden floors and patchwork tiling create a contemporary, rustic-chic look throughout. Chef Tom Blake (formerly of the *River Cottage Canteen*) supports West Country suppliers in his 'fresh, simple' dishes – 'a model of what local and organic food should be'; meals are served in a conservatory dining room, or alfresco in the courtyard. The bar has locally brewed beer and cider, newspapers and open fires; light meals and snacks are available throughout the day. Ramps. Bar, restaurant (closed Sun eve; 3 dining areas); large garden and courtyard. Free Wi-Fi. 'Easy listening' background music. Children (special menu), and dogs (in one room) welcomed. 8 bedrooms. Per room B&B £85–£130, D,B&B from £165.

SOUTH MOLTON Devon
Map 1:C4

ASHLEY HOUSE, 3 Paradise Lawn, EX36 3DJ. Tel 01769-573444, www.ashleyhousebedandbreakfast.com. Nicky Robbins offers B&B accommodation in this brick-built former gentleman's residence in the centre of a small market town. Handsomely restored, the house has an interesting history, and features on the South Molton Heritage Trail: a blue plaque is dedicated to Lord Samuel Widgery, the Lord Chief Justice of England from 1971 to 1980. High-ceilinged rooms have been elegantly furnished with antiques, contemporary pieces and original photography and artwork; they have a fireplace and countryside views. Devonshire breakfasts include home-made preserves, eggs from resident hens, fruit and vegetables from the garden, and locally sourced bacon and sausages. Breakfast/sitting

room (wood-burning stove; classical background music). Free Wi-Fi. Large garden. Resident dog. Parking. 3 bedrooms. Per person B&B £75–£105. Closed New Year.

SOUTHPORT Merseyside
Map 4:E2

THE VINCENT, 98 Lord Street, PR8 1JR. Tel 01704-883800, www.thevincenthotel.com. Transformed from a former cinema by local restaurateur Paul Adams, this large, fashionable hotel near the train station has a striking glass facade, and a buzzing bar and restaurant within. Alan Richmond is the manager. Decorated in restful tones, bedrooms vary in size; some have an adjoining lounge and balcony. The penthouse suite has fantastic views over the town. Sushi and other international dishes are served in the *V-Cafe*, which has outdoor seating (open early until late; Andrew Carter is the chef). Members' bar; background music. Free Wi-Fi. Spa; gym; beauty treatments. Civil wedding licence; function facilities. Valet parking. Children welcomed. 59 bedrooms (3 suitable for &.). Per room B&B £103–£218, penthouse £695, D,B&B £109–£244.

STAMFORD Lincolnshire
Map 2:B3

THE BULL AND SWAN AT BURGHLEY, High Street, St Martins, PE9 2LJ. Tel 01780-66412, www.thebullandswan.co.uk. There are quirky bedrooms and British bistro dinners at this refurbished old coaching inn, in a medieval market town. Full of history, the ancient stone building served as both a staging post for coaches on the Great North Road, and as the alleged venue of the

Honourable Order of Little Bedlam, a riotous gentlemen's drinking club founded in 1684. Today, it is managed by James Chadwick for Hillbrooke Hotels. Attractive bedrooms, given the pseudonyms of Little Bedlam members, are furnished with carved dark wood furniture, crisp linen and smart fabrics; one room has a freestanding bath. New chef Luke Holland cooks informal modern dishes using produce from local suppliers; set-course meals for early diners; Sunday roasts. 'Excellent' breakfasts include yogurt, fresh berries, kippers, and eggs Benedict and Royale. Dogs have their own room-service menu. The town is a short stroll across the river; Burghley House can be reached via a cross-country walk. 2 bars (background music), 2 dining areas. Free Wi-Fi. Courtyard garden with seating. Parking (narrow entrance). Children (£20 per night; special menu), and dogs (in 3 rooms) welcomed. 7 bedrooms. Per room B&B £80–£150, D,B&B £140–£200.

STOWMARKET Suffolk
Map 2:C5

BAYS FARM, Earl Stonham, IP14 5HU. Tel 01449-711286, www.baysfarmsuffolk. co.uk. Deep in the countryside, on the outskirts of a peaceful village, this 'attractive, tastefully modernised' 17th-century farmhouse is run as a B&B by Stephanie and Richard Challinor. The beautiful two-acre grounds (included in the National Gardens Scheme) have an orchard, a wildflower garden, and vegetable and fruit gardens, as well as plenty of comfortable seating; guests may relax in the pavilion, which has its own heating, lighting and iPod docking station. Overlooking the gardens, the

'charming' bedrooms have a large bed and lots of little extras (fresh flowers, coffee machine, DVD-player); the Hayloft Suite is in a converted building with a balcony. A communal breakfast is served in the former dairy, the oldest part of the house, at a time to suit guests; bread, marmalade and jams are home made. A supper menu and snacks are available; licensed. Drawing room (open fire), dining room (background music). Free Wi-Fi. Garden. 4 miles NE of Stowmarket. 4 bedrooms (1 in separate building). Per room B&B £80–£125.

STRATFORD-UPON-AVON
Warwickshire
Map 3:D6

CHURCH STREET TOWNHOUSE, 16 Church Street, CV37 6HB. Tel 01789-262222, www.churchstreet townhouse.com. A short walk from the Royal Shakespeare Theatre, this 400-year-old building, with low ceilings and beams, has an all-day brasserie, a lively bar and comfortable modern bedrooms. It is managed by David Mackinnon for City Pub Company (East). Rooms vary in size, but all have a large bed, TV/ DVD-player, iPod dock and period features; complimentary champagne, port, fresh milk and nibbles are provided. Andrew Taylor's menus use local produce in season; heavy drapes, armchairs, and a candelabra on each table give the restaurant a Victorian intimacy. 2 bars (18th-century bread oven; background music), restaurant. Free Wi-Fi. 12 bedrooms. Per room B&B £110–£200. D,B&B from £137.50 per person.

WHITE SAILS, 85 Evesham Road, CV37 9BE. Tel 01789-550469, www. white-sails.co.uk. Within walking distance of Anne Hathaway's cottage and gardens, this comfortable B&B on the outskirts of Stratford has new owners, Tim and Denise Perkin. 'High standards' are maintained in the bedrooms and bathrooms; additional comforts include bathrobes, an iPod docking station with DAB radio, and a silent fridge with a supply of fresh milk. Guests may help themselves to complimentary sherry and coffee in the lounge. 'We had a very comfortable stay.' Lounge, dining room (background music). Free Wi-Fi. Garden with summer house. Bike storage. 1 mile W of centre (on a bus route). 4 bedrooms. Per room B&B £100–£125.

SWINBROOK Oxfordshire
Map 3:D6

THE SWAN INN, near Burford, OX18 4DY. Tel 01993-823339, www. theswanswinbrook.co.uk. By a bridge over the River Windrush, in a 'picture-perfect' rural setting, this lovely old inn has 'charm in buckets'. It is owned by the Dowager Duchess of Devonshire (Debo Mitford), who was brought up in the village; Nicola and Archie Orr-Ewing (see *The King's Head Inn*, Bledington, main entry), who run it, have styled it 'beautifully', paying homage to the Mitford sisters with family photographs and memorabilia. The bar and restaurant are a series of interconnected rooms with mismatched wooden tables and chairs; a recently added wood-and-glass extension opens on to the garden, where chickens roam freely. The bedrooms are in converted stables: 'Our compact, modern room was handsomely styled, with a large, comfortable bed and – hurray – no countryside twee.' Seasonal,

traditional English food with a modern edge is cooked by chef Matthew Laughton. Bar, restaurant. Large garden, orchard. Children welcomed. 11 bedrooms (6 in the stables; 5 in riverside cottage; 1 suitable for &). Per room B&B £100–£180, D,B&B £145–£165. 2-night min. stay at weekend. Closed Christmas Day.
25% DISCOUNT VOUCHERS

TEIGNMOUTH Devon
Map 1:D5

THOMAS LUNY HOUSE, Teign Street, TQ14 8EG. Tel 01626-772976, www.thomas-luny-house.co.uk. A short walk from the town and quay, John and Alison Allan's 'immaculate' B&B is approached via a walled courtyard set back from the street. Arriving guests are offered tea or coffee with home-made cake in the spacious drawing room, which stretches the length of the house, or in the secluded, south-facing garden. Elegant bedrooms are well equipped with books, magazines, fresh flowers and assorted sundries. A daily newspaper is provided at breakfast. 2 lounges, breakfast room; garden. Free Wi-Fi. No background music. Parking. 4 bedrooms. Per person B&B £40–£75.

TETBURY Gloucestershire
Map 3:E5

OAK HOUSE NO.1, The Chipping, GL8 8EU. Tel 01666-505741, www.oakhouseno1.com. In a well-manicured Cotswolds market town, this fine Georgian house is run as a luxurious B&B by interior designer and art collector Gary Kennedy, with Nicola MacWilliam. The strikingly decorated public rooms are filled with antiques, paintings, photographs and intriguing artefacts; individually styled bedrooms range from the sumptuous Cavalier Room to the eclectic Prince's Suite and more modern Garden View Suite. A complimentary afternoon tea is served at a time to suit guests; communal breakfasts are praised. Sitting room, dining room. Free Wi-Fi. Background jazz. Walled garden. Luxury picnic hampers. Beauty treatments. Wellingtons and thick socks supplied for walkers wanting to explore the countryside. Babies, and children over 11, welcomed. 4 bedrooms. Per room B&B £275–£325.

THORPE MARKET, Norfolk
Map 2:A5

THE GUNTON ARMS, Cromer Road, NR11 8TZ. Tel. 01263 832010, www.theguntonarms.co.uk. 'A very relaxed place', this old, red-gabled inn on the edge of a deer park is run as a characterful pub-with-rooms by art dealer Ivor Braka and his artist wife, Sarah Graham. The 'vibrant' interior is filled with unusual pieces and artwork ranging from Stubbs engravings to a Tracey Emin neon sign. Within the inn's flint walls, public areas have stone-flagged floors, roaring fires, mounted antlers on wood-panelled walls. 'Lovely' bedrooms have handmade wallpaper, Turkish rugs, antique furniture; 'plenty of storage' and good lighting; 'a double washbasin and a huge retro bathtub in the bathroom'. No television; instead, a Roberts radio 'in colours to match the decor'. Each of the two large lounges has a television; guests may help themselves to juice, tea and coffee in a downstairs pantry. The dining room – 'like a medieval banqueting hall' – serves 'chunks of meat' (steaks, Barnsley chops, sausages, etc.) and potatoes on a grill set over a huge open fire; bread is fresh from the oven. Stuart Tattersall is chef. 2 lounges, bar, restaurant, pantry. Free Wi-Fi. Background music. Children, and dogs (£10 per night) welcomed. Per room B&B £95–£185 (2-night min. stay at weekends). Dinner from £35.

THURNHAM Kent
Map 2:D4

THURNHAM KEEP, Castle Hill, ME14 3LE. Tel 01622-734149, www.thurnhamkeep.co.uk. Amanda Lane extends a friendly welcome, with tea and freshly made scones, to B&B guests arriving at her childhood home, a 'very impressive' Edwardian house on the North Downs. At the end of a long drive, it is in extensive grounds, with views over the Weald of Kent. 'Beautiful' rooms are traditionally furnished; two have a huge original Edwardian bath. Communal breakfasts include home-made jams, honey from the garden's bees, and eggs from resident free-range hens. Supper is available, by arrangement; plenty of pubs nearby. Oak-panelled sitting room (wood-burning stove), conservatory, dining room; terrace (alfresco breakfasts); snooker room (in the old chapel). Free Wi-Fi. Background music (weekend eve only; 'easy listening'/ classical/jazz). 7-acre terraced garden: heated outdoor swimming pool (June–early Sept); pond; kitchen garden; dovecote; summer house; tennis, croquet. Parking. 3 bedrooms. Per room B&B £130-£160.

TISBURY Wiltshire
Map 2:D1

THE COMPASSES INN, Lower Chicksgrove, SP3 6NB. Tel 01722-

714318, www.thecompassesinn.com. A typical English country pub, Susie and Alan Stoneham's thatched 14th-century inn has low ceilings, huge beams, a crackling log fire, and plenty of nooks and crannies. It is in an area of outstanding natural beauty, and is a good base for country walks and visits to Longleat, Stonehenge and Wilton House. In the main bar and adjacent dining room, chef Dave Cousin serves a regularly changing menu of seasonal dishes alongside traditional pub grub. All vegetables are from a local farm; there is an extensive wine list. Accessed separately from the pub, simply furnished, country-style bedrooms vary in size and decor; each has a hospitality tray and a modern bathroom. Bar, dining room. Free Wi-Fi. No background music. Garden. Small function facilities. Children (baby monitor, babysitting, baby food), and dogs welcomed. 4 bedrooms (plus adjacent 2-bed cottage). Per room B&B £65–£85 (2-night min. stay on summer and bank holiday weekends). Dinner from £24.50.

TITCHWELL Norfolk
Map 2:A5
BRIARFIELDS, Main Road, PE31 8BB. Tel 01485-210742, www.briarfieldshotelnorfolk.co.uk. Popular with birdwatchers, golfers, walkers, families and dog-owners, this flint-built hotel on the north Norfolk coast has expansive views of the sea and salt marshes, and exclusive (seasonal) access to Titchwell reserve and beach. It is managed by Bradley Williams. Bedrooms are neatly decorated and spacious; some overlook the RSPB reserve. Guests have use of the cosy snug (exposed beams, open fire), the sheltered courtyard (with fish pond) and the decked terrace. Chef Richard Bargewell's dishes are based on local and home-smoked produce; Sunday roasts; afternoon teas. 3 lounges; 5-acre garden. Free Wi-Fi. Background music. Children (special menu; play area), and dogs welcomed. 23 bedrooms (8 in converted outbuilding; 3 family rooms). Per person B&B £52.50–£125, D,B&B £72.50–£150 (2-night min. stay in summer).

TOLLARD ROYAL Wiltshire
Map 2:E1
KING JOHN INN, SP5 5PS. Tel 01725-516207, www.kingjohninn.co.uk. In a lovely village on the Wiltshire/Dorset border, this roadside pub has been updated by owners Alex and Gretchen Boon in modern country style. The open-plan bar and dining area has large black-and-white photographs, and comfy sofas by an open fire; chef Simon Trepess cooks a daily changing menu of 'relaxed' dishes using much local and seasonal produce. Alfresco dining is in the terraced garden; on fine days, there may be barbecues on the Victorian-inspired pavilion. Five smart, well-designed bedrooms are accessed via a steep, narrow staircase; three are in the converted coach house opposite. 'We really enjoyed breakfast': fresh orange juice, 'proper' toast, 'delicious' pots of warm granola with poached berries and yogurt. Bar, restaurant; wine shop. Garden (outdoor functions; music licence). Free Wi-Fi. On Cranborne Chase; 6 miles W of Shaftesbury. 8 bedrooms (some on ground floor; plus 2/3-bed self-catering cottage). Per room B&B from £140. Dinner from £20.

TOTNES Devon
Map 1:D4
ROYAL SEVEN STARS, The Plains,
TQ9 5DD. Tel 01803-862125,
www.royalsevenstars.co.uk. In the
centre of this bohemian town, Anne
and Nigel Way's hotel occupies a 'very
interesting' 17th-century coaching inn
with an imposing original facade, and a
cobbled front terrace. Inside, there is
a bright, modern interior and a lively
atmosphere: it is a popular events venue,
and its restaurant and bars are well
patronised by local residents. Margaret
Stone is the manager. Bedrooms vary in
size and decor; the largest have a spa
bath in the bathroom. Light bar meals
are available all day; in the old stables
at the end of the courtyard, chef John
Gallagher serves brasserie dinners
('easy listening' background music).
'All met a good standard.' Lounge,
2 bars (log fires in winter), TQ9 brasserie
and grill, champagne bar; terrace
(alfresco dining); balcony. Free Wi-Fi.
Civil wedding licence; business
facilities; ballroom. Parking. Children
and dogs welcomed. 21 bedrooms
(quietest at back). Per room B&B single
£91–£122, double £125–£156. Dinner
from £18.95.

TRESCO Isles of Scilly
Map 1: inset C1
NEW INN, TR24 0QQ. Tel 01720-422849,
www.tresco.co.uk. 'A very good stay.'
Near the beach and harbour, the only
pub on Robert Dorrien-Smith's
private, car-free island is a hub of the
community. It is run with 'very pleasant'
staff, and managed by Robin Lawson.
Decorated with nautical memorabilia,
the informal bars and restaurant are
popular with visitors to the timeshare

cottages on the island; music, beer and
cider festivals are held. Accommodation
is 'basic, clean and comfortable'.
'Excellent' traditional English cooking
features local fish and Tresco beef; Alan
Hewitt is the new head chef. Residents'
lounge, 2 bars (background music),
pavilion, restaurant, patio (alfresco
eating); garden. Outdoor heated
swimming pool. Children welcomed.
16 bedrooms (some with terrace, some
with sea views). Per person B&B £55–
£120. Dinner from £44.

TROUTBECK Cumbria
Map 4: inset C2
BROADOAKS, Bridge Lane, LA23 1LA.
Tel 015394-45566, www.broadoaks
countryhouse.co.uk. There is a 'lovely
warm feel' at Tracey Robinson's
'stunning' 19th-century house, standing
in extensive landscaped grounds with
views towards Windermere. Andrea
Carter is the manager. Bedrooms are
individually styled (some are compact);
some have striking modern wallpaper,
others traditional Victorian windows,
yet others an antique roll-top bath in the
bathroom. Canapés are taken in the
music room before dinner; in Oaks
restaurant, chef Sharon Elders serves
a regularly changing menu of classic
dishes (with vegetarian options) using
much local produce. Popular as a
wedding venue. Music room (vintage
Bechstein piano; log fire), bar,
restaurant. Free Wi-Fi. Background
music. 7-acre grounds; stream. Civil
wedding licence. Free membership at
nearby spa. 19 bedrooms (some on
ground floor; 5 in coach house;
3 detached garden suites, 5 mins' walk
from house). Children, and dogs (in
some rooms; £25 per night) welcomed.

Resident cockapoo, Molly. Per room B&B £130–£305, D,B&B £160–£345.

TUNBRIDGE WELLS Kent
Map 2:D4
HOTEL DU VIN TUNBRIDGE WELLS, 13 Crescent Road, TN1 2LY. Tel 08447-489266, www.hotelduvin.com. Facing Calverley Park, this outpost of the du Vin group occupies an 18th-century Grade II listed sandstone mansion in a Georgian spa town. Some of the smart, handsomely furnished bedrooms overlook the park; all have a well-stocked minibar. Reliable bistro dishes are served in the informal dining room (pictures, paintings, restored fireplaces); alfresco meals may be taken on the garden terrace with views across the park. Bar, bistro, tea lounge; private dining room. Free Wi-Fi. No background music. Function facilities. 1-acre garden: terrace (alfresco dining); vineyard; boules. Close to the station. Limited parking. Children and dogs welcomed. 34 bedrooms (4 in annexe). Per room B&B £185–£259, D,B&B £185–£400.

ULLSWATER Cumbria
Map 4: inset C2
INN ON THE LAKE, Glenridding, Penrith, CA11 0PE. Tel 01768-482444, www.lakedistricthotels.net. There are 'fabulous' lake and mountain views from this 'wonderful' hotel standing in extensive grounds on the shores of Lake Ullswater. It is managed by Gary Wilson, with staff who 'could not have been nicer or more helpful'. Decorated in contemporary style, bedrooms are of a good size; they have tea- and coffee-making facilities, bottled water and biscuits. Morning coffee, lunch and afternoon tea may be taken in the elegant orangery or the lounge bar and terrace; both have expansive views of the landscaped gardens. A daily-changing menu of 'superb' modern European dishes is served in the *Lake View* restaurant (smart casual dress requested); local real ales and informal pub meals are taken in the *Ramblers* bar in the grounds. Lounge, bar, restaurant, orangery; lakeside terrace (alfresco dining). Lift. Gym, spa bath, sauna; 15-acre grounds: croquet, 9-hole golf course (seasonal); children's outdoor play area; private jetties. Free Wi-Fi. Background music. Civil wedding licence; conference/function facilities. Parking. Children, and dogs (in some rooms) welcomed. 47 bedrooms. Per room B&B £188–£324, D,B&B £256–£389. Dinner £32.

VENTNOR Isle of Wight
Map 2:E2
OCEAN VIEW HOUSE, 46 Zig Zag Road, PO38 1DD. Tel 01983-852729, www.oceanviewhouse.co.uk. At the top of a steep hill overlooking Ventnor, Sarah Smith's 'gorgeous' B&B has 'beautiful views'. It is 'a wonderful, relaxing place' where visitors in search of 'privacy and relaxation' are well catered for: they have a separate entrance, and can come and go as they please. Two of the neat, modern bedrooms have a balcony with panoramic sea views; the terraced garden has hammocks and decked areas with sunshades and cushions. From Nov to Mar, a home-cooked dinner is available, by arrangement (from £8.95); there are takeaway menus, and tableware for picnics in a small dining area. A 'delicious' breakfast is served in

the bedroom. The town and beach are a short downhill stroll away (guests returning on foot catch their breath on a bench halfway, or take a bus or taxi back up). Picnic hampers available (from £8). In-room massage treatments can be arranged. Free Wi-Fi. No background music. Garden. Street parking. 1 mile N of town centre. 4 bedrooms. Per person B&B £75–£110. 2-night min. stay preferred.

THE ROYAL HOTEL, Belgrave Road, PO38 1JJ. Tel 01983-852186, www.royalhoteliow.co.uk. 'We enjoyed our stay.' Liked for its 'olde-worlde charm', this traditional seaside hotel close to the seafront and town centre is owned by William Bailey and managed by Philip Wilson. Gracious country house-style bedrooms have rich fabrics; eight have recently been refurbished. Chef Steven Harris's award-winning seasonal menus are served in the elegant *Appuldurcombe* restaurant (closed for lunch Oct–June, except Sun); lunch and afternoon tea can be taken in the colonial-style conservatory, or on the cliff-top terrace, which has glorious panoramic views. Lounge, bar, *Riviera* terrace (alfresco dining); conservatory. Lift to some rooms. Ramp. Background music; resident pianist during peak-season weekends. Free Wi-Fi in public areas. Civil wedding licence; function rooms. 2-acre subtropical grounds: heated outdoor swimming pool (May–Sept), children's play area. In-room massages and beauty treatments. Sandy beach nearby (hilly walk). Picnic hampers available. Parking. Children welcomed (baby-listening facilities; children's high tea). Dogs welcomed (charge). 53 bedrooms (1 suitable for &.).

Per room B&B £185–£285, D,B&B £265–£365. 2-night min. stay at peak weekends. Closed 2 weeks in Jan.

WALLINGTON Northumberland Map 4:B3

SHIELDHALL, Morpeth, NE61 4AQ. Tel 01830-540387, www.shieldhallguest house.co.uk. In a beautiful setting overlooking the National Trust's Wallington estate, this stone house was once owned by the family of Capability Brown. It stands amid gardens and parkland with a stream, woodland and natural meadow. It is run as a B&B by welcoming owners Celia and Stephen Gay, who converted the farmstead and decorated it with antiques, original art, and furniture handcrafted by Stephen and his sons. Bedrooms (named after the wood used for their furniture and fittings) open on to a central courtyard; Oak has a panelled four-poster bed. Celia Gay serves traditional Aga-cooked four-course dinners by arrangement, using home-grown vegetables and fresh eggs from her own hens. Daughter Sarah manages. Library, 'secret' bar, dining room. Free Wi-Fi. No background music. 4 bedrooms (all on ground floor). Per person B&B £40–£49, D,B&B £70. Closed Christmas, New Year.

WARTLING East Sussex Map 2:E4

WARTLING PLACE, Herstmonceux, nr Hailsham, BN27 1RY. Tel 01323-832590, www.wartlingplace.co.uk. 'All in all, a very pleasant stay.' Opposite a lovely church and a pub, Rowena and Barry Gittoes's tastefully furnished B&B is in a Grade II listed former rectory in a tiny village mentioned in the Domesday Book. The Georgian building stands in 'delightful' landscaped gardens filled with many subtropical plants and shrubs, on the edge of the Pevensey Levels nature reserve. Inside, there are interesting prints and pictures on the walls, and comfortable seating in the large lounge. 'Great' breakfasts are served at a long mahogany table or can be taken in the room. An evening meal or late supper is available, by arrangement. Drawing room, dining room (honesty bar, CD-player). Free Wi-Fi. No background music. 3-acre garden. Parking. Children welcomed; dogs allowed in cottage suite. 4 bedrooms (plus 2-bedroom self-catering cottage; suitable for &). Per room B&B £125–£165 (2 people sharing). Dinner £35.

WATERGATE BAY Cornwall
Map 1:D2
WATERGATE BAY, On the beach, TR8 4AA. Tel 01637-860543, www.watergatebay.co.uk. On a two-mile stretch of sandy beach, this large, extended hotel has its own on-site surf school (the Extreme Academy), and plenty of outdoor activities for families and the less adventurous. The leisure complex, Swim Club, has a 25-metre ocean-view infinity pool, a fitness studio and treatment rooms (open to day members); a boardwalk leads to the beach. Inspired by the coast, bedrooms have dark wood flooring, bright colours and stripy fabrics; many face the sea. There are many eating options: new restaurant *Zacry's* specialises in contemporary American cuisine; *The Living Space* (stunning coast views) has sharing platters, seasonal salads and hearty dishes; menus at *The Beach Hut* feature steaks, burgers and shellfish. Mark Williams is the manager. Lounge,

3 restaurants; terrace, sun deck. Free Wi-Fi. Background music in restaurants. Indoor/outdoor pool. Surf school: waterskiing, paddlesurf, power kiting, etc. Children (special meals, organised games, entertainment), and dogs (in some rooms, £15 per night charge) welcomed. 69 bedrooms (family suites; 2 suitable for &). Per room B&B £135–£395, D,B&B £180–£440.

WATERMILLOCK Cumbria
Map 4: inset C2
RAMPSBECK, Lake Ullswater, nr Penrith, CA11 0LP. Tel 01768-486442, www.rampsbeck.co.uk. On the shores of Lake Ullswater, this whitewashed 18th-century Lakeland country house stands in 18 acres of mature grounds with stunning views over the lake and the fells. It is owned by John Brooksbank. Traditionally furnished, the comfortable drawing room has an ornate ceiling and a marble fireplace. Afternoon tea and light meals can be taken on a terrace in warmer months. Most of the 'elegant' bedrooms face the lake or garden. Chef Ben Wilkinson cooks refined modern British dishes; Sunday lunches. 3 lounges, bar, restaurant (no children under 10 in the evening). Free Wi-Fi. No background music. Garden (croquet). Fishing, sailing, windsurfing. Civil wedding licence; function facilities. Parking. Children, and dogs (in 3 rooms) welcomed. 19 bedrooms. Per person B&B £79.75–£165, D,B&B £129.75–£215.

WEDMORE Somerset
Map 1:B6
THE SWAN, Cheddar Road, BS28 4EQ. Tel 01934-710337, www.theswanwedmore.com. In a lovely village, this popular

pub-with-rooms (Draco Pub Company) has 'smart', modern bedrooms, and a bustling bar and dining room where snacks, drinks and home-made cake are served all day. Bedrooms come in Small, Medium and Big; each has freshly ground coffee and a cafetière, a stash of old-fashioned sweets, and 'super' toiletries. There are newspapers, fires and local ales in the pub (Pimm's and home-made lemonade in summer); in the informal restaurant, chef Tom Blake (formerly of the *River Cottage Canteen*) cooks 'very good', unfussy dishes using Somerset produce in season, and locally reared meat. Breakfast, with home-cured bacon and freshly baked bread, is served till 11 am. Bar (wood-burning stove), restaurant (closed Sun eve). Terrace; garden (wood-fired oven and barbecue). Free Wi-Fi. DVD library. 'Eclectic' background music. Function facilities. Parking. Children welcomed. 6 bedrooms. Per room B&B £85–£125. Dinner from £28.

WEST LULWORTH Dorset
Map 2:E1
BINDON BOTTOM, Main Road, Lulworth Cove, BH20 5RL. Tel 01929-400256, www.bindonbottom.com. Ideally placed for coastal and countryside walks, this stone-built Victorian country house at the bottom of Bindon Hill is owned and run by Clive and Lisa Orchard. Country cottage-style rooms have charming features such as a Victorian fireplace, or an elegant bay window with views across farmland hills; all are well equipped with guidebooks, fresh milk, local biscuits, organic toiletries and a wind-up eco torch (there are no street lights in the village). Organic breakfasts, cooked by Clive Orchard, are ordered

the night before; vegetarians and vegans are well catered for. Restaurants nearby. Lulworth Cove is minutes away. Breakfast room (no background music). DVD library. Free Wi-Fi. Children over 12 welcomed. 5 bedrooms. Per room B&B £85–£110. 2-night stays preferred.

WESTON-SUPER-MARE Somerset
Map 1:B6
BEACHLANDS HOTEL, 17 Uphill Road North, BS23 4NG. Tel 01934-621401, www.beachlandshotel.com. Close to the beach, overlooking sand dunes and a golf course, this family-friendly hotel is run by welcoming owners Charles and Beverly Porter. Comfortable, simply furnished bedrooms have tea- and coffee-making facilities; some have a veranda opening on to the secluded garden. A daily changing menu is served in the dining room; special diets are catered for. 4 lounges, bar, restaurant; private dining; background music. Free Wi-Fi. 10-metre indoor swimming pool, sauna. Garden. Civil wedding licence; function/conference facilities. Parking. Children welcomed (baby-listening service; high tea; swimming lessons by arrangement). 20 bedrooms (some on ground floor; some family rooms; 1 suitable for &). Per room B&B single £67–£108.25, double £133.75–£144.25.

WHEATHILL Shropshire
Map 3:C5
THE OLD RECTORY, Bridgnorth, WV16 6QT. Tel 01746-787209, www.theoldrectorywheathill.com. Izzy Barnard's charming country B&B, in a handsome Georgian house, stands in extensive gardens with free-range chickens and ducks. Guests like the

many delightful touches: home-made scones or cake on arrival, wild flowers throughout the house, knitted cosies on the boiled eggs at breakfast. The drawing room has family photographs, sofas, and a roaring fire in cold weather; comfortable bedrooms have fresh flowers, books and plenty of treats (a decanter of sherry; home-made biscuits or flapjacks tied with a ribbon). A candlelit three-course dinner or light supper is available on request (BYO bottle); breakfast has jams and compotes from home-grown summer fruit, local sausages and home-cured bacon, and freshly squeezed orange juice. On a bridleway amid acres of riding country (maps and route cards to borrow); horses welcomed. Drawing room, dining room; sauna (in the cellar). Boot room. Loose boxes; tack room. Free Wi-Fi. No background music. In-room treatments by arrangement. Children, and dogs (£10 per night) by arrangement; horses welcomed (£20 per night). Resident dogs and cat. 7-acre gardens (ancient cedar tree). 7 miles E of Ludlow. 3 bedrooms. Per room B&B single £65–£105, double £80–£125. Dinner £30.

WHITSTABLE Kent
Map 2:D5
THE FRONT ROOMS, 9 Tower Parade, CT5 2BJ. Tel 01227-282132, www. thefrontrooms.co.uk. A short harbourside walk from the centre, this stylish B&B is run by friendly owners Julie Thorne and Tom Sutherland in their discreet, restored Victorian town house. Decorated in heritage whites, the light, airy rooms have a Victorian cast iron bed and cosy blanket throws; thoughtful extras include bathrobes, a hot-water bottle and a complimentary minibar. A continental breakfast, ordered the night before, is served in a room doubling as a modern photography gallery; guests in Room 3 may have breakfast on their balcony. Books, magazines, DVDs and board games are available to borrow; the hosts are happy to make recommendations for restaurants, walks and places to visit. Lounge/breakfast room/gallery. Free Wi-Fi. Background music. A short walk into town; bicycles for hire. 3 bedrooms. Per room B&B £120–£150 (2-night min. stay at weekends).

WIGMORE Herefordshire
Map 3:C4
PEAR TREE FARM, HR6 9UR. Tel 01568-770140, www.peartree-farm. co.uk. On the edge of a small village with castle ruins, Jill Fieldhouse and Steve Dawson's 17th-century stone-built farmhouse has charming bedrooms and romantic bathrooms with candles, bath oils and fluffy bathrobes. The welcoming hosts provide afternoon tea; home-cooked dinners, using local and free-range produce, are available on Friday and Saturday evenings, by arrangement. Guests may choose from a selection of wines, or bring their own bottle (£6 corkage). There is a wide variety at breakfast, including kedgeree, devilled kidneys, fruit from the garden, and Steve Dawson's organic, home-baked bread. An early-morning tea or coffee tray is delivered to the room. Sitting room (log fire, books, music), dining room; 2-acre garden. Free Wi-Fi. No background music. 7 miles from Ludlow; good walks from the doorstep. 2 resident dogs. 3 bedrooms (1 with private bath; 1 on ground floor). Per room B&B £105. D,B&B £90 per person. 2-night min. stay. Closed Christmas.

WILMSLOW Cheshire
Map 4:E3
KINGSLEY LODGE, 10 Hough Lane,
SK9 2LQ. Tel 01625-441794, www.
kingsleylodge.com. Immaculately
designed by Jeremy Levy and Cliff
Thomson, this luxurious B&B is in an
enlarged and remodelled 1950s Arts and
Crafts house, in a peaceful residential
area. Handcrafted antiques sit
comfortably with more modern pieces;
elegant bedrooms have fresh flowers,
scented candles and original works of
art. There are a formal parterre, ponds,
a pine wood and a seating deck with a
water cascade in the large landscaped
gardens. Lounge (honesty bar),
breakfast room; patio. Free Wi-Fi
(in public areas). DVD library. No
background music. Parking. Close to
Manchester airport. 6 bedrooms. Per
room B&B single £110–£189, double
£210–£330.

WILTON Wiltshire
Map 2:D2
THE PEMBROKE ARMS, Minster Street,
SP2 0BH. Tel 01722-743328, www.
pembrokearms.co.uk. Opposite the
entrance to Wilton House, seat of the
Earls of Pembroke, this Georgian
building was recently extensively
refurbished by Hillbrooke Hotels, and
is back in the hands of Ido Davids,
who runs it with his wife, Alison.
Public areas are simply decorated;
bedrooms are 'Indian colonial' in
style, with an ornate bedhead and
colourful fabrics. The eclectic menu has
plenty of vegetarian options. Lounge
(wood-burning fire), bar, restaurant.
2-acre garden. Free Wi-Fi. No
background music. Wedding/function
facilities. Shooting parties: gun and dog

room. Children welcomed. 8 bedrooms.
Per room B&B £65–£170, D,B&B
£80–£210.

WINCANTON Somerset
Map 2:D1
HOLBROOK HOUSE, BA9 8BS. Tel.
01963-824466, www.holbrookhouse.
co.uk. Returning guests praise the
relaxed atmosphere and friendly staff at
this historic Georgian country house
and spa, once a gentleman's residence, in
the heart of the Wessex countryside. It is
owned by John and Pat McGinley; son
Darren is the manager. In the main
house and walled garden, bedrooms
are traditionally furnished; all have
bathrobes, fresh fruit and views of the
surrounding woodlands and pastures. In
the *Cedar* restaurant overlooking the
grounds, chef James Forman serves
British dishes; light meals are taken in
the *Stables* bar. Wincanton racecourse
is nearby. Popular with summer
weddings. Lounges, bar, restaurant
(closed lunch Mon–Thurs). Background
music in public areas. Free Wi-Fi.
Private dining rooms. Civil wedding
licence; business/function facilities.
20-acre grounds: lawns, streams, grass
tennis court. Spa (indoor swimming
pool, hot tub, sauna, steam room);
treatment rooms; nail bar; health club
(exercise classes). Children welcomed.
21 bedrooms (some in walled garden).
Per room B&B £150–£220, D,B&B
£230–£300.

WINCHESTER Hampshire
Map 2:D2
THE OLD VINE, 8 Great Minster Street,
SO23 9HA. Tel 01962-854616,
www.oldvinewinchester.com. Opposite
the cathedral green, Ashton Gray's

small, design-conscious hotel is in a Grade II listed 18th-century inn, and 'perfectly situated' for both spiritual sustenance and shopping therapy. Elegant, well-furnished bedrooms have designer fabrics, a sleigh bed and a mix of antique and modern furniture; a top-floor suite has impressive views of the cathedral. Hampshire produce is showcased in the oak-beamed restaurant, where an open fire burns in cool weather; the bar has real ales, a small, flower-filled patio and a bright conservatory. Bar ('easy listening' background music), restaurant. Free Wi-Fi. Children welcomed (no under-6s in restaurant and bar). Parking permits supplied for on-street parking. 6 bedrooms (2-bedroom self-catering apartment with garage in annexe). Per room B&B £120–£195, D,B&B (Mon–Thurs) £160–£190.

THE WYKEHAM ARMS, 75 Kingsgate Street, SO23 9PE. Tel 01962-853834, www.wykehamarmswinchester.co.uk. Packed with character, this 18th-century former coaching inn is managed by Jon Howard for Fullers Brewery, and run with enthusiastic, friendly staff. There are cosy nooks and crannies embellished with pictures, ale mugs and memorabilia; well-equipped bedrooms (with a spacious bathroom) are above the pub, reached via a narrow staircase, or in a 16th-century building opposite. Modern British food and pub classics are cooked by Gavin Sinden and served in the wood-panelled restaurant, where old school desks are repurposed as dining tables. 2 bars (local ales), 2 dining rooms, function room; small garden. Background music at breakfast. Free Wi-Fi (in public areas). Children over 12 welcomed. Parking. 14 bedrooms (7 in annexe). Per room B&B £99–£169, D,B&B £104–£180.

25% **DISCOUNT VOUCHERS**

WINDERMERE Cumbria
Map 4: inset C2
CEDAR MANOR, Ambleside Road, LA23 1AX. Tel 015394-43192, www.cedarmanor.co.uk. A 200-year-old cedar tree stands in the walled gardens of this 19th-century hotel, which is within an easy walk of the lake and village. Caroline and Jonathan Kaye are the hands-on owners. The award-winning interior has designer fabrics and handmade furniture. Some bedrooms have original arched windows, others a canopy or four-poster bed; a romantic, eco-friendly suite in the coach house has a lounge with a Juliet balcony, a full entertainment system and a luxurious bathroom. The restaurant focuses on seasonal, locally sourced produce; menus include a list of local suppliers. 2 lounges, dining room (light background music during meals). Free Wi-Fi. Bicycle storage; electric bike hire. Small weddings. Children welcomed. 10 bedrooms (1 suite in coach house). Per room B&B £125–£385, D,B&B £204–£464 (2-night min. stay at weekends). Closed 15–27 Dec.

25% **DISCOUNT VOUCHERS**

WOODBRIDGE Suffolk
Map 2:C5
THE CROWN, The Thoroughfare, IP12 1AD. Tel 01394-384242, www.thecrownatwoodbridge.co.uk. Near the Deben estuary, this white-painted 16th-century coaching inn (decorated with Nantucket overtones) is in the centre of a thriving market town.

It is run by chef/patron Stephen David for the Suffolk-based TA Hotel Collection. In the chic, glass-roofed bar, a wooden sailing skiff suspended from the ceiling makes a striking feature; the bustling dining and drinking areas are popular with locals. Bright bedrooms are styled in neutral tones and shades of grey; modern lighting is 'excellent throughout'. Stephen David shares the modern European, brasserie-style cooking with Luke Bailey; meals are served in two informal dining rooms, at a communal table in the bar, or on sofas in front of the fire. Fixed-price dinners available. Cocktails and Suffolk brews. Background music; monthly jazz evenings. Bar, 4 dining areas; courtyard garden. Free Wi-Fi. Private dining. Children welcomed. Parking. 10 bedrooms. Per room B&B £120–£180, D,B&B from £170.

WOODSTOCK Oxfordshire
Map 2:C2

THE FEATHERS, 16–20 Market Street, OX20 1SX. Tel 01993-812291, www.feathers.co.uk. In the centre of a 'handsome' market town, this privately owned town house hotel occupies a row of buildings (formerly a sanatorium, shops and cottages) on the edge of the Blenheim estate. Traditional features are offset with vibrant colours and bold wallpapers; bedrooms are reached by a series of winding staircases – 'an intimate experience'. 'Our high-ceilinged room was of a good size, with an enormous sleigh bed, a desk and table, an armchair and adequate storage; the superb bathroom had excellent lighting and under-floor heating. No tea or coffee, but guests are invited to take complimentary afternoon tea and

morning coffee in the room or the lounge.' In the restaurant, tables are 'smartly laid' for 'sophisticated dinners'; informal meals are served in the bar. 'Afternoon tea is taken seriously.' Study, *Courtyard* gin bar, restaurant. Jazz/'easy listening' background music. Free Wi-Fi. Function facilities. Picnic hampers. Free long-term parking within walking distance. Children and dogs welcomed. 21 bedrooms (5 in adjacent town house; 1 suitable for &; 1 suite has private steam room). Per room B&B single (Mon–Thurs) £129–£159, double £199–£319. Dinner from £40.

WOOTTON COURTENAY Somerset
Map 1:B5

DUNKERY BEACON COUNTRY HOUSE, Exmoor, TA24 8RH. Tel 01643-841241, www.dunkerybeaconcountryhouse.co.uk. In the heart of Exmoor, this immaculate Edwardian hunting lodge is the home of chef/proprietor John Bradley and his wife, Jane. There are dramatic views across the moor and toward the summit of Dunkery Beacon from the country-style bedrooms, the elegant veranda and the lounge; night skies, unpolluted by artificial light, can be viewed through a Newtonian reflector telescope. John Bradley's imaginative cooking focuses on locally sourced produce; special diets are catered for. Lounge (log-burning stove), *Coleridge* restaurant (background music; open to non-residents; closed Sun–Tues); drying room. ¾-acre garden. Free Wi-Fi (limited in bedrooms). Parking. Dogs welcomed in 2 rooms. 8 bedrooms (1 on ground floor). Per room B&B £80–£130, D,B&B £127–£177 (2-night min. stay at weekends). Closed Jan–mid-Feb.
25% DISCOUNT VOUCHERS

WORCESTER Worcestershire
Map 3:C5
THE MANOR COACH HOUSE, Hindlip
Lane, Hindlip, WR3 8SJ. Tel 01905-
456457, www.manorcoachhouse.co.uk.
'Top notch.' Terry and Sylvia Smith's
fine 1780s house sits in attractive
gardens ('a bird lover's paradise') in a
semi-rural location two miles from the
city centre. It is a good base for walking
the Worcester and Birmingham canal.
Simply furnished bedrooms are in a
renovated outbuilding next to the main
house. They are well equipped; one
room has kitchenette facilities. Generous,
locally sourced breakfasts can be taken
in the garden in fine weather. Afternoon
tea. Breakfast room. 1-acre garden. Free
Wi-Fi. No background music. Parking.
Children welcomed, by arrangement.
5 bedrooms (private courtyard; 2 family
rooms; 1 suitable for &). Per room B&B
single £55, double £80.

WROXTON Oxfordshire
Map 2:C2
WROXTON HOUSE HOTEL, Silver
Street, OX15 6QB. Tel 01295-730777,
www.bw-wroxtonhousehotel.co.uk. 'We
love to visit as often as we can.' On the
edge of a picturesque village three
miles west of Banbury, this 'exquisite'
thatched-roof manor house, dating back
to 1649, is ably run as a Best Western
hotel by the Smith family. It has many
original features (inglenook fireplace,
oak beams) and characterful bedrooms;
those in the new wing are more modern.
'The place is spotless, staff are excellent
in every aspect, and rooms are
constantly kept to a high standard.'
Daily-changing contemporary menus
are served by head chef Steve Mason-
Tocker; biscuits, jam, marmalade and

chutney are all home made. 2 lounges,
bar, *1649* restaurant; terrace. Free Wi-
Fi. Background music. 2 private
function rooms. Civil wedding licence.
Parking. Children welcomed. 32
bedrooms (7 on ground floor; 3 in
adjoining cottage). Per room B&B single
£70–£112, double £89–£235. 2-night
min. stay at weekends.

YORK North Yorkshire
Map 4:D4
BAR CONVENT, 17 Blossom Street,
YO24 1AQ. Tel 01904-643238,
www.bar-convent.org.uk. 'Unlike any
other hotel in which I have stayed.' By
the historic city walls at Micklegate Bar,
a five-minute walk to the centre, this
quirky and interesting Grade I listed
Georgian building houses England's
oldest active convent (founded in 1686).
It has a 'magnificent' glass-roofed
entrance hall, an 18th-century domed
chapel and a library full of fascinating
antique Catholic texts. The simply
decorated bedrooms have 'wickedly'
comfortable beds and communal self-
catering facilities. It is managed by
James Foster. Sitting rooms (on each
floor, with TV), games room (small
snooker table, board games); licensed
café. Meeting rooms; museum; shop;
chapel (Catholic weddings); function
facilities. Lift to 1st and 2nd floors. Free
Wi-Fi. No background music. ½-acre
garden. 20 bedrooms (12 with nearby
bathroom facilities; some suitable for &).
Per room B&B (continental) single £37–
£42, double £86–£96. Dinner £17. Closed
Sun; Easter; 18 Dec–18 Jan.

THE BLOOMSBURY, 127 Clifton,
YO30 6BL. Tel 01904-634031,
www.bloomsburyhotel.co.uk.

'Exceptionally helpful' hosts Steve and Tricia Townsley run this B&B in their 'welcoming, comfortable family home', a Victorian house in a leafy neighbourhood close to Clifton Green. Guests reach the centre via a scenic river walk or a short bus ride; on-site parking is a 'bonus'. 'Spotless, very quiet' bedrooms are traditionally furnished and have efficient lighting. 'Good' breakfasts use fresh local produce and home-made preserves; dietary requirements are catered for, by arrangement. Sitting room, dining room (optional background music); terrace; flowery courtyard; 'secret garden'. Free Wi-Fi. Parking. Within a mile of the city. Children welcomed. Resident dog, Harvey. 6 bedrooms (1 on ground floor). Per person B&B £37.50–£45. 2 people sharing; 2-night min. stay on Sat. Closed 23 Dec–10 Feb.
25% DISCOUNT VOUCHERS

DEAN COURT, Duncombe Place, YO1 7EF. Tel 01904-625082, www.deancourt-york.co.uk. Right by the Minster, this Best Western hotel is formed from three separate dwellings built in 1865 to house the clergy. David Brooks is the manager. Bedrooms are 'comfortable'; windows in the front-facing rooms have secondary glazing to dampen the sound of ringing bells. The 'attractive' dining room has 'splendid' views over the west end of the Minster; *The Court* café/bistro, which serves light meals and snacks, frequently has live entertainment. 'Good' breakfasts. 2 lounges, bar, *D.C.H.* restaurant (closed for lunch Mon–Fri), café/bistro. Free Wi-Fi. Background music. Lift (no access to 4 rooms). Ramp. Civil wedding licence; conference facilities. Valet parking; electric vehicle charging point.

Children welcomed (cots, baby-listening; special menu). 37 bedrooms (family rooms; 3 suitable for &.). Per room B&B £95–£250, D,B&B £125–£300. 2-night min. stay preferred.

THE GRANGE, 1 Clifton, YO30 6AA. Tel 01904-644744, www.grangehotel. co.uk. Just outside the city walls, Vivien and Jeremy Cassel's traditional hotel is in a Grade II listed Regency town house. Jackie Millan is the new manager. It has classically furnished bedrooms (some small), and two modern restaurants (open to non-residents). Traditional English cuisine is served in *The Ivy*; in the original brick-vaulted cellars, the informal *Brasserie* has grilled meats, sharing platters and sandwiches. Will Nicol is chef. Lounge, 2 bars, *The Ivy* restaurant (dinners only Mon–Sat; Sun lunch; closed Sun eve), *Brasserie* (closed Sun lunch). Free Wi-Fi. Background music. Ramps. Civil wedding licence; function facilities. Limited parking on busy road. Children, and dogs (charge) welcomed. 36 bedrooms (some on ground floor). Per room B&B £90–£370, D,B&B £119–£428.
25% DISCOUNT VOUCHERS

MOUNT ROYALE, The Mount, YO24 1GU. Tel 01904-628856, www. mountroyale.co.uk. Owned by the Oxtoby family for more than 40 years, this traditional hotel, formed from two Grade II listed William IV houses, stands near the racecourse and Micklegate Bar. 'The antique-filled entrance hall has a calming atmosphere. The staff, many long-serving, take a genuine interest in their guests.' Although it is on a busy road, the one-acre garden is 'an oasis of peace'; guests appreciate the heated outdoor swimming pool (open May–Sept). In *Oxo's Restaurant on the Mount*, chef Russell Johnson serves 'Yorkshire portions' of English dishes with French influence. Lounge, bar, function rooms, beauty centre. Free Wi-Fi. Background music ('we would have appreciated a more soporific choice'). Civil wedding licence. Children (and dogs) welcomed. 24 bedrooms (some on ground floor; best in garden annexe). Per room B&B single £95, double £125–£265. Dinner £35.

SCOTLAND

ABERDEEN
Map 5:C3

ATHOLL HOTEL, 54 King's Gate, AB15 4YN. Tel 01224-323505, www.atholl-aberdeen.co.uk. Guests like the comfortable bedrooms, friendly staff and traditional Scottish meals at this privately owned hotel, in a tranquil residential neighbourhood within easy reach of the city centre. Gordon Sinclair is the manager. Simply decorated bedrooms have tea- and coffee-making facilities; some rooms are large enough to accommodate a family. A frequent bus goes to and from the city centre; the airport is a 15-minute drive away. Lounge, bar, restaurant; patio. Free Wi-Fi. No background music. Wedding/function facilities. Parking. Children welcomed. 34 bedrooms (some suitable for &). Per room B&B single £70–£145, double £100–£160. Dinner £25.

ACHILTIBUIE Highland
Map 5:B1

SUMMER ISLES, by Ullapool, IV26 2YG. Tel 01854-622282, www.summerisles hotel.com. Reached by a single-track road that winds past lochs, around mountains and beside the sea, this former 19th-century fishing inn 'in a remote spot' has 'amazing' views to the Summer Isles and the Hebrides. It is owned by Terry and Irina Mackay; Chris and Julia Webb manage, with 'charming, attentive' staff. Simply furnished accommodation is spread across the hotel and converted outbuildings; a three-bedroom cottage on the hillside is available out of season for self-catering. A visitor this year found a room for disabled guests 'excellent, with the best shower we have experienced'. In the candlelit restaurant, chef Alan White serves leisurely five-course tasting menus using much produce from nearby Achiltibuie Gardens; his modern Scottish dishes, served at 7.30 pm, are 'outstanding'. 'Excellent' informal meals and a good selection of whiskies are taken in the bar. Brown trout fishing on the hill lochs can be arranged. Bar (occasional live music), lounge (pre-dinner canapés), restaurant, library. Free Wi-Fi. Children, and dogs (in some rooms; not in dining room or lounge) welcomed. 13 bedrooms (10 in annexe and cottage; 1 suitable for &). Per room B&B £165–£330. Dinner £59. Closed Nov–Mar.

ARINAGOUR Argyll and Bute
Map 5:C1

COLL HOTEL, Isle of Coll, PA78 6SZ. Tel 01879-230334, www.collhotel.com. On a small Hebridean island, Kevin and Julie Oliphant's white-painted hotel stands in large gardens with views across a lovely bay to Staffa, Iona, Jura and the Treshnish Isles. It is a lively hub: locals and visitors are drawn to the cosy bars, with their open fires in winter, and to the *Gannet* restaurant, where Julie Oliphant and chef Graham Griffiths cook simple dishes using local fish and seafood, and island produce. Guests are welcomed with tea or coffee and home-made shortbread on arrival; simply furnished bedrooms (four with sea views) have a book on birds and a glow-in-the-dark skyscope. (No light pollution; astronomy workshops in the autumn and winter months.) Complimentary pick-up from and return to the ferry pier. Lounge, 2 bars (darts, pool table), 2 restaurants. Free Wi-Fi. No background music. Garden (decking, plenty of seating; pétanque). Bicycles available to borrow (BYO helmet). Helipad. Children welcomed (special menu). 6 bedrooms. Per room B&B single £55–£65, double £100–£125. Dinner £20–£30 (house parties only at Christmas and New Year).

BALLYGRANT Argyll and Bute
Map 5:D1
KILMENY COUNTRY HOUSE, Isle of Islay, PA45 7QW. Tel 01496-840668, www.kilmeny.co.uk. 'Nothing short of excellent.' On a working farm, Margaret and Blair Rozga's handsomely furnished 19th-century house is in an elevated position with 'spectacular views' over the Islay countryside. The hosts 'make guests feel relaxed from the minute they arrive', and offer tea and home-baked cakes. 'Definitely not to be missed', evening meals (Tues and Thurs only) include drinks and canapés before, and petits fours afterwards. 2 sitting rooms; garden. Free Wi-Fi. No background music. On the edge of a village, 4 miles from the ferry terminal at Port Askaig. Children over 5 welcomed. 5 bedrooms (2 on ground floor, with walk-in

shower). Per room B&B £90–£158. Dinner £32 (by arrangement; BYO wine). Closed Dec–Mar.

BRAE Shetland
Map 5: inset A2
BUSTA HOUSE, ZE2 9QN. Tel 01806-522506, www.bustahouse.com. On the secluded shores of Busta Voe, this characterful small hotel has creaky floors, an open peat fire and an extensive selection of malt whiskies. It is owned and run by Joe and Veronica Rocks, personable hosts who will regale guests with the house's fascinating history – one that links a shipwreck, an illegitimate child, an envious cousin and a ghost. The house, with parts that date back to 1588, has a quirky layout and lots of stairs; traditionally furnished (even old-fashioned) bedrooms overlook the gardens or the harbour. Generous portions at dinner; informal meals are taken in the lounges. 2 lounges, bar/dining area, *Pitcairn* restaurant (background music). Free Wi-Fi; computer available. Garden. Wedding facilities. Children welcomed. 22 bedrooms. Per room B&B £115–£160. Dinner £35.

BRODICK North Ayrshire
Map 5:E1
AUCHRANNIE HOUSE HOTEL, Isle of Arran, KA27 8BZ. Tel 01770-302234, www.auchrannie.co.uk. There are many diversions at the Johnston family's child-friendly island enterprise, which includes a resort with three restaurants, two leisure clubs and two hotels. Standing in 'lovely' landscaped gardens, the *Auchrannie House Hotel* occupies a 19th-century country house with modern bedrooms and 'plush lounges to

relax in'. Richard Small is the manager. A contemporary bar/brasserie serves informal meals all day; *Brambles* has grills and West Coast seafood; the seasonal (Mar–Oct) *eighteen69* conservatory restaurant serves an extensive menu of Scottish-themed tapas. 'Everything you would expect in a country house.' A complimentary bus service operates between the resort and the ferry terminal. Bar, 3 restaurants; spa (indoor pool, steam room, spa bath; gym). Free Wi-Fi. Background music. Parking. Children (play barn, external play and picnic area, library), and dogs welcomed. 28 bedrooms (plus accommodation in the modern spa resort; also 30 self-catering lodges). Per room B&B £99–£224, D,B&B £129–£254.

CUMNOCK East Ayrshire
Map 5:E2
DUMFRIES HOUSE LODGE, KA18 2NJ. Tel 01290-429920, www.dumfrieshouse lodge.com. Part of the 2,000-acre Dumfries House estate, built by Robert Adam for the Earl of Dumfries, this 18th-century factor's house has been turned into a 'luxurious' B&B with cosy lounge areas, and bedrooms filled with antiques. It is managed by Mark Robson for the Prince's Trust. 'We were encouraged to treat the beautifully furnished house as our country home.' Many parts of the original building have been incorporated into the renovated guest house: there are two 'pretty' drawing rooms, a laundry room, and a kitchen where guests can prepare hot drinks and snacks. Bedrooms and bathrooms are decorated in modern country house style; further accommodation was being added in a lodge and cottages nearby as the *Guide*

went to press. House tours can be booked. Free Wi-Fi. No background music. Children welcomed. 22 bedrooms (9 in Factor's House; 1 suitable for &; plus 2 self-catering cottages). Per room B&B £70–£135. Closed Christmas.

DALKEITH Midlothian
Map 5:D2
THE SUN INN, Lothianbridge, EH22 4TR. Tel 0131-663 2456, www.thesuninnedinburgh.co.uk. In a handsomely refurbished former coaching inn, chef/proprietor Ian Minto and his family run this 'down-to-earth' gastropub-with-rooms standing in five acres of wooded grounds close to the banks of the River Esk. A guest in 2013 found it 'charming (though it is beside a railway viaduct); good for a short stay'. The 'busy', praiseworthy dining room serves 'very good' modern interpretations of pub classics using much Scottish produce; the covered courtyard has barbecues and spritzers in the summer. 'Good-sized portions; we enjoyed some of the best fish we have had in a while.' Stylish bedrooms have DVDs, a Roberts radio and home-made biscuits; the quietest face away from the street. Edinburgh city centre is 20 mins' drive away. Bar, restaurant (modern background music); garden. Free Wi-Fi. Parking. 5 bedrooms (1 suite with copper bath). Per room B&B single £70–£100, double £85–£150. Dinner from £28. Closed 26 Dec and 1 Jan.

DERVAIG Argyll and Bute
Map 5:D1
KILLORAN HOUSE, Isle of Mull, PA75 6QR. Tel 01688-400362, www.killoranmull.co.uk. In a remote

northern area of Mull, Janette and Ian McKilligan's purpose-built small hotel stands on a hillside with panoramic views over Dervaig and Loch Cuin. Binoculars are provided in the well-proportioned sitting room on the first floor, where tea and cake are served to arriving guests. Pre-dinner drinks may be taken on the balcony in fine weather; chef Ian McKilligan's well-executed, daily-changing set dinners are served in the conservatory. Pristine bedrooms vary in size. Sitting room, study, conservatory dining room ('easy listening' background music). Free Wi-Fi. 1¾-acre garden. Parking. 1½ miles SW of Dervaig. 5 bedrooms (1 on ground floor suitable for &.). Per person B&B £62.50–£92. 2-night min. stay. Dinner £25–£36. Closed Nov–Mar.

DORNOCH Highland
Map 5:B2
2 QUAIL, Castle Street, IV25 3SN. Tel 01862-811811, www.2quail.com. Golf enthusiasts Michael and Kerensa Carr run this 'very pleasant, comfortable and quiet' B&B in their mellow stone house close to the cathedral and the Royal Dornoch Golf Club (Michael Carr, who trained at The Ritz, is executive chef there). The house is traditionally decorated with tartan carpets and inherited furniture and antiques; bedrooms have a wood or iron bedstead. A 'delicious' breakfast is served at an agreed time from 7 am ('for those with early tee times'). The beautiful stretch of sandy beach is a short distance away. Lounge/library, dining room. Licensed. Free Wi-Fi. Occasional background music. 'Babes in arms' and children over 10 welcomed. 3 bedrooms. Per room B&B single £70–£100, double £75–£120.

DUNDEE
Map 5:D3
DUNTRUNE HOUSE, Main Wing, Duntrune, DD4 0PJ. Tel 01382-350239, www.duntrunehouse.co.uk. In extensive gardens with woodland walks and gorgeous scenery, welcoming hosts Olwyn and Barrie Jack offer tranquil B&B accommodation in their restored 19th-century manor house. Traditionally furnished bedrooms have views over the grounds to Fife and beyond; all are equipped with bathrobes, organic toiletries and a well-considered hospitality tray. Chef Mathew Defranco's home-cooked dinners, available by arrangement, use much organic produce grown in the grounds. Breakfast is taken communally; there is good variety, including home-made muesli and jams, local honey, and fresh garden fruit in season. Sitting room, dining room; 8-acre garden. Free Wi-Fi. No background music. Laundry facilities. Parking. Children welcomed. Activity courses (painting, yoga, Bellyfit; sauna and beauty treatments) nearby. 3 bedrooms (1 on ground floor; plus a self-catering flat). Per person B&B £42.50–£62.50. 2-night min. stay. Dinner £15–£27.50. Closed Nov–Mar.

EDINBANE Highland
Map 5:C1
GRESHORNISH HOUSE, by Portree, Isle of Skye, IV51 9PN. Tel 01470-582266, www.greshornishhouse.com. In secluded grounds that once belonged to the local laird, this elegant white-painted house (Georgian with Victorian additions) is beside a loch in a remote corner of Skye. There is a country house feel, with squashy sofas and log fires in the public rooms; staying here is 'like visiting

friends'. Bedrooms, named after Scottish islands, have 'gorgeous' views of the loch or beautiful garden; a daily-changing tasting menu, cooked by Glyn Musker, is served in the candlelit dining room. In summer 2014, Neil and Rosemary Colquhoun, the owners, put the house up for sale. Drawing room, bar, conservatory, dining room (non-residents welcome, closed Mon), billiard room. Free Wi-Fi (limited). No background music. Parking. Children welcomed; dogs by arrangement. 17 miles NW of Portree. 6 bedrooms (plus 2 attic rooms). Per person B&B £70–£100, D,B&B £105–£135. 2-night min. stay.

EDINBURGH
Map 5:D2
THE BALMORAL, 1 Princes Street, EH2 2EQ. Tel 0131-556 2414, www.thebalmoralhotel.com. A doorman in a kilt, cloak and ghillie brogues welcomes guests to this grand Victorian building in the centre of the city. Once one of the great railway hotels, it is today a luxury enterprise (Rocco Forte Hotels) with understated modern bedrooms and a *Michelin*-starred restaurant. Franck Arnold is the manager. Guests have many options of eating, drinking and lounging areas: the well-regarded *Number One* restaurant has modern European tasting menus; the lively *Hadrians* brasserie is ideal for informal eating; afternoon tea is taken under the glass dome and Venetian chandelier of the *Palm Court*; the whisky bar has tweed sofas and more than 400 malts, blends and vintages. Drawing room, 2 bars, restaurant, brasserie. Wi-Fi (charge; free if room is booked via the hotel's website). Background music. 15-metre indoor pool. Spa (treatment rooms, sauna, gym, exercise studio). Room service; 24-hour concierge. Wedding/conference facilities. Valet parking. Children welcomed. 188 bedrooms (3 suitable for ♿). Per room B&B £267–£772. Dinner £68–£75.

BROOKS HOTEL EDINBURGH, 70–72 Grove Street, EH3 8AP. Tel 0131-228 2323, www.brooksedinburgh.com. Close to the Edinburgh International Conference Centre in the west end of the city, this 1840s stone building has been restyled inside with a mix of classic and contemporary furnishings. It is owned by Andrew and Carla Brooks (see also *Brooks Guesthouse*, Bristol, main entry). Half-panelled bedrooms are simply decorated in pastel shades; the lounge has an open fire, vintage leather seating and a chandelier. Scottish breakfasts include haggis and tattie scones. No evening meals. Emma Loane is the manager. Lounge (honesty bar), breakfast room; private dining room. Free Wi-Fi. Background music. Courtyard garden. Small conference facilities. Paid parking nearby (£12 per day). Children welcomed (cots). 46 bedrooms (some in annexe; 1 suitable for ♿). Per person B&B £27–£75 (2 people sharing). Closed Christmas.

94DR, 94 Dalkeith Road, EH16 5AF. Tel 0131-662 9265, www.94dr.com. Paul Lightfoot and John MacEwan run this modern B&B in their restored Victorian town house; helpful hosts, they assist with restaurant, theatre and concert bookings, car hire and guided tours. Decorated with verve, contemporary bedrooms (Couture, Bespoke or Tailored) have panoramic views of the Salisbury Crags and Arthur's Seat, or over the walled gardens towards the Pentland hills. In the orangery, breakfasts use organic local produce and include a daily special; breakfast boxes can be eaten in the room. Ten minutes by bus from the centre; bicycles are available to borrow. Lounge, drawing room, breakfast room (classical/jazz/'easy listening' background music). Free Wi-Fi. Walled garden. Children welcomed (books, DVDs, games, Xbox). Resident labradoodle, Molli. 6 bedrooms. Per person B&B £45–£95. 2-night min. stay on Sat in high season. Closed 5–20 Jan.

ONE ROYAL CIRCUS, EH3 6TL. Tel 0131-625 6669, www.oneroyalcircus.com. Susan and Mike Gordon's stylish modern B&B stands on a World Heritage-listed crescent in the heart of the fashionable New Town neighbourhood. Guests like the relaxed atmosphere: they are given a key to the front door and have the run of the Georgian town house. Beyond the discreet entrance, there are vintage French posters, a disco ball, a baby grand piano, and an eclectic mix of antique and modern pieces; the best of the spacious, individually styled bedrooms overlook the elegant private gardens across the street. Breakfast has lots of choice, including granola, fruit salad, pancakes and a full Scottish. Kitchen, lounge (bar), drawing room. Free Wi-Fi. No background music. Pool room (with Bonzini Babyfoot table), gym; key access to private gardens. Wedding facilities. Children welcomed (books, games; babysitting by arrangement). 5 bedrooms (plus a 1-bedroom apartment). Per room B&B from £130.

PRESTONFIELD, Priestfield Road, EH16 5UT. Tel 0131-225 7800, www.prestonfield.com. Next to Holyrood Park, this grand Baroque home owned by James Thomson (see also *The Witchery by the Castle*, Edinburgh, in the Shortlist, below) stands in 20 acres of private grounds. 'An orgy for the eyes and senses', it is opulently decorated, and has gilded furniture, swags, velvets and brocades, leather-panelled rooms, wood-burning stoves, and black-kilted staff; seductive bedrooms, each with views over parkland, have antiques, remarkable beds, and a bottle of chilled champagne on arrival. 'Excellent' food is served in the glamorous *Rhubarb* restaurant. 2 drawing rooms, salon, whisky bar; 4 private dining rooms. Free Wi-Fi. Background music. Terraces, 'Gothic' tea house. Lift. Wedding/function facilities. Parking. Children and dogs welcomed. 23 bedrooms (5 suites; 1 suitable for &). Per room B&B £295, D,B&B from £365.

THE SCOTSMAN, 20 North Bridge, EH1 1TR. Tel 0131-556 5565, www.thescotsmanhotel.co.uk. The former offices of the *Scotsman* newspaper have been 'sympathetically restored and adapted' to house this 'stylish and tasteful' luxury hotel. Many features of the spectacular 1905 building have been preserved, such as a hand-carved wooden balcony, ornate ceilings and an impressive Italian marble staircase. Bedrooms are well equipped with an Edinburgh Monopoly board game, *Scotsman* newspaper, Scottish shortbread and complimentary shoe-shine service. 'Our enormous room had plenty of storage space and a lavishly appointed bathroom; three large windows had distant views of the sea; pity about the low lighting.' Extensive breakfasts. Drawing room, breakfast room, bar/brasserie; lift, ramps. Free Wi-Fi. Background music. Cinema; health spa (16-metre swimming pool, sauna, gym, treatment rooms; juice bar, café). Wedding/conference facilities. Children welcomed. 69 bedrooms (2 suitable for &). Per room B&B £184–£424.

SOUTHSIDE GUEST HOUSE, 8 Newington Road, EH9 1QS. Tel 0131-668 4422, www.southsideguesthouse.co.uk. Near the Meadows and Holyrood Park, Franco and Lynne Galgani's 'friendly' B&B is in a terrace of Victorian houses, and has lovely views over Edinburgh. It is within easy walking distance of restaurants, pubs and shops; a bus-stop is nearby. Colourful, modern bedrooms have comfortable seating; one, with a four-poster bed, also has a fireplace and a private terrace. Breakfast includes vegetarian options, a daily special and Buck's Fizz. Breakfast room (light classical background music). Free Wi-Fi. Limited parking. Children over 8 welcomed. 8 bedrooms. Per room B&B £90–£180.
25% DISCOUNT VOUCHERS

TIGERLILY, 125 George Street, EH2 4JN. Tel 0131-225 5005, www.tigerlily edinburgh.co.uk. A sense of fun permeates this stylish hotel filled with spirited prints, revolving glitter balls and chic modern fireplaces. It occupies a Georgian town house on a street popular for shopping and nights out; its two opulent, lively bars have mirrored walls and chandeliers. Bedrooms –

ranging from good-sized doubles to a high-ceilinged suite with a contemporary four-poster bed – are individually styled; all have organic fruit and fresh flowers. 2 bars (resident DJs), restaurant (background music); lift. Free Wi-Fi. Complimentary access to gym and pool, opposite. Children welcomed (cots; babysitting by arrangement). 33 bedrooms (some smoking). Per room B&B £175–£300.

20 ALBANY STREET, 20 Albany Street, EH1 3QB. Tel 0131-478 5386, www.20albanystreet.co.uk. Guests are welcomed with tea, home-made cake and a wee dram of Highland malt whisky at Denise Walker's centrally, yet peacefully, located B&B. The elegantly furnished Georgian town house has spacious bedrooms with a large bed and bathroom; shortbread is a thoughtful extra. Served at a time to suit guests, sumptuous breakfasts have a seasonal fruit salad, freshly baked croissants, a full Scottish and a daily fish dish. Drawing room, dining room. Free Wi-Fi. Background music at breakfast. Parking available (charge). Resident dog, Rolo. 3 bedrooms. Per room B&B £129–£189.

21212, 3 Royal Terrace, EH7 5AB. Tel 0845 22 21212, www.21212restaurant. co.uk. Paul Kitching and Katie O'Brien's award-winning restaurant-with-rooms is in a restored Grade A listed town house, at the end of a Georgian terrace. Pre- and post-dinner drinks can be taken in the glamorous drawing room, which retains many original features; oversized windows give good views across Royal Terrace and its gardens to the Firth of Forth and beyond. In the restaurant, Paul Kitching has a *Michelin* star for his creative cooking; diners can watch him and his team of seven chefs at work in the open kitchen. On the upper floors, large, sleek bedrooms have an ample seating area and plenty of storage. Drawing room, restaurant (closed Sun, Mon); private dining rooms. Free Wi-Fi. Children over 5 welcomed. 4 bedrooms. Per room B&B £95–£325. Dinner £49–£69. Closed 10 days in Jan; 10 days in summer.

THE WITCHERY BY THE CASTLE, Castlehill, EH1 2NF. Tel 0131-225 5613, www.thewitchery.com. In two 16th- and 17th-century buildings by the gates of Edinburgh Castle, this theatrical restaurant-with-suites overlooks the Royal Mile. It is owned by James Thomson (see *Prestonfield*, Edinburgh, in the Shortlist). It has candlelit rooms, secret doors, and nooks and crannies; sumptuous Gothic-style accommodation is decorated with antique velvet drapes and gold-laced brocade. The new Turret Suite has a tapestry-lined entrance, a collection of stags' antlers, an oak-panelled bathroom and exceptional views over the rooftops. A bottle of champagne is presented on arrival; in the morning, a breakfast hamper is delivered to the room. 2 restaurants: *The Witchery* and *The Secret Garden* (Douglas Roberts is chef; background music); terrace. Free Wi-Fi. 9 suites. Per room B&B £325–£350, D,B&B from £400.

FORT WILLIAM Highland
Map 5:C1
THE LIME TREE, The Old Manse, Achintore Road, PH33 6RQ. Tel 01397-701806, www.limetreefortwilliam.co.uk.

Overlooking Loch Linnhe and the hills beyond, this former manse near the town centre has been 'imaginatively converted' into a small hotel, restaurant and regional art gallery hosting exhibitions from touring national collections. The owner, David Wilson, is an artist; his 'exciting' work is displayed in both the hotel and the gallery. Most of the modern rustic bedrooms have lovely loch views; the cosy lounges have open fires. Chef William MacDonald cooks modern European food with a Scottish slant. 3 lounges (a map room has 'books and guides to help guests plan their journeys'), restaurant (background music); gallery; garden with seating area. Free Wi-Fi. Drying room; bicycle storage. Children, and dogs (£5 charge) welcomed. 9 bedrooms (in main house and extension). Per room B&B £80–£120. Dinner £29.95.

GATESIDE Fife
Map 5:D2
EDENSHEAD STABLES, by Falkland, Cupar, KY14 7ST. Tel 01337-868500, www.edensheadstables.com. Guests like the warm welcome from amiable hosts Gill and John Donald at their peaceful B&B, in converted Georgian stables at the foot of the Lomond hills. The pink-stone building stands in wooded grounds that lead down to the River Eden; the gardens are regularly visited by goldfinches, robins, woodpeckers, and a heron fishing in the river. B&B accommodation is in comfortable, traditionally furnished bedrooms; the sitting room has French doors that open on to a patio. Served between 7.45 am and 8.45 am, communal breakfasts use locally sourced produce; hot dishes are cooked to order. Lounge (magazines,

guidebooks), dining room. Free Wi-Fi. No background music. 3-acre grounds. Golf, and cycle routes nearby; safe storage for equipment. Children over 14 welcomed. Resident dogs. 3 bedrooms (all on ground floor). Per person B&B from £46. 2-night min. stay in summer. Dinner £30 (by arrangement, for groups of 4–6; BYO wine). Closed Dec–Mar.

GLASGOW
Map 5:D2
BLYTHSWOOD SQUARE HOTEL, 11 Blythswood Square, G2 4AD. Tel 0141-248 8888, www.blythswoodsquare.com. 'A comfortable and glamorous place to stay', this modern hotel (part of the Town House Collection) occupies an 'imposing' Victorian building on a 'splendid' garden square. 'Elegantly furnished, the hotel is contemporary, rich and stylish; the opulent marble bathrooms give the bedrooms a real touch of luxury.' The restaurant and lively cocktail bar are 'busy all day and evening'; champagne afternoon teas are served in the salon. 'Great' breakfasts. Salon, 3 bars, restaurant; private screening room. Free Wi-Fi. Background music. Lift. Spa (2 relaxation pools, treatment rooms, rasul mud chamber, relaxing lounge, café). Valet parking (from £27.50 for 24 hours). Children (special menu), and dogs (in some bedrooms; £30 charge) welcomed. 100 bedrooms (some suitable for &). Room only £120–£300. Breakfast £12.50–£16.50.

15GLASGOW, 15 Woodside Place, G3 7QL. Tel 0141-332 1263, www. 15glasgow.com. Shane and Laura McKenzie have won a design award for the restoration of their town house B&B in a Victorian terrace. Original fireplaces, intricate cornicing, working wooden shutters, stained glass and oak panelling have been retained. Modern, pared-down bedrooms, decorated in cool shades of silver, grey and caramel, are spacious and comfortable, with tall windows, high ceilings and mood lighting; Tunnock's teacakes are a welcome gesture. Breakfast is brought to the room at an arranged time. A short walk from the city centre; the University of Glasgow and the museums are close by. Lounge (classical radio background music); garden. Free Wi-Fi. Parking. Children welcomed. 5 bedrooms. Per person B&B £50–£85. min. 3-night stay for advance bookings.

GLENDEVON Perth and Kinross
Map 5:D2
THE TORMAUKIN HOTEL, FK14 7JY. Tel 01259-781252, www.tormaukinhotel. co.uk. Welcoming owners Dave and Lesley Morby run their charming small hotel in a refurbished 18th-century drovers' inn surrounded by Perthshire countryside. Simply furnished bedrooms retain many original features, such as a beamed ceiling or stone fireplace; two new rooms, in chalets on a slope behind the main house, have a terrace and outdoor seating. Chef Martin Cowan uses much locally reared beef and lamb, and locally sourced fish and game in his well-regarded menus. Lounge, bar, restaurant, conservatory; patio. Free Wi-Fi. Background music. Parking. Children, and dogs (£10 charge) welcomed. 13 bedrooms (some on ground floor; 4 in adjoining stables block, 2 in chalets). Per room B&B £70–£100. Dinner £23.

GRANTOWN-ON-SPEY Highland
Map 5:C2

THE DULAIG, Seafield Avenue, PH26 3JF. Tel 01479-872065, www.thedulaig. com. 'A great place to stay.' In a rural position, Carol and Gordon Bulloch's 'utterly luxurious' B&B is in an Edwardian house, a ten-minute walk from town. The Bullochs are 'fun' and provide lots of 'small and thoughtful' touches; freshly baked treats are left daily by the 'cake fairy' in the spacious, elegant bedrooms. Extensive, 'top-of-the-line' breakfasts use home-grown produce and eggs from the Bullochs' flock of free-range Black Rock hens. Packed lunches available. 'The gardens are spectacular, and even include tame wildlife.' Drawing room, dining room (optional background music), veranda; secluded garden (pond, summer house). Free Wi-Fi; computer available. Parking (garage for motorbikes and cycles). 3 bedrooms. Per person B&B £77.50–£87.50.

GULLANE East Lothian
Map 5:D3

GREYWALLS, Muirfield, EH31 2EG. Tel 01620-842144, www.greywalls.co.uk. In a crescent-shaped stone house designed by Sir Edwin Lutyens, this hotel is ideally placed for golfers: it overlooks the 9th and 18th holes of Muirfield golf course; nine other courses are nearby. Interiors remain faithful to the Edwardian period; individually styled bedrooms have antique furnishings. Classical French cuisine is served in *Chez Roux* restaurant; lighter meals are taken in the lounge or, in mild weather, on the terrace. Delightful walled gardens (attributed to Gertrude Jekyll) have secluded seating, arches, 'rooms' and vistas. Bar/lounge, drawing room, library, *Chez Roux* restaurant (open to non-residents). Free Wi-Fi. No background music. Treatments. 4-acre garden (hard and grass tennis courts, croquet lawn, putting green). Wedding/function facilities. Children, and dogs (in cottages only) welcomed. 23 bedrooms (some in cottage nearby). Per room B&B £240–£335. Dinner £30–£45.

INNERLEITHEN Scottish Borders
Map 5:E2

CADDON VIEW, 14 Pirn Road, EH44 6HH. Tel 01896-830208, www.caddonview.co.uk. Set in mature grounds, this handsome Victorian house is run as a guest house and licensed restaurant by Stephen and Lisa Davies. There is a country house atmosphere: the cosy drawing room has a log fire, books, maps, magazines and games; tea and home-baked cake are served to arriving guests. Some bedrooms have pretty floral wallpaper; others are more simply decorated. Stephen Davies's two-and three-course Scottish menus are served in the candlelit dining room (closed for dinner on Sun, Mon; room snacks available). Drawing room, dining room (background music). Free Wi-Fi (signal strength varies). Picnics available. Storage for bikes and fishing gear. Parking. Children, and dogs (only in 1 bedroom; £5 per night charge), welcomed. 8 bedrooms. Per room B&B £50–£110, D,B&B £75–£160.

INVERNESS Highland
Map 5:C2

MOYNESS HOUSE, 6 Bruce Gardens, IV3 5EN. Tel 01463-233836, www.moyness. co.uk. On a quiet residential street, this 'very good' B&B is within walking distance of the town centre and the

River Ness. The Victorian villa, which was formerly the home of Scottish Renaissance author Neil M Gunn, has been restored by Jenny and Richard Jones; individually styled bedrooms are named after Gunn's works. 'Good' breakfasts include Speyside haggis and whole kippers. The hands-on hosts are happy to advise on restaurants and activities in the area. Sitting room, dining room; ½-acre garden. Free Wi-Fi. No background music. Parking. Children over 6 welcomed. 6 bedrooms (1 family room). Per room B&B £69–£110. Closed Christmas.

ROCPOOL RESERVE, 14 Culduthel Road, IV2 4AG. Tel 01463-240089, www.rocpool.com. A ten-minute walk from the centre, this sophisticated hotel has magnificent views towards the mountains of Cairngorms national park. It has modern bedrooms, a split-level cocktail bar and a *Chez Roux* restaurant, where Javier Santos is chef. Sleek rooms have a large bed, a flat-screen TV, and a Tassimo drinks machine for coffees and hot chocolates; some have a private balcony or outdoor hot tub. David Robertson is the manager. The hotel is part of the ICMI group; sister hotels include *Inverlochy Castle*, Fort William (see main entry), and *Greywalls*, Gullane (see above). Children are well provided for with lots of activities: quad biking, go-carting, archery, ice skating and riding, all by arrangement. Lounge, *r* bar, *Chez Roux* restaurant; terrace. In-room massages and treatments can be arranged. Free Wi-Fi. Background music. Wedding/conference facilities. Parking. Children welcomed (Xbox, board games, DVDs; kids' menu). 11 bedrooms (plus 3 serviced apartments

in the West End). Per room B&B £195–£395, D,B&B £250–£460.

TRAFFORD BANK GUEST HOUSE, 96 Fairfield Road, IV3 5LL. Tel 01463-241414, www.traffordbankguesthouse.co.uk. Once the home of the Bishop of Moray and Ross-shire, this bay-windowed, sandstone Victorian house has been furnished by interior designer Lorraine Pun with a mix of antique and contemporary pieces, including interesting sculptures in the mature garden. Large bedrooms are equipped with sherry and organic toiletries. Breakfast, ordered the evening before, 'hits all the right buttons', with home-made scones and oatcakes. Ten minutes' walk from the centre. 2 lounges, conservatory; garden. Free Wi-Fi. No background music. Children welcomed. 5 bedrooms. Per room B&B £98–£128. Closed mid-Nov–mid-Dec.

IONA Argyll and Bute
Map 5:D1

ARGYLL HOTEL, PA76 6SJ. Tel 01681-700334, www.argyllhoteliona.co.uk. 'Perfect in every way for a spiritual pilgrimage.' On a 'magical' island, this hotel and restaurant, once a modest croft house, has been welcoming visitors for nearly 150 years. Today, it is owned and run in an 'unpretentious and laid-back' manner by two couples, Wendy and Rob MacManaway, and Katy and Dafydd Russon. Jann Simpson is the manager. There are fires in the lounge and the 'convivial' dining room; simply furnished bedrooms overlook the Sound of Iona, or the courtyard and garden. 'Really delicious' seasonal meals are cooked by Richard Shwe on the 1920s Aga; vegetables come fresh from the organic kitchen garden; marmalades, chutneys, scones, shortbreads and brownies are all home made (special diets catered for). 3 lounges, television room, dining room ('easy listening' background music; open to non-residents). No TV or telephone in rooms. Free Wi-Fi (in lounges, dining room). Organic kitchen garden. Children and dogs welcomed. 17 bedrooms (7 in annexe). Per room B&B (continental) single from £60, double £75–£165. Closed Nov–late Mar (except 2–21 Mar). Dinner £30.

KELSO Scottish Borders
Map 5:E3

THE CROSS KEYS, 36–37 The Square, TD5 7HL. Tel 01573-223303, www.cross-keys-hotel.co.uk. 'Highly recommended.' On a picturesque square in a historic Borders town, the 'delightful' Becattelli family still run this hotel after more than 30 years. Bedrooms in the 18th-century coaching inn vary in size and shape; interconnecting family rooms, with a shared bathroom, are available. The *Oak Room* restaurant serves 'excellent' modern Scottish and Mediterranean dishes cooked by head chef Brian Crawford; good vegetarian choices. Popular with groups. Lounge, *No. 36* bar, restaurant; ballroom. Free Wi-Fi. Background music. Lift. Ramp. Wedding/function/conference facilities. Parking. Children welcomed. 26 bedrooms. Per room B&B £89.50–£155, D,B&B £109.50–£175. Closed Christmas.

KILMARTIN Argyll and Bute
Map 5:D1

DUNCHRAIGAIG HOUSE, Lochgilphead, PA31 8RG. Tel 01546-510396, www.dunchraigaig.co.uk. Opposite a group of standing stones in an area rich in prehistoric sites, this B&B is run by 'hands-on and competent' hosts Cameron Bruce and Lynn Jones. Bedrooms, decorated in 'relaxing' colours, have views of the stones or of woodland at the back (from which deer or the 'resident' pine marten may emerge). Breakfast, taken communally or at separate tables, includes eggs from resident hens, and fruit from the garden; muffins or rolls are baked daily. 'Interesting' walks from the garden gate; packed lunches (£5). Cupcake-decorating workshops. Lounge (books, games, information), dining room; ½-acre garden. Free Wi-Fi. No background music. Parking. 1 mile south of village, 7 miles N of Lochgilphead. 5 bedrooms. Per room B&B £30–£50. Closed Dec–Mar.
25% DISCOUNT VOUCHERS

KINCLAVEN Perth and Kinross
Map 5:D2

BALLATHIE HOUSE, Stanley, nr Perth, PH41 4QN. Tel 01250-883268, www.ballathiehousehotel.com. 'A wonderful place.' Visitors return again and again to the Mulligan family's 'impressive' 19th-century house in 'fabulous' grounds, on the west bank of the River Tay. The hotel has long been associated with salmon fishing; display cabinets in the public rooms showcase 'monster' fishing trophies. Public areas have old-style grandeur, sporting prints and open fires; country house-style bedrooms have period features and views of the river or surrounding countryside. Chef Scott Scorer's menus have trout and salmon from local rivers, and home-grown herbs; Jody Marshall is the manager. Drawing room, bar, restaurant; private dining rooms.

Free Wi-Fi. No background music. Wedding/function facilities. Golf, fishing, shooting, sled-dog racing by arrangement. Children, and dogs (£20 charge) welcomed. 53 bedrooms (16 in riverside building reached via a lit garden pathway; 12 in Sportsman's Lodge). Per person B&B £110–£135, D,B&B £150–£175; Sportsman's Lodge per person from £60.

KINLOCHLEVEN Highland
Map 5:D2
TIGH NA CHEO, Garbhein Road, PH50 4SE. Tel 01855-831434, www. tigh-na-cheo.co.uk. Surrounded by mountains, Martin and Jacqui Clark's comforting B&B is at the head of Loch Leven, three minutes from Kinlochleven, the penultimate halt on the West Highland Way. Walkers, bikers and cyclists are heartily welcomed; secure storage is available. Experienced walkers themselves, the hosts ('charming, friendly and helpful') understand the importance of well-equipped rooms, soothing baths and hearty Scottish breakfasts; they also offer maps and guidebooks, a pick-up and drop-off service into town, and much useful local knowledge. Lounge, drying room; terrace; 1-acre garden. Limited parking. 9 bedrooms (1 suitable for &). Per room B&B single £40, double £60–£74. Closed Nov–mid-Mar.

LOCHINVER Highland
Map 5:B1
INVER LODGE HOTEL, Iolaire Road, IV27 4LU. Tel 01571-844496, www. inverlodge.com. There are gorgeous views from each bedroom in this purpose-built hotel surrounded by dramatic nature. Owned by Robin Vestey, it is managed by Nicholas Gorton. The foyer lounge has comfortable sofas, an open fire and picture windows; daily-changing menus are served in the *Chez Roux* restaurant. Walkers, climbers and birdwatchers have much diversion; stalking on local estates can be arranged. Lounge, bar, restaurant. Free Wi-Fi. No background music. Snooker table; sauna; massages and treatments available. ½-acre grounds (salmon and trout fishing). Children and dogs welcomed. 21 bedrooms (some on ground floor; 1 suitable for &). Per room B&B £225–£335, D,B&B £300–£410. Closed Nov–Mar.

LOCHRANZA North Ayrshire
Map 5:D1
APPLE LODGE, Isle of Arran, KA27 8HJ. Tel 01770-830229, www.applelodgearran.co.uk. Near the ferry to the Kintyre peninsula, Jeannie and John Boyd's small guest house is in a white-painted Edwardian manse surrounded by beautiful countryside; deer and eagles are often sighted. Warm and welcoming, the Boyds have embellished their home with paintings, embroidery and antique furniture. Each bedroom is named after an apple variety and has an old fireplace; the Apple cottage, a self-contained suite with a sitting room and kitchen, has French doors opening on to the garden. Jeannie Boyd serves a three-course, no-choice dinner menu (not Tues, or in July, Aug; no licence, BYO). 'Hearty' breakfasts. Lounge, dining room; garden. Free Wi-Fi. No background music. 4 bedrooms (1 on ground floor). Per person B&B £39, D,B&B £64. 3-night min. stay. Closed mid-Dec–mid-Jan.

LOCKERBIE Dumfries and Galloway
Map 5:E2
THE DRYFESDALE, Dryfebridge,
DG11 2SF. Tel 01576-202427, www.
dryfesdalehotel.co.uk. Standing in
parkland, this member of the Best
Western hotel group occupies an 18th-
century manse at the end of a long drive
bordered by beech trees. All the
bedrooms have views of the grounds
and surrounding countryside; garden
suites have French windows opening
on to a private patio. There are daily
specials in the bar/brasserie, and any of
130 malt whiskies to be enjoyed in
front of a log fire. Easy access from the
motorway. Lounge, bar, restaurant. Free
Wi-Fi. Background music. Wedding/
function/conference facilities. 5-acre
grounds (9-hole putting green). Children
welcomed; dogs by arrangement. 29
bedrooms (some suitable for &). Per
room B&B £125–£145, D,B&B £175–
£190. Closed Christmas.

MELROSE Scottish Borders
Map 5:E3
BURT'S, Market Square, TD6 9PL. Tel
01896-822285, www.burtshotel.co.uk.
In a listed 18th-century building, the
Henderson family's 'excellent' small
hotel is in a pretty market town on the
banks of the River Tweed. It attracts
anglers and other outdoorsy guests keen
on the many rural pastimes – walking,
cycling, stalking, game shooting –
available on the doorstep. The
restaurant specialises in local game and
fish; the bar has a dedicated whisky
menu and 'good' beer. 'Excellent main
courses and superb desserts.' 'Immaculate'
bedrooms (some may be small) are
decorated with tartan cushions and
blankets. 2 lounges, bistro bar,

restaurant (closed for lunch Mon–Fri);
¼-acre garden. Free Wi-Fi. Background
music. Parking. Wedding/function
facilities. Children welcomed (no under-
8s in restaurant); dogs by arrangement.
20 bedrooms (some recently
refurbished). Per room B&B single £72,
double from £133. D,B&B from £92 per
person. Closed Christmas.

THE TOWNHOUSE, Market Square,
TD6 9PQ. Tel 01896-822645,
www.thetownhousemelrose.co.uk. The
stylish little sister to *Burt's* (see entry,
above), this modern hotel stands across
the town square from its older sibling. It
is owned by the Henderson family, who
run it with 'extremely pleasant and
helpful staff'. Well-appointed rooms
vary in size and facilities; one is large
enough to accommodate a family.
Scottish fusion dishes are served in the
brasserie and more formal restaurant;
'the sticky toffee pudding was to die
for'. 'Excellent' breakfasts. Good
walking nearby. Brasserie (background
music), restaurant (table d'hôte menus),
conservatory, patio/decked area; ramps.
Free Wi-Fi. Wedding/function facilities.
Parking. Children welcomed.
11 bedrooms (1 family room). Per room
B&B single from £95, double £130–£147.
D,B&B from £90 per person. Closed for
1 week mid-Jan.

MOFFAT Dumfries and Galloway
Map 5:E2
HARTFELL HOUSE & THE LIMETREE
RESTAURANT, Hartfell Crescent,
DG10 9AL. Tel 01683-220153,
www.hartfellhouse.co.uk. On the edge
of town, this listed Victorian home,
built of local stone, is in a rural setting
overlooking the surrounding hills. It is

run as a guest house and restaurant by Robert Ash. Traditionally decorated rooms retain some original features; bedrooms have a memory foam mattress, Freeview TV and Scottish biscuits. Chef Matt Seddon serves 'high standard' British dishes in the restaurant, which is popular with locals. There is home-baked bread at breakfast. Lounge, dining room (classical background music); garden. Free Wi-Fi (in public areas); computer available. Secure bike storage. Parking. Children welcomed. 7 bedrooms (plus self-catering cottage). Per room B&B £65–£75, D,B&B £115–£125. Closed Christmas. Restaurant closed Sun (except by arrangement), Mon.

NAIRN Highland
Map 5:C2
SUNNY BRAE, Marine Road, IV12 4EA. Tel 01667-452309, www.sunnybraehotel.com. 'A pleasing stay, and good value for money.' Facing the green and promenade of a seaside town on the Moray Firth, this small hotel has been extended to provide a glass-fronted lounge that enjoys the 'panorama of the sea'. It has been run by the Bochel family for 16 years; son John (the chef) is now in charge, with his wife, Rachel, as manager. Seasonal Scottish cooking with an international influence is served in the bright dining room; there is an extensive wine list as well as a selection of 100 malt whiskies to choose from. Four of the bedrooms face the sea; others overlook the garden, which has a hedged lawn and flowerbeds. Breakfasts are praised. Lounge, dining room ('easy listening' background music); terrace; ½-acre garden. Ramp. Free Wi-Fi. Parking. Children welcomed. 8 bedrooms

(1 suitable for &). Per room B&B £80–£170. Dinner £30. Closed Nov–Feb.

OBAN Argyll and Bute
Map 5:D1
ALT NA CRAIG HOUSE, Glenmore Road, PA34 4PG. Tel 01631-564524, www.guesthouseinoban.com. In an elevated position on the western coast, Sandy and Ina MacArthur's turreted stone-built Victorian house has glorious seascape views across Oban Bay to the isles of Mull, Kerrera and Lismore. Attractive modern bedrooms (some with sea views) are decorated with feature wallpaper and rich colours; they are well equipped with a flat-screen TV, an iPod docking station and locally baked biscuits or shortbread. Breakfast has plenty of Scottish options, including kippers, locally smoked haddock and Stornoway black pudding. The hospitable hosts have much local knowledge to share, and are happy to recommend restaurants and places to visit. 15 mins' walk into town. Breakfast room. Free Wi-Fi. No background music. 3-acre wooded grounds. Parking. 6 bedrooms (1 on ground floor). Per room B&B £120–£150.

GREYSTONES, 13 Dalriach Road, PA34 5EQ. Tel 01631-358653, www.greystonesoban.co.uk. In a Scottish baronial mansion, up a short, steep slope in town, this B&B has magnificent views of the bay and across to the Isle of Mull. It is owned by Mark and Suzanne McPhillips. The house has been thoughtfully decorated: period features such as stained-glass windows, moulded ceilings and an impressive wooden staircase provide an interesting backdrop for understated modern furnishings and contemporary art. Most of the minimalist bedrooms have sea views; the chic bathrooms are spacious. Breakfast in the turreted dining room includes kedgeree, frittata with spinach and Parmesan, and porridge with whisky and brown sugar. Sitting room (books), dining room; ½-acre garden. Free Wi-Fi. No background music. Parking. 5 bedrooms. Per room B&B £110–£160. Closed Christmas, New Year.

PEAT INN Fife
Map 5:D3

THE PEAT INN, Cupar, KY15 5LH. Tel 01334-840206, www.thepeatinn.co.uk. Chef/patron Geoffrey Smeddle and his wife, Katherine, run this restaurant-with-rooms in a whitewashed 17th-century former coaching inn, in a hamlet six miles from St Andrews. Bedrooms are in *The Residence*, an adjoining building (umbrellas provided); seven are split level, with a gallery sitting room. Bathrooms have recently been upgraded. In the candlelit restaurant, Geoffrey Smeddle's award-winning cooking is based on French cuisine, using local ingredients. A continental breakfast is brought to the room. Lounge, restaurant. Garden. Children welcomed. 8 suites (all on ground floor in annexe). Per room B&B £195–£225, D,B&B from £335 (includes tasting menu). Closed Christmas; 1–8 Jan.

PEEBLES Scottish Borders
Map 5:E2

HORSESHOE INN, Eddleston, EH45 8QP. Tel 01721-730225, www.horseshoeinn. co.uk. Just outside a market town in the Tweed valley, this restaurant-with-rooms occupies a former village inn where Princess Margaret is rumoured to have danced on the tables. Mark Slaney is the manager. The restaurant, in a low, white building, is an elegant room, with pillars, antique polished-wood tables and original works of modern art; pre-dinner drinks are served in the cosy lounge (flagstone floor, deep sofas, wood-burning stove). Chef Alistair Craig's modern British dishes use 60-day-aged beef from nearby farms, local honey and apples, and vegetables and herbs from the kitchen garden. Comfortable accommodation is behind the restaurant, in a converted Victorian school house. Walks from the front door. Lounge, restaurant; private dining room; small garden. Free Wi-Fi. Background music. Parking. Children over 5, and dogs (in some rooms; £10 per day) welcomed. 8 bedrooms. Per room B&B £120–£140, D,B&B £180–£200. Closed 2 weeks Jan; 2 weeks Sept.
25% DISCOUNT VOUCHERS

PERTH Perth and Kinross
Map 5:D2

THE PARKLANDS, 2 St Leonard's Bank, PH2 8EB. Tel 01738-622451, www.theparklandshotel.com. In an elevated position above South Inch Park, this hotel, in a Victorian stone-built house, is convenient for both town and station. It has been run for more than ten years by Penny and Scott Edwards. Its two restaurants, *63@Parklands* and the informal *No. 1 The Bank Bistro* (overseen by executive chef Graeme Pallister), focus on seasonal Perthshire produce. Contemporary interiors have abstract art, feature wallpaper and brightly upholstered armchairs; simple bedrooms are enlivened by colourful fabrics. Lounge,

bar, 2 restaurants; private dining room; terrace (alfresco dining); garden leading to park. Free Wi-Fi. Light background music. Wedding/function facilities. Parking. Children and dogs welcomed. 15 bedrooms (4 on ground floor; 1 family room). Per person B&B £54.50–£89.50, D,B&B £65.50–£97.50.
25% DISCOUNT VOUCHERS

Sᴜɴʙᴀɴᴋ Hᴏᴜsᴇ, 50 Dundee Road, PH2 7BA. Tel 01738-624882, www.sunbankhouse.com. Set in large landscaped gardens, this traditionally furnished hotel is in a Victorian house overlooking the River Tay and the city. It is run in a friendly, hospitable fashion by Remo and Georgina Zane. Remo Zane cooks uncomplicated à la carte dinners, often with an Italian influence (bookings advised); sandwiches and snacks are served till late in the lounge. Plentiful breakfasts have lots of choice; packed lunches and picnics are available on request. A short walk from the centre. Lounge/bar, restaurant (light background music); terrace; garden. Free Wi-Fi. Wedding/function facilities. Parking. Children welcomed. 9 bedrooms (some on ground floor; 2 suitable for &). Per person B&B £45–£79, D,B&B £70–£99.

PITLOCHRY Perth and Kinross
Map 5:D2
Eᴀsᴛ Hᴀᴜɢʜ Hᴏᴜsᴇ, by Pitlochry, PH16 5TE. Tel 01796-473121, www.easthaugh.co.uk. Guests like the thoughtful touches at the McGown family's small hotel, a turreted stone house set in two acres of gardens in Highland Perthshire. Decorated in tartan and toile de Jouy, comfortable bedrooms (some may be small) have

home-baked shortbread and fresh milk; one has a fireplace and a four-poster bed. Sporty visitors may fish for salmon and trout on the River Tay (the fishing lodge has a barbecue and cooking facilities); stalking and shooting on nearby estates is regularly arranged. Chef/proprietor Neil McGown's menus feature fish and game in season (often caught by McGown himself); meals are served in the restaurant or cosy bar. Lounge, bar, restaurant (background jazz); patio; ramps. Free Wi-Fi. 2-acre grounds; river beat. Wedding/business facilities. Parking. Children welcomed; dogs by arrangement. 13 bedrooms (2 suitable for &; 5 in a converted 'bothy' beside the hotel), plus 2 self-catering cottages. Per room B&B £99–£229; D,B&B £119–£259. Closed Christmas.

Pɪɴᴇ Tʀᴇᴇs, Strathview Terrace, PH16 5QR. Tel 01796-472121, www.pinetreeshotel.co.uk. 'We can't wait to go back for a longer stay.' A short walk from town, Valerie and Robert Kerr's Victorian hillside mansion is set in peaceful woodland, where roe deer and red squirrels roam amid the pine trees. 'Warm and welcoming', public areas have cosy seating, half-panelled walls and an open log fire; comfortable bedrooms are traditionally furnished. Overlooking the gardens, the restaurant serves 'beautiful' Scottish-influenced dishes cooked by Cristian Cojocaru; special diets are catered for. 2 lounges, bar, restaurant; soft background music. Free Wi-Fi (in lounge only). 7-acre grounds. Parking. Dogs welcomed (charge). ¼ mile N of town. 23 bedrooms (3 on ground floor in annexe). Per person B&B £52–£74, D,B&B £72–£94.

TORRDARACH HOUSE, Golf Course Road, PH16 5AU. Tel 01796-472136, www.torrdarach.co.uk. A small stream runs through the thickly wooded grounds of this raspberry-red house built in 1901, which has 'astounding' views over the gardens and the Perthshire Highlands. New owners Susanne Wallner, who is Austrian, and Graeme Fish, a golf professional, took over the B&B at the end of 2013. Rooms retain a blend of modern furniture and antiques, with contemporary art on the walls; a new bedroom was recently added. Guests can watch red squirrels from the new breakfast conservatory while enjoying home-made marmalade, jams and granola, porridge with a dash of whisky, and Dunkeld hot-smoked salmon. Sitting room, breakfast room; comprehensive bar service; 1-acre garden. Free Wi-Fi. No background music. Parking. Golf clubs and bicycle storage. Golf packages; reservations for tee times and green fees can be arranged. 7 bedrooms (1 in 'bothy' behind the house). Per room B&B £88–£104. 2-night min. stay at weekends. Closed mid-Nov–mid-Feb.

PORT APPIN Argyll and Bute
Map 5:D1
THE PIERHOUSE, PA38 4DE. Tel 01631-730302, www.pierhousehotel.co.uk. 'Absolute bliss.' At the end of a winding single-track road, this 'pretty little building' stands beside Loch Linnhe, in a 'beautiful' setting with 'spectacular views to the Isle of Lismore and the mountains beyond'. 'Cosy and warm', the informal hotel and restaurant, once the 19th-century pier master's residence, are owned and run by Nick and Nikki Horne. Contemporary bedrooms are in a modern, purpose-built block; many have views over the loch to the islands of Lismore and Shuna. 'We had the most comfortable bed, with wonderful pillows; we could hear the gentle lap of the waves from just outside the window.' The restaurant overlooks the original pier, and the local fishermen bringing in their catch. 'The food was all very good, from breakfast to bar meals to the excellent seafood at dinner.' *Ferry* bar (wood-burning stove), snug, restaurant (Laura Milne is chef); terrace. Free Wi-Fi. Celtic and 'easy listening' background music. Sauna; treatments available. Wedding facilities. Yacht moorings for visitors. Parking. Children (special menu), and dogs welcomed. 12 bedrooms (3 family triple rooms). Per room B&B £85–£225.

ST ANDREWS Fife
Map 5:D3
RUFFLETS, Strathkinness Low Road, KY16 9TX. Tel 01334-472594, www.rufflets.co.uk. In a creeper-covered 1920s turreted mansion that was built for the widow of a Dundee jute baron, this 'extremely welcoming' family-owned hotel is liked for the 'excellent service'. Stephen Owen is the manager. Antique furnishings are set against contemporary fabrics and wallpaper; the drawing room and lounge have roaring fires. Individually styled bedrooms are spread across the main house, and the lodge and gatehouse in the 'beautiful' ten-acre grounds; two characterful rooms have extra seating space in the turret. A modern Scottish daily changing table d'hôte menu is served in the elegant *Terrace* restaurant. Drawing room, library, music room, bar, restaurant (background music). Free Wi-Fi.

Gardens. Wedding/function facilities. Children and dogs welcomed. 1 mile from the centre. 24 bedrooms (3 in gatehouse; 2 in lodge; 2 family rooms; 1 suitable for &), plus 3 self-catering cottages. Per room B&B £170–£395, D,B&B £230–£455.

SANQUHAR Dumfries and Galloway
Map 5:E2

BLACKADDIE HOUSE, Blackaddie Road, DG4 6JJ. Tel 01659-50270, www.blackaddiehotel.co.uk. In 'an enchanting setting' on the banks of the River Nith, Jane and Ian McAndrew's small hotel is in a 'beautiful' 16th-century stone-built manse. Traditionally furnished bedrooms overlook the gardens or the hills of Dumfries and Galloway. Ian McAndrew, who uses good-quality local ingredients wherever possible, has received a *Michelin* star for his past cooking; in the elegant dining room, he serves daily-changing menus of 'tastebud-popping' dishes. 'Each course was like a work of art, beautifully presented, perfectly cooked.' On the edge of the village. Bar, library, conservatory; 2-acre garden. Free Wi-Fi (ground-floor rooms only). 'Easy listening' background music. Wedding/function facilities. Cookery school; fishing and photography breaks. Parking. Children (cots), and dogs (in some rooms) welcomed; good riverbank walks. 7 bedrooms (1 river suite). Per room B&B £120–£220, D,B&B £224–£324.
25% DISCOUNT VOUCHERS

SCOURIE Highland
Map 5:B2

EDDRACHILLES HOTEL, Badcall Bay, IV27 4TH. Tel 01971-502080, www.eddrachilles.com. At the head of Badcall Bay, in 'lovely, extensive grounds along the seashore', this relaxing, traditionally furnished hotel is in an 18th-century manse. It is run by 'knowledgeable' owners Isabelle and Richard Flannery, who provide 'excellent details on local attractions and walks'. Isabelle Flannery's cooking has a French slant and focuses on seafood from the bay, fish from Kinlochbervie, and Lochinver and Highland meat; a smokehouse in the grounds provides the restaurant with smoked fish and meats. (Vegetarians and special diets are catered for.) Lunch and dinner are served in the conservatory overlooking the garden and the bay. Reception, breakfast room, restaurant (extensive wine list; open to non-residents), bar (over 100 single malt whiskies); classical background music. Free Wi-Fi (in public areas); computer available. 4-acre garden. Parking. Children welcomed (high tea at 6 pm for under-6s). 11 bedrooms. Per person B&B £55, D,B&B £74. Closed Oct–Mar.

SKEABOST BRIDGE Highland
Map 5:C1

THE SPOONS, 75 Aird Bernisdale, Isle of Skye, IV51 9NU. Tel 01470-532217, www.thespoonsonskye.com. On a working croft overlooking Loch Snizort, 'perfect hosts' Marie and Ian Lewis have decorated their stylish B&B with original works by local artists; bedrooms have cashmere and sheepskin throws, a DVD/CD-player and a Nespresso coffee machine. Lavish breakfasts, locally sourced and home made, are taken communally, and include granola, home-baked bread, smoked fish, honey from the hive and freshly laid eggs from the house's own hens. Afternoon tea has freshly baked treats. Good walks from the door. Sitting room (wood-burning stove), dining room. Free Wi-Fi. No background music. 7-acre grounds (sheep, ducks, geese). 3 bedrooms (1 on ground floor). Per room B&B £140–£160. 2-night min. stay preferred. Closed Nov–20 Mar.

SLEAT Highland
Map 5:C1
DUISDALE HOUSE, Isle of Skye, IV43 8QW. Tel 01471-833202, www. duisdale.com. In a stunning setting within extensive gardens and woodland, Anne Gracie and Ken Gunn have transformed a Victorian hunting lodge into a small, hospitable hotel; they also own *Toravaig House* nearby (see main entry). Decorated in a modern style, bedrooms have bold prints and wallpaper; some overlook the gardens or loch, while others have views across to the Highlands beyond. Seasonal local produce from Skye and the Highlands is served in the restaurant; Peter Cullen is the new chef. *The Chart Room*, overlooking the Sound of Sleat, is a relaxing place for pre-dinner drinks and casual dining; afternoon tea can be taken by the log fire in the lounge or outside on the south-facing deck. Guests may book days out on the hotel's luxury yacht (Apr–Sept), with lunch and champagne included (whales, dolphins, seals and seabirds optional). Lounge, bar, restaurant, conservatory. Free Wi-Fi. Background music. Wedding facilities. 35-acre grounds (10-person garden hot tub). Children welcomed. 18 bedrooms (2 family rooms; 1 garden suite suitable for &). Per person B&B £73.50–£165, D,B&B £99–£210.

SPEAN BRIDGE Highland
Map 5:C2
SMIDDY HOUSE, Roy Bridge Road, PH34 4EU. Tel 01397-712335, www. smiddyhouse.com. Guests receive 'a warm welcome' at Robert Bryson and Glen Russell's 'beautifully decorated' restaurant-with-rooms; afternoon tea is provided in the garden room, or sherry and home-made shortbread later in the evening. In a village along the scenic West Highland rail route, the house is well situated for trips to the mountains or lochs, or for travellers en route to the Isle of Skye. 'Imaginative and delicious' dinners use much Scottish produce, including scallops from the Isle of Mull, salmon from Wester Ross and Highland game; there are 'excellent' vegetarian options. Scottish breakfasts. Golf, mountain bike trails nearby. Garden room, *Russell's* restaurant (booking essential; closed Sun pm, Mon, Tues Nov–Mar). Free Wi-Fi. Classical background music. Parking. 4 bedrooms (plus self-catering accommodation in adjacent building, *The Old Smiddy*). Per room B&B £85–£115, D,B&B £165–£185. Closed Christmas, restaurant open.

STIRLING
Map 5:D2
POWIS HOUSE, FK9 5PS. Tel 01786-460231, www.powishouse.co.uk. Approached through wrought iron gates, Jane and Colin Kilgour's impressive 18th-century mansion stands in mature ten-acre grounds of lawns, woodland and pasture, beneath the Ochil hills. Carefully restored bedrooms (Thistle, Heather, Hazel) have a Georgian fireplace, polished flooring and handmade Harris Tweed curtains

and bed throws; a bowl of fresh fruit is provided. Ample breakfasts are served in the sun-filled dining room, and include eggs from the Kilgours' hens. 4 miles NE of town. Sitting room (open fire, board games, DVDs), dining room. Free Wi-Fi. No background music. Terrace; garden (ha-ha; listed shafted stone sundial). Parking. Children welcomed. 3 bedrooms (plus 2 gypsy caravans and a shepherd's hut in the grounds). Per room B&B £90–£100. Closed Nov–Mar.

STRACHUR Argyll and Bute
Map 5:D1

THE CREGGANS INN, PA27 8BX. Tel 01369-860279, www.creggans-inn.co.uk. With 'breathtaking' views over Loch Fyne, this 'extremely welcoming' white-painted inn is run by Gill and Archie MacLellan. It has simply decorated, pretty bedrooms and a popular bistro and restaurant. Books and binoculars are available to borrow in the lounge, and there is a handsome rocking horse for younger visitors. Two moorings are available to guests arriving by boat. 2 lounges, bar/bistro ('easy listening' background music), restaurant; 2-acre garden. Free Wi-Fi. Unsuitable for &. Wedding/function facilities. Children and dogs welcomed. Resident dog, Hector. 14 bedrooms. Per person B&B £50–£110, D,B&B £80–£140.

STRATHYRE Perth and Kinross
Map 5:D2

AIRLIE HOUSE, Main Street, nr Callendar, FK18 8NA. Tel 01877-384247, www.airliehouse.co.uk. Warm, welcoming hosts Jacquie and Ray Hill run this small B&B in their early 1900s Scottish villa. Surrounded by countryside and rolling hills in the Trossachs and Breadalbane area of Scotland's first national park, it is well placed for walking the Rob Roy Way. Most of the spacious, simply furnished bedrooms have views of Ben Sheann or the hillside beyond the river. Praiseworthy breakfasts. Sitting room (library; log fires in winter), dining room, drying room. Free Wi-Fi. Background music. Parking. Children welcomed; 'well-behaved' dogs by arrangement. Resident dog, Poppy. 4 bedrooms (3 with views; 1 & friendly). Per person B&B single from £45, double from £32.

SWINTON Scottish Borders
Map 5:E3

THE WHEATSHEAF, Main Street, TD11 3JJ. Tel 01890-860257, www.wheatsheaf-swinton.co.uk. Opposite the village green, Chris and Jan Winson's cosy, stone-built country roadside inn has cottage-style bedrooms and a popular restaurant serving 'really good' food. John Forrestier, the French chef, specialises in fish and seafood direct from Eyemouth harbour, and prime Scottish beef sourced from local Borders livestock; when in season, wild salmon, venison, partridge, pheasant, woodcock and duck are added to the menu. One of three comfortable seating areas, the Fish Lounge, has fish-print wallpaper, fly rods adorning the walls, and a detailed map of salmon beats on the River Tweed. Extensive wine cellar; large collection of single malt whiskies. Lounge/bars, 3 dining areas; small beer garden. Ramps. Free Wi-Fi. Background music. Function facilities. Children (cots), and dogs (in 3 rooms) welcomed. 10 bedrooms (3 in annexe,

20 yds from main house; 1 suitable for
(&). Per person B&B £99–£119. Dinner
£32. Closed Christmas.

TARBERT Western Isles
Map 5:B1

HOTEL HEBRIDES, Pier Road, HS3
3DG. Tel 01859-502364, www.hotel-
hebrides.com. Beside the harbour,
Angus and Chirsty Macleod's 'boxy'
modern hotel is 'adroit and stylish'
inside. Visitors and locals throng the
lively bar; there are 'good food and
friendly service' in the informal
Pierhouse restaurant. 'Smallish'
bedrooms are bright and well equipped.
Near the 'spectacular' white sandy beach
at Luskentyre Bay, the hotel is also a
convenient base for touring the Western
Isles; boat trips can be taken to St Kilda
and other islands. *Mote* bar (open for
lunch and dinner), restaurant
(background music; closed Nov–Mar).
Free Wi-Fi. Small conference facilities.
Parking. Children welcomed (special
menu). 21 bedrooms (some small). Per
person B&B £65–£85, D,B&B £90–£95.

TAYNUILT Argyll and Bute
Map 5:D1

ROINEABHAL COUNTRY HOUSE,
Kilchrenan, PA35 1HD. Tel 01866-
833207, www.roineabhal.com. Beside a
tumbling stream, Roger and Maria
Soep's homely and welcoming country
guest house is in an isolated spot in the
wild glens of Argyll, close to Loch Awe.
It is well placed for visits to Inveraray,
Glencoe, Fort William and Kintyre;
from the nearby port of Oban, ferries
offer transport to Skye, Mull, Iona and
the outer islands. Individually styled
bedrooms, all with good views, have
fresh flowers and shortbread. Breakfast

includes locally smoked kippers,
porridge and home-made bread; light
supper platters of Scottish produce
are available, by arrangement (£25).
Lounge, dining room, covered veranda;
2-acre garden. Free Wi-Fi. No
background music. Ramp. Children and
pets welcomed; resident dog. 18 miles E
of Oban. 3 bedrooms (1 on ground floor
suitable for (&). Per person B&B £55–£80.
Closed Nov–Easter.
25% DISCOUNT VOUCHERS

TOBERMORY Argyll and Bute
Map 5:D1

GLENGORM CASTLE, PA75 6QE. Tel
01688-302321, www.glengormcastle.
co.uk. Perched peacefully on a cliff-top,
this fairytale building with turrets and
towers (completed in 1863) affords
glorious views over the Sound of Mull
to the Western Isles beyond. Guests are
free to roam the 5,000-acre estate, on
which owners Tom and Marjorie
Nelson raise Highland cattle and sheep.
Inside, there are books, board games
and complimentary whisky to be
enjoyed by the open fires. Massive
rooms and bathrooms overlook the sea
or front lawns; satisfying Scottish
breakfasts are taken communally at a
large oak table. Main hall, library,
dining room; coffee shop; farm shop.
Free Wi-Fi (in public areas). No
background music. Packed lunches
available. Fishing; guided walks.
Children (cots provided) and dogs
welcomed; resident cat and spaniels.
4 miles from Tobermory. 5 bedrooms,
plus 6 self-catering cottages). Per room
B&B £130–£210. Closed Christmas,
New Year.
25% DISCOUNT VOUCHERS (excl.
July, Aug)

THE TOBERMORY HOTEL, Main Street, PA75 6NT. Tel 01688-302091, www. thetobermoryhotel.com. On the harbour front in a 'very pretty town', this 'cosy', 'perfectly pleasant' hotel occupies a row of colourful converted fishermen's cottages with 'good views' over the water. Ian and Andi Stevens are the 'very friendly' owners. The 'old-fashioned' public rooms have maps, guidebooks, original art, local beers and malt whiskies, and 'plenty of knick-knacks'; simply furnished bedrooms (some compact) are 'comfortable and light'. 'Good' breakfasts have locally smoked haddock and kippers. Packed lunches. The hotel was for sale as the *Guide* went to press. 2 lounges, bar, restaurant (closed Mon). Free Wi-Fi. Background music. Wedding/conference facilities. Children and dogs welcomed. 16 bedrooms (most with sea view, 1 suitable for &.). Per room B&B single £40–£65, double £85–£128. Closed early Nov–late Mar.

TONGUE Highland
Map 5:B2
THE TONGUE HOTEL, IV27 4XD. Tel 01847-611206, www.tonguehotel.co.uk. 'A fine hotel in a truly spectacular area.' 'Wild and wonderfully remote', this small hotel is in a former Victorian sporting lodge in a sleepy coastal village beneath Ben Loyal. It is run by Lorraine and David Hook with a team of 'friendly and helpful' local staff. 'It is a homely and characterful place; traditional decor, dark furniture and tartan fabrics suit the hunting-lodge atmosphere.' With seascape and landscape views, bedrooms have fruits, sweets and a decanter of sherry; many also retain an old fireplace or marble washstand. Simple Scottish fare is

served in the restaurant, beside a cosy fire. 'Dinner was better than we might have expected, and served in substantial portions. We enjoyed a delicious, tender rare venison; a dense, home-made tomato soup came with good, home-made caraway brown bread.' Breakfast is ordered the night before; there are home-made compotes, granola and muesli, and porridge with cream and heather honey ('whisky available to add'). Bar, restaurant; therapy room. Free Wi-Fi (in public areas only). Background music. Wedding facilities. Children welcomed. 19 bedrooms. Per person B&B £45–£55, D,B&B from £82.

TORRIDON Highland
Map 5:C1
THE TORRIDON, Annat, by Achnasheen, IV22 2EY. Tel 01445-791242, www. thetorridon.com. 'Wildly beautiful.' At the end of a single-track road, this luxury hotel is on a wooded estate by the side of a vast sea loch. It is run by owners Rohaise and Daniel Rose-Bristow. The hotel occupies a former shooting lodge; the 'lovely' reception rooms have big open fireplaces, leather sofas, moulded plaster ceilings and panelling. Glamorous, well-equipped bedrooms vary in size and style; the best have views of the loch (the rest overlook the mountains or grounds). Chef David Barnett's French-inspired menus are based on Scottish produce such as grouse, fish and seafood, and moorland venison; herbs, vegetables and fruit are from the garden. The family-friendly *Torridon Inn* is also on the estate. Complimentary activities range from gorge scrambling and archery to guided walks at sunrise and sunset. Drawing room, whisky bar (more than 350 malts), dining room (classical

background music). Free Wi-Fi. Wedding facilities. 58 acres of parkland; walled garden. Children welcomed. 10 miles SW of Kinlochewe. 18 bedrooms (1 on ground floor; suitable for &; 1 deluxe suite in adjacent cottage; dogs allowed). Per room B&B £235–£360. Dinner £55. Closed Jan, Mon–Wed Nov–Mar.

UIG Western Isles
Map 5:B1
AUBERGE CARNISH, 5 Carnish, HS2 9EX. Tel 01851-672459, www.aubergecarnish. co.uk. Guests admire the 'stunning views' from Richard and Jo-Ann Leparoux's purpose-built beachside guest house, in a 'spectacular location' on a working croft perched above Uig Sands. Modern bedrooms are styled in calming natural shades and have window seating for watching the ever-changing sea- and skyscapes; there is original local artwork on the walls. In a restaurant filled with natural light, Richard Leparoux serves 'superlative' 'Franco-Hebridean' dishes that feature local ingredients in season (dietary requirements are catered for). Breakfast has home-baked bread and home-made marmalade; guests may take their morning coffee on the decked terrace. Trips and day cruises to St Kilda. Dining room (open to non-residents), lounge (wood-burning stove; jazz/classical background music); patio. Free Wi-Fi. 4 bedrooms (1 suitable for &; plus 1-bedroom self-catering cottage). Per person B&B £65–£75, D,B&B £100–£110. Closed Dec–Jan.

ULLAPOOL Highland
Map 5:B2
RIVERVIEW, 2 Castle Terrace, IV26 2XD. Tel 01854-612019, www. riverviewullapool.co.uk. In a 'good

location' close to shops, eating places and the harbour, this small, good-value B&B is run by friendly hostess Nadine Farquhar. 'Very clean and comfortable' bedrooms are decorated in a bright, modern style; guests have a chocolate on the pillow at night. The open-plan lounge has DVDs and board games; 'wonderful', hearty breakfasts are served at a time to suit guests. A microwave, crockery and cutlery are made available to guests; packed lunches on request. Open-plan lounge/dining room/library. Free Wi-Fi. Drying facilities. Complimentary use of leisure centre with pool. Off-street parking. 3 bedrooms. Per person B&B from £30 (credit and debit cards not accepted). Closed Nov–Jan and for Loopallu (Sept).

THE SHEILING, Garve Road, IV26 2SX. Tel 01854-612947, www.thesheiling ullapool.co.uk. Beside Loch Broom, Iain and Lesley MacDonald's comfortable, modern B&B in lovely gardens enjoys stunning views over the bay and the mountains beyond. Large bedrooms have complimentary sherry and sweets; an open fire burns in the lounge, where guests are provided with books, games, magazines and newspapers. Highland breakfasts, served in a bright room overlooking the loch, have local sausages, and porridge with honey and cream. The town centre is ten mins' walk away; five mins to the ferry for the Hebrides. Sitting room, dining room; Sportsman's Lodge (guest laundry, drying room; sauna, shower; bike store). Free Wi-Fi. No background music. 1-acre garden; patio; fishing permits. Parking. Children welcomed. 6 bedrooms (2 on ground floor). Per person B&B £35–£42.50. Closed Nov–Mar.

ABERGELE Conwy
Map 3:A3

THE KINMEL ARMS, St George, LL22 9BP. Tel 01745-832207, www. thekinmelarms.co.uk. In a tranquil hamlet in the Elwy valley, Lynn and Tim Watson's Victorian inn has a 'relaxed' atmosphere. Modern bedrooms are 'finished to a high standard, displaying the artistic temperament of the hosts' (Tim Watson's artwork is displayed on the walls); each has a large bed, and French windows that open on to a decked balcony or patio. The bar and conservatory restaurant are popular with locals; brasserie-style menus champion seasonal produce and local fish and meat. A continental breakfast is taken in the room. Good walks. Bar (real ales, wood-burning stove), restaurant (closed Sun, Mon). Free Wi-Fi. Background music. Small garden. Parking. 4 bedrooms. Per room B&B £115–£175. Dinner from £35.

CAERNARFON Gwynedd
Map 3:A2

PLAS DINAS COUNTRY HOUSE, Bontnewydd, LL54 7YF. Tel 01256-830214, www.plasdinas.co.uk. Set in 15-acre grounds, this 17th-century Grade II listed building, once the country home of the Armstrong-Jones family, is packed with history; new owners Neil Baines and Marco Soares have filled it with antiques, portraits and memorabilia. Bedrooms are individually designed with vintage and modern furniture; all have a hospitality tray with ground coffee, hot chocolate, home-made biscuits and a selection of teas. Guests take drinks in front of a roaring log fire in winter or on the terrace in warm weather. Drawing room, restaurant (closed Sun, Mon; background music); gun room. Free Wi-Fi. Civil wedding licence. Parking. Well-behaved dogs welcomed, by arrangement; resident dogs, Malta and Blue. 10 bedrooms (1 on ground floor). Per room B&B £89–£249 (2-night min. stay at weekends). Dinner £30. Closed Christmas.

CARDIFF Cardiff
Map 3:E4

HOTEL ONE HUNDRED, 100 Newport Road, CF24 1DG. Tel 07916-888423, www.hotelonehundred.com. 'Perfect for short stays in Cardiff', this small budget hotel, run by brother-and-sister team Charlie and Abi Prothero, is close to the city centre, with shops, pubs and good eating places just around the corner. The renovated Victorian town house is decorated in a 'warm, modern' style; 'comfortable' bedrooms have hot drinks and biscuits, and a DVD-player with access to a movie library. Pre-dinner drinks may be taken on the decked terrace; a continental breakfast buffet has Welsh cakes, yogurts, pastries and freshly ground coffee. Breakfast room (background music), lounge (honesty bar); decked terrace. Free Wi-Fi. DVD library. Some self-catering facilities (guest fridge, microwave, plates, cutlery, glasses). Access to nearby fitness and leisure club (£8). Limited on-site parking. Children welcomed. 7 bedrooms (1 on ground floor). Per room B&B (3% charge on all card payments) £50–£80. Cooked breakfast £5.

JOLYON'S AT NO. 10, 10 Cathedral Road, CF11 9LJ. Tel 029-2009 1900, www. jolyons10.com. There is a youthful, 'laid-back vibe' at Jolyon Joseph's small hotel, occupying a Victorian villa near Sophia Gardens. The decoration is bright and eclectic throughout: gold-painted armchairs, crystal chandeliers, swathes of leopard print, grand walnut wardrobes, tasselled four-poster beds. The lively bar (deep sofas, log fire) is a popular local venue for afternoon tea and late-night drinks. Breakfast, with Glamorgan sausages, is served until 10 am (later at weekends). Opposite the Millennium Centre. Lounge, bar (occasional live music); terrace. Free Wi-Fi. Background music. Conference/function facilities. Parking. 7 bedrooms (1 on ground floor). Per room B&B £64–£134.

COLWYN BAY Conwy
Map 3:A3
ELLINGHAM HOUSE, 1 Woodland Park West, LL29 7DR. Tel 01492-533345, www.ellinghamhouse.com. Peacefully located in a leafy conservation area, Ian Davies and Chris Jennings's traditionally furnished B&B is in a late Victorian villa, a short walk from the town and the sea. Spacious bedrooms have a 'wonderful' bathroom; they are well equipped with bathrobes, a DVD-player, biscuits and fruit. Wholesome breakfasts are taken in a colourful, elegant room furnished in period style. Lounge (DVD library), dining room. Garden. No background music. Free Wi-Fi. Parking. Children welcomed (cots); dogs by arrangement (£5 per night). 5 bedrooms. Per room B&B from £79. Closed Jan.

CONWY Conwy
Map 3:A3
CASTLE HOTEL, High Street, LL32 8DB. Tel 01492-582800, www.castlewales.co.uk. In a World Heritage town, this centrally located old coaching inn is run by the Lavin family as a hotel and restaurant. It stands on the site of a Cistercian abbey; parts of the building, once two hostelries, date back to the 1400s. The quirky interior has characterful nooks, crannies and creaky floors; public rooms are furnished with antiques, and paintings by Victorian artist John Dawson Watson. Bedrooms vary in size; some have castle views. In the restaurant, head chef Andrew Nelson promotes local seafood, and Welsh produce from artisan suppliers. Bar, lounge, *Dawsons* restaurant. Free Wi-Fi. Background music. Treatment room. Courtyard garden (alfresco dining). Parking (narrow entrance). Children (special meals), and dogs (charge) welcomed. 27 bedrooms (1 with 16th-century four-poster bed; some on ground floor). Per person B&B £65–£135. Dinner £30–£40.

COWBRIDGE Vale of Glamorgan
Map 3:E3
THE BEAR, 63 High Street, CF71 7AF. Tel 01446-774814, www.bearhotel.com. Dating to the 12th century, this characterful coaching inn is in a lovely market town, 20 minutes' drive from Cardiff; a handy local bus service goes straight to the city centre. There is a relaxed atmosphere: visitors may call in throughout the day for breakfast, snacks, more formal meals and popular traditional Sunday roasts, served until 9 pm. Bedrooms are bright and cheerful; some have a beamed ceiling, four-poster bed or chandelier. Chef Richard Bowles's 'satisfying' dishes are served in a variety of dining areas: *Cellars* restaurant, with its stone-vaulted ceiling; *Teddies Grill* bar; the lounge, by a fire; and alfresco in

the courtyard. Lounge, 2 bars (real ales), restaurant. Free Wi-Fi. Background music. Civil wedding licence; conference facilities. Parking. 33 bedrooms (some in annexe; plus 1- and 2-bedroom apartments a short walk away). Per room B&B single £80, double £110–£140. Dinner from £25.

CRICKHOWELL Powys
Map 3:D4

THE MANOR, Brecon Road, NP8 1SE. Tel 01873-810212, www.manorhotel. co.uk. The birthplace of Sir George Everest in 1790, this white-painted 18th-century manor house is owned by Glyn and Jess Bridgeman and Sean Gerrard; Catherine Lloyd is the manager. 'Comfortable, with good facilities', it is in 'an excellent location' in the Brecon Beacons national park. The bistro has views over a valley and the River Usk; 'high-quality' British dishes are cooked by chef Andre Kerin, using locally reared, organic meat and poultry, mainly from the family farm, seven miles away. Lounge, bar, bistro (background music/radio). Free Wi-Fi. Leisure suite (10-metre indoor swimming pool, sauna, steam room, whirlpool, gym). Civil wedding licence; conference facilities. Children and dogs welcomed. ¼ mile from town. 23 bedrooms. Per room B&B £90–£165, D,B&B £150–£225. Closed Christmas.
25% DISCOUNT VOUCHERS

DOLGELLAU Gwynedd
Map 3:B3

FFYNNON, Love Lane, LL40 1RR. Tel 01341-421774, www.ffynnontownhouse. com. In a small market town at the foot of Cadair Idris, this Victorian Gothic house began as a rectory and later served as a convalescent home and cottage hospital. Today, it is a stylish guest house run by owners Debra Harris and Steven Holt. Period features, such as an Adam fireplace and stained-glass windows, have been retained; well-decorated, modern bedrooms have a walk-in drench shower or spa bath, flat-screen TV, DVD-player and iPod docking station. Lounge (background music), dining room, butler's pantry (honesty bar; room-service menu); drying room. Free Wi-Fi. ½-acre garden: patio; hot tub; play area. Small function facilities. Parking. Children welcomed (high tea, baby-listening; PlayStation). Steps and level changes; steep, narrow approach. 3 mins' walk to town. 6 bedrooms. Per person B&B £72.50–£100. 2-night min. stay at weekends. Closed Christmas.
25% DISCOUNT VOUCHERS

LAUGHARNE Carmarthenshire
Map 3:D2

BROWNS HOTEL, King Street, SA33 4RY. Tel 01994-427688, www.browns-hotel. co.uk. A favourite watering hole of Dylan Thomas, this renovated 18th-century inn helps keep the poet's memory alive with memorabilia and a library of Thomas-related reading material. Jon Tregenna is the manager. Colourful rooms are modern, with an interesting mix of 1950s furnishings, exposed stonework and beams, and modern facilities (HDTV, digital radio, iPod docking system); some are decorated with photographic wall murals. Light bites and snacks are available in the Grade II listed bar; nearby, *The New Three Mariners* pub-with-rooms (under the same management) has real ales and stone-baked pizzas. Substantial breakfasts.

Reading room, bar (traditional Welsh ales). Free Wi-Fi. 'Gentle' background music. Children and dogs welcomed. Parking. 14 bedrooms. Per room B&B single £75–£85, double £95–£140.

LLANDDEINIOLEN Gwynedd
Map 3:A3

TY'N RHOS, Seion, LL55 3AE. Tel 01248-670489, www.tynrhos.co.uk. 'Most enjoyable.' Stephen and Hilary Murphy's 'relaxed and friendly' hotel is on a secluded farmstead in rolling countryside: sheep and cattle graze in the fields beyond the gardens, while families of ducks, coots and moorhens paddle on two small lakes. Named after wild flowers, bedrooms are in the creeper-covered house or the courtyard; some have patio doors opening on to the garden and ornamental pond. The large, 'very comfortable' conservatory has good views of the garden, and across to Anglesey. Stephen Murphy's 'delicious' cooking makes use of local ingredients, and vegetables and herbs from the garden. Lounge (wood-burning fire; board games), bar, *Garden View* restaurant (open to non-residents), conservatory. Free Wi-Fi (in public areas and some rooms only). Background music/radio. Parking. Children welcomed; dogs (in some rooms, £5 per night) by arrangement. 4 miles from Bangor and Caernarfon. 19 bedrooms (7 in 2 annexes; 1 family suite). Per room B&B £85–£165. 2-night min. stay at peak weekends. Dinner £37.50.

LLANDUDNO Conwy
Map 3:A3

ESCAPE, 48 Church Walks, LL30 2HL. Tel 01492-877776, www.escapebandb. co.uk. Close to the promenade, Sam

Nayar's unusual B&B, in a white-stucco Victorian villa, has a traditional facade and a cool, urban interior: contemporary and vintage furnishings and fabrics are set against a backdrop of oak panelling, stained glass and period fireplaces. Modern bedrooms are imaginatively designed: one has a floating bed, another a coastal look with deckchair stripes; the Loft, set over three levels, has a wall-mounted fireplace, and a body-drier in the shower room. Up-to-date technology in the rooms includes a flat-screen TV, Blu-ray-player and iPod docking station; guests may borrow from a DVD library. Josh Simonds is the manager. Welsh breakfasts. Lounge, breakfast room; honesty bar. Free Wi-Fi. Background music. Children over 10 welcomed. 9 bedrooms. Per room B&B £89–£140. Closed Christmas.

LLANDYRNOG Denbighshire
Map 3:A4

PENTRE MAWR, LL16 4LA. Tel 01824-790732, www.pentremawrcountryhouse. co.uk. Visitors like the 'welcoming, homely atmosphere' at Graham and Bre Carrington-Sykes's guest house, on a 400-year-old farmstead. Accommodation is in country house-style bedrooms in the main house, two cottage suites next door, and luxury canvas lodges in the grounds, each with an outdoor hot tub on a private terrace. The hosts also produce 'great' home-cooked dinners; bread, cakes and other treats are baked daily. Sitting rooms, gallery, café, restaurant. Free Wi-Fi. No background music. 2-acre grounds: walled garden; solar-heated saltwater swimming pool. Dogs welcomed; resident dogs. Falconry demonstrations are 'a highly recommended adventure'. Wedding facilities. 11 bedrooms (3 in main house; 2 suites in cottage; 6 lodges). Per person B&B £75–£115, D,B&B £100–£140.

LLANGOLLEN Denbighshire
Map 3:B4

GALES, 18 Bridge Street, LL20 8PF. Tel 01978-860089, www.galesofllangollen. co.uk. On one of the oldest streets in Llangollen, this quirky hotel has a wine bar and restaurant, and a wine and gift shop in its Reception area. It is run by oenophile Richard Gale and his family. Comfortable bedrooms are above the bar in the Georgian town house, and in an older, timber-framed building opposite; some are large enough to accommodate a family. In the informal, wood-panelled restaurant, chef Daniel Gaskin prepares daily-changing menus of simple, home-cooked food. Bar/restaurant (extensive wine list; closed Sun); courtyard. Free Wi-Fi. Background music. Conference facilities. Parking. Children welcomed. 15 bedrooms (1 suitable for &). Per room B&B (continental) single £60, double £80. Cooked breakfast £5, dinner £23.

MANORHAUS LLANGOLLEN, Hill Street, LL20 8EU. Tel 01978-860775, www. manorhausllangollen.com. In a small town close to Offa's Dyke, this stylish restaurant-with-rooms occupies a smartly renovated Victorian town house. Christopher Frost and Gavin Harris are the owners. Modern bedrooms (some compact) take inspiration from the striking geometric fabrics of the Melin Tregwynt wool mill; they are simply but well equipped with a tea/coffee-machine, iPod docking station and bathrobes. A weekly-changing dinner menu is served in the informal restaurant; seasonal cocktails use Welsh spirits such as Brecon gin and Penderyn whisky. Bar, restaurant (closed Mon/Tues); rooftop hot tub. Free Wi-Fi. Background music. Parking permits supplied. Children over 12 welcomed. 6 bedrooms. Per room B&B single £82.50–£125.50, double £115–£180. Dinner £26–£32.50.

LLANWRTYD WELLS Powys
Map 3:D3

LASSWADE COUNTRY HOUSE, Station Road, LD5 4RW. Tel 01591-610515, www.lasswadehotel.co.uk. 'We were impressed.' There are 'superb' views of the Cambrian Mountains, Mynydd Epynt and the Brecon Beacons from Roger and Emma Stevens's small hotel and restaurant, in a traditional Edwardian house on the edge of the UK's smallest town. Friendly and helpful, the hosts follow a green agenda; discounts are offered to guests using public transport. Roger Stevens uses mainly organic ingredients from local farms for his 'excellent' daily-changing menus; vegetarian and special diets are catered for. Breakfast is served in the conservatory with views over the River Irfon. Drawing room (log fire), restaurant, conservatory; function room. Free Wi-Fi. No background music. Small garden; patio. Parking. Children (high teas on request; no under-8s in restaurant), and dogs (in kennels provided) welcomed. 8 bedrooms. Per room B&B £70–£120, D,B&B £140–£170. Closed Christmas.

MONTGOMERY Powys
Map 3:C4

THE CHECKERS, Broad Street, SY15 6PN. Tel 01686-669822, www.thecheckersmontgomery.co.uk. Overlooking the town square, this 'charming' restaurant-with-rooms is in an old coaching inn 'brought tastefully up to date' by sisters Kathryn and Sarah Francis, and Sarah's husband, Stéphane Borie. Modern bedrooms (some with low ceilings and doorways) are cosy, and equipped with a large bed, home-made biscuits and the latest gadgetry; some bathrooms have a freestanding bath. Stéphane Borie has a *Michelin* star for his seasonal classic French dishes; a seven-course tasting menu is available. Breakfast has local sausages and bacon, and home-made brioche toast. Lounge/ bar, restaurant; small terrace. Free Wi-Fi (signal variable). No background music. Chef's masterclasses. Children welcomed, by arrangement. 5 bedrooms (1 accessed via the roof terrace). Per room B&B £125–£170. Dinner from £50, tasting menu £75. Closed Christmas; 2 weeks in Jan; 1 week in autumn.

MUMBLES Swansea
Map 3:E3
PATRICKS WITH ROOMS, 638 Mumbles Road, SA3 4EA. Tel 01792-360199, www.patrickswithrooms.com. There are views across Mumbles Bay from this informal restaurant-with-rooms on the promenade. It is owned and run by two husband-and-wife teams, Catherine and Patrick Walsh, and Sally and Dean Fuller. The husbands are the chefs in the well-regarded restaurant, which is busy with locals on the weekends; monthly menus feature home-grown and Welsh produce, including laver bread and foraged sloe berries. Children are made very welcome with toys, books, DVDs, skateboards, and plenty of pasta on request; interconnecting rooms are ideal for a family. Breakfast, with home-baked bread, may be taken

in the room. Lounge/bar, restaurant. Free Wi-Fi. Background music. Gym. Greenhouse. Civil wedding licence; meeting room. On-street parking (can be difficult at peak times). Children welcomed (cots, high chairs, baby monitors, DVDs; playground across the road). 16 bedrooms. Per room B&B £115–£175. Dinner £40.

NARBERTH Pembrokeshire
Map 3:D2
CANASTON OAKS, Canaston Bridge, SA67 8DE. Tel 01437-541254, www.canastonoaks.co.uk. In lovely landscaped gardens, with walks down to ponds and the river beyond, David and Eleanor Lewis run their relaxed B&B in converted barns designed and built by Pembrokeshire craftsmen. Homely bedrooms have views of the countryside and are equipped with a TV, DVD-player, iPod dock, and a refrigerator stocked with drinks; some have their own sitting room or patio. Good walks from the front door; 3 miles from Narberth. Dining room. Free Wi-Fi. Parking. Children welcomed (cots, high chairs). 7 bedrooms (all on ground floor; 2 suitable for &; 1 family room). Per room B&B £90–£180.

NEWPORT Pembrokeshire
Map 3:D1
Y GARTH, Cae Tabor, Dinas Cross, SA42 0XR. Tel 01348-811777, www. bedandbreakfast-pembrokeshire.co.uk. 'Well worth a return visit.' Popular with walkers, Joyce Evans's 'faultless' B&B lies midway between Newport and Fishguard, and a short distance from the Pembrokeshire Coastal Path. Welsh cakes and a pot of tea are offered on arrival. Brightly decorated bedrooms

have little extras such as fresh flowers, local handmade chocolates and a mini-fridge; all have distant views of the sea or open countryside. Generous Pembrokeshire breakfasts are ordered the evening before. Convenient for the ferry to Rosslare. Lounge, dining room (background music); patio with seating. Free Wi-Fi. Parking. 3 bedrooms. Per person B&B £45–£55. Closed Christmas. **25% DISCOUNT VOUCHERS**

NEWTOWN Powys
Map 3:C4

THE FOREST COUNTRY GUEST HOUSE, Gilfach Lane, Kerry, SY16 4DW. Tel 01686-621821, www.bedandbreakfast newtown.co.uk. In the Vale of Kerry, this family-friendly B&B is owned by Paul and Michelle Martin. Run on eco-conscious lines, the Victorian country house has solar panels for heating water, and photovoltaic cells for generating electricity. Rooms have views of the undulating countryside or the large garden; breakfasts include locally sourced, organic produce and eggs from the Martins' free-range hens. The B&B is a five-minute drive from Newtown, and well located for exploring the Marches area of Mid Wales. Drawing room (books, games, laptop, piano), dining room; kitchenette. Free Wi-Fi. No background music. Games room (pool, table football, table tennis); toy box; DVDs. 4-acre garden; play area with forest fort; tennis. 3 miles SE of Newtown (train and bus stations). Secure bicycle storage. Children, and dogs (in kennels) welcomed; stabling available. Resident dog and cat; chickens and sheep. 5 bedrooms (plus 4 holiday cottages in outbuildings). Per room B&B £75.

SAUNDERSFOOT Pembrokeshire
Map 3:D2

ST BRIDES SPA HOTEL, St Brides Hill, SA69 9NH. Tel 01834-812 304, www.stbridesspahotel.com. On the Coastal Path overlooking Carmarthen Bay, with 'very good views' of the harbour and up the coast, Andrew and Lindsey Evans have created a relaxed, modern hotel with 'good' spa facilities and a gallery of contemporary Welsh art. Minimalist, with a chic maritime theme, bedrooms (Good, Better, Best) are light and airy; most have a sea view and a balcony. B&B guests receive a complimentary 90-minute session in the thermal suite and hydro pool, and unlimited access to the fitness suite. Dinners are served in the *Cliff* restaurant or less formal *Gallery* bar; for alfresco meals, a large decked terrace 'would have a wow factor on a summer's day'. 'Dinner and breakfast were excellent.' Sister eateries *The Mermaid* and *The Marina* are down by the harbour. Bar, sitting area, restaurant. Lift. Spa (steam room, salt room, rock sauna, adventure shower, ice fountain and a hydro pool with sea views). Gallery. Free Wi-Fi. Background music. Parking. Children welcomed (special menu). Function facilities. 34 bedrooms (1 suitable for ♿), plus six 2-bedroom apartments (pets allowed in some apartments). Per room B&B £160–£310.

WHITEBROOK Monmouthshire
Map 3:D4

THE CROWN AT WHITEBROOK, NP25 4TX. Tel 01600-860254, www.crownatwhitebrook.co.uk. Six miles south of Monmouth, in a small village in the wooded Wye valley, this former 17th-century drovers' inn is run as a restaurant-with-rooms by Raymond Blanc-trained chef/proprietor Chris Harrod. Rooted in French gastronomy, his dishes use local ingredients, and foraged herbs and mushrooms. The elegant bedrooms have a pared-back contemporary look; all have views across the rolling countryside. Lounge, restaurant (closed Mon); terrace; garden. Free Wi-Fi. Background music. Parking. Children welcomed. 8 bedrooms. Per room B&B £115–£140, D,B&B £198–£250 (midweek). Dinner £48–£54; tasting menus.

CHANNEL ISLANDS

ST MARTIN Guernsey
Map 1: inset E5
BELLA LUCE HOTEL, La Fosse, GY4 6EB. Tel 01481-238764, www.bellalucehotel. com. Down tranquil, leafy lanes, this beautifully restored manor house (Small Luxury Hotels of the World) has a spa, and an outdoor pool with loungers and sofas in lush, walled gardens. It is owned by Luke Wheadon; Michael McBride is the manager. Understated bedrooms (some small) have magazines, bathrobes and slippers; some have a modern four-poster bed. Bathrooms are luxurious. Overlooking the courtyard garden, the award-winning restaurant has candles and log fires at night; in summer, French windows open on to a sunny terrace for alfresco dining. Bistro food is served in the intimate bar. Chef Sebastian Orzechowski includes ingredients from artisanal producers, and herbs from the kitchen garden in his modern European dishes. Lounge, bar, *Garden Room* restaurant, cellar lounge (extensive wine list; background music). Free Wi-Fi. Garden (alfresco dining); courtyard.

Swimming pool (heated in summer), spa. Civil wedding licence; function facilities. 2 miles to St Peter Port; rock beach 5 mins' walk. Parking. Children welcomed (special menu). 25 bedrooms (2 on ground floor; some family rooms). Per room B&B from £135. Dinner from £30. Closed 2 weeks in Jan.

ST PETER PORT Guernsey
Map 1: inset E5
LA COLLINETTE HOTEL, St Jacques, GY1 1SN. Tel 01481-710331, www. lacollinette.com. Close to the seafront and centre, the Chambers family have run their welcoming hotel, with cottages and apartments, for almost 50 years. The white-painted house, decked with window boxes, has bright, modern rooms; most have views over the grounds and distant views of Guernsey to the north. In the grounds, the self-catering cottages and apartments have a terrace or balcony overlooking the gardens. The picturesque harbour nearby has access to the surrounding islands (and tax-free shopping). Bar, restaurant (brasserie menu; seafood and local produce); background music. Free Wi-Fi. DVD library. Conference facilities. Garden; heated swimming pool; gym; massages. Children welcomed (teddy bear gift; children's pool; play area). 30 bedrooms (plus 15 self-catering cottages and apartments). Per person B&B £60–£90. Dinner from £15.

THE DUKE OF RICHMOND, Cambridge Park Road, Les Cotils, GY1 1UY. Tel 01481-726221, www.dukeofrichmond. com. Close to the harbour, this large hotel (Red Carnation Hotels) overlooks a quiet park, and has fine views over the town to the neighbouring islands of

Herm and Sark beyond. Lukas Laubscher is the manager. Its glitzy interior has bold wallpapers and fabrics, mirrored furniture, chandeliers and decorative mirrors; the *Leopard* bar and restaurant runs wild with animal prints. Children are well provided for with DVDs, toy basket, board and card games, bathtime treats and robes; dogs have their own treats as well. Dining options range from formal to relaxed alfresco. Lounge, bar, restaurant, conservatory; terrace. Background music. Free Wi-Fi. Outdoor heated pool. Wedding/function facilities. Children, and dogs (in 2 rooms) welcomed. 73 bedrooms. Per room B&B £155–£410, D,B&B £220–£475.

LA FRÉGATE, Beauregard Lane, Les Cotils, GY1 1UT. Tel 01481-724624, www.lafregatehotel.com. There are 'fantastic' views of neighbouring islands and, on a clear day, the coast of France from this 18th-century manor house perched high above the town. It is managed by Simon Dufty. The hotel has simply styled, well-equipped bedrooms; most have a balcony or terrace. Decorated in blue and white, the restaurant has a fresh, coastal look and fine vistas; drinks and lunches are served alfresco on the sea-view terrace. Chef Neil Maginnis's menus are strong on local fish, shellfish and home-grown vegetables and herbs. Lounge/bar (light background music), restaurant; terrace; *The Boardroom* and *The Orangery* (function/conference facilities). Free Wi-Fi. Terraced garden. 2 mins' walk from centre. Children welcomed. 22 bedrooms (all with sea views; some with balcony). Per person B&B from £90. Dinner £33.50–£40.

BALLINTOY Co. Antrim
Map 6:A6
WHITEPARK HOUSE, 150 Whitepark Road, BT54 6NH. Tel 028-2073 1482, www.whiteparkhouse.com. Above the spectacular sandy beach of Whitepark Bay, this crenellated 18th-century house in a lovely garden is four miles east of the Giant's Causeway. It is run as a cosy B&B by Bob and Siobhan Isles, who have decorated their home with art, artefacts and souvenirs from their travels around the world; 'the attention to detail and comfort is exemplary'. Warm and welcoming, the Isleses offer guests tea and home-baked goodies on arrival; they are happy to advise on restaurants and places to visit. Bedrooms, with bathrobes and a hot-water bottle, have views of the garden or the sea; bathrooms are large. Irish breakfasts (vegetarians catered for). 'Delightful' sitting room (peat fire), conservatory. Free Wi-Fi. No background music. 3 bedrooms. Per room B&B £80–£120.

BALLYCASTLE Co. Mayo
Map 6:B4
STELLA MARIS. Tel 00 353 96-43322, www.stellamarisireland.com. 'We enjoyed sitting in the splendid conservatory, where we had the additional pleasure of watching dolphins frolicking in the bay.' In former times a Coast Guard regional headquarters and, latterly, a convent, this white-painted building on Bunatrahir Bay was restored and transformed into a small hotel by 'warmly welcoming' owners Frances Kelly and her husband, Terence McSweeney (a keen golfer and

sportswriter). It has simply furnished rooms named after famous golf courses; most look out to the Atlantic Ocean. The 'lovely' bar has fireplaces, old prints and golf memorabilia; in the restaurant, Frances Kelly serves a daily-changing menu of modern dishes. Lounge, bar, restaurant, conservatory. Free Wi-Fi. Quiet Irish background music. Ramp. Wedding facilities; 3-acre grounds. Sandy beach nearby. Parking. Children welcomed, by arrangement; small dogs in 1 room. 1½ miles W of Ballycastle. 11 bedrooms (1 on ground floor, suitable for &). Per person B&B €75–€125, Dinner £35–£40. Closed Oct–20 Apr.

BALLYVAUGHAN Co. Clare
Map 6:C4

GREGANS CASTLE HOTEL. Tel 00 353 65-707 7005, www.gregans.ie. Simon Haden and Friederieke McMurray's 'magical' 18th-century country house stands in tranquil grounds with views across the Burren to Galway Bay. Public rooms have antiques, sofas and jugs of garden flowers; bedrooms, decorated with elegant fabrics and original art, have seats for admiring the views. Some rooms have direct access to the garden. Chef David Hurley serves 'creative' modern Irish and European dishes; an early dinner for children is available by arrangement. Donkeys, ducks and a pony roam the extensive grounds. Drawing room, bar (background jazz, classical), restaurant (closed Sun). Free Wi-Fi. 15-acre grounds: ornamental pool; croquet. No TV. Wedding facilities. Children (no under-5s in dining room at night), and dogs (in 2 bedrooms) welcomed. 21 bedrooms (some on ground floor). Per room B&B €215–€255, D,B&B €325–€370. Closed 3 Nov–mid-Feb.

BELFAST
Map 6:B6

THE OLD RECTORY, 148 Malone Road, BT9 5LH. Tel 028-9066 7882, www.anoldrectory.co.uk. There is a friendly atmosphere at Mary Callan's homely guest house, in a 19th-century rectory close to the centre and the university. Visitors appreciate the many thoughtful touches: the drawing room has games, and books on Irish history, architecture and culture; comfortable bedrooms have books, magazines and biscuits. During the cooler months, guests are offered a complimentary hot whiskey in the evening. Award-winning breakfasts have lots of choice, including Irish smoked salmon, wild boar sausages, and porridge with cream, honey and Irish Mist liqueur; raspberry jam, whiskey marmalade and soda bread are all home made. A small supper menu is available Mon to Fri. Ten mins' walk to Lagan Meadows (river walks). Drawing room. Garden. Free Wi-Fi. No background music. Parking. Children welcomed. 5 bedrooms (1 on ground floor). Per room B&B single £45–£55, double £84–£86. Closed Christmas.

RAVENHILL HOUSE, 690 Ravenhill Road, BT6 0BZ. Tel 028-9020 7444, www.ravenhillhouse.com. Hospitable hosts Roger and Olive Nicholson greet B&B guests with tea, coffee and biscuits at their restored Victorian house two miles from the centre. Bedrooms have locally handcrafted furniture; the sitting room has a computer for guests' use and local-interest books. Breakfasts include freshly baked Irish wheaten bread and home-made granola and muesli (plus good vegetarian options). The Nicholsons share tips about the city. Shops, pubs,

restaurants and a park within walking distance. Sitting room, dining room; small garden. Free Wi-Fi. Occasional background music; Radio 3 at breakfast. Parking. Children welcomed.
5 bedrooms (1 on ground floor). Per room B&B single £55–£60, double £80–£95. Closed early July; mid-Dec–Feb.

BUSHMILLS Co. Antrim
Map 6:A6
BUSHMILLS INN, 9 Dunluce Road, BT57 8QG. Tel 028-2073 3000, www. bushmillsinn.com. Dating in part to the 17th century, this higgledy-piggledy old coaching inn and adjoining mill house has a grand staircase, a 'secret' library, and a web of interconnecting cosy snugs with turf fires, oil lamps and ancient wooden booths. It is hospitably run by Alan Dunlop and friendly staff. Traditional Irish music is performed in the *Gas* bar, lit by original gas lights; movies are screened on Thursday nights. The restaurant (modern Irish cuisine) overlooks the garden courtyard. Drawing room, restaurant, gallery, oak-beamed loft; patio; 2-acre garden. Free Wi-Fi. Conference facilities; 30-seat cinema; treatment room. Parking. Children welcomed (family rooms; cots). 2 miles from the Giant's Causeway. 41 bedrooms (some on ground floor; spacious ones in mill house, smaller ones in inn). Per room B&B £128–£398. Dinner £40–£45.

CALLAN Co. Kilkenny
Map 6:D5
BALLAGHTOBIN COUNTRY HOUSE. Tel 00 353 56-772 5227, www.ballaghtobin.com. Remotely situated, Catherine and Mickey Gabbett's 18th-century ancestral home is in informal gardens within a 500-acre farm producing cereals and Christmas trees (wood chips power the boiler for heating and hot water). There is a ruined Norman church opposite. Fourteen generations of the Gabbett family have lived on the site of the house; today, the hospitable owners delight in welcoming B&B guests. Refurbished country house-style rooms are decorated in soothing colours and furnished with paintings and antiques; generous breakfasts are served at a large table in the elegant dining room. Drawing room, dining room, study, conservatory. Free Wi-Fi. No background music. Tennis, croquet, clock golf. Children and dogs welcomed. 10 miles from Kilkenny. 3 bedrooms. Per person B&B from €50. Closed Nov–Mar.

CARLINGFORD Co. Louth
Map 6:B6
GHAN HOUSE. Tel 00 353 42-937 3682, www.ghanhouse.com. By a 'pretty' medieval village, this listed Georgian house with views across Carlingford Lough is run in 'hands-on' style by Paul Carroll and his mother, Joyce, with friendly staff. Traditionally furnished rooms have family antiques alongside modern equipment (iPod dock, flat-screen Internet-enabled TV); garden annexe rooms have views of the mountains beyond. There is a grand piano in the 'very elegant' dining room, where chef Stephane Le Sourne's menus are based on the abundant supply of shellfish from the lough, and vegetables and herbs from the kitchen garden. Breakfast has home-made jams and marmalade, and home-baked bread. Sitting room, bar, restaurant (3 dining areas; closed Mon, Tues in low season).

Free Wi-Fi. 'Easy listening' background music. Civil wedding licence. Cookery school. 3-acre garden. Parking; bicycle storage. Children, and dogs (in stables only) welcomed. 12 bedrooms (8 in annexe). Per person B&B €75–€95, D,B&B €105–€130.

CASTLEBALDWIN Co. Sligo
Map 6:B5
CROMLEACH LODGE, Lough Arrow. Tel 00 353 71-916 5155, www.cromleach.com. In a tranquil position in the hills above Lough Arrow, Moira and Christy Tighe's hotel is surrounded by 'beautiful' Sligo scenery. Spacious, traditionally decorated bedrooms are in the main house, with views over the water; more modern rooms, some with a private balcony, are in a purpose-built block accessible via enclosed walkways (some rooms are 'a considerable distance' from the public areas). In the restaurant overlooking the lough and mountains, chef Lanka Fernando's modern Irish dishes are praised; sandwiches and light meals are served in the bar. The hosts are keen walkers and are happy to provide information on the best routes for varying abilities. Lounge, bar, restaurant; spa (sauna, steam room, outdoor whirlpool; treatment rooms). Free Wi-Fi (in public rooms only). Background music. 30-acre grounds: forest walks, private access to Lough Arrow (fishing, boating, surfing), hill climbing. Wedding/function facilities. Good walks from the front door; packed lunches available. Children and dogs welcomed (dog-grooming parlour). 57 bedrooms (1 suitable for &). Per room B&B €80–€200. Dinner €50. Closed Mon and Tues, May–June, Sept–Dec; Christmas.

COBH Co. Cork
Map 6:D5
KNOCKEVEN HOUSE, Rushbrooke. Tel 00 353 21-481 1778, www.knockeven house.com. On the outskirts of town, Pam and John Mulhaire's B&B is in a double-fronted Victorian house in well-kept gardens; displays of magnolias, azaleas and camellias can be seen from the spacious bedrooms. Richly furnished rooms have high ceilings and large windows; guests are served home-made scones and afternoon tea or coffee in the comfortable drawing room. Generous breakfasts are taken at a large mahogany table; Pam Mulhaire cooks three-course dinners on the Aga, by arrangement. Drawing room, dining room. 2-acre grounds. Free Wi-Fi. Classical background music. Children welcomed. 1 mile from town. 4 bedrooms. Per person B&B €50, D,B&B €85.

CORK Co. Cork
Map 6:D5
CAFÉ PARADISO, 16 Lancaster Quay. Tel 00 353 21-427 7939, www.cafeparadiso.ie. Within easy walking distance of the centre, this vegetarian restaurant-with-rooms is owned by acclaimed chef and cookbook writer Denis Cotter, who runs it with Geraldine O'Toole. Tempting enough for non-vegetarians, his inventive meat-free dishes are based on seasonal, organic produce from the nearby Gort na Nain Farm (visits arranged). Dinner is served from 5.30 pm, in the quayside restaurant. Upstairs, the spacious bedrooms have an iPod dock, coffee machine and supply of board games and books; no TV. Breakfast, with baked pastries, yogurt, granola, farmhouse cheeses, preserves and juice, is served in the room. Free Wi-Fi. Background

music. Restricted parking. 2 bedrooms (1 faces the river). Per person D,B&B €100. Closed Sundays; Christmas.

DONEGAL Co. Donegal
Map 6:B5

HARVEY'S POINT, Lough Eske. Tel 00 353 74-972 2208, www.harveyspoint.com. The Bluestack Mountains provide the backdrop for the Gysling family's country hotel, on the shores of Lough Eske. In the main house, spacious, traditionally decorated bedrooms have dark wood furnishings and oriental rugs; lakeshore suites, accessed via a separate entrance, have a private terrace and outdoor seating overlooking the water. Fresh milk, fruit and biscuits are delivered to all rooms daily. The restaurant was refurbished in 2014 to include an open kitchen, where guests can watch the chefs at work; huge windows in the dining room have lovely views of the lake. Activity breaks (fishing, canoeing, golf, walks, archery) available. Lounge, drawing room, bar (turf fire), restaurant (closed Sun–Tues, Nov–Mar), ballroom (resident pianist; Irish/classical background music). Summertime cabaret dinners June–Oct. Free Wi-Fi. Beauty treatments; massage. Lift; ramps. Civil wedding licence; conference facilities. 20-acre grounds. Children (babysitting, early supper), and dogs (in some bedrooms) welcomed; stabling and grazing for horses available. 4 miles from town. 64 bedrooms (8 lakeside suites). Per room B&B €198–€298. 2-night min. stay at weekends.

DUBLIN
Map 6:C6

ARIEL HOUSE, 50–54 Lansdowne Road, Dublin 4. Tel 00 353 1-668 5512, www.ariel-house.net. The McKeown family renovated three Victorian town houses to form their B&B hotel in leafy Ballsbridge, close to the Aviva stadium and the RDS showgrounds. It is managed by Deidre McDonald. Period features such as stained glass and iron railings have been retained; bedrooms in the main building have high ceilings, an original fireplace and plasterwork. Eight smaller bedrooms in an extension at the back face the private garden. 'Imaginative and excellent' breakfasts are 'served with some flair' (until 11 am at weekends). Drawing room, dining room; garden. Free Wi-Fi. Classical background music. Limited parking. Children welcomed. 37 bedrooms (some with a four-poster bed). Per room B&B €69–€190. Closed Christmas.

THE CLIFF TOWNHOUSE, 22 St Stephen's Green, Dublin 2. Tel 00 353 1-638 3939, www.theclifftownhouse.com. Once home to one of the oldest private members' clubs in Ireland, this handsome Georgian house opposite St Stephen's Green is now a stylish town house hotel and seafood and oyster restaurant. It is run by owner Barry O'Callaghan; Siobhan Ryan is the manager. It is decorated in pleasing heritage shades, and furnished with a mix of antique and modern pieces. Bedrooms have reproduction period prints and Donegal tweed blankets; some of the marble bathrooms have a quirky hip bath and vintage fittings. Most deluxe rooms overlook the green. In the smart restaurant, with its high ceilings and leather booths, chef Sean Smith's menus showcase local seafood (Galway oysters, native lobster, dressed Yawl Bay crab) and hearty salads. Bar, restaurant (pre- and post-theatre service); private dining room. Free Wi-Fi. 'Subtle' background music. Wedding function facilities. Children welcomed. 9 bedrooms. Per room B&B from €163. Dinner €28–€70. Closed Christmas.

WATERLOO HOUSE, 8–10 Waterloo Road, Dublin 4. Tel 00 353 1-660 1888, www.waterloohouse.ie. On a peaceful residential street in a 'very central' location near St Stephen's Green, Evelyn Corcoran's comfortable B&B is well liked for the 'helpful' service and 'good' breakfasts. Some of the traditionally furnished bedrooms are compact, though 'more than adequate' for a short stay. Served in the dining room or adjoining conservatory, breakfasts have a 'catch of the day', home-made traditional Irish soda bread, and fresh and stewed fruit. Lounge (classical background music), dining room, conservatory; garden. Free Wi-Fi. Lift; ramp. Parking. Children welcomed. 19 bedrooms (some family rooms; some suitable for &). Per room B&B single €99–€109, double €139–€155.

DUNFANAGHY Co. Donegal
Map 6:A5
THE MILL, Figart. Tel 00 353 74-913 6985, www.themillrestaurant.com. Overlooking a 'lovely' lake, on the outskirts of a small resort town, this former 19th-century flax mill is run as an unpretentious restaurant-with-rooms by Susan Alcorn and her husband, Derek. She is the granddaughter of Frank Egginton, the watercolour artist, whose work is displayed throughout. There are plenty of comfortable lounging facilities; dinner orders are taken in the conservatory overlooking the lake, or in the 'atmospheric' drawing

room, which has an open fire on cool evenings. Bedrooms are simply furnished. Guests, who are asked to arrive after 4 pm, are offered a cup of coffee or tea and home-made shortbread. Derek Alcorn, the chef, uses local produce for his 'imaginative' modern Irish menus, ending with coffee and petits fours (served 7 pm–9 pm, Tues–Sun; popular with non-residents; booking is advisable). Breakfast, with home-made breads and preserves, is 'excellent'. Free Wi-Fi (limited). Background music. Garden. Children welcomed. ½ mile W of town. 6 bedrooms. Per person B&B €48–€63. Dinner €41. Closed Jan–mid-Mar.

GALWAY Co. Galway
Map 6:C5
THE G HOTEL, Wellpark. Tel 00 353 91-865200, www.theghotel.ie. A dramatic light installation hangs in the double-height atrium of this style-conscious Philip Treacy-designed hotel overlooking Lough Atalia; elsewhere in the hotel, there are glamorous, dimly lit corridors, a mirrored bar, candy-coloured furnishings and original artworks. It is managed by Triona Gannon for Edward Hotels. Spacious bedrooms are decorated in calm shades; rooms overlooking the Zen garden are 'particularly quiet and private'. The clubby restaurant has European-inspired dishes; light lunches, afternoon tea and informal dinners are taken in any of the three distinctively designed lounges. Cocktail bar, 3 lounges, *gigi's* restaurant; spa (indoor swimming pool, sauna, steam room, treatments); bamboo Zen garden. Free Wi-Fi. Background music. Lift. Wedding/function facilities. Parking. On the outskirts of town.

Children welcomed (milk and cookies on arrival, DVD and games library; babysitting). 101 rooms. Per room B&B €140–€600. Dinner €29.50–€46.50.

GLASHABEG Co. Kerry
Map 6:D4

GORMAN'S CLIFFTOP HOUSE. Tel 00 353 66-915-5162, www.gormans-clifftop house.com. An open turf fire and a pot of tea await guests on cool days at this comfortable guest house and restaurant, in a 'splendid location' on the Dingle peninsula. It is run by Síle and Vincent Gorman, whose family have fished and farmed this area for generations. Spacious, modern bedrooms, each with a seating area, have sea or mountain views; all are well equipped with books, a DVD-player and tea- and coffee-making facilities. There are huge picture windows overlooking the harbour and ocean from the restaurant; here, Vincent Gorman's 'very good' dinners use much local and home-grown produce. Breakfast has home-baked bread, organic compotes and yogurt, and a good variety of hot dishes. Walks from the front door. Lounge, library, restaurant (closed Sun; lighter meals available for staying guests). Free Wi-Fi. Classical and traditional Irish background music. 4-acre garden, bogland and cliff. Children welcomed. Resident dog, Molly. 8 bedrooms (1 family room). Per room B&B €110–€150. Open some weekends and by arrangement Oct–Mar.

GLASLOUGH, Co. Monaghan
Map 6:B6

CASTLE LESLIE. Tel 00 353 47 88100, www.castleleslie.com. 'Everything was excellent.' In 1,000 acres of rolling countryside, ancient woods and lakes, this luxury hotel remains in the hands of the Leslie family, who founded the estate in the 1660s. It is managed by Brian Baldwin. Rooms in the main house are furnished in sumptuous country house style with antiques and old paintings; there is much interesting family history here. Near the main gate, the *Lodge* has been sympathetically restored and extended to include the restaurant, spa and further accommodation. Drawing room, bar, breakfast room, *Snaffles* restaurant (5-course menus; Andrew Bradley is chef); conservatory, billiard room, library, cinema. Free Wi-Fi. Background music in *Lodge* only. Spa (treatment rooms, relaxation area; outdoor hot tub). Civil wedding licence. Equestrian centre; fishing, boating, kayaking, clay-pigeon shooting, falconry, walking trails, picnics. Children welcomed (special menu). 6 miles from Monaghan. 126 bedrooms (29 in the *Lodge*, 12 in stable mews, 12 in cottages with self-catering facilities). Per person B&B €80–€135, D,B&B €115–€190. Closed Christmas.

INIS MEÁIN Co. Galway
Map 6:C4

INIS MEÁIN RESTAURANT AND SUITES, Aran Islands. Tel 00 353 86-826 6026, www.inismeain.com. On the most remote of the three Aran Islands (a stronghold of Irish culture), this 'stunning' modern stone-and-glass building is designed to blend into the native terraced stone fields; there are panoramic views to Galway Bay and the mountains of Connemara. It is run as a restaurant-with-rooms by Ruairí de Blacam and his wife, Marie Thérèse, who offer a 'gentle and warm' welcome.

Based on a philosophy of Elemental Eating, Ruairí de Blacam's four-course menus use hyper-local ingredients (lobster and crab caught by island fishermen from traditional currachs; vegetables grown in the shelter of stone); dinner is served at 8 pm. Minimalist suites are decorated in muted colours with wooden floors and modern furnishings; each has a large bed, a living space, large windows and an outdoor seating area. Guests are provided with bicycles, fishing rods and swimming towels. A breakfast box is delivered to the suite. 45-min ferry from Ros a' Mhíl; flights from Connemara airport. Restaurant. 3-acre grounds. Free Wi-Fi. Background Irish music, in evening. Children welcomed. 5 bedrooms. Per room B&B €440–€660. 2-night min. stay. Closed Oct–Apr.

KANTURK Co. Cork
Map 6:D5

GLENLOHANE HOUSE. Tel 00 353 29-50014, www.glenlohane.com. Surrounded by acres of landscaped gardens, meadows and fields, this handsome 18th-century country house has belonged to the Sharp-Bolster family for 11 generations. It is filled with heirlooms and family memorabilia. Desmond and Melanie Sharp-Bolster and their son, Gordon – all motorcycle enthusiasts – delight in sharing their home's interesting history; guests are encouraged to enjoy the house 'as if staying with friends'. Tastefully furnished bedrooms are spacious and light; the red-walled library has comfortable seating and is a cosseting place in which to read or relax beside the open fire in the evenings. Three-course dinners (by arrangement) are taken with the family. Drawing room, library, dining room. 250-acre gardens and parkland (chickens, peacocks, sheep, horses). Free Wi-Fi. No background music. 1½ miles E of town; plenty of pubs and restaurants. Glenlohane Vintage Show in summer. Resident cat and dogs. 3 bedrooms (plus 2-bedroom self-catering cottage nearby). Per person B&B €90. Dinner €50.

KENMARE Co. Kerry
Map 6:D4

BROOK LANE HOTEL. Tel 00 353 64-664 2077, www.brooklanehotel.com. Una and Dermot Brennan's small, friendly hotel is in a pretty heritage town on the bay, and an ideal base for exploring the Ring of Kerry. Superior bedrooms are simply decorated in earth tones; deluxe rooms have bold colours and striking wallpaper. Chef Brendan Scannell's modern Irish dishes are served in the bistro; a sister restaurant, *No. 35*, is a 15-minute walk away. Extensive Irish breakfasts. Library, bar/restaurant; private dining room; ½-acre garden. Free Wi-Fi (in public areas). Background music. Lift. Wedding/conference facilities. Golf, walking, cycling. Parking. Children welcomed. 20 bedrooms (1 suitable for &), plus 2-bedroom apartment. Per person B&B €50–€90, D,B&B €85–€130. Closed Christmas.
25% DISCOUNT VOUCHERS

KILKENNY Co. Kilkenny
Map 6:D5

ROSQUIL HOUSE, Castlecomer Road. Tel 00 353 56-772 1419, www.rosquilhouse. com. Phil and Rhoda Nolan are the welcoming owners at this 'pleasing, modern' guest house, 20 minutes' walk from the 'well-kept and interesting town'. Good-sized bedrooms are simply and smartly furnished; a comfortable sitting room has books to borrow. Breakfast is praised: bread, scones and cakes are home baked; fruit compotes, jam and granola are home made; hot dishes are cooked to order. Lounge; small garden. Free Wi-Fi. No background music. Close to Kilkenny Golf Club. Children and dogs welcomed. Resident dog. 7 bedrooms (1 suitable for &), plus *The Mews* self-catering apartment. Per person B&B from €35.

KILLARNEY Co. Kerry
Map 6:D4

THE BREHON, Muckross Road. Tel 00 353 64-663 0700, www.thebrehon.com. 'Absolute relaxation.' Next to Killarney national park, the O'Donahue family's large, modern spa hotel is run with 'fantastic attention to detail' by staff who 'serve with pride and professionalism'. Spacious bedrooms have a marble bathroom with a separate shower and bath. Chef Chad Byrne serves international cuisine and traditional Irish dishes in *Danú* restaurant; afternoon tea and post-dinner drinks can be taken in the lounge beside an open fire. Young guests have complimentary access to the Aquila Club leisure centre at the neighbouring *Gleneagles Hotel*. 'Truly a gem.' Lounge, bar, restaurant; private dining room. Room service. Spa (12-metre indoor Vitality pool, crystal steam room, herb sauna, tropical showers, ice fountain, kubel dusche, spa bath; fitness centre; Thai-style massages and treatments). Free Wi-Fi. Background music. Lift. Wedding/function facilities. ½ mile from town centre; INEC is close by. Parking. Children welcomed. 123

bedrooms (family suites). Per room B&B €109–€149. Dinner from €27.

THE DUNLOE, Beaufort. Tel 00 353 64-664 4111, www.thedunloe.com. Surrounded by stunning scenery overlooking the Gap of Dunloe, this 'magical' luxury hotel stands in its own extensive estate, with gardens, farmland and the ruins of the 12th-century Dunloe Castle, now restored, which guests can explore. It is managed by Jason Clifford, who 'simply thinks of everything'. Children are made very welcome: there are movie nights and a kids' club in the summer, and many other facilities (playground, games room, indoor tennis; pony riding). There is complimentary fishing on the River Laune; the kitchen will prepare and cook guests' catch for their dinner. 3 lounges, bar, *Garden café*, *Oak* restaurant; 64-acre grounds. Free Wi-Fi in lobby. Background music. Heated indoor pool; tennis courts; sauna, steam room; treatment rooms; gym. Wedding/function facilities. Children and dogs welcomed. 102 bedrooms (20 smoking; 1 suitable for &). Per room B&B €180–€260. D,B&B per person €145–€185. Closed mid-Oct–mid-Apr.

KINSALE Co. Cork
Map 6:D5

THE OLD PRESBYTERY, 43 Cork Street. Tel 00 353 21-477 2027, www.oldpres.com. Packed with fascinating memorabilia, Philip and Noreen McEvoy's rambling B&B, on a quiet street in the centre of town, is in a 200-year-old house that was once a priests' residence attached to the nearby St John the Baptist church. Bedrooms have stripped pine furniture, antiques and a brass or cast iron bed; some superior rooms have a balcony. The hosts are warmly welcoming; Philip McEvoy, a professional chef, cooks substantial breakfasts using organic produce (vegetarian options available). Lounge, dining room; patio. Free Wi-Fi. Classical/Irish background music. Parking. Children welcomed. 9 bedrooms (3 suites; 2 self-catering). Per room B&B €90–€160. Closed Nov–Feb.

LAHINCH Co. Clare
Map 6:C4
MOY HOUSE. Tel 00 353 65-708 2800, www.moyhouse.com. In extensive grounds with mature woodland and a river, this white-painted 19th-century country house has spectacular views over Lahinch Bay. Caroline Enright is the manager. Bedrooms are individually decorated; the Signature suite has a private conservatory, and an original well in the bathroom. In the drawing room, guests help themselves from the honesty bar in front of an open fire; Matthew Strefford's daily changing five-course tasting menus are served in the candlelit conservatory restaurant overlooking the ocean. Praiseworthy breakfasts include home-made bread and granola. Library, drawing room, restaurant (background music; closed Sun, Mon low season). Free Wi-Fi; computer provided. 15-acre grounds. Children welcomed. Resident dog. 9 bedrooms. Per room B&B €165–€360. Dinner €55. Closed Nov–Apr.

LISNASKEA Co. Fermanagh
Map 6:B5
WATERMILL LODGE, Kilmore Quay South, BT92 0DT. Tel 028-6772 4369, www.watermillrestaurantfermanagh.com.
In mature gardens beside Lough Erne, French chef and keen fisherman Pascal Brissaud's restaurant-with-rooms is in a picturesque thatched house, with accommodation in an adjacent building. Comfortable bedrooms have access to a little patio with a table and chairs, and views of 'fabulous scenery'. In the smartly rustic restaurant, Pascal Brissaud cooks with local produce, fish from the lough, and vegetables and herbs from his garden; his 'delicious' food has a Gallic slant. 'Superb' breakfasts have fresh croissants and baguettes. Traditional Irish Sunday roasts. Restaurant (background music). Free Wi-Fi. Civil wedding licence. Fishing breaks and holidays can be arranged. Children (special menus), and small dogs welcomed. 7 bedrooms. Per room B&B single £59, double £95. Dinner £25.
25% DISCOUNT VOUCHERS

LONGFORD Co. Longford
Map 6:C5
VIEWMOUNT HOUSE, Dublin Road. Tel 00 353 43-334 1919, www.viewmount house.com. The former home of the Earl of Longford, this restored Georgian house is run as a 'wonderful' guest house and restaurant by Beryl and James Kearney. Less than a mile from the town centre, it sits in large landscaped gardens adjoining Longford Golf Club. Colourful, individually decorated bedrooms have an antique bed and country views; the former kitchen, with its vaulted ceiling, is now a cosy sitting room with chesterfields in front of an open fire. The old stables in the grounds have been converted into the smart, candlelit *VM* restaurant; chef Gary O'Hanlon's seasonal Irish dinners

have a modern twist (served 6.30 pm–9 pm, Wed–Sat). Reception room, library, sitting room, breakfast room, restaurant (background music); courtyard. Free Wi-Fi. 4-acre gardens (Japanese garden, knot garden, orchard). Wedding facilities. Children welcomed. 12 bedrooms (7 in modern extension; some on ground floor). Per person B&B €60–€75, D,B&B €115. **25% DISCOUNT VOUCHERS**

MAGHERAFELT Co. Londonderry
Map 6:B6

LAUREL VILLA TOWNHOUSE, 60 Church Street, BT45 6AW. Tel 028-7930 1459, www.laurel-villa.com. The atmosphere at Eugene and Gerardine Kielt's elegant B&B is decidedly literary, with a rich collection of Seamus Heaney memorabilia on display, and comfortable bedrooms named after Ulster poets. A breakfast of fresh fruit salad and an Ulster fry is served in the wood-panelled dining room; Gerardine Kielt's afternoon teas, with home-baked cakes and scones, are legendary. Eugene Kielt, a Blue Badge guide, arranges poetry readings and tours of 'Heaney country'; he also holds a large collection of local genealogical and historical materials, and provides an ancestry-tracing service. 2 lounges, dining room. In the centre of town. Free Wi-Fi. No background music. Children welcomed. 4 bedrooms. Per person B&B single £60, double £40–£45.

MOYARD Co. Galway
Map 6:C4

CROCNARAW COUNTRY HOUSE. Tel 00 353 95-41068, www.crocnaraw.co.uk. 'A terrific hostess', Lucy Fretwell runs this homely guest house in her traditional Georgian country home. Close to Ballinakill Bay, the house is set in 20 acres of wooded gardens and meadows. Individually decorated bedrooms are quaint and 'full of light'; one has an old-fashioned claw-footed bath. Afternoon tea with home-made scones and strawberry jam is taken in front of the peat fire in the drawing room; three-course dinners use locally sourced fish and meat, and vegetables, salads and fruits from the kitchen garden and orchard. Generous breakfasts include home-made Irish bread. Fully licensed. Fishing, angling, pony trekking, golf nearby. Dining room, drawing room, snug; garden, orchard. Free Wi-Fi. No background music. Children (no babies) welcomed; dogs allowed in some bedrooms. 4 bedrooms. Per person B&B €35–€58. Dinner €35. Closed Nov–May. **25% DISCOUNT VOUCHERS**

NEWPORT Co. Mayo
Map 6:B4

NEWPORT HOUSE. Tel 00 353 98-41222, www.newporthouse.ie. There is a mellow elegance at this grand Georgian country house overlooking the estuary of the River Newport: its traditionally decorated public rooms are filled with intricate mouldings, oil paintings, bronzes and statuary; the high-ceilinged drawing rooms have bookcases, 'lived-in' sofas and open fires. It is owned by Kieran Thompson; Catherine Flynn, the manager, is 'the heart and soul of the place'. In the dining room overlooking the gardens and the river, guests praise long-serving chef John Gavin's six-course menus, which include produce from the fishery, garden and farm, home-smoked salmon and 'delicious' home-baked bread. Free Wi-Fi (in public areas and some bedrooms). No background music. Children, and dogs (in courtyard bedrooms) welcomed. 14 bedrooms (4 in courtyard). Per person B&B €95–€140, D,B&B €160–€205. Closed Nov–late Mar.

NEWTOWNARDS Co. Down
Map 6:B6
BEECH HILL COUNTRY HOUSE, 23 Ballymoney Road, Craigantlet, BT23 4TG. Tel 028-9042 5892, www.beech-hill.net. In the Holywood hills, close to Belfast, Victoria Brann's white Georgian-style house is ideally placed for Belfast City Airport and the ferries. The stunning entrance hall, painted a vivid red, has a chandelier and fresh flowers; elsewhere in the colourful, imaginatively decorated B&B are interesting antiques and period pieces. Bedrooms are spacious, with panoramic views over the north Down countryside. Water is heated by solar power; extensive breakfasts use locally sourced produce. Drawing room, dining room, conservatory. Free Wi-Fi. No background music. Parking. Dogs welcomed. 3 bedrooms (on ground floor; *The Colonel's Lodge* is available for self-catering). Per person B&B £50–£60.

PORTSTEWART Co. Londonderry
Map 6:A6
THE YORK, 2 Station Road, BT55 7DA. Tel 028-7083 3594, www.theyork portstewart.co.uk. Overlooking the sea, this contemporary restaurant-with-rooms has 'pleasant' staff and 'spacious, well-equipped' bedrooms. Several rooms have sea views; superior suites have a private balcony overlooking the water. Pub classics and a daily special (Tuesday grills, Thursday curries, etc)

are served in the 'busy' *York Grill Bar* restaurant. Bar, dining room (piano, jukebox); terrace/conservatory. Free Wi-Fi. Lift. Small wedding/function facilities. Children welcomed. 8 bedrooms (1 suitable for ᕯ). Per room B&B single £79 (Sun–Thurs), double £115. Dinner from £22.

RAMELTON Co. Donegal
Map 6:B5
FREWIN, Rectory Road. Tel 00 353 74-915 1246, www.frewinhouse.com. On the outskirts of a historic Georgian port, Regina and Thomas Coyle's carefully restored Victorian rectory stands in mature wooded grounds. Decorated 'with flair', the family home has stained-glass windows, an elegant staircase, and antiques. Three of the spacious country house-style bedrooms have their own sitting room; bathrooms are compact. Regina Coyle greets B&B guests with afternoon tea, served by a big open fire in the cosy library; the sumptuous breakfasts are praiseworthy and taken communally at a large table. Candlelit dinners are by arrangement. Sitting room, library, dining room; 2-acre garden. Free Wi-Fi. No background music. Children welcomed. 4 bedrooms (1 with private bathroom; plus 1-bedroom cottage in the grounds). Per person B&B €55–€75. Dinner €45.50. Closed Christmas.

RATHNEW Co. Wicklow
Map 6:C6
HUNTER'S HOTEL, Newrath Bridge. Tel 00 353 404 40106, www.hunters.ie. Said to be the oldest remaining inn in Ireland, this former coaching inn, in two acres of beautiful gardens on the banks of the River Vartry, retains all the

charms of a former age. Currently run by brothers Richard and Tom Gelletlie, it has been in the same family for five generations. Bedrooms have antiques, prints and creaking floorboards; many overlook the gardens. The public areas are traditionally decorated, and have chintzy sofas, polished brass and open fires. In warm weather, the garden is a pleasant place in which to take afternoon tea and drinks. Set lunch and dinner menus are based on traditional Irish/continental cooking and freshly picked garden produce. Sitting room, lounge, bar, restaurant; garden. Free Wi-Fi. No background music. Children, and dogs (by arrangement) welcomed. 16 bedrooms (1 suitable for &). Per person B&B €65–€95, D,B&B €85–€125. Closed Christmas.
25% DISCOUNT VOUCHERS

RECESS Co. Galway
Map 6:C4
LOUGH INAGH LODGE, Connemara. Tel 00 353 95-34706, www.loughinagh lodgehotel.ie. In a 'spectacular' position, this 'lovely, peaceful' lodge overlooking the lough is surrounded by the Twelve Bens and Mam Turk mountain ranges. It is run with 'a pleasant informality' by owner Máire O'Connor and manager Dominic O'Morain. Each of the country house-style bedrooms has a comfortable seating area; all have stunning views of the lough and the mountains. Chef Julie Worley's 'delicious' four-course Irish country menus, served in the elegant dining room, feature seafood and wild game; a good bar menu is also available. Good walks, fishing. Sitting room, bar, library, dining room. Free Wi-Fi. No background music. 5-acre grounds. Wedding facilities. Children and dogs

welcomed. 13 bedrooms (4 on ground floor). Per room B&B €130–€180. Dinner €50. Closed mid-Dec–mid-Mar.

STRANGFORD Co. Down
Map 6:B6
THE CUAN, 6–10 The Square, BT30 7ND. Tel 028-4488 1222, www.thecuan.com. Guests like the warm welcome and personable service at Peter and Caroline McErlean's guest house, in a conservation village on the shores of Strangford Lough (a World Heritage site). Spacious, comfortable bedrooms are simply furnished; some overlook the village square. The restaurant specialises in locally sourced seafood, including langoustines freshly caught from the lough; at breakfast, Peter McErlean's home-baked scones are praised. 2 lounges, bar, restaurant (traditional background music). Wedding/function facilities. Free Wi-Fi. Live music events in the summer. Children welcomed. 9 bedrooms (1 suitable for &), plus 1 self-catering cottage. Per person B&B £42.50–£65, D,B&B £58–£80.

THOMASTOWN Co. Kilkenny
Map 6:D5
BALLYDUFF HOUSE. Tel 00 353 56-775 8488, www.ballyduffhouse.ie. On the banks of the River Nore, Brede Thomas's 'outstanding' B&B is filled with 'real style and friendliness'. The handsome Georgian house is in a 'fabulous situation' amid farmland and gardens; inside, spacious, traditionally decorated bedrooms have views of the river or rolling parkland. Hot drinks and biscuits are taken in the book-lined library; 'delicious' breakfasts are served in the dining room. Lounge, library

(open fire), dining room. Free Wi-Fi. No background music. Fishing, canoeing. 1 hour from Dublin. Children welcomed; pets allowed by arrangement. 6 bedrooms. Per person B&B €50.

WATERFORD Co. Waterford
Map 6:D5

FOXMOUNT COUNTRY HOUSE, Passage East Road. Tel 00 353 51-874308, www.foxmountcountryhouse.com. On a working dairy farm, Margaret and David Kent's creeper-covered 17th-century house stands in extensive gardens of manicured lawns, mature trees and a profusion of azaleas and rhododendrons. B&B accommodation is in homely, 'well-decorated' rooms overlooking the grounds or herb garden. Tea and home-made scones are served in the drawing room beside an open fire; guests are welcome to bring their own wine and aperitifs. Full Irish breakfasts include eggs from the farm, and compotes and preserves made from home-grown fruit; bread is home baked. Dining room, drawing room. 4-acre grounds. Free Wi-Fi. No background music. Children welcomed; dogs stay in kennels in the grounds. 2 miles S of the city. 4 bedrooms. Per person B&B €55–€60. Closed mid-Sept–mid-Mar.

WATERVILLE Co. Kerry
Map 6:D4

BUTLER ARMS. Tel 00 353 66-947 4144, www.butlerarms.com. Five generations of the Huggard family have run this 'friendly' hotel since 1915, in a little village along the Wild Atlantic Way. 'It is a well-run place; the management are highly visible at all times.' Bedrooms are 'simple, clean and unfussy'; most have views towards Ballinskelligs Bay. The restaurant specialises in seafood and locally sourced meat; light meals and sharing platters are taken in the 'lively' *Fishermen's Bar*, popular with locals. Good walks; bicycles for hire; fishing, shooting, horse riding and surfing can be arranged. Golf nearby. 'Excellent' value. Lounge, bar, restaurant; garden. Free Wi-Fi. Background music. Wedding/function facilities. Parking. Children (family rooms), and dogs welcomed. 36 bedrooms (1 suitable for ♿). Per room B&B €100–€280. Closed Oct–Apr.

WESTPORT Co. Mayo
Map 6:C4

ARDMORE COUNTRY HOUSE, The Quay. Tel 00 353 98-25994, www.ardmore countryhouse.com. 'We had a warm welcome.' With 'excellent' views over Clew Bay, the Hoban family's yellow-painted hotel and restaurant is a short walk from the lively town and harbour. David Hoban is the manager; 'staff are pleasant and helpful throughout'. Traditionally and comfortably furnished, most of the 'fine, spacious and well-equipped' rooms have a large sleigh bed, separate walk-in shower and bath, and views of Croagh Patrick and the bay. As chef, Pat Hoban specialises in locally caught fish and shellfish; Noreen, his wife, is the friendly front-of-house. Sitting room, bar, dining room. Free Wi-Fi (variable signal). Classical background music. 1½-acre garden. Small conference facilities; available for exclusive hire. Parking. Children welcomed. 13 bedrooms (some on ground floor). Per room B&B €90–€160, D,B&B €140–€200. Closed Nov–Mar.

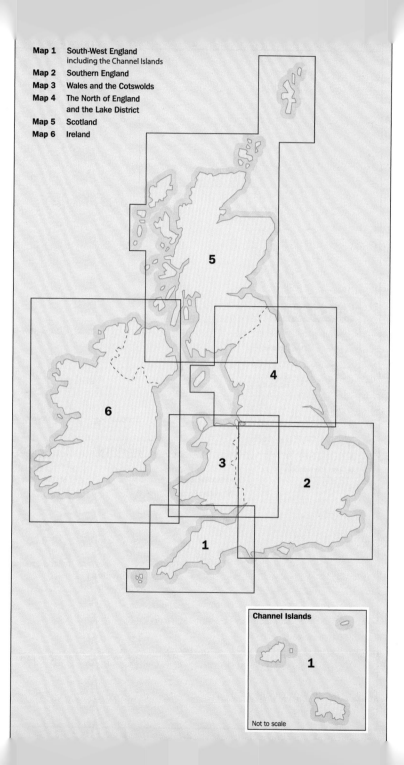

Map 1   South-West England
including the Channel Islands
Map 2   Southern England
Map 3   Wales and the Cotswolds
Map 4   The North of England
and the Lake District
Map 5   Scotland
Map 6   Ireland

5

4

6

3

2

1

Channel Islands

1

Not to scale

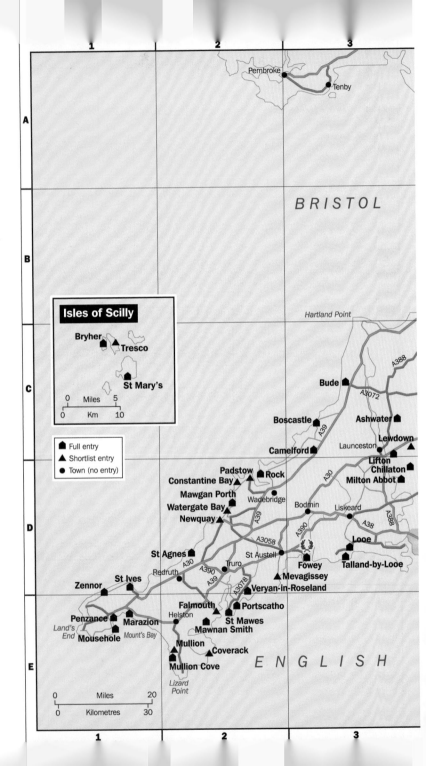

Isles of Scilly

Bryher
Tresco
St Mary's

0   Miles   5
0   Km   10

■ Full entry
▲ Shortlist entry
● Town (no entry)

BRISTOL

ENGLISH

Pembroke
Tenby

Hartland Point

Bude
Boscastle
Ashwater
Lewdown
Camelford
Launceston
Lifton
Chillaton
Milton Abbot

Padstow
Rock
Constantine Bay
Mawgan Porth
Wadebridge
Watergate Bay
Newquay
Bodmin
Liskeard
Looe
A3058
St Austell
Talland-by-Looe
St Agnes
Fowey
Redruth
Truro
Mevagissey
Zennor
St Ives
Veryan-in-Roseland
Falmouth
Portscatho
Penzance
Marazion
Helston
St Mawes
Land's
End
Mousehole
Mount's Bay
Mawnan Smith
Mullion
Coverack
Mullion Cove
Lizard
Point

A388
A3072
A39
A30
A390
A39
A30
A390
A38
A388
A39
A3078

0   Miles   20
0   Kilometres   30

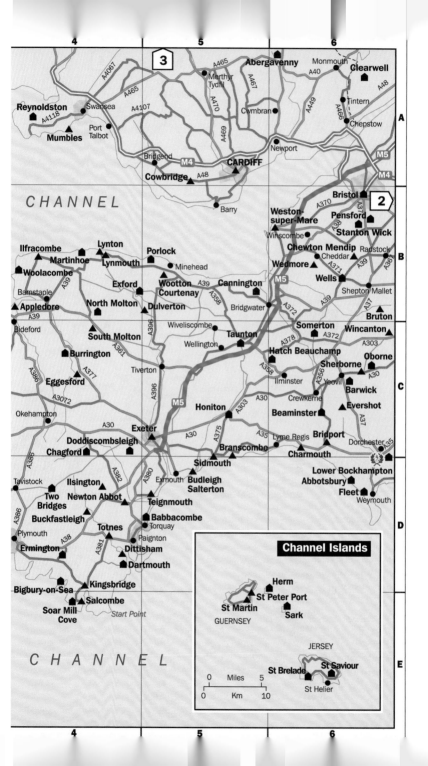

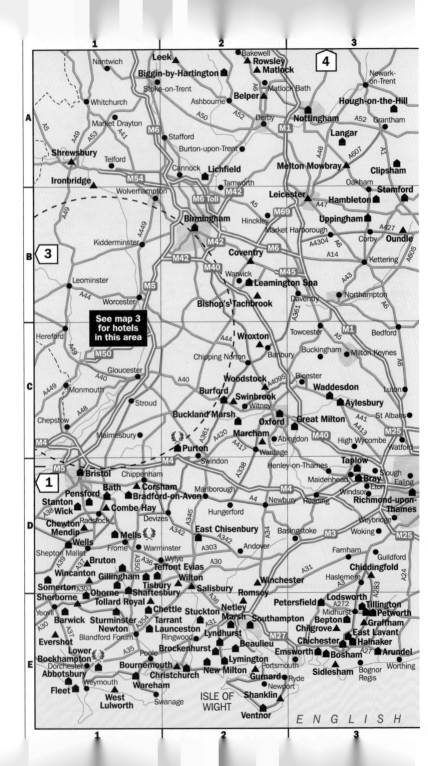

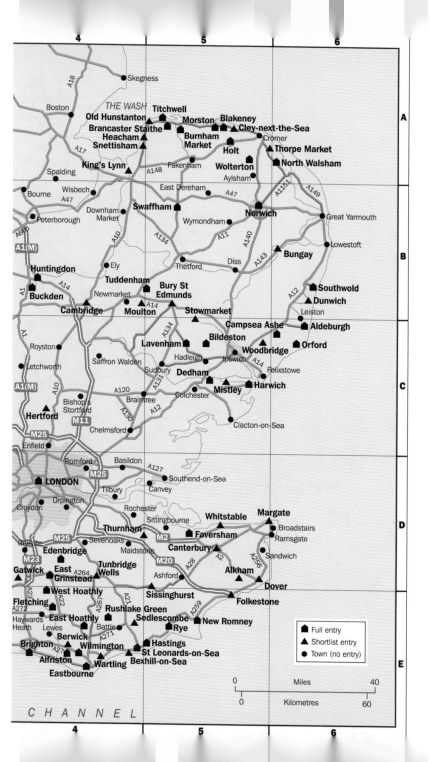

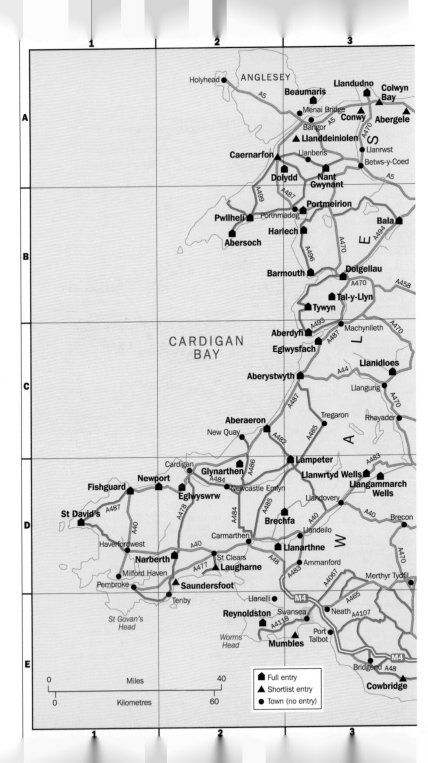

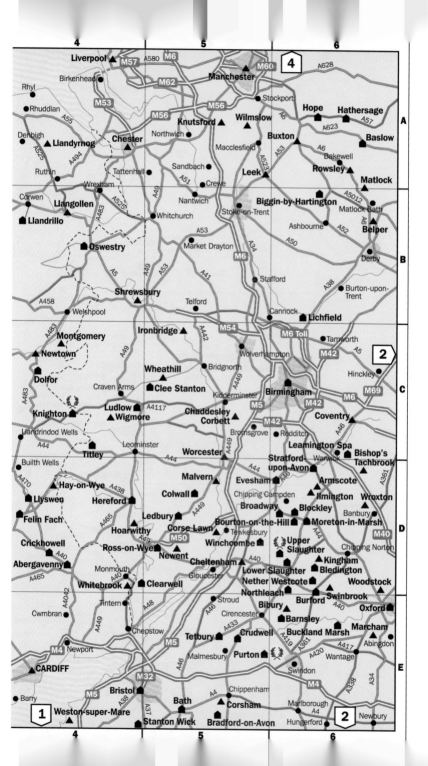

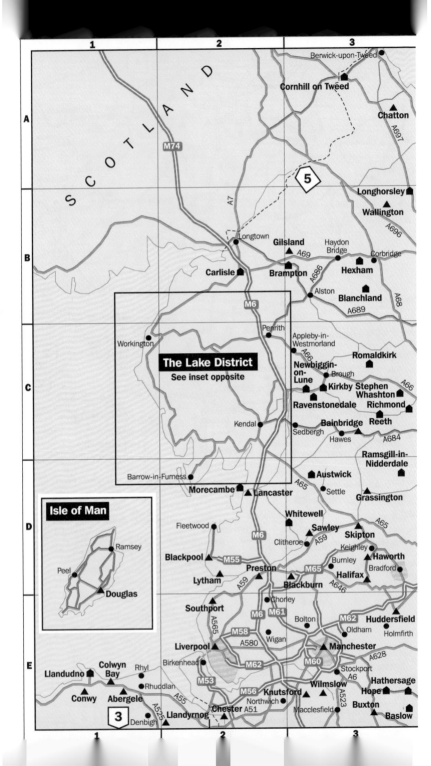

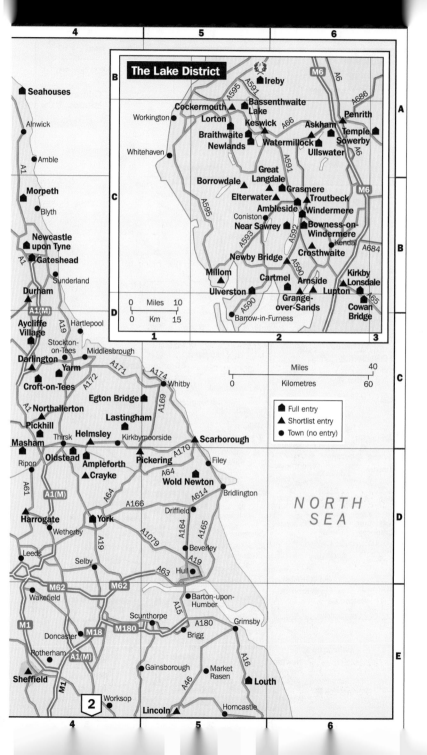

The Lake District

Ireby
M6 A6 A686

Workington
Cockermouth
Lorton
Bassenthwaite Lake
Keswick
Penrith
Askham
Temple Sowerby
Braithwaite
Newlands
Watermillock
Ullswater
Whitehaven
Great Langdale
Borrowdale
Grasmere
Elterwater
Troutbeck
Ambleside
Windermere
Coniston
Near Sawrey
Bowness-on-Windermere
Kendal
Newby Bridge
Crosthwaite
Millom
Cartmel
Arnside
Kirkby Lonsdale
Ulverston
Grange-over-Sands
Lupton
Barrow-in-Furness
Cowan Bridge

0   Miles   10
0   Km   15

Seahouses
Alnwick
Amble
A1
Morpeth
Blyth
Newcastle upon Tyne
Gateshead
Sunderland
Durham
A1(M)
Aycliffe Village
Hartlepool
Stockton-on-Tees
Middlesbrough
Darlington
Yarm
Whitby
Croft-on-Tees
Egton Bridge
Northallerton
Lastingham
Pickhill
Thirsk
Helmsley
Kirkbymoorside
Scarborough
Masham
Oldstead
Ripon
Ampleforth
Pickering
Filey
Crayke
Wold Newton
Bridlington
Harrogate
Driffield
Wetherby
York
A1(M)
Leeds
Selby
Beverley
Hull
M62
M62
Wakefield
Barton-upon-Humber
M1
Scunthorpe
Grimsby
Doncaster
M18
M180
Brigg
Rotherham
A1(M)
Sheffield
Gainsborough
Market Rasen
Louth
Worksop
Lincoln
Horncastle

NORTH SEA

Miles   40
Kilometres   60

Full entry
Shortlist entry
Town (no entry)

2

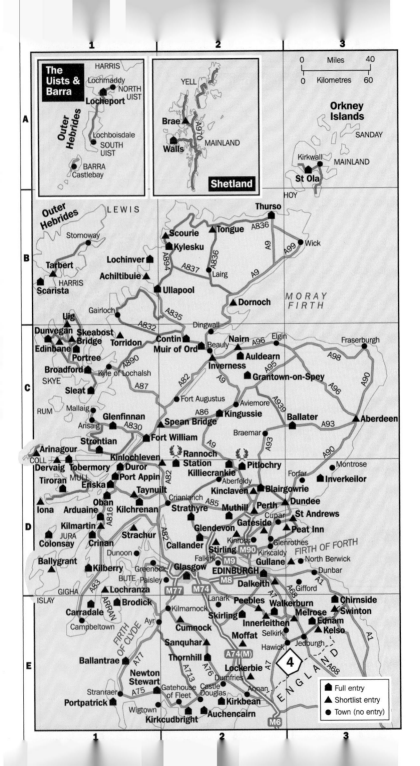

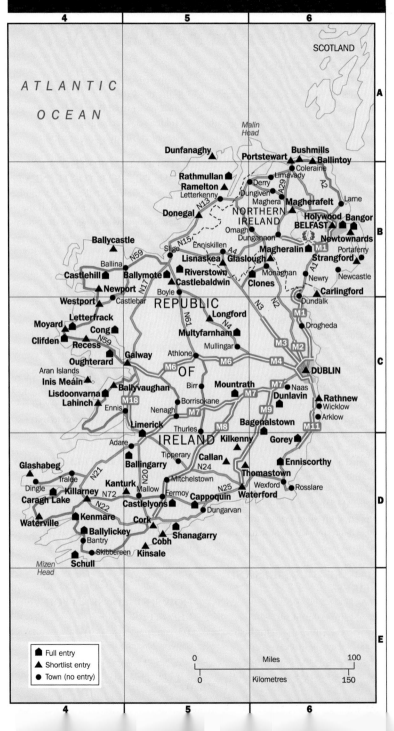

FREQUENTLY ASKED QUESTIONS

HOW DO YOU CHOOSE A GOOD HOTEL?

The hotels we like are relaxed, unstuffy and personally run. We do not have a specific template: our choices vary greatly in style and size. Most of the hotels in the *Guide* are family owned and family run. These are places where the needs and comfort of the guest are put ahead of the convenience of the management.

YOU ARE A HOTEL GUIDE – WHY DO YOU INCLUDE SO MANY PUBS AND B&BS?

Attitudes and expectations have changed considerably since the *Guide* was founded in the 1970s. Today's guests expect more informality, less deference. There has been a noticeable rise in the standards of food and accommodation in pubs and restaurants. This is demonstrated by the number of such places suggested to us by our readers. While pubs may have a more relaxed attitude than some traditional hotels, we ensure that only those that maintain high standards of service are included in our selections. The best B&Bs have always combined a high standard of accommodation with excellent value for money. Expect the bedrooms in a pub or B&B listed in the *Guide* to be well equipped, with thoughtful extras. B&B owners invariably know how to serve a good breakfast.

WHAT ARE YOUR LIKES AND DISLIKES?

We like
* Flexible times for meals.
* Two decent armchairs in the bedroom.
* Good bedside lighting.
* Proper hangers in the wardrobe.
* Fresh milk with the tea tray in the room.

We dislike
* Intrusive background music.
* Stuffy dress codes.
* Bossy notices and house rules.
* Hidden service charges.
* Packaged fruit juices at breakfast.

WHY DO YOU DROP HOTELS FROM ONE YEAR TO THE NEXT?

Readers are quick to tell us if they think standards have slipped at a hotel. If the evidence is overwhelming, we drop the hotel from the *Guide* or perhaps downgrade it to the Shortlist. Sometimes we send inspectors just to be sure. When a hotel is sold, we look for reports since the new owners took over, otherwise we inspect or omit it.

WHY DO YOU ASK FOR 'MORE REPORTS, PLEASE'?

When we have not heard about a hotel for several years, we ask readers for more reports. Sometimes readers returning to a favourite hotel may not send a fresh report. Readers often respond to our request.

WHAT SHOULD I TELL YOU IN A REPORT?

How you enjoyed your stay. We welcome reports of any length. We want to know what you think about the welcome, the service, the building and the facilities. Even a short report can tell us a great deal about the owners, the staff and the atmosphere.

HOW SHOULD I SEND YOU A REPORT?

You can email us at editor@goodhotelguide.com. Or you can write to us at the address given on the report forms at the back of the *Guide*.

Please send your reports to:

The *Good Hotel Guide*, Freepost PAM 2931, London W11 4BR

NOTE: No stamps needed in the UK.

Letters/report forms posted outside the UK should be addressed to:

The *Good Hotel Guide*, 50 Addison Avenue, London W11 4QP, England, and stamped normally.

Unless asked not to, we assume that we may publish your name. If you would like more report forms please tick ☐

NAME OF HOTEL: _____

ADDRESS: _____

_____

Date of most recent visit: _____ Duration of stay: _____

☐ New recommendation   ☐ Comment on existing entry

REPORT:

Please continue overleaf

I am not connected directly or indirectly with the management or proprietors

Signed: _____

Name: (CAPITALS PLEASE) _____

Address: _____

            _____

Email address: _____

Please send your reports to:

The *Good Hotel Guide*, Freepost PAM 2931, London W11 4BR

NOTE: No stamps needed in the UK.

Letters/report forms posted outside the UK should be addressed to:

The *Good Hotel Guide*, 50 Addison Avenue, London W11 4QP, England, and stamped normally.

Unless asked not to, we assume that we may publish your name. If you would like more report forms please tick ☐

NAME OF HOTEL: _____

ADDRESS: _____

_____

Date of most recent visit: _____ Duration of stay: _____

☐ New recommendation   ☐ Comment on existing entry

REPORT:

Please continue overleaf

I am not connected directly or indirectly with the management or proprietors

Signed: _____

Name: (CAPITALS PLEASE) _____

Address: _____

_____

Email address: _____

Please send your reports to:

The *Good Hotel Guide*, Freepost PAM 2931, London W11 4BR

NOTE: No stamps needed in the UK.

Letters/report forms posted outside the UK should be addressed to:

The *Good Hotel Guide*, 50 Addison Avenue, London W11 4QP, England, and stamped normally.

Unless asked not to, we assume that we may publish your name. If you would like more report forms please tick ☐

NAME OF HOTEL: _____

ADDRESS: _____

_____

Date of most recent visit: _____ Duration of stay: _____

☐ New recommendation   ☐ Comment on existing entry

REPORT:

Please continue overleaf

I am not connected directly or indirectly with the management or proprietors

Signed: _____

Name: (CAPITALS PLEASE) _____

Address: _____

_____

Email address: _____

INDEX OF HOTELS BY COUNTY

(S) indicates a Shortlist entry

ALPHABETICAL LIST OF HOTELS
(S) indicates a Shortlist entry

A

Abbey Bath (S) 477

Abbey Penzance 241

Abbey House Abbotsbury 68

Abbots House Charmouth (S) 490

Acorn Inn Evershot (S) 502

Ael y Bryn Eglwyswrw 397

Airds Port Appin 363

Airlie House Strathyre (S) 577

Albannach Lochinver 355

Alma London (S) 464

Alt na Craig House Oban (S) 571

Ampersand London (S) 464

Angel Abergavenny 384

Apple Lodge Lochranza (S) 569

Apsley House Bath 87

Aquae Sulis Bath (S) 477

Ardanaiseig Kilchrenan 348

Arden Stratford-upon-Avon 275

Ardmor House Edinburgh 333

Ardmore Country House Westport (S) 602

Argyll Iona (S) 567

Ariel House Dublin (S) 593

Artist Residence Penzance (S) 529

Arundell Arms Lifton 194

Ashley House South Molton (S) 541

Ashmount Country House Haworth (S) 507

Ashton Lancaster (S) 514

Askham Hall Askham 76

Aspen House Hoarwithy (S) 509

At the Chapel Bruton (S) 486

Atholl Aberdeen (S) 557

Atlantic St Brelade 427

Auberge Carnish Uig (S) 580

Auchrannie House Brodick (S) 558

Augill Castle Kirkby Stephen 186

Austwick Hall Austwick 77

Aynsome Manor Cartmel 130

B

B+B Belgravia London (S) 464

B&B Rafters Marcham (S) 521

Balcary Bay Auchencairn 317

Ballaghtobin Country House Callan (S) 591

Ballathie House Kinclaven (S) 568

Ballinkeele House Enniscorthy 446

Ballyduff House Thomastown (S) 601

Ballymaloe House Shanagarry 462

Ballyvolane House Castlelyons 440

Ballywarren House Cong 444

Balmoral Edinburgh (S) 561

Bar Convent York (S) 555

Barley Bree Muthill 357

Barnacle Hall Coventry (S) 496

Barnsley House Barnsley 82

Barrasford Arms Hexham (S) 509

Barton Grange Preston (S) 530

Bath Priory Bath 88

Battlesteads Hexham 178

Bay Coverack (S) 497

Bay Horse Ulverston 294

Bay Tree Burford (S) 487

Bays Farm Stowmarket (S) 542

Beach Bude 122

Beach House Looe 197

Beachlands Weston-super-Mare (S) 550

C